THE OXFORD HANDBOOK OF

HESIOD

THE OXFORD HANDBOOK OF

HESIOD

Edited by

ALEXANDER C. LONEY

and

STEPHEN SCULLY

OXFORD

UNIVERSITY PRESS

OXFORD
UNIVERSITY PRESS

Oxford University Press is a department of the University of Oxford. It furthers
the University's objective of excellence in research, scholarship, and education
by publishing worldwide. Oxford is a registered trade mark of Oxford University
Press in the UK and certain other countries.

Published in the United States of America by Oxford University Press
198 Madison Avenue, New York, NY 10016, United States of America.

CIP data is on file at the Library of Congress
ISBN 978-0-19-020903-2

1 3 5 9 8 6 4 2

Printed by Sheridan Books, Inc., United States of America

To our children—Audra, Hope, and Neil Loney and Benjamin, Katherine, and Chiara Scully—and to the future students of τὰ Ἡσιόδου.

Contents

PART IV HESIOD FROM BYZANTIUM TO MODERN TIMES

Acknowledgments

We are greatly indebted to our students for the help and care they have given to the preparation of this volume. In particular, we wish to acknowledge Katherine Baylis, Daniel Bennett, Suzanna Hersey, and Jessica Johnson, supported by the G. W. Aldeen Memorial Fund at Wheaton College, and Gideon Breslaw and Elizabeth Higgins, supported by the Undergraduate Research Opportunities Program in the College of Arts and Sciences at Boston University. We also must thank Suzanna Levey at Boston University, who in a directed study contributed greatly to the project.

Notes on Contributors

Joseph A. Almeida is professor of classics and legal studies and director of the Great Books of Western Civilization Honors Program at Franciscan University of Steubenville.

Egbert J. Bakker is the Alvan Talcott Professor of Classics at Yale University. His main interest is the combination of linguistic and literary perspectives on archaic Greek poetry. His last two books are *The Meaning of Meat and the Structure of the Odyssey* (Cambridge University Press, 2013) and *Authorship and Greek Song: Authority, Authenticity, and Performance* (ed., Brill, 2017).

Lilah Grace Canevaro is Leverhulme Early Career Fellow in Classics at the University of Edinburgh. She is author of *Hesiod's Works and Days: How to Teach Self-Sufficiency* (Oxford University Press, 2015), and coeditor of *Conflict and Consensus in Early Greek Hexameter Poetry* (Cambridge University Press, 2017). She has published in the fields of classical reception and comparative literature and has begun to test out cognitive approaches to didactic poetry. She is currently working on a book project on *Women of Substance in Homeric Epic: Objects, Gender, Agency* (Oxford University Press, forthcoming, 2018) and is exploring ways in which the new materialisms can be integrated into classical study.

Radcliffe G. Edmonds III is the Paul Shorey Professor of Greek in the Department of Greek, Latin, & Classical Studies at Bryn Mawr College. His research focuses on Greek religion and mythology, especially ideas of the underworld and afterlife, as well as on Platonic philosophy, ritual, and magic, and on various topics relating to Orphica, including the Derveni papyrus and the gold tablets. He has published *Myths of the Underworld Journey: Plato, Aristophanes, and the "Orphic" Gold Tablets* (Cambridge University Press, 2004) and *Redefining Ancient Orphism: A Study in Greek Religion* (Cambridge University Press, 2013). He has also edited a volume of essays entitled *The "Orphic" Gold Tablets and Greek Religion: Further Along the Path* (Cambridge University Press, 2011) and a volume of essays, *Plato and the Power of Images* (Brill, 2017, coedited with Pierre Destrée). His current project is a study of the category of magic, *Drawing Down the Moon: Magic in the Ancient Greco-Roman World* (Princeton University Press, forthcoming).

Marcus Folch is associate professor of classics at Columbia University. His work focuses on ancient Greek literature and philosophy, performance in antiquity, and incarceration in the ancient world. He is the author of *The City and the Stage: Performance, Genre, and Gender in Plato's Laws* (Oxford University Press, 2015), as well as articles and chapters on ancient literary criticism, the dialogue between ancient Greek philosophy and the poetic tradition, and classical reception in the twentieth century. He is currently at work on a book entitled *Bondage, Incarceration, and the Prison in Ancient Greece and Rome: A Cultural and Literary History*.

José M. González is associate professor of classical studies at Duke University and coeditor of *Greek, Roman, and Byzantine Studies*. His research interests bear on Greek literature (Homer to Nonnos), the intellectual history of classical antiquity, Aristotle, ancient rhetoric and literary criticism, ritual theory, and performance studies. His publications include *The Epic Rhapsode and His Craft: Homeric Performance in a Diachronic Perspective* (Harvard University Press, 2013), and the edited volume *Diachrony: Diachronic Studies of Ancient Greek Literature and Culture* (De Gruyter, 2015). He is currently writing a monograph on the Hesiodic poetic tradition.

Jeffrey Henderson is the William Goodwin Aurelio Professor of Greek Language and Literature, and former dean of the College and Graduate School of Arts and Sciences, at Boston University. He is best known for his pioneering work on the language and history of sexuality, on Greek drama (especially comedy) and politics, and for his editions and translations of Aristophanes. Since 1999 he has been the general editor of the Loeb Classical Library, and he was elected to the American Academy of Arts and Sciences in 2011.

Thomas E. Jenkins is professor of classical studies at Trinity University in San Antonio, TX. He is a past fellow of Harvard University's Center for Hellenic Studies and the American Council on Education, with research that cuts across a wide swathe of disciplines, including classics, theater, film, and gender studies. He was the winner of the inaugural Paul Rehak award for best article in LGBT studies in classics, on Lucian's *Dialogues of the Courtesans*; he is also the author of *Antiquity Now: The Classical World in the Contemporary American Imagination* (Cambridge University Press, 2015). His goofy stage adaptation of Plautus's *The Haunted House* premiered in 2013.

Joshua T. Katz is Cotsen Professor in the Humanities, professor of classics, and a member (and former director) of the Program in Linguistics at Princeton University, where he has been teaching since 1998. Widely published in the languages, literatures, and cultures of the ancient world, from India to Ireland, he has recently written on such subjects as wordplay in Vergil, the morphology of the Greek pluperfect, and Old Norse pederasty. He has a long-standing fascination with archaic Greek poetry, and the chapter in the present volume is part of a series of studies aimed at showing how much there is to learn about Homer and Hesiod from examining them from an Indo-European perspective.

Hugo H. Koning is a lecturer at Leiden University. His main interests are early epic, mythology and Herodotus. He is the author of *Hesiod: The Other Poet; Ancient Reception of a Cultural Icon* (Brill, 2010). He is currently working (with Glenn Most) on an edition of ancient exegetical texts on the *Theogony* and editing a volume (with Leopoldo Iribarren) on Hesiod and the pre-Socratics.

Stephanie Larson is professor of classics and ancient Mediterranean studies at Bucknell University, specializing in Boiotian studies and literature. Her dissertation (University of Texas, Austin) and later book, *Tales of Epic Ancestry: Boiotian Collective Identity in the Late Archaic and Early Classical Periods* (Stuttgart, 2007), explore the intersection of myth, material culture, and ethnic identity. For almost three decades Professor Larson has lived off and on in Greece, and in the last several years she has co-directed an excavation on the Ismenion Hill in Thebes, Boiotia. Additional interests include gender identities in ancient and modern Greece, Sappho, early Greek mythology, and Herodotus.

Adam Lecznar teaches modules in Greek language and literature at University College London and Royal Holloway and works on the reception of ancient Greek literature and philosophy in the modern period. His research focuses primarily on the work of Friedrich Nietzsche and his influence on later visions of the classical world. He has published on classical themes in the work of Nietzsche and Joyce and recently completed work on his first monograph project, *Dionysus after Nietzsche: Five Studies in Tragedy, Philosophy and Modernity*, for Cambridge University Press.

Alexander C. Loney is associate professor of classical languages at Wheaton College. Previously he was an American Council of Learned Societies New Faculty Fellow in Classics and a fellow of the Whitney Humanities Center at Yale University. He has written articles on Homer, Hesiod, and Greek lyric poetry, and has a monograph forthcoming with Oxford University Press, titled *The Ethics of Revenge and the Meanings of the Odyssey*.

Suzanne Lye is assistant professor in the Department of Classics at the University of North Carolina at Chapel Hill. She received her AB from Harvard University, where she studied organic chemistry and the history of antibiotics. After receiving her PhD in classics from the University of California, Los Angeles, she was awarded a postdoctoral fellowship at Dartmouth College. Her current research focuses on conceptions of the afterlife in ancient Greek underworld narratives from Homer to Lucian. She has published on ancient epic, ancient magic and religion, ancient representations of gender and ethnicity, ancient and modern pedagogy, and classical reception. Additionally, she has contributed to several digital humanities initiatives through Harvard's Center for Hellenic Studies, including the Homer Multitext Project.

Richard P. Martin is the Isabelle and Antony Raubitschek Professor in Classics at Stanford University, where he has taught Greek, Latin, and Irish literature for the past seventeen years. Previously he taught for eighteen years at Princeton University. His works on Greek poetry and myth include *Healing, Sacrifice, and Battle: Amechania and Related Concepts in Early Greek Poetry* (1983); *The Language of Heroes: Speech and Performance in the Iliad* (1989); *Classical Mythology: The Basics* (2016); and *Mythologizing Performance* (forthcoming). Hesiodic poetry has been the topic of several of his articles: "Hesiod, Odysseus, and the Instruction of Princes," *Transactions of the American Philological Association* 114 (1984); "Hesiod's Metanastic Poetics," *Ramus* 21 (1992); and "Hesiod and the Didactic Double," *Synthesis* (La Plata, Arg.) 11 (2004). The sociology of Greek comedy was the focus of his 2014 Sather Lectures at the University of

California, Berkeley. Martin's ongoing project on Homeric religion examines the interface between historically attested cult practices and the poetic representation of gods, heroes, and rituals. He holds an AB (in classics and Celtic studies) and an AM and PhD (in classical philology) from Harvard University.

Mitchell Miller, former Dexter Ferry Professor in Philosophy, is professor emeritus at Vassar College. In addition to his work on Plato and the pre-Socratics, he has long-term interests in late medieval philosophy, Descartes and Leibniz, and nineteenth- and twentieth-century continental thought. He has published two books on Plato, *Plato's Parmenides: The Conversion of the Soul* (Princeton University Press, 1986; Penn State UP pap., 1991) and *The Philosopher in Plato's Statesman* (Martinus Nijhoff, 1980; reissued with "Dialectical Education and Unwritten Teachings in Plato's *Statesman*," Parmenides Publishing, 2004), a wide-ranging array of essays on Plato, and studies of Hesiod ("'First of All,'" *Anc Phil* 21 2001]) and Parmenides ("Ambiguity and Transport," *OSAP* 30 [2006]). In recent years he has concentrated on the *Sophist* ("What the Dialectician Discerns," *Anc Phil* 36 [2016]); the *Philebus* ("A More 'Exact Grasp' of the Soul," in *Truth*, ed. K. Pritzl, CUAP 2010); and, as the context for inquiry into Plato's "so-called unwritten teachings," the notion of "the longer way" to the Good and a more "precise grasp" of the city, the soul, and (he argues) the cosmos that Plato has Socrates project at *Republic* 435c-d and 504b-e. For more, go to http://pages.vassar.edu/mitchellmiller/.

Stephanie Nelson is associate professor of classical studies at Boston University and currently director and dean of the core curriculum. She has her BA from St. John's College in Annapolis, MD, and her MA and PhD from the University of Chicago. She teaches widely in Greek and Latin literature and in the classical tradition and has written on subjects ranging from Hesiod to Aristophanes to translation from the classics. She is the author of *God and the Land: The Metaphysics of Farming in Hesiod and Vergil* (Oxford University Press, 1998) and of a work on Greek comedy and tragedy, *Aristophanes' Tragic Muse: Comedy, Tragedy and the Polis in Classical Athens* (Brill, 2016). She has also written on and given numerous talks on the relationship of Joyce's *Ulysses* and the *Odyssey* and is currently at work on a monograph on the subject.

Tom Phillips is supernumerary fellow in classics at Merton College, Oxford. He is the author of *Pindar's Library: Performance Poetry and Material Texts* (Oxford University Press, 2016). His current research focuses on lyric poetry, Hellenistic poetry, and ancient scholarship.

Benjamin Sammons has published numerous articles on early Greek literature, as well as two books, *The Art and Rhetoric of the Homeric Catalogue* (Oxford University Press, 2010) and *Device and Composition in the Greek Epic Cycle* (Oxford University Press, 2017). He has taught at Penn State University, New York University, and Queens College in the City University of New York.

Stephen Scully is professor of classical studies at Boston University. He has written on Homer, Hesiod, Greek tragedy, Plato, Freud's antiquities, and aspects of reception.

Translations include *Plato's Phaedrus* (Focus Publishing, 2003; now distributed by Hackett Publishing) and, with Rosanna Warren, *Euripides' Suppliant Women* (Oxford University Press, 1995; now in *The Complete Euripides*, vol. III, 2010), and recent publications include the introduction to George Chapman's *Homer's Hymns and Other Homerica* (Princeton University Press, 2008); "Englished Homer from Chapman to Walcott," *Arion* 17 (2009); *Hesiod's Theogony: From Near Eastern Creation Myths to Paradise Lost* (Oxford University Press, 2015); and "Dryden's *Aeneis*," in *Virgil and His Translators* (Oxford University Press, forthcoming).

H. A. Shapiro is the W. H. Collins Vickers Professor of Archaeology, Emeritus, in the Department of Classics at Johns Hopkins University. He is the author of several books on Greek archaeology, myth, and religion, including *Art and Cult under the Tyrants in Athens* (1989), *Personifications in Greek Art* (1993), *Myth into Art: Poet and Painter in Classical Greece* (1994), and *Re-fashioning Anakreon in Classical Athens* (2012). He has also curated exhibitions of Greek art at the New Orleans Museum of Art (*Greek Vases from Southern Collections*, 1981) and the Onassis Cultural Center in New York (*Worshipping Women: Ritual and Reality in Classical Athens*, 2008).

Alan H. Sommerstein is emeritus professor of Greek at the University of Nottingham. He has produced editions with commentary of Aeschylus's *Eumenides* (Cambridge University Press, 1989) and *Suppliants* (Cambridge University Press, forthcoming), on all the plays of Aristophanes (Warminster/Oxford, 1980–2003), and on Menander's *Samia* (Cambridge University Press, 2013). His recent books include *Aeschylean Tragedy* (2nd ed., London, 2010); the coauthored volumes *Oath and State in Ancient Greece* (Berlin, 2013) and *Oaths and Swearing in Ancient Greece* (Berlin, 2014); and two volumes of collected essays, *Talking about Laughter* (Oxford University Press, 2009) and *The Tangled Ways of Zeus* (Oxford University Press, 2010). He is editor of the forthcoming *Wiley-Blackwell Encyclopedia of Greek Comedy*.

Charles Stocking is assistant professor in the Department of Classical Studies and a core faculty member of the Centre for the Study of Theory and Criticism at the University of Western Ontario. He is also an associate member of the research center ANHIMA (Anthropologie et histoire des mondes antiques) in Paris. He is the author of *The Politics of Sacrifice in Early Greek Myth and Poetry* (Cambridge University Press, 2017), as well as various articles on archaic Greek poetry, Greek religion, and ancient athletics. He is currently at work on several projects that explore the impact of classical philology on continental philosophy and modern cultural history.

David W. Tandy is professor of classics emeritus at the University of Tennessee and visiting professor of classics at the University of Leeds. He is the author of *Warriors into Traders* (Berkeley, 1997) and of a translation (with commentary) of *Works and Days* (Berkeley, 1996), and has coedited or cowritten several other books, including *Ancient Greece, a Political, Social, and Cultural History*, 4th ed. (Oxford University Press, 2018). He has published articles and chapters on the economies and economic histories of the

Near East and pre-Hellenistic Greece, as well as on Homer, Hesiod, lyric poets, Lysias, Skopas, Virgil, and Beowulf.

Helen Van Noorden is the Wrigley Fellow and senior lecturer in classics at Girton College, University of Cambridge, and affiliated lecturer in the Faculty of Classics. Her undergraduate and graduate degrees come from Trinity College, University of Cambridge, and she held a junior research fellowship at Clare College. She is the author of *Playing Hesiod: The "Myth of the Races" in Classical Antiquity* (Cambridge University Press, 2014), and her publications continue to explore ancient legacies of Homeric and Hesiodic epic, especially Hellenistic and later didactic literature, philosophy, and "apocalyptic" writing. She is currently occupied with the later Sibylline Oracles and is coediting a large volume on eschatology in antiquity. Broader research interests include cultural interaction and concepts of authorship in antiquity.

Jessica Wolfe is professor of English and comparative literature at the University of North Carolina at Chapel Hill and articles editor of *Renaissance Quarterly*. She is the author of two books, including, most recently, *Homer and the Question of Strife from Erasmus to Hobbes* (University of Toronto Press, 2015), and has published essays and articles on Renaissance writers, including Erasmus, Spenser, Milton, Shakespeare, Chapman, Hobbes, and Thomas Browne, as well as on the Renaissance reception of Homer. She is currently working on an edition of Thomas Browne's *Pseudodoxia Epidemica* for the forthcoming *Complete Works of Thomas Browne* (Oxford University Press) as well as on a biography of the Renaissance poet, playwright, and translator George Chapman.

David Conan Wolfsdorf is professor of philosophy at Temple University. He is the author of *Trails of Reason: Plato and the Crafting of Philosophy* (Oxford University Press, 2008), *Pleasure in Ancient Greek Philosophy* (Cambridge University Press, 2013), as well as many articles and chapters in ancient philosophy. He is currently editing a volume, *Early Greek Ethics*, on philosophical ethics in the fifth and early fourth centuries BCE, and he is completing a nonhistorical philosophical work, *On Goodness*, on the meanings of "good" and "goodness" and the metaphysical implications of the semantic results.

Ioannis Ziogas is assistant professor at Durham University. He is the author of *Ovid and Hesiod: The Metamorphosis of the Catalogue of Women* (Cambridge University Press, 2013). He coedited (with M. Skempis) *Geography, Topography, Landscape: Configurations of Space in Greek and Roman Epic* (DeGruyter, 2014) and (with P. Mitsis) *Wordplay and Powerplay in Latin Poetry* (DeGruyter, 2016). He is currently working on a monograph on law and love in Ovid.

Niccolò Zorzi is assistant professor in Byzantine civilization at the Department of Linguistic and Literary Studies of the University of Padua (Italy). His research focuses on Byzantine historiography and rhetoric (*La "Storia" di Niceta Coniata, Libri I–VIII*, Venice 2012), Byzantine literacy, Byzantine culture and humanism, and the long-lasting relationship between Byzantium and Venice. He is a member of the editorial board of the *Byzantinische Zeitschrit*.

CHAPTER 1

....

INTRODUCTION

....

STEPHEN SCULLY AND ALEXANDER C. LONEY

THE time for a *Handbook of Hesiod* is ripe. In the last decade there have been at least thirteen major publications on Hesiod's poetry or its reception. These include important commentaries on the *Works and Days* (hereafter *WD*) (Ercolani 2010) and on the proem of the *Theogony* (hereafter *Th*) (Pucci 2007), a new edition and translation of the Hesiodic scholia (Cassanmagnago 2009), and a much-enriched Loeb in two volumes (Most 2006–2007). There are also two groundbreaking reception studies of Hesiod's works, broadly considered (Koning 2010, Montanari et al. 2009), as well as multiple studies that focus on the reception of individual songs (the *Th*: Scully 2015; the *WD*: Canevaro 2015; Hunter 2014; and Van Noorden 2014; the *Catalogue of Women*: Ormand 2014). Other studies consider Hesiod in relation to classical Greek poetry (Stamatopoulou 2017), to Plato (Boys-Stones and Haubold 2010), and to Ovid's *Metamorphoses* (Ziogas 2013). A number of important studies prepared the way for this onrush of publications on Hesiod and the reception of his works, including *Hesiod's Askra* (Edwards 2004), *Hesiod's Cosmos* (Clay 2003), a study on the narrative of the *Th* (Stoddard 2004), studies on farming and the *WD* (Nelson 1998 and Marsilio 2000), and a study on the *Catalogue of Women* and its reception (Hunter 2005). (And forthcoming are commentaries on the *Th* and *WD* in the Cambridge Greek and Latin Classics series.) Approaching one publication per year on average over twenty years rivals the number of books written on Homer, Hesiod's more-famous competitor, in the same time frame. It seems fair to say that with this flurry of recent activity, excitement for this archaic Greek songmaker and his legacy has reached a fever pitch not witnessed since the time of the Alexandrian librarians over two thousand years ago.

This volume aims to combine chapters on Hesiod's poetry and its milieu with others examining the reception of his songs over two and half millennia, from shortly after their conception to contemporary comic books. This Handbook is not intended as a complete survey or catalog of all of Hesiod's works or themes but is conceived as a guide through this terrain, much of which has not been extensively chartered previously. It is designed to offer an introduction and to be a reference guide to Hesiod by raising wide-ranging and complex issues, but it is not meant to be exhaustive in identifying all questions and answers. We expect it to be of use for students, as well as a starting point for further research.

Too often, handbooks rely on senior experts who have already determined and articulated their ideas. In the hope of adding fresh insights to the study of Hesiod and his reception, we have brought together twenty-nine junior and senior scholars, many of whom, while experts in their fields, are looking at Hesiodic questions or Hesiodic reception for the first time. Such is the case with a scholar like Egbert J. Bakker, who here has the opportunity to refocus his extensive study of Homer and Homeric poetics through a Hesiodic lens. The same is true for scholars like Jeffrey Henderson and David Conan Wolfsdorf in their study of Attic comedy and Hellenistic philosophy through the lens of Hesiodic themes and poetics. Similarly, more junior scholars like Benjamin Sammons, Marcus Folch, and Tom Phillips have turned their prior studies on Homeric catalogs, Plato, and Pindar to include Hesiod within those contexts.

The first section of the Handbook—on Hesiod and his archaic Boiotian context—focuses on historical questions. Some basic issues are still subject to dispute. Hugo H. Koning writes on the "Hesiodic question"; Stephanie Larson on the social and political conditions of his Askra in seventh-century BCE Boiotia; David W. Tandy on Hesiod's scheme of production in the context of the growing influence of an expanding urban *basilēes*. How one addresses these issues informs how one understands the nature of Hesiod's poetry. The Handbook does not intend to resolve these disputes or argue for any single point of view, but it does hope to give a critical picture of the sorts of answers that have been attempted.

Some take Hesiod's famous self-references at face value, reading them as testimonials of an historical figure, as argued by scholars like M. L. West and Hermann Fränkel, who saw in Hesiod early signs of authorial self-consciousness and self-representation; others see them as rhetorical indicators of an oral bard in live performance: see Joshua T. Katz, Richard P. Martin, José M. González, and Benjamin Sammons in this volume. Some believe that these self-references and Hesiod's self-correcting indicate written compositions (West 1966; Most 2006), while others see them as further evidence of performance art in an oral medium.

Related questions concern what many take to be Hesiod's intensely local focus on the village of Askra and surprising silence regarding the larger settlement of nearby Thespiai, particularly in the *WD* in political terms (see in this volume Tandy; Larson detects a pro-Theban sentiment). By contrast, as recognized by Herodotus, Hesiod's theology is thoroughly Panhellenic, particularly in the *Th*. However, as Martin and Bakker argue in this volume (see also Nagy 1990: 36–82) this Panhellenism is the end product of an evolution from local theogonic narratives in what may be described as a diachronic, agonistic process. Hesiod's vision of the divine world prevailed over alternative theologies promulgated by other competing, oral poets. (See Radcliffe G. Edmonds III in this volume on one such group of alternatives, the Orphics.) Also, the depictions of *basilēes* in the two poems differ dramatically, with the *Th* (80–93) presenting an idealized image of "kings"/"judges," descended from Zeus, who with straight judgments and soft voices quell social unrest in the agora, while in the *WD* (202–341) they dispense crooked judgments and threaten to bring Zeus's punishment down upon a polis. Some regard the moral injunctions of constraint and justice (*dikē/Dikē*) in the *WD* as absent in Hesiod's earlier *Th* (J. A. Almeida in this volume); others see signs of balance and restraint at the beginning of creation in the *Th* that prefigure Zeus's balanced political innovations at the end of the poem (Mitchell Miller in this volume); and still others see Zeus's creation of Olympus and his giving birth to *Dikē* as Zeus's attempt to create a new social order of communal harmony designed to overcome earlier generations of familial violence (esp. Scully 2015).

Koning's chapter, "The Hesiodic Question," alludes to the more famous "Homeric question." This question encompasses not just *who* the poet was, but *how* the epics bearing his name were composed and written down. Since the paradigm-shifting work of Milman Parry (1971, in the collective works published posthumously by Adam Parry) and Albert Lord (1960), it is almost universally agreed that the Homeric poems came out of a tradition of oral poetry, and in particular, that certain features discernible in the diction and construction of the poems owed their existence to that history. Study of the oral composition of the Homeric poems has overshadowed that of Hesiodic ones— for understandable reasons, seeing as the evidence we possess for the performance of Homer in antiquity outweighs that of Hesiod. Plato mentions the rhapsodic performance of Hesiod (*Ion* 531a1–4; *Laws* 658d) and indicates that—at least in the classical era—performers specialized in one poet. But such testimony—which at any rate is the limit of our extant textual evidence—only goes so far. Scholars of oral poetry including Parry have often contrasted the supposedly productive phase of epic composition by *aoidoi* with the merely re-productive phase by *rhapsodoi*. But the *Th* represents its composer, "Hesiod," as a *rhapsodos*, in contrast to the *Odyssey*'s depiction of *citharodoi*, like Demodokos, performing heroic epics. The same features of diction that indicate oral composition in Homer are present in similar ratios in Hesiod as well (Pavese 1998). Hesiod is just as silent on the technology of writing as Homer. Therefore, the same range of views on the extent of Homer's orality—from fully literate poet (West, Most) to completely oral poet, even as a metonym for the oral tradition itself (Nagy, González, Bakker)—is represented in views on Hesiod's orality.

It seems likely that a festival served as the occasion for the original performance of the *Th*. (However, "original" is a fraught term when speaking of oral performance, as Bakker discusses in this volume.) On the basis of comparative evidence, Bakker suggests a New Year's festival (more extensively argued by West 1966). Given the *Th*'s similarity in genre to a hymn (to Zeus), it seems likely it would have been performed in circumstances similar to those of the longer *Homeric Hymns*. (Hesiod famously says he performed a *hymnos*—perhaps the *Th*?—at Chalcis [*WD* 656–57]; cf. frag. 357 M-W.) The *WD*, on the other hand, is perhaps harder to place (see Canevaro 2015: 11–13), though its gnomic and parabolic aspects are more appropriate in a sympotic context. The original performance conditions of Hesiod's poetry may be unrecoverable. An earlier generation of scholars was more intent on uncovering the underlying oral nature of how the poems were composed, principally through studying the degree of their formularity (e.g., Notopoulos 1960; Edwards 1971). The results of such studies showed the poems to be as formulaic as Homer's and therefore equally as oral. More recent scholars have examined how oral composition affects our interpretation of the poems. To wit, Bakker, González, and Martin in this volume each focuses on how the language of the poems reveals the interactive situation of performer before audience (see esp. Bakker). González argues that this performer in the *WD* is constructing the very audience he is addressing, through shared ridicule of a deserving target: Perses. And Martin argues that Hesiod's diction, though broadly similar to Homer's, differs in ways that mark competitive oral traditions.

In this volume we seek to explore various ways that Hesiod's poetics may be distinguished from that of other Greek poets, especially Homer's. Identifying what might be considered a characteristic of epic catalog poetry, Stephen Scully discusses how Hesiod, as a stylist and a thinker, "speaks through" his personified abstractions in catalog lists and endless etymological puns. To a much greater extent than in Homeric phrasing, these stylistic traits draw attention to individual words. Furthermore, Hesiod is particularly artful in interweaving the personified names in his (in)famous genealogical lists with the common nouns and verbs of the surrounding narrative, giving the impression that the gods named in the lists pulsate throughout the action. Joshua T. Katz discusses Hesiod as "an Indo-European poet" who taps into a deep tradition of metaphoric associations, but who is also as interested in the sound of a line of poetry as its signification. Benjamin Sammons examines the way Hesiod interworks different modes of poetry: the *Th* transitions from genealogical and catalogic poetry to narrative as its emphasis shifts from generations of creation to Zeus's creation of Olympus. Alexander C. Loney shows how Hesiod's poetry is concerned with the various temporal modes that structure his universe. These temporalities are ways of viewing and modes of being in the world, and they interact with one another in complex and even paradoxical ways. Hesiod's poetry is animated by the tension between synchrony and diachrony, between permanence and development. Suzanne Lye explores Hesiod's famous misogyny in the context of a poet anxious about exerting some form of authority in the context of his own powerlessness. (On the legacy of Hesiod's misogyny in contemporary receptions, see also Thomas E. Jenkins in this volume.)

Thematic elements also make Hesiod an important author, not only for what he says himself but also for his pervasive influence, both positive and negative, on later writers, in poetry and prose, ranging across a wide array of genres and periods. Because he describes the iconic moment of divine inspiration, Hesiod became the defining exemplum of the divinely inspired singer, an important point of reference throughout antiquity up through the Renaissance. The source of his inspiration, the Muses, are the subject and addressee of the proem to the *Th*, the so-called "Hymn to the Muses" (1–115). This passage is an important early account of the Muses' birth and activity, lengthier and more detailed than anything we find on them in Homer. Homer's muse is anonymous; Hesiod is our first source for the names of the canonical nine and the name of their mother, Mnēmonsynē (Memory).

As the earliest Greek visionary of an idealized social order (Olympus) and a political thinker interested in questions of justice and social harmony, Hesiod was the ancient authority for a wide spectrum of writers, ranging from Solon, Xenophanes, Heraclitus,

Parmenides, and Pindar in the archaic period; to Aeschylus, Aristophanes, Prodicus, Plato, and Xenophon in the classical period; to the Stoics, the euhemeristic writers, Lucian, and the Christian apologists in Hellenistic and Roman times. Equally important were his complex depictions of male and female interrelationships, both within the family and as part of the social fabric of Olympus. The importance of this story is increasingly receiving attention, but much of it is told in bits and pieces, and there is more to be said on all counts. Contemplation of origins—natural, divine, social, and political—is an integral aspect of Hesiod's poetics (see in this volume Loney and Miller).

Furthermore, the *Th*, when combined with *Catalogue of Women* (attributed to Hesiod at least until Hellenistic times), offered a continuous mythic narrative of the world from its beginnings to the age of heroes and the Trojan War that proved increasingly important for universal histories and especially for Ovid, as Ioannis Ziogas illustrates in this volume. The poems become a touchstone for theological reflection, not only in polytheistic antiquity, but also for early Christian apologists and later for Renaissance and early modern Christian writers, including Milton and his telling of a Christian creation epic (see Jessica Wolfe in this volume). Helen Van Noorden in this volume outlines Hesiod's reception among second sophistic and early Christian writers. Perhaps the most important act of reception in the period is the text known to us as "The Contest (*Certamen*) of Homer and Hesiod," which stages a poetic duel between the two greatest epic bards of archaic Greece. In the final stage of the contest, Hesiod quotes *WD* 383–92 on the proper time for agricultural labor and wins on the verdict of the king Panedes:

> The king crowned Hesiod saying that it was just (*dikaion*) that he who exhorts men to farming (*geōrgian*) and peace (*eirēnēn*) win, and not he who goes in detail through wars and slaughter.
>
> (*Certamen Homeri et Hesiodi* 207–10, trans. Loney)

This association of peace and farming with Hesiod (here opposed to Homer's penchant for martial themes) results from the popularity of the *WD*, but as Van Noorden shows, the whole corpus of his works served as sources for scholar-writers like Plutarch and Athenaeus to exploit for discussion on topics as abstruse as kinds of drinking cups. The corpus of poems by "Hesiod" once included more than the *Th* and *WD*. Though only three complete longer poems attributed to Hesiod have come down to us—and one, the *Shield of Herakles*, is a falsely attributed, fifth-century BCE poem—many other poems that we know only in fragments were once attributed to him. These include not only the influential *Catalogue of Women*, but also poems on such abstruse topics as bird omens: an *Ornithomanteia* (on the wider corpus, see Cingano 2009; Stamatopoulou 2017: 6–13). While these sundry minor poems did contribute to the ancients' sense, from the classical through the imperial periods, of what constituted Hesiodic poetry, Hesiod was always best known as the author of the *Th* and the *WD*, although in Pausanias's time local Boiotians regarded the *WD* alone as authentic (Scully 2015: 153).

Of these two, the *WD*, with its stern moralizing tale and easily extracted gnomic exempla, was the more popular, leading to what Richard Hunter has called a distinctive and insistent "Hesiodic voice" of didacticism and practical wisdom (2014: 124). Central to that voice is the poem's concern with "justice" and "laws." Hesiod sings:

Zeus has drawn up this *nomos* (law) for humans:

> that fish and beasts and birds
> devour one another because they have no justice,
> but to humans he has given justice, which is by far
> the best thing . . .

(*WD* 274–80, trans. Scully)

In this poem that concern often takes the form of fierce censure—of his brother's transgressions, of corrupt kings, of the devastating moral decline of the Fifth Age of Man (the Iron Age into which Hesiod was born), and of Pandora's unleashing of pains and tolls upon man. These themes, told in the first person and ripe with moralizing maxims, linked the poem with an emerging sympotic tradition, first in verse in the archaic period and later in prose in the Roman imperial age.

It is for similar reasons that Virgil could build upon the poem in his own moralizing study of farming and the hard lot of humankind, and Christians in the Renaissance turned to the poem less for its treatise on farming than as a manual for better living. Seeing the WD both as a precursor to Virgil's Georgics and as a proto-Christian manual, George Chapman is the first to give the English-speaking world a taste of Hesiod, writing on the title page of his translation of the WD (1621): "Translated Elaborately out of the Greek: Containing Doctrine of Husbandrie, Moralitie, and Pietie; with a perpetuall Calendar of Good and Bad Dates; Not Superstitious, but necessarie (as farre as naturall Causes compeil) for all Men to observe, and difference in following their affaires." In note 48 of his translation, Chapman even characterizes Hesiod's views as "truly religious and right Christian." For the Georgic tradition and Hesiod in the context of Chapman and Christian humanism in the sixteenth and seventeenth centuries, see Stephanie Nelson and Jessica Wolfe in this volume.

Evidence of reception can take many forms, ranging from an artist's, writer's, or thinker's direct engagement with a text by citation, translation, or adaptation, to a more conceptual engagement by allusion, periphrasis, or summary. Or one might react to the ideas or point of view in a text; especially with the passage of time, readings might pass through an intermediary work (or works) that serve as a window to an older source. Also, with the passage of time reception can blend with what might more appropriately be called a study of the classical tradition, which, as Michael Silk, Ingo Gildenhard, and Rosemary Barrow have recently written (2014: 5), "subsumes not only direct engagements with antiquity, but engagements with earlier engagements" and tends to raise questions of value, perceived positively or negatively. Finally, reception must also include scholarly output in the form of manuscripts and commentaries (see Niccolò Zorzi and Jessica Wolfe in this volume).

Reception studies offer their own form of readings, even as they reveal shifting values and views of the world in later eras. In the case of Hesiod, the earliest signs of reception began less than a century after he lived, as new waves of poets and art forms responded to the authoritative Hesiod, even as the Greek world was rapidly changing with the (further) development of the Greek polis, the rise of class conflict, and an increasing disparity between the rich and poor with the introduction of money into the Greek economy. There is no single or simple answer to how we understand the reception of Hesiod's poems in this changing world. In this volume, J. A. Almeida offers a chapter on *dikē* in Hesiod's *WD* and Solon; Tom Phillips on Pindar's sophisticated and vivifying engagement with his fellow Boiotian poet; Alan H. Sommerstein on the varying portraits of Prometheus and Pandora in Greek tragedy and their profound influence on Aeschylus; and Jeffrey Henderson on the comic poets' engagement with Hesiod, from direct allusion and echo to story patterns, ideas, themes, and style. Two other chapters look at relatively understudied and vast topics: Radcliffe G. Edmonds III on Hesiod in relation to the Orphic tradition and H. A. Shapiro in relation to archaic art.

This period was also a time of intellectual tumult, marked most dramatically by a new class of thinkers whom Aristotle called the *physikoi* ("those concerned with the nature of things") to distinguish them from *theologoi* ("theologians") like Hesiod and from those who speak "mythically" like Homer (Aristotle, *Metaphysics* III.4, 1000a). In this volume, essays range from Mitchell Miller's discussion of the ways pre-Socratic writers like Anaximander and Xenophanes both depart from and appropriate Hesiod in their own search for the divine and cosmic order, to Marcus Folch's study of Hesiod's reception among fourth-century BCE prose writers, with an expansive study of Hesiod in relation to Plato's *Laws*. David Conan Wolfsdorf expands that focus by exploring the diverse ways the Peripatetics, Epicureans, and Stoics variously used or ignored Hesiod. In Alexandria and among scholar poets, interest in both the *Th* and *WD* blossomed, as Lilah Grace Canevaro illustrates with her focus on the learned literary culture of Alexandria.

Not all stories of reception are positive. Even in the sixth century BCE, figures like Xenophanes, intensely aware of the limits and sources of human understanding, struggled with the idea of anthropomorphic gods and the belief in a late-born god, like Zeus, as ruler of the universe. Miller in this volume argues that as pre-Socratic writers like Anaximander and Xenophanes saw in the archaic period, Hesiod himself had already suggested a process by which to de-anthropomorphize the great cosmic gods and to replace named gods with personified abstractions. Conversely, Orphic theogonies and cosmogonies, even as they adhered to the Hesiodic structure of creation, depicted a more supreme, more transcendent, and more transgressive Zeus, ostentatiously deviating from the standard model to outdo Hesiod's authoritative version of creation and Zeus (Edmonds in this volume). But for most Greeks, criticism of anthropomorphic deities intensified with time, especially with the rise of monotheistic beliefs, most popularly exemplified by Stoic philosophical monotheism, which replaced traditional views of Zeus and of polytheism with a single, all-powerful god who created and ruled a morally coherent and rational universe.

Movement toward a cosmic monotheism can even be detected in Orphism, which came to imagine Zeus as the first, last, and middle of all things and even embraced the opposites of beginning and end, male and female, fire and water, earth and air, and so on (cf. Edmonds pp. 237–39 in this volume). Yet as Folch (p9. 322–23 in this volume) wisely cautions us, even in the rising rationalism of the fourth century BCE there were as many *receptions* of Hesiod as there were institutions and media in which the poems were transmitted. Even then the Greeks could regard Hesiod as a contemporary who animated philosophical, literary, and political debates.

The Greeks also became increasingly concerned with mythic accounts of the gods in conflict with one another. In what Plato would come to describe as a war between poetry and philosophy, already in the archaic period Xenophanes complained:

> Both Homer and Hesiod attributed all those things to the gods
> which in the human world are considered shameful and blameworthy:
> to steal, to commit adultery, and to deceive one another.
>
> (DK B11, trans. Scully; cf. Mitchell Miller, p. 214 in this volume)

From the *Th*, the Greeks were particularly critical of stories of sons warring against fathers: for example, Zeus's defeat of his father Kronos becomes a touchstone of moral criticism (cf. Aristophanes, *Clouds* 905; Aeschylus, *Eumenides* 640–41; see Folch in this volume, pp. 318–19 on Plato). Of less concern were stories of male violence against female deities: for example, Zeus's swallowing Metis.

Theagenes of Rhegium, also in the sixth century BCE like Xenophanes, was among the first to attempt to rescue such stories from ridicule by using *allegoresis* ("the act of saying one thing so as to imply another"), a mode of interpretation that typically regarded the surface, mythological meaning of a story as defective and a riddle in need of decoding. While introduced early on among Greek apologists, this approach is notably absent from the pre-Socratics, Plato (although see Folch, p. 322 in this volume), Aristotle, and the Epicureans, as Most has shown (2016: 59–72), but it was a popular strategy among Orphic critics in the early fourth century BCE, as the anonymous Derveni commentator openly acknowledges: "Orpheus' poetry is strange and riddling for people. But he did not intend to tell captious riddles but momentous things in riddles" (Derveni Papyrus 7.4–7) (see Edmonds, p. 232 in this volume). The import of Orphic myth, this commentator insists, lies in the decoder revealing the wisdom hidden in the riddling surface. Stoics similarly favored such readings, searching beneath the mytheme of divinely inspired poetry to uncover a philosophical, theological, moralistic, historical, or naturalistic truism (see Wolfsdorf, pp. 352–54 in this volume).

Neoplatonists, in particular, continued this tradition (again, see Edmonds), as exemplified by Proclus in the fifth century CE. Proclus sought to reconcile how Plato both admired inspired poets like Hesiod, Homer, and Orpheus and yet also attacked them for their stories, especially about the gods. Proclus agreed with Plato that such poets had no place in the educational system and must be kept from children, but he argued that skilled readers capable of grasping the secret meanings of these stories could see that both an inspired poet and the philosopher were defensible:

[They were equally] thoughtful and knowledgeable contemplator[s] of the divine beings, both of them teaching the same things about the same things, and both interpreters of the same truth about reality, participating in the procession of the same god and taking their places in the same chain.

(*In Platonis rempublicam*, as translated by Lamberton 2012: 61)

Referring to the Greek succession myth in the same essay, he writes that for

those capable of following on the uphill path of contemplation, we shall not find it impossible to incorporate . . . the binding of Kronos, or the castration of Ouranos into the irrefutable body of wisdom about the gods. . . . The mystical apprehension of the divine would not, after all, come about in entirely alien receptacles, and so, when we tell those who have experienced such spectacles that . . . the bonds of Kronos show the union of the whole creation with the intellective and paternal transcendence of Kronos—and that the castration of Ouranos points to the separation of the Titanic chain from the essential ordering of the universe—in saying all this, we may well be telling a familiar story, referring the theatrical and the fictional [in the myths] to the intellective contemplation of the gods.

(Lamberton, 81–83)

Such defenses also proved useful to save Hesiod and Homer from a relentless Christian mockery of the archaic, mythical representation of the gods and remained highly influential in shaping interpretations of Greek epic poetry in late antiquity, Byzantium, the Middle Ages, and well past the Renaissance (see Zorzi, p. 421; Wolfe, pp. 432–34; Adam Lecznar, pp. 448–49 in this volume).

In antiquity, another popular mode of reading was to reveal the "true meaning," the *etymologia*, of a god's name (theonym) and epithets. Unlike allegory, which required substituting a hidden meaning of a storyline for a surface one, the true nature of a god is already partially exposed in his name(s) and epithets. Often in antiquity, an author would employ one mode of interpretation or the other, but not both. In the *Cratylus*, for example, Plato draws heavily on etymology but not allegory; the same is true for most ancient grammarians. The Derveni author and the Stoics stand out for combining both modes, although subordinating etymology to allegory, using it "to provide a kind of supplementary proof" (Most 2016: 72). Distinct as they are, both approaches "echo a common philosophical theme running from the Pythagoreans to Plato to the Cynics to Epicurus: conventional culture manifests psychological corruptions; philosophy endeavors to purify the mind and to redirect motivation and action," as Wolfsdorf writes (p. 354).

In his penchant for punning and etymologizing divine names, we see Hesiod himself deploying such tactics, especially in the *Th*, as if the etymology of a word revealed a story of origin or the essence of character. So, for example, he derives both Aphrodite's name and a number of her epithets from his story of her sea birth: Aphrodite, "because she was nurtured / in the *aphros* (foam)"; *Cytherea* "because she reached [the island of] Cytherea"; Cyprus-born "because she was born on Cyprus washed by many waves"; and *philommēdēs* ("lover of genitals") "because she sprang from [Ouranos's] *mēdea* (genitals)" (*Th* 195–200). With a similar attention to the efficacy of names and perhaps drawing on Greek cult names, Hesiod frequently recycles the names of deified abstractions (like Dike, Eirene, Eris, Kratos, and Bia) into the commonplace nouns of his narrative, giving the sense that the narrative itself is pulsating with divinity. We also sense with these abstractions how a composer of songs is moving toward philosophy, using the technique of personification to assemble the building blocks of logical argument, turning mythic story into something approaching political science and political allegory (in this volume, see Scully, pp. 85–92, Sammons, pp. 98–99, 101; and Miller, pp. 218–19).

Even as allegory continues to be a frequent mode of interpretation, the nature of that allegorizing has shifted significantly in the modern era, a shift that marks an embrace of the surface meaning rather than an escape from it. Friedrich Nietzsche was one such figure exemplifying this shift, as we can see in these comments on the Greek succession myth:

> Let us imagine the air of Hesiod's poems difficult to breathe as it is, still thicker and darker and without any of the things to alleviate and cleanse it which poured over Hellas from Delphi and numerous seats of the gods: let us mix this thickened Boeotian air with the dark voluptuousness of the Etruscans; such a reality would then *extort* from us a world of myths in which Uranus, Kronos and Zeus and the struggles of the Titans would seem like a relief; in this brooding atmosphere, combat is salvation and deliverance, the cruelty of the victory is the pinnacle of life's jubilation.
>
> ("Homer's Contest," unpublished essay written in 1872,
> now in Nietzsche 2010: 175)

So read, the surface narrative of myth is not something to be explained away but to be embraced for its strength and bravery in illuminating the dark and irrational forces inherent in the human condition. And symbol, so read, rather than being a pathway to esoteric meaning, served as a key to expose, or decode, that the "meaning" of the myth was the narrative itself.

Attention to the surface meaning of myths continues in many forms of twentieth-century interpretation. In this volume we look at two such approaches. In the first, Scully explores how Sigmund Freud turned to classical myth in the first half of the twentieth century to reveal the hidden forces at work in the human unconscious. In addition to borrowing from Greek myth to name human complexes, Freud felt that only myth—what he called "our mythology" (1933: 95)—could describe what he felt were primal instincts (one libidinal, the other aggressive) underlying the dynamic conflicts between the ego, id, and superego. Giving these "mythical entities" Greek names, he labeled them, a bit misleadingly, Eros and Thanatos (Love and Death). Freud's scientific reputation has fallen sharply in the last fifty years, but he stands out as one of the most influential thinkers of the twentieth century.

In the second example, Charles Stocking explores how the anthropologist Claude Lévi-Strauss, relying on the language of formal linguistics and mathematics, turned to myth in the second half of the century to identify the hidden structures, tensions, and logic of social organization. Like Freud, he utilized a pattern of binary oppositions that organize fundamental dichotomies between nature and culture, life and death, male and female, and so on, in an effort to make life coherent and intelligible. In this system, cultures create myths to mediate these polarities and logical contradictions: "The purpose of myth," Lévi-Strauss wrote, "is to provide a logical model capable of overcoming a contradiction" (1963: 229).

For Freud, Greek myth, but not Hesiod, was an important guide, although one can detect Hesiodic themes resurfacing in fascinating ways in his own narrative of the creation of civilization. Lévi-Strauss drew from mythic narratives in the Americas and only sparingly, and then not very convincingly, engaged with Greek myth. But in both cases numerous classicists have been inspired by and responded to these theoretical approaches in their own treatments of Greek myth, with a special focus on Hesiod. For instance, Richard Caldwell has supplemented the absence of Hesiod in Freud with his own psychoanalytic reading of the *Th*, while scholars such as Jean-Pierre Vernant, Marcel Detienne, and Pietro Pucci engaged in structuralist debates through Hesiodic poetry in a manner that extended far beyond Lévi-Strauss (for references, see chapter 29).

Different as both systems are on the surface—one concerned "with the irrational impulses of the unconscious," the other "with the rational structures with which the human mind tends to organize reality," as Charles Segal writes (1978: 129)—they both are reductionist theories and require a trained eye to decode symbolic language, whether it be of dreams or myth, and to bring subsurface tensions to the light of day for analysis. In this sense, Freud and Lévi-Strauss employ their own forms of allegory, namely that the mythic narrative tells *another story*, which requires the symbol-interpreter to analyze and systematize. But the difference between their approach and the traditional, classical approach is that instead of seeking to save the myth by saying that it in fact means something contrary to the surface story, these approaches embrace that narrative for itself, finding its dark and violent components central to interpretation. Like allegorical readings, these approaches, as various as they are, are dependent on symbols, but unlike allegory they seek to understand the symbols within a text as a complex interweaving of components, unlocking the underlying meaning of the narrative itself.

Within the past fifty years we have witnessed a major shift in attention from the *WD* to the *Th*, a shift that is most pronounced if we compare the relative attention and weight given to the two poems in the Renaissance. When scholars in the West first became aware of Hesiod, the predominance of attention was on the *WD*, both for its Christian-like sensibilities and as a precursor of Vergil's *Georgics* (see Nelson and Wolfe in this volume). A humanist like Erasmus regarded the *Th* as essential reading:

> One must also learn the genealogy of the gods, as stories of every sort are filled with them. After Hesiod, Boccaccio transmitted this account with more aplomb (*foelicius*) than might be expected for his time.
>
> (*De ratione studii* LP 523 [1511], trans. Scully; cf. McGregor 1978: 674)

But he also felt a deep disdain for polytheism, especially in its violent Hesiodic and Homeric form:

> The gentiles (*gentes*) prefer to worship evil spirits (*daemonia*) rather than the true God, because [a believer of the true god] detests all baseness but [the gentiles] favor vices and nourish corrupt desires; nor are they offended when such gods are engaged in entertainments and tales, the types of which no good man would want for his son or wife—or even his servant.
>
> (*De linguae usu et abusu* LB 705 [1525], trans. Scully; cf. Fantham 1989: 336–37)

In the tradition of Xenophanes, Lucian, and the Christian apologists, Erasmus is especially horrified by events told in the *Th* and draws on this poem when condemning Greek religion, as the continuation of the passage from *Lingua* shows:

> Such gods are pleasing to [the gentiles] because under such deities, it is permitted, with impunity, as they think, to associate with harlots, to commit adultery, to deceive, to thieve, to seize tyranny, and to excite sedition as Jupiter [*sic*] is said to have done when he seized kingship, having dethroned and de-manned his father (*exacto et execto patre*), and as the other gods did when, moved by sedition, they drove out Jupiter along with his backers. Perhaps you would not easily find this kind of blasphemy among Christians today, although it is monstrous that it be found at all. For certainly it is found; nor is the great severity of laws able to heal or check this raging of the tongue.
>
> *De linguae usu et abusu* LB 705, continued

Living at the same time as Luther's challenge to the Church, Erasmus certainly acknowledged the possibility of Christian misdeeds, but there can be no mistaking the scorn he felt for a pagan religion that reeked with violence among its gods. As it did for many in antiquity, the *Th* provided fodder for that scorn. By contrast, on numerous occasions in his *Adagia*, Erasmus cites "Hesiod" (meaning the author of the *WD*) for his sage advice, including the famed adage that virtue dwells with hardship. A century later George Chapman, relying on Spondanus's and Melanchthon's Christianizing commentaries when translating the *WD* into English for the first time, regarded *The Georgicks of Hesiod* (1618) as a manual for better living. But the *Th* would not be rendered into English until the early eighteenth century, in the time of Alexander Pope, when Thomas Cooke translated it into heroic couplets (1728).

Almost 400 years since Chapman's translation of the *WD*, the story of reception has shifted greatly. By the early twenty-first century (in no small measure due to the importance of myth for Nietzsche, Freud, Lévi-Strauss, and later structuralists) interest has shifted to the *Th,* an interest further enhanced by the discovery in the 1950s of parallel creation stories from the Near East. Even the interest in the *WD* has shifted to its myths (Pandora and Prometheus, the Five Races of Man), its parables (like the nightingale and the hawk), and the window it affords upon agrarian, eighth-century BCE life in mainland Greece. We see this shift in the final chapter of this volume.

The surface meaning of Hesiod's poetry remains the focus for the popular reception of Hesiod in the twentieth and twenty-first centuries, as Thomas E. Jenkins analyzes. The products that result from these engagements with Hesiod tend to focus on a select set of passages with memorable narratives, such as the myth of Pandora. Many of these products are now directed at young readers and viewers, and though the surface narrative of Hesiod in these retellings is the center of attention, a kind of supplementary meaning can still be discerned. Often these myths receive a moralizing interpretation suitable to a young audience and sometimes an explicitly revisionist interpretation suitable to contemporary mores. (Such child-friendly revisionism has had its critics too, as Jenkins notes.) In more adult-oriented receptions of Hesiod, modern social anxieties—from environmentalism to the ethics of imprisonment—can be felt, and Hesiodic myths continue to serve as morality tales, if more subtle ones. But in contrast to many ancient Greeks and to Renaissance figures like Erasmus, Jenkins shows how people of all ages in recent times delight in the spectacle of gods and demigods at war with each other. No doubt, others in antiquity, as also Milton later did in *Paradise Lost*, took pleasure in Hesiod's virtuosic telling of these combats. In short, Hesiod's poetry has always been appreciated on multiple levels, and so it remains to this day.

References

Boys-Stones, G. R., and J. H. Haubold, eds. 2010. *Plato and Hesiod*. Oxford.

Canevaro, L.G. 2015. *Hesiod's Works and Days: How to Teach Self-Sufficiency*. Oxford.

Cassanmagnago, C., ed. and trans. 2009. *Esiodo: Tutte le opere e i frammenti con la prima traduzione degli scolii*. Milan.

Chapman, G., trans. and comm. 1618. *The Georgicks of Hesiod*. London.

Cingano, E. 2009. "The Hesiodic Corpus." In *Brill's Companion to Hesiod*, edited by F. Montanari, A. Rengakos and Ch. Tsagalis, 91–130. Leiden, Netherlands.

Clay, J. S. 2003. *Hesiod's Cosmos*. Cambridge.

Edwards, A. T. 2004. *Hesiod's Askra*. Berkeley.

Edwards, G. P. 1971. *The Language of Hesiod in Its Traditional Context*. Oxford.

Erasmus, D. 1515. *De ratione studii*. In *Opera Omnia Desiderii Erasmi*, edited by J.-C. Margolin, vol. 1, part 2. Amsterdam, 1971. = LP 521–30, in reference to *Erasmi Opera Omnia*, edited by J. Clericus. Leiden, 1703–1706. Tr. B. McGregor, "On the Method of Study." In *Collected Works of Erasmus*, edited by C. R. Thompson, 24:665–91. Toronto, 1978.

Erasmus, D. 1525. *De linguae usu et abusu*. In *Opera Omnia Desiderii Erasmi*, edited by J. H. Waszink, vol. 4, part 1a. Amsterdam, 1989. = LP 656–754, in reference to *Erasmi Opera Omnia*, edited by J. Clericus. Leiden, 1703–1706. Tr. E. Fantham, "The Tongue." In *Collected Works of Erasmus*, edited by E. Fantham and E. Rummel, 29:262–412. Toronto, 1989.

Ercolani, A., ed. and comm. 2010. *Esiodo: Opere e giorni*. Rome.

Fraenkel, H. 1973. *Early Greek Poetry and Philosophy: A History of Greek Epic, Lyric, and Prose to the Middle of the Fifth Century*. Translated by M. Hadas and J. Willis. New York.

Freud, S. 1933. *New Introductory Lectures on Psycho-analysis*. Vol. 22 of *Standard Edition of the Complete Psychological Works of Sigmund Freud*. 1956–1974. 24 vols. Translated under the general editorship of J. Strachey. London.

Hunter, R. 2005. *The Hesiodic Catalogue of Women: Constructions and Reconstructions*. Cambridge.

Hunter, R. 2014. *Hesiodic Voices: Studies in the Ancient Reception of Hesiod's Works and Days*. Cambridge.

Koning, H. 2010. *Hesiod: The Other Poet; Ancient Reception of a Cultural Icon*. Mnemosyne Supplement 325. Leiden, Netherlands.

Lamberton, R., trans. and notes. 2012. *Proclus the Successor on Poetics and the Homeric Poems: Essays 5 and 6 of His Commentary on the Republic of Plato*. Atlanta,GA.

Lévi-Strauss, C. 1963. *Structural Anthropology*. Translated by C. Jacobsen and B. G. Schoepf. New York.

Lord, A. 1960. *Singer of Tales*. Cambridge, MA.

Marsilio, M. S. 2000. *Farming and Poetry in Hesiod's Works and Days*. Lanham, MD.

Montanari, F., A. Rengakos, and Ch. Tsagalis, eds. 2009. *Brill's Companion to Hesiod*. Leiden, Netherlands.

Most, G. W., ed. and trans. 2006–2007. *Hesiod I, Theogony, Works and Days, Testimonia; II, The Shield, Catalogue of Women, Other Fragments*. 2 vols. Cambridge, MA.

Most, G. W. 2016. "Allegoresis and Etymology." In *Canonical Texts and Scholarly Practices: A Global Comparative Approach*, edited by A. Grafton and G. W. Most, 52–74. Cambridge.

Nagy, G. 1990. *Greek Mythology and Poetics*. Ithaca, NY.

Nelson, S. 1998. *God and the Land: The Metaphysics of Farming in Hesiod and Vergil*. New York.

Nietzsche, F. (1997) 2010. *On the Genealogy of Morality*. Edited by K. Ansell-Pearson. Translated by C. Diethe. Cambridge.

Notopoulos, J. A. 1960. "Homer, Hesiod and the Achaean Heritage of Oral Poetry." *Hesperia* 29: 177–97.

Ormand, K. 2014. *The Hesiodic Catalogue of Women and Archaic Greece*. Cambridge.

Parry, A., ed. 1971. *The Making of Homeric Verse: The Collected Papers of Milman Parry*. Oxford.

Pavese, C. O. 1998. "The Rhapsodic Epic Poems as Oral and Independent Poems." *Harvard Studies in Classical Philology* 98: 63–90.

Pucci, P., ed. and comm. 2007. *Inno Alle Muse: (Esiodo, Teogonia, 1–115)*. Pisa, Italy.

Scully, S. 2015. *Hesiod's Theogony From Near Eastern Creation Myths to Paradise Lost*. Oxford.

Segal, C. 1978. "Pentheus and Hippolytus on the Couch and on the Grid." *Classical World* 72: 129–48.

Silk, M., I. Gildenhard, and R. Barrow. 2014. *The Classical Tradition: Art, Literature, Thought*. Malden, MA.

Stamatopoulou, Z. 2017. *Hesiod and Classical Greek Poetry: Reception and Transformation in the Fifth Century BCE*. Cambridge.

Stoddard, K. 2004. *The Narrative Voice in the Theogony of Hesiod*. Mnemosyne Supplement 255. Leiden, Netherlands.

Van Noorden, H. 2014. *Playing Hesiod: The "Myth of the Races" in Classical Antiquity*. Cambridge.

Ziogas, I. 2013. *Ovid and Hesiod: The Metamorphosis of the Catalogue of Women*. Cambridge.

West, M. L., ed. and comm. 1966. *Hesiod: Theogony*. Oxford.

West, M. L., ed. and comm. 1978. *Hesiod: Works and Days*. Oxford.

PART I

HESIOD IN CONTEXT

CHAPTER 2

···

THE HESIODIC QUESTION

···

HUGO H. KONING

INTRODUCTION

THERE is no such thing as a Hesiodic Question. Whereas modern Homeric scholarship has focused from the beginning on fundamental issues like the historicity and identity of the poet, the authorship and chronological order of his poems, the method of composition, and the process of codification (in short, all those questions that together make up the Homeric question), Hesiod had to do without. The main reason for this somewhat uneven treatment is rather straightforward: Hesiod tells us everything we need to know. Hesiod's father, we are told, moved from Aeolian Cymae for financial reasons and settled in Boeotian Ascra (*Works and Days* [hereafter *WD*] 633–40), where his son apparently started his professional life as a shepherd. While minding his flocks, Hesiod was transformed into a poet by the Muses (*Theogony* [hereafter *Th*] 22–35) and composed the *Th*; later, he presumably combined poetic with agricultural activities and composed the *WD*. Hesiod's career flourished sometime during the so-called Lelantine War, since he delivered the winning performance at the funeral games of the Euboean king Amphidamas (*WD* 654–59). Going beyond such basic information as time and place, Hesiod also tells us he has a brother, Perses, a shady character who is averse to hard work and keen on getting Hesiod's part of the inheritance (*WD* 27–42 and elsewhere).

This wealth of biographical information has been taken at face value during the longest part of modern Hesiodic scholarship, contrasting as it does so sharply with Homer's near-complete anonymity. Hesiod became the first "Mensch von Fleisch und Blut" (Wilamowitz 1928: 161), a convenient stopover in the development from the anonymous Homer to the (supposedly) abundantly self-referential lyric poets. Recent scholarship, however, has cast doubt on virtually everything we thought we knew about Hesiod. Perhaps the most important insight triggering this development was that Hesiod's works should be regarded as the products of oral poetry, not created by one historical person having a daytime job as a farmer. Hoekstra (1957) was one of the first to point to the oral quality of Hesiod's works, which was supported by the studies of Edwards (1971) and Janko (1982), among others.[1]

A more nuanced appraisal of Hesiod's self-referential remarks has now reduced formerly held certainties to hypotheses. It thus seems necessary again to ask who Hesiod was, when and where he lived, which poems he composed, and in what order. These matters are discussed below, but first we turn briefly to ancient views.

ANCIENT VIEWS

In antiquity no one seriously doubted the autobiographical information in the *Th* and *WD*. Hesiod was thus regarded as an ancient but historical poet who once lived in Boeotia, suffering from familial issues and the hardships of a farmer's life. Further aspects of his life were provided by a rather detailed ancient biography,[2] which dutifully tells us of his successful career as a poet but afterward focuses on his violent death: while staying in Locris, Hesiod was (rightfully or not) accused of seducing the sister of his hosts, who subsequently killed him. They cast his body into the sea, but it was miraculously brought back to shore by dolphins, so that it could receive a proper burial. The bones of the deceased Hesiod were thought to have healing powers, so much so that his remains were relocated from Locris to Orchomenus to end a virulent plague (Pausanias 9.38.3–4). These anecdotal data, together with some other considerations, suggest that Hesiod was regarded as a *heros*, perhaps with special knowledge concerning the afterlife (for Hesiod's heroization see, e.g., Scodel 1980 and Beaulieu 2004). There is evidence that there was a cult for him on or around Mt. Helicon (cf. Bershadsky 2011).

The ancients paired Hesiod and Homer, putting them in a league of their own in terms of age, genre, scope, and authority. They pictured them as traveling the land to perform their poems—not as bards, however, since the Greeks were unaware of the oral nature of their poems and the concomitant practice of composition-in-performance, but as ancient rhapsodes. The obvious affinity between Hesiodic and Homeric poetry led to a common belief that the poets themselves may have been kinsmen (cf. Koning 2010: 40–42). The important question of priority was subject to serious debate: some believed Hesiod was older (a minority view), while most experts believed that Hesiod was younger; scholiasts occasionally suggest that Hesiod depends on Homer for some of his ideas, and Alexandrian scholars (especially Eratosthenes) considered Hesiod's supposedly more detailed geographical knowledge a sign of posteriority. But most Greeks assumed they were roughly contemporary (and even met in a poetic competition, an idea suggested by Hesiod himself), placing them both in some *illud tempus* at the fountainhead of tradition.[3]

The Greeks almost universally believed Hesiod composed both the *Th* and the *WD*; references to his authorship abound. In Pausanias's day, some Boeotian purists (living around Mt. Helicon) accepted only the *WD* as authentic (even deleting the proem). Most Greeks regarded the *Catalogue of Women* (hereafter *Catalogue*) as composed by Hesiod;

the *Shield* was approached with considerably more skepticism. Some ten other minor poems were occasionally attributed to Hesiod, and although they never reached canonical status, their connection to Hesiod was not forgotten. This situation contrasts rather sharply with Homer, who was at first similarly credited with many minor productions and even some cyclic poems, but from the fourth century BCE onward he was known only for the *Iliad* and the *Odyssey*. Because of Homer's growing reputation, he became more and more "exclusive," whereas all kinds of didactic material were "clustered under Hesiod's name, with little competition from other candidates."[4]

Of the two major Hesiodic poems, the *Th* was seen as composed first. There are no sources on the chronology of the other poems ascribed to Hesiod.

WHO WAS HESIOD?

To many scholars Hesiod's autobiographical remarks are credible enough. For instance, his encounter with the Muses (*Th* 22–35), which led to his initiation as a poet, is generally regarded as a true (although romanticized, or perhaps dreamlike) experience. Similarly, the migration of Hesiod's father from Cymae to Ascra can be seen as an actual, historical event (for why else, scholars argue, would one disclose that one's father was a poor man?); the same goes for Hesiod's voyage to Euboea to participate in the funeral games of Alcidamas, where he presumably performed his *Th* and won (too falsifiable to be untrue) and for his status as a farmer, whose *WD* was meant as an "almanac" of sorts to instruct people on such agricultural activities as plowing, sowing, and harvesting (see *WD* 448–92). There is nothing inherently unreliable or inconsistent about such personal claims, so why not simply trust our narrator?[5]

It is Hesiod's no-good brother who problematizes this reasonable approach. Hesiod accosts him nine times in the *WD* and presents injunctions, reproaches, and pieces of advice that are difficult to reconcile with a singular historical situation. For instance, we understand that Perses has acquired a larger part of the inheritance through bribery (*WD* 37–41), but we hear later on that he is destitute and forced to go around begging (*WD* 394–404); moreover, his appearance in the poem is unsettlingly on and off. The Perses situation caused some scholars to suppose several original poems dealing with different historical situations, later united by a rather careless redactor; others downplayed the problem by arguing, with West, that "Perses is a changeable figure that Hesiod stations in his poem as he chooses" (West 1978: 40)—and this still allows one to maintain that Perses was a historical person.

Needless to say, this second line of approach puts a greater strain on historicist interpreters than the other autobiographical remarks.[6] But there is another option, and that is to regard Perses as fictitious, an interpretation already offered by the scholiast. In this view, Perses is part of the poet's persona and made subject to the rhetorical strategy of Hesiod's work. Inventing a morally challenged brother allows one to offer advice to an equal, with greater hope, perhaps, of the injunctions actually "being stored up in the heart."[7] With Perses fictionalized, the road is open to consider other biographical data in terms of poetic strategy. The father's migration, for instance, could be a way to present oneself as an outsider, allowing the narrator to be more outspoken (cf. Martin 1992). It has also been remarked that many of the names in the autobiography are transparent: "Hesiod" could be taken to mean "he who emits the voice"; his village, "Ascra," translates as "barren oak" (emphasizing the roughness of the *condition humaine* in the Iron Age and the concomitant necessity to work hard); and "Perses" means "Wrecker." Too much, perhaps, to count as coincidence.

The de-historization of Hesiod is part of a larger trend to break with a view of the author as poetically clumsy and naïve, inserting traditional material in a rather unorganized whole, association being his primary structuring principle. The careful crafting of a unique and rhetorically effective persona is part of this new Hesiod, a powerful poet who is in absolute control of his subject matter.[8] This poet is also fully aware of his status as a poet; his self-representation often has (meta)poetical import. One scholar posits, for instance, that "Hesiod treats the farmer's agricultural life as analogous to his own virtuous life as a poet, in that agricultural and poetic excellence both entail intelligent mastery of oneself and one's work, and a special understanding of the justice of Zeus" (Marsilio 2000: 15).

This new Hesiod seems especially bent on establishing his own genre, setting his own poetic project apart from the other type of epic poetry, Homeric heroic epic. A strong (and in my view, convincing) case at hand is a metapoetical reading of a part of the so-called *nautilia*, an episode in the *WD* (618–94) that focuses on seafaring. Hesiod tells us there that he has little firsthand experience in the field of sea travel, since he has only once crossed from Aulis to Euboea, a meager sixty-five meters. He reminds us that this is the same Aulis at which the Greeks of a bygone age once assembled their fleet to sail to Troy, a heroic endeavor that contrasts sharply with Hesiod's own adventure. Many details of this passage, also known as Hesiod's *sphragis* (646–62), can be read metaphorically so as to constitute a "declarative program about poetry" (Rosen 1990: 100), a deliberate opposition to Homeric epic, which is compared to the dangerous enterprise of sailing on the open sea. A similar reading can successfully be applied to Hesiod's differentiation of two kinds of Eris ("Strife," *WD* 11–26), one leading to war and conflict (and heroic epic) and the other to the hard work necessary for approaching the wealth and abundance of one's neighbor (Hesiod's kind of poetry).

Obviously, purely historical interpretations of Hesiod's self-referential remarks on the one hand, and rhetorical/metaphorical readings on the other, are essentially incompatible, though not strictly speaking mutually exclusive. I believe that as in the case of Homer, there must have been a historical poet giving a definite form to Hesiod's poems, a form close to the one we now possess;[9] the internal allusions, the pervasive poetic persona, the careful structure of the poems and their thematic interdependence, the metapoetic passages, and the awareness of other poetic traditions are enough (in my opinion) to prove this. Other scholars, however, argue for multiple authorship, or in a more extreme fashion, are opposed to the notion of a "unitext" of oral poetry altogether.[10]

In my view, the autobiographical information discussed here was part of the traditional material that was given its final shape by a single mind. That means that Hesiod's personal revelations are better understood rhetorically than historically; it is impossible for us to determine the exact proportion between historicity and rhetorical fiction. At the moment the poems were committed to writing,[11] the autobiography was a key factor to unify the corpus and identify the poems as Hesiod's. What we find there is a conscious and assertive poetic voice, claiming a distinct part of the epic tradition for himself; in fact, this very act of stepping forward in the poems already distances this type of epic from Homer's poems.

This, in my view, is about as close as we can get to answering the question "Who was Hesiod?" Naturally, this does not mean that we cannot pinpoint the time and place of the final composition of the poems. However, we need to rely on other data.

WHEN AND WHERE?

There are roughly six categories of data that scholars have used to date Hesiod, that is, to establish the time of the solidification of the Hesiodic poems: (1) references to historical events, (2) ancient sources on Hesiod's date, (3) the sociopolitical reality of Hesiod's world, (4) Eastern influences, (5) verbal echoes and imitations, and (6) linguistic data. These approaches vary considerably in terms of quantity and objectivity of the data; conclusions are seldom undisputed.

The first category of data is relatively empty; the most interesting clue we have is Hesiod's self-avowed participation in the funeral games of Alcidamas, a Chalcean hero who according to the ancients fell during the Lelantine War, a conflict between Chalcis and Eretria.[12] The problem, however, is that the date and duration of this war are heavily disputed, with dates ranging from the late eighth to the early sixth centuries BCE. This uncertainty makes this clue for a *terminus post quem* for the WD rather useless. Other possibly historical events include a reference to the sanctuary of Delphi (*Th* 499), the decoration of Pandora's diadem (*Th* 578–84), and Hesiod's supposed geographical expertise, but none of these is very precise.[13]

The second category, ancient dates, contains much more information. Numerous ancient scholars tried their hand at finding a suitable date for Hesiod, their efforts varying from rather sketchy ("400 years before my own time," Herodotus) to more precise (766 BCE, Eusebius). Needless to say, they arrive at very different conclusions; Matt Kõiv, in a thorough article dealing with exactly this problem, distinguishes no less than seven separate dates (2011: 373–74). It all depends on what particular events or persons Hesiod is synchronized with; examples are the Ionian migration, the lawgiver Lycurgus, and of course, the problematic Lelantine War (the ancients holding onto the same straws as modern scholars). Hesiod is often coupled with other poets, such as Eumelus and Arctinus, and especially with Homer. As we have already seen, the ancients disagree on whether he was earlier, later, or (largely) contemporaneous.

Ancient datings of Hesiod are problematic for modern scholars because they are all speculative and imprecise. Ancient dates tend to be relative to other events and figures that are undatable or historically suspect themselves. The actual arguments for a specific dating are generally speaking either unknown to us (as in Herodotus's statement) or invalid by modern standards (such as datings depending on the assumption that Stesichorus was Hesiod's son). Kõiv concludes that Hesiod "was a floating figure who could have been placed, with or without Homer, at any time between the Ionian migration and the reign of Gyges" (2011: 374). That leaves us with a time span of about 150 years after the Trojan War to the early seventh century BCE.

The third category is Hesiod's sociopolitical climate. It has been obvious to scholars that the world evoked by Hesiod, especially in his *WD*, is quite different from that in the *Iliad* and *Odyssey*. This has generally been taken to mean that Hesiod's poems were composed later. Such reasoning, aimed only at relative dating, taking Homer as its point of departure, is problematized by important considerations, such as the possibility of deliberately archaizing passages and its perhaps overly teleological view. Most important, differences between Hesiod and Homer have also often been explained in terms of another geographical location or social status. The worlds offered by Homer and Hesiod should thus, according to this line of reasoning, be seen as complementary rather than successive; one is produced by an Ionian enlightened spirit singing of the glory of war for the aristocracy, the other by a sullen *Festlandsgriechen* concerned with the everyday realities of regular folk (see Koning 2010: 28–32 for some references).

Be that as it may, numerous scholars believe that Hesiod was younger than Homer because they see traces of historical development in his poems, either in the field of sociopolitics or that of the "history of ideas." An example from the latter field is Hesiod's concept of justice. According to Gagarin (1973), justice is a relatively unimportant theme in the Homeric poems, its primary meaning being "settlement." In Hesiod, however, that meaning is "extended" to cover "(rule of) law" as well, and as such is rather more abstract (given its deification in the *WD*). Connected to this is the common notion that Hesiod's gods are of a higher moral fiber than Homer's (Finley 1972: 141 being one to voice this widespread belief).

More often, development is seen in the context of social, economic, and political change in the Greek world. From the beginning of the twentieth century onward, scholars have focused on what is different from Homer—and this has uniformly been labeled "new," placing Hesiod in a more "advanced" stage of civilization. For example, the Homeric clan system that distributes the land among the extended family is being replaced by a smaller family system depending on direct heirs. There appear to be no centrally organized redistributive systems; instead excess produce is shipped, a sign of the rising importance of sea trade,[14] and there is a growing hostility toward aristocratic rule (some scholars going so far as to proclaim Hesiod a revolutionary).[15] Placing Hesiod in his historical context is immensely important for the understanding of his poetry. As a dating strategy, however, it is imprecise—any date between 730 and 650 BCE fits well.

The fourth category of data deals with Eastern influence on the Hesiodic poems. Scholars like West, Walcot, and Burkert have amply demonstrated that certain passages in the *Th* and *WD* display significant similarities to narratives from the eastern part of the Mediterranean basin.[16] For instance, the backbone of the *Th*, its tale of divine succession, shows a remarkable affinity with a Hurrian myth on the rise to power of the Storm-god Teshub. In theory, such Eastern tales can provide us with *termini postquem* for the Hesiodic poems, but as a *direct* source, they are far too old to be of use in dating Hesiod.

It is possible that Hesiod came to know parts of such ancient mythology during a historical phase commonly known as "the orientalizing period" (ca. 750–650 BCE), characterized by an influx of Eastern artistic, religious, and literary ideas and forms. But tracing such influence is in all cases speculative due to a lack of knowledge concerning the contact between the peoples involved. More important, besides the striking similarities focused on by scholars, there are always numerous differences. This makes it virtually impossible to conclude that Hesiod inherited some theme from another source and subsequently adapted it to his own needs and to exclude the possibility that *both* texts reshape "common and revolving clusters of mythical ideas" (Csapo 2005: 78).

The fifth category of data consists of the earliest influence of Hesiod on Greek poetry. Greek imitations and adaptations are usually considered a reliable *terminus antequem*, since we have a considerably firmer historical grasp of the earliest poets who echo Hesiodic lines. References to Hesiod have been found in, for example, Archilochus, Tyrtaeus, and Semonides, thus providing a *terminus antequem* of about 650 BCE (cf. West 1966: 40). We should acknowledge here that the simple model of lyric poetry borrowing from the epic mother genre has come under pressure in recent scholarship; sometimes, a case can be made that both Hesiod and the lyric poet may be referring to some general pool of ideas and ways of expressing them. Generally speaking, however, lyric references to Hesiod are numerous and pertinent enough to allow the hypothesis that archaic poets were familiar with Hesiodic poetry by around 650 BCE, though not necessarily in a fixed form.

The sixth and final category is linguistic evidence, sometimes regarded as the "hardest" kind because of the quantifiable data used. From Hoekstra (1957) onward, scholars have attempted to date the composition of the Hesiodic poems with the use of linguistic phenomena that are proven or most likely to show linear development. Statistical analysis is applied to such data to provide insights into relative chronology. To be sure, this approach needs to be handled with great care; sometimes the amount of relevant data is dangerously small, and one has to be aware of occasional pitfalls like deliberate archaisms. But an integral study of several criteria avoids such problems and can produce statistically acceptable results.

That is exactly the modus operandi in the thorough and influential study by Richard Janko (1982, updated in 2012), which will here serve as an example. Janko takes all archaic epic poetry of suitable length as his corpus (differentiating among *Th*, *WD*, *Catalogue*, and *Shield*) and applies a total of ten criteria to it (expanded to fourteen in the 2012 article); examples are the use of digamma, the occurrence of the genitive in -οιο, and the length of the accusative plurals of a- and o-stems. The outcome of Janko's analysis is remarkable in terms of consistency and, hence, reliability: almost all criteria support the

same pattern of relative chronology.[17] The *Iliad* and *Odyssey* are seen to be the most conservative poems, and Janko notes a considerable temporal gap before the composition
of the *Th* and *WD*, with the latter slightly more advanced than the former, almost to the
same degree that the *Odyssey* shows signs of further development than the *Iliad*. Janko
estimates that this difference is no more than about twenty to thirty years, allowing for
a hypothesis that both poems are the work of a single person, "whose diction advanced
with his age" (Janko 1982: 82).

The linguistic approach adopted by Janko and others is relative and yields no absolute dates; educated guesses arrive at ca. 700–690 BCE for the *Th* and ca. 670–660 BCE
for the *WD*. This tentative conclusion both is rather specific and relies on the most solid
of all arguments that we have discussed, and it does not contradict the findings of any
of the other five approaches. I can think of no reason why we should not accept these
dates. (In fact, they concur rather nicely with the most recent position of West [2012],
who downplays linguistic and statistical evidence, reconstructing a completely different
relative chronology, but still arrives at a range of 680–660 BCE for the Hesiodic poems.)

Linguistic evidence also comes into play when determining the *place* of composition
of Hesiodic poetry. Needless to say, those taking Hesiod's autobiography seriously naturally believe that his poems were composed somewhere in Boeotia; the poet himself says
he lives in Ascra, close to Mt. Helicon (describing the place as "evil in winter, distressful
in summer, not ever fine," *WD* 640). This could be used to contrast Hesiod once more
to the obviously Ionian poetry of Homer. Scholars like Notopoulos and Pavese consequently argued for a typically Boeotian *language* in Hesiod, largely unaffected by Ionian
poetry. The ubiquity of Ionicisms in Hesiod's poems, however, invalidates this position.
As Edwards and Janko (among others) have demonstrated, Hesiodic diction is over-
whelmingly similar to Homeric diction, so much so that we must conclude that they
are part of the same tradition. There are very few Boeoticisms and remarkably few non-
Homeric features in Hesiod's poems, and in some respects Hesiod's language is even
more Ionian than Homer's. In other words, the Homeric and Hesiodic traditions are
intertwined and must have shared a certain part of their development.

When we assume that Hesiod actually lived in Boeotia (as Edwards and Janko do), we
must conclude that Ionian epic was so predominant as to preclude any other dialect for
the composition of epic hexameter poetry. If we assume that Hesiod's autobiographical
remarks are rhetorical rather than true in a literal sense, we need not pinpoint him in the
direct vicinity of Mt. Helicon (a location that, as some scholars have felt obliged to say, is
in fact rather lovely and hardly qualifies for Hesiod's harsh description).

WHAT POEMS?

Of all major and minor works attributed to the poet, Hesiodic authorship is nowadays
undisputed for the *Th* and *WD*. This certitude in modern scholarship is to a considerable
degree based on the (near-)unanimity of ancient sources, varying from sixth-century

BCE references to the opinions of Alexandrian scholars. The manuscript tradition leaves no uncertainties. The language, diction, style, and meter of both poems are very much alike. And the two poems are thematically related as well, both even containing (different versions of) one and the same tale, that of Prometheus and Pandora.

Recent scholarship has stressed the thematic kinship of the poems, arguing for a large degree of interdependence between the *Th* and *WD*. The best example of this approach is provided by the influential study of Jenny Strauss Clay, *Hesiod's Cosmos* (2003). Clay argues that both poems are mainly concerned with the *condition humaine* and the role played by the gods in establishing it, but that they take a different perspective: "Only from combining both perspectives does the full pathos of the human condition emerge" (2003: 128). The far-reaching thematic unity of the poems is attributed to an overarching *design*: the *Th* and *WD* are meant to be appreciated and can only be fully understood *together*. This final step is not one all scholars are willing to take, but most readers (myself included) generally believe that the thematic overlap and references between the two poems are sufficient proof for single authorship.

As regards the chronological order of the two poems, modern scholars generally agree with the ancient view that the *Th* was composed before the *WD*. The two main arguments are often left implicit: it seems to make sense to mention one's transformation into a poet in the first of one's poems, and similarly to explain the birth of the universe before discussing the way mankind can successfully find a place to live in it. Naturally, Hesiod invites this sensible approach, telling us that the Muses transformed him and immediately ordered him to sing of the gods. Linguistic evidence supports the idea of the *WD* as being slightly more advanced. It thus seems fair to conclude that the poems developed simultaneously, but that the *WD* was committed to writing slightly later than the *Th*.

Thematically speaking, the natural place for the *Catalogue* is between the *Th* and the *WD*, dealing with the heroes and heroines who flourished in the period after the gods established the world as it is and before the dreadful Iron Age of normal humans. Moreover, the end of the *Th* seems to clear the way for the *Catalogue*, mentioning liaisons between gods and human beings that lead to semidivine offspring. Nevertheless, most scholars—when not dodging the question—believe the *Catalogue* was not composed by Hesiod; oft-heard stylistic or genre-related arguments, however, are hardly decisive. On the other hand, content-based arguments supporting Hesiodic authorship are rather weak as well; the evidence is too little and the claim too large. Linguistic evidence, surprisingly, points to a less advanced stage than the *Th* and *WD*, but the data may be warped by the fragmentary nature of the text (see Janko 1982: 85–87). A unanimous verdict on the matter is not forthcoming; but if the *Catalogue* was not composed by Hesiod, it must have been very close to the Hesiodic tradition.

The *Shield* is a different matter altogether; it is quite certainly not Hesiod's, regardless of what ancient scholars believed. The language is considerably more advanced than that of the other poems; the narratological signature is decidedly different (containing, for instance, a disproportionate number of speeches and similes); and the style made one scholar think of "pulp" art, informed by the adage of "more is more" (Martin 2005: 164).

Linguistic evidence, possible historical references, and influence on vase painting put the composition of the *Shield* at roughly 575 BCE, a century later than the other poems.

Many other poems circulated under Hesiod's name; it was presumably their instructional nature that caused them to become attached to the supposed grand master of didactic poetry. Their titles are *Great Ehoeae* (perhaps an expansion of the *Catalogue*), *Melampodia, Aegimius, Wedding of Ceyx, Katabasis of Theseus and Peirithous, Precepts of Chiron, Great Works* (perhaps partly the same as the *WD*), *Astronomy, Ornithomanteia, Idaean Dactyls,* a *Dirge* for a supposed *eromenos* of Hesiod called Batrachus, and *Potters*. Only fragments of these works remain, and nothing much can be said about their authorship and date of composition.

CONCLUSION

The preceding discussion—brief as it may be—demonstrates that Hesiod is just as entitled to a "question" as Homer. In fact, the autobiographical remarks in the *Th* and *WD* pose an interpretative challenge that makes the Hesiodic Question even more riddling and intriguing. The poems, composed in roughly their present form at the beginning of the seventh century BCE, show a remarkable similarity to the Homeric poems in terms of language and dialect mixture. This indicates a remarkable unity and continuity of the archaic epic hexameter tradition. On the other hand, there is a distinctly Hesiodic voice discernible in both the *Th* and *WD*, either rooted in historical truth or constructed for rhetorical purposes. In either case, this voice is spoken by a sophisticated and self-conscious poet weaving his own fabric in the epic megatext, using traditional language for a unique branch of poetry. This poet is beyond our reach, in much the same way as Homer, but he is an unmistakably different poet, who should be studied in his own right.

NOTES

1. Janko (1982: 41) discussing Homer, Hesiod, and the Homeric Hymns concludes that "there is no evidence against their being oral compositions in the fullest sense of the term." Other scholars believe Hesiod composed with the aid of writing; see, e.g., West (1981) and Most (1993).
2. Contained in the *Certamen Homeri et Hesiodi*, which provides the most elaborate account of Hesiod's life. See Lefkowitz (1981: 1–11) for a survey of all ancient biographical information on Hesiod. Ancient biography is notoriously unreliable and implausible, at least in a historical or literal sense; anecdotal information does tell us much on how the poet was viewed and evaluated.
3. See Koning (2010: 40–46).
4. Cingano (2009: 95). His article on the authenticity of the Hesiodic corpus covers ancient views as well.

5. One example of this approach is provided by West in his commentaries to the *Theogony* (1966) and *Works and Days* (1978); a more recent example is the remark of Cassio (2009: 179) that "to all appearances Hesiod was a real person."

6. See the influential article by Clay (1993) on Perses's function as a foil and didactic instrument.

7. *WD* 274 and elsewhere. Cf., e.g., Martin (2004) and Canevaro (2015: 89–99).

8. A critical point in the rehabilitation of Hesiod as a poet is Hamilton (1989). Recent scholars sometimes explain Hesiodic traits traditionally regarded as weak points as intentional and poetically successful. For instance, Nelson (1996) argues that the *WD*'s "section on farming may fail as agricultural instruction simply because this is not what it is intended to do" (45); Hesiod does not tell us what farming is but "how it feels" (48). Similarly, Canevaro (2015: 220) explains the "jumble" of the *WD* as "an ideal didactic tool," created to encourage the addressee to think for oneself and "to spur the student on to higher-level learning."

9. Cf. Cassio (2009: 192): "Hesiod's text was recited in a linguistic shape extremely similar to the one we have."

10. Nagy is the most fervent adherent of seeing early oral poetry as a multitext; see Nagy (2000) in general and, more specifically on Hesiod, Nagy (2009: esp. 295).

11. How we should envisage this process is a matter that is and probably will remain unclear to us; the poet may have done the writing himself, or he could have dictated it to an amanuensis.

12. I am leaving aside a possible reference in the *Shield* to the First Sacred War; see Janko (1986).

13. See West (1966: 41); he claims these references point to a *terminus post quem* of about 750.

14. See the studies of, e.g., Trever (1924); Burn (1936); Millet (1984); Tandy and Neale (1996).

15. See Koning (2010: 273–75) for a brief discussion and references.

16. Notable studies are, apart from West's introduction to his editions of Hesiod, Walcot (1966); Burkert (1992, 2004); West (1997).

17. See Jones (2010) for a detailed criticism of Janko's method and assumptions; see also West (2012) for a more general critique of the linguistic method.

References

Beaulieu, M. C. 2004. "L'Héroisation du Poète Hésiode en Grèce Ancienne." *Kernos* 17: 103–17.

Bershadsky, N. 2011. "A Picnic, a Tomb, and a Crow." *Harvard Studies in Classical Philology* 106: 1–45.

Burkert, W. 1992. *The Orientalizing Revolution: Near Eastern Influence on Greek Culture in the Early Archaic Age*. Cambridge, MA.

Burkert, W. 2004. *Babylon, Memphis, Persepolis: Eastern Contexts of Greek Culture*. Cambridge, MA.

Burn, A. R. 1936. *The World of Hesiod*. New York.

Canevaro, L. 2015. *Hesiod's Works and Days: How to Teach Self-Sufficiency*. Oxford.

Cassio, A. C. 2009. "The Language of Hesiod and the Corpus Hesiodeum." In *Brill's Companion to Hesiod*, edited by F. Montanari, A. Rengakos, and C. Tsagalis, 179–201. Leiden, Netherlands.

Cingano, E. 2009. "The Hesiodic Corpus." In *Brill's Companion to Hesiod*, edited by F. Montanari, A. Rengakos, and C. Tsagalis, 91–130. Leiden, Netherlands.

Claus, D. B. 1977. "Defining Moral Terms in the *Works and Days*." *TAPA* 107: 73–84.

Clay, J. S. 1993 "The Education of Perses: From Mega Nepios to Dion Genos and Back." In *Mega Nepios: Il Destinatario Nell'Epos Didascalico*, edited by Schiesaro, A., P. Mitsis, and J. Strauss Clay, 23–33. Pisa.

Clay, J. S. 2003. *Hesiod's Cosmos*. Cambridge.

Csapo, E. 2005. *Theories of Mythology*. Oxford.

Dowden, K. 2004. "The Epic Tradition in Greece." In *The Cambridge Companion to Homer*, edited by R. Fowler, 188–205. Cambridge.

Edwards, G. P. 1971. *The Language of Hesiod in Its Traditional Context*. Oxford.

Finley, M. I. 1972. *The World of Odysseus*. London.

Gagarin, M. 1973. "Dike in the Works and Days." *Classical Philology* 68: 81–94.

Hamilton, R. 1989. *The Architecture of Hesiodic Poetry*. Baltimore, MD.

Hoekstra, A. 1957. "Hésiode et la Tradition Orale." *Mnemosyne* 10: 193–225.

Janko, R. 1982. *Homer, Hesiod and the Hymns: Diachronic Development in Epic Diction*. Cambridge.

Janko, R. 1986. "The Shield of Heracles and the Legend of Cycnus." *Classical Quarterly* 36: 38–59.

Janko, R. 2012. "πρῶτόν τε καὶ ὕστατον αἰὲν ἀείδειν: Relative Chronology and the Literary History of the Early Greek Epos." In *Relative Chronology in Early Greek Epic Poetry*, edited by Ø. Andersen and D. D. Haug, 20–43. Cambridge.

Jones, B. 2010. "Relative Chronology Within (an) Oral Tradition." *Classical Journal* 105: 289–318.

Kirby, J. T. 1992. "Rhetorics and Poetics in Hesiod." In *Essays on Hesiod*, edited by A. N. Athanassakis, 11–33. *Ramus* 21: 34–60.

Kõiv, M. 2011. "A Note on the Dating of Hesiod." *Classical Quarterly* 61: 355–77.

Koning, H. H. 2010. *Hesiod: The Other Poet. Ancient Reception of a Cultural Icon*. Mnemosyne Supplement 325. Leiden, Netherlands.

Lefkowitz, M. 1981. *The Lives of the Greek Poets*. Baltimore, MD.

Marsilio, M. S. 2000. *Farming and Poetry in Hesiod's "Works and Days"*. Lanham, MD.

Martin, R. 1992. "Hesiod's Metanastic Poetics." In *Essays on Hesiod*, edited by A. N. Athanassakis, 11–33. *Ramus* 21: 11–33.

Martin, R. 2004. "Hesiod and the Didactic Double." *Synthesis* 11: 31–53.

Martin, R. 2005. "Pulp Epic: The *Catalogue* and the *Shield*." In *The Hesiodic Catalogue of Women: Constructions and Reconstructions*, edited by R. Hunter, 153–75. Cambridge.

Millett, P. 1984. "Hesiod and His World." *Proceedings of the Cambridge Philological Society* 30: 84–115.

Morpurgo Davies, A. 1964. "'Doric' Features in the Language of Hesiod." *Glotta* 42: 138–65.

Most, G. W. 1993. "Hesiod and the Textualization of Personal Temporality." In *La Componente autobiografica nella poesia greca e Latina fra realtà e artificio letterario: Atti del Convegno Pisa, 16–17 maggio 1991*, edited by G. Arrighetti and F. Montanari, 73–92. Pisa, Italy.

Nagy, G. 2000. "Review of West." *Bryn Mawr Classical Review* 9: 12.

Nagy, G. 2009. "Hesiod and the Ancient Biographical Traditions." In *Brill's Companion to Hesiod*, edited by F. Montanari, A. Rengakos, and C. Tsagalis, 271–311. Leiden, Netherlands.

Nelson, S. 1996. "The Drama of Hesiod's Farm." *Classical Philology* 91: 45–53.

Notopoulos, J. A. 1960. "Homer, Hesiod and the Achaean Heritage of Oral Poetry." *Hesperia* 29: 177–97.

Pavese, C. O. 1998. "The Rhapsodic Epic Poems as Oral and Independent Poems." *Harvard Studies in Classical Philology* 98: 63–90.

Rosen, R. M. 1990. "Poetry and Sailing in Hesiod's *Works and Days*." *Classical Antiquity* 9: 99–113.

Rutherford, I. 2009. "Hesiod and the Literary Traditions of the Near East." In *Brill's Companion to Hesiod*, edited by F. Montanari, A. Rengakos, and C. Tsagalis, 9–35. Leiden, Netherlands.

Scodel, R. 1980. "Hesiod Redivivus." *Greek, Roman, and Byzantine Studies* 21: 301–20.

Scodel, R. 2014. "Prophetic Hesiod." In *Between Orality and Literacy: Communication and Adaptation in Antiquity*, edited by R. Scodel, 56–76. Leiden, Netherlands.

Tandy, D., and W. Neale. 1996. *Hesiod's "Works and Days": Introduction, Translation and Commentary for the Social Sciences*. Berkeley, CA.

Trever, A. A. 1924. "The Age of Hesiod: A Study in Economic History." *Classical Philology* 19: 157–68.

Troxler, H. 1964. *Sprache und Wortschatz Hesiods*. Zürich.

Walcot, P. 1966. *Hesiod and the Near East*. Cardiff, UK.

West, M. L., ed. and comm. 1966. *Hesiod: Theogony*. Oxford.

West, M. L., ed. and comm. 1978. *Hesiod: Works and Days*. Oxford.

West, M. L. 1981. "Is the *Works and Days* an Oral Poem?" In *I Poemi Epici Rapsodici non Omerici e la Tradizione Orale*, edited by C. Brillante, M. Cantilena, and C. Odo Pavese, 53–73. Padua, Italy.

West, M. L. 1997. *The East Face of Helicon: West Asiatic Elements in Greek Poetry and Myth*. Oxford.

West, M. L. 2012. "Towards a Chronology of Early Greek Epic." In *Relative Chronology in Early Greek Epic Poetry*, edited by Ø. Andersen and D. D. Haug, 224–41. Cambridge.

Wilamowitz-Moellendorff, U. von. 1928. *Hesiodus Erga*. Berlin.

CHAPTER 3

....

SEVENTH-CENTURY MATERIAL CULTURE IN BOIOTIA

....

STEPHANIE LARSON

THE material culture of seventh-century BCE Boiotia rivals the better-studied regions of Lakonia and Attika in myriad ways: Boiotian poleis and other population centers dotted the landscape throughout the region; Mycenaean remains were widespread and surely still visible in the seventh century BCE in many urban centers as well as in the country-side; regional and local sanctuaries were well-known even outside Boiotia; and Thebes, as the largest urban center, produced inscriptions and built complexes whose remains testify to its significance as a regional power at the time. The Catalogue of Ships of course testifies to many archaic and classical predecessors of the poleis, which Hansen, in his detailed inventory, numbers at sixty-five in Boiotia (1996: 73–74).

In light of the present volume, in what follows I discuss a number of significant sites and material remains from Boiotia relevant to the Hesiodic corpus: Askra and the Valley of the Muses; seventh-century BCE Thebes and its sanctuaries of Apollo Ismenios and Herakles; and a brief look at artistic trends in the region. These remains situate Hesiod's Boiotia at the forefront of artistic production in the seventh century BCE and also con-firm Boiotian interests in emphasizing ties to the past.

Hesiod's criticism of the weather conditions in Askra is well-known and not inaccu-rate (*Works and Days* 639–40 [hereafter *WD*]): the canonical site for the acropolis of ancient Askra lies atop a low hill in the eastern Helicon range, which separates this area of Boiotia, the Thespike, from the southwestern area of the region. Like much of inte-rior Boiotia, Askra is cold and windy in the winter and oppressively hot in the summer, without any respite from a sea breeze. The topographer Wallace took pains to exonerate Askra from the ill repute of its bad weather, but there really is no reason to sugarcoat the temperature extremes of central Boiotia (1974: 8–9).

Askra sits opposite the Valley of the Muses, and the extant fourth-century BCE ashlar tower on Askra's acropolis (known as *Pyrgaki* in modern Greek) can easily be seen as one approaches the sanctuary. The site was first identified by Leake with the help of descriptions by Pausanias and Strabo (Leake 1835, II: 490–506; Pausanias 9.28–29; Strabo 9.2.25). The earliest material remains from Askra consist in Geometric and early archaic pottery from the acropolis and lower city area, although traces of a polygonal wall near the acropolis tower were observed by Fossey in his topographical research (Fossey 1988: 142–43).

Bintliff and Snodgrass surveyed the Valley of the Muses intensively and revealed many archaeological sites of both prehistoric and classical dates; they concluded that Askra had been quite a small community with some dependence upon Thespiai ca. 700 BCE (Bintliff 1996: 197) and should be counted as only one among many small hamlets and farmsteads of the valley area (Bintliff 1996: 194–95). Freitag also considers Askra a dependency within the larger territory of Thespiai (2000: 159–70). Edwards argues that in Hesiod's time Askra was for the most part autonomous from Thespiai and subordinate only in judicial matters brought to Thespiai voluntarily (2004: 30–79); while valuable, this argument does not sufficiently address the issue of polis formation and conurbation in Boiotia and throughout central Greece in the early archaic period. Further, Hesiod uses the term *polis* himself at *WD* 222 and 227: What kind of social structure does Hesiod describe in these lines generically, if not a larger nearby community with some control over a smaller community's affairs? Unfortunately the archaeology of Thespiai can never be recovered because of careless excavations throughout the ancient city in the nineteenth century; surface survey, however, shows habitation of some kind at Thespiai from the early Helladic through the Roman periods (Fossey 1988: 137–38).

That said, Hesiod's notable omission of Thespiai from his corpus likely reflects a complicated relationship between Thebes and Thespiai in this early period. Much like Tanagra, which lies on the other side of Boiotia and closer than Thebes to the main eastern sea route of central Greece, Thespiai could control sea trade and travel through its proximity to the far western area of Boiotia and its ports on the Corinthian gulf. This geography alone likely contributed to a certain sense of Thespian self-reliance and Theban unease toward the valley communities, the latter of which may be reflected in Hesiod's marginalization of Thespiai in his work. With this slight, Hesiod also perhaps offers a Thebanocentric riposte to the *Iliad's* Catalogue of Ships, in which Thespiai appears prominently in sixth position in the list of the twenty-nine Boiotian places included in the Boiotian section (Homer, *Iliad* 2.498), whereas the Thebans, notably designated only as the Hypothebai, are listed sixth to last (505). In contrast, in the *WD* Hesiod omits Thespiai from the discussion entirely, and in his section on the "Ages of Man" chooses to emphasize the legends of Kadmos, Oedipus, and Thebes's famed seven gates alongside the tradition of the Trojan expedition (*WD* 161–65). Perhaps anti-Thespian sentiments ran high in Askra around 700 BCE.

Like Thespiai, the sanctuary of the Muses today offers little evidence for activity ca. 700–500 BCE. Most remains, in fact, date from the Hellenistic period and later, both because of the intense spoliation of the sanctuary in antiquity and also because of careless excavations there and errors in archaeological reports of the nineteenth century. Excavated objects and features reputed to have originated at various locations on and around the site cannot be truly verified in terms of find-spot, since the early excavation records from the site are very poor or nonexistent, as Mojsik notes (forthcoming: 5–6, 19–20); furthermore, modern assumptions trend toward positivistic interpretations of the antiquity of cult worship of the Muses in the valley and are often based on retrojection of later sources into these early centuries. Some of the early archaeological material from the site can just as easily be linked to simple habitation and farming of the area, as opposed to verifiable cult activity (Mojsik forthcoming: 7–9, 20; Bintliff, Howard, and Snodgrass 2007: 136).

The sanctuary of the Muses is associated with one piece of relevance in discussing the early life of the site but more importantly for understanding the early production of victory *lebetes* in Boiotia ca. 700 BCE. A rim fragment from a *lebes*, a large, deep bowl often given as a victory prize in athletic contests together with a tripod for display, reputedly came from the sanctuary. Jeffery (1961: 91) dates this particular piece by letter forms to the seventh century BCE, which is within the realm of possibility, since many other fragments of such victory vessels emerged on the Athenian Acropolis with inscriptions in late-seventh-century Boiotian lettering. Although early epigraphists suggested a link between the *lebes* inscription from the Valley of the Muses and Hesiod's dedicatory tripod won in the Chalkidian funerary games of Amphidamas (*WD* 654–59; the inscription: [ℎιαρον ϵ]μι το Ἑλιϙōν[ιο - - -], "I am sacred to Helikonios . . ."), it is enough to acknowledge the widespread existence of such inscribed vessels from the region during the seventh century BCE. Their display on the Acropolis and possibly in the sanctuary of the Muses, as well as their specific mention in the *WD*, testifies to the appeal of Boiotian contests in Attica and also to the production of victory inscriptions within Boiotia during the seventh century BCE. Aside from the extant *lebetes* from Boiotia, Paplexandrou has wondered if Hesiod's own tripod dedication could be seen as a "revolutionary gesture," motivated by his need to proclaim as unassailable his claims to divinely inspired authority and poetic prowess, and "tantamount to the foundation rite of a famous and important sanctuary," since strictly Geometric tripods have appeared only at more well-known Panhellenic sites such as Olympia and Delphi. Extant tripods appear in Boiotia only in the sixth century BCE (Papalexandrou 2008: 255–56). If we accept Hesiod's dedication of a tripod in the Valley of the Muses ca. 700 BCE as a potential reality, then Boiotian *lebes* production and the site of the sanctuary of the Muses take on added significance in light of the dearth of extant contemporary tripod remains from the region.

Hesiod's altar of Zeus is not and likely never will be securely located, although various scholars who insist on an identification link the altar with the chapel of Saint Elias on Helikon above Hippokrene (Wallace 1974: 23–24). The Helikon massif and the Hippokrene spring are linked through myth to Askra, the former having been the site of a sacrifice by the famed heroes Otos and Ephialtes, and the latter having been founded by them (Pausanias 9.29.1). Although only Pausanias attests to this relationship, his account exemplifies the kind of antiquity that the Helikonian mountains and the area associated with Hesiod were thought to have had in later times. Many streams identified with Hesiod still flow from the area near Hippokrene atop Helicon (Aravantinos

1996: 187; Wallace 1974: 14–21 for details). In reflecting on his visits there, Aravantinos describes an archaic wall and possibly an archaic building (judged by masonry style; 1996: 191). At Hippokrene itself (accepted as the modern Kryopegadi by both modern and early topographers [Wallace 1974: 16–17]), Pausanias mentions seeing selections from *WD* inscribed on lead there, and the medium of such a tribute may indicate an early date for such a display, although we will never know (Pausanias 9.31.4).

Thebes offers a wealth of evidence from the seventh century BCE, since, as is well-known, Thebes was a thriving center in the Bronze Age and was continuously inhabited from Neolithic times, although as elsewhere in Greece, the sub-Mycenaean period saw a substantial population decrease. By 700 BCE Thebes was flourishing again and likely served as the most prominent and centralized community of Boiotia; Thebes also lies quite close to Askra and would have been, as it is today, a commercial hub for both Thespiai and Hesiod's more rural community. Thebes is a challenging city for excavation, since most systematic explorations must naturally occur within the modern city and thus in sporadic plots at random locations and often in response to modern construction needs. But the fact that so much fascinating evidence has been unearthed at these accidental locations testifies to the layers waiting to be explored by future scholars. Aside from a number of cemeteries north of the city beginning ca. 800 BCE, the most important Theban sites for the purposes of this volume are the sanctuary of Ismenian Apollo and the sanctuary of Herakles.

The sanctuary of Ismenian Apollo sits on a low hill outside ancient Thebes to the southeast of the Electra gate. The site served as the main civic sanctuary for the city, at least by the time of Pindar, some of whose poems involve the locale and the celebration of the *daphnephoria*, the procession in which a young Theban aristocratic boy carrying various ritual objects decorated with laurel processed to the sanctuary, accompanied by a civic parade, to dedicate a tripod to the god (Pausanias 9.10.4; Papalexandrou 2008: 257–58; Finglass 2007: 27–34; Schachter 2000: 99–119).

According to the earliest excavations on the site of the Ismenion hill, the first temple to Apollo Ismenios was built in the Geometric period, around the same time as the sanctuary of Artemis Orthia at Sparta. The hill's first excavator, Keramopoullos, speculated that this first temple lay on a slightly different southwest-northeast orientation from the later two temples on the site. Mixed deposits of Geometric and Mycenaean sherds, bronzes, pieces of poros, and other stones came to light, all damaged by fire and associated with what he saw as the deliberate destruction of this first temple around 700 BCE. Because of this destruction and later expansion on the site, not much can be said about this putative first building, except that it would likely have been constructed of mud brick and wood with a plaster finish. A larger second temple, now Doric in part, was built on the same spot and finished ca. 600 BCE. The chronology between these two constructions is almost impossible to determine, as Keramopoullos acknowledges (1917: 66–79), and debate has continued about the veracity and chronology of these early buildings (e.g., Pharaklas 1996: 33–57; Kountouri 2014: 222, 229).

Whether or not we provisionally accept Keramopoullos's hypothesis, however, one of the most interesting questions about the building of the first temples on the Ismenion hill during this period pertains to the existence of six Mycenaean chamber tombs in the western area of the hill, over which the extant classical foundations for the third and final temple rest. Exploring these features of the hill, Keramopoullos (1917: 33, 80–98) provides an excellent top plan of the tombs and the temple foundations. Given the veneration that Mycenaean tholoi and chamber tombs received elsewhere in Greece during the Geometric period, it seems odd that the Thebans would choose to construct a cult building to their civic deity on top of such remains. Perhaps they were unaware of the existence of the Mycenaean tombs when the first temple was built, as Keramopoullos suggests (1917: 79). If so, the Thebans chose the hill to situate their temple to Apollo for its proximity to the Theban acropolis (Kadmeia) and for its height: low enough for ease of access from the city but high enough to accent the temple's visibility from the civic center.

That the Geometric Thebans could have been unaware of the Mycenaean burials on the hill seems unlikely, however, for a number of reasons. Many of the hills surrounding Thebes held Mycenaean cemeteries, and given their concentration near the city, it is difficult to imagine that the Thebans of Hesiod's time would not have been aware of these areas (for the Mycenaean cemeteries, see Aravantinos and Fappas 2009: 90–115). Two hills in particular close to the Kadmeia still must have been well-known earlier burial sites: the Amphion hill tumulus and the so-called Tomb of the sons of Oedipous, the latter of which shows an interesting double *dromos*. Both tombs lie in the northern area of Thebes (see Symeonoglou 25, 272–74 [Amphion] and 54, 305 [sons of Oedipous]). One would have expected other Mycenaean tombs on the other hills in the area, and one may even have been able to see traces of them above ground during later periods. Certainly the archaic Thebans who constructed the second temple were aware of the existence of the chamber tombs on the Ismenion Hill, since its polygonal foundations visible even today cut deep into the area of the tombs. It seems to defy credulity to suggest that those who built the first temple in the area remained ignorant of the previous funerary use of the hill.

If we accept that the Geometric Thebans were aware of the tombs' presence, then we must conclude that they built their civic temple to Apollo over the tombs on purpose. They very easily could have located the temple more to the east on the hill to avoid the tombs in the west, shoring up the sloping bedrock in the east with deep foundations in the same way that they did in the west for the archaic and classical temples. Furthermore, the western edge of the archaic and classical temple platforms also lies nearly in the direct center of the line of tombs. If the builders were aware of the tombs and had wanted to protect them or avoid them, they could also have situated the temple platform further to the south, since the Ismenion hill extends comfortably at least fifteen meters further in that direction from the projected edge of the current temple. In this way they would have circumvented at least some of the northernmost tombs. But the builders did not choose to avoid the more complicated task of constructing a massive temple directly atop the tombs, and so the western foundations of the archaic temple, possibly following its predecessor on the site, was built along the north-south line of the Bronze Age tombs. Purposefully situating the temple atop such a number of Mycenaean burials and in close alignment with them suggests that the Thebans were interested in linking their local Apollo with the general idea of the past and with those they perceived to have previously inhabited the citadel.

In Hesiod's Thebes, then, a civic center that most inhabitants of Boiotia must at some point have at least seen towering over southeastern Thebes, inhabitants memorialized their imagined Bronze Age ancestors by setting their main civic sanctuary upon their graves. My speculation about the pro-Theban slant in the *WD* may indicate a certain level of Theban success in promoting an illustrious vision of its ancestry, since there Hesiod sets Kadmos and the tradition of Oedipus in the same category as the Trojan expedition. Outside Thebes, too, we find similar Boiotian attempts at linking themselves to the Bronze Age past through myth, literature, and symbol in the late sixth and early fifth centuries BCE, as I have demonstrated elsewhere (Larson 2007).

The Ismenion hill in Thebes is also linked to a number of significant epigraphic *testimonia*. Most famously, Herodotus visited the site and presents a number of early tripod dedications inscribed with what he calls καδμήια γράμματα, "Phoenician letters" (Herodotus 5.59). He discusses the inscriptions in his exegesis of the Phoenician migration to Athens via Boiotia and uses the Phoenician inscriptions from the Ismenion as proof of Phoenician migration to the region. Herodotus also includes the inscription as evidence for Phoenician importation of the alphabet to Greece, and he does not mention other sites in Boiotia with such inscriptions, even though he denotes Boiotian Tanagra as the specific area in which Phoenicians first were allotted land (5.57).

The veracity of Herodotus's account and these inscriptions has often been questioned (e.g., West 1985: 289–95), as has always been a trend in Herodotean scholarship, and his reports of autopsy also raise the issue of how thoroughly the story of the Phoenician alphabet's arrival through Boiotia was believed in general (Hornblower 2013: 179, after Dewald 1987: 155–59; West 1985: 289–94). The only trace of such a stone to survive on the Ismenion hill is a cutting in the bedrock for a square stone base outside the eastern face of the temple to Apollo and to the immediate right of the entrance area. Given the personae cited by Herodotus as erecting these stones (e.g., Laodamas, son of Eteokles, and Amphitryon, mortal father of Herakles), it seems undeniable that these dedications were concocted relics linking early Thebans to legends from the heroic past (West 1985: 292; Schachter 1981–1994 I: 82 and n5). At the same time, that Herodotus saw pieces that appeared to date from earlier centuries and were associated with heroic figures of Thebes quite probably indicates their existence at an earlier time than his fifth-century BCE visit. That is to say, perhaps Phoenician inscriptions, but certainly inscriptions with early forms of lettering, were displayed at the Theban Ismenion during the seventh century BCE, since the earliest post–Bronze Age archaeological remains on the Ismenion hill predate Hesiod's time. That Herodotus cites surviving inscriptions verbatim elsewhere in his *Histories* lends credence to his citation of inscribed stones at the Ismenion in Thebes (e.g., Hdt. 5.77 and *IG* I³ 501 among others; Larson 2007: 150–52, 159; even West [1985: 283–85] cannot convincingly find fault with Herodotus's reading of *IG* I³ 501). Recent epigraphical work from Thebes also confirms Herodotus's trustworthiness on things Boiotian and the historian's visit to the Ismenion (Papazarchadas 2014: 242, 247).

In sum, we can reasonably say that Herodotus saw archaic inscriptions at the Ismenion that tied the civic sanctuary of contemporary Thebes to the Theban (and non–Trojan War) heroic past, particularly through the local figures of Herakles and Oedipus, and as Papalexandrou remarks (2008: 258–59), these tripod dedications at the shrine of the civic god legitimized these figures as powerful Theban ancestors. The tripod dedication as a symbol of power, prestige, or sovereignty held fast in later centuries throughout Boiotia, and it is in the early archaic period that we can situate its beginnings. The ritual procession associated with the erection of such tripods, the *tripodephoria*, can also be set within this period (see Schachter 1981–1994: I:83; Papalexandrou 2008: esp. 257–77).

One extant inscription from Boiotia helps in locating early inscriptions in the region and perhaps even at the Ismenion hill: the much-discussed Mantiklos Apollo, a small cast bronze warrior statuette with a dedication inscribed along its legs (MFA 03.997; *CEG* 326; Lazzarini 1976: no. 795). Dated to the first quarter of the seventh century BCE , the figurine displays one of the earliest Greek inscriptions from the mainland, written in Boiotian script with somewhat irregular and early "spidery" lettering (Day 2010: 37; Jeffery [1961] 1990: 90). The statuette's style is also Boiotian, as first remarked after its discovery in the late nineteenth century and as maintained since then (Papalexandrou 2005: 85). Because of the various associations between the Ismenion and tripod dedications, as well as the inscription on the statuette which names Apollo, the piece has often been linked, perhaps erroneously, to the Ismenion; it is reported that the original art dealer had specified only that the statuette came "from Thebes" (Jeffery [1961] 1990: 90; see also Day 2010: 35). Papalexandrou has suggested that the Mantiklos Apollo was a tripod attachment (2005: 96n146, 1997), which is an attractive suggestion but will remain difficult to prove because of the preservation of the lower half of the piece. Day argues that the inscription on Mantiklos's legs would have been read or partially read, and that the presence of Homeric metrical vocabulary common also to other inscriptions would have made Mantiklos's dedication easier to perform by the limited audience that would have had access to the statue after its dedication (Day 2010: 37–48, esp. 43–44 on possible levels of reading and literacy in Thebes). Regardless of Mantiklos's function as a tripod attachment or a statuette encouraging speech acts, the statuette's presence in Thebes and possibly at the Ismenion indicates the early presence of written dedications in Thebes in sacred contexts. That so many inscribed dedications appear in the first half of the sixth century BCE across Boiotia further corroborates the relatively advanced development of writing in the region by the late seventh century BCE.

Recent excavations in Thebes have brought to light the nearby and contemporaneous sanctuary of Herakles, a cult site founded in the second half of the eighth century BCE outside the Elektra gate of the city (Aravantinos 2014: 155 and 196). This early date for the foundation of this site is of extreme importance given the dearth of evidence from Geometric Thebes from stratified contexts (Kountouri 2014: 228). The Herakleion also provides enough evidence from the seventh and early sixth centuries BCE to indicate its continued importance and renown during Hesiod's time and through 500 BCE. The Herakleion encompassed worship of a variety of Theban mythical personae connected to the hero but was primarily dedicated to Herakles. A multitude of inscribed objects,

FIGURE 3.1. Lebes fragment from the Theban Herakleion with dedication to Herakles (Thebes Mus. inv. 46854a-b). Permission Archaeological Museum of Thebes.

many of which date to the seventh century BCE, came to light (see Aravantinos 2014: nos. 1a–5, 43, 45, where dates are specified). The excavated area of the sanctuary itself is small but crammed full of hearths, altars, a peribolos wall, an empty tomb, a pseudo-"house," and a well (for an aerial plan and description, see Aravantinos 2015: 88, 90; 2014: 156). The ceramic material, much of it of Boiotian and Theban manufacture, and other small finds were densely deposited (Aravantinos 2014: 194). Aravantinos has identified the site with absolute certainty via a multitude of inscribed dedications to Herakles, such as a late-seventh-century BCE lebes fragment with a clear dedication to Herakles inscribed on it (figure 3.1).

Interestingly, a dedication to Apollo Ismenios was also discovered, which may indicate a cultic relationship between the two sites alongside the contemporaneous dates for the establishment of the sanctuaries in the southeastern area of Thebes outside the Elektra gate (Aravantinos 2014: 202 [for the dedication], 2015: 103).

The Herakleion is of immense importance for Thebes during the eighth and seventh centuries BCE, in part because of a number of important finds, only one of which I include, but which demonstrate the sanctuary's significance and further our understanding of Boiotia and Thebes at the forefront of artistic production in the seventh century BCE. The piece (figure 3.2), a fragmentary *dinos* (mixing bowl), depicts a late Geometric scene that has been identified as the centaur Nessus abducting Deinareia while being shot with arrows from the opposite side of the vase, now broken.

Kalliga dates this piece to the opening decades of the seventh century BCE (2015: 112). Visible on the broken edge of the *dinos* is the top portion of a bow and an arrow pointed slightly downward, as it would be when the archer secures it for drawing. Also visible is the front of a foot; this figure has surely correctly been identified as Herakles. Placed in the seventh century BCE, this piece offers one of the most secure narrative scenes from early Greek art from Herakles's mythology. Moreover, in her discussion of the vase's painting, Kalliga argues for Attic influence but ultimately Theban production (2015: 112); she categorizes the piece as Geometric with strong Boiotian late Geometric traditional motifs (personal communication to author fall 2016; contra Morris 2014). It seems more than likely, then, that the Boiotian artist selected the scene of Nessos, Deianeira, and

FIGURE 3.2 Late Geometric *dinos* depicting Herakles, Nessos, and Deianeira. (Thebes Museum inv. 43488). Permission Archaeological Museum of Thebes.

Herakles because of the intended dedication of the *dinos* at the sanctuary of Herakles (Morris 2014: 100). If these analyses are correct, then this piece from the Herakleion situates early Thebes as a site for production of narrative in ceramics in the seventh century BCE. Corroborating this local production in and near Thebes are two Geometric bell figurines, which came to light as part of a pit deposit near Thebes and are identified as local products on the basis of their clay and other objects within their assemblage (Kountouri 2014: 223–27). The local significance of the legend of Herakles is of course well-known and is corroborated by this vase, and in the context of this important piece it is worth mentioning that contrary to Homer, Hesiod too pays particular attention to Herakles, both in *Ehoiai* and in the *Theogony* (289, 314–19, 332, 534–34, 943, 950–55, 982–83), thereby further accentuating the fame of Thebes in his work, as opposed to any other Boiotian community.

We also find important sculptural contributions near but outside Thebes, most notably at Plataia and Akraiphia, two Boiotian communities with vastly different later relationships to Thebes. From Plataia come two stone tripods sculpted from local stone and imitating bronze tripods of the type discussed above so important to our understanding of seventh-century BCE Boiotia. The stone tripods are decorated with linear incisions resembling but not as exact as Geometric patterns, and Pharaklas dates them to not late in the seventh century BCE (1970: 175–78). From Akraiphia near Lake Hylike in northeast Boiotia come a number of early sculptures and inscriptions from the sanctuary of Apollo Ptoios, a regional Boiotian sanctuary during the eighth and seventh centuries BCE and a more international one in the sixth century BCE (see Schachter 1981–1994: 54; Larson 2014: 420–26). From here come large fragments of dark marble kouroi and korai, accepted as Boiotian products, together with decorative pieces from perirrhanteria, all well-published and similar enough to each other to be known as products of the "Boiotian school" (Kokkorou-Alevra 2014: 10–17). On one kore fragment from this sanctuary we find a dedication to Apollo concluded with an artist's signature, a personal mark that should most likely be included among the three earliest artists' signatures from Greece (Hurwit 2015: 3–4 and 163n5). This evidence thus places Boiotia firmly among those regions producing fine art—sculpture, ceramics, and vase painting—in the seventh century BCE. Given the Nessus fragment from Thebes and the artist's signature from the Ptoion, we might even say that Boiotia, particularly Thebes and its environs, stood at the vanguard of early Greek art during the time of Hesiod.

In later centuries, of course, Hesiod was immortalized as the poetic son of Boiotia, with his tomb reported by Pausanias at Orchomenos (Pausanias 9.38.3). Wallace suggests that Hesiod's relics were taken from Lokris and placed in the Mycenaean tholos at Orchomenos in the fifth century BCE (1985: 168), although neither the chronology nor the veracity of the placement of Hesiod's remains will likely ever be accurately traced. Tales of Hesiod's repatriation seem to have been well-established by Plutarch's time, if not before (Wallace 1985: 165–67; 170n1), and we can thus note the widespread fame of Boiotia's legendary poet in Boiotia for at least a millennium after the canonization of his corpus. Most important, however, is that we can place the Hesiodic corpus within the framework of a vibrant central Boiotian sanctuary and art scene, one that produced monumental sculpture, tripod dedications in both metal and stone, evidence for local workshops and individual artists, and some of the earliest narrative art on the Greek mainland.

References

Aravantinos, V. 1996. "Topographical and Archaeological Investigations on the Summit of Helicon." In *La Montagne des Muses*, edited by A. Hurst and A. Schachter, 185–92. Geneva.

Aravantinos, V. 2010. *The Archaeological Museum of Thebes*. Athens.

Aravantinos, V. 2014. "The Inscriptions from the Sanctuary of Herakles at Thebes: An Overview." In *The Epigraphy and History of Boeotia: New Finds, New Prospects*, edited by N. Papazarchadas, 149–210. Leiden, Netherlands.

Aravantinos, V. 2015. "*Το Τέμενος του Ηρακλέους στη Θήβα.*" In *Αρχαιολογικές Σύμβολες*, vol. 3, *Βοιωτία και Εύβοια*, edited by Σ. Οικονόμου, 85–106. Athens.

Aravantinos, V., and I. Fappas. 2009. "*Τα μυκηναϊκά νεκροταφεία των Θηβών: προκαταρκτικό σχέδιο μελέτης.*" In *Ubi Dubium Ibi Libertas: Studies in Honor of Professor Nikolaos Pharaklas*, edited by Ch. Loukos, K. Xifaras, and K. Pateraki, 87–122. Rethymnon, Greece.

Bintliff, J. 1996. "The Archaeological Survey of the Valley of the Muses and Its Significance for Boeotian History." In *La Montagne des Muses*, edited by A. Hurst and A. Schachter, 193–224. Geneva.

Bintliff, J., P. Howard, and A. Snodgrass. 2007. *Testing the Hinterland: The Work of the Boeotia Survey (1989–1991) in the Southern Approaches to the City of Thespiai*. Exeter, UK.

Day, J. 2010. *Archaic Greek Epigram and Dedication: Representation and Reperformance.* Cambridge.

Dewald, C. 1987. "Narrative Surface and Authorial Voice in Herodotus' *Histories.*" *Arethusa* 20: 147–70.

Edwards, A. 2004. *Hesiod's Ascra.* Berkeley, CA.

Finglass, J. 2007. *Pindar: Pythian Eleven.* Cambridge.

Fossey, J. 1988. *Topography and Population of Ancient Boiotia.* Chicago.

Freitag, K. 2000. *Der Golf von Korinth: Historisch-topgraphische Untersuchungen von der Archaik bis in das 1. Jh.v. Chr.* Munich.

Hansen, M. 1996. "An Inventory of Boiotian Poleis in the Archaic and Classical Periods." In *Introduction to an Inventory of Poleis,* edited by M. Hansen, 73–116. Copenhagen, Denmark:.

Hornblower, S., ed. and comm. 2013. *Herodotus: Book Five.* Cambridge.

Hurwit, J. 2015. *Artist Signatures in Ancient Greece.* Cambridge.

Jeffrey, L. H. 1961. *The Local Scripts of Archaic Greece.* Oxford.

Kalliga, K. 2015. "Ιερά δώρα: κεραμικά αναθήματα από δύο Βοιωτικά ιερά." In Αρχαιολογικές Σύμβουλες, volume Γ, Βοιωτία και Εύβοια, edited by S. Oikonomou, 107–23. Athens.

Keramopoullos, A. 1917. Θηβαϊκά. Athens.

Kokkorou-Alevra, G. 2014. Entries I.1.2–I.1.5 in "Αγάλματα Γυναικεία,." In Κατάλογος Γλυπτών. Εθνικό Αρχαιολογικό Μουσείο I.1. Γλυπτά των αρχαϊκών χρόνων από τον 70 αιώνα εως 480 π. X, edited by G. Despinis and N. Kaltsas, 1–90. Athens.

Kountouri, E. 2014. "Γεωμετρική Θήβα: τα δεδομένα από τις σύγχρονες έρευνες." In 100 Χρόνια Αρχαιολογικού Έργου στη Θήβα, edited by B. Aravantinos and E. Kountouri, 213–29. Athens.

Larson, S. 2007. *Tales of Epic Ancestry: Boiotian Collective Identity in the Late Archaic and Early Classical Periods.* Stuttgart.

Larson, S. 2014. "Thebes in the *Odyssey's* 'Catalogue of Women.'" In *Theban Resonances in Homeric Epic,* edited by C. Tsagalis, 412–27. Trends in Classics 6.2. Berlin.

Lazzarini, M. 1976. *Le formule delle dediche votive nella Grecia arcaica.* Rome.

Leake, W. 1835. *Travels in Northern Greece II.* London.

Mojsik, T. Forthcoming. *From Hesiod's Tripod to Thespian Mouseia: Archaeological Evidence for Early Cult Activity in the Thespian "Valley of the Muses".*

Morris, S. 2014. "Artists in Motion: Proto-attic and Related Pottery of the Seventh Century BC." In *Egrapsen kai Epoiesen: Studies in Greek Pottery and Iconography in Honour of Professor Michalis Tiverios,* edited by P. Valavanis and E. Manakidou, 95–104. Thessaloniki, Greece.

Papalexandrou, N. 1997. "Listening to the Early Greek Images: The 'Mantiklos Apollo' Reconsidered." *American Journal of Archaeology* 101: 345–46.

Papalexandrou, N. 2005. *The Visual Poetics of Power: Warriors, Youths, and Tripods in Early Greece.* Lanham, MD.

Papalexandrou, N. 2008. "Boiotian Tripods: The Tenacity of a Panhellenic Symbol in a Regional Context." *Hesperia* 77: 251–82.

Papazarchadas, N. 2014. "Two New Epigrams from Thebes." In *The Epigraphy and History of Boeotia: New Finds, New Prospects,* edited by N. Papazarchadas, 223–51. Leiden, Netherlands.

Pharaklas, N. 1970. "The Stone Tripods from Plataea." *Annual of the British School at Athens* 65: 175–78.

Pharaklas, N. 1996. Θηβαϊκά. Athens.

Schachter, A. 1981–1994. *Cults of Boiotia.* Bulletin of the Institute of Classical Studies Supplement 38, vol. 1.

Schachter, A. 2000. "The Daphnephoria at Thebes." In *Presenza e funzione della città di Tebe nella cultura greca: Atti del convegno internazionale (Urbino, 7–9 luglio 1997)*, edited by O. Bernadini, 99–119. Pisa, Italy.

Symeonoglou, S. 1985. *The Topography of Thebes from the Bronze Age to Modern Times*. Princeton, NJ.

Wallace, P. 1974. "Hesiod and the Valley of the Muses." *Greek Roman and Byzantine Studies* 15: 5–24.

Wallace, P. 1985. "The Tomb of Hesiod and The Treasury of Minyas at Orchomenos." In *Proceedings of the Third International Conference of Boiotian Antiquities*, edited by J. Foseey, and H. Giroux, 165–71. Amsterdam, Netherlands.

West, S. 1985. "Herodotus' Epigraphical Interests." *Classical Quarterly* 35: 278–305.

CHAPTER 4

....

IN HESIOD'S WORLD

....

DAVID W. TANDY

THE goal of this chapter is to provide a backdrop and analysis of Hesiod's world. Although we see precious little of the mortal world in the *Theogony* (hereafter *Th*), what we do see there does not contradict what we see in *Works and Days* (herefter *WD*). There are community leaders from a nearby polis in both poems called *basilēes*, in the *Th* highly regarded and effective, in *WD* less so on both counts. A close look at Hesiod's relationship with the *basilēes* reveals much about *WD*. What did the world of Hesiod's audience look like? Can we discern what his social and economic standing was? Who controlled production and its distribution in markets and by trade? Where did Hesiod's world fit into the bigger picture of the Aegean and eastern Mediterranean? Let us frame things with a look at this last question and then focus on Hesiod's farm; then we will look at his relations with the *basilēes*, who appear to have played important roles in Hesiod's and the region's connections to the framing outside world.

When Hesiod's (or "Hesiod's")[1] father left Aeolian Kyme[2] for Ascra in the second half of the eighth century BCE, there was a new energy coursing through the Aegean. In response to population growth and state formations, there was intensification and extensification of agricultural production. While Hesiod's father looked for a new place to live and raise a family, other Greeks sought their fortunes abroad: first Euboeans to Pithekoussai and other points west, then Corinthians, who appear to have become the leading players in the west by the end of the eighth century BCE. Mainland Greeks participated in the eighth- and seventh-century BCE east-west trade corridor along coastal Thrace from Torone to Troy. Fully developed engagement with the Near East after 700 BCE accomplished an integration of the Aegean with the outside world that was fuller than at any time since the eve of the catastrophe that marked the end of the Mycenaean Bronze Age.

Eastern goods had been flowing into the Aegean, especially to Lefkandi and Athens, since the ninth century BCE, and later into other settlements, especially Eretria and then Corinth. We cannot say that prosperity, as it worked its way unevenly through mainland Greece, had reached Hesiod's village of Ascra in the Valley of the Muses, which was connected to the world outside it, but as we shall see, this connection was economically and culturally flimsy as well as politically perilous. In fact, Hesiod's account of his life in seventh-century BCE Boeotia is in one important sense an account of the political and economic integration of Ascra into the reality of the nearby polis of Thespiae,[3] now just beginning to flex its regional political muscle.

HESIOD'S QUOTIDIANALITIES AND THE MEANS OF PRODUCTION

Hesiod tells us a lot about his farm and his life on and around it. After a long abandonment, Ascra had been resettled shortly before ca. 900 BCE (Bintliff and Snodgrass 1985b: 5); by the time of Hesiod's father's arrival, the best plots of land would have been spoken for, forcing him to take an available parcel in the Valley of the Muses at the east foot of Mt. Helikon, in or near Ascra, a "substantial village" (Snodgrass 1985: 90; although still quite smaller than its classical descendant, which was home to 1,500–1,600 souls [Bintliff et al. 2007: 148]), eight kilometers west of Thespiae, precisely what Strabo reports (9.2.25: ὅσον τεττaράκοντα σταδίους, "around forty stadia"). Ascra was the lone settlement at the time in the valley, according to the Boeotia Survey (Bintliff and Snodgrass 1985a: 129; further discussion in Bintliff et al. 1999).

Hesiod's household (*oikos*) was near Ascra town. In his fields Hesiod grew grains, mostly wheat (lower yields but more nourishing) and barley (higher yields but less nourishing), as well as vegetables (which he does not mention), vines, and olive and fruit trees. In good years there would be a surplus (a "cash crop"), but there is nothing in Hesiod's presentation of his farm that suggests that a surplus was a regular outcome or even a reasonable expectation; nevertheless, it appears always to be the goal. His large animals (bovids) would probably have grazed common pastureland (Hesiod mentions a cow "fed in the woods" at 591), while his goats and sheep would have found fodder on his fallow land when not being pastured on higher ground (e.g., at *Th* 23).

The *oikos* was, at least since the start of the first millennium BCE, the essential unit of Greek life. This is clearly the case in the Homeric epics, the great heroes each having an *oikos* of usually stupendous magnitude, both in number of personnel and productive capacity. Ordinary people in the epics have more modest setups, but all persons belong or work for *oikoi*. There are many people living on Hesiod's *oikos*. He has a son, from which we may infer that he has a wife. If we assume that he follows his own advice, we can further infer that he has a slave woman who follows his plough and keeps his house in order (405–6); another (the same?) woman works in the house (603–4). A male (free?) laborer takes a turn at the plough (445–46); he or a different man (called a *dmōos*, "slave") covers the seeds as Hesiod ploughs his field (469–70). From the outside, there is the occasional dependent laborer who is resident seasonally (600–603) and the irregular hiring of a friend (370). In addition to the slaves already mentioned, there are others (or the same two men?) who build granaries (502–3), help with the reaping and processing (573, 597), and plough the harvested field for fallow (607–8). This leads to a total of seven to nine persons; in addition, there may be unmentioned sons or daughters, slaves (perhaps two or more), and seasonal or part-time workers. From this roster we may conclude that Hesiod's *oikos* needed to be big enough to support ten to twelve full-time people.

How big was the farm? It was certainly larger than a "family farm." The size of the late Attic zeugite farm, which is presumed to have fed four adults and children, is generally agreed to have been in the range of 9 to 13.5 acres (Burford-Cooper 1977: 168–70; Amouretti 1986: 205; Gallant 1991: 86–87; Foxhall 1992: 157; Bintliff et al. 2007: 145–48; Halstead 2014: 61). Victor Hanson (1995: 107) preferred "five to fifteen acres";[4] by the simple arithmetic of about 2 acres per person, Hans van Wees (2013: 227) has recently suggested a size of about 20 acres.[5] With additional acreage for fruit and olive trees, providing his population with grains as well as vegetables, fruit and oil, and wine, the farm may be thought to be about 25 acres. A farm this size would grow what Hesiod says he grows and would feed the residents we have counted. It would also provide, in good years and with vigorous management, a surplus for storage and market, more on which below.

Let us pause and contemplate what we are to make of the size of Hesiod's farm. This is no family farm; it is twice the size of a family farm. Hesiod (436–37) recommends (and so presumably uses) a pair of mature (nine-year-old) male bovids to plough with. This betrays a commitment to "extensive surplus-generating agriculture" (Halstead 2014: 60–61); if his ambition were limited to subsistence and autarchy, Hesiod could have used cows for ploughing. He also would not have had so many extrafamilial persons in residence. But, he tells us,

> ῥεῖα δέ κεν πλεόνεσσι πόροι Ζεὺς ἄσπετον ὄλβον·
> πλείων μὲν πλεόνων μελέτη, μείζων δ' ἐπιθήκη.

Easily would Zeus give unquenchable prosperity to more persons. The care of more hands is more, and the surplus is greater. (379–80)

Both the extra dependent laborers on the farm and Hesiod's ability to bring in extra labor as needed were important factors in the mobilization of human labor[6] for reaping and harvesting, another characteristic of extensive surplus-producing agriculture (Halstead 2014: 121).

Recognition of this type of agricultural regime allows us to see in fact a close parallel between Hesiod's life and that of the happy *basileus* on the Shield of Achilles in the *Iliad*, where the *basileus* admires the happiness of his gathered workers during the reaping of the grains:

> ἐν δ' ἐτίθει τέμενος βασιλήϊον· ἔνθα δ' ἔριθοι
> ἤμων ὀξείας δρεπάνας ἐν χερσὶν ἔχοντες.
> δράγματα δ' ἄλλα μετ' ὄγμον ἐπήτριμα πῖπτον ἔραζε,
> ἄλλα δ' ἀμαλλοδετῆρες ἐν ἐλλεδανοῖσι δέοντο.
> τρεῖς δ' ἄρ' ἀμαλλοδετῆρες ἐφέστασαν· αὐτὰρ ὄπισθε

παῖδες δραγμεύοντες ἐν ἀγκαλίδεσσι φέροντες
ἀσπερχὲς πάρεχον· βασιλεὺς δ' ἐν τοῖσι σιωπῇ
σκῆπτρον ἔχων ἑστήκει ἐπ' ὄγμου γηθόσυνος κῆρ.
κήρυκες δ' ἀπάνευθεν ὑπὸ δρυΐ δαῖτα πένοντο,
βοῦν δ' ἱερεύσαντες μέγαν ἄμφεπον· αἱ δὲ γυναῖκες
δεῖπνον ἐρίθοισιν λεύκ' ἄλφιτα πολλὰ πάλυνον

On it [Hephaistos] placed an estate of a *basileus*, where workers (*erithoi*) were harvesting, holding sharp sickles in their hands. Some handfuls were falling in rows to the ground along the furrow, while others the sheafbinders were binding in ropes. Three sheafbinders stood right there, while behind them boys, gathering handfuls and stacking them in the crooks of their arms, were handling them over energetically. Among them in silence at the furrow stood a *basileus*, scepter in hand, delighting in his heart. Heralds, separately under an oak, were busy with the meal, and they were attending to a great ox they had sacrificed; and the women sprinkled the lunch for the laborers (*erithoi*) with much white barley. (*Iliad* 18.550–60)

Note how similar is Hesiod's description of his role as supervisor of his workers (here called *dmoes* and *erithoi*, as on the Shield):

δμωσὶ δ' ἐποτρύνειν Δημήτερος ἱερὸν ἀκτὴν
δινέμεν, εὖτ' ἂν πρῶτα φανῇ σθένος Ὠρίωνος,
χώρῳ ἐν εὐαεῖ καὶ ἐυτροχάλῳ ἐν ἀλωῇ.
μέτρῳ δ' εὖ κομίσασθαι ἐν ἄγγεσιν· αὐτὰρ ἐπὴν δὴ
πάντα βίον κατάθηαι ἐπάρμενον ἔνδοθι οἴκου,
θῆτά τ' ἄοικον ποιεῖσθαι καὶ ἄτεκνον ἔριθον
δίζησθαι κέλομαι· χαλεπὴ δ' ὑπόπορτις ἔριθος·

Urge your slaves (*dmoes*) to thresh out Demeter's holy grain, whenever the might of Orion first appears, in an airy place and on the well-rolled threshing floor. With a measuring scoop give heed to [storing] it well in vats. When you have put away all of your sustenance under lock inside your *oikos*, I exhort you to put your worker (*thes*) out of the *oikos* and to search for a hired girl (*erithos*) without a child; a hired girl (*erithos*) with a baby at her breast is hard. (597–603)

We see here, in parallel to the Homeric *basileus*, Hesiod's careful supervision of his workers and his ability to mobilize workers when they are needed (when Orion rises) and to cast off dependent labor when the labor is no longer needed.[7] Here is the place to compare Laertes's farm in the *Odyssey*, where he lives with an elderly slave and his wife and six sons as well as unnumbered slaves or forced laborers (*dmoes anankaioi: Odyssey* 24.210) who eat and sleep outdoors; consider too the rich suitor Eurymachus's offer to the disguised Odysseus of a one-year contract as an agricultural laborer, which has the ring of an offer often made (*Odyssey* 18.357–61). It is easy to see through these vignettes that Hesiod has much in common with these Homeric *basilees*.

It was de Ste. Croix's considered opinion that Hesiod saw himself as a peer of the *basilees* in Thespiae, and he had no difficulty lumping together Hesiod and Theognis, "a class-conscious aristocrat if ever there was one."[8] I agree with him at this point in this essay—there will be an additional, contradictory assessment later—because it is impossible not to observe that Hesiod has much more in common with his addressees and the *basilees* in the polis than with those whose dependent labor Hesiod exploits: hired men and women, slaves. There is no getting around the fact that in *WD* Hesiod is addressing people no different than himself; he is addressing neither his dependent laborers nor the few specialists on the landscape (the potter and the carpenter at 25, the smith in his forge at 493, perhaps even the ploughman at 445–46). Nevertheless, Hesiod's awareness of the chasm between the class of nondependents to which he belongs and those on the other side is betrayed by his concern for the working conditions of his dependents; note his tired slaves' "poor knees" (608: φίλα γούνατα) and his sense of justice: prosperity should not be achieved at the cost of others' misfortune (321–26), an attitude that underlies the contradiction in his relations with Thespiae and Ascra.[9]

Hesiod's interest in work is not only as a spectator. It is an old but valuable commonplace to remark on the hard work that Hesiod advocates to his fellow producers. The word Hesiod uses for work is *ergon*, which was also used as a word for farm. Everyone with a successful farm works hard:

ἀλλὰ σύ γ᾽ ἡμετέρης μεμνημένος αἰὲν ἐφετμῆς
ἐργάζευ, Πέρση, δῖον γένος, ὄφρα σε Λιμὸς
ἐχθαίρῃ, φιλέῃ δέ σ᾽ ἐυστέφανος Δημήτηρ (300)
αἰδοίη, βιότου δὲ τεὴν πιμπλῇσι καλιήν·
Λιμὸς γάρ τοι πάμπαν ἀεργῷ σύμφορος ἀνδρί·
τῷ δὲ θεοὶ νεμεσῶσι καὶ ἀνέρες ὅς κεν ἀεργὸς
ζώῃ, κηφήνεσσι κοθούροις εἴκελος ὀργήν,
οἵ τε μελισσάων κάματον τρύχουσιν ἀεργοὶ (305)
ἔσθοντες· σοὶ δ᾽ ἔργα φίλ᾽ ἔστω μέτρια κοσμεῖν,
ὥς κέ τοι ὡραίου βιότου πλήθωσι καλιαί.
ἐξ ἔργων δ᾽ ἄνδρες πολύμηλοί τ᾽ ἀφνειοί τε,
καί τ᾽ ἐργαζόμενος πολὺ φίλτερος ἀθανάτοισιν. (309)

ἔργον δ᾽ οὐδὲν ὄνειδος, ἀεργίη δέ τ᾽ ὄνειδος. (311)
εἰ δέ κεν ἐργάζῃ, τάχα σε ζηλώσει ἀεργὸς
πλουτεῦντα· πλούτῳ δ᾽ ἀρετὴ καὶ κῦδος ὀπηδεῖ.

But you, ever mindful of our bidding, get to work, Perses, glorious offspring, in order that Hunger may detest you, and revered, goodly crowned Demeter may be fond of you and fill your granary with sustenance. For Hunger is an entirely natural companion for a man who is a non-worker; gods and also men resent him who lives as a non-worker, in temperament like the stingless drones who wear away the labor of the bees by eating, non-workers that they are. Let it be important to you to keep your own works properly organized so that your granaries may become full of seasonal sustenance. It is from works that men are many-sheeped and rich, and the man who works is much dearer to the deathless ones. . . . Work is no reproach; not-working is a reproach. If you work, the non-worker will quickly envy you as you become wealthy. Success and renown attend upon wealth. (*WD* 298–309, 311–13)

Hesiod leaves little to the imagination elsewhere as well (382): ὧδ' ἔρδειν, καὶ ἔργον ἐπ' ἔργῳ ἐργάζεσθαι, "do these things, and pile work upon work upon work." Work is constant and must be done at the right time.[10] Hesiod performs much manual labor himself, as implied in the exhortations to his fellow growers, but it is also clear that after "*ergon* is best," his next mantra was surely εὐθημοσύνη γὰρ ἀρίστη / θνητοῖς ἀνθρώποις, κακοθημοσύνη δὲ κακίστη, "good management is best for mortal people, while bad management is worst" (471–72).[11]

SURPLUS PRODUCTION

Let us follow what happens to Hesiod's surplus should he generate one. Hesiod's commitment to extensive surplus agriculture means it is his goal to grow as much as possible and prepare to transport the surplus out of his *oikos* into his community as well as overland to the sea, where he can move it locally in his own small ship (624–26, 630–32), thus participating in the eternal rhythm of Mediterranean cabotage (Horden and Purcell 2000), or farther along in another man's vessel (643).[12] If he had knowledge of a nearby shortage, he might take his surplus in his own ship. (Hesiod's absurd remark that he has never been to sea except once, to compete at Chalkis [650–57], is contradicted by his detailed instructions on small-ship maintenance [622–29] and the description of his own cabotage.) It would appear otherwise that he would put his excess into the ship of another man, who would take it out tramping or to a specific destination based on knowledge that *he* possessed.[13] It is a curious omission—we will return to this below—that Hesiod makes no mention of taking production to market locally.

Hesiod speaks of his seafaring as one *ergon* among many *erga* (Mele 1979: 40–46, 53–57; Tandy 1997: 75, 212–14); in winter he even hangs his steering oar over the fireplace (45, 629)! He must have taken his surplus by wagon to the Gulf of Corinth, probably to the harbor at Kreusis. He would have traveled there via Thespiae on the Haliartos-to-Kreusis road (Farinetti 2011: 160); there is an old stone road, possibly Mycenaean, that runs from Thespiae to Kreusis, clearly indicated in Buck (1979: iv, map 2) (see description in Pritchett 1965: 54–55; discussion in Tandy 1997: 213). (Lake Kopais was too marshy to navigate in anything other than a canoe,[14] and the rivers to the Euboeic Gulf were not navigable.) Hesiod advises keeping most of one's surplus at home (689–90) and being careful about putting too much production in one's wagon (692–93), which reflects his aversion to risk, as he makes sure that he has plenty of grain in storage and that his wagon will survive to roll another day. It is this same risk aversion that we see when he tells his listeners to admire a small ship but put the surplus in a big ship, while adding that the more one loads on the ship the larger will be one's *kerdos* ("profit"), weather permitting (643–45).[15] We may be getting an archaeological glimpse of this type of trade in the recently excavated shipwrecks off southwestern Anatolia from the late seventh and early sixth centuries BCE, ships that operate regionally but have clearly multiple sources from which they are drawing their mostly agricultural wares for sale elsewhere (Greene, Lawall, and Polzer 2008; Greene, Leidwanger, and Özdaş 2011). These may be the very sort of "big" ship that Hesiod talks about.

Let me finish this part of the discussion by asking: What about autarchy? Isn't Hesiod supposed to be a paragon of Greek self-sufficiency and subsistence? It is becoming clear, in the study of archaic Greeks both at home and on the colonial trails, that the "notional autonomous individual" is a "phantom"; the reality of Hesiod's world is not so much a landscape of independent producers as it is one dominated by "people-devouring *basilēes*" (*Iliad* 1.231), upon whom many are dependent (thus Purcell 2005: 116). Archaic agriculturalists such as Hesiod sought "maximum productivity and profit-seeking, extreme exploitation of labor" (van Wees 2009: 450). Hesiod and everyone else in his position was by necessity maximizing production as a strategy against the bad years (or decisions) that could lead to debt and land alienation or other conditions of dependency like the one Perses found himself in. In other words, the annual cycle of agricultural battle was fought as much against the elements as it was against the social world in which one found oneself. There must have been a great variety of mechanisms by which these maximizers distributed their surpluses before they reached their sell-by dates. There is evidence of reciprocal distribution within the community: "Take good measure from a neighbour, and pay it back well, with the same measure, or better if you can, so that you may later find him reliable should you need him" (349–51), and no doubt further afield; there were opportunities to sell at a distance, as we just saw. But especially striking, given that Hesiod must in social terms have been tied to, even allied with, the *basilēes* in Thespiae, is that Hesiod was taking his surplus away from Ascra but *not to Thespiae*, a sign that there was tension between Ascra and Thespiae in addition to the affinities between those who were powerful in Thespiae and those who were independent, for the most part, in the valley.

We may draw the following conclusions: Hesiod is in control of his production because he owns or controls his land; he is overseeing an extensive agricultural regime that generates surpluses derived specifically and entirely from slave and dependent or forced labor; thus Hesiod's is a slave economy.[16] That is why Hesiod is able to observe that "the care of more hands is more, and the surplus is greater" (380), which in turn reveals the ample availability of labor (in spite of a sparse population), for the gain to a farmer from hiring extra labor (the marginal product of labor) is only efficient if workers have few options and so wages are low (see note 6). It is necessary then to conclude, perhaps counterintuitively given the animus that he feels for the *basilēes*, that Hesiod should be lumped together with the very *basilēes* for whom he has no good things to say in *WD* but whom he identified as godlike in the *Th*. Only the *basilēes* and the free farmers of the Hesiodic ilk are not dependent; they belong to a class to which everyone else in Hesiod's world does not.

HESIOD'S PERIPHERALITY, PEASANT
THEORY, AND THE MEANS OF ALLOCATION

Let us turn to Hesiod's animus toward the center. There is a deep division between Thespiae and Ascra, according to Hesiod. What happened that Hesiod's attitude could be so changed between the *Th* and *WD*? If in fact the *Th* is the *hymnos* (657) performed by Hesiod at the funeral games of Amphidamas the War-Wise (654–56), we would expect the approach we have there to the *basilées* who would have been in attendance. Funeral games aside, we are told in *WD* that there has been a falling out between Hesiod and his brother Perses; they fought over the *klēros* that they inherited partibly from their father, with Perses then successfully pursuing more from Hesiod's share (35–39). Perses at some point lost his share by an unclear mechanism, but it is clear that the *basilées* in the agora in Thespiae were complicit in that loss by making a ruling or a judgment (*dikē*), and it looks as if debts (*chrea*: 404, 647; Tandy and Neale 1996: 39–42) played a critical role in Perses's predicament. Hesiod considers Perses's time spent in the agora as explaining both Perses's further pursuit of the family wealth as well as his loss of his own share of it (27–39). That is the specific reason for Hesiod's dissatisfaction with the *basilées* in Thespiae.

There is also an important ideology-driven structure in place in Hesiod's world that helps to explain this poor opinion of the *basilées*. Many scholars have seen in Hesiod's world a typically peasant setting: a community of autarchic and reciprocal, agricultural small-production units. This is well documented over many locations and times: Robert Redfield (1953, 1956) was the Anglophone pioneer in peasant studies, and Eric Wolf was influential later and remains so today, emphasizing the role of the emergence of the state, which I call the "center," as the sine qua non of the emergence of a peasantry (Wolf 1966: 11). E. K. L. Francis (1945) first brought the analysis of the peasant as autarchic smallholder to bear on Hesiod; Paul Millett, who has become the common referent for Hesiod qua peasant, showed that the society of Hesiod is coherently peasant but that the expected domination from the city is not quite in place: "links beyond the οἶκος normally extended no further than the local community" (Millett 1984: 91). The lack of agreement between yes-peasant (e.g., Millett 1984; Tandy and Neale 1996) and no-peasant (e.g., Hanson 1995: esp. 98; Edwards 2004: 2–5; Osborne 2009: 139; van Wees 2009: esp. 450, 464) may be due to the mixing of two issues: (1) whether "peasant" is the correct term to use (see Edwards 2004: 4–5) and (2) whether we identify in Hesiod's world the domination of the center (as Millett does not). What defines a peasant is the relationship between this group that is away from the center and those who are at the center of the broader economic and social formation. Autarchy *appears* to be an outstanding characteristic of this group of outsiders, but that is primarily because of the group's commitment qua group and its resolve to maximize its independence from the center. But everywhere we look there are rich peasants and poor peasants. Dependence of the outsiders on the center first develops and then grows as the gravity of the center grows, but there is also a fierce, counteractive streak of independence that enables the peasants to be totally or nearly independent in terms of production. The result is the illusion of autarchy.

The tension spikes and the division widens when the outsiders are forced to reckon with those in the center. This can happen in many ways, but two are happening here in the Valley of the Muses: the center is expanding its political influence through the judicial pronouncements of the *basilēes*, and the center seems to be controlling a local agricultural market that is bringing bad results for those in the valley seeking outlets for their production. There is, of course, a difference between the peasant producing cash crops and the peasant looking for opportunities to move occasional surpluses, but it is only a difference of degree, for the structure and the advantage held by the center are the same in both scenarios; this advantage, great or small, firms up the structural division between central power and the peasantry. This is what we are seeing in *WD*.[17]

Even if he is a peasant, Hesiod as an intensive, surplus-generating agriculturalist needs outlets for his strategic overproduction, be that via external outlets, as we have already seen, or through neighborly social storage:

> εὖ μὲν μετρεῖσθαι παρὰ γείτονος, εὖ δ' ἀποδοῦναι,
> αὐτῷ τῷ μέτρῳ, καὶ λώιον αἴ κε δύνηαι,
> ὡς ἂν χρηίζων καὶ ἐς ὕστερον ἄρκιον εὕρῃς.

> Take good measure from a neighbour, and pay it back well, with the same measure, or better if you can, so that you may later find him reliable should you need him. (349–51)

As a (relatively) small-unit producer, albeit bigger than average, Hesiod clearly feels a typical peasant bond with his addressees to fight the unwelcome influence of the polis. The size of his farm and the size of many of his neighbors' farms may mean that they have much in common with the *basilēes* in Thespiae, who may or may not have estates much larger than some of the farms in Ascra; this is reflected in the division of Ascra's labor between owners and the dependent laborers of many (lower) statuses. But the typical peasant animosity toward the city and town creates a second division as well as a contradiction, perhaps what we should expect; this second division overlies the first. These simultaneous divisions may explain why there has been both agreement and disagreement since antiquity about Hesiod's social status. He and his successful peers in the Valley of the Muses are not dependent on the polis, but it would appear that they are resistant to it, having developed or being in the process of developing strategies for bringing their surplus goods not to Thespiae, but to the sea. The common strength of the *basilēes* and Hesiod is control over the means of production (although the *basilēes* in Thespiae have some sort of juridical control/influence over land use or ownership). The issue that divides them is control over the means of allocation: the *basilēes* would have control over the market in Thespiae, and those out in the valley must be aware of this and are acting accordingly.

Hesiod and persons like him (his audience) are able to control their own means of production as long as their luck holds and they do not acquire debt, which along with partible inheritance (which split Hesiod's father's property in half) is the only apparent way to lose control over one's land. *Basilēes* influence land use; recently they have begun to extend their power outward by issuing *dikai* that affect land use on the periphery, and thus they can execute land alienation by these *dikai* and/or via *chrea*. But this does not appear to have led to greater control over the means of production. These *basilēes*, so admirably limned in the *Th* (80–93), are not friends of the weak, but it does not appear that Hesiod and hard-working people like him have much to worry about. Hesiod and other hard-working growers are not dependent on the polis at Thespiae or the *basilēes* there; he and others like him are quite free to make their own choices about production and allocation. If one is seeking justice, especially in a dispute over property, one must go sometimes (always?) to Thespiae to get it, and in this regard we may say that Ascra is a village (*kōmē*) that is dependent on Thespiae, the polis, perhaps only recently. Another whiff of dependence can be sniffed when we realize that Hesiod's emphasis on taking his surplus production to sea instead of to market in Thespiae is an acknowledgment by him of the constant potential of domination from the center.[18]

It seems a risky matter for independent, nonleading agriculturalists to separate themselves from the power of the *basilēes*—in this scenario Hesiod's world is narrowly peasant—as we see with his situation with Perses; presumably it was Perses's hanging out in the agora that got him into destitution, but we must not forget also that it was hanging out there that seems to have got things to go his way with the family inheritance. The power center has no control over Hesiod, according to Hesiod. There is no forcing of goods to market in Thespiae, as Hesiod appears free to take his surplus to market outside the immediate vicinity, namely to the coast, where he puts it on a ship.

Who Are the *Basilēes* of Thespiae?

Peter Rose (2012: 181) makes the valuable observation that in the *Th* the *basilēes* have admirable qualities in common, plurally, but the performance for which they are admired is a solo one. They plurally come from Zeus with the blessing of the Muses (*Th* 96, 80–82), but when they act and one of them receives admiration, the *basileus* is acting as an individual (*Th* 84–87, 91–92). By contrast, in *WD* the *basilēes* are always plural and are addressed as if they are collectively or even conspiratorially responsible for the events (*dikai*) that are driving a wedge between the polis and the village (*kōmē*).

The *basilēes* in *WD* are not only of a different number than those in the *Th*. The *WD basilēes*, who act in the poem only in matters of property, may even have evolved into or were in the process of becoming an institutionalized body: a board of decision makers and/or executors of the decisions of others. The old term *basileus*, a surviving rubric of power from the Bronze Age *qa-si-le-u*, morphed at Athens into a political title carried by the *archōn basileus*; such an institutional rubric survived in many other poleis (Carlier 1984). As for the plural, a transition from a status or office of *basileus* to a board of *basilēes* is documented at several locations,[19] such as at Mytilene, where their remit included overseeing the disposition of property in exilic contexts (their responsibilities are listed in *Inscriptiones Graecae* XII.2 6 1–21 [late fourth century BCE], conveniently translated in Heisserer 1980: 124–25). Coincidentally, the *basilēes* who are implicated in Perses's problems appear to have a specific involvement with land transfers.[20]

These *basilēes* also appear to control the agora, where property losses (and gains) occur (*WD* 29–34) and near which should be located the Thespiae market into which production from the hinterlands should come for distribution.[21] It is through allocation that Hesiod's world is connected, as it has always been, with the broader context of the Aegean and the eastern Mediterranean with which this chapter began. Let us date Hesiod to about 700 BCE and into the seventh century BCE (see note 1); this is not controversial, as Martin West (e.g., 1997: 276–333) and others have made clear how much Near Eastern material has made its way into the Hesiodic poems. This can be attributed narrowly to Hesiod's father's life experiences, both at home in Kyme and on the sea lanes, looking for a decent living. While it seems profitable to consider the geographical knowledge of Archilochus and Alcaeus (Tandy 2004), the results are less than that with Hesiod, who in any case is certainly drawing more on the materials of his poetic tradition than on personal experience. For while it is extremely unlikely that his only trip on the sea was the seventy-five-meter one he took to Chalkis, it is more likely that he never did more than hug the shores of the Corinthian Gulf.[22] The Greeks in touch with the wider world were not Boeotians and certainly were not from the Valley of the Muses. Contemporary Greeks were busy settling and expanding their presence in Magna Graecia and the northern Aegean in Hesiod's lifetime, but Hesiod reveals no knowledge of this. The Neo-Assyrians in the last quarter of the eighth century BCE completed their utter domination of western Asia by taking into vassalage and other forms of dependence all the kingdoms of Asia as far west as Cilicia and even Pamphylia; Babylon fell dramatically in 689, but Hesiod does not refer to any of this. Life in the Valley of the Muses is not entirely isolated from those Greeks who *are* in touch with the outside world: in the last third of the eighth century BCE, primarily Euboean but also Corinthian influences come to bear on Boeotian Geometric ceramics (Coldstream 2003: 201, 377–78; 2008: 469–70). But the closest significant Near Eastern material to the Valley of the Muses is a late eighth-century BCE bronze libation bowl from North Syria found in a wealthy woman's grave in Tragana in east Lokris—this is the extent of reasonably direct contact with the outside world (Onasoglou 1981: 50, pl. 21; Kourou 2008: 330–35).[23] The snapshot in *WD* of the way the independent Boeotians of the eighth and seventh centuries BCE lived has a narrow field of vision that is in agreement with the archaeological record.

THE IDEOLOGICAL NACHLEBEN
OF *WORKS AND DAYS*

The ancient reception of Hesiod has been given excellent scholarly attention in recent years (Boys-Stones and Haubold 2010; Koning 2010; Hunter 2014; Canevaro 2015; Van Noorden 2015). Although the *Th* offers praise of gods and *basilées*, it is the didactic *WD* that survives in many more quotations (as is jaw-droppingly clear when comparing the upper registers of the *apparatus critici* in West's editions [1966, 1978]). No attention is paid to the division between polis insiders and those outside; Richard Hunter (2014: ch. 3) surveys the adaptations of *WD* in the aristocratic symposium, where interests are predictable. But we must remember that most of Hesiod's advice is in support of surplus-producing agriculture, precisely an important interest of many of those who held positions of economic and social strength in the ancient world—men like Xenophon, whose understanding of and devotion to large-scale agriculture, Amouretti (1986: 233) reminds us, are revealed in his focus on optimizing yields through good labor management.[24] The voices of peripheral growers, on the wrong side of the divide between Thespiae and the Valley of the Muses, are not what will interest later Greeks such as the likes of Xenophon, son of Gryllos.

The poem's afterlife, however, should not distract us from seeing *WD* for what it is: a song that documents two great social/economic divisions, one between those who control production and those who do not, the other between the urban forces that control allocation and are extending their interests outward and the ones who have to deal with that. This pair of divisions generated an uneven but unsurprising reception.

FURTHER READING

On agricultural technique, see Amouretti (1986) and Tandy and Neale (1996). On grain productivity and consumption, see Foxhall and Forbes (1982) and Moreno (2007). On settling disputes in early Greece, see Gagarin (1986).

NOTES

1. This chapter, not the place to debate whether Hesiod is a real person, a persona, or an abstraction, proceeds on the assumption that Hesiod/"Hesiod" is describing a real world around him, be it his own or someone else's; it must be comprehensible to his audience. Martin (1992) provides an excellent discussion of Hesiod's personal details as an outsider so as to make his "metanastic" advice more effective (although the adoption of such a strategy does not mean that his personal narrative is not true). Taken one step further, it does not matter whether Perses or Hesiod's father is real; rather, it matters that the audience recognized them as representative or emblematic of lived experiences in the eighth

and seventh centuries BCE. Every point on the scholarly spectrum between total fiction and totally reliable, true account is discussed in Stoddard (2004: 1–33).

Most scholars place Hesiod after Homer and have him composing in about 700 BCE or in the first part of the seventh century BCE. (West would place him before Homer, but he moves the *Iliad* into the middle half of the seventh century [2011: 17–19] and the *Odyssey* to after 630 [2014: 35–41].) For a more comprehensive dating of early epic see West (2012). Kõiv shows that based primarily on the testimonial evidence Hesiod can be placed "anywhere within the period from the late eighth to the early sixth century" (2011: 377).

2. *WD* 636. Unless indicated otherwise, all references are to *WD*. Translations are adapted from my translation in Tandy and Neale (1996). Other translations from the Greek are mine. All the geographical references to mainland Greece can be conveniently found in Talbert (2000: map 55).

3. Hesiod does not name the polis that is making his life complicated. The two candidates are Thespiae, located about eight kilometers east of Ascra, and Haliartos, nearly as close due north. Farinetti makes it clear that to the south of Haliartos there were no hamlets or villages—it is an archaeological "empty zone" (Farinetti 2011: 153, fig. 7), which suggests a lack of influence by Haliartos in that direction. In contrast, to the west of Thespiae there is a "densely scattered landscape" in the direction of Ascra, defined by Farinetti as "definitely one of the second-rank settlements" of the *chōra* of Thespiae (2011: 161). The eastward thrust of the valley from Helikon also invites us to look in that direction. Strabo says that Ascra was in the *chōra* of Roman Thespiae, which is a coincidence rather than a confirmation.

4. Hanson (1995: ch. 3) would also have us believe in a yeoman Hesiod of small means and vigorous energy, but this just does not seem possible.

5. This number can be reached by complicated arithmetic, also. If ten persons require about six thousand pounds of grain annually—this would include putting aside one-sixth for next year's seed and some amounts for animal fodder—and an acre yields about six hundred pounds of grain per acre, Hesiod needs ten acres under grains. If he is running a three-field rotation, with one-third of his land lying fallow each year, Hesiod needs fifteen acres; if he is on a two-field system, he needs twenty acres. Add the acreage for vines, fruit trees, and greens, and he needs twenty-five, perhaps thirty acres. There is more detailed arithmetic in Tandy and Neale (1996: 27–31).

6. Morris (2015: 63–64), speaking of farmers universally, is correct to question the wisdom of hiring extra hands when laborers had attractive options from which to choose, but under the circumstances in the Valley of the Muses, labor appears to have been inexpensive and, as Hesiod says, more hands mean more surplus. Witold Kula, in his neglected study of the feudal Polish peasantry, concluded that "the families of rich peasants are those which have the most members . . . , not larger because they are richer, but on the contrary, richer because they are larger" (1976: 72).

7. As many have pointed out, the Greek at 603, θῆτά τ' ἄοικον ποιεῖσθαι, can mean both "make your *thēs* homeless" and "take on a *thēs* with no home"; this ambiguity neatly covers these two most important requirements of labor management, the abilities to mobilize labor when needed and to shed it when not.

8. De Ste. Croix (1981: 278), where he takes pains to emphasize that not having enough substance to leave a good inheritance to more than one son (376–78; exactly what happened to Hesiod's father) is what haunts especially those at the bottom of the high-wealth stratum.

9. This is how I read it. Others may suspect the sympathy to be false.

10. There is a chart of farming activities according to the star signs Hesiod refers to in West (1978: 253) and an even more illuminating chart of the ancient year's agricultural works according to our modern months in Foxhall (2007: 127, fig. 5.4).

11. Van Wees (2013: 227–28) emphasizes that the vast majority of the work to which Hesiod refers is undertaken by slaves and other dependent laborers, not by Hesiod himself; Rose (2012: 183–84) takes exception to a similar remark by van Wees about Hesiod's "rhetoric of toil" (2009: 447). Hesiod certainly does not see his management work as less important or less work-like than the labor undertaken by his many dependents.

12. Hesiod's ship, with its bilge-plug (626), was a ship with a deck, more elaborate than a dugout canoe (see note 14) but hardly competition for what appears to be the standard twenty-oared, thick-masted merchant vessel of the time, the *phortis eureia* (*Odyssey* 9.323), the type of ship Telemachus borrows from Noëmon for his trip to visit Nestor and Menelaos (*Odyssey* 1.280; 2.212, 387).

13. "Another man's ship" (νηῦς ἀλλοτρία) is found at *Odyssey* 9.535; 11.115; 24.301.

14. The Greeks must have used dugout canoes to negotiate marshy, very shallow waters. These would not so easily survive archaeologically, and their users would have no reason to leave us written testimony regarding them. Dugouts were in use in Egypt for thousands of years before Hesiod, even in the Neolithic in Holland (Casson 1971: 8, references in n20); we have Bronze Age lead models of dugouts from Naxos (Renfrew 1967: 5, 18, pl. 3 [see esp. no. 20]). Hippocrates (*De aere aquis et locis* 15.6) describes the use of μονόξυλα (sc. πλοῖα) on canals by Phasians; Xenophon (*Anabasis* 5.4.11) refers to the canoes that he encounters in the east as πλοῖα μονόξυλα; and Plato (*Laws* 956a3), Aeschines (2.124.3), and Aristotle (*History of Animals* 553b11) use this same term to describe these small boats without any need to elaborate beyond denotation.

15. A larger ship is more likely to survive its venture. In this early cost-benefit analysis, Hesiod urges his listeners to keep most of a surplus at home where it is safe (690), but put what one does send out on a large ship, not a small one.

16. For more on slaves in *WD*, see Harris (2012: 361).

17. In an excellent, thorough essay, Tony Edwards (2014) pursues this division with the tools of philology, articulating clearly the ethical geographical opposition between the polis, the agora, idleness, and crooked *dikai* on the one hand, and the *kōmē*, the farm (*ergon*), work (*ergon*), and straight *dikai* on the other.

18. Edwards (2004: 176–84, 2014) and I agree that Hesiod wants to settle the dispute with his brother αὖθι (35) "right here," that is, not in the agora of the polis but in the *kōmē*, Ascra, where the *dikai* are straight. I cannot understand Hesiod's world without Hesiod accepting that there will be conflict between Thespiae and Ascra, between center and edges, always. Edwards would find a rhetorical solution by capturing "Perses within the limits of the village both spatially and morally while simultaneously eliminating the city from the land-scape" (2004: 178).

19. The board of *basilēes* at Mytilene was active during Pittakos's *aisymneteia* (Theophrastus, fr. 97 Wimmer) in the first decade of the sixth century BCE. There was a board of *basilēes* at Kyme in the fourth century BCE and perhaps much earlier whose remit is not known (Plutarch, *Moralia* 291E–292A, presumably drawing on Aristotle). This unusual pattern of plural Aeolic *basileis* at Mytilene and Kyme may have some bearing on an inquiry into why Hesiod's father, when he left Kyme under unknown circumstances, ended up in the Valley of the Muses. Apart from the many *basilēes* in the *Iliad* and *Odyssey*, the only other pluralities of *basilēes* that I know of are the Hesiodic ones; the largely symbolic *basileis* at

the Panionia (βασι)λέας σκηπτούχους [*Princeton Epigraphical Project (Priene)* 11.17; 350–323 BCE]); the otherwise unknown oligarchy at Erythrai called the Basilidai (Aristotle, *Politica* 1305b.18–22; early [ἐν ἀρχαίοις χρόνοις]); and the *basileis* who presided over the *boulē* at Chios (*Supplementum Epigraphicum Graecum* 35 923 B.14–15; ca. 400 BCE).

20. Such a board was in place by the 510s at nearby Thebes, as we see in a new inscription that indicates that a local board of *prorarchoi* (= *phrourarchoi*) oversaw the auction of confiscated properties (Matthaiou 2014: 215–20); the phrourarchs may well have had a hand in the confiscations themselves. Matthaiou offers a commentary on specific aspects of this text, which is not yet published. There is a primus inter pares among the phrourarchs, whose work appears to be guaranteed or at least supported by a council, a βολά; this is superficially reminiscent of the arrangements at Phaeacia (*Odyssey* 8.390–91). *Omnibus dictis*, it may be the case that Hesiod calls his *basilées* in Thespiae what he does because *basileus* is the epic-Ionic, hexameter rubric in his poetic tradition (thus Carlier 1984: 411).

21. This is not the place to take up the thorny issue of how early we can be confident that the agora was as much a market as it was a place of political assembly. See most recently and not optimistically Canevaro (2017).

22. The predominance of Asian rivers, including the Aeolic Kaïkos and the Hermos, in the catalog of rivers at *Th* 338–45 finds its best explanation in Hesiod's father qua source, while Hesiod's knowledge, e.g., of the *omphalos* at Delphi (fr. 33a.26), is not surprising given its proximity to the valley (just on the other side of Helikon) and his acquaintance with those traders who knew the Gulf of Corinth intimately, not to mention his access to recitations by those from whom he learned his poetic craft.

23. There are also, in Hesiod's lifetime, a few imported beads at Orchomenos, two siren attachments from the same cauldron at Ptoion, and a solitary scarab at Thebes (Murray 2017: 110, table 2.6).

24. Xenophon praises orderliness (*taxis*) at great length in the *Oeconomicus* (8.3–20): orderliness means everything is in its proper place, the result of good and close management. In the *Cyropaedia* (8.5.7), things run most smoothly when everything can be found precisely where it should be located; he says there that εὐθημοσύνη—Hesiod's very term for "good management" (471)—is καλὸν ἐπιτήδευμα, "a good practice," ἐν οἰκίᾳ, "in the house."

References

Amouretti, M.-C. 1986. *Le pain et l'huile dans la Grèce antique: De araire au moulin*. Paris.

Bintliff, J., P. Howard, and A. Snodgrass. 1999. "The Hidden Landscape of Prehistoric Greece." *Journal of Mediterranean Archaeology* 12: 139–68.

Bintliff, J., P. Howard, and A. Snodgrass. 2007. *Testing the Hinterland: The Work of the Boeotia Survey (1989–1991) in the Southern Approaches to the City of Thespiai*. Cambridge.

Bintliff, J., and A. Snodgrass. 1985a. "The Cambridge/Bradford Boeotian Expedition: The First Four Years." *Journal of Field Archaeology* 12: 123–61.

Bintliff, J., and A. Snodgrass. 1985b. "The Development of Settlement in South-West Boeotia." In *La Béotie Antique*, edited by P. Roesch and G. Argoud, 49–70. Paris.

Boys-Stones, G., and J. Haubold, eds. 2010. *Plato and Hesiod*. Oxford.

Buck, R. 1979. *A History of Boeotia*. Alberta, BC.

Burford-Cooper, A. 1977. "The Family Farm in Greece." *Classical Journal* 73: 162–75.

Canevaro, L. 2015. *Hesiod's Works and Days: How to Teach Self-Sufficiency*. Oxford.

Canevaro, M. 2017. "How to Cast a Criminal out of Athens: Law and Territory in Archaic Attica." In *Violence and Community: Law, Space and Identity in the Ancient Eastern Mediterranean World*, edited by I. K. Xydopoulos, K. Vlassopoulos, and E. Tounta, 50–71. London.

Carlier, P. 1984. *La Royauté en Grèce avant Alexandre*. Strasbourg, France.

Coldstream, J. N. 2003. *Geometric Greece, 900–700 BC*. 2nd ed. Oxford.

Coldstream, J. N. 2008. *Greek Geometric Pottery*. 2nd ed. Bristol, UK.

de Ste. Croix, G. E. M. 1981. *The Class Struggle in the Ancient Greek World*. Oxford.

Duplouy, A. 2006. *Le Prestige des Élites: Recherches sur les modes de reconnaissance sociale en Grèce entre les xe et ve siècles avant J.-C.* Paris.

Edwards, A. 2004. *Hesiod's Ascra*. Berkeley, CA.

Edwards, A. 2014. "The Ethical Geography of Hesiod's *Works and Days*." In *Geography, Topography, Landscape: Configurations of Space in Greek and Roman Epic*, edited by M. Skempis and I. Ziogas, 95–136. Berlin.

Farinetti, E. 2011. *Boeotian Landscapes. A GIS-based Study for the Reconstruction and Interpretation of the Archaeological Datasets of Ancient Boeotia*. Oxford.

Foxhall, L. 1992. "The Control of the Attic Landscape." In *Agriculture in Ancient Greece*, edited by B. Wells, 155–59. Stockholm, Sweden.

Foxhall, L. 2007. *Olive Cultivation in Ancient Greece: Seeking the Ancient Economy*. Oxford.

Foxhall, L., and H. Forbes. 1982. "Σιτομετρεία: The Role of Grain as a Staple Food in Classical Antiquity." *Chiron* 12: 41–90.

Francis, E. 1945. "The Personality Type of the Peasant according to Hesiod's *Works and Days*." *Rural Sociology* 10: 275–95.

Gagarin, M. 1986. *Early Greek Law*. Berkeley, CA.

Gallant, T. 1991. *Risk and Survival in Ancient Greece: Reconstructing the Rural Domestic Economy*. Cambridge.

Gallego, J. 2007. "Farming in the Ancient Greek World: How Should the Small Free Producers Be Defined?" *Studia Humaniora Tartuensia* 8 (8.A.3): 1–21.

Gallego, J. 2012. "La Formación de la Pólis en la Grecia Antigua: Autonomía del campesinado, subordinación de las aldeas." *Trabajos y Comunicaciones* 38: 133–51.

Greene, E., M. Lawall, and M. Polzer. 2008. "Inconspicuous Consumption: The Sixth-Century B.C.E. Shipwreck at Pubuç Burnu, Turkey." *American Journal of Archaeology* 112: 685–711.

Greene, E., J. Leidwanger, and H. Özdaş. 2011. "Two Early Archaic Shipwrecks at Kekova Adası and Kepçe Burnu, Turkey." *International Journal of Nautical Archaeology* 40: 60–68.

Halstead, P. 2014. *Two Oxen Ahead: Pre-Mechanized Farming in the Mediterranean*. Oxford.

Hanson, V. 1995. *The Other Greeks: The Family Farm and the Agrarian Roots of Western Civilization*. New York.

Harris, E. 2012. "Homer, Hesiod, and the 'Origins' of Greek Slavery." *Revue d'Études Anciennes* 114: 345–65.

Heisserer, A. 1980. *Alexander the Great and the Greeks: The Epigraphic Evidence*. Norman, OK.

Horden, P., and N. Purcell. 2000. *The Corrupting Sea: A Study of Mediterranean History*. Oxford.

Hunter, R. 2014. *Hesiodic Voices: Studies in the Ancient Reception of Hesiod's Works and Days*. Cambridge.

Kõiv, M. 2011. "A Note on the Dating of Hesiod." *Classical Quarterly* 61: 355–77.

Koning, H. H. 2010. *Hesiod: The Other Poet; Ancient Reception of a Cultural Icon*. Mnemosyne Supplement 325. Leiden, Netherlands.

Kourou, N. 2008. "The Evidence from the Aegean." In *Beyond the Homeland: Markers in Phoenician Chronology*, edited by C. Sagona, 305–64. Leuven, Belgium.

Kula, W. 1976. *An Economic Theory of the Feudal System*. London.

Martin, R. 1992. "Hesiod's Metanastic Poetics." *Ramus* 21: 11–33.

Matthaiou, A. 2014. "Four Inscribed Bronze Tablets from Thebes: Preliminary Notes." In *The Epigraphy and History of Boeotia: New Finds, New Prospects*, edited by N. Papazarkadas, 211–22. Leiden, Netherlands.

Mele, A. 1979. *Il commercio Greco arcaico. Prexis ed emporie*. Naples.

Millett, P. 1984. "Hesiod and His World." *Proceedings of the Cambridge Philological Society* 210: 84–115.

Moreno, A. 2007. *Feeding the Democracy: The Athenian Grain Supply in the Fifth and Fourth Centuries BC*. Oxford.

Morris, I. 2015. *Foragers, Farmers, and Fossil Fuels: How Human Values Evolve*. Princeton, NJ.

Murray, S. 2017. *The Collapse of the Mycenaean Economy: Imports, Trade, and Institutions 1300–700 BCE*. Cambridge.

Onasoglou, A. 1981. "Οι γεωμετρικοί τάφοι της Τραγάνας στην ανατολική Λοκρίδα." *Archaiologikon Deltion* 36: 1–57.

Osborne, R. 2009. *Greece in the Making*. 2nd ed. Oxford.

Pritchett, W. K. 1965. *Studies in Ancient Greek Topography, Part 1*. Berkeley, CA.

Purcell, N. 2005. "Colonization and Mediterranean History." In *Ancient Colonizations: Analogy, Similarity and Difference*, edited by H. Hurst and S. Owen, 115–39. London.

Redfield, R. 1953. *The Primitive World and Its Transformation*. Ithaca, NY.

Redfield, R. 1956. *Peasant Society and Culture*. Chicago.

Renfrew, C. 1967. "Cycladic Metallurgy and the Aegean Early Bronze Age." *American Journal of Archaeology* 71: 1–20.

Rose, P. 2012. *Class in Archaic Greece*. Cambridge.

Scott, J. 1976. *The Moral Economy of the Peasant: Rebellion and Subsistence in Southeast Asia*. New Haven, CT.

Snodgrass, A. 1985. "The Site of Askra." In *La Béotie Antique*, edited by P. Roesch and G. Argoud, 87–95. Paris.

Stoddard, K. 2004. *The Narrative Voice in the Theogony of Hesiod*. Mnemosyne Supplement 255. Leiden, Netherlands.

Talbert, R., ed. 2000. *Barrington Atlas of the Greek and Roman World*. Princeton, NJ.

Tandy, D. 1997. *Warriors into Traders*. Berkeley, CA.

Tandy, D. 2004. "Trade and Commerce in Archilochos, Sappho, and Alkaios." In *Commerce and Monetary Systems in the Ancient World: Means of Transmission and Cultural Interaction*, edited by R. Rollinger, C. Ulf, and K. Schnegg, 183–94. Stuttgart, Germany.

Tandy, D., and W. Neale. 1996. *Hesiod's Works and Days: Introduction, Translation and Commentary for the Social Sciences*. Berkeley, CA.

Van Noorden, H. 2015. *Playing Hesiod: The "Myth of the Races" in Classical Antiquity*. Cambridge.

van Wees, H. 2009. "The Economy." In *A Companion to Archaic Greece*, edited by K. Raaflaub and H. van Wees, 444–67. Oxford.

van Wees, H. 2013. "Farmers and Hoplites: Models of Historical Development." In *Men of Bronze: Hoplite Warfare in Ancient Greece*, edited by D. Kagan and G. Viggiano, 222–55. Princeton, NJ.

West, M. L., ed. and comm. 1966. *Hesiod: Theogony*. Oxford.

West, M. L., ed. and comm. 1978. *Hesiod: Works and Days*. Oxford.

West, M. L. 1997. *The East Face of Helicon: West Asiatic Elements in Greek Poetry and Myth*. Oxford.

West, M. L. 2011. *The Making of the Iliad: Disquisition and Analytical Commentary*. Oxford

West, M. L. 2012. "Towards a Chronology of Early Greek Epic." *Relative Chronology in Early Greek Epic Poetry*, edited by In Ø. Andersen and D. Haug, 224–41. Cambridge.

West, M. L. 2014. *The Making of the Odyssey*. Oxford.

Wolf, E. 1966. *Peasants*. Englewood Cliffs, NJ.

CHAPTER 5

....

THE PREHISTORY
AND ANALOGUES OF
HESIOD'S POETRY

....

JOSHUA T. KATZ

But why linger? Why stay in this world of oak and tree and rock?

(Taylor 2016: 13)

ON the assumption that Homer sits at the head of the Greek tradition, the first question in Western literature—*the* Homeric question, as it were—is found almost at the start of the *Iliad*. Directly after the short proem (1.1–7), the poet asks about the cause of the quarrel between Achilles and Agamemnon that will be the theme of the entire poem: τίς τάρ σφωε θεῶν ἔριδι ξυνέηκε μάχεσθαι; (1.8), "Who of the gods brought together these two to contend in strife?" It is a straightforward question with a straightforward answer, one that is given without delay in the next verse in a four-word clause that is as clipped and syntactically unadorned as anything one can find in Greek literature: Λητοῦς καὶ Διὸς υἱός (1.9), "the son of Leto and Zeus." Hesiod, too, poses a question early in the *Theogony* (hereafter *Th*). However, it takes a rather different form: ἀλλὰ τίη μοι ταῦτα περὶ δρῦν ἢ περὶ πέτρην; (35), which might be translated as something like "But what are these things about a tree or a rock to me?" Unlike the one in the *Iliad*, this question is anything but straightforward and receives no explicit answer. While it does not immediately follow the lengthy proem of the *Th* (1–115), sometimes referred to as the "Hymn to the Muses," it likewise falls at a juncture: specifically, between the account of the poet's *Dichterweihe* at the hands of the Muses and the description of the birth and poetic qualities of these nine goddesses, the daughters of Mnemosyne and Zeus.[1]

Hesiod's enigmatic question appears most recently as the epigraph of American poet Tess Taylor's *Work & Days: Poems*, which I have borrowed in turn as the opening words of this chapter. I linger over it because the disjunctive prepositional phrase about tree or rock provides a striking laboratory for looking in miniature at the Indo-European prehistory and Near Eastern analogues of Hesiod's two great poems, the *Th* and the *Works and Days* (hereafter *WD*), both of which a few scholars, most prominently M. L. West (see, e.g., 2012), regard as older than the *Iliad*. An excellent laboratory—but, as so often, the results, which for reasons of space will largely concern the *Th*, are not always conclusive.

As it happens, the question in *Iliad* 1.8, which looks at first glance to be a mundane bit of Greek, contains a feature that most readers will find surprising: the opening sequence of interrogative plus particle, τίς ταρ (thus West 1998: 4, in place of τίς τ᾽ ἄρ), which one might (over-)translate as "who on earth?," reflects one of a number of "small-scale borrowings" in Homer from across the Bosporus (Bachvarova 2016: 427).[2] In principle, τίς ταρ and *kuiš tar* in (Cuneiform) Luvian—it has been suggested that this language, closely related to the better-known Hittite, is what the Trojans spoke[3]—could be exact cognates, with both going back to $*k^w is \; t\underset{.}{r}$ in Proto-Indo-European, the reconstructed "mother tongue" from about fifty-five hundred years ago that has given rise to such now-different languages as Greek, Luvian, Sanskrit, Latin, and English.[4] However, τίς ταρ is instead probably a Western Anatolianism, "an areal feature common to both languages at the geographical point of their contact" (Watkins 1995: 151), namely Troy (in present-day terms, Hisarlık, in the far northwest of Turkey). My aim here is not to defend this hypothesis but rather to show two things: first, that the extraordinary can lie beneath the surface of the seemingly ordinary; and second, that it is sometimes very difficult to determine whether a linguistic, stylistic, or literary feature in archaic Greek resembles a feature in another Indo-European language because both descend from a long-gone common source (Proto-Indo-European) or rather because the two languages have rubbed up against each other in historical time (e.g., in Aeolis).

Scholarship on the relationship between Greece and the East—especially the Near East, but also lands from the Caucasus to Gandhara—has flourished over the past half-century.[5] On the Near Eastern background of Hesiod in particular there is a significant body of secondary literature, with some aspects of his poetry probably to be attributed to direct borrowing from Hittite or Luvian but much of it indebted to the influence of such mutually unintelligible non-Indo-European languages of second- and early first-millennium BCE Asia Minor as Akkadian, Hurrian, and Ugaritic. Pride of place goes here to two publications from 1966: Peter Walcot's *Hesiod and the Near East* and West's remarkable commentary on the *Th*, both of which give due attention to prior scholarship; other important contributions include Penglase (1994), West (1997: 276–333 and index s.v. "Hesiod"), and Rutherford (2009), the last of which packs tremendous punch in only a few pages. As its expansive title suggests, the latest large-scale contribution, Scully (2015), considers an exceptionally broad range of texts: *Hesiod's "Theogony": From Near Eastern Creation Myths to "Paradise Lost"*. Recent years have seen an explosion in work on Hesiod, with monographs and substantial essays appearing at an astonishing clip. Some take a Near Eastern perspective on Hesiod; others read him "as such," that is to say, as a product of the eighth- or seventh-century BCE Greek world; and most consider the reception history of his oeuvre. (The chapters in Montanari, Rengakos, and Tsagalis 2009 cover all three perspectives.) Surprisingly, however, there have been almost no sustained efforts to comment on Hesiod as an Indo-European poet.[6] An obvious desideratum for the modern study of Hesiod is, therefore, a holistic understanding of how Indo-European prehistory and Near Eastern analogues contribute together to the formation of Hesioidic language and thought. It is my contention, which I illustrate in what follows through close attention to a single verse, that there is no Greek author who has more per line to tell us about how Greek became Greek.

Let us return, then, to ἀλλὰ τίη μοι ταῦτα περὶ δρῦν ἢ περὶ πέτρην;. The phrase, on which see above all West (1966: 167–69), is not isolated in Greek—or at least the connection between tree and rock is not—though it is never otherwise found with the preposition περί "around, about" (and the accusative case), much less with περί repeated. Consider Homer, who uses repeated ἀπό "from" (and the genitive): in Book 22 of the *Iliad*, Hector says of Achilles, οὐ μέν πως νῦν ἔστιν ἀπὸ δρυὸς οὐδ᾽ ἀπὸ πέτρης | τῷ ὀαριζέμεναι (126–27), "it is in no way possible now to woo/converse with him from tree or from rock,"[7] while in Book 19 of the *Odyssey*, Penelope says to her disguised husband, ἀλλὰ καὶ ὧς μοι εἰπὲ τεὸν γένος, ὁππόθεν ἐσσί. | οὐ γὰρ ἀπὸ δρυός ἐσσι παλαιφάτου οὐδ᾽ ἀπὸ πέτρης (162–63), "But even so tell me your race, where you are from. For you are not from a tree, spoken long ago, or from a rock." Furthermore, Plato employs variants of the schema "δρυ- and/or πετρ-" on three occasions: *Apology* 34d, *Republic* 544d, and *Phaedrus* 275b–c.[8] In the first two, he paraphrases the *Odyssey*, on the latter occasion with repeated ἐκ "from, out of" (ἐκ δρυός . . . ἢ ἐκ πέτρας . . . γίγνεσθαι, "born from tree or from rock") instead of the semantically very similar ἀπό. The passage from the *Phaedrus*, which has no prepositions but does present δρῦς and πέτρα in the genitive (as the objects of ἀκούειν "to hear"), is rather different in content (though also suggesting an interest in where a person may hail from):

οἱ δέ γ᾽, ὦ φίλε, ἐν τῷ τοῦ Διὸς τοῦ Δωδωναίου ἱερῷ δρυὸς λόγους ἔφησαν μαντικοὺς πρώτους γενέσθαι. τοῖς μὲν οὖν τότε, ἅτε οὐκ οὖσι σοφοῖς ὥσπερ ὑμεῖς οἱ νέοι, ἀπέχρη δρυὸς καὶ πέτρας ἀκούειν ὑπ᾽ εὐηθείας, εἰ μόνον ἀληθῆ λέγοιεν· σοὶ δ᾽ ἴσως διαφέρει τίς ὁ λέγων καὶ ποδαπός. οὐ γὰρ ἐκεῖνο μόνον σκοπεῖς, εἴτε οὕτως εἴτε ἄλλως ἔχει;

They used to say, friend, that the first oracular words came from an oak in the temple of Dodonian Zeus. In fact, the people at that time, not being as wise as you young folk, were content in their simplicity to hear an oak and a rock, provided only that they spoke the truth. But to you does it perhaps make a difference who the speaker is and where he comes from, for you do not consider only whether or not he speaks the truth?

What Socrates says to Phaedrus seems to be of particular relevance to our understanding of Hesiod. First of all, the word δρῦς here means specifically "oak." In a number of archaic Indo-European traditions, this is the tree of the storm (or high) god, including Zeus (see, e.g., West 2007: 248 and index s.v. "oak"), at whose oracular sanctuary at Dodona priests are said to have interpreted the rustling of the leaves of a mantic oak (see, e.g., Parke 1967: 13) and who has already been mentioned by name four times in the *Th* (11, 13, 25, and 29) and will next appear in the verse immediately after the question under discussion (36). In addition, the passage from the *Phaedrus* addresses prophetic truth, a matter it would be easy to connect to what is arguably the most controversial passage in archaic Greek poetry, found just a few verses earlier in Hesiod's *Dichterweihe*: ἴδμεν ψεύδεα πολλὰ λέγειν ἐτύμοισιν ὁμοῖα, | ἴδμεν δ᾽ εὖτ᾽ ἐθέλωμεν ἀληθέα γηρύσασθαι (*Th* 27–28), "We know to tell many lies similar to true things; we also know to speak the truth, if we want to."[9]

It is widely acknowledged that ἀλλὰ τίη μοι ταῦτα περὶ δρῦν ἢ περὶ πέτρην; has Near Eastern parallels in the realm of prophecy and oracles and, further, that these are of interest to the Hellenist in that they help explain what the phrase means,[10] why Hesiod would have chosen to speak of two prominent features of the natural world, and (perhaps most of all) why he would have chosen to speak of them exactly here. A list of studies just from recent years would be long, but the most important ones are O'Bryhim (1996), López-Ruiz (2010: 56–83 and 205–10), and Forte (2015). Forte, relying heavily on the first two, as well as on Indo-European-based work by Gregory Nagy (see below), builds especially on a thirteenth-century BCE text from the Ugaritic Ba'al Cycle found at Ras Shamra (in present-day northern Syria) in which two divine messengers of the storm god Ba'al rush to the goddess Anat and recount to her "a word of tree and murmur of rock" (*rgm* | ʿ . *w* . *lḫšt* . *ʾabn*; KTU³/ CAT I.3 iii 22–23)[11] and on various pieces of iconographic evidence, above all a cylinder seal from the middle Bronze Age that appears to depict the same scene, with—until now inexplicably—a tree shooting forth from Ba'al's mouth (BM 132824).

The idea of a connection between *Th* 35 and the Ugaritic passage goes back to Dirlmeier (1955: 25–26) and has been regularly repeated in Hesiodic scholarship since West (1966: 168). Forte's insight is that both have to do with " '*speech* from tree and/ or rock' "—or, in the proverbial words of the fourteenth-century metropolitan bishop Macarius Chrysocephalus, δρυὸς καὶ πέτρας λόγοι (*Corpus paroemiographorum Graecorum* 2, p. 158)—"distinct from a more general phrase of 'tree and/or rock' that has been thoroughly addressed elsewhere."[12] By insisting, with Nagy (1974, 1990), that " 'trees and rocks' are generally associated with lightning and thunder" and that " 'word of tree and murmur of rock' is a metaphorical representation of these phenomena," expressing (and perhaps even imitating; cf. Forte 2015: 15–16, with n32) "the divine voice of the storm-god at the height of his power" (Forte 2015: 14), this scholar has considerably advanced our understanding of Hesiod.

Still, for all that he is right to highlight the Near Eastern analogues of phrases about trees/oaks and rocks in Homer, Hesiod, and Plato, Forte underplays the Indo-European dimension, perhaps because these two perspectives appear to be antithetical. But they are not, or at least not necessarily.[13] In the case of Homer's τίς ταρ, for instance, both words are of Proto-Indo-European heritage, though it seems likely that their combination in Greek is a more-recent borrowing. Or to take a much larger, and Hesiodic, example, it has long been known that the myth of Typhoeus (cf., e.g., *Th* 820–80) made its way into Greece from Asia Minor, but much of the Greek vocabulary here owes more than a little to the proto-language; see Watkins (1995: 455) for a careful statement of the complicated dance between inheritance and borrowing, with reference to the use by Hesiod and other Greek authors of the noun ἱμάς and verb ἱμάσσω "(to) bind, lash" in connection with the monster's battle with Zeus, who subdues him and throws him into Tartarus before becoming king of the gods.[14] Not incidentally, and of particular interest for what follows, Goslin (2010) compares the extraordinary range of sounds that Typhoeus makes in the *Th* with the thundering of his adversary, suggesting that the Muses' sweet song could not have arisen without this sonic clash.[15]

As far as the Indo-European background of our Hesiodic question is concerned, we should keep in mind three things. First, there are potentially pertinent examples throughout the Indo-European world of the seemingly universal collocation "sticks and stones," and Janda (1997: 157) has reconstructed the earliest Proto-Indo-European formula as "*$druh_2$ & *$peru\bar{o}r$." Second, the Avestan phrase *draoca pauruuąnca*, "in tree and in rock," found twice in each of two *Yašts* (13.99 = 19.85), conjoins cognates of both δρῦς and πέτρη[16] and is thus likely of special importance for our understanding of *Th* 35, all the more so since the context is a poet/priest/seer's quest for and discovery of nothing less than Truth.[17] And third, scholars, including Nagy (1974, 1990), have made excellent use of evidence from such traditions as Baltic and Slavic, notably the name of the storm god (e.g., Lithuanian *Perkúnas* and Old Russian *Perunŭ*), to emphasize the multifaceted connections in archaic Indo-European languages and cultures among storm god, oak, "thunderstones," and lightning—so this is by no means a purely Near Eastern nexus.[18] That said, while ἀλλὰ τίη μοι ταῦτα περὶ δρῦν ἢ περὶ πέτρην; is Indo-European in form— the words themselves are all based on inherited linguistic ingredients—it is not entirely, and very likely not even primarily, so in substance. Perhaps further work will tease out its larger Indo-European implications.

Although Hesiod's question resists easy translation and interpretation, both synchronically and diachronically, we can now understand better how it functions as a rhetorical pivot. It is clear that in terms of content, it bridges verses 1–34 (in particular the material that has to do with prophecy; see above) and the "second beginning" that follows:[19] verse 36 restates the name of Zeus, so prominent in what precedes, and also contains the phrase Μουσάων ἀρχώμεθα, "let us begin from the Muses," which directly repeats the first and third words of the poem as a whole: Μουσάων ... ἀρχώμεθ' (1). What has not been recognized, despite intensive discussion of Hesiod's sounds, especially in the proem of the *Th*,[20] is that Hesiod's question is also a pivot between descriptions that run the sonic gamut. At the one end is the vocalic melodiousness of Zeus's daughters (περικαλλέα ὄσσαν ἱεῖσαι, "sending forth very beautiful divine utterance"; 10[21]), a capacity that they exceptionally grant to the shepherd-turned-poet Hesiod, whom καλὴν ἐδίδαξαν ἀοιδήν (22), "they taught beautiful song" and ἐνέπνευσαν δέ μοι αὐδὴν | θέσπιν (31–32), "into whom they breathed godly voice." (See Katz 2013a, esp. 21–23, for what I mean by "vocalic.") At the other end is the harshly consonantal crashing of Ζηνὸς ἐριγδούποιο (41), "loud-thundering Zeus" himself, whose voice is explicitly contrasted with the "sweet" and "lily-like" tones of his daughters (39–43):

φωνῇ ὁμηρεῦσαι, τῶν δ᾽ ἀκάματος ῥέει αὐδὴ
ἐκ στομάτων ἡδεῖα· γελᾷ δέ τε δώματα πατρὸς
Ζηνὸς ἐριγδούποιο θεᾶν ὀπὶ λειροέσσῃ

σκιδναμένη, ἠχεῖ δὲ κάρη νιφόεντος Ὀλύμπου
δώματά τ᾽ ἀθανάτων· αἱ δ᾽ ἄμβροτον ὄσσαν ἱεῖσαι

They harmonize in sound; and their tireless voice flows sweet from their mouths; and the halls of their father, loud-thundering Zeus, rejoice in the goddesses' lilied voice as it spreads out; and the peak of snowy Olympus resounds, and the halls of the deathless ones. They, sending forth undying divine utterance, ...

An only slightly less explicit contrast between the Muses' song and Zeus's *Sturm und Drang* comes a bit later (68–72):[22]

αἳ τότ᾽ ἴσαν πρὸς Ὄλυμπον, ἀγαλλόμεναι ὀπὶ καλῇ,
ἀμβροσίῃ μολπῇ· περὶ δ᾽ ἴαχε γαῖα μέλαινα
ὑμνεύσαις, ἐρατὸς δὲ ποδῶν ὕπο δοῦπος ὀρώρει
νισομένων πατέρ᾽ εἰς ὅν· ὁ δ᾽ οὐρανῷ ἐμβασιλεύει,
αὐτὸς ἔχων βροντὴν ἠδ᾽ αἰθαλόεντα κεραυνόν

Then they [sc. the Muses] went toward Olympus, exulting in beautiful voice, in immortal song; and around them as they sang the black earth resounded, and from under their feet a lovely noise rose up as they went to their father. He is king in the sky, himself holding thunder and the blazing thunderbolt.

Note that Zeus is ἐρίγδουπος, "loud-thundering" (the cluster -γδ- adds expressive noise to the basic form ἐρίδουπος), while the δοῦπος, "noise, din" of the Muses is ἐρατός, "lovely."

An appreciation of these different forms of speech helps explain a phonologico-semantic aspect of the structure of the first half of the proem. According to Tsagalis (2009: 134), "[t]he cryptic pitch of line 35 . . . is an attempt to tell the audience to tune in to an interpretive wavelength, which is difficult to locate, yet essential if the Hesiodic *Theogony* is to be fully understood"; one of my goals in the present chapter is to help locate Hesiod's sonic wavelength—or, rather, wavelengths. For each subsection (i: vv. 1–21; ii: vv. 22–34; and iv: vv. 36–52—with the stand-alone pivotal question iii: v. 35 between the last two), consider especially the first verse and the end of the final verse and concentrate on the words that denote sounds as well as on the sounds themselves.

The poem opens thus:

Subsection i (vv. 1–21)

Μουσάων Ἑλικωνιάδων ἀρχώμεθ᾽ ἀείδειν (1), "from the Heliconian Muses let us
begin to sing"

. . .

. . . *ὄσσαν ἱεῖσαι* (10), "sending forth divine utterance"

. . .

. . . *αἰὲν ἐόντων* (21), "of [the race of the gods who]
always are."

Then comes the *Dichterweihe*:

<u>Subsection ii (vv. 22–34)</u>

αἵ νύ ποθ᾽ Ἡσίοδον καλὴν ἐδίδαξαν ἀοιδήν (22), "and once they [sc. the Muses] taught Hesiod beautiful song"

. . .

Μοῦσαι Ὀλυμπιάδες, κοῦραι Διὸς αἰγιόχοιο (25), "the Olympian Muses, daughters of aegis-bearing Zeus"

. . .

. . . αὐδήν (31), "voice"

. . . ἐόντα (32), "[the things that] are"

. . . αἰὲν ἐόντων (33), "of [the race of the gods who] always are"

. . . αἰὲν ἀείδειν (34), "always to sing."

There follows the pivotal question—

<u>Subsection iii (v. 35)</u>

ἀλλὰ τίη μοι ταῦτα περὶ δρῦν ἢ περὶ πέτρην; (35), "But what are these things about a tree or a rock to me?"

—and, after that, we return to a greater description of the Muses:

<u>Subsection iv (vv. 36–52)</u>

τύνη, Μουσάων ἀρχώμεθα, ταὶ Διὶ πατρί (36), "come now, from the Muses let us begin, who for Father Zeus"

. . .

. . . ἐόντα (38), "[the things that] are"

. . . αὐδή (39), "voice"

. . .

. . . ὄσσαν ἱεῖσαι (43), "sending forth divine utterance"

. . . ἀοιδῇ (44), "in song"

. . .

. . . ἀοιδῆς (48), "of song"

. . .

Μοῦσαι Ὀλυμπιάδες, κοῦραι Διὸς αἰγιόχοιο (52), "the Olympian Muses, daughters of aegis-bearing Zeus."

A number of features that bring together sound and meaning will immediately strike the attentive reader and will presumably have struck the attentive listener in the age of oral performance:

(1) The poem opens with the Muses, who reappear, again as the first word, in the last verse of the whole section under discussion (52), which is repeated from 25; they are also nearly the first word of another verse that starts a subsection, 36, though there they are preceded by the curious pronominal/exhortative form τύνη ("hey you!/come now!"), on which see below.

(2) The poem, for which Goslin (2010: 355–56) provides a helpful "taxonomy of voice," also opens with singing: the last word of verse 1. And, indeed, there is a lot of song: the last word of 22 (the start of the second subsection), the last word of 34 (the end of the second subsection), and also the last word of 44 and 48.

(3) Whatever deep etymological connection between ἀείδειν, "to sing"/ἀοιδή, "song" and αὐδή, "voice" may or may not exist (in my view there probably is none), it is clear that there is a synchronic connection between the words, which means that two more verses end in this way: 31 (v.l. ἀοιδήν) and 39.

(4) Also regularly closing verses is a participle of the verb "to be," ἐοντ-: 21 (the end of a subsection), 32, 33, and 38.

(5) Yet another important word here is αἰέν, "always," which directly precedes the participle in verses 21 (the end of the first subsection) and 33 and the verb "to sing" in 34 (the end of the second subsection).

What are we to make of this? A tremendous number of final words begin with a vocalic hiatus, as though to emphasize the melodiousness of the Muses'—and, in consequence, Hesiod's—vowels.[23] Especially striking is the chiastic and augmentative sequence in verses 31–34, in the *Dichterweihe* and immediately before the question: "voice—are—always are—always to sing." No wonder, then, that

(6) the formula ὄσσαν ἱεῖσαι (10 and 43, plus 65 and 67), "sending forth divine utterance" is often said to be an etymological gloss on Ἡσίοδος, the poet's name, which is made explicit in verse 22 (the start of the second subsection).[24]

Among the reasons to care about all this is the matter of the Indo-European background of Hesiod's poetry. It has occasionally been suggested that some of the ways in which early Greek hymns start are formally indebted to the Near East (see, e.g., West 1997: 170–73), but a recent study by Metcalf (2015: 130–53) concludes that neither openings of the type found in the *Th* ("Let me Sing of *N*") nor those of the type found in the *WD* ("Sing of *N*!") owe anything to Sumerian, Akkadian, or Hittite material. Rather, both Μουσάων Ἑλικωνιάδων ἀρχώμεθ᾽ ἀείδειν (*Th* 1), "from the Heliconian Muses let us begin to sing" and Μοῦσαι Πιερίηθεν, ἀοιδῇσι κλείουσαι | . . . ἐννέπετε (*WD* 1–2), "O Muses from Pieria, glorifying in songs, . . . tell!" are Indo-European to the core, and as I have tried to demonstrate in a series of papers on how Greek epic poems begin, in the first place in one titled "Gods and Vowels" (Katz 2013a), there are a number of remarkable features just beneath the synchronic surface that the incipits of Hesiod's two poems, the two Homeric epics, and many of the *Homeric Hymns* have in common. For example, the very first word of these works often reflects the resonant Proto-Indo-European root **men-*, "think, engage in *men*tal activity"—cf. Μοῦσα; μνήσομαι, "let me remember" (*Homeric Hymn* (3) *to Apollo*); and μῆνιν, "wrath" (*Iliad*)—and there is also a heavy emphasis on the root **h₂weid-*, "sing," as in the vowel-heavy ἀϵ/οιδ-.[25] Such openings, which in both form and function resemble the Indic sacred syllable *om*, emphasize both poetic melody and poetic memory—no coincidence when the two most important functions of the Proto-Indo-European bard were singing and the mental activity of committing information to memory (see, e.g., Watkins 1995: 68–84, esp. 68–69; West 2007: 33–35). Carolina López-Ruiz opens her paper "How to Start a Cosmogony: On the Poetics of Beginnings in Greece and the Near East" with the words of the Hellenistic Jewish sage Ben Sira, "The beginning of any work (is) a word, / and the beginning of any deed is a thought" (2012: 30), but it turns out that, in Indo-European poetry, the beginning is both word and thought.

In all of this, verses 35–36 stand out. For one thing, the last word of nearly every verse of the *Dichterweihe* is vowel-initial (22, 24–27, and 29–34), a tendency that is picked up again from 37 (37–39, 42–48, and 51–52)—whereas 35 closes with πέτρην and 36 with πατρί. Furthermore, the stand-alone question in 35 is phonologically isolated from what has preceded, and the only material in 36 that is familiar is Μουσάων ἀρχώμεθα, which is exceptionally located in the less-prominent middle of the verse. My suggestion is that, as far as sounds are concerned, 35–36 are a bridge between the Muses' vocalic melodiousness, which they probably learned from their mother, Μνημοσύνη, "Memory" (whose name likewise goes back to **men-* and who is named at the start of verse 54, just after the last of the subsections treated above), and the harsh consonants of their loud-thundering father, Zeus, sounds they may be able to make themselves (perhaps as part of telling tales that only resemble true things?) but not the ones that the poet or the tradition emphasizes. It may be added that while the Muses τέρπουσι Διὸς νόον (51), "delight the mind of Zeus" (note that τερπ- Διός is phonetically reminiscent of Διὶ πατρί), Zeus himself is described elsewhere in Hesiod (*WD* 52) and in Homer (e.g., *Iliad* 1.419) with the epithet τερπικέραυνος. This consonant-heavy compound synchronically means "delighting [τερπι-] in the thunderbolt [κεραυνός]," but there is a good chance that it has been linguistically deformed from something like **perkʷi-peraunos*, "having a striking thunderstrike," where the first element is immediately relatable to the name of the Lithuanian storm god *Perkúnas* (and to Latin *quercus*, "oak," assimilated from "**percus*") and the second to his Slavic equivalent, *Perunŭ* (see above).[26]

One last look at verses 35–36 will make clear what I mean:

ἀλλὰ τίη μοι ταῦτα περὶ δρῦν ἢ περὶ πέτρην;
τύνη, Μουσάων ἀρχώμεθα, ταὶ Διὶ πατρί.

If it is acceptable at some level to read the ends of verses 31–34 vertically as "voice—are—always are—always to sing," then there is no reason not to keep going in the same way, which yields the immediately following "rock—father Zeus." In a society in which prophetic rocks are associated with a high god, in which Zeus owes his birth to his mother Rhea's ruse with a μέγαν λίθον (*Th* 485, acc.), "great stone" (see, e.g., Bassi 2016: 33–39), and in which there are both natural and artificial "aniconic representations of Zeus as a stone" (Cook 1914: 520n2), it would hardly be surprising if a (folk-)etymological association between the nouns πατήρ and πέτρη had (an almost Lucretian, but in the first place oral) resonance: the Muses always sing sweetly of their father, who himself crashes about. Furthermore, by using the epithet "father," Διὶ πατρί ("Zeus' most ancient title"; West 1966: 170),[27] Hesiod not only employs a fine Indo-European touch (cf. Vedic *dyàuṣ pítar* and Latin *Iuppiter*) but highlights the harsh oral stops of Zeus's thunder: if we leave aside the resonant Μουσάων ἀρχώμεθα, which picks up the start of the poem, all the words in verse 36 begin with a dental or labial oral stop—T/D or P, respectively—and the one that begins with a P has a following T; there is, of course, a similar emphasis on these same sounds in 35, and not just in the final word.[28]

What of the preposition περί? A curiosity about verse 35, noted above, is that Hesiod uses this preposition plus the accusative rather than ἀπό (or ἐκ) and the genitive.[29] Much ink has been spilled over this, and most people cite the statement of West (1966: 169) that "[a]nyone who attempts to explain . . . Hesiod's expression . . . should in future take note of the fact that περί with the accusative in early epic always has a local sense; so that the phrase is not simply 'about', i.e. concerning, tree and rock, but 'round.'" It is surely wise not to be too strict about this (see Nagy 1990: 199n122; Clay 2003: 53n12; López-Ruiz 2010: 81; also Forte 2015: 9), but in any case we now see that there is quite another set of reasons—phonetic reasons—for Hesiod's choice of περί.[30] One is that περί, with its P and its R and also its final I, combines with πέτρην to make an especially nice phonetic play on ταὶ Διὶ πατρί. Another is that the accusative δρῦν has a dental stop, an R, and a final N, so the combination of περὶ δρῦν plus περὶ πέτρην provides further emphasis on the same sounds. And finally, it will be noted that the one word in verse 36 that I have not yet analyzed, the unusual subsection-opening τύνη, picks up phonetically on the almost immediately preceding δρῦν ἤ. The sequence -ŪNĒ- is found in Hesiod only here, in the two other—and likewise verse-initial—instances of τύνη (*WD* 10 and 641; see below), and in most case-forms of nouns in -σύνη, of which there are not many instances in Hesiod (see Wyss 1954: 29–30), with the only verse-initial examples being the name of the Muses' memorial mother, Μνημοσύνη, in *Th* 54 and 915, plus the paradoxical juxtaposition of the former with λησμοσύνην (55, acc.), "forgetfulness."

Forte (2015: 2n3) writes of περὶ δρῦν ἤ περὶ πέτρην that "[t]he scholarly emphasis on the 'proverbial' nature of the phrase is somewhat imprecise in my view, given that proverbs usually connote a particular maxim or practical truth for which I see no evidence here." Be that as it may, proverbs are often rhetorically balanced and "jingly,"[31] and it is easy to see that Hesiod's close attention to phonetic form makes this an exceptionally good and balanced jingle.[32] And there is truth in it, too, as well as folk-etymological knowledge that resembles truth. As I hope to have shown, Hesiod's question looks both backward and forward, in ways that go beyond what anyone has so far noticed. Looking to both the Muses and their father, Zeus, to the melodies of the former and the thunder of the latter, the question encapsulates in just a few syllables Hesiod's new role as mouth-piece at the head of the simultaneously Indo-European- and Near Eastern-based tradition of Greek poetry. But he is also very much his own mouthpiece: by naming himself in verse 22; by etymologizing his own name (ὄσσαν ἱεῖσαι; see above) while at the same time instantiating the vowel-filled speech of the Muses; by making the question in 35 personal (μοι "to me"); and by adding a marked form of the second-person plural pro-noun in 36 (τύνη, literally "you") to address himself—the last a pronoun that, as al-ready noted, he will go on to use twice more, in the same metrical position, in the WD, once at the end of the proem and both times referring to his brother Perses—Hesiod inaugurates his poetic career with a stress on the (apparently) biographical as well as on the sorts of deeper literary and cultural effects that lead scholars today to examine Indo-European prehistory and Near Eastern analogues.

Nagy (1990: 199; cf. 1974: 125) writes that Hesiod's question in verse 35 is "the equiva-lent of asking why he has lingered at the beginning of beginnings. 'Why am I still going around, as it were, the proverbial oak or rock? Let me proceed at last by starting out again!'" Have I now lingered too long myself? Maybe so—but careless forays into Proto-Indo-European territory and into Asia Minor are perilous. Many Indo-Europeanists are reluctant to acknowledge the limitations of reconstruction and downplay the very real dangers that can arise when one "finds" cultural material that suits one's prejudices; while the remark of Doniger O'Flaherty (1979: 2, 1980: 151) that "Proto-Indo-Europe, the country east of the asterisk, is a never-never land" is more witty than true, it behooves us to do things right, and that means proceeding with deliberation. As for Greece and the Near East, one does not need to cite the debacle that is *Black Athena* to know that "[i]n language and onomastics as in art it is too easy to pull a parallel of some sort out of the Near Eastern hat and our tests must be rigorous" (Boardman 1966: 87). If there were more space, I would continue, not neglecting the *WD*, and I would point out such poten-tial Indo-European nuggets as the taboo on urinating while standing up facing the sun (*WD* 727);[33] assess claims like the one of Zanker (2009) that a "stor[y]...in the [Sanskrit epic] *Mahābhārata* and the tale that inspired the Fable of the Hawk and Nightingale [*WD* 202–12] both had a common ancestor..., which originated in Mesopotamia" (23); and further explore the idea that Hesiod looks westward, too, giving us, in a curious turn of phrase at *Th* 1013, our first Greek mention of King Latinus (see Katz 2010b: 80–83). But such things—new beginnings—are for other works and for other days.[34]

Notes

1. Some editions (e.g., Solmsen 1990) put a paragraph break right after verse 35, others (e.g., West 1966; Most 2006) right before.
2. For the argument advanced in this paragraph, see Watkins (1995: 150–51), extended by Katz (2007); see also Reece (2009: 217–30).

3. The controversial idea that Trojan is Luvian is associated above all with Watkins (1986, 1995: 144–51) and Starke (1997: 456–59 and passim). Bachvarova (2016: 361–62) provides the latest assessment.

4. The best introduction to the Indo-European languages is Fortson 2010 (ταρ makes a cameo appearance on p. 150).

5. See, e.g., West (1971, 1997), Burkert (1992, 2004), Morris (1992), Bezantakos (2006), López-Ruiz (2010), Haubold (2013), Metcalf (2015), Bachvarova (2016), and Currie (2016: 147–222), as well as the papers in Collins, Bachvarova, and Rutherford (2008).

6. The partial exception is Woodard (2007), which has in common with the present chapter that it considers both the Near Eastern and the Indo-European sources of myth in Hesiod; my own interest here is as much in Hesiod's poetics as in the content of his words.

7. A few verses earlier, Hector asks himself a question that begins ἀλλὰ τίη μοι ταῦτα (122), "but why to me these things . . . ?," which occupies the same metrical position as οὐ μέν πως νῦν ἔστιν (up to the penthemimeral caesura). Leaving aside the would-be hiatus between ταῦτα and ἀπό, we can easily stitch the first half of verse 122 to the second half of 126 (~ Th 35).

8. The collocation πέτρας καὶ δρῦς (acc. pl.) appears in Sophist 246a, but the two terms are in the opposite order from the usual and I do not believe that this is part of the set. We also find examples in Plato and elsewhere of "λιθ- and/or ξυλ-" (e.g., λίθους καὶ ξύλα, "stones and sticks"; Plato, Gorgias 468a, acc.), a "Paarformel" that Janda (1997: 90) says is "die jüngere und . . . auf die Prosa beschränkt." For a reckoning of the Greek evidence from Homer and Hesiod to Nonnus via Plutarch (Moralia 608c; see Alexiou 1998), see Janda (1997: 68–90).

9. See Katz and Volk (2000) for the idea that the immediately preceding verse—ποιμένες ἄγραυλοι, κάκ' ἐλέγχεα, γαστέρες οἶον (26), "shepherds who dwell in the fields, worthy of reproach, mere bellies"—provides us with the earliest Greek example of the Near Eastern practice of belly-prophecy.

10. The alert reader may have wondered how exactly to interpret the translation I gave in the opening paragraph: "But what are these things about a tree or a rock to me?" West (1966: 169) concludes, "It is best to acknowledge that the truth is lost in antiquity"; in his own translation of a couple of decades later he opts for "But what is my business round tree or rock?" (West 1988: 4). Other renderings include "[B]ut why do I have these things around the oak or around the rock?" and "But why do I have these things about the oak or about the rock?" (Nagy 1974: 125 and 1990: 182 and 199, respectively); "But what are such things to me, round tree and round rock[?]" (Watkins 1995: 161); and "But what is this to me, about an oak or a rock?" (Most 2006: 5, with the comment in n3: "A proverbial expression, possibly already so for Hesiod; its origin is obscure but its meaning here is evidently, 'Why should I waste time speaking about irrelevant matters?'"). López-Ruiz (2010: 82–83) writes, "If I had to paraphrase verse 35 . . . , the result would be something like this: 'Why am I digressing about these mysterious/arcane and divine things, that is, about where my special knowledge of the origin of the world and the gods came from?'"

11. The translation is that of Forte (2015: 12 and passim), adapted from Smith and Pitard (2009: 71 and 202). For commentary on the difficult Ugaritic lines and their surrounding context, see Smith and Pitard (2009: 225–34) and Forte (2015: 22–25 and passim).

12. Thus Forte (2015: 2; emphasis in original). Already O'Bryhim (1996), besides mentioning Zeus's oak at Dodona (see above), gives examples of Greek prophetic interpretation via the sounds of trees (arbores locutae; Pliny, Natural History 17.243) and stones (Orphic

Lithica 360–75); he also describes Semitic oracular trees (often oaks) and stones (including baetyls). In his discussion of the Ugaritic text, Janda (1997: 164) mischievously remarks, "*Saxa loquuntur.*" For Macarius, see West (1966: 168) and Watkins (1995: 162).

13. An interesting exercise is to go through West (1997; on the Near Eastern background of early Greek poetry) and West (2007; on Indo-European elements in Greek and other poetry), see which passages are discussed in both places, and try to evaluate in each case whether this scholar has contradicted himself or the picture is complicated. Compare Rutherford (2009: 20–21).

14. Watkins (1992, 1995: 448–59) emphasizes the indebtedness of the Greek version of the story to the (Hatto-)Hittite Myth of Illuyankas, a serpent with whom the storm god engages in an epic battle, whereas West (1997: 300–4) considers a range of parallels, most of them ultimately non-Indo-European, including the Hurro-Hittite Song of Ullikummi, a gigantic stone monster, and the Sumero-Akkadian epic of the "storm bird" Anzû; see Rutherford (2009: 9–14 and passim), as well as Scully (2015: 54–55). For further Indo-European thoughts on and around the myth of Typhoeus and its analogues, including on the Hittite word *illuyankaš* and the Greek name $T\nu\varphi\omega\epsilon\acute{\nu}\varsigma/T\nu\varphi\hat{\omega}\nu$, see Katz (1998, 2005).

15. See Lamberterie (1998) for an Indo-European-based account of $\gamma\lambda\acute{\omega}\sigma\sigma\eta\sigma\iota$ $\delta\nuο\varphi\epsilon\rho\hat{\eta}\sigma\iota$ $\lambda\epsilon\lambda\iota\chi\mu\acute{ο}\tau\epsilon\varsigma$ (*Th* 826), "licking with their dark tongues," said of Typhoeus's hundred snaky heads; the perfect participle has a cognate in Indic (*Rig Veda* 10.79.3), and Lamberterie shows that it means "non pas 'léchant (quelque chose)', mais 'agitant une langue lécheuse' ou 'donnant des coups de langue'" (384–85)—an excellent meaning for this in every way multilingual monster.

16. For the etymology of the latter word and its connection (not immediately obvious) to forms elsewhere in Indo-European, see Meier-Brügger (1980).

17. For the Avestan comparison, see Jochem Schindler *apud* Watkins (1995: 162–64); see also in great detail Janda (1997: 23–49). Forte (2015) relegates the evidence to two footnotes, writing that "[t]here appears to be no element of speech in the Avestan passage, which indicates that it likely is not semantically related to the Greek phrase in question" (7–8n9; see also 2n2). I am confident that there is more to say.

18. Fortson (2010: 26) briefly describes what the Proto-Indo-European "god of thunder and lightning" had to do with both trees/oaks and stones; see in detail West (2007: 238–55). In Greece, "[t]he thunder-god's functions were taken over . . . by the great sky-god, Zeus" (West 2007: 243; see also 247–49).

19. See Schmoll (1994) on verse 35 as a bridge. López-Ruiz (2010: 80) argues that it "does not simply have the rhetorical function of changing topics and linking the previous and following sections, [but] it encapsulates the whole previous passage."

20. See above all Pucci (2007). For the proem of the *WD*, see West (1978: 136–42), Watkins (1995: 98–101), and Katz (2013a: 15–21).

21. For ὄσσα as "divine utterance," compare Collins (1999).

22. Cook (1925: 829; footnotes omitted) observes that "[t]he modern mind, steeped in Semitic thought, readily conceives thunder as the voice of God. But this was not a classical conception. Thunder was at most an ominous sound preceding divine speech"; see also Goslin (2010: 365).

23. Note that words beginning $\alpha\epsilon(\iota)$-, $\alpha\iota$-, $\alpha o(\iota)$-, and $\alpha\nu$- show up in this spot, though not all of them have a hiatus.

24. On the etymology and folk-etymological associations of Hesiod's name, see Meier-Brügger (1990).

25. See Katz (2013a, rev. version: forthcoming-a), as well as Katz (2013b, forthcoming-b).

26. See Nagy (1974: 126–28, 1990: 194–95), as well as West (2007: 244). Compare also Watkins (1995: 343n1).

27. We have already seen πατρὸς | Ζηνός (40–41), but the two words may not function as a unit here ("the halls of their father, loud-thundering Zeus" rather than "the halls of loud-thundering father Zeus"); they are in the non-canonical order; and Ζηνός is obviously a neologism vis-à-vis the inherited genitive Διός.

28. In Katz (2013a: 13–14) I comment on the striking vocalic nature of the paradigm nom. Ζεύς, gen. Διός, etc. and the way the forms play themselves out in the proem of the WD. My emphasis here, by contrast, is not on Zeus's name but on the sounds he himself makes, his thunderous nature—a change of perspective aided by the addition of the word for "father."

29. Reversing the order of the objects (cf. note 8 above), Plutarch uses the preposition διά and the genitive at *Moralia* 1083d: διὰ πέτρας καὶ διὰ δρυὸς ὁρᾶν, "to see through rock and tree," i.e., "s[e]h[en] durch alles hindurch" (Janda 1997: 84).

30. For a metrical perspective on the placement of forms of δρυ- in archaic epic, both with and without a preceding περί, see Watkins (1995: 161n7).

31. Compare Greene (2012: 763, "Jingle" (L. Perrine, T. V. F. Brogan, and E. J. Rettberg) and esp. 1122–23, "Proverb" (D. Hoffman)), with references.

32. See Watkins (1995: 21–49) and West (2007: 58–59 and 75–119) for comments on Indo-European poetic stylistics, including phonetic play; see also Katz (2010a).

33. Adducing evidence from the Indic *Atharva Veda*, Watkins (1995: 14 and 152) highlights this as an Indo-European formula; West (1997: 217) provides further support for the taboo in Greece and India, though writing that "the conjunction of words ['urinate upright'] is too natural to be claimed as a poetic or ritual formula" (n78). Scodel (2017: 83–85) considers Hesiod's comments on toilet practices to be highly personal and "eccentric" (84).

34. My thanks go to Teddy Fassberg for inspiring me to build this chapter around *Th* 35.

References

Alexiou, E. 1998. "'Οὐκ ἀπὸ δρυὸς οὐδ᾽ ἀπὸ πέτρης': Plutarch *Consolatio ad uxorem* 608C und die Umdeutung eines Homerverses." *Mnemosyne* 51: 72–75.

Bachvarova, M. R. 2016. *From Hittite to Homer: The Anatolian Background of Ancient Greek Epic*. Cambridge.

Bassi, K. 2016. *Traces of the Past: Classics between History and Archaeology*. Ann Arbor, MI.

Bezantakos, N. P. 2006. "Ἡσίοδος καὶ Ἀνατολή." In Μουσάων ἀρχώμεθα: Ὁ Ἡσίοδος καὶ ἡ ἀρχαϊκὴ ἐπικὴ ποίηση, edited by N. P. Bezantakos and Ch. K. Tsagalis, 21–138. Athens, Greece.

Boardman, J. 1966. "An Orient Wave [review of *Hellenosemitica: An Ethnic and Cultural Study in West Semitic Impact on Mycenaean Greece* (1965), by M. C. Astour]." *Classical Review* 16: 86–88.

Burkert, W. 1992. *The Orientalizing Revolution: Near Eastern Influence on Greek Culture in the Early Archaic Age*. Translated by M. E. Pinder and W. Burkert. Cambridge, MA. (Revised from German original of 1984.)

Burkert, W. 2004. *Babylon, Memphis, Persepolis: Eastern Contexts of Greek Culture*. Cambridge, MA. (Revised from Italian original of 1999.)

Clay, J. S. 2003. *Hesiod's Cosmos*. Cambridge.

Collins, B. J., M. R. Bachvarova, and I. C. Rutherford, eds. 2008. *Anatolian Interfaces: Hittites, Greeks and Their Neighbours. Proceedings of an International Conference on Cross-cultural Interaction, September 17–19, 2004, Emory University, Atlanta, GA*. Oxford.

Collins, D. 1999. "Hesiod and the Divine Voice of the Muses." *Arethusa* 32: 241–62.

Cook, A. B. 1914. *Zeus: A Study in Ancient Religion*. Vol. 1, *Zeus God of the Bright Sky*. Cambridge.

Cook, A. B. 1925. *Zeus: A Study in Ancient Religion*. Vol. 2, *Zeus God of the Dark Sky (Thunder and Lightning)*. Cambridge.

Currie, B. 2016. *Homer's Allusive Art*. Oxford.

Dirlmeier, F. 1955. "Homerisches Epos und Orient." *Rheinisches Museum* 98: 18–37.

Doniger O'Flaherty, W. 1979. "Sacred Cows and Profane Mares in Indian Mythology." *History of Religions* 19: 1–26.

Doniger O'Flaherty, W. 1980. *Women, Androgynes, and Other Mythical Beasts*. Chicago.

Forte, A. S. W. 2015. "Speech from Tree and Rock: Recovery of a Bronze Age Metaphor." *American Journal of Philology* 136: 1–35.

Fortson, B. W. IV. 2010. *Indo-European Language and Culture: An Introduction*. 2nd ed. Malden, MA.

Goslin, O. 2010. "Hesiod's Typhonomachy and the Ordering of Sound." *Transactions of the American Philological Association* 140: 351–73.

Greene, R., ed. 2012. *The Princeton Encyclopedia of Poetry and Poetics*. 4th ed. Princeton, NJ.

Haubold, J. 2013. *Greece and Mesopotamia: Dialogues in Literature*. Cambridge.

Janda, M. 1997. *Über "Stock und Stein": Die indogermanischen Variationen eines universalen Phraseologismus*. Dettelbach, Germany.

Katz, J. T. 1998. "How to Be a Dragon in Indo-European: Hittite *illuyankaš* and Its Linguistic and Cultural Congeners in Latin, Greek, and Germanic." In *Mír Curad: Studies in Honor of Calvert Watkins*, edited by J. Jasanoff, H. C. Melchert, and L. Oliver, 317–34. Innsbruck, Austria.

Katz, J. T. 2005. "To Turn a Blind Eel." In *Proceedings of the Sixteenth Annual UCLA Indo-European Conference, Los Angeles, November 5–6, 2004*, edited by K. Jones-Bley, M. E. Huld, A. Della Volpe, and M. R. Dexter, 259–96. Washington, DC.

Katz, J. T. 2007. "The Epic Adventures of an Unknown Particle." In *Greek and Latin from an Indo-European Perspective*, edited by C. George, M. McCullagh, B. Nielsen, A. Ruppel, and O. Tribulato, 65–79. Cambridge.

Katz, J. T. 2010a. "Inherited Poetics." In *A Companion to the Ancient Greek Language*, edited by E. J. Bakker, 357–69. Malden, MA.

Katz, J. T. 2010b. "Linguistics." In *The Oxford Handbook of Roman Studies*, edited by A. Barchiesi and W. Scheidel, 77–92. Oxford.

Katz, J. T. 2013a. "Gods and Vowels." In *Poetic Language and Religion in Greece and Rome*, edited by J. V. García and A. Ruiz, 2–28. Newcastle upon Tyne, UK.

Katz, J. T. 2013b. "The Hymnic Long Alpha: Μούσας ἀείδω and Related Incipits in Archaic Greek Poetry." In *Proceedings of the 24th Annual UCLA Indo-European Conference, Los Angeles, October 26th and 27th, 2012*, edited by S. W. Jamison, H. C. Melchert, and B. Vine, 87–101. Bremen, Germany.

Katz, J. T. Forthcoming-a. "Gods and Vowels." In *Sound and the Ancient Senses*, edited by S. Butler and S. Nooter. London. (Revised version of Katz 2013a.)

Katz, J. T. Forthcoming-b. "Μῆνιν ἄειδε, θεά and the Form of the Homeric Word for 'Goddess.'" In *Language and Meter*, edited by D. Gunkel and O. Hackstein. Leiden, Netherlands.

Katz, J. T., and K. Volk. 2000. "'Mere Bellies': A New Look at *Theogony* 26–8." *Journal of Hellenic Studies* 120: 122–31.

Lamberterie, C. de. 1998. "Langues de feu (Grec hésiodique λελιχμότες : sanskrit védique ririhvás-)." In *Mír Curad: Studies in Honor of Calvert Watkins*, edited by J. Jasanoff, H. C. Melchert, and L. Oliver, 373–90. Innsbruck, Austria.

López-Ruiz, C. 2010. *When the Gods were Born: Greek Cosmogonies and the Near East.* Cambridge, MA.

López-Ruiz, C. 2012. "How to Start a Cosmogony: On the Poetics of Beginnings in Greece and the Near East." *Journal of Ancient Near Eastern Religions* 12: 30–48.

Meier-Brügger, M. 1980. "Griechisch πέτρᾱ, πέτρος." *Zeitschrift für Vergleichende Sprachforschung* 94: 122–24.

Meier-Brügger, M. 1990. "Zu Hesiods Namen." *Glotta* 68: 62–67.

Metcalf, C. 2015. *The Gods Rich in Praise: Early Greek and Mesopotamian Religious Poetry.* Oxford.

Montanari, F., A. Rengakos, and C. Tsagalis, eds. 2009. *Brill's Companion to Hesiod.* Leiden, Netherlands.

Morris, S. P. 1992. *Daidalos and the Origins of Greek Art.* Princeton, NJ.

Most, G. W., ed. and trans. 2006. *Hesiod: Theogony, Works and Days, Testimonia.* Cambridge, MA.

Nagy, G. 1974. "*Perkúnas* and *Perunъ.*" In *Antiquitates Indogermanicae: Studien zur indogermanischen Altertumskunde und zur Sprach- und Kulturgeschichte der indogermanischen Völker. Gedenkschrift für Hermann Güntert zur 25. Wiederkehr seines Todestages am 23. April 1973,* edited by M. Mayrhofer, W. Meid, B. Schlerath, and R. Schmitt, 113–31. Innsbruck, Austria.

Nagy, G. 1990. *Greek Mythology and Poetics.* Ithaca, NY.

O'Bryhim, S. 1996. "A New Interpretation of Hesiod, 'Theogony' 35." *Hermes* 124: 131–39.

Parke, H. W. 1967. *The Oracles of Zeus: Dodona, Olympia, Ammon.* Cambridge, MA.

Penglase, C. 1994. *Greek Myths and Mesopotamia: Parallels and Influence in the "Homeric Hymns" and Hesiod.* London.

Pucci, P., trans. and comm. 2007. *Inno alle Muse (Esiodo, Teogonia, 1–115).* Pisa, Italy.

Reece, S. 2009. *Homer's Winged Words: The Evolution of Early Greek Epic Diction in the Light of Oral Theory.* Leiden, Netherlands.

Rutherford, I. 2009. "Hesiod and the Literary Traditions of the Near East." In *Brill's Companion to Hesiod,* edited by F. Montanari, A. Rengakos, and C. Tsagalis, 9–35. Leiden, Netherlands.

Schmoll, E. A. 1994. "Hesiod's *Theogony*: Oak and Stone Again." *Scholia* 3: 46–52.

Scodel, R. 2017. "The Individual Voice in *Works and Days.*" In *Voice and Voices in Antiquity,* edited by N. W. Slater, 74–91. Leiden, Netherlands.

Scully, S. 2015. *Hesiod's Theogony: From Near Eastern Creation Myths to Paradise Lost.* Oxford.

Smith, M. S., and W. T. Pitard, trans. and comm. 2009. *The Ugaritic Baal Cycle.* Vol. 2, *Introduction with Text, Translation and Commentary of KTU/CAT 1.3–1.4.* Leiden, Netherlands.

Solmsen, F., ed. 1990. *Hesiodi Theogonia, Opera et Dies, Scutum.* 3rd ed. Oxford.

Starke, F. 1997. "Troia im Kontext des historisch-politischen und sprachlichen Umfeldes Kleinasiens im 2. Jahrtausend." *Studia Troica* 7: 447–87.

Taylor, T. 2016. *Work & Days: Poems.* Pasadena, CA.

Tsagalis, C. 2009. "Poetry and Poetics in the Hesiodic Corpus." In *Brill's Companion to Hesiod,* edited by F. Montanari, A. Rengakos, and C. Tsagalis, 131–77. Leiden, Netherlands.

Walcot, P. 1966. *Hesiod and the Near East.* Cardiff, UK.

Watkins, C. 1986. "The Language of the Trojans." In *Troy and the Trojan War: A Symposium Held at Bryn Mawr College, October 1984,* edited by M. J. Mellink, 45–62. Bryn Mawr, PA. (Reprinted in C. Watkins, *Selected Writings,* edited by L. Oliver, 2:700–17. Innsbruck, Austria, 1994.)

Watkins, C. 1992. "Le Dragon hittite Illuyankas et le géant grec Typhôeus." *Comptes Rendus de l'Académie des Inscriptions et Belles-Lettres,* 319–30. (Reprinted in C. Watkins, *Selected Writings,* edited by L. Oliver, 3: 775–86. Innsbruck, Austria, 2008.)

Watkins, C. 1995. *How to Kill a Dragon: Aspects of Indo-European Poetics.* New York.

West, M. L., ed. and comm. 1966. *Hesiod: Theogony.* Oxford.

West, M. L. 1971. *Early Greek Philosophy and the Orient.* Oxford.

West, M. L., ed. and comm. 1978. *Hesiod: Works & Days.* Oxford.

West, M. L., trans. 1988. *Hesiod: Theogony and Works and Days.* Oxford.

West, M. L. 1997. *The East Face of Helicon: West Asiatic Elements in Greek Poetry and Myth.* Oxford.

West, M. L., ed. 1998. *Homeri Ilias.* Vol. 1, *Rhapsodias I–XII continens.* Stuttgart, Germany.

West, M. L. 2007. *Indo-European Poetry and Myth.* Oxford.

West, M. L. 2012. "Towards a Chronology of Early Greek Epic." In *Relative Chronology in Early Greek Epic Poetry,* edited by Ø. Andersen and D. T. T. Haug, 224–41. Cambridge.

Woodard, R. D. 2007. "Hesiod and Greek Myth." In *The Cambridge Companion to Greek Mythology,* edited by R. D. Woodard, 83–165. Cambridge.

Wyss, U. 1954. *Die Wörter auf -σύνη in ihrer historischen Entwicklung.* Aarau, Switzerland.

Zanker, A. T. 2009. "A Dove and a Nightingale: *Mahābhārata* 3. 130. 18–3. 131. 32 and Hesiod, *Works and Days* 202–213." *Philologus* 153: 10–25.

PART II

HESIOD'S ART

CHAPTER 6

....

HESIODIC POETICS

....

STEPHEN SCULLY

THE ancient Greeks and Romans, viewing Hesiod and Homer as the two finest singers of ancient *epea*, frequently imagined them in a poetic face-off. In terms of poetics, this contest seems simultaneously natural and surprising: natural because both of them composed in the artificial "song dialect" and highly formulaic medium of epic, and surprising because Homer's long, heroic poetry differed so greatly in voice, theme, length, structure, and style from Hesiod's much shorter narrative poetry or from his didactic poetry. Four major songs were attributed to Hesiod for much of antiquity, but in this chapter I concentrate on the *Theogony* (hereafter *Th*) and the *Works and Days* (hereafter *WD*).

The important question of whether Homer or Hesiod "took advantage" of writing unfortunately remains unanswerable. By the end of the eighth century BCE the Greeks had developed an alphabetic writing system that was used, among other things, to record hexameter verses on drinking cups, but it is unknown if Hesiod or Homer was literate or employed this new technology when composing (even assuming that these figures were historical authors). Nor has it been clearly explained how writing might have aided composition at this time. If Hesiod and Homer did not commit their songs to writing, they may have either recited them to scribes or had them memorized by rhapsodes, who retained the songs (perhaps still in a somewhat fluid state) for a period of time before transcription. Some take Hesiod's act of naming himself as proof of writing, as a singer before a live audience would feel no such need, while others see the name Hesiod (perhaps meaning Songsender) as a generic descriptor of the traditional persona of the poem's composer. Regardless of the method of stabilization of the composition, it is crucial to recognize, as numbers of scholars now have, that oral composers could memorize extensive sections of a song and "creatively" employ formulaic expression for artistic effect (Jensen 1980: 112–24; Rutherford 2012: 115). It is thus on this principle of controlled artistic expression that I consider various stylistic features in Hesiod, with reference to Homer.

VOICE AND THEME

In narrative voice and theme, the *Th* and the *WD* differ one from another as much as they do from the *Iliad* and *Odyssey*. As are Homer's songs, the *Th* is told almost exclusively in the third person, except for the memorable moment when the singer identifies himself by name and then turns to the first person to describe an encounter with the Muses as he was shepherding his flock on Mt. Helicon (22–35). Even in hymnic epic, nothing comes close to this extensive "autobiographical" intrusion. Numerous details in this epiphany are striking, including the use of enjambment to recount the making of Hesiod's "voice / divine" (the human voice, αὐδή, made divine in the bridge from verse 31 to 32; perhaps imitated by Milton: "What in me is dark / Illumine," in *Paradise Lost* i. 26–27). Also striking is the Muses' unparalleled gift of a σκῆπτρον, a staff of religious and political bearing, rather than a lyre, to the shepherd turned singer (30–31). Much in this scene goes unexplained, but collectively it bestows upon Hesiod an authority to speak of primordial beginnings and Zeus's political rise to power that culminates in the Olympian acclamation that he be "king and ruler of the immortals" (883–85). It is no less striking in this epiphanic encounter that after the Muses reveal that they know how to tell true tales or false tales that sound true (27–28), neither they nor Hesiod then assures the audience that the story about to be told is indeed truthful. After this duly famous personal account, the *Th* reverts back to a Homeric-like, third-person narration.

After a very short proem (sometimes in antiquity thought to be spurious) (1–10), the *WD*, by contrast, is told almost entirely in the first person, as the narrator describes a bitter quarrel with his brother, Perses (last mentioned at 641) and offers phrases of gnomic wisdom. Even the invocation to the Muses and Zeus, called upon to "give ear" and "straighten verdicts with justice" (9), concludes with the first-person voice of the narrator: "I should like to speak of true things to Perses" (10). At times this voice easily aligns itself with the Muses' voices: "I shall tell you the mind of aegis-bearing Zeus / for the Muses taught me to sing a hymn of great beauty" (661–62), but often it speaks with self-assured independence: "You great fool, Perses, with my clear-headed thoughts I shall address you" (σοὶ δ' ἐγὼ ἐσθλὰ νοέων ἐρέω, μέγα νήπιε Πέρση) (286). Even when narrating stories like the Five Ages of Man, the "I" prevails: "Would that I did not live among men of the fifth age, but had died before or been born afterwards" (174–75). Others in this volume (Koning, Bakker, Gonzalez) discuss whether this voice should be considered autobiographical or "fictive," in the manner of performative oral poetry.

Even with its local, first-person orientation, the song is far from being parochial, as it expands to include fables and mythic accounts of the Five Ages of Man, Prometheus contending with Zeus, and the creation of Pandora. With such vistas, the *WD* attains something approaching the *Th*'s and Homer's universal themes. Also expanding upon its initial focus, the song concludes with a calendar (of sorts) of a farmer's year.

The afterlives of the *Th* and the *WD* reflect their different voices. Only occasionally do later authors draw actively from both. Already in the archaic period, the moralizing indignation and first-person narrative of the *WD* enter into the emerging sympotic tradition, appealing to poets like Alcaeus, Theognis, and the Aesop-tradition. The *Th* with its genealogies, story of cosmic evolution, and broad political themes, by contrast, was likely performed at festivals and athletic games, appealing to a different set of authors and genres, including writers of the *Homeric Hymns*; Pre-Socratics like Heraclitus, Parmenides, and Empedocles; and poets like Pindar, Aeschylus, and Aristophanes, not to mention Orphic rhapsodists and cosmologists like Epimenides and Pherecydes. Among Greek authors, only Solon and Plato draw significantly from both songs, and among Roman authors, only Ovid does so, especially in the *Metamorphoses*. These divergences can also be mapped out for all periods of reception up to the Renaissance and beyond. (See Canevaro, Van Noorden, and Lecznar in this volume.)

LENGTH AND FORM

Compared to Homer's monumental compositions (the *Iliad* being over fifteen thousand verses and the *Odyssey* over twelve thousand), Hesiod's songs are short (roughly one thousand verses each). Even in this shortened form, neither displays Homer's narrative tautness. Aristotle makes the important observation that of all archaic epic only the *Iliad* and the *Odyssey* are constructed around a single, unified action, comprising a whole with a beginning, middle, and end (paraphrased from *Poetics* 1451a and 1459a–b). Hesiod's compositions have never been praised for their formal organization. On the contrary, Alexandrian scholar/poets, and those influenced by them, admired and imitated Hesiod's narratives expressly for being nonlinear and discontinuous.

The organization of the *WD* is fluid, perhaps self-consciously so. Recent discussions of its structure include those by Lilah Grace Canevaro, who speaks of a loose tethering of detachable elements (2015: passim, see esp. 21–33, 83–89, 221–29), and Jenny Strauss Clay, who speaks of an increasingly darkening vision and narrowing of horizons from city to household to body (2003: 31–48). The *Th* follows a more predictable trajectory, telling an evolutionary tale from the earliest births (Chaos, Earth, Tartara, Eros, Erebos, and Night) to Zeus's creation of a permanent and stable political order on Olympus, but it tells this tale in a curious way, making it, like the *WD*, a difficult storyline to follow. The song's many extended genealogies (and the ordering of those genealogies) and its numerous digressions seem to confound a clean narrative arc. Upon reflection, however, we realize that each of these digressions relates to Zeus's rise to power, his reign, or efforts to tame a violent world.[1] Half of these stories occur before Zeus's birth is even narrated (457–58), and all occur before the Olympians make Zeus their king (881–85). Even the story of

Zeus's birth anticipates his future prowess: Rhea bore "μητιόεις Zeus, father of gods and men, / by whose thunder the wide earth is shaken" (457–58). The *Th*'s long proem (1–115), much of it in praise of Zeus (47–74), is also striking in comparison to other creation stories, which simply begin at the beginning of things.

As structured, the *Th* frames a story of evolution and change (the theogonic story) with one of permanence and stability (i.e., Zeus's rule), or, in Platonic terms, a story of "being" frames one of "becoming."[2] If we regard the *Th* less as a creation story and more as a hymn to Zeus (which in some ways it certainly is), then its structure and many digressions to Zeus throughout appear less discontinuous and suggest something approaching design, as Hesiod subordinates and recasts the story of evolution and succession into a hymnic praise of Zeus and *his* creation. From this perspective, beginning, middle, and end are one, with the *Th*'s central theme consistently before the reader even as one hears a story of evolution and genealogy. As such, the *Th*, like Homer's poems, may be said to enfold a vast amount of material around a central, dominant theme.

With its attention on the king of the gods, the *Th* resembles a hymn to Zeus (Cornford 1952: 202–13; Pavese 1998: 86), although this song exceeds in length even the longest of the *Homeric Hymns* at least twofold. The oldest of these, the *Hymn to Aphrodite* (no. 5), probably composed less than a century later than the *Th*, comprises 293 verses, while the longest and also the newest of them, the *Hymn to Hermes*, is 580 verses. The *Th*, by comparison, is close to 1,000 verses and perhaps more tightly composed than often supposed. As Homer's poems stood out from all other heroic narratives not only for their compositional unity and thematic focus but also for their monumental length, so one might conjecture that the *Th* stood apart from other hymnic creation stories not only for its unity of design, but also for its exceptional length.

STYLE, NARRATIVE, AND GENEALOGICAL LISTS

Hesiod's and Homer's poetic (and artificial) language draws from the same centuries-old oral tradition, rich in specifically epic vocabulary and formulaic phrases. Like all dialects, this one was continually evolving and refashioning itself. Stylistically, the two practitioners appear on the surface to have had much in common, except that Hesiod was invariably regarded as the inferior craftsman. In antiquity, Horace and pseudo-Longinus marveled at Homer's narrative force, expressive range, and emotional subtlety, while they have little to say about Hesiod's style. In our own time, Hesiod's style is also sometimes ridiculed: "It is as if an artisan with big, awkward fingers were patiently, fascinatedly imitating the fine seam of the professional tailor" (West 1966: 73), and his use of formulae found wanting: "Old formulas from the Ionian tradition, even when not varied, are combined with each other in a clumsy, redundant, or colourless manner" (Kirk 1960: 66).

Similarities in Hesiod's and Homer's formulaic usage are readily apparent, especially in the case of shared epithets for the gods, but even in these likenesses there are noteworthy distinctions. Zeus, for example, is τερπικέραυνος (delighting in thunder) in the *Iliad, Odyssey,* and the *WD,* but not in the *Th;* Gaia is πελώρη (wondrously large, perhaps also with the sense of monstrous) in the *Th,* but nowhere else in epic poetry. Even with common epithets, individual songs can use them with special distinction. For example, the epithet μητίετα, historically most likely a vocative form used as a nominative, indicative of long-standing usage, and referring exclusively to Zeus's μῆτις, appears widely in archaic epic (*Iliad* [15 times], *Odyssey* [3 times], *Th* [5 times], *WD* [1 time], and the *Homeric Hymns*), but its usage in the *Th* stands out. With the poem's characteristic attention to etymologies, Hesiod uses the common formulaic phrase μητίετα Ζεύς just four verses after he has narrated the dramatic story of Zeus ingesting Μῆτις, "in order that the goddess would advise him about good and evil" (900). In such instances, it is tempting to see Hesiod giving μητίετα its origin story. He may similarly be mindful of this story when he uses the epithet μητιόεις (all-wise, skillful) for Zeus (*Th* 2 times; cf. *WD* 3 times), a less common epithet that in Homer is only used for "skillful drugs" (*Odyssey* 4.227).

In the *Th* especially, the storyline elegantly interweaves the personified names in genealogical lists with the corresponding lowercase words (nouns, verbs, and adjectives) in the surrounding narrative. A similar phenomenon is also evident in Iliadic catalogic lists, such as for example in the way the personified figure Φιλότης (Sexual Intercourse) on Aphrodite's girdle (14.216) reappears as a lowercase noun, φιλότης, throughout the immediate narrative, delightfully integrating the catalog figure of Sexual Intercourse with the subsequent narrative concern with such intercourse. Such interweaving of names in lists with the surrounding narrative may indeed be a distinctive stylistic feature of catalog poetry in archaic hexameter poetry. More evidence would tell. One consequence of such interweaving is to draw attention to individual words. Hesiod's unrelenting pleasure in (penchant for?) etymological wordplay, punning, and deified abstractions (many of which he surely made up) has a similar effect. Our previous analysis of Hesiod's treatment of μητίετα and μητιόεις also helps illustrate the point: to a much greater extent than is evident in Homeric poetry, Hesiodic style draws attention to individual words. The examples help illustrate a pervasive distinction between Hesiodic and Homeric use of epic diction.

In the *Th,* examples of such attention to individual words and interplay between catalogic lists and surrounding narrative abound. In one instance, the gods' names appear to emerge out of a narrative description, as if "virtually summoned" into existence, to quote from William Thalmann's graceful description of this phenomenon.[3] For example, immediately following a lovely description of the Muses singing and dancing on their way up the slopes of Olympus to Zeus's home, we learn their names, most of which, we see, have already been intimated in the preceding description. It is worth noting in this context that the *Th* is the earliest poem to name the Muses individually or to give them a genealogy. First, Hesiod's narrative:

> ἔνθά σφιν λιπαροί τε **χοροὶ** καὶ δώματα καλά,
> πὰρ δ' αὐτῆς Χάριτές τε καὶ Ἵμερος οἰκί' ἔχουσιν
> ἐν **θαλίης·** ἐρατὴν δὲ διὰ στόμα ὄσσαν ἱεῖσαι
> **μέλπονται,** πάντων τε νόμους καὶ ἤθεα κεδνὰ
> ἀθανάτων **κλείουσιν,** **ἐπήρατον** ὄσσαν ἱεῖσαι.
> αἳ τότ' ἴσαν πρὸς Ὄλυμπον, ἀγαλλόμεναι **ὀπὶ καλῇ,**
> ἀμβροσίῃ **μολπῇ·** περὶ δ' ἴαχε γαῖα μέλαινα
> **ὑμνεύσαις, ἐρατὸς** δὲ ποδῶν ὕπο δοῦπος ὀρώρει
> νισομένων πατέρ' εἰς ὅν· ὁ δ' **οὐρανῷ** ἐμβασιλεύει

Here is where their shining **dance places** and beautiful homes are,
And next door to them the Graces and Desire have their houses,
in joyous **festivities**; the Muses send forth a **lovely** voice from their mouths
as they **sing and dance** and **glorify** the laws and the cherished customs
of all the immortals, sending forth their **lovely voice.**
Exalting in their **lovely voice** and ambrosial **dance,** they go
to Olympus, the black Earth echoing all 'round as
they hymned, and a **lovely** din rose under their feet as they made
their way to their father who reigns as king in **heaven.**   (63–71)

Then, his list of the Muses' individual names:

> ταῦτ' ἄρα Μοῦσαι ἄειδον Ὀλύμπια δώματ' ἔχουσαι,
> ἐννέα θυγατέρες μεγάλου Διὸς ἐκγεγαυῖαι,
> **Κλειώ** τ' **Εὐτέρπη** τε **Θάλειά** τε **Μελπομένη** τε
> **Τερψιχόρη** τ' **Ἐρατώ** τε **Πολύμνιά** τ' **Οὐρανίη** τε
> **Καλλιόπη** θ'· ἣ δὲ προφερεστάτη ἐστὶν ἁπασέων.

These are the things that the Muses who have their homes on Olympus sing,
the nine daughters conceived from mighty Zeus:
Glory, Happily Delighting, **Festivity/Blooming,** and **Song-and-Dance,**
Delighting in the Chorus, **Lovely, Hymning Many,** and **Heavenly,**
and **With-Lovely-Voice,** the oldest of them all.   (75–79)

The two Muses who are not overtly prefigured in the narrative—Happily-Delighting (Euterpe) and Delighting-in-the-Chorus (Terpsichore)—have already made an appearance in the mention of the Muses *delighting* the mind of Zeus (*Th* 51) and their *dance places* (*Th* 63). In the story's movement from narrative to genealogical list, we sense commonplace words leaping into divine beings.

The interplay between genealogy and storyline works just as smoothly in the opposite direction, when a list of names prefigures the words in the narrative to follow. A case in point is the genealogical list of Eris and her children (with no mention of a male partner):

αὐτὰρ Ἔρις στυγερὴ τέκε μὲν Πόνον ἀλγινόεντα
Λήθην τε Λιμόν τε καὶ Ἄλγεα δακρυόεντα
Ὑσμίνας τε Μάχας τε Φόνους τ' Ἀνδροκτασίας τε
Νείκεά τε Ψεύδεά τε Λόγους τ' Ἀμφιλλογίας τε
Δυσνομίην τ' Ἄτην τε, συνήθεας ἀλλήλῃσιν,
Ὅρκόν θ', ὃς δὴ πλεῖστον ἐπιχθονίους ἀνθρώπους
πημαίνει, ὅτε κέν τις ἑκὼν ἐπίορκον ὀμόσσῃ·

And then hateful **Discord** gave birth to grievous Pain,
and **Forgetfulness** (Lethe), Hunger, and tearful Griefs,
and Fightings, Battles, Murders, and Man-Killings,
and Quarrels and **Lies** (Pseudea), Words, and Double-Words,
and Bad Governance (Dusnomia) and Ruin (Ate), two sisters who go together,
and Oath, who especially brings suffering for earth-bound
humankind, whenever someone willfully swears a false oath.   (226–32)

Immediately following is the narrative description of Nereus, fathered by Pontos (Sea) (with no mention of a female partner):

Νηρέα δ' ἀψευδέα καὶ ἀληθέα γείνατο Πόντος
πρεσβύτατον παίδων· αὐτὰρ καλέουσι γέροντα,
οὕνεκα νημερτής τε καὶ ἤπιος, οὐδὲ θεμίστων
λήθεται, ἀλλὰ δίκαια καὶ ἤπια δήνεα οἶδεν·

Pontos begot **Nereus**, one who **does-not-lie** and **does-not-forget** [i.e. is **truthful**],
the oldest of his children; moreover they call him the old man
because he is both unerring and gentle; **nor does he forget**
ordinances but knows just and gentle counsels.   (233–36)

The sequence of Eris's children in itself tells us something about Hesiod's art. Discord first introduces Pain to the world (226), a general term manifest in a number of different ways (each expressed in a full verse of names), ranging from (a) Forgetfulness, Hunger, and Griefs (perhaps understood here in agricultural terms) (227); to (b) Wars and Man-Killings, as suggested by all the children listed in verse 228; to (c) political conflict, as suggested by the children: Quarrels, Lies, Words, or Double-Words (229). This triad of Pains—agricultural, military, and political—is aptly summarized by Eris's two daughters who never part company: Bad Governance (Dusnomia) and Ruin (Ate). Together, they abstractly summarize both the kind of society that generates these individual maladies and the consequences of them (230). While they affect farming, war, and social discord, the sequence of the list suggests that they are most manifest in political conflict. Hunger, or famine, suggests that the first cause of pain stems from agricultural neglect and the economic grief that comes from it. Forgetfulness in this context may refer to a farmer's failure to attend to Zeus's weather signs, as described at *WD* 491, but it can also be associated with falsehood and the disregard of the law (cf. *WD* 268–69 and *Th* 233–36). Manslayings, Wars, Battles, and Murders are another form of pain, with the emphasis here especially on the conflicts that exist between cities. The following verse turns to the pain within the city in the form of political upheaval. Quarrels, Lies, Words (Logoi), and DoubleWords (Amphillogiai) suggest the agitation of competing words in the ἀγορή, in contrast to the like-minded concord of a community at one with itself

Eris's child Oath comes last and holds an ambiguous status, as he is both an expression and a guarantee of a faithful adherence to one's word, but when that promise is forsworn, as here, the social fabric is riddled with conflict. In this context, Oath is a worthy child of Discord. But even when Oath is honored, he remains painful and hateful, as suggested by his habitation far from Olympus, deep below the highways of Earth, under the watchful eye of "dread, hateful Styx" (cf. 775–76 and 805).[4]

In the narrative that follows, the verbs and adjectives describing Nereus's gentle manner set him apart, point by counterpoint, from the list of Discord's politically disruptive offspring. Here, the interplay between deified abstractions and narrative depends as much on etymology as on personified abstractions. The effect is the same: attention to single terms. Hesiod's choice of the word *does-not-lie*, ἀψευδέα, is rare in Greek, found only here in Hesiod's extant works, and once in Homer as a proper name (Ἀψευδής, *Iliad* 18.96). (It will not reappear in extant Greek for another two hundred years.) There is every reason to suppose that Hesiod chose it deliberately, to contrast with Eris's Ψευδέα (Lies). In like manner, in contrast to Eris's Lethe (Forgetfulness), Nereus is ἀ-ληθέα, truthful, a word Hesiod here suggests means *does-not-forget*. As if to underscore his etymology of ἀληθέα, he repeats this verbal echo, saying that Nereus *does not forget* (οὐδὲ / λήθεται) ordinances. Words built off of root ληθ- appear only three times in the *Th*, two of them being here, first as Eris's child and then as the verb negated (or we can suppose a third instance of the root ληθ- in this ten-verse stretch, if we follow Hesiod's derivation of ἀληθέα). (The only other instance of ληθ- is at verse 28, when the Muses are said to tell lies like truths.) It has even been proposed that Nereus's name is here interpreted as deriving from Ne-Eris, "Not-Discord" (Merkelbach 1956), though Hesiod also plays on the verbal likeness between Nereus and νημερτής ("unerring"). The language of this passage flows from the genealogical list that precedes it.

In addition to drawing attention to individual words, this stylistic feature wonderfully energizes both list and narrative description, as the names of gods seem to pulsate through the everyday language of common nouns, verbs, and adjectives. The case of the Muses' names being summoned out of the narrative is a delightful touch, but the verbal play in the case of Eris and Nereus offers a basic civics lesson. If Bad Governance is characterized by Forgetfulness, Lies, Quarrels, and a plurality of Words, Nereus offers a paradigm of political leadership: not-lieing, always telling the truth, not forgetting ordinances (θέμιστες), being gentle, and knowing just and gentle counsels. The child Good Governance (Eunomia)—the pointed antithesis of Discord's Dusnomia—will not be born until near the end of the poem, when Zeus beds down with Themis (Custom/Law/Ordinance) and they together bring into the world the three Horai (Seasons): Eunomia, Justice (Dike), and Social Peace (Eirene) (*Th* 901–3). We have to wait close to seven hundred verses for Zeus and Themis to produce these deities, but at this point in the poem we have already been introduced to the essential contrast between good and bad governance, in the contrast between Nereus and Eris's children.

Explanation of proper names is certainly Homeric, as well, as in the example of Astyanax, "Lord of the City," the Trojan name for Hektor's and Andromache's son (*Iliad* 6.403), but the *Th* never seems to tire of the habit. The *unerring* (νημερτής) Nereus is a case in point, as are the Horai (Seasons), who "mind" (ὡρεύουσι) the works of men (*Th* 901–2), a pun difficult to capture in English. Such *figurae etymologicae* both draw attention to the proper noun and underline the sense that a name captures a being's essence.

Hesiod's explanation of terms is a further instance of his eye falling on the word. There is not one Eris but two, he says in the *WD*, and then he proceeds to inform his reader of that difference (*WD* 11–26). In the *Th*, this lexical focus can take the form of words curiously juxtaposed or of words evolving in meaning; what is playful also has point. Calling a woman a καλὸν κακόν, a beautiful evil (*Th* 585), draws attention to both "beautiful" and "evil." To use the same word, μήδεα, first for genitals (at the first stage of evolution) (180, 188), and then for Zeus's *plans* (545, 559, 561), is another example of focalization upon a word. The same is true when the word for *sexual intercourse*, φιλότης, comes to describe Zeus's *social intercourse*, or *alliance* (e.g., when he asks the monstrous Hundred-Handers to "remember his kindly friendship" and to stand with the Olympians against the Titans [651]). This moment of reimagining φιλότης and seeing it afresh is underscored by its new epithet, ἐνηής (kindly or gentle), only here with φιλότης in extant Greek. In the context of this new form of alliance, the Hundred-Handers also praise Zeus for his exceptional understanding and intelligence, praise that sets this φιλότης apart from the erotic form, which "overpowers the mind and thoughtful counsel of gods and men" (121–22). At moments like this in the poem, we see words evolving, like the universe itself, away from the physical and sexual toward the political and orderly. A similar shift is evident in the movement from Cronus's crooked μῆτις (18, 137, passim) and Prometheus's shifty and crooked μῆτις (511, 521, 546) to Zeus μητιόεις (457, 286) and μητίετα (56, 520, 904, 914), by which he can differentiate good from evil (899). In Hesiod's art, the shifting meaning of words, style, and content work together to plot the trajectory of the poem and bring out the poem's political and philosophical themes.

In short, Hesiod's style is didactic, a quality of style that is often underappreciated. While Hesiod and Homer draw from the same poetic medium, little in Homer parallels Hesiod's focus on individual terms, a point most critics of Hesiod's style miss.

All these aspects of Hesiod's art bedevil modern-day editors and translators as they have to decide whether or not to capitalize a word. Both to Hesiod's audience, who heard the poem rather than read it, and to later Greeks, who only knew letters of one size, this modern editorial difficulty would most likely never have been felt. But modern conventions inevitably distort our appreciation of a passage when in one instance Gaia (being a goddess) is capitalized and in another instance she appears as a lowercase, common noun. When the minuscule script was introduced in the Byzantine period, editors were forced to decide whether to write Γαῖα or γαῖα, or to choose between Βίη and Κράτος (Styx's children given to Zeus at *Th* 385) or βίη and κράτος (or κάρτος), the force and might Zeus uses to defeat the Titans or Typhoeus. Before the Byzantine invention, both the goddess and the common noun would have been written ΓΑΙΑ, and there would have been little reason to distinguish between them. Are we to suppose Hesiod's hearers and readers before the ninth century CE saying to themselves: "Oh, there, Might and Force are Styx' children and gods, but here they are descriptive, common nouns."

It might be simple enough for a modern editor to capitalize Might and Force at all times, but what is one to do when the name of a god like Νείκεα (a plural noun) elsewhere appears in the singular (νεῖκος), and that god's sibling, Ψεύδεα, in the same passage appears as a verb, ψεύδηται? Such is the case at Th 782–83: ὁππότ' ἔρις καὶ νεῖκος ἐν ἀθανάτοισιν ὄρηται, /καί ῥ' ὅστις ψεύδηται Ὀλύμπια δώματ' ἐχόντων ("whenever discord and quarrel arise among the immortals / and one of those with homes on Olympus lies"). In this context, editors understandably print ἔρις and νεῖκος as lowercase nouns and obviously print the verb ψεύδηται in lowercase letters, but an attentive member of the audience hearing the words ἔρις, νεῖκος, and ψεύδηται in close succession at 782–83 might recall that Ἔρις gave birth to Νείκεα and Ψεύδεα earlier at 225–30, and so might we as attentive readers. With Hesiod's many deified abstractions, such movement from god to verb is common enough: the Muses Κλειώ and Μελπομένη (77) follow the verbs μέλπονται (66) and κλείουσιν (67). Or consider the phrase κάρτει νικήσας, words referring to Zeus "having conquered [his father] by might" (73). Mindful that Κάρτος (Strength, an alternate form of Κράτος) is brother of Νίκη (Victory) and that the two are Styx's children who are said to stand at all times by Zeus's side (388 and 401), one might be tempted to capitalize Κάρτος at Th 73, but one can hardly also capitalize the participle νικήσας in this phrase. But such is Hesiod's art. The post-Hesiodic distinction between upper- and lowercase letters muffles the resonance of these associations. The same, I would say, is true when we hear that Hera ἤρισεν (raged) (928) against her husband for giving birth to Athena, as if Night's child Ἔρις has entered Olympus, albeit in verbal form (and in spite of the injunction that Olympians be punished for ten years if they introduce ἔρις to Olympus). How are we to represent these wordplays on the page? Such are the choices modern editors have to make, and it has the effect of quieting the poem and of diminishing the sensation that the *narrative* is alive with divinities. The problem is only intensified in translation.

Short of returning the entire text to capital letters, there is no easy solution to this orthographic problem. But the effect of our printing conventions is secularizing, declaring for the reader that god is present in one instance but not in another. Hesiod's remarkably innovative and original use of formulaic expression in his rather un-Homeric but brilliant uses of personifications, punning, and changing definitions of words contributes artfully to the poem's storyline.

While the *Th* and *WD* differ in voice and have divergent afterlives, they often complement each other in terms of language and seem self-consciously interconnected. (See also Ziogas in this volume.) Particularly interesting is the way the *Th*'s genealogies "inform" the narrative in the *WD*. Witness the description of the "just polis" at *WD* 225–37: "for them the city is in perpetual bloom and the people in it blossom" (τοῖσι τέθηλε πόλις, λαοὶ δ'ἀνθέουσιν ἐν αὐτῇ) (*WD* 227). Compare it to "blooming Eirene" (Εἰρήνην τεθαλυῖαν) at *Th* 902. Also in the just city, child-nurturing peace (εἰρήνη) abounds, but war and hunger (λιμός) are kept away, and ruin (ἄτη) is absent. Here, men work as if they were at festivities (θαλίαι), and Dike appears as δίκας, δίκαιος. The just city teems with the common nouns and verbs of Zeus's children, with Themis, Δίκη, and Εἰρήνη (with Εὐνομίη implied throughout), and with Eurynome, in their child Θαλίη (Aglaia [Merriment] and Euphrosyne [Well-mindedness] are no less implied), while Eris's children, war (here πόλεμος), ἄτη, and λιμός, are kept at bay.

Consider as well the description of Pandora. Adjectives in the *Th* and the *WD* describing the first woman dovetail with the names in the *Th* of Night's and Eris's children. As "destructive Night" and "hateful Discord" brought Κῆρες (Specters of Death), Old Age, Πόνος (Labor/Pain), Ψεύδεα (Lies), and Λόγοι (Words) (*Th* 218, 225, 226, 229) into the universe, so the "destructive race of women" (*Th* 591) (bracketed by West, and others), "gave men the κῆρες (the specters of death), made them *grow old*, and introduced them to diseases and πόνος" (*WD* 90–3). Furthermore, Hermes set ψεύδεα and wily λόγοι in her (*WD* 78). As Night's Nemesis is a "burden to mortal men" (*Th* 223), so Pandora is a "burden to men" (*WD* 82; *Th* 592). Like Night's Philotes, she also introduces males to sex, albeit a sexuality that is socially regulated by marriage. In short, what the children of Night and Eris do for the universe, the first mortal woman does for mortal man.

It is difficult to know what to make of these correspondences and echoes across these two poems. On the surface, the gods' two gifts to humankind (the Muses' gift, which allows kings to bring peace and concord to the city, and the gift of woman, which brings discord and hardship at home) appear contradictory. Regarding the creation of woman, Jenny Clay (2003: 125) argues that Zeus's sole intent was "to rid Olympus of noxious forces and foist them on mankind." From these verbal echoes, however, we might imagine a different scenario, which comes into focus only if we read the two poems together, namely, that with the creation of Pandora, humans can follow the trajectory of the gods as detailed in the *Th*: born into a world of familial strife, mortal man may find concord and blooming fecundity in the ἀγορή (*Th*) and the just city (*WD*). It takes the two songs together for this picture to emerge, and in neither of them is the story made explicit. If Hesiod had any or all of these patterns in mind, he does not say so directly.

How, if at all, did ancient readers and writers respond to the Hesiodic interplay of proper name into the fabric of the nouns and verbs in the narrative? Among poets, Ovid appears to imitate this feature the most fully (as Ziogas notes in this volume). Witness Ovid's play on the word *amor* as it metamorphosizes, appearing now as god, now as a common noun, now as a verb or participle in *Metamorphoses* I.452–567. It is less clear if the ancient rhetoricians also recognized this quality of Hesiod's art.

Some ancient readers looked upon Hesiod's many genealogies with annoyance. Some scholia, critical of genealogies in Homer, identify them as a Hesiodic χαρακτήρ (character) (cf. Schroeder 2006: 139–47 and 160; Canevaro in this volume). Similarly, Quintilian is clearly impatient with the many lists of names in Hesiod's poems (*in nominibus est occupata*), presumably when thinking of the *Th* and the *Catalogue of*

Women. But others, when discussing genealogical hymns, praised the *Th* (in contrast to the Orphic hymns) for its purity or cleanness (καθαρότης) and moderation (συμμετρία) in periphrases (cf. the fourth-century CE rhetorician Menander Rhetor).

In general terms, stylists saw Hesiod's poetry as a worthy example of the "middle" or smooth style—in company with poets like Sappho, Anacreon, and Euripides—distinguished for its polish, elegance, and musicality, or, in the words of ancient grammarians, for being sweet (τὸ γλυκύ) and pleasing (τὸ ἡδύ). Dionysius of Halicarnassus (during the time of Caesar Augustus) in particular praises Hesiod's poetry for its delightfulness or pleasantness (ἡδονή), smoothness of names (ὀνομάτων λειότης) (some translate "smoothness of words"), and harmonious composition (σύνθεσις ἐμμελής) (*De Imitatione* 2.2). He also praises Hesiod for his finely meshed expressions, effectively fitting and interweaving words together (*De compositione verborum* 6.114). No doubt paraphrasing these Greek sentiments in Latin, Quintilian finds Hesiod's smoothness of expression and arrangement (*levitas verborum et compositionis*) worthy of approval and his didactic maxims (*praecepta sententiae*) (in the *WD*) useful, but he says that Hesiod rarely soars, and he complains, as noted previously, that much of his work is filled with names (*Institutio Oratoria* 10.1.52; cf. 12.10.58–59). Yet it is not always easy to know exactly what the ancients meant by these terms. Richard Hunter (2009: 253–56; 2014: 286–89) has attractively drawn the link between the critics' words characterizing Hesiod's style and those Hesiod himself uses to describe the gentle and honeyed manners by which just kings talk to their people when issuing "straight judgments" (*Th* 80–93). It is also interesting to think of these terms in relation to the graceful interplay between proper names and epithets in his genealogical lists, and perhaps even in his distinctive interweaving of verbs, nouns, and adjectives in his narrative with the proper names of his genealogical lists.

NOTES

1. The six major digressions are Heracles freeing the world of monsters (289–332), Styx aligning with Zeus (383–403), Zeus honoring Hecate (411–52), Zeus freeing the Cyclopes (501–6), Zeus's clash with Prometheus and the creation of woman (520–616), and exile for those who bring discord to Olympus (775–806).
2. On beginning and ending with Zeus, see also Rengakos (2009: 209); on genealogy and arrangement, see Pucci (2009: 46–47); Rengakos (2009: 204); Brown (1953); Hamilton (1989); Clay (2003: 9–30); and Sammons in this volume. On the *Theogony* ending at *Th* 950–55, see Scully 92015: 191n52). For criticism of the *Th*'s design, see West (1966: 37–39).
3. Thalmann (1984: 123); cf. West (1966: ad loc. 76). For Hesiod's artful arrangement of names within a genealogy, see Faraone (2013; but like many he fails to consider how catalogs relate to their surrounding narrative). Cf. Koning (2010: 227–33); Pucci (2009: 39–41); Rengakos (2009: 203–12); and Sammons in this volume.
4. Cf. Brown (1953: 86–87). Faraone (2013: 295), misleadingly I believe, identifies Oath as "the most painful" and most significant of Eris's children, as indicated by the name occupying the last position. (For Oath helping to ensure Olympian social cohesion, see 775–76 and 805.) The list of Eris's children reaches its crescendo, more likely, in the figures of Dusnomia and Ate, capped by the phrase συνήθεας ἀλλήλησιν, both forces antithetical to Zeus's and

Themis's Eunomia (*Th* 902). Only sometimes (pace Faraone 2013) do first- and last-named children signify prominence, and only sometimes does an epithet signify prominence. Cf. "Eunomia, Dike and blooming Eirene (Social Peace)" (*Th* 902), where abstract principle is first named, followed by essential elements; here the middle-named Dike (without epithet) vies with Eunomia for primacy. Similarly, in "Brontes (Thunder), Steropes (Lightning) and strong-spirited Arges (Bright)" (*Th* 140), the third name (with epithet) is relatively unimportant; Arges is not even named at *Th* 707 = 854. Often, as at *Th* 922, Behaghel's law applies: the longest name is named last—Hebe, Ares, Eileithyia—where the troublesome, sole male, Ares is in the middle.

References

Brown, N. O., trans. 1953. *Hesiod's Theogony*. Indianapolis, IN.

Canevaro, L. G. 2015. *Hesiod's Works and Days: How to Teach Self-Sufficiency*. Oxford.

Clay, J. S. 2003. *Hesiod's Cosmos*. Cambridge.

Cornford, F. M. 1952. *Principium Sapientiae: The Origins of Greek Philosophical Thought*. Cambridge.

Faraone, C. 2013. "The Poetics of the Catalogue in the Hesiodic *Theogony*." *TAPA* 143: 293–323.

Hamilton, R. 1989. *The Architecture of Hesiodic Poetry*. Baltimore, MD.

Hunter, R. 2009. "Hesiod's Style: Towards an Ancient Analysis." In *Brill's Companion to Hesiod*, edited by F. Montanari, A. Rengakos, and C. Tsagalis, 253–69. Leiden, Netherlands.

Hunter, R. 2014. *Hesiodic Voices: Studies in the Ancient Reception of Hesiod's Works and Days*. Cambridge.

Jensen, M. S. 1980. *The Homeric Question and the Oral-Formulaic Theory*. Copenhagen, Denmark.

Kirk, G. S. 1960. "The Structure and Aim of the *Theogony*." Entretiens sur l'Antiquité classique 7. Hésiode et son influence. 63–107. Geneva.

Koning, H. H. 2010. *Hesiod: The Other Poet. Ancient Reception of a Cultural Icon*. Mnemosyne Supplement 325. Leiden, Netherlands.

Merkelbach, R. 1956. "Konjekturen zu Hesiod." *Studi Italiani di Filologia Classica* 27–28: 286–301.

Pavese, C. O. 1998. "The Rhapsodic Epic Poems as Oral and Independent Poems." *Harvard Studies in Classical Philology* 98: 63–90.

Pucci, P. 2009. "The Poetry of the *Theogony*." In *Brill's Companion to Hesiod*, edited by F. Montanari, A. Rengakos, and C. Tsagalis, 37–70. Leiden, Netherlands.

Rengakos, A. 2009. "Hesiod's Narrative." In *Brill's Companion to Hesiod*, edited by F. Montanari, A. Rengakos, and C. Tsagalis, 203–18. Leiden, Netherlands.

Rutherford, I. 2012. "The *Catalogue of Women* within the Greek Epic Tradition: Allusion, Intertextuality and Traditional Referentiality." In *Relative Chronology in Early Greek Epic Poetry*, edited by Ø. Anderson, and D. T. T. Haug, 152–67. Cambridge.

Sammons, B. 2010. *The Art and Rhetoric of the Homeric Catalogue*. Oxford.

Schroeder, C. M. 2006. "Hesiod in the Hellenistic Imagination." PhD thesis, University of Michigan.

Scully, S. 2015. *Hesiod's Theogony, from Near Eastern Creation Myths to Paradise Lost*. Oxford.

Thalmann, W. G. 1984. *Conventions of Form and Thought in Early Greek Epic*. Baltimore, MD.

West, M. L., ed. and comm. 1966. *Hesiod: Theogony*. Oxford.

CHAPTER 7

··

HESIOD'S *THEOGONY* AND THE STRUCTURES OF POETRY

··

BENJAMIN SAMMONS

In poems as in buildings, structure is an artifact that points back to the original construction of a thing and points forward to its enduring stability. Structures both signal the skill of the builder and guarantee the continuing reliability and usefulness of what has been built. They may also contribute to its grace, but here a distinction must be drawn, since some structures are intentionally concealed, while others are meant to be seen and therefore become an element of outward design as well as inner stability. Rafters may be hidden or exposed. Columns bear weight, but set along the perimeter they become fundamental to the stately aesthetic of the ancient temple. And to this we must add yet a third category, the column that does not bear weight—for some structures are merely ornamental and contribute primarily to a poem's outward design.

Hesiod's *Theogony* (hereafter *Th*) is rife with structures; indeed, it seems almost to be overstructured. This should not surprise us, since structure is not just an outward feature of the poem, but one of its primary subjects. For the poem recounts the construction of the cosmos and the structures that underlie *its* coherence and enduring stability, from the actual physical structure of the world around us to the distinctly political structures of the gods who now govern it. The poem's aggressive display of its own structures suggests an identification of its stability with the stability of the cosmos the poem describes (Pucci 2009: 46–47). Perhaps for this reason the *Th* gestures to its own production, and exposes its own maker, far more explicitly than any other early Greek poem; it must be shown as well how its maker Hesiod was himself made a singer, and what supports him in this role (cf. Clay 2005: 52).

The most obvious poetic structure of the *Th* is the catalogue. Indeed, the poem is routinely named as the epitome of catalogue poetry in the Greek tradition. Catalogue was a well-established structure in the early Greek poetic tradition and is fundamentally linked to other types of epic narrative attested already in Homer's *Iliad*. In Homer, catalogue can be anything from a concealed structure, underlying passages of "catalogic" narrative, to a stately display that is both utilitarian and graceful, to something that has a largely thematic significance (Sammons 2010: 7–12). Hesiodic poetry, however, seems to have a particularly close association with the catalogue form. While it would be an exaggeration to say that Hesiod was recognized primarily as a "catalogue poet" in antiquity, there is no doubt that the permeable Hesiodic corpus was particularly welcoming to works showing the polymathic, systematizing tendency associated with the form (cf. Koning 2010: 233–35). But what is a catalogue, and in what sense can Hesiod be seen as the consummate "catalogue poet"?

A catalogue can be defined as a verbal list containing a number of items in entries, the basic form of an entry requiring nothing more than the naming of an item, though it may contain any amount of additional, elaborative information (Sammons 2010: 8–10). In its most basic form catalogue can be contrasted with narrative, in that the order in which items are named is not determined, whereas narrative, even when analyzable as a series of vignettes, follows a set sequence. In practice, there is considerable overlap between catalogue and narrative. The *Th* is not just a catalogue poem, but a genealogical poem, and there is a difference between pure catalogue and genealogy: genealogy is a rudimentary narrative form ("x begat y, y begat z") presenting a temporal and causal sequence, whereas pure catalogue is merely a list ("x, y, z"). Nevertheless, genealogical narrative is very close to catalogue—one might even call it "catalogic" narrative—and a genealogy may become a pure catalogue whenever numerous offspring are to be listed for one set of parents. Moreover, it is clear that the simple list underlies the large-scale construction of the *Th*: genealogical lines are taken up separately; each consists of a rubric under which many offspring are listed and briefly described; and these family trees themselves are being listed, with one taken up asyndetically when another is complete, resulting in leaps through time that would be inadmissible in the narrative-dominant epic tradition of Homer.

Other works attributed to Hesiod show a similar balance and integration of the catalogue form with other structuring principles. Hesiod was considered the consummate catalogue-poet not only because he composed works that consisted only of catalogues, nor even because the form is particularly pervasive in works attributed to him, but also because of the virtuosity with which he integrated the catalogue into larger compositions. A good example is the so-called *Catalogue of Women* or, by its alternative title, the *Ehoiai*. Both titles suggest a poem that is essentially a catalogue; the latter implies in particular a list of exemplary women, each introduced with the expression "or such a one as . . ." (ἢ οἵη). Indeed, we can see from the fragments that some portions of the poem were introduced in this way. Yet the accepted reconstruction of the poem shows that the larger governing principle was that of genealogy—the poem traced major genealogical stemmata, sometimes moving vertically, sometimes horizontally within them, while the great family trees themselves are being dealt with in order, very much on the same system just described for the *Th* (West 1985: 46–50; Rengakos 2009: 204, 213–14). The *Catalogue*, too, was full of narrative segments, and the Hesiodic "Shield of Heracles" perhaps shows how a single "entry" in the larger catalogue could be spun out into freestanding epic poem.[1] Yet there was also a larger historical movement in the poem, which traced the heroic age from its beginnings until the Trojan War. The fact that this final subject was introduced with a catalogue of Helen's suitors, probably in direct allusion to the *Iliad*'s Catalogue of Ships, shows how pure catalogue, catalogic narrative, and a larger historical narrative all worked together (Cingano 2005). Yet the poet could do other things with the catalogue form, for example in his didactic works; the *Works and Days* (hereafter *WD*) shows a mixed format, with increasing reliance on catalogic format as the poem progresses (cf. Verdenius 1962: 154–57; West 1978: 44–46; Ercolani 2010: 44–46). The first part of the poem is built around the drama of Hesiod's quarrel with his brother Perses. Around the middle of the poem, Hesiod launches into a series of precepts on the subject of farming (414–617, the "works" of its traditional title), using the calendar to provide a chronological frame for his various instructions. Yet the poet could still resort to presenting his advice in the form of a bare list, as is particularly clear from the somewhat disorderly list of "days" with which the poem ends (756–828, on which see Lardinois 1998). Like the *Th*, the *WD* is interspersed with narrative segments, some of which may in turn take catalogic form, as with the famous "Ages of Man" (109–201, on which see Van Noorden 2014). The catalogic tendencies of such "wisdom literature" can, in turn, give us some insight into the likely format of lost didactic works such as the *Precepts of Chiron* or the poem on *Bird Omens* appended to some ancient copies of the *WD* (cf. West 1985: 23; Most 2006: lxii). While a similar variety of catalogic passages can be seen in Homer, what seems to set Hesiodic poetry apart is that it not only relies on the catalogue form but revels in it. We are, with Hesiod, never far from lapsing into the basic form of a list, and the poet makes no secret of this; rather, it becomes the outward sign of his inspired state, privileged knowledge, and poetic virtuosity.

While Homeric poetry can give the impression of a narrative interspersed with catalogues, the *Th* seems at first glance to present the opposite picture, that is, of a catalogue-poem interspersed with narrative digressions. The digressive character of many narrative passages is suggested by the fact that they are often "spun" from an item or name mentioned in a larger catalogic context. As we shall see, stories about Aphrodite, Prometheus, or Styx are told at the point where these figures are mentioned in the course of the genealogies, though the stories themselves may be anachronous relative to the progress of the genealogical framework itself, opening the door to many striking juxtapositions (cf. Rengakos 2009: 204). Yet readers of the *Th* rightly hesitate to acknowledge that the narrative passages, which tell the tale of divine succession leading to the ultimate kingship of Zeus, are truly subordinate to the genealogies except in a purely formal sense. One common metaphor is that the catalogues are the bones of the poem, the narrative passages the flesh—or vice versa (West 1966: 31; Hamilton 1989: 5–9; Nünlist 2007: 44). In fact, the poem is not quite so easy to pin down. Particularly in the first half of the poem, narrative passages are shorter and present the character of arbitrary digressions. Yet as the poem progresses, free alternation of catalogue and narrative blurs the sense that one predominates over the other, as in an Escher print where background and foreground get confused. No single structure dominates in the *Th*; the poem itself is dynamic in this regard and changes its form over time just like the evolving cosmos it describes.[2]

In the lengthy proem to the *Th*, Hesiod displays a fine sense of what the catalogue form can achieve and how it can be combined with other structures. For example, lines 11–21, indirectly reporting the hymn sung by the Muses as they dance on Mt. Helicon, seem to represent a kind of reverse *Th*, beginning with Zeus, Hera, and the other Olympians (11–15); moving on to the Titans (16–19); and ending with the "cosmic" gods Gaia, Earth, and Night (20). The Muses, then, sing a hymn that proceeds through a catalogue of gods; it is evidently not genealogical and therefore can have an order that is the reverse of Hesiod's poem, with the obvious benefit that the gods who deserve immediate praise (Zeus and the Olympians, who currently rule the cosmos) come first, and the other gods come after. Another performance of the Muses is described at lines 44–52. It seems to have three parts: (1) praise of the "race of gods" from the beginning (ἐξ ἀρχῆς) and proceeding in a genealogical fashion (44–46); (2) then (δεύτερον αὖτε) a celebration of the preeminence and power of Zeus (47–49); and (3) then (αὖτις δέ) a song, for the pleasure of Zeus, about the race of men and Giants (50–52). Here we can envision a poem in which the praise of Zeus occupies the middle and is flanked on either side by genealogies that extend from the beginning of the world to (we can presume) the heroic age. Finally, in the invocation proper, Hesiod describes the song he would like the Muses to sing for him now (104–15): a genealogical account of the race of the gods, beginning with the children of Gaia and Ouranos (106), then those of Night and Pontos (107); the divine origin of the physical cosmos, including rivers, sea, stars, and heaven (108–10), and the other gods born from these (111); and an account of how the gods divided up their various honors (*timai*) and now hold Olympus (112–13). None of these possible *Theogonies* exactly corresponds to the one Hesiod produces, not even the last one.[3] But in these passages we can see Hesiod exploring possibilities of what his poem can be. The first exploits the intransitive nature of a pure catalogue poem by putting the Olympians first, naturally because they are of first importance. The second possibility shows a concern for an element that is thematically necessary but, within the context of a catalogue poem, formally superfluous: praise of Zeus, which could perhaps be placed in the central position between two genealogical catalogues comprising gods on the one hand and humans and giants on the other. Finally, the poem Hesiod invokes from his Muse will certainly feature genealogical catalogues, but ought also to include an account of how the present divine rulers obtained possession of Olympus and how the gods in general divided honors among themselves. That is to say, Hesiod's poem will also include a narrative element, but how this will be worked into the larger framework of the catalogue poem is not made clear (cf. Hamilton 1989: 12–14). At this point Hesiod is more interested in showing the difficulty of his task than in forecasting how he will execute it (cf. Schwabl 1963: 397–403). It is clear at any rate that he cannot accomplish all he wishes through the catalogue format alone. But before we take a closer look at the narrative element of the *Th*, it is worthwhile to look more closely at all that the poet *can* do with the catalogue form.

The pure catalogue or "bare list," consisting of little more than names and epithets, may seem at first to hold little interest beyond the virtuoso performance required for its delivery; in fact, it can be given a thematic shape that reflects that of the

larger work. Brown (1953: 86–87; cf. Faraone 2013: 309–10) observes that in the catalogue of Nereids (243–62), the goddesses' names (all etymologically transparent)
show a progression from more general positive qualities to those that have a particular
bearing on the society of humans. At first the names reflect general properties of the
sea (e.g., Galene, Glauke, and Kymothoe), then names appear that specifically evoke
sailing (e.g., Kymodoke and Kymatolege, who are able to calm the winds and waves,
and Pontoporeia); the final names reflect various social virtues embodied in their father Nereus—hence the names in the final set have nothing to do with the sea but much
to do with human society (Protomedea, Laomedea, Themisto, etc.). The diminution
in the number of names per line draws due attention the last-named group (Faraone
2013: 307–8). It is notable that the catalogue of Nereids in Homer's *Iliad*, though it
includes many of the same names, has a completely different order that does not reveal
any such progression (Faraone 2013: 317–18; cf. Butterworth 1986: 39–43). The almost
allegorical "message" conveyed by Hesiod through the names of the Nereids would
serve no function in the Iliadic passage, but is quite at home in the *Th*, where similar etymological play can be observed in the listing of the Oceanids (346–70; Brown 1953: 85–
86) and of the Muses themselves (77–79; cf. Solmsen 1949: 40–41). Hesiod plays here
with the idea of a catalogue of beings as something that can express the evolution of a
primordial world into the world we inhabit. One can see a still more complicated example in the catalogue that lists the progeny of Night (211–32). Night's own children
consist mostly of general or cosmic ills such as death, fate, doom, deceit, and old age,
along with the Hesperides and Fates. The poet then names the offspring of Night's last
child, Strife (Eris), whose brood includes a number of social pathologies specific to the
lives of humans (e.g., battles, murders, quarrels, lies, lawlessness, and Oath). As with
the catalogue of Nereids, there is a progress from general features of the cosmos to the
specific conditions of human life (Brown 1953: 85–86; Solmsen 1949: 28–30). Hence,
while it is often noted that the *Th* does not recount the creation of humankind, the poet
finds ways to depict the evolution of the world in which humans find themselves. This
also serves to remind the audience, even in the midst of the most catalogic passages of
the *Th*, that the poem has a historical dimension that will extend to their own time.

Beyond such allegorical nuances, catalogues can be used to develop paradigmatic
patterns that reflect on the larger context. Again, the children of Night offer a rudimentary example, since the entities named are almost uniformly negative, distressing,
and destabilizing, and this reflects thematically on the story of Kronos's overthrow
of his father that immediately precedes the passage (Clay 2005: 19, 96). More complicated examples involve the establishment of paradigmatic narrative forms. In the
midst of listing the offspring of various Titans, Hesiod recounts how each of the sons
of Iapetos was punished by Zeus (506–34). This leads to a major narrative digression
on Prometheus (535–616, on which see below), but one could think of it more precisely as a paradigmatic catalogue of figures punished by Zeus, of which the entry for
Prometheus is greatly elaborated with narrative material (cf. Muellner 1996: 82–87;
Loney 2014: 506–10). The timeless character of each punishment recalls the catalogue
of sinners in the Odyssean *Nekyia* (*Odyssey* 11.576–600). Yet the Hesiodic passage is

far more pointed than the Homeric one, since the paradigmatic fate of the sons of Iapetos, punished opponents of Zeus, helps Hesiod keep the primacy of Zeus before our eyes even while he executes his genealogical aims. Another example can be found in the offspring of Phorkys and Keto (270–336). Clay (1993) has drawn attention to the many peculiarities of this generation of "monsters," who seem to toe the line between mortal and immortal. The catalogue forecasts that most of these monsters (Cerberus, Hydra, Chimaera, Sphinx, Nemean Lion, and Pegasus) will be killed or subdued by mortal heroes (Perseus, Bellerophon, and Heracles). As Clay argues, the passage becomes a paradigm for the fraught boundary between mortal and immortal and suggests a confusion of boundaries that are otherwise clear-cut in the world of the poem (1993, esp. 112–13; cf. Hamilton 1989: 30–32; Pucci 2009: 57–58). The allusion to the future exploits of heroic monster-slayers also points to a further reordering of the cosmos after the arrival of humans. It has often been asked why Phorkys and Keto, not extraordinary themselves, should have been so unlucky in their offspring, but we should look rather to Hesiod's use of the catalogue form as a medium for accumulation of examples and establishment of desired themes (cf. Thalmann 1984: 25–26; Schwabl 1970).

Both examples above also show how the execution of a genealogical catalogue can introduce juxtapositions and anachronies that seem, at first glance, accidental but that are surely fundamental to the implied historical narrative that Hesiod always keeps before our eyes (cf. Stoddard 2004: 126–61). The catalogue of Iapetids (506–34) leads to a narrative digression on the story of Prometheus (535–616), ending with the creation of Pandora, and this in turn is suggestively juxtaposed with a narrative recounting Zeus's victory over the Titans (617–725). Similarly, the progeny of Phorkys and Keto, which we may imagine as belonging to one of the more primordial "levels" of the divine genealogies, bring us into a series of brief allusions to the age of the heroes, directly before Hesiod takes a step back, genealogically, with the catalogue of the offspring of Tethys and Ocean (Nünlist 2007: 39–40).

Hesiod also will exploit the ordering of items to convey, or forestall, a particular meaning. Consider, for example, the catalogue of the children of Gaia (126–53): it begins, as we might expect, with the birth of various geographical features of the world we know, that is, Ouranos, mountains, the sea, and Pontos (126–32). Then, with Ouranos, Gaia gives birth to the set of gods later named "Titans," a list that ends with Kronos, "most fearsome of their sons, who hated his father" (132–38). Then Hesiod names the Cyclopes, who gave the thunderbolt to Zeus, and finally the "Hundred-Handers," Kottos, Briareus, and Gyges, who will play a crucial role in the victory of Zeus over the Titans (139–53; cf. 617ff.). The listener naturally presumes that Hesiod lists these three sets of progeny in the order of their birth: the first gods listed are indeed of a primordial order relative to the others. But there is an artful touch in listing the Titans before the Cyclopes and Hundred-Handers. They are thus placed in the middle, between the primordial gods who will eventually turn against them and the gigantic beings who are destined to become allies of Zeus; within the seemingly arbitrary ordering of the catalogue, therefore, they are enveloped by hostile forces.[4] Though the catalogue is followed by a narrative explaining Kronos's overthrow of Ouranos (154–210), at this very first appearance Kronos is already hemmed in by allies of Zeus.

Alternation of catalogue and narrative, another feature of the *Th* that can appear free or disorganized at first glance, is also conducive to such thematic effects. An excellent example can be seen in the narrative episode just mentioned, the story of Kronos's overthrow of Ouranos (154–210). It is introduced quite loosely, with a γάρ that must be referred to some fifteen lines earlier, that is, to the mention of Kronos's hatred for his father rather than the interposed account of the Cyclopes and Hundred-Handers. Nevertheless, a detailed narrative follows until the moment that Kronos tosses his father's severed genitals into the sea. Then we suddenly have a new catalogue, since the drops of blood and the genitals themselves produce their own offspring. From the blood and Gaia are born the Erinyes, Giants, and Melian nymphs (183–87). From the genitals and sea, the goddess Aphrodite is born (188–206). This last entry is then elaborated with an extended description of the goddess's birth, her arrival among the gods, and the honors that she enjoyed from the beginning (ἐξ ἀρχῆς), sixteen verses in all (190–206) in comparison with the twenty-seven verses (154–81) devoted to Kronos's achievement. But what is really noticeable here is that the narrative of Kronos's defeat of Ouranos is left strangely unfinished; there is no celebratory account of his accession to power, no account of his reconciliation (if any) with the other gods, no account of how honors were distributed under his rule. Rather, the poet follows up on Aphrodite's birth with a brief remark on how the "Titans" received this pejorative appellation from their deposed father (207–10), and then moves on to an extensive catalogue of the children of Night (211–25). We have, therefore, a narrative (overthrow of Ouranos) that leads into a catalogue (offspring born from the genitals of Ouranos), which leads in turn to a new narrative digression (birth and introduction of Aphrodite), followed immediately by a new catalogue (children of Night). The original narrative on Kronos's overthrow of his father feels strangely incomplete. But this is surely not because of sloppiness or disorganization on Hesiod's part; just as with the "sandwiching" of the Titans within the earlier catalogue segment, the upshot is that the poet avoids praising the Titans and alludes indirectly to their eventual defeat—Aphrodite is, after all, one of the Olympians, and notably obtains her honors quite independently of Kronos's new regime.

As in many Homeric catalogues, then, narrative elaboration of particular entries is a key device for controlling the thematic shape of the larger work. But in Hesiod this is no static device; rather, it becomes more elaborate and more structurally fundamental as the poem progresses. To take another example: while running through the offspring of various Titans, Hesiod returns to Styx, recently named as the last of the children of Ocean and Tethys (383–403; cf. 361). She gives birth to four children, all of allegorical significance: Rivalry (*Zēlos*), Victory (*Nikē*), Power (*Kratos*), and Violence (*Biē*). Hesiod then describes in a digression how Styx assigned her children to be the neighbors and constant companions of Zeus. By a common device discussed below, this leads retrospectively to an account of how Zeus, before his accession to power, called a meeting of the gods and promised that all could retain their *timai* or obtain new ones if they joined him in his struggle against the Titans. Since Styx first answered the call, she is among the most honored of the immortals under the present regime. The digression occupies some seventeen verses (386–403), after which the poet returns to his genealogical catalogue of the offspring of the Titans. It introduces a significant anachrony, since Zeus's distinctly political strategy for achieving power is described well before even Kronos's more brutal methods have been explained, let alone his overthrow by Zeus. The topic of Zeus's power is introduced already in the allegorical play with which Hesiod names Styx's children (Solmsen 1949: 33–34; Loney 2014: 523–24). The consequence is that the poet interpolates a reference to Zeus's rise to power directly into the center of this larger genealogical frame, which is also practically the center of the *Th* itself. One should recall here the poem imagined at lines 44–47, in which praise of Zeus occupied the center, flanked on either side by two major genealogical movements. Our poet is indeed working on such an arrangement, but not in the way implied there.

Narrative passages grow longer and more elaborate as the poem progresses, eventually separating from and swamping the catalogic framework in a kind of crescendo effect. The relatively brief enumeration of the children of Rheia and Kronos (itself part of the larger catalogic account of the children of the Titans) immediately gives way to the extensive narrative description of Rheia's deception of her husband, Zeus's upbringing in Crete, the device whereby Kronos is made to vomit up Zeus's brothers and sisters (unfortunately a deeply corrupt passage), and how Zeus released the Hundred-Handers whom Kronos had imprisoned. In all the narrative occupies forty-eight verses (459–506), whereas the catalogue recounting the Olympians' birth occupied only six (453–58). Immediately the poet takes up the catalogic thread with the offspring of Iapetos and Klymene, but as noted previously, this catalogue becomes a paradigmatic list of figures who opposed Zeus and were imprisoned: Menoitios, Atlas, and finally Prometheus. The punishment of Prometheus is retrospectively explained with a narrative going back to the distribution of portions at Mykone, continuing through to the theft of fire and the creation of Pandora, and returning at last to its starting point with the punishment of Prometheus. In all, narrative occupies eighty-one verses (535–616), catalogue roughly nineteen (506–25).[5] Indeed, the tale of Prometheus dwarfs its catalogic context and arguably ceases to be felt as a digression. Nevertheless, as with the story of Styx, it exploits the larger catalogic frame to create a significant anachrony through which we see Zeus handling a challenge to his authority before his actual rise to power has yet been fully narrated.

It is worthwhile taking a closer look at how the narrative movements discussed thus far show a development over the course of the poem. The device Hesiod uses to introduce these is typical: the particle γάρ ("for") is used to explain a previously mentioned fact; this can involve a step back through a causal chain of events, which then must be retraced to bring us back to the starting place. Homer himself uses the device at the very beginning of the *Iliad*, where, in order to explain Apollo's responsibility for the withdrawal of Achilles, he introduces a retrospective narrative recounting Chryses's attempt to ransom his daughter, the plague, and the quarrel of Achilles and Agamemnon (Bakker 1997: 112–15, with more Homeric examples). The tale of Kronos's overthrow of his father is introduced with the phrase "for (γάρ) as many as were born from Gaia and Ouranos were hateful to their father from the beginning . . ." (155–56). I have already noted the rather awkward placement of this introduction and the strangely unfinished character of the narrative itself. The fact that Styx's children reside near Zeus must be explained: "For thus did Styx plan it on that day when . . ." (389–90). The narrative that follows recounts how Zeus summoned the gods to Olympus and persuaded them to fight for him with a promise that they could keep their existing honors or earn new ones; since Styx was the first to answer the invitation, she is particularly honored. The tale of Prometheus begins with an extended description of his punishment, which must then be explained: "For when the gods and mortals chose their portions at Mykone . . ." (535–36). What follows traces the chain of events from Prometheus's trick to Zeus's response in concealing fire from mortals, Prometheus's theft of fire, and the creation of Pandora (cf. Nünlist 2007: 41–42). The longest narrative segment, that of Zeus's final battle with the Titans (617–728), is appended directly to the end of the Pandora story with no γάρ or other device to mark it as a formal digression.[6] This creates a striking effect whereby Zeus's defeat of Prometheus is juxtaposed, we would imagine in anachrony, with his defeat of the Titans (Muellner 1996: 87). It also marks the moment at which the genealogical portion of the poem has "caught up" with the narrative element, which no longer represents a forecast of what is to come but is finally happening in narrated time. It marks the moment, in other words, where the catalogue poem becomes an epic poem, and not coincidentally the narrative that follows is one of battle and victory (cf. Rengakos 2009: 211; Most 2006: xxxiii). It would be fair to say that narrative, as a poetic structure, is something that grows and evolves along with the cosmos itself. From small beginnings it becomes the dominant mode.

This method of allowing narrative to become the dominant mode only gradually also allows for a variety of anachronies and juxtapositions. In retrospect, the tale of Zeus's rise to power is actually rather fragmentary and not entirely coherent; some have argued that more than one version is at work (see, e.g., Fränkel 1975 98–101 and the discussion of Rowe 1983: 131–32). But by interpolating these narrative elements within the larger framework of a huge catalogue of the gods—itself, outside of the continuous genealogical passages, not tied to chronological sequence—the poet is able to complete his genealogies while narrating Zeus's rise at intervals throughout the poem, from its beginning (proem), to the middle (offspring of Styx), to the end (Titanomachy). Moreover, essential and distinctly political aspects of Zeus's rule are set out long before the rather ponderous account of the Olympians' "world war" with the Titans (cf. Scully 2015: 34–36, 77). This final narrative corresponds to one of the requests Hesiod made to his Muses in the proem (113), where he had also asked for an account of the gods' division of *timai* among themselves (112). Although the poem he recites does not include an *exhaustive* account of each god's honors, it does touch on the topic in various places, once again by using narrative digressions within the genealogical framework. The answer, it turns out, is not really a simple one: many gods, like Aphrodite, apparently enjoyed their honors "from the beginning" and were merely confirmed in their privileges when Zeus defeated the Titans. Others, like Styx, acquired new honors in the watershed that followed Zeus's victory. For this topic, as it turns out, digression within the genealogical framework is a more useful device than any continuous narrative account.

It is difficult to pin down the real ending of the *Th*. With Zeus's defeat of the Titans, it would seem that the poem, as defined in the invocation to the Muses at 104–15, is complete. And yet this passage is followed in our text by several more: (1) a list of the denizens of Tartarus (729–819); (2) a detailed narrative of Zeus's final battle with the Earth-born monster Typhoeus (820–80); (3) a list of Zeus's dalliances with goddesses and human women and the resulting offspring (886–929); (4) a more generalized catalogue of divine and heroic births involving various Olympian gods as well as Zeus (930–62); (5) a new catalogue, with separate invocation of the Muses, detailing goddesses who consorted with mortals and the resulting offspring (963–1020); and (6) an invocation, without catalogue, asking the Muses to sing about the "tribe of women" (1020–22), clearly in reference to a separate work, the Hesiodic *Catalogue of Women*. In between the second and third passages are some lines briefly noting the re-distribution of *timai* after the defeat of the Titans (881–85); this may well mark the end of the poem since it corresponds to the last item mentioned in the invocation.

While few scholars accept all of the passages listed above as original to the *Th*, how much of this material is accepted depends on how much and what kind of artistry one expects from the poet. In my view, the most attractive passage to save for our *Th* is the account of Tartarus. Despite the primacy of the narrative mode by the end of the poem, one should like some catalogic element to balance things off at the end. This need could, of course, be satisfied with the passages numbered 3–5 above, but these bring with them a sense of open-endedness rather than closure. The description of Tartarus is catalogic, as can be seen especially in its use of anaphora (West 1966: 357), but it is quite unlike any of the preceding catalogues in that it describes both the denizens and the topography of Tartarus. While the genealogical catalogues with which the poem began were organized chronologically, the catalogic description of Tartarus is organized spatially, showing that the poetic catalogue can organize space as well as it can organize time (Stoddard 2004: 137–43). It is a brilliant signal that the evolutionary progress of the cosmos has reached its end, and now its physical shape takes a concrete form, with the Olympians taking their place aloft and others taking their place below. Figures featured earlier as being somehow important to Zeus's rise to power—the Titans (728–35), a son of Iapetos (745–47), the river Styx (775–806), the Hundred-Handers (815–19)—now appear again and for the last time, having found their place in Zeus's newly ordered cosmos (cf. Thalmann 1984: 39–40; Fränkel 1975: 104–7).

Whatever view one takes on the end of the poem, or indeed on the issue of interpolation in the *Th* as a whole, it is not hard to see why the *Th* should have been more susceptible to this kind of "multiformity" than poems like the *Iliad* and *Odyssey*. Ancient readers as well as modern ones could get the impression that the poem consisted of a loose alternation of narrative and catalogue elements that could be extended ad nauseam (Kirk 1962: 67–68). In fact the alternation of poetic structures in the poem stands in a carefully designed tension that ensures the stability of both poem and universe. Those who extended the *Th* did so because it seemed ideally extensible; they did not notice that the poem as they found it constituted a dynamic and evolutionary, but also a closed and teleological, discourse.

FURTHER READING

Thalmann (1984) offers a wealth of observations on poetic structures in the *Th* in comparison with other early Greek hexameter poems, including forms not discussed in my essay, such as "ring-composition." Kelly (2007) also situates the poetic forms of the poem within the broader tradition, with particular emphasis on large-scale doublets and their relation to closure. Muellner (1996) offers a richly nuanced "metonymic" reading of the *Th*, setting form and content in a dynamic relation with one another. For detailed and sometimes minute appreciation of poetic forms in Hesiod, Schwabl's articles and his 1966 "Unitarian analysis" of the poem are useful both for study and reference. For the form of Hesiodic catalogues the best recent discussion is that of Faraone (2013). Minton (1962) shows how Hesiod's special relationship with the Muses is connected with his role as a maker of catalogues.

NOTES

1. There is, however, considerable controversy concerning the date and character of this poem, as well as its affiliation with the *Catalogue of Women*; for a thought-provoking discussion see Martin (2005).
2. For this very reason the term "digression" seems more apt for some passages than for others. Narrative elaboration on the birth of Aphrodite or Styx's acquisition of honors appears more "digressive," while major episodes of the so-called succession myth may appear less so, and the tale of Prometheus stands somewhere in between (both literally and figuratively). My argument is precisely that within the poem itself narrative evolves from a subordinate element to a freestanding one. Muellner (1996: 80–91) offers a similar discussion of the essentially "digressive" but constantly evolving character of the *Th*'s narrative segments.
3. The invocation proper (i.e., 104–15) corresponds to our *Th* in naming as the three major genealogical sequences the offspring of Gaia, Night, and Pontos, but as we shall see the story of the rise of the Olympian gods and their division of honors is presented in a more complicated way than implied in the invocation, which gives the impression that the narrative element will come in after the genealogies are complete. In fact, Hesiod artfully blends the two elements. It should also be noted that the invocation (as opposed to the proem as a whole) does not fully signal the *Th*'s relentless focus on Zeus.
4. For a similar reading see Thalmann (1984: 12–14) and the important remarks of Muellner (1996: 76–80). For the alliance of Zeus with the Hundred-Handers, recommended to him by a friendly Gaia, see 616ff. Some editors have bracketed lines 139–53 as an interpolation, but it will not do for the Hundred-Handers and Cyclopes to have no proper birth within the genealogies. The fact that the γάρ of line 154 must be referred to the content of 138 protects rather than impugns the passage, because one cannot see why this segue should have been left alone by the supposed interpolator. Moreover, since 154 relates to all the Titans, whereas 138 relates only to Kronos, the transition would be awkward even if the one line followed immediately upon the other. The conventional device whereby γάρ is used to introduce

a retrospective narrative seems to become more precise and sophisticated as the *Th* itself develops into a narrative of Zeus's rise to power (see pp. 102–3).

5. I leave 526–34 (on Heracles's eventual rescue of Prometheus) out of consideration not because it is bracketed by some editors, but because it would be difficult to assign either to the catalogic or the narrative section; obviously if genuine it serves as a segue between the two.

6. That is to say, the tale of Prometheus is clearly digressive in that it is essentially a narrative elaboration on the last-mentioned "item" in the catalogue of the Iapetids, appended there as an explanation (γὰρ ὅτε, 535), whereas the account of the Titanomachy is introduced quite independently of the genealogical context, with an explanation of the imprisonment of the Hundred-Handers, last mentioned almost five hundred verses earlier among the children of Gaia at 149–53.

REFERENCES

Bakker, E. 1997. *Poetry in Speech: Orality and Homeric Discourse.* Ithaca, NY.

Brown, N. O., trans. 1953. *Hesiod's Theogony.* New York.

Butterworth, J. 1986. "Homer and Hesiod." In *Studies in Honour of T. B. L. Webster,* edited by J. H. Betts and J. R. Green, 1:33–45. Bristol, UK.

Cingano, E. 2005. "A Catalogue within a Catalogue: Helen's Suitors in the Hesiodic *Catalogue of Women* (frr. 196–204)." In *The Hesiodic Catalogue of Women: Constructions and Reconstructions,* edited by R. Hunter, 118–52. Cambridge.

Clay, J. S. 1993. "The Generation of Monsters in Hesiod." *Classical Philology* 88: 105–16.

Clay, J. S. 2005. *Hesiod's Cosmos.* Cambridge.

Ercolani, A. 2010. *Esiodo: Opere e giorni.* Rome.

Faraone, C. A. 2013. "The Poetics of Catalogues in the Hesiodic *Theogony.*" *TAPA* 143: 293–323.

Fraenkel, H. 1973. *Early Greek Poetry and Philosophy: A History of Greek Epic, Lyric, and Prose to the Middle of the Fifth Century.* Translated by M. Hadas and J. Willis. New York.

Hamilton, R. 1989. *The Architecture of Hesiodic Poetry.* Baltimore, MD.

Hésiode et son influence. 1962. Entretiens sur l'antiquité classique, vol. 7. Fondation Hardt. Vandoeuvres-Genève.

Hunter, R., ed. 2005. *The Hesiodic Catalogue of Women: Constructions and Reconstructions.* Cambridge.

Kelly, A. 2007. "How to End an Orally-Derived Epic Poem." *TAPA* 137: 371–402.

Kirk, G. S. 1962. "The Structure and Aim of the Theogony." In *Hésiode et son Influence,* 63–95. Vandoeuvres-Genève.

Koning, H. H. 2010. *Hesiod: The Other Poet: Ancient Reception of a Cultural Icon.* Mnemosyne Supplement 325. Leiden, Netherlands.

Lardinois, A. 1998. "How the Days Fit the Works in Hesiod's *Works and Days.*" *American Journal of Philology* 119: 319–36.

Loney, A. C. 2014. "Hesiod's Incorporative Poetics in the *Theogony* and the Contradictions of Prometheus." *American Journal of Philology* 135: 503–31.

Martin, R. P. 2005. "Pulp Epic: The *Catalogue* and the *Shield.*" In *The Hesiodic Catalogue of Women: Constructions and Reconstructions,* edited by R. Hunter, 153–75. Cambridge.

Minton, W. W. 1962. "Invocation and Catalogue in Hesiod and Homer." *TAPA* 93: 188–212.

Montanari, F., A. Rengakos, and C. Tsagalis, eds. 2009. *Brill's Companion to Hesiod.* Leiden, Netherlands.

Most, G. W., ed. and trans. 2006. *Hesiod: Theogony, Works and Days, Testimonia*. Cambridge, MA.

Muellner, L. 1996. *The Anger of Achilles: Mênis in Greek Epic*. Ithaca, NY.

Nünlist, R. 2007. "Hesiod." In *Time in Ancient Greek Literature: Studies in Ancient Greek Narrative*, edited by I. J. F. de Jong and R. Nünlist, 2:39–52. Leiden, Netherlands.

Pucci, P. 2009. "The Poetry of the *Theogony*." In *Brill's Companion to Hesiod*, edited by F. Montanari, A. Rengakos, and C. Tsagalis, 37–70. Leiden, Netherlands.

Rengakos, A. 2009. "Hesiod's Narrative." In *Brill's Companion to Hesiod*, edited by F. Montanari, A. Rengakos, and C. Tsagalis, 203–18. Leiden, Netherlands.

Rowe, C. J. 1983. "'Archaic Thought' in Hesiod." *Journal of Hellenic Studies* 103: 124–35.

Sammons, B. 2010. *The Art and Rhetoric of the Homeric Catalogue*. New York.

Schwabl, H. 1963. "Afbau und Struktur des Prooimions des Hesiodischen Theogonie." *Hermes* 91: 385–415.

Schwabl, H. 1966. *Hesiods Theogonie, eine unitarische Analyse*. Graz, Austria.

Schwabl, H. 1970. "Aufbau und Genealogie des hesiodischen Ungeheuerkatalogs." *Glotta* 174–84.

Scully, S. 2015. *Hesiod's Theogony: From Near Eastern Creation Myths to Paradise Lost*. Oxford.

Solmsen, F. 1949. *Hesiod and Aeschylus*. Ithaca, NY.

Stoddard, K. 2004. *The Narrative Voice in the Theogony of Hesiod*. Mnemosyne Supplement 255. Leiden, Netherlands.

Thalmann, W. G. 1984. *Conventions of Form and Thought in Early Greek Epic Poetry*. Baltimore, MD.

Van Noorden, H. 2014. *Playing Hesiod: The "Myth of the Races" in Classical Antiquity*. Cambridge.

Verdenius, W. J. 1962. "Aufbau und Absicht der Erga." In *Hésiode et son Influence*, 111–59. Vandoeuvres-Genève.

West, M. L., ed. and comm. 1966. *Hesiod: Theogony*. Oxford.

West, M. L., ed. and comm. 1978. *Hesiod: Works and Days*. Oxford.

West, M. L. 1985. *The Hesiodic Catalogue of Women: Its Nature, Structure and Origins*. Oxford.

CHAPTER 8

···

HESIOD'S TEMPORALITIES

···

ALEXANDER C. LONEY

WHEN Hesiod encountered the Muses beneath Helicon, they inspired him with a new poetic voice (*Theogony* [hereafter *Th*] 31–34):

> ἐνέπνευσαν δέ μοι αὐδὴν
> θέσπιν, ἵνα κλείοιμι τά τ' ἐσσόμενα πρό τ' ἐόντα,
> καί μ' ἐκέλονθ' ὑμνεῖν μακάρων γένος αἰὲν ἐόντων,
> σφᾶς δ' αὐτὰς πρῶτόν τε καὶ ὕστατον αἰὲν ἀείδειν.

> They breathed into me a voice,
> a divine one, in order that I might glorify both what will be and what was before,
> and they bade me to hymn the race of the blessed ones who are eternal
> and to sing ever of themselves first and last.

Though the first line could be syntactically complete on its own, ending with αὐδὴν, Hesiod elaborates with an enjambed adjective, θέσπιν; his new voice will not be human but divine. The purpose of this superhuman voice is to put the entire sweep of the history of cosmos and its eternal gods into finite, temporally bound human speech. Hesiod has been granted a divine perspective on the cosmos that encompasses both the future and the past (32). What about the present? If we compare the formula that occupies the second half of that line to similar phrases, we find it is a shortened way to describe the universe in a three-part temporal structure including the present: the Muses, who are the source of Hesiod's perspective on time, sing of "what is, what will be, and what was before" (τά τ' ἐόντα τά τ' ἐσσόμενα πρό τ' ἐόντα, 38). (Despite this statement, the future seems to be absent from the *Th*—but see the final section below.) Hesiod thus makes the temporal structure and scope of his poetry prominent by putting it in this brief summary of his divinely inspired song. Further references to time in the opening "Hymn to the Muses" (1–115) underscore this point. In the hymn, Hesiod selects the appropriate beginning and ending points for his song—namely, the Muses (1, 34, 36)—who in their turn elect to begin either with Zeus (11) or, "from the beginning" (ἐξ ἀρχῆς, 45), with Gaia and Ouranos (106), and when the myth begins in earnest, Hesiod will proceed ἐξ ἀρχῆς (115), with Chaos born "first of all" (πρώτιστα, 116). Hesiod sequences the succession of divine births (45–50). He arranges Zeus's begetting of the nine Muses over nine nights (56–57), which is followed by a relatively lengthy two-line reference to their period of gestation (58–59). All this shows that Hesiod is deeply concerned with temporality.

But we may note an apparent paradox. How can beings who "always exist" (αἰὲν ἐόντων) be born and their generation be a subject of song? Furthermore, how can divine rulers, who cannot pass away, be superseded by new ones? These two problems point to a fundamental tension in how Hesiod conceptualizes time. On the one hand, Hesiod represents his present reality as a universe governed by unchanging and unchallenged divinities, chiefly Zeus. But on the other hand, this static present has a genealogy. The current universe is a telos. But like every telos, it is a final, stable state that resulted from a development over time from more rudimentary beginnings. This progressive development, moreover, is cyclical. As one generation succeeds another, a pattern takes shape that will lie behind the presently unchallenged order. This tension between the secure, unchanging present and the dynamic force that propelled the universe to reach this telos animates Hesiod's poetry and provides suspense for his audience. This is suspense not about the ultimate conclusion; the present reality of the cosmos cannot be different than it is, of course. It is suspense about the process of how this inevitable end came about. How did the universe move from primordial origins to the orderly present, with Zeus triumphant over all his rivals? How does this present order endure in the face of the same forces that brought it into being? Hesiod thus operates with a double vision. First, he can view the universe from a removed, synchronic perspective, seeing a present that is a telos and an unchanging reality. Connected with this temporal mode are various etiologies. Second, Hesiod can also view his universe internally and diachronically, seeing a cyclical reality full of patterns of change and development. Connected with this temporal mode are also notions of seasonality. At important points throughout the poems, this second temporality undercuts the first, undoing potentially stable moments; propelling the narrative onward; and, in an apocalyptic section of the *Works and Days* (hereafter *WD*) (174–201), even threatening to do away with Hesiod's and his audience's own present.

This essay outlines the structure and tensions of temporality in Hesiod's poetry. Broadly speaking, there are two overarching groups of temporalities. Within both of these groups, there is a set of different but related temporalities. In the first group, which I have brought together under the heading "synchronic," are ways of viewing the world as an unchanging state or telos. These include omnipresent, etiological, and teleological temporalities. In the second group, which I have brought together under the heading "diachronic," are ways of viewing the world as a process without a final state in focus. These include seasonal and cyclical temporalities. However, it must be noted that this grouping is not a strict dichotomy, only a general tendency to view time in two more or less opposed ways. And of more interest is the way these different temporalities interact. Often the same event or narrative can be viewed using multiple temporalities, which draw out underlying tensions in the poems. In what follows I examine each temporality in turn and then analyze how they interact.

Synchronic Temporality 1: Omnipresent

The omnipresent type of synchronic temporality emphasizes an unchanging state as an ongoing present reality. Whereas the other two synchronic temporalities in my analysis assume an external perspective, this sort of temporality is internal. More precisely, there is nothing external to it, since it imagines the universe as constituted by a single, unbroken present, uniting the subject, singer, and audience of song in a single time.

Consider the Muses, who are the subject of the beginning of both the *Th* and the *WD*. The temporal reference of the opening is not the past, not the Muses' birth, for instance, though this will be mentioned. Rather, the poems begin in the present, to be precise, at the moment of performance. They describe the current activity of Muses during the performance of the song itself. The Muses "occupy" (ἔχουσιν, *Th* 2) mount Helicon and "dance" (ὀρχεῦνται, 4) around a sacred spring and altar on the mountain. They "delight" (τέρπουσι, 37, 51) Zeus as they "sing" (κλείουσιν, 44, 67; μέλπονται, 66); Zeus's palace "laughs" (γελᾷ, 40) and Olympus "resounds" (ἠχεῖ, 42) with their song. The Muses' "tireless voice flows" (ἀκάματος ῥέει αὐδή, 39); being gods, they will never become exhausted and will be able to sing eternally. To call their voice ἀκάματος is to place it in the same category as Atlas's hands (519, 747), the heavenly fire that Prometheus stole (563, 566), and ever-watchful Argos's spirit (frag. 294.3 MW). These are things that neither tire nor rest but are in a constant state of activity.[1] Thus, each time a singer utters the invocation of *Th* 115—"tell me these things" (ταῦτά μοι ἔσπετε)—or similar invocations (e.g., *WD* 2), he is bringing before his audience a song that is already being sung on Olympus. (See Stoddard 2004: 129–35 for a similar interpretation.)

In the *WD*, Hesiod quickly passes from the Muses to the object of their song of praise: Zeus. The language of 3–8 is reminiscent of the "attributive" section of a hymn (see Janko 1981: 10–12). Zeus, like the Muses, is described in an ongoing present tense (5–8): he "strengthens" (βριάει), "oppresses" (χαλέπτει), "reduces" (μινύθει), "straightens" (ἰθύνει), and "withers" (κάρφει). Like the Muses and other divinities, he "dwells" (ναίει) in his particular abode. Even in passages that describe past events, such descriptions of activities of the gods appear in the present tense, which adds a degree of prolepsis as well. Hesiod interjects into his account of the birth of the primordial deities a reference to how the immortals "occupy" (ἔχουσι, *Th* 118, 794) Olympus. Such present tense verbs describing immortals abound in Hesiod and are too numerous to go through in detail. A few noteworthy cases include the description of the two Erises (*WD* 12–16); Eros, who "dominates" the minds and wills of all gods and men (δάμναται, *Th* 122); and perhaps the best example, Hekate, whom Zeus made a helper for humans and who "even now . . . gives happiness" (καὶ γὰρ νῦν . . . ὄλβον ὀπάζει, *Th* 416–20). (See also Nünlist 2007: 45–46.)

Similar to these "attributive" descriptions, we find Hesiod regularly describes the gods in terms of the eternity of their being. As I mentioned in connection with

Th 33, the gods are a "race" (γένος)—just as humans, from gold to iron, are "races"—defined by the particular temporality of their lives: the gods constitute a "sacred race of immortals who exist forever" (ἀθανάτων ἱερὸν γένος αἰὲν ἐόντων, *Th* 21). This temporality is opposed to human life: the gods are the "*un*-dying" (ἀ-θάνατοι, ἄμ-βροτοι). While human lives end and are thus naturally cyclical, divine lives never end, never even age; note how the other Gorgons are distinguished from the mortal Medusa by virtue of their being "undying and un-aging" (ἀθάνατοι καὶ ἀγήρῳ, *Th* 277; cf. *Th* 305; Homer, *Iliad* 12.323). Thus, gods' existence has a degree of eternal presentness, which is most clear in "attributive" descriptions. This presentnesss, however, does not preclude change. A god like Kronos may rule for a time but later be imprisoned (and still later be released to have eternal honors, if *WD* 173a–e is genuine). Indeed, the gods' susceptibility to change, despite their eternity, is part of the tension between the different temporalities of the poem. The immortal essence of the gods can be seen even at an anatomical level, as Ouranos's severed skin (*Th* 191), Zeus's feet (842), and Prometheus's liver (524) are called "immortal." In the last example, this immortality has the effect of extending Prometheus's suffering endlessly. Just as his bonds "restrain" (ἐρύκει, 616)—note again the present tense—Prometheus is bound to the eternal present in which all immortals live.[2] Although Hesiod sharply divides immortals from mortals, a few humans do become gods (Semele, Ariadne, Herakles). But their new condition as "immortal" or "unharmed and ageless" (*Th* 949, 955) only underscores the distance from their former condition.

Synchronic Temporality 2: Etiological

As I wrote in the preceding section, "attributive" present tenses highlight the continuity between the mythical past and the audience's present. The past, therefore, is not "merely the time prior to the present" but, as Vernant writes, "is its very source"; "the past is an integral part of the cosmos" (1983: 79–80). Continuities between past and present are evident in the way the present condition of the universe can be explained by originating events in the past. This is an "etiological" temporality, wherein a present, stable state is seen as the enduring outcome of an original "cause," what in later Greek thought is called an *aitia*. This temporality is synchronic because it "establishes a timeless continuity from the moment of origins to the present day."[3] For example, as Hesiod tells the myth, after Kronos vomited up the stone that Rhea had tricked him into swallowing in place of Zeus, Zeus took it and made it an enduring monument to his victory (*Th* 498–500):

τὸν μὲν Ζεὺς στήριξε κατὰ χθονὸς εὐρυοδείης
Πυθοῖ ἐν ἠγαθέῃ, γυάλοις ὕπο Παρνησσοῖο,
σῆμ' ἔμεν ἐξοπίσω, θαῦμα θνητοῖσι βροτοῖσι.

Zeus fixed it in the earth of wide ways
in holy Pytho, down the vales of Parnassos,
to be a sign thereafter, a marvel for mortal men.

The stone is a σῆμα because it points to the story of Zeus's triumph. Whenever a visitor to Delphi encounters the stone in its unchanging permanence, it creates for him a link between his own present world and the mythic past. Zeus was here; he stuck *this* stone in *this* spot of ground. According to Pausanias (10.24.6), even the better part of a millennium after Hesiod, there was a stone at the site believed by some to be the very same one Kronos swallowed. An etiology of this sort does not eliminate the temporal distance between the primordial past and the present, but it makes that past contiguous with the present. It gives the mythical past a permanent meaning—a fixity of significance well-symbolized in Zeus's fixing the stone in the earth. This sort of significance can only be found by adopting a removed, synchronic perspective, where no further developments in the story can occur to change its meaning.

Other cases of etiology operate similarly. Just to note a few examples, evil has its origin in Pandora's jar (*WD* 90–105); note the transition into present tenses at line 100, marking these evils the same today as when in an earlier time (πρίν, 90) they first escaped. The power of good winds "is from Typhoeos" (ἐκ δὲ Τυφωέος ἔστ', *Th* 869). The physical universe has its organization as a result of the birth and conflict of the gods (esp. *Th* 116–210). As is common in myth, the same present reality can be explained by multiple, incompatible causes; one particular evil—the need to toil—has two (three, if we include Pandora) different origin stories. It comes as a result of Zeus's anger over Prometheus's trick at Mekone (*WD* 47–50, *Th* 562–64) and as a result of the decline from golden to iron races (106–201).[4] Alternatively, one myth can explain multiple present realities: Prometheus's story in the *Th* accounts for the division of meat and bones in sacrifice (556–57), the domestication of fire (562–69), and the race of women and the evils they bring to men (590–612). In these cases, we tend to find a principle of original precedent. The first instance sets a pattern that endures in the present; for example, sacrificial ritual reenacts Prometheus's trick.[5] Closely related to such etiologies are Hesiod's genealogies. This is the most common sort of origin story in Hesiod. The family relations among various divine abstractions explain how they have come to function as they do in the present world, where virtues like Justice (Δίκη) or vices like Bad Government (Δυσνομίη) are the same now as they were when they were born (see Scully and Sammons in this volume). Similarly, humans in Hesiod's own present day call the gods by the names and epithets that they obtained at their birth or when they acquired their roles: Aphrodite, for example, acquired her name and epithets Kythereia, Kyprogenes, and Philommedes by virtue of how and where she was born (*Th* 188–206). In summary, etiological temporality is synchronic because it assumes an external perspective, viewing time as a contiguous unit. This unit is differentiated into a past and present, which nonetheless remain inextricably linked, the former as the source of the latter.

Synchronic Temporality 3:
Teleological

At its core, the *Th* resembles a hymn to Zeus, as Scully has recently argued (2015: 30–49). It narrates Zeus's rise to power and the inauguration of his reign of justice over the other gods and humans. The *WD* assumes that conclusion and teaches humans how to live in the world so ordered (Clay 2003: 1–11). On further reflection, we see that the telos of Zeus's accession is already presupposed in the *Th*, before it is narrated. In the proem, the Muses sing (71–74):

> ὁ δ' οὐρανῷ **ἐμβασιλεύει**,
> αὐτὸς ἔχων βροντὴν ἠδ' αἰθαλόεντα κεραυνόν,
> κάρτει νικήσας πατέρα Κρόνον· **εὖ** δὲ ἕκαστα
> **ἀθανάτοις διέ**ταξε νόμους καὶ ἐπέφραδε **τιμάς**.

> He **reigns** in heaven,
> having himself the thunder and blazing lightning,
> having defeated with might his father Kronos. **Well** in each detail,
> he **distributed** the laws and ordained **the honors among the immortals**.

Hesiod also forecasts this final divine hierarchy when he describes the Muses' song as having Zeus at the head of the list of the gods (11–21) and as depicting Zeus succeeding Gaia and Ouranos to be the mightiest of the gods (47–49). After Hesiod narrates how Zeus defeats all his foes and obtains his rule, he summarizes it in an echo of the earlier prediction (883–85):

> δή ῥα τότ' ὤτρυνον **βασιλευέμεν** ἠδὲ ἀνάσσειν
> Γαίης φραδμοσύνῃσιν Ὀλύμπιον εὐρύοπα Ζῆν
> **ἀθανάτων**· ὁ δὲ **τοῖσιν εὖ διεδά**σσατο **τιμάς**.

> Then they urged wide-seeing Olympian Zeus
> **to reign** and rule over **the immortals**, by the prophecies of Gaia.
> And he **well distributed the honors among them**.

Note the verbal parallels: ἐμβασιλεύει/βασιλευέμεν, εὖ/εὖ, ἀθανάτοις/ἀθανάτων … τοῖσιν, διέ/διε, τιμάς/τιμάς. The conclusion to the poem is exactly what was promised. The *telos* is always in view from Hesiod's external vantage point, and he alludes to it several times throughout the narrative (e.g., 141, 399, 411–13, 457–58, 488–91, 504–6; see also Rengakos 2009: 209–10; Scully 2015: 34–35). Considered retrospectively from Hesiod's present, this telos seems preordained. There are some indications in the text that a trajectory toward stability and order was inherent in the cosmos from the beginning; for instance, Gaia gave birth to Ouranos "in order that there be an ever-secure seat for the blessed gods" (ὄφρ' εἴη μακάρεσσι θεοῖς ἕδος ἀσφαλὲς αἰεί, 128). (The subject of εἴη is ambiguous.) But this sense of inevitability might be a product of Hesiod's ex post facto point of view, as I discuss in the final section.

We find a similarly teleological view when Hesiod refers to Zeus's justice for evil men. Hesiod exhorts Perses to reject outrageousness (ὕβρις) and pursue justice (δίκη), because justice wins out "in **the** end" (ἐς **τέλος**, *WD* 213–18; cf. 5–7, 294, 333–34). Though those who do wrong may seem to prosper in the present moment, when the total picture of crimes and punishments comes into view from a removed, final perspective, justice will be done. This means that an evil man effectively does evil to himself (265–66). Zeus, who can see all (267)—that is, take a synoptic and synchronic vantage point—guarantees this outcome. Hesiod's focus on ultimate justice in an *eschaton* has parallels in apocalyptic literature.

Teleological temporality is much like etiological temporality in that both adopt a removed perspective, viewing the span of time as a whole. The main difference is that the teleological places emphasis on an inevitable conclusion, while the etiological places emphasis on the origin of an observed present reality. In both cases, past and present come together under a single aspect.

Diachronic Temporality 1: Seasonal

Perhaps the most conspicuous temporal feature of Hesiod's poetry is the calendric structure of the second half of the *WD*. From 383 to its end, the poem contains a farrago of purportedly practical instructions for agricultural and seafaring life. (Hamilton 1989: 47 sees four main divisions: the agricultural year [381–617], instructions on seafaring [618–94], general advice [695–764], and the lucky days [765–828].) It may be ultimately futile to attempt to find a unity to these passages. But one particular theme recurs: the need to find the right moment, the kairos (694):

μέτρα φυλάσσεσθαι· **καιρὸς** δ' ἐπὶ πᾶσιν ἄριστος.

Guard measures; **the right moment** is best for everything.

Humans need to take care to observe the right moment because of the nature of the current world under Zeus (483–84):

ἄλλοτε δ' ἀλλοῖος Ζηνὸς νόος αἰγιόχοιο,
ἀργαλέος δ' ἄνδρεσσι καταθνητοῖσι νοῆσαι.

There is one sort of mind to Aegis-bearing Zeus at one time, another at another.
His mind is difficult for mortal men to know.

As Zeus governs it, the world favors a particular sort of action for a particular time and disfavors others. In the present era of iron, it is difficult to determine which action is appropriate when—difficult, but not impossible. Hesiod's task is to identify the proper moment for each action amid changing circumstances.[6]

The predominant sphere of activity that Hesiod concentrates on is agriculture. Temporal clauses involving astronomical phenomena, animal activity, and the like serve to identify the moment for action. When the sun's heat lessens, rain comes, and Sirius changes its course (414–19); at that time, cut wood, it is a "seasonable work" (ὥρια ἔργα, 422). Sometimes the temporal clauses become rather lengthy and ornate, as if the season for the work is the focus of attention, rather than the work—for example, the glowing, pastoral description of summer (582–88). This need to identify a proper time shades into other spheres as well. The passage quoted above—"The right moment (*kairos*) is best for everything"—serves as a bridge between the advice on seafaring and more general "lifestyle" advice. Immediately following, Hesiod advises a "seasonable" (ὥριος, 697) marriage, when a man is himself "in season" (ὡραῖος, 695), not much younger or older than thirty, and his wife is in her fifth year since puberty (695–98). In this way, the different sections of the *WD* are united under this theme. In the section on seafaring, Hesiod advises to "wait for the proper season for sailing" (ὡραῖον μίμνειν πλόον, 630; cf. 665). Hesiod even frames his famous allusion to the muster at Aulis for the Trojan War in this way. The full effect of his programmatic reworking of the episode as merely another occasion when sailors needed to observe the calendar and await the opportune time is often missed. There is no hint of the traditional features of unusual adverse winds, child sacrifice, or an angry god (West 1978: ad 652); the Achaeans were merely "waiting through the winter" (μείναντες χειμῶνα, 652). The Trojan War becomes just another instance of trying to identify the right moment for everyday action. Finally, the much-maligned final section, the "Days," is perhaps the section most obviously linked with a concern to identify the right moment for an action; for example, the thirteenth of the month is the day to oversee one's farm (767). The section (and the poem) ends with a programmatic statement of the fittingness of different days for different people (824–26), thematically and verbally echoing 483–84.

Hesiod's interest in identifying the right moment for an action is also important in the first half of the *WD*. Given the farmer's hardscrabble life, which requires much more than one day's labor out of the whole year (42–44), there is a right and a wrong time for quarrels (30–34; see Jones 1984: 31). In the *Th* as well, the succession plot advances as gods pick the right moment to act. The best example is when Zeus forestalls threat from Metis. Detienne and Vernant (1978: 14, 20–21, 65–68, passim) have taken the encounter as a programmatic example of *mētis*—a "cunning intelligence" of seizing opportunity, kairos. Gaia and Ouranos inform Zeus that his first wife, Metis, "was going to give birth" (ἤμελλεν τέξεσθαι, 898) "first" (πρώτην, 895) to a wise and powerful daughter and "then" (ἔπειτ', 897) to a son who would supplant him as king. Knowing this, Zeus acts "beforehand" (πρόσθεν, 899) and swallows Metis. With the help of Gaia and Ouranos, he decisively selects the right moment between the "first" and "then": after he has impregnated Metis, so that his most loyal child, Athena, could be born (from his head), but before a dangerous son could be born.

Seasonal time—or what we could call "kairological" time—is a diachronic mode of temporality, because it views events unfolding from an internal perspective.[7] A subject experiences a period of time and identifies the right moment *as* it comes. It is similar to teleological time, insofar as both conceptualize a period of time that leads to a certain outcome. But teleological time views events only from after that outcome, whereas seasonal time sees the outcome as a point along a stretch of time that has both a before and an after. A telos is typically inevitable and enduring; a kairos, contingent and passing. And one can view the same events using both temporal lenses: Zeus's defeat of the threat

from Metis is both the inevitable telos of the *Th* (when viewed externally) and an opportunity that Zeus seizes successfully (when viewed internally). I return to this distinction
in the final section.

DIACHRONIC TEMPORALITY 2: CYCLICAL

The final temporal mode to discuss is cyclical temporality. The calendrical portion of
the *WD* can, as a whole, be viewed cyclically. It follows a pattern that begins and ends
in autumn with plowing (383–84, 615–17). The calendar begins when "the year moves
back around again" (αὖτις δὲ περιπλομένου ἐνιαυτοῦ, 386; cf. *Th* 184; Homer, *Iliad* 23.833,
Odyssey 1.16, 11.248). Time turns in a circle so that the same event (e.g., the grape harvest) repeats or a similar event occurs like an echo of the first (e.g., a son follows his father). To take a simple example, near the beginning of the *Th*'s cosmogony, Night gives
birth to Day (124) and in this way inaugurates the cyclical pattern observed every day
thereafter: dark gives way to light, then light to dark, in endless cycles.

The best example of cyclical temporality is the "myth of the races" (*WD* 106–201).
Five races of humans succeed one another. The first three and the fifth are named after
metals: gold, silver, bronze, and iron. As these metals are progressively less valuable, so
each race is progressively worse. The fourth race is an exception, called the "heroes" and
better than the bronze race that precedes it. And for the fifth race of iron, Hesiod's own,
he predicts an apocalypse. Vernant (1983: 3–72) has produced the most influential analysis of the temporality of the passage. For Vernant, however, the cyclical pattern is just
the starting point for a paradigmatic structural analysis, which privileges a synchronic
system of binary oppositions over the progression of the myth through time (see esp. 9).
The temporal structure of the passage is complex. Each "race" (γένος), like an individual
human, has its lifespan. Each is first made by the gods (109–10, 127–28, 143–44, 157–58),
except for the iron race, which evidently descends from the heroes (though the disputed
lines 173d–e account for its origin). Then each race lives for a certain time. Three races
have lives of idiosyncratic temporalities because of peculiar patterns of aging: the gold
live only in the prime of life (they die in their sleep, apparently before succumbing to old
age: 116); the silver live for one hundred years as children and then soon die (130–34); and
the iron, in the future, will be born already old (181). Finally, each dies (121, 140, 156, 166,
180) and, with the exception of the bronze and iron races, obtains an afterlife (122–26, 141–
42, 167–173). For the first four races—the iron race follows a different pattern—Hesiod
bookends his account with their origin and their death. In this way, the races are like a
succession of generations. This is a pattern also apparent in the *Th*, which has three generations of successive divine rulers: Ouranos, Kronos, and Zeus. In fact, Hesiod links the
myth of the races to the divine succession by dating the golden race to Kronos's reign (111)
and makes Zeus responsible for both the end of the silver and iron races (138, 180) and the
origin of the bronze and heroic races (143, 156). In the myth of the races, then, we have,
five sequences that, with some variation, follow the same pattern, repeating as cycles.[8]

Cyclical temporality is a diachronic and internal mode of temporality because it views events from a posture within a cycle or series of cycles. It necessarily implies points of time along that cycle or series of cycles other than one adopted by the viewer; hence, as I discuss in more detail below, Hesiod's statement about being at a point within the fifth race of men (occupying an internal perspective) from which he can see other cycles before and after himself (174–76). Cyclical temporality has obvious affinities to seasonal time, especially as the perhaps most common example of cyclical time is the yearly cycle of the seasons. The key difference is that seasonal time emphasizes a single "right time," whereas cyclical time does not posit such a moment. Indeed, cyclical time emphasizes the opposite: no one moment or age is special. Every narrative of ascent is followed by one of descent, night follows day, and death follows life. Such is the implication of some of the most famous invocations of cyclical temporality in Greek literature, for example, Homer's "generation of the leaves" simile (*Iliad* 6.146–49) and Herodotus's programmatic statement on the fate of cities (1.5).

THE INTERACTION AND TENSIONS OF TEMPORALITIES

This scheme of five temporalities is not meant to be exhaustive, only to outline the modes most important in Hesiod. Next I show how these modes can operate simultaneously and interact with one another, beginning with this last example, the myth of the races.

In addition to cyclical temporality, the myth displays other temporal modes as well. As previously mentioned, the myth is etiological, explaining the misery of the current race of iron. There are also aspects of omnipresent temporality, with the afterlives of the golden, silver, and heroic races (122–26, 141–42, 167–173); note the transition from past to present tenses.

The most sophisticated interaction in the myth is between teleological and cyclical temporalities. It is generally agreed that the myth constitutes a narrative of decline, from metals of higher value and races of greater virtue to those of lesser. (A significant minority, however, drawing attention to features like the better race of heroes, dispute this characterization; see Most 1998, among others.) The myth therefore operates with a negative teleology, descending toward a nadir. The result of this decline is that Zeus "will destroy this generation too" (Ζεὺς δ' ὀλέσει καὶ τοῦτο γένος, 180)—a starker description of their death than any other generation experienced. This reverses the *Th*'s positive teleology of progress. Whereas the *Th* virtually culminates in the birth of divinities who secure positive social relations of humans—Εὐνομίη, Δίκη, and Εἰρήνη ("Good-Governance, Justice, and Peace," 901–3)—the myth of the races concludes when humans are abandoned by divinities who similarly maintain society by restraining vices—Αἰδώς and Νέμεσις ("Shame and Indignation," 199–200). This parallel strongly implies that the myth of the races, as Hesiod tells it, declines to a telos, albeit one projected into the future, which Hesiod can foresee by adopting an external perspective.

At the same time, Hesiod implies another conclusion—or rather, continuation—to the myth, one based on cyclical temporality in a brief, but marked, first-person interjection. In the face of the coming nadir of evil, Hesiod is led to wish he lived in a different era (174–75):

> μηκέτ' ἔπειτ' ὤφελλον ἐγὼ πέμπτοισι μετεῖναι
> ἀνδράσιν, ἀλλ' ἢ πρόσθε θανεῖν ἢ ἔπειτα γενέσθαι.

> Would that I did live among the fifth
> men, but either earlier had died or were born later.

To wish to have lived earlier among humans of a better race—perhaps the golden or the heroic—is easy enough to understand. But to wish to live later requires some explanation. This interpretation is contested (see Verdenius 1985: 105), but it would seem that Hesiod expects another, better race to follow his own race of iron. A cyclical temporality allows Hesiod to expect this and provides a template for imagining in just what ways such a race might be better. Although there are a few historical elements to Hesiod's imagined earlier races (like the use of bronze), they are essentially constructed by modifying aspects of the present and retrojecting them into the past. A cyclical temporality operates on a principle of symmetry, where each cycle echoes other cycles in the sequence. Each cycle is similar but, importantly, not identical to the others. For example, I have already mentioned how all the races are born and die, but the humans of the golden race die a better death, as if going to sleep (116). In fact, Hesiod constructs the paradisiacal life of the golden race by negation, by obliquely referring to the hard life of his present and correcting it. The golden race had an "**un**caring spirit" (ἀκηδέα θυμόν, 112); its members lived "**apart from and without** toil and misery" (νόσφιν ἄτερ τε πόνων καὶ ὀιζύος, 113); "worthless old age was **not** upon them" (οὐδέ τι δειλὸν γῆρας ἐπῆν, 113–14); the earth produced crops "**un**grudging" (ἄφθονον, 118). Life "under Kronos" (ἐπὶ Κρόνου, 111) is an inversion of the present (see Versnel 1993: 89–135). The present miserable race is therefore logically, though not temporally, prior to the golden race. A future, better race would be a similarly improved version of the present cycle. (Other races similarly reflect one another through what they lack, though they are not uniformly better than the present; for example, the race of bronze lacks the use of iron [151].)

Viewed this way, the cyclical temporality of the myth of the races undercuts its negative teleology. It provides an escape from the narrative of social decline into bestiality. On a straightforward reading, lines 174–75 and 180 predict certain destruction, and consequently Hesiod does not foresee this escape for himself, but only for another, sixth race of humans (Krafft 1963: 116). Other scholars have read these lines as minatory: destruction could be avoided if the current humans of iron reformed their ways along the lines Hesiod teaches (Clay 2003: 81–99; Ercolani 2010: 193–94; Scodel 2014). In either case, the cyclical return of a better race—whether a new one or a reformed version of the present one—disrupts the teleological temporality of inevitable decline.

A second example, this time from the *Th*, also illustrates the interaction and potential conflict between teleological and cyclical temporality. As discussed previously, Hesiod composed his *Th* with a positive teleology in mind, with Zeus installed as permanent ruler of the ordered cosmos. But upon closer investigation, we find a cyclical pattern of one generation overthrowing the previous one. As Kronos succeeds Ouranos, and Zeus Kronos, these cycles develop progressively toward a cosmos of greater order. But the revolutions as one cycle turns into the next produce crises that threaten the order of the cosmos. When Zeus uses his full might in his battle with the Titans, he sets the universe ablaze (687–710). Hesiod compares the resulting conflagration to the primal joining of Ouranos and Gaia, before the earth and sky were separated and thus put into order (702–5), as if the very organization of the universe might come apart.

The cyclical pattern of the succession myth also threatens its teleology in another way. There are numerous parallels among the different narratives of gods who represent a threat to the ruling god, some successful—Kronos, Zeus—some unsuccessful—Prometheus, Typhoeus, Metis (see Detienne and Vernant 1978: 57–130; Thalmann 1984: 38–45; Muellner 1996: 52–93). Given the inherent form of cyclical temporality, these similarities among cycles are to be expected. For instance, Ouranos, when his children are born, hides them back inside Earth; Kronos, when his are born, hides them inside himself. Gaia advises first Kronos how to take revenge on Ouranos, then Rhea how to do so on Kronos. Kronos defeats his father through cunning and force; Zeus does the same to his. There are subtle verbal echoes that further underscore the parallelism: "vengeance" (τίσιν/τεισαίμεθα/τείσαιτο, 165, 210, 472) runs throughout, and Kronos's "reaping" (ἤμησε, 181) Ouranos's genitals resonates with Kronos's later "disgorging" (ἐξήμησε, 497) the stone Rhea used to trick him. This pattern suggests that Zeus too would face a challenge from a son and lose his rule—as indeed Gaia and Ouranos warn (891–94), just as they had warned Kronos (461–65). Thus, the structure of recurrence inherent in cyclical temporality becomes an obstacle on the path to the telos of Zeus's reign, creating suspense for the audience about how this forecasted end will be achieved. From Hesiod's removed, teleological point of view, the conclusion of the poem is never in doubt; after all, Hesiod's own present seemed obviously to him to be a universe under Zeus. However, the many proleptic references within the narrative to Zeus's reign may be actually retrospective interpretations of events from Hesiod's own point of view after Zeus's accession. From an internal point of view, it may be that the narrative's telos was uncertain, that under the pressure of cyclical temporality, the succession could have turned out differently. In the event, Zeus does succeed—not by attempting to stop the cyclical progression of new generations of gods, as Ouranos and Kronos had tried to do and failed, but by taking on and transforming that cyclical progression for a teleological purpose. He ingests Metis, who, as the mother of his prophesied deposer, represents the force of cyclical temporality. (We may also note a more general pattern here in which female goddesses tend to promote disruptive, cyclical temporality and male gods tend to promote orderly, teleological temporality.) Zeus intervenes before Metis can give birth and takes on himself the role of birthing the next generation, producing from his head Athena, his strongest ally. At the end of the *Th*, as Stephen Scully has recently put it (2015: 27), Zeus "thwarts time" and creates on Olympus "a space set apart." Olympus becomes a harmonious place produced by a teleological process, yet free from diachronic change. If there is any reference to the future in the *Th* (as lines 32 and 38 would lead us to expect to find), it is on Olympus, where we find an omnipresent temporality that extends the current order indefinitely into the future.

Conclusion

I have shown the different sorts of temporality that operate in Hesiod's poetry and how they interact. These temporalities fall under two general headings—synchronic and diachronic—that are sometimes at odds with one another. At a more abstract level, as Stephen Scully has written in this volume regarding the *Th* (see p. 84), "a story of 'being' frames one of 'becoming.'" This dynamic between stability and change, telos and evolution, is a key part of Hesiod's artistry.

Further Reading

Hesiod's temporality has not previously received the systematic discussion I presented here, but there has been some earlier work on various aspects of it. The narratological aspects of time in Hesiod have received some attention (Stoddard 2004: 126–61; Nünlist 2007; Rengakos 2009). Some ancient readers saw in Hesiod a story about the origin of time itself: a popular false etymology derived Kronos from *chronos*, "time" (ps.-Aristotle, *On the Cosmos* 401a; ps.-Clement, *Homilies* 6.5; Cicero, *On the Nature of the Gods* 2.25); both Near Eastern influences (López-Ruiz 2010: 151–70) and Orphic cosmogonies (see Edmonds in this volume) aligned Kronos with *chronos*, a divinized Time. (For a modern attempt to make this connection, see Tralau forthcoming.) Some modern scholars have focused on the initial *Chaos* (Mondi 1989: 37–41) or Zeus's accession (Philippson 1966) as the origin of time. The myth of the races has received the most attention from scholars interested in temporality (see above). The two studies that pursue an argument the most similar to my own in this chapter are Clay (2003: esp. 17–18), who is concerned with new generations threatening old ones, and Purves (2004), who shows how time is "stored" in jars or underground.

Notes

1. There is only one other use of this word in Hesiod, where it describes the feet of Typhon (824). In this case, the reference is not obviously being made to an object in constant activity and perhaps is a generic reference to his strength. Nonetheless, given that, outside Hesiod, Typhon is usually imagined as having snakes for feet (see Goslin 2010: 358n22), the reference here might just allude to or be derived from that tradition, where describing writhing snakes as "restless" would be appropriate.

2. I develop this point in Loney (2014: 509–11).
3. Kowalzig (2007: 27); see further Kowalzig (2007: 24–32), whose analysis of etiological myths notes also the continuity of place and of objects into the present, both of which are important in my first example. See also Parker (2011: 26–27, 199–200); Seaford (2012: 5, 38–39).
4. A fourth origin for hard labor may be found in Πόνος being born of Ἔρις (*Th* 226).
5. Similarly, Stocking (2017: 27–54, esp. 39) argues that the smoke from the burnt offering reenacts Zeus's anger.
6. See Jones (1984: esp. 323). Canevaro (2015: 199) argues that Hesiod promotes his own skill in the face of this difficulty, answering 483–84 at 661–62.
7. On kairos and "kairological" (sometimes called "kairotic") as a mode of temporality, see Sipiora and Baumlin (2002). Hesiod is the first to use the word, though the concept was known to Homer (Rinon 2008), as was the cognate adjective καίριος, used in a spatial sense (e.g., *Iliad* 3.185). The most influential modern theorists of kairological temporality are Paul Tillich (1948: 32–54) and Martin Heidegger (see esp. 1988: 286–91 on Aristotle and Heidegger's translation of kairos as *der Augenblick*).
8. Vernant (1983: 6) argues that the myth as a whole represents a cycle, in which the sequence of races would repeat in reverse order. Most scholars have not accepted this aspect of his interpretation. (For Vernant's view of cyclical temporality, see esp. 1983: 57–60.) Some scholars in arguing against a future sixth race have outright denied that Hesiod uses cyclical temporality, e.g., Verdenius (1985: 105). But irrespective of the status of a sixth race, the first five races by themselves constitute five temporal cycles, a fact Vernant does not emphasize in his presentation.

REFERENCES

Canevaro, L. G. 2015. *Hesiod's Works and Days: How to Teach Self-Sufficiency*. Oxford.
Clay, J. S. 2003. *Hesiod's Cosmos*. Cambridge.
Detienne, M., and J.-P. Vernant. 1978. *Cunning Intelligence in Greek Culture and Society*. Translated by J. Lloyd. Sussex, UK.
Ercolani, A., ed. and comm. 2010. *Opere E Giorni*. Roma.
Goslin, O. 2010. "Hesiod's Typhonomachy and the Ordering of Sound." *TAPA* 140: 351–73.
Hamilton, R. 1989. *The Architecture of Hesiodic Poetry*. Baltimore, MD.
Heidegger, M. 1988. *The Basic Problems of Phenomenology*. Translated by A. Hofstadter. Bloomington, IN.
Janko, R. 1981. "The Structure of the Homeric Hymns: A Study in Genre." *Hermes* 109: 9–24.
Jones, N. F. 1984. "Perses, Work 'in Season,' and the Purpose of Hesiod's '*Works and Days*.'" *Classical Journal* 79: 307–23.
Krafft, F. 1963. *Vergleichende Untersuchungen zu Homer und Hesiod*. Göttingen.
Kowalzig, B. 2007. *Singing for the Gods. Performances of Myth and Ritual in Archaic and Classical Greece*. Oxford.
Loney, A. C. 2014. "Hesiod's Incorporative Poetics in the *Theogony* and the Contradictions of Prometheus." *American Journal of Philology* 135: 503–31.
López-Ruiz, C. 2010. *When the Gods Were Born: Greek Cosmogonies and the Near East*. Cambridge, MA.
Mondi, R. 1989. "*XAOΣ* and the Hesiodic Cosmogony." *Harvard Studies in Classical Philology* 92: 1–41.

Most, G. W. 1998. "Hesiod's Myth of the Five (or Three or Four) Races." *Proceedings of the Cambridge Philological Society* 43: 104–127.

Muellner, L. 1996. *The Anger of Achilles: Mênis in Greek Epic.* Ithaca, NY.

Nünlist, R. 2007. "Hesiod." In *Time in Ancient Greek Literature: Studies in Ancient Greek Narrative*, edited by I. J. F. de Jong and R. Nünlist, 2:39–52. Leiden, Netherlands.

Parker, R. 2011. *On Greek Religion.* Ithaca, NY.

Rengakos, A. 2009. "Hesiod's Narrative." In *Brill's Companion to Hesiod*, edited by F. Montanari, A. Rengakos, and C. Tsagalis, 203–18. Leiden, Netherlands.

Philippson, P. 1966. "Genealogie als mythische Form." In *Hesiod*, edited by E. Heitsch, 651–87. Wege der Forschung vol. 44. Darmstadt, Germany.

Purves, A. 2004. "Topographies of Time in Hesiod." In *Time and Temporality in the Ancient World*, edited by R. M. Rosen, 147–68. Philadelphia, PA.

Rinon, Y. 2008. *Homer and the Dual Model of the Tragic.* Ann Arbor, MI.

Scodel, R. 2014. "Prophetic Hesiod." In *Between Orality and Literacy: Communication and Adaptation in Antiquity*, edited by R. Scodel, 56–76. Mnemosyne Supplement 367. Leiden, Netherlands.

Scully, S. 2015. *Hesiod's Theogony: From Near Eastern Creation Myths to Paradise Lost.* Oxford.

Seaford, R. 2012. *Cosmology and the Polis: The Social Construction of Space and Time in the Tragedies of Aeschylus.* Cambridge.

Sipiora, J. E., and P. Baumlin, eds., 2002. *Rhetoric and Kairos: Essays in History, Theory, and Praxis.* Albany, NY.

Stocking, C. 2017. *The Politics of Sacrifice in Early Greek Myth and Poetry.* Cambridge.

Stoddard, K. 2004. *The Narrative Voice in the Theogony of Hesiod.* Mnemosyne Supplement 255. Leiden, Netherlands.

Thalmann, W. G. 1984. *Conventions of Form and Thought in Early Greek Epic.* Baltimore, MD.

Tillich, P. 1948. *The Protestant Era.* Translated by J. L. Adams. Chicago.

Tralau, J. Forthcoming. "Hesiod, Uranos, Kronos, and the Emasculation at the Beginning of Time." *Classical World* 111.

Verdenius, W. J., ed. and comm. 1985. *A Commentary on Hesiod, Works and Days vv. 1–382.* Leiden, Netherlands.

Vernant, J.-P. 1983. *Myth and Thought Among the Greeks.* London.

Versnel, H. S. 1993. *Inconsistencies in Greek and Roman Religion.* Leiden, Netherlands.

West, M. L., ed. and comm. 1978. *Hesiod: Works and Days.* Oxford.

CHAPTER 9

....

HESIODIC THEOLOGY

....

RICHARD P. MARTIN

WHAT would seventeenth-century Christianity look like if our sole guides were *Paradise Lost* and *Paradise Regained*? The Miltonic poems are obviously dramatic fantasies spun from some biblical narratives. Their purpose, point of view, expectations regarding audiences, and even reliance on a notionally unchanging theology result from centuries of contestation and influences—not least that of classical epic, including Hesiodic (Porter 1993: 43–82; Scully 2015: 171–83).

The two major surviving poems attributed to Hesiod must be read like Milton's, as compelling fictions embedded in a poetic tradition, fed by religious notions: supernatural beings, divine rewards and punishments, and a morality backed up by divine authority. But like Milton's texts, they are not "religious" in the manner of the Bible. The *Theogony* (hereafter *Th*) and *Works and Days* (hereafter *WD*) were never sacred; their representation of the world of gods was not canonical. Apart from some marginal inscribed objects and papyri, inherently "sacred" literature does not survive from ancient Greek (Henrichs 2003). The closest approximations are hymns, mostly fragmentary shorter praise songs, particularly to Apollo or Dionysos. A hypertrophied form of this genre, the so-called *Homeric Hymns*, like the poetry of Hesiod or Homer provides vivid narratives about the deeds of gods amid mortals, but these long hexameter compositions are equally "secular" if one applies to them the criteria defining sacred texts (e.g., respect accorded to a text thought to be preserved verbatim, incorporation of the text into a system of rituals and codified beliefs, transmission by way of accredited interpreters, indications of divine authorship or origination).

In short, concepts derived from institutionalized monotheistic religions only hinder the interpreter of Hesiodic "theology." Ancient Greek usage of the term denoted speculation about divinity rather than systematic investigation. Thus, Hesiod is included by Aristotle among philosophically unsophisticated *theologoi* (*Metaphysics* 3.1000a9–10), while the Platonic Socrates criticizes Hesiodic stories and Homeric verses about the violence of gods as he tries to wrestle verbal art into more normative patterns (*tupoi*) conducive to virtue (*Republic* 2.378d–379a; cf. 378a):

> "It's the founders' job to know the forms (*tupoi*) in which the poets must tell their stories (*muthologein*), from which, if they compose, they must not deviate; but it is not the job of the founders themselves to write stories (*muthous*)."
>
> "And rightly so," he [Adeimantus] said. "But on this specific point, what would be the model for a story about matters divine (*theologia*)?"
>
> "Something like this, I suppose," I said: "I think you should always present a god as he really is, whether you are writing about him in epic, lyric or tragedy."
> (Emlyn-Jones and Preddy 2013: 201)

The passage elides *muthologein*, "making up stories with authoritative force" (less precisely, "tell stories"), and *theologia*, "speech about the gods," in a manner that reflects philosophical bias against poetic treatments of the supernatural. For the thinkers of the later fifth century BCE, Hesiod and Homer were makers of *muthoi*, a shifting term originally indicating a type of public speaking implying authority. By the classical period *muthos* was already close to meaning "lie" (Martin 2013; Detienne 1986). A similar prejudice undergirds Socrates's interrogation of the traveling reciter Ion. Although Ion purports to specialize only in the interpretation of Homer (rather than Hesiod as well), it is clear that Plato seeks to denigrate all myth-making propagated through rhapsodic performance (Hunter 2012: 89–108).

THEOLOGY IN PERFORMANCE

A revealing detail enables us to retroject into the sixth century BCE this infamous struggle between poetry and philosophy, while offering further insight into the composition of the "theological" poetry of Hesiod. Xenophanes of Colophon (ca. 570–467 BCE), in later tradition an Ionian precursor of philosophy, was a poet (Diogenes Laertius 9.18, derived partially from the satirist Timon of Phlius, ca. 320–230 BCE):

> Xenophanes, the son of Dexius or, according to Apollodorus, of Orthomenes, from Colophon, is praised by Timon. At any rate he says: "Xenophanes, moderately free of vanity, censorious of Homer's deceit" ("Ξεινοφάνη θ' ὑπάτυφον Ὁμηραπάτην ἐπικόπτην"). . . . He wrote in hexameters as well as elegiac and iambic poems against Hesiod and Homer, censuring (ἐπικόπτων) what they said about the gods. But he also recited (ἐρραψῴδει) his own works. (Gerber 1999: 409)

Literally, Xenophanes "rhapsodized" his own work. Three hexameter lines demonstrate that his criticism of earlier poets was thematically identical to the later Platonic critique (fr. 11 DK):

Homer and Hesiod have attributed to the gods
all sorts of things which are matters of reproach and censure among men:
theft, adultery, and mutual deceit. (Lesher 1992: 23)

Xenophanes used Hesiod's own medium to attack his view of divinity, so that their interaction resembles an asynchronous rhapsodic contest. The relationship could represent a continuation of actual sociopoetic practices extending back several generations. Approaching Hesiodic "theology" in terms of agonistic composition-in-performance helps explain features that have dismayed interpreters, including apparent contradictions, both within the Hesiodic corpus and in comparison with the *Iliad* (hereafter *Il*) and *Odyssey* (hereafter *Od*) (cf. Loney 2014).

Several pieces of evidence point to such an agonistic environment for Hesiodic composition and transmission. First, there is the *Contest of Homer and Hesiod*, dating in its present form to the era of the emperor Hadrian, but enclosing an earlier work by Alcidamas (fourth century BCE), ultimately rooted in a rhapsodic context from the sixth century BCE (Richardson 1981; Nagy 2009a: 297–304). This prosimetric piece stages a competition at funeral games held for Amphidamas of Chalcis in Euboea. Homer maintains the upper hand during a series of increasingly elaborate verbal challenges that resemble sympotic entertainments (Collins 2004). But Hesiod is adjudged the winner on the basis of his peace-loving *WD*. Before proceeding to tell of the victor's subsequent murder, the *Certamen* notes his dedication of a tripod marked with a couplet (13):

Hesiod dedicated this to the Muses of Helicon,
having defeated in song at Chalcis the godly Homer (West 2003: 341)

The *WD* gives a complementary picture of the poet's personal religiosity, connecting this dedicatory moment with Hesiod's original poetic initiation as recounted in the proem of the *Th*, when the poet recalls a journey to games at Chalkis (*WD* 655–62):

[A]nd there, I declare, I gained victory with a hymn, and carried off a tripod with handles. This I dedicated to the Heliconian Muses, where they first set me upon the path of clear-sounding song. (Most 2006: 141)

The *WD* version, although similar to the later verses (compare ὕμνωι νικήσας ἐν Χαλκίδι θεῖον Ὅμηρον and ὕμνῳ νικήσαντα φέρειν τρίποδ᾽ ὠτώεντα), does not specify Homer as his rival, while the *Certamen* version says nothing about the Muses' earlier role in Hesiod's career. Yet another passage (fr. 357 MW) adds a surprising touch to a multiform of this Euboean agonistic scenario, with Hesiod speaking:

In Delos then for the first time Homer and I, bards, sang,
stitching together our song with new hymns (ἐν νεαροῖς ὕμνοις ῥάψαντες ἀοιδήν),
of Phoebus Apollo with his golden sword, whom Leto bore. (Most 2007: 355)

This time the event takes place at the pan-Ionian cult center of Delos.[1] But the agonistic aspect has been shaded over in favor of collaborative composition. Read literally, it sounds as though Homer and Hesiod *together* "stitched" a song by joining two or more previously unperformed hymns (for *humnos* as textile metaphor, see Nagy 2000). This recalls chaining techniques, whereby one singer starts off and the next elaborates the song, adding details or episodes. The presentation of Hesiod's interaction with Homer in the *Certamen* argues for precisely such expansion (albeit on a smaller scale). In addition, the *Homeric Hymn to Apollo* splices together "Hesiodic" and "Homeric" styles, suggesting such collaboration (Martin 2000).

What does it mean for Hesiodic "theology" that—as the *WD* observes (26)—"beggar begrudges beggar and poet poet" (καὶ πτωχὸς πτωχῷ φθονέει καὶ ἀοιδὸς ἀοιδῷ)? Quite simply, how this corpus presents divinity is contingent: not immobile dogma, but fluid fiction made in the face of other authoritative assertions (*muthoi*). Thus, Hesiodic poetry is metonymic for Greek religion taken as a whole, characterized as it is by flexibility, localness, and openness to change in details and interpretation (Parker 2011; Kindt 2012). Hesiodic treatments of the divine surely reacted to or anticipated points made by competing traditions, in particular the Epic Cycle and verse attributed to the mythical Orpheus (Martin 2001). The only available full corpus, however, is that of Homer. Comparison can bring out the essentials of each.

HESIOD, NOT HOMER

In an excursus during his account of Egypt, Herodotus credits Homer and Hesiod with forming the Greek religious imagination (2.53):

> Where each of the gods arose from, or whether all had always existed, and what they were like in form, they [the Greeks] did not know until yesterday or the day before, one might say. For I reckon that Hesiod and Homer existed not more than four hundred years before me, and it is they who taught the Greeks the origin of the gods (*theogoniē*), gave the gods their titles (*epōnumiai*), distinguished the honors due them (*timai*) and their skills (*tekhnai*), and indicated their forms. (Martin)

While this may seem a counterintuitive claim (and was eventually hijacked by Christian apologists like Athenagoras to dismiss the pagan gods), in terms of the sociology of religious practice, it makes sense. Rituals, sacrifices, processions, and other gestural components of Greek religion were mute unless complemented by discourse, which formed a parallel, yet equally influential, expressive track. While a community might worship Zeus and Athena in a certain manner (e.g., by making sacrifices to them simultaneously), only a verbal supplement (what we might call "myth") would explain their kinship, how Athena came to be, what her range of patronage was, and so forth.

Poeticized with compelling plot lines, such lore became for early Greeks a powerful means for thinking about the supernatural.

Because traditional poetry encapsulates its main themes in recurrent phrases or "formulae," one should rightly begin to contrast Hesiodic and Homeric religious expression at this microlevel. A full appraisal cannot be carried out here and remains a desideratum. But from a sample examination of one basic category—phrases that occur in Hesiod and feature the noun for "god(s)"—the conclusion emerges that the two poetic corpora, while sharing a number of phrases, differ in some telling ways. The dictional differences point us toward the central role of females in the two wholly extant Hesiodic poems (and the fragmentary *Catalogue of Women*). Specifically, Homeric verse knows the formula "gifts of the gods" (*Il* 3.65 and 20.265, θεῶν ἐρικυδέα δῶρα; cf. *Il* 20.268, δῶρα θεοῖο; *Od* 7.132, θεῶν ἔσαν ἀγλαὰ δῶρα). But nowhere does it contain the phrase "gift(s) of the *goddesses*," which by contrast can be found in Hesiod (*Th* 103, ταχέως δὲ παρέτραπε δῶρα θεάων). The line-final genitive plural does occur thirty-seven times in Homer, all but three of these in the fixed phrase *dia theaōn*, "splendid among goddesses." But it is never associated with "gifts." The key importance of the Muses in the opening section of the *Th* underlies the Hesiodic version, but it is worth observing the patterning of this genitive "of goddesses" elsewhere in the poem; out of seven other instances, four come within that phrase shared with Homeric diction, the fixed line-final *dia theaōn* (*Th* 376, 969, 1004, 1017), but three occur in distinctly non-Homeric phrases (240, τέκνα θεάων; cf. 366, θεάων ἀγλαὰ τέκνα; 965, θεάων φῦλον). These latter phrases relate to the role of goddesses in reproduction, admittedly a theme less likely to occur in Homeric poetry.[2] Yet the masculine or unmarked plural form does occur there, in a phrase similar to the "gifts of gods" (*Od* 11.631, Θησέα Πειρίθοόν τε, θεῶν ἐρικυδέα τέκνα; cf. θεῶν ἐρικυδέα δῶρα as above).

The reproduction theme co-occurs with another variation, this time in the Hesiodic epithet system for Zeus. The common nominative formula "father of gods and men" is a leitmotif, describing Zeus twenty-one times in Hesiod and fifteen times in Homer (a corpus more than ten times as large). But the accusative equivalent (θεῶν πατέρ᾽ ἠδὲ καὶ ἀνδρῶν), which occurs three times in Hesiod, never appears in Homer. Closer investigation shows that this object-formula for Zeus occurs in the *Th* in a description of the Muses' praise (47) and in the narration of Rheia's childbearing and subsequent quest to conceal the eventual father of gods (457, 468). As with the previous example, differences in content and theme generate formulaic variations between Homer and Hesiod. We must not be misled into thinking that one or the other poet consciously made such variations. Instead, any theological point one might be tempted to make about the relative agency of Zeus in Hesiod must acknowledge that Homeric poetry simply does not relate the birth of any gods.

Other Hesiodic expressions emphasize aspects of the gods that Homeric poetry suppresses or handles differently. For example, fourteen times in Homer the gods are described as "gods always existing" (θεοὶ αἰὲν ἐόντες, e.g., *Il* 1.290, and with case variations of the line-final phrase, e.g., *Od* 1.263, 3.147). The phrase exists in the Hesiodic word-hoard (used in genitive at *Th* 801, εἰνάετες δὲ θεῶν ἀπαμείρεται αἰὲν ἐόντων; cf.

fr. 296.2), as does the phrase θεῶν αἰειγενετάων, "of gods eternal" (*Th* 548, 893, 993, and fr. 283.3), found in the same metrical slot in its seven Homeric occurrences. But non-Homeric phrases *not* using the word *theoi* are prominent in Hesiod, expressing the same idea of eternity: "the holy race of the ever-existing deathless ones" (*Th* 21 and 105, ἀθανάτων ἱερὸν γένος αἰὲν ἐόντων) or a variant "race of the ever-existing blessed ones" (*Th* 33, μακάρων γένος αἰὲν ἐόντων; cf. *WD* 718, μακάρων δόσιν αἰὲν ἐόντων). Hesiod speaks a slightly different poetic dialect.

Deeper currents, however, might produce such surface ripples. Homeric poetry, it turns out, never speaks of a "race" (*genos*) of the gods (unlike Hesiod), reserving that noun instead for the "race of heroes," and then only in the proleptic passage foretelling the eventual destruction of the Achaean wall (*Il* 12.23, ἡμιθέων γένος ἀνδρῶν). The Homeric narrator's unexpected wide-angle view into deep time at this moment closely resembles the cosmic perspective of the *WD*. It cannot be accidental that the "divine race of heroes" (ἀνδρῶν ἡρώων θεῖον γένος) is commemorated in the Hesiodic Myth of the Races with very similar wording and with precise reference to the wars at Thebes and Troy (*WD* 156–60). Put another way, what is a given for the Hesiodic view of divine beings—that each category of heroes and gods has its own *genos*, but they come from the same source (*WD* 108)—is missing from the epic perspective. The Homeric vision prefers to suppress any hint of parallel evolutionary development that would unite "races" of gods and men, in favor of a tragic dramatization of the gap between the categories.

This marks the passage describing Zeus's relations with Mētis ("cunning intelligence") that raises the possibility of uniting the two "races" under one head. Here, a unique combination of words (at least as contrasted with Homeric usage) expresses the threat that the goddess will bear a rival to Zeus's power, "a son, a king of gods and of men" (*Th* 897, παῖδα θεῶν βασιλῆα καὶ ἀνδρῶν). The same phrase refers to Zeus himself at 923 (μιχθεῖσ' ἐν φιλότητι θεῶν βασιλῆι καὶ ἀνδρῶν). Zeus therefore has not just a (pseudo-) biological role as "father" of gods and men, but an overtly political role as *basileus* (cf. Kronos, too: *Th* 486). Homeric poetry, in stark contrast, never uses either "king of gods" or "king of men," let alone this pairing. This is the effect on diction of yet another *Th* theme—the sovereignty of heaven—as well as the larger complex involving "kings" within the *WD*. Rather than involving a radically different theological idea, the contrasting Hesiodic phrase opens up a new angle of vision, unexplored by the Homeric focus on heroes.[3]

One final example suffices to underscore the meaningfulness of such dictional variations. At *Th* 46, 633, and 664, the gods are called "givers of good things" (θεοὶ δωτῆρες ἐάων). The first occurrence comes within the Muses' song, while the second is tacitly also a praise-formula within a hymn: the *Th* itself, celebrating the greatness of Zeus. Whether or not "givers of good things" continues an Indo-European formula, cognate with a phrase in Sanskrit (long maintained, but see Katz 2010: 361), it is unsurprising to find the singular of this formula in another praise context, the shorter *Homeric Hymn to Hermes* (18.12, χαῖρ' Ἑρμῆ χαριδῶτα διάκτορε, δῶτορ ἐάων). More unusual is the near complete absence of this seemingly innocuous phrase from Homeric poetry. Keeping in mind the tragically fraught relationship between humans and gods in Homeric theology, we might call this absence purposeful; in the *Il* and *Od* the gods are emphatically *not* trustworthy "givers of good things." It is significant that one of the three places where the archaic word (*h*)*eaōn* does occur is in the very scene that characterizes Zeus as only a *partial* giver of good, as Achilles instructs Priam concerning the urns of good and evil (*Il* 24.527–33):

> There are two urns that stand on the door-sill of Zeus. They are unlike for the gifts they bestow: an urn of evils, an urn of blessings (ἐάων).
>
> If Zeus who delights in thunder mingles these and bestows them on man, he shifts, and moves now in evil, again in good fortune. But when Zeus bestows from the urn of sorrows, he makes a failure of man, and the evil hunger drives him over the shining earth, and he wanders respected neither of gods nor mortals. (Lattimore 2011: 511)

There could be no sharper contrast between the uncomplicated Hesiodic predication "givers of goods" and this scenario, in which Zeus instead of unmixed "good" doles out either straight-up evils or a distressing mixture. Confirming this divide between an idyllic Olympian realm of good-giving divinities and the "real" world of epic, the only other two places where the phrase "gods givers of good things" appears are in the song of Demodocus concerning Olympian adultery. The guffawing male spectators of the trapped Ares and Aphrodite are so described (*Od* 8.325), and Hermes (once again) is singled out (8.335, Ἑρμεία Διὸς υἱέ, διάκτορε, δῶτορ ἐάων). Within Homer, then, the only way to deploy the formula about the gods as "givers of good" is to set it in an explicitly unreal "mythological" entertainment, as if to underscore the impossibility of the notion in the hard-bitten epic world.

THE ENDS OF HESIODIC THEOLOGY

Oral-poetic competition provides the outer framework for the *Th*, helping to explain motives and mechanisms for contrastive theological visions. But there is also an elaborate framing device *within* the text that meditates on the very act of making declarations about gods. The narrator proposes in the style of hymns, "Let us begin to sing from the Heliconian Muses" (*Th* 1), and proceeds to describe their activity, through a combination of timeless present-tense verbs and punctual aorists or progressive imperfects, a characteristic style of Greek hymns attempting to combine a deity's eternal features with a time-bound narrative of divine deeds (Clay 1989: 22–29; see also Loney in this volume, pp. 111–12). The Muses "possess" Helicon and "dance" there around a fountain and altar of Zeus; they "performed" choral dances and "were moving" down the mountain while singing a hymn (*steikhon, Th* 10; *humneusai*, 11). The opening lines thus artfully merge a mortal's here-and-now performance with the Muses' eternal song, a catalog of Olympian gods starting with Zeus (11), then moving backward in cosmic time with Titans (Themis, 16; Iapetos and Kronos, 18) to primeval deities (Gaia, Okeanos, Night, 20).

The next section of the proem (22–34) narrates in hymnic style a one-time deed: how the Muses taught Hesiod the art of song as he pastured sheep on the slopes of Helicon. The audience has been prepared because the composer's own hymnic style has already been closely aligned with the praise-song of the Muses during their mist-enshrouded descent in the previous section. We imagine the (one-time or recurrent?) descent as targeting an encounter with "Hesiod" (as the narrator significantly names himself in the third person; Nagy 2009b: 287–88). Essential for the "theological" constructions of the poem are the tone of the Muses' proclamation, the purport of their direct speech, and the purpose that Hesiod derives from their literal "inspiration" (*enepneusan . . . audēn*, 31, "they breathed a divine voice"). Rather than address Hesiod directly, the Muses call the group of shepherds "ignoble disgrace, mere bellies," in the mocking register of *iambos* poetry.[4] The Muses then claim to be able to "say many false things similar to genuine ones" but also (when they wish) "to proclaim true things." Whether or not this speech highlights the gap between divine and mortal worlds (Stoddard 2004: 87) or empowers the poet to lie, the Muses' next gesture (gifting Hesiod with a "scepter" of laurel) clearly raises him above the level of a "mere belly" (presumably saying anything to get fed) and instead gives him a career purpose: to sing of the gods "but always to sing of themselves first and last." The very first line of the poem, naming the Muses, demonstrates that the poet has followed their command.

This instruction by the Muses sets the entire *Th* within the sphere of divine patronage. Just as Hesiod is recruited to sing about them, so the Muses have the eternal task of hymning their father Zeus (48). The poet performs as a solo singer the task that the Muses perform as a chorus of nine like-minded daughters (Nagy 2009b: 282–84). The third section of the proem (35–74) describes the sweet sounds and therapeutic effects of their song and dance, backtracking to tell of their conception. The burden of their song is the power Zeus used to overcome Kronos, leading to distribution of honors (*timai*) to the immortals (71–74), a preview of the upcoming *Th*. Three Muses bear names highlighting their praise relationship with Zeus: Ourania (Zeus as sky-god); Kleio ("Glorifying"), and Polymnia ("Many Hymning"). Calliope, the most prominent, bridges the royal power of Zeus and mortal kings by giving the latter fluent speech to resolve disputes (80–92; Martin 1984). As the proem had earlier aligned the solo performer and his divine patronesses, so now the Muses' regard unites singers, players, and kings (93–97). The analogy is implicit: as the Muses praise Zeus, so mortal poets honor kings.

The underlying praise-contract that we can trace within the *Th* proem does not necessarily destabilize the subsequent theological narrative in the poem, the story of Zeus's violent rise to permanent power. Yet the extended proem *does* highlight that story's rhetorical nature: the song is an assertion *about* power *by* beneficiaries of it. In this regard, it is comparable to two other theogonic discourses. When the newborn Hermes first tries out his tortoiseshell lyre, his song is improvised, resembling party jests, detailing his own surreptitious conception (*Homeric Hymn to Hermes* 54–61):

The god sang beautifully to it, impromptu, experimentally [ἐξ αὐτοσχεδίης πειρώμενος] as young men at dinners make ribald interjections: (he sang) about

Zeus son of Kronos and fair-shod Maia, how they used to talk love in companionable intimacy, and declaring his own renowned lineage. He also celebrated the servants of the nymph, and her splendid home, the tripods disposed about it and the unending cauldrons. (West 2003: 117–19)

If not a demolition of theogonic hymns, the spectacle of Hermes celebrating his own divine birth while elevating the quality of his home furnishings exposes the self-interest beneath this genre. Later in the poem, Hermes sings another, less comical theogony, of a distinctly un-Hesiodic strain.[5] This, too, is explicitly self-interested, part of the calculated exchange that frees Hermes from compensating Apollo for stolen cattle. In sum, the two "theogony" scenes might recall rival rhapsodic traditions (not unlike a contest between divine brothers).

Distribution of honors, a major theme in Hesiod's *Th*, prompts an instructive contrast with the *Il*. Zeus commands Poseidon to desist from fighting, claiming to be older and stronger (*Il* 15.181–82), an assertion that matches the *Th*. But Poseidon relies on a different theogonic memory to justify his resistance, saying he is "of equal honor with Zeus and Hades" (*homotimos*, 15.186) because each received his portion by *the shaking of lots* (189, ἕκαστος δ᾽ ἔμμορε τιμῆς; 190, ἔλαχον; 191, παλλομένων)—not, that is, through Zeus's personal dispensation. In effect, Poseidon's alternate *muthos*, like the version sung by Hermes, undercuts the Zeus-centered version that resembles the *Th*. The "theological" contestation arising from conditions of rhapsodic competition are thus thematized in the *Il* when gods dispute their own histories.

A final example from the same section of the poem places theogonic material clearly within the realm of rhetoric. Bent on a deception of Promethean proportion (*Il* 14.160, ἐξαπάφοιτο Διὸς νόον; cf. *Th* 537, Διὸς νόον ἐξαπαφίσκων), Hera lies first to Aphrodite, then to Zeus, about visiting her foster parents Okeanos and Tethys (14.200–5; cf. 14.301–4):

Since I go now to the ends of the generous earth, on a visit to Okeanos, whence the gods have risen [θεῶν γένεσιν] and Tethys our mother who brought me up kindly in their own house, and cared for me and took me from Rheia, at that time when Zeus of the wide brows drove Kronos underneath the earth and the barren water. I shall go to visit these, and resolve their division of discord (Lattimore 2011: 323).

As has long been recognized, Hera's remark that Okeanos and Tethys are the source of the gods contradicts the *Th*, in which the aquatic couple are Titans, the *second* divine generation (Clay 2003: 16, 22). In Hesiod, they are merely parents of rivers and nymphs, most prominently Styx (*Th* 337–70). The phrase θεῶν γένεσιν never occurs in Hesiod, where, in marked contrast, the "race of gods" (θεῶν γένος), of which the Muses sing, descends directly from Gaia and Ouranos (*Th* 44–45; Janko 1994 181–82). This theogonic rhetoric is even more revealing, however, given evidence from Plato's *Cratylus* (402B) that an "Orphic" poem featured a motif close to Hera's version (West 1983: 182–90; extensive discussion at Nagy 2009a: 250–91):

Orpheus, too, says:

> Fair-flowing Ocean was the first to marry,
> and he wedded his sister Tethys, daughter of his mother. (Fowler 1926: 69).

Hesiodic myth-making, therefore, emerges in a new light after one observes how theogonies are "weaponized" for rhetorical purposes. That the "theogonies" of Hermes, Poseidon, or Hera might also echo myths from actual performance repertories of "Orphic" or other poetry lends them additional resonance (as with *Od* responses to such material; see Martin 2001).

THEOGONY AND DIACHRONY

Homeric poetry can also clarify how Hesiod's supernatural design employs a perspective essentially at odds with epic. Put briefly, the latter is synchronic in orientation, the former diachronic.[6] (For another perspective, see Loney in this volume, pp. 115–18.) The four poems in question form a spectrum, *Il* and *Th* at the extremes with *WD* and *Od* occupying the midpoint. To take the endpoints first: divine action in the *Il* is a largely opaque process, at least to the mortals affected. Prayer, sacrifice, and supplication can influence it, but divine favoritism, accumulated obligations, and sheer jealousy negate any advantage that humans gain. The "will of Zeus" (*Dios boulē*) dominates the action from the very start. Because Zeus owes a favor to Thetis (a theogonic allusion), he intervenes to honor Achilles, sparking resistance from Hera and Athena. Apollo and Aphrodite, with other Olympians, variously motivated, are on the Trojan side. As a result, a full-scale "theomachy" erupts (Bks. 20–21). Whereas the *Th* depicts a united front of Olympians led by Zeus against older Titans, the *Il* descends into intragenerational warfare.

With few exceptions, the Olympian system seen in epic matches that painfully established through struggles in the *Th*. Epithets are largely shared. Hera is "mistress" (*potnia*, e.g., *Il* 1.551; cf. *Th* 11), Artemis is "arrow-pouring" (*Il* 5.447; cf. *Th* 14.), Apollo is Phoebus (*Il* 15.256; cf. *Th* 14), Athena is "grey eyed daughter of Zeus" (*Th* 13; *Il* 10.553), and Poseidon is "earth shaker, earth holder (*Th* 15 = *Il* 13.43). What we do not see in Hesiod are the typical actions that illustrate these epithets. On the whole, the deeds of the gods are reserved for epic or the *Homeric Hymns* to enact. The Titans, a major component of the *Th*, are by contrast mostly absent from Homeric poetry. Themis merits mention in a prayer by Telemachus (*Od* 2.68) and makes a cameo appearance, welcoming Hera on Olympus after she has been threatened by Zeus (*Il* 15.87–112). In the latter, Themis signifies the stability that Zeus created according to the *Th* (partly by wedding her and creating the Seasons and Destinies; *Th* 901–6). It is therefore mythically appropriate that Hera at this juncture in the *Il*, although incensed, urges her fellow Olympians to yield to the chief god. A similar domestication in the *Il* highlights, by contrast, Aphrodite's status in the *Th*. She is a rather skittish daughter of the obscure Dione (*Il* 5.370–425), far from the all-powerful force of nature antedating the epoch of Zeus (*Th* 190–206). Only when answering Helen's mockery with threats does a flash of the cosmic Aphrodite emerge, the overpowering divinity whom Eros and Himeros (Desire) have escorted since birth (*Il* 3.413–17).

In the *Th*, energy is never lost; discarded body parts and blood can generate Aphrodite, Erinyes, Giants, and Ash-Tree nymphs (*Th* 185–87). Unlike epic, the *Th* emphasizes the enduring role of even the earliest supernatural beings; again, the diachronic dimension predominates. The displaced sky-god Ouranos remains available as counselor when his castrating son Kronos learns he himself will be overthrown, and Rheia seeks advice from her two parents (*Th* 461, 470). The first half of the *Th* details meticulously the pre-Olympian origins of all surviving cosmic features. Gaia (Earth) and Eros (the force of attraction) are productive divinities, while the other two ungenerated original beings, Tartarus, far below earth, and Chaos ("Gap"), represent spaces to be filled. From the latter emerges (without reproduction) the particularized feminine deity, Night, and the more abstract male principle of darkness (*Erebos*). Their union creates another pairing of abstraction with specific instantiation: Shining Brightness (*Aithēr*) and Day (*Th.* 116–25). The many children of Night might be dismissed as ad hoc personifications were it not for the worship of some in ancient cults (e.g., Moirai at Olympia and Nemesis at Rhamnous; Pausanias 5.15.5; 1.33.2).

Night's brood (211–25) are bound together by associative logic. Death and Sleep are both characterized by loss of consciousness; Blame (*Mōmos*) causes Distress (*Oizus*) and Indignation (*Nemesis*). The category of destructive forces such as Strife (*Eris*) overlaps with that of boundary-setting notions, such as Old Age (*Gēras*) and Destinies (*Moirai*), a triplet that expresses human fate as a process of spinning (*Klōthō*), apportioning (*Lachesis*), and snipping a thread (*Atropos*). It is through this underlying idea of ultimate limitation, as well, that the Hesperidae and the "tribe of Dreams" belong to Night's clan, for both are located at the ends of the earth, the former "beyond glorious Okeanos" (215), the latter alongside its streams (*Od* 24.11–12).[7]

This passage is shaped by two poetic techniques that not only permeate the *Th* but are inextricable from its "theological" thinking: catalogs and the specification of locale. Adopting genealogy as the primary metaphor for cosmic evolution naturally leads to the creation of family trees. Specific branches—whether determined by the culture or the poet—express fundamental beliefs about reality. In Hesiod, the descendants of Night are kept separate from the Pontids, who come from the open sea (*Pontos*), a child of Gaia produced without intercourse (132) in contrast to the cosmic river Okeanos, whom she bore to Ouranos. Lies (229, *Pseudea*) are descendants of Night; by contrast, Pontus produced Nereus the "unerring and true" (233, *apseudea kai alēthea*). The polarity of truth and deception may create this genealogical divide, but further branchings express less clearly related aspects. The Pontids eventually include Iris, the gods' messenger; the Harpies; the Graiai and their sisters the Gorgons (living near the Hesperidae); and a series of threatening monster-types: Echidna, Chimera, the Nemean lion, the Hydra, Cerberus, and Geryoneus. Most beautiful of this impressive family are the fifty daughters of Nereus (240–64), whose mellifluous names mirror a mariner's ideal sea. The list's exuberant delight in sound may raise a basic question for much Hesiodic material: Is this a tour de force display of the poet's global knowledge or a theological statement acceptable to an audience?[8] Nereids possessed individual cults (e.g., Thetis, Amphitrite, Dōtō Galēnē) and were also worshipped collectively (Pausanias 7.1.8). But the above dichotomy is itself questionable. Worshippers most likely singled out Nereids according to local customs that varied widely among the roughly eight hundred archaic city-states. But even when praying and dedicating to "the Nereids," it is implausible that anyone recited all their names catalogically. The paradox of Greek religion is that poetry and cult live in synergy, the former supporting but also creating the latter. The subsequent long catalog of the family of Okeanos (337–63) makes explicit this complementarity. After listing many rivers and man-nurturing water nymphs, the poet pauses (363–70):

> [T]here are many others as well. For there are three thousand long-ankled daughters of Ocean who are widely dispersed and hold fast to the earth and the depths of the waters, everywhere in the same way, splendid children of goddesses; and there are just as many other loud-flowing rivers, sons of Ocean, to whom queenly Tethys gave birth. The names of them all it is difficult for a mortal man to tell, but each of those who dwell around them knows them. (Most 2006: 33)

In short, the authoritative poet conspicuously yields to the local "epichoric" knowledge of his widely dispersed audiences concerning their own worship, while nevertheless demonstrating his own awareness of a vast cosmos of divinity (Nagy 2009b: 275–76).

Localization distinguishes the Okeanid and Pontid catalogs from the obscure brood of Night. The Nile and Peneius Rivers occupy real space; Blame and the Destinies do not. Remarkably, even the monstrous descendants of Pontus are localized, albeit in less accessible spots. Geryoneus died "in sea-girt Erythea" (290), Echidna dwells "among the Arima" (304), and the Hydra haunts Lerna (314). Here, one is at the intersection of cosmology and epic legend. Highlighted throughout the Pontid catalog are future fatalities at the hands of heroes (and by extension, in heroic epics): Perseus (280), Bellerophon (325), and especially Heracles (316–18, 332; cf. 527–34). Theological confidence flows from heroes. The cosmos presents insuperable abstract phenomena (e.g., Strife) that are impossible to pin down (although gods indulging in them can be temporarily exiled; *Th* 782–804). Yet it also puts forth containable threats, no matter how difficult (*amēkhanon*, describing Cerberus at 310). By being enabled to overcome the latter, through courage and divine help, heroes enable us to face, if never fully beat, the former.

THEOGONIC EPIC AND AFTERMATH

The *Th* epicizes as much as the *Il* theologizes. Neither mode can claim priority, just as ancient aporia over the relative ages of "Homer" and "Hesiod" suggest their mutual dependence. In this light, Zeus's conquest of the Titans and Typhoeus corresponds to Achilles's demonstration of fighting power (*aristeia*). Whereas the hero's brilliant display (Bk. 20–22) ultimately triggers his death, the god's establishes the enduring pattern for human-divine relations. Overcoming rivals from his father's generation (*Th* 687–720), Zeus blasts the final monstrous threat to his regime (820–68). But his success depends, apart from control over incendiary thunderbolts, on the primeval Gaia, who recommends recruiting the powerful Hundred-Handers, hitherto bound beneath Earth by Ouranos (617–86, 711–20). Once more, diachrony asserts its importance. That divine sovereignty results from such political rewards and bargaining with the old regime is further underlined by the story of Styx. Through her own strategizing (389, *ebouleuse*) with advice from her father Okeanos, she obtains for her children (Rivalry, Victory, Supremacy, and Force) the honor of residing with Zeus, while she herself is made into the great oath-guarantor of the gods (383–403). Zeus's swallowing of his first wife, Mētis ("Cunning Intelligence"), another Okeanid, literalizes the incorporation of older cosmic forces whose powers he seeks to neutralize. Having this goddess within, he obtains wisdom about good and evil (886–900). His subsequent refashioning of the world requires serial impregnations (the first, with Mētis, producing Athena through Zeus's own head); these introduce into the cosmos harmony and order in the form of the Seasons (Lawfulness, Justice, Peace), the Graces, and the Muses, among other offspring (901–29). The summation of Zeus's new dispensation is his treatment of Hekate, detailed in a hymnic digression (411–52). Her honor (*timē*) operates on earth, sky, and sea; from her, when invoked before sacrificial acts, *timē* and happiness come to mortals; and thanks to Zeus, she retains the privileges she held among the Titans "according to the division first made from the beginning" (425). The list of those whom Hekate aids, from assembly speakers to athletes, fishermen to cattle breeders, has suggested that this closely reflects popular religious beliefs (Clay 2003: 131–37).

The theme of a contested "division" (*dasmos*) of privileges and honors, the heart of the struggle between Agamemnon and Achilles in the *Il*, has cosmic precedent in the Hesiodic story of Prometheus, the third major victory of Zeus. If his martial conquests are like an Achillean *aristeia*, Zeus's punishment of his rival, the son of Iapetos, more closely foreshadows the manipulative brilliance of Odysseus (whose regular epithet, *polymētis*, makes him Zeus-like: "having much cunning intelligence"). Irked by Prometheus's unfair sacrificial division at a feast (544, *heterozēlōs diedassao*), Zeus sees through the trick and yet chooses *intentionally* (551) the worse portion from two offered him, thus determining the format of meat sacrifices for all time: mortals set aside "white bones" for gods but consume roasted meat (related to deeper themes; see Stocking 2017). The *Th* explicitly makes Zeus plan long-term harm for mortals (552) and narrates the result: Zeus hiding fire; Prometheus stealing it back; Zeus creating the "beautiful bad thing" Pandora, source of the "race of women," that will become a (necessary) bane for men (561–611).

It is the complex saga of Prometheus and Pandora that aligns the theological outlook of the *Th* with the *WD*. The latter works out in detail the consequences of Zeus's plan that mortals pay a price (perhaps as collateral damage with their benefactor

Prometheus, although the rationale is never stated; see Clay 2003: 100–28). The poem posits a prelapsarian age akin to the *Th*'s divine-human commensality predating Prometheus's division (535–37; cf. *WD* 108, gods and humans have the same source). [9] But its main lesson is that livelihood and justice, in the here and now, are hard to come by. Zeus, with an atavistic addiction to concealment (like Ouranos and Kronos), hides not children but fire (*WD* 50) and the means of living (*bios*, *WD* 42, 47). Pandora's threat, too, is hidden, her lovely outside concealing "a dog's mind and thievish character" (67), leading her to open the storage jar that in turn conceals all woes for mortals (69–105).

The theology of the *WD*, however, holds out one hope (like Elpis under the jar's lid; *WD* 95) not expressed in the *Th*. It is not Pandora qua first woman who is to be faulted not for mortal fragility, but for intelligence failure. Prometheus's warning to his brother Epimetheus not to take such gifts went unheeded. Mythical fraternal advice becomes the analog for the poem's realistic frame. Hesiod's brother, Perses, has the opportunity to redeem, at least partially, Epimetheus's original lack of forethought (Martin 2004). By listening to his brother and putting his mind to work, he can survive and even prosper (293–319). The link between such productive mindfulness and the poem's great overarching theme of Justice (*Dikē*) depends on the implicit assumption (a subsistence economy's) that not possessing one's own proper share must engender thievish appropriations (cf. *WD* 314–34). Maintaining a just proportion in all things means respecting *right division*, a theme foregrounded by the brothers' litigation over inheritance (33–41). This entails choosing the right one of the two Strifes (*Erides*), choosing the spirit of zealous competition rather than conflict (11–26). Zeus hid this, as well, in the earth (18–19)—but the burial is beneficial.

Two much-discussed Hesiodic fables encapsulate the diptych that has been painted thus far. The so-called Myth of the Races depicts, at first sight, a degenerate world, with three divinely created races symbolized by metals (gold, silver, bronze) successively dying off between the time of Kronos and that of the fourth generation, of the demigod heroes that disappeared just before Hesiod's own Iron Age (*WD* 109–76). The diachronic "myth" asserts a powerful synchronic message concerning the abiding structural opposition of Dikē and Hubris (Vernant 1965; Nagy 1979: 151–69). At the same time, it shows the gods weighing in on the positive side of this polarity—a theological point that the *Th* leaves obscure. Not only does Zeus transform the gold generation into benign guardians of justice roaming the earth (*WD* 121–26; cf. 252–55), honor the ungrateful silver (140–42), and give immortality to the heroes (166–73). Despite the near annihilation of Justice by Hubris envisioned as the result of Iron Age lawlessness, the poet insists that Dikē *does* win (217–24), the just city flourishes (225–37), and Zeus will (probably) not let the unjust ultimately succeed (271–73).

In the poet's theological imagination, divine Dikē herself, when harmed, "proclaims (*gēruet'*) the unjust mind of human beings" so that Zeus can take revenge (260). This image of urgent ethical enunciation is key to the second fable, a coded message (*ainos*) to the "kings" (alternating with Perses as addressees). In the fable we hear only the hawk speak, boasting of his overpowering force to the weeping nightingale held firmly in his grasp: "You are going wherever I shall carry you even if you are a singer" (*WD* 208). But the encoded allegory runs counter to the hawk's hubris: might is *not* right. Instead, we must listen to the actual medium of the poet Hesiod that frames this communication. A higher form of moral articulation activates the divinely inspired poetry that Hesiod learned from the Muses, the power "to proclaim (*gērusasthai*) true things" (*Th* 28).[10]

FURTHER READING

Lamberton (1988) remains the best concise introduction to the major Hesiodic questions. Clay (2003) meticulously surveys previous work, providing important new suggestions. Nagy (2009a) summarizes his crucial arguments relevant to compositional contexts and broader treatment of the divine. Pucci (1977) analyzes the ontological status of the Muses' communication. Solmsen (1949) is important for questions of theology and Lloyd-Jones (1983) for theodicy. Excellent, relevant essays in Montanari et al. (2009), Blaise et al. (1996), and Heitsch (1966) have helpful bibliographies.

NOTES

1. In the *Certamen* (18) Homer, after losing to Hesiod in Chalkis, sings a hymn at Delos, without mention of a contest.
2. On unique aspects of Hesiodic cosmology arising from incorporation of the female, see Park (2014).
3. Shared phrases using forms of *theos* include *WD* 139, 257, "gods who hold Olympus" cf. *Od* 12.337); *Th* 400, "gods' great oath" (cf. *Od* 2.377); fr. 176.4, "dear to the blessed gods (cf. *Od* 1.82); and fr. 211.3, "dear to the deathless gods" (cf. *Il* 20.347).
4. The iambic touch confirms the Muses' mastery of every genre. On their speech see Nagy (2009b: 276–77) and Stoddard (2004: 73–85); on the similarity to Archilochus's initiation see Nagy (2009b: 307–308).
5. He begins not with the Muses but with their mother, Mnemosyne, claiming her as patroness (ἢ γὰρ λάχε Μαιάδος υἱόν); rather than chiefly praising Zeus, who wins sovereignty and distributes honors, he tells how each god received his portion (*moiran*), as if such awards were automatic, and he praises the rest of the gods "according to seniority," which presumably subordinates Zeus to preceding generations.
6. I use this term to make a different point from Mondi (1984), with whom, however, I am in agreement as to diachronically distinct oral-poetic traditions generating inconsistencies.
7. Similarly, Eris, daughter of Night, produces individual instantiations of Strife (*Th* 226–32), from Toil (*Ponos*), to disputes, to Oath (generator of disputes when broken).
8. On the polarity truth/lies in early Greek thought, see Detienne (1996). The ring-composition, whereby the Nereid *Nemertēs* is named last (262), foregrounds this aspect (cf. 235).
9. The larger issue of divine-human relations in Hesiod is analyzed at length in Clay (2003, 2005).
10. On the fable, see Clay (2003: 39), with further bibliography. On the variant reading *muthēsasthai*, "make a *muthos*," at *Th* 28 see Nagy (2009b: 280).

References

Blaise, F., P. Judet de la Combe, and P. Rousseau, eds. 1996. *Le Métier du mythe: Lectures d'Hèsiode*. Lille, France.

Clay, J. S. 1989. *The Politics of Olympus: Form and Meaning in the Major Homeric Hymns*. Princeton, NJ.

Clay, J. S. 2003. *Hesiod's Cosmos*. Cambridge.

Clay, J. S. 2005. "The Beginning and End of the Hesiodic *Catalogue of Women* and Its Relation to Hesiod." In *The Hesiodic Catalogue of Women: Constructions and Reconstructions*, edited by R. Hunter, 25–34. Cambridge.

Collins, D. 2004. *Master of the Game: Competition and Performance in Greek Poetry*. Washington, DC.

Detienne, M. 1986. *The Creation of Mythology*. Translated by M. Cook. Chicago. Originally published as *L'invention de la mythologie* (Paris, 1981).

Detienne, M. 1996. *The Masters of Truth in Archaic Greece*. 2nd ed. Translated by J. Lloyd. Cambridge, MA. Originally published as *Maîtres de vérité dans la Grèce archaïque* (Paris, 1994).

Emlyn-Jones, C., and W. Preddy., eds. and trans. 2013. *Plato, Republic*. Vol. 1. Cambridge, MA.

Fowler, H. L., ed. and trans. 1926. *Plato: Cratylus, Parmenides, Greater Hippias, Lesser Hippias*. Cambridge, MA.

Gerber, D., ed. and trans. 1999. *Greek Elegiac Poetry: From the Seventh to the Fifth Centuries BC*. Cambridge, MA.

Heitsch, E., ed. 1966. *Hesiod*. Darmstadt, Germany.

Henrichs, A. 2003. "'Hieroi Logoi' and 'Hierai Bibloi': The (Un)Written Margins of the Sacred in Ancient Greece." *Harvard Studies in Classical Philology* 101: 207–66.

Hunter, R. 2012. *Plato and the Traditions of Ancient Literature: The Silent Stream*. Cambridge.

Janko, R. 1994. *The Iliad: A Commentary, Books 13–16*. Vol. 4. Cambridge.

Katz, J. 2010. "Inherited Poetics." In *A Companion to the Ancient Greek Language*, edited by E. J. Bakker, 357–69. Chichester, UK.

Kindt, J. 2012. *Rethinking Greek Religion*. Cambridge.

Lamberton, R. 1988. *Hesiod*. New Haven, CT.

Lattimore, R., trans. 2011. *The Iliad of Homer*. Introduction and Notes by Richard Martin. Chicago, IL.

Lesher, J. H. 1992. *Xenophanes of Colophon: Fragments; A Text and Translation with a Commentary*. Toronto.

Lloyd-Jones, H. 1983. *The Justice of Zeus*. Berkeley, CA.

Loney, A. C. 2014. "Hesiod's Incorporative Poetics in the *Theogony* and the Contradictions of Prometheus." *American Journal of Philology* 135: 503–31.

Martin, R. P. 1984. "Hesiod, Odysseus, and the Instruction of Princes." *TAPA* 114: 29–48.

Martin, R. P. 1989. *The Language of Heroes: Speech and Performance in the Iliad*. Ithaca, NY.

Martin, R. P. 2000. "Synchronic Aspects of Homeric Performance: The Evidence of the *Hymn to Apollo*." In *Una nueva visión de la cultura griega antigua hacia el fin del milenio*, edited by A. M. González de Tobia, A. M., 403–32. La Plata, Argentina.

Martin, R. P. 2001. "Rhapsodizing Orpheus." *Kernos* 14: 23–33.

Martin, R. P. 2004. "Hesiod and the Didactic Double." *Synthesis* 11: 31–53.

Martin, R. P. 2013. "The 'Myth before the Myth Began." In *Writing Down the Myths*, edited by J. F. Nagy, J. F., 45–66. Cursor Mundi 17, Turnhout, Belgium.

Mondi, R. 1984. "The Ascension of Zeus and the Composition of Hesiod's *Theogony*." *Greek, Roman, and Byzantium Studies* 25: 325–44.

Montanari, F., C. Tsagalis, and A. Rengakos, eds. 2009. *Brill's Companion to Hesiod*. Leiden, Netherlands.

Most, G., ed. and trans. 2006. *Hesiod I: Theogony, Works and Days, Testimonia*. Cambridge, MA.

Most, G., ed. and trans. 2007. *Hesiod II: The Shield, Catalogue of Women, Other Fragments*. Cambridge, MA.

Nagy, G. 1979. *The Best of the Achaeans*. Baltimore, MD.

Nagy, G. 2000. "Homeric *humnos* as a Rhapsodic Term." In *Una nueva visión de la cultura griega antigua hacia el fin del milenio*, edited by A. M. González de Tobia, 385–401. La Plata, Argentina.

Nagy, G. 2009a. *Homer the Classic*. Washington, DC.

Nagy, G. 2009b. "Hesiod and the Ancient Biographical Traditions." In *Brill's Companion to Hesiod*, edited by F. Montanari, A. Rengakos, and C. Tsagalis, 271–311. Leiden, Netherlands.

Park, A. 2014. "Parthenogenesis in Hesiod's *Theogony*." *Preternature: Critical and Historical Studies on the Preternatural* 3: 261–83.

Parker, R., 2011. *On Greek Religion*. Ithaca, NY.

Porter, W. M. 1993. *Reading the Classics and Paradise Lost*. Lincoln, NE.

Pucci, P. 1977. *Hesiod and the Language of Poetry*. Baltimore, MD.

Richardson, N. J. 1981. "The Contest of Homer and Hesiod and Alcidamas' *Mouseion*." *The Classical Quaterly* 31: 1–10.

Richardson, N. J. 1993. *The Iliad: A Commentary, Books 21–24*. Vol. 6. Cambridge.

Scully, S. 2015. *Hesiod's Theogony: From Near Eastern Creation Myths to Paradise Lost*. Oxford.

Solmsen, F. 1949. *Hesiod and Aeschylus*. Ithaca, NY.

Stocking, C. 2017. The Politics of Sacrifice in Early Greek Myth and Poetry. Cambridge.

Stoddard, K., 2004. *The Narrative Voice in the Theogony of Hesiod*. Mnemosyne Supplement 255. Leiden, Netherlands.

Vernant, J.-P. 1965. "Le mythe hésiodique des races: Essai d'analyse structural." In *Mythe et pensée chez les Grecs*, 19–47. Paris.

West, M. L. 1983. *The Orphic Poems*. Oxford.

West, M. L., ed. and trans. 2003. *Homeric Hymns, Apocrypha, Lives*. Cambridge, MA.

CHAPTER 10

··

HESIOD IN PERFORMANCE

··

EGBERT J. BAKKER

THE poems of the Hesiodic corpus were, like all poetic compositions and traditions of archaic Greece, disseminated and transmitted through performance. By this we mean primarily that Hesiod was performed qua Hesiod as part of a literary "canon" by professional performers called "rhapsodes." In the classical period the Hesiodic poems were part of the rhapsodic repertoire alongside the *Iliad* and *Odyssey* (e.g., Plato, *Ion* 531a2–9; *Republic* 600d5–6; *Laws* 658d6–8). Since Homer was performed at the large public religious festivals, such as the Panathenaia in Athens and the Asklepieia at Epidauros, we may infer that Hesiod was also. Rhapsodic contests go back to the sixth century BCE, and although only Homer is mentioned in our sources (e.g., Herodotus 5.67.1), there is no reason to doubt that Hesiod was already part of the rhapsodes' repertoire then (on the rhapsodic performance of Homer and Hesiod, see Koning 2010: 46–51).

It would seem natural to assume that rhapsodic performance was merely a stage in the transmission of Hesiod, something that was extrinsic to the "real" works composed by the poet Hesiod. Various strands of scholarship would set apart the rhapsodic Hesiod (or Homer) from the "original" poet, for example, when scholars look for an original poet's life and times as the key to his works' meaning, or when rhapsodic performance is set as a reproductive stage against the creative stage of genuine oral composition (e.g., Parry 1971: 337, Kirk 1976: 126–27). But there are reasons for assigning more importance to the rhapsodic performance of Homer and Hesiod. For one thing, we would probably not have Hesiod—or Homer, for that matter—without the wide Panhellenic diffusion of rhapsodic transmission over a period of various centuries, which provided a solid basis for textual transmission. And more important, for the purposes of a discussion of Hesiod as performance it is more productive to see the relation between "Hesiod" and the rhapsodic tradition as something more interesting and complex than the simple recitation of the compositions of an "original" poet.[1] The poet and the biographical features associated with him (such as Hesiod's encounter with the Muses or his dispute with his brother) may be less an independent reality preceding rhapsodic performance than a persona created in and through performance (cf. Nagy 1990: 36–81; Martin 1992: 14–15).

Hesiod and Homer complement each other well as interlocking components of the rhapsodic repertoire; against epic's representation of an age of heroes, Hesiod on the one hand places the birth of the gods and the cosmos in a remote, preheroic, past and on the other hand depicts matters of justice and human conduct in the audience's own time, the Iron Age, thus temporally framing and encapsulating the Homeric heroic universe. (This means that the *Theogony* [hereafter *Th*] and *Works and Days* [hereafter *WD*] are themselves complementary to each other, a central point in Clay 2003.) These two mainstays of the rhapsodic repertoire sometimes seem to have formed a canonical triad with Archilochus, the poet of abuse and invective, whose oeuvre is complementary to both Homer's and Hesiod's.[2]

PERFORMING JUSTICE

The juxtaposition with Homer is a productive way of looking at the performance of Hesiod, as demonstrated later in this chapter. But let us first ask whether there are ways in which we can look beyond rhapsodic performance into the "prehistory" of the Hesiodic tradition. What are possible occasions for its performance? We know that there is a link between the reenactment of cosmogonic myths and seasonally occurring rituals of renewal. The Babylonian *Enûma Eliš*, for example, was performed on the fourth day of the New Year festival, and a similar connection is attested for other cultures as well (Auffahrt 1991; López-Ruiz 2010: 182). Typically, the poem to be performed on such occasions is a celebration of the supreme god's power and will contain the narrative of how he established his reign through a victory over a previous generation of gods. This is of course also the theme of the Hesiodic *Th*, but, although the performance of some proto-*Th* at local or regional Dark Age or early archaic festivals of renewal is inherently likely, we do not have direct evidence for it.

Equally widespread in archaic cultures is wisdom poetry, and the Near East provides a variety of parallels for Hesiod. The most pertinent of these for a study of the *WD* are those that involve a recipient of the poet's precepts, someone who has misbehaved or even done injustice to the speaker (West 1997: 307). This interaction may be a stylization of real situations of conflict, in which proverbs or other expressions of received wisdom can be uttered in order to reach a resolution. In the *Th* (80–93) it is the wise king, endowed with the gift of speech received from the Muses, who is presented as such a performer of wisdom; he may well be thought of as mastering a body of poetic wisdom utterances through which he resolves the conflict.[3] In the *WD* it is the speaker, Hesiod "himself," who settles the dispute, interspersing his discourse with gnomic utterances, which may well have been established proverbs in the language. An example is verse 347: "Esteem is the share of him whose share is a decent neighbor" (ἔμμορε τοι τιμῆς ὅς τ' ἔμμορε γείτονος ἐσθλοῦ, cf. 319, 579, and 825).

The conflict that constitutes the *WD* is one between the speaker and his brother Perses. Hesiod urges his brother to "settle on the spot" (αὖθι διακρινώμεθα νεῖκος, *WD*

35), which, as we shall see, means "in and through the performance of the poem." The two have divided their inheritance between them (κλῆρον ἐδασσάμεθ, 37), and it is usually held that Perses has now taken more than his share (*WD* 37–38). But that interpretation is not necessary, and the poem's points work just as well, perhaps better, if Perses has done harm to third parties:

> ἤδη μὲν γὰρ κλῆρον ἐδασσάμεθ' ἄλλα τε πολλὰ
> ἁρπάζων ἐφόρεις (*WD* 37–38)

> We have now divided our lot and <in addition/at the same time> you
> carried many other things that you had snatched

Just as in the *Th*, the "kings" are available as judges to settle the case. They have lost all moral authority, however, after they have been "honored" by Perses, presumably by accepting gifts, which earns them the epithet "gift-eating" (δωροφάγους, 39). But Hesiod makes sure that the case is tried in the court of the highest judge of all, the supreme god Zeus himself (*WD* 9–10):

> κλῦθι ἰδὼν ἀίων τε, δίκῃ δ' ἴθυνε θέμιστας
> τύνη· ἐγὼ δέ κε Πέρσῃ ἐτήτυμα μυθησαίμην

> Hearken by seeing and hearing, and straighten the laws with your justice,
> you god, so that I can proclaim to Perses things that are grounded in reality.

These lines come at the end of a short proem in which the Muses are invoked to sing of Zeus, the ultimate dispenser of fame among mortals. The poem thus begins as a hymn to Zeus, in a way that lends authority to the composition and its performer, who shows he has access to the divine and to the proper poetic means to evoke it. But in a twist the presence of the supreme god is then used as the backdrop for the juridical and moral issues to be addressed. Zeus will enforce justice, but this is not something that will happen in the future, beyond the confines of the poem and its performance. It will happen *now*, in and through the poem. The *WD* is not merely a poetic performance; it is also an extended performative speech act, an utterance that accomplishes its semantic content in and through being uttered (for this concept, see Austin 1975: 4–5).

As the poem unfolds, the speaker adopts various roles, from arbitrator in the quarrel (νεῖκος, 35), to prophet and seer, to preceptor, just as the main addressee, Perses, turns from being defendant into an object of rebuke, to blend finally with the generic "you" of an impersonal audience as the recipient of moral and agricultural advice. In other words, the poem resolves the conflict that prompted its existence, letting justice (δίκη) prevail over transgression and aggression (ὕβρις), thus effecting justice not merely through pleading or persuasion, but performatively, in and through the act of being uttered, that is, performed.

The performative reading may resolve an issue that has perplexed some readers, namely that Perses is rebuked one last time in the course of this progression, when Hesiod tells him that he will not help him out now that he has come once more begging at his door, having failed to sow and reap his crops properly (*WD* 396–97). Perses's new role as beggar has been found irreconcilable with the earlier Perses who hobnobs with the kings themselves.[4] But we should follow the poem's performative progression. By the time we reach verse 396 the dispute has been resolved in Hesiod's favor. The rebuke occurs just after the beginning of the *WD* proper (381–83), the industrious farmer's life in accordance with the seasons as the right way to acquire wealth. The improper ways of doing this have now been discredited. By putting Perses on trial in the very act of performing the poem—and winning the case—Hesiod has shown how wealth should never be acquired. Perses is now deprived of the social context in which he could become rich unjustly and unsustainably.

The new situation shows Perses for what he is: a lazy and ineffectual farmer, who can only become a social parasite, as he fails to carry out the proper "works." And the greedy and corrupt "kings," participants in a trial they are eager to settle to their advantage, melt away once the trial is over; the last address to them occurs at verse 263, in the context of divine retribution for misdeeds. Hesiod, who is entrusted with the scepter (*Th* 30), the symbol of god-given authority, has (like a good "king") had recourse to divine justice and wisdom in settling the dispute, acquiring a voice that will resound far beyond the original occasion.

FROM EPICHORIC TO PANHELLENIC

Thus the poem, which starts with a confrontation between the speaker, Perses, and the "kings," ends with a situation in which its named addressee, Perses (last mentioned at verse 641 in a context of neutral advice, not litigation or rebuke), becomes a member of an unspecific and generic audience. The *WD*, in other words, not only resolves in performance the juridical issue that prompts its utterance; it also reenacts its development from specific to generic, from local into global, from epichoric into Panhellenic. The "kings," βασιλῆς, have no place in the civic context of the Panhellenic festivals in which Hesiod was to be performed.[5] But conversely, the careful lack of detail on the *neîkos* among Hesiod, his brother, and the "kings" cannot be the faithful representation of a local dispute; it foreshadows the strategy of Panhellenism to make a given situation or version of a myth as widely distributable as possible, by avoiding elements that could make it irrelevant or unacceptable to a given local community.

The *Th* provides a similar "internal reenactment" of the transition from epichoric to Panhellenic (Nagy 1990: 57). The poem opens emphatically with the "Heliconian Muses" (*Th* 1):

Μουσάων Ἑλικωνιάδων ἀρχώμεθ᾿ ἀείδειν

From the Heliconian Muses let us start our song.

That is, the Muses, the song's programmatic starting point,[6] are local, not Panhellenic, and the programmatic verb for "beginning" can perhaps be taken in the loaded sense of *"beginning* with/from the Heliconian Muses—but *not* ending with them." Alternatively, we may place emphasis on the toponym "Heliconian" (note that the epithet "Heliconian" prominently occupies the second slot of a rising tricolon that bridges the main caesura). When they descend from the mountain,[7] they encounter the poet as he is tending his herds and call on him to enter his vocation as visionary poet and seer. This *Dichterweihe* is often compared to the experience of the biblical prophet Amos, who was likewise called away from his sheep (Amos 1.1). But whereas the text of the prophet goes on to rebuke and admonish precisely identified kings and nations, thus passing on a historical snapshot to the canon of which he will be a part, Hesiod's kings remain unspecific and generic, whether they are the object of rebuke, as in the *WD*, or the object of praise, as in the *Th* (80–93). And Helicon is not the deictic center of the poem, but rather its starting point or launching pad. The Muses' *descent* from Helicon, when they sing a song that starts with the Olympians and recedes back in time to the primordial gods, will be followed by their *ascent* of Olympus (68–71), when they sing the song of the world in reverse order, starting with the primordial gods and ending with Zeus and the Olympians (44–52). This is the song they sing *after* calling Hesiod to his vocation, the song that serves as a divine model for the Panhellenic *Th*.

Deixis in Performance

The Muses' song as they arrive on Olympus pleases Zeus as he is rejoicing in his victory over his father Kronos and in the way he has arranged the world by assigning each god his or her specific and stable sphere of influence (*Th* 71–75):

> ὁ δ' οὐρανῷ ἐμβασιλεύει,
> αὐτὸς ἔχων βροντὴν ἠδ' αἰθαλόεντα κεραυνόν,
> κάρτεϊ νικήσας πατέρα Κρόνον· εὖ δὲ ἕκαστα
> ἀθανάτοις διέταξε νόμους καὶ ἐπέφραδε τιμάς.
> <u>ταῦτ' ἄρα</u> Μοῦσαι ἄειδον Ὀλύμπια δώματ' ἔχουσαι

> and he reigns supreme in the sky,
> holding the thunder himself and the blazing lightning bolt,
> having defeated his father Kronos by force. And well in every respect
> has he arranged the laws for the immortals and shown them their privileges.
> <u>That</u> is what the Muses sang, who have their dwellings on Olympos.

It is easy to miss the importance of the pronoun ταῦτ'(α). In the archaizing epic idiom that the *Th* is following, this is not an anaphoric pronoun that refers back to what was said earlier. The demonstrative pronoun οὗτος in the language of Greek epic is a truly deictic element. There is a clear division of labor between οὗτος as deictic and ὁ as anaphoric; the situation in which οὗτος has subsumed the function of ὁ, which in its turn has bleached into being the definite article, does not apply to the language of epic (Bakker 1999: 4–5, 2005: 75–77). As deictic marker, οὗτος indicates that a speaker considers something so close to his interlocutor as to be within the latter's mental or even physical grasp. The pronoun thus conveys that the thing pointed at is shared information in the interaction with the addressee.[8]

The pronoun occurs throughout the *Th* and typically when Hesiod refers to a reality that is the result of Zeus's or the Olympians' actions, and that is therefore a constitutive element of the universe he and his audience share. "Sing of these events to me, Muses" (ταῦτά μοι ἔσπετε Μοῦσαι, 114) sings Hesiod, referring to the division of the gods' prerogatives (τιμαί, 112), just as in the extract cited above (74–75); "this is the prerogative she holds from the beginning and which has been allotted to her as her share among humans and the immortal gods" (ταύτην δ' ἐξ ἀρχῆς τιμὴν ἔχει ἠδὲ λέλογχε | μοῖραν ἐν ἀνθρώποισι καὶ ἀθανάτοισι θεοῖσι, 203–4), about Aphrodite and her power, a fact of the universe that was established well before Zeus's ascension to his reign, or even before his birth, but that is now a piece of knowledge of the world as Hesiod and his audience know it; this audience-oriented deixis pertains also to Atlas, who holds the heavens on his shoulders at the edges of the earth: ταύτην γάρ οἱ μοῖραν ἐδάσσατο μητίετα Ζεύς, "for that is the share that Zeus has assigned to him" (520). The poet may have special understanding of how the world has come about, but the reality he explains is common to all humans and a matter of the face-to-face interaction between a performer and his audience.

A situation in which text-external, interpersonal deixis (οὗτος) is always preferred over text-internal anaphora (ὁ) is the conclusion of catalogs, a typical and expected feature of cosmogonic poetry. The list of the fifty Nereids, for example, which runs over twenty lines, is rounded off as follows (*Th* 263–64):

αὗται μὲν Νηρῆος ἀμύμονος ἐξεγένοντο
κοῦραι πεντήκοντα, ἀμύμονα ἔργα ἰδυῖαι

These are born from blameless Nereus,
fifty maidens, knowing blameless works

And similarly, an impressive list of nymphs, daughters of Okeanos and Tethys, concludes: αὗται δ' Ὠκεανοῦ καὶ Τηθύος ἐξεγένοντο, "these are born from Okeanos and Tethys" (*Th* 362). The religious and experiential relevance of these cataloged sea and river goddesses is perhaps less important than the performer's pride in (and his audience's admiration of) the mnemonic prowess he has just demonstrated, which would be reflected in the choice of the interactive deictic: "There you have them. I did it!" It is no coincidence that the Homeric Catalogue of Ships ends in the same way (*Iliad* 2.760; οὗτοι ἄρ' ἡγεμόνες Δαναῶν καὶ κοίρανοι ἦσαν, "these, then, were the leaders of the Danaans and their lords") in a rare case of the Homeric narrator using the deictic (Bakker 2005: 80).

The Hesiodic performance, then, can draw attention to what is produced in and through the narrative, but it can also draw attention to itself, to the performer and the song. This involves an even more powerful deictic marker.

The Muses' address of Hesiod is introduced in the following way (*Th* 24–25):

τόνδε δέ με πρώτιστα θεαὶ πρὸς μῦθον ἔειπον,
Μοῦσαι Ὀλυμπιάδες, κοῦραι Διὸς αἰγιόχοιο

Some scholars might want to take the deictic pronoun τόνδε with μῦθον, but there are various problems with this reading. First, the hyperbaton between τόνδε and μῦθον is quite extreme and not easy to parallel in epic Greek. Second, μῦθον is an integral part of the formula πρὸς μῦθον ἔειπον (which occurs thirty-three times in Homer) and intimately bound up with the verb, being nested between the verb and its preverb ("they *mûthon*-addressed"); in none of the Homeric instances is the very bound accusative functioning as a real, independent, direct object that can be modified by other elements elsewhere in the verse (the only other example of the formula in Hesiod is *WD* 206: τὴν ὅ γ' ἐπικρατέως πρὸς μῦθον ἔειπεν). Third, and perhaps most important, the combination *τόνδε μῦθον "this *mûthos* here," is unparalleled in epic: the deictic would impart a "hereness" and physicality to the speech that is possible only when it is conceived as a written artifact.[9]

We may therefore consider the other reading, in which τόνδε is taken with με, which would involve a striking (self-)pointing to the physical presence of the performer. The deictic ὅδε is aligned with the first person, just as οὗτος is aligned with the second person, but beyond this semantic difference there is a pragmatic contrast, a difference in information status: whereas οὗτος presents information as accessible to the addressee and therefore "known," ὅδε presents information as not (yet) accessible to the interlocutor and so new or newsworthy (cf. Bakker 2010: 152–57). Such a self-presentation suits a performer reporting on a mystic experience that placed a shepherd's life on a wholly new footing, and who now addresses an audience with a newfound authority: "Me here, I am the one the goddesses personally addressed."

The *WD* has a similarly striking way of typifying itself through deictic markers. As we saw, the dispute between Hesiod and Perses needs to be settled in and through the context of the poem's performance (ἀλλ' αὖθι διακρινώμεθα νεῖκος, "but let us settle our dispute here and now," 35). This is the juridical case of which the kings want to be the judges (*WD* 37–39):

ἤδη μὲν γὰρ κλῆρον ἐδασσάμεθ', ἀλλά τε πολλὰ
ἁρπάζων ἐφόρεις μέγα κυδαίνων βασιλῆας
δωροφάγους, οἳ τήνδε δίκην ἐθέλουσι δικάσσαι.

We have now divided our lot and you
carried many other things that you had snatched, paying major tribute to the kings
who devour gifts, and who now want to pronounce a verdict in this present case.

The δίκη, as we saw, is nothing other than the *WD* itself, but in referring to it with τήνδε δίκην the poet is not referring to the poem qua work without further ado (as, for example, Herodotus does with ἱστορίης ἀπόδεξις ἥδε, reifying his work and presenting it to the reader as a monument); the τήνδε δίκην refers to the work *in context*, the poem in the act of being performed (see also Calame 2004: 418–19). The two remaining instances of τήνδε δίκην equally present the present case as something in progress, and equally with respect to the kings, whose verdict, δίκη, it will turn out to be—within the wider context of divine observation and vengeance (e.g., *WD* 248–51):

> ὮΩ βασιλῆς, ὑμεῖς δὲ καταφράζεσθε καὶ αὐτοὶ
> <u>τήνδε δίκην</u>· ἐγγὺς γὰρ ἐν ἀνθρώποισιν ἐόντες
> ἀθάνατοι φράζονται ὅσοι σκολιῇσι δίκῃσιν
> ἀλλήλους τρίβουσι θεῶν ὄπιν οὐκ ἀλέγοντες.

> Oh, you kings, you, consider yourselves too
> <u>this case</u>; close by, here among humans,
> the immortals are observing all those who with crooked judgments
> are wearing each other out, paying no heed to the vengeance of the gods.

That is, the poem and its speaker open up to the possibly hostile attention of the kings, but not without confirming that they themselves are scrutinized in a higher court of justice. The poem's self-contextualization is a layered affair.

In all this there is no reason to suppose that the performer's admonitions are the faithful representation, or even a stylized representation, of a real trial. Nor are we to suppose that Hesiod and Perses are historical figures, in spite of substantial scholarly assumption, from antiquity onward, that they are (recently Scodel 2012: 113). Instead, what happens in the performance of the *WD* is a matter of mimesis.

Hesiodic versus Homeric Mimesis

Plato virtually founded the literary discipline of narratology by having Socrates introduce the distinction between diegesis and mimesis in a discussion of how poetry ought to be presented in the ideal polis (*Republic* 392d5–6), after a discussion of poetry's content and subject matter; after dealing with *what* poetry should and should not say, Socrates proposes to move on to *how* poets should present their content. Applied to the study of modern written narrative, the distinction between diegesis and mimesis comes down to the opposition between the discourse of a novel's narrator and that of the characters whom the narrator "quotes" as part of the total strategy of presentation. But Plato is discussing the rhapsodic performance of Homer in the public space of the polis, not literary novels, and this gives mimesis an entirely different conceptual load (393c5–6):

οὐκοῦν τό γε ὁμοιοῦν ἑαυτὸν ἄλλῳ ἢ κατὰ φωνὴν ἢ κατὰ σχῆμα μιμεῖσθαί ἐστιν
ἐκείνου ᾧ ἄν τις ὁμοιοῖ;

Now making oneself similar to someone else either in one's voice or in one's gestures
is doing a *mimēsis* of the person one makes oneself similar to, no?

In other words, mimesis is a matter of *impersonation*, a theatrical affair, which aligns
the rhapsode with the *hupokritēs*, the actor in theater, who plays roles in tragedy and
comedy (cf. Plato, *Ion* 532d7, 536a1; *Republic* 373b7, 395a8; see also Herington 1985: 10–15).

In thinking how Plato's conception of mimesis and diegesis might apply to Hesiod,
we may begin by noticing that direct speech in the *Th* is far sparser than in Homer; there
are no long, passionate speeches, no elaborate exchanges. Conversations are short, with
"turns" of no more than two or three lines, as between Gaia and Kronos (164–66; 170–72) or
Prometheus and Zeus (548–49; 559–60); the longest speeches are that of Zeus in the struggle
with the Titēnes (644–53) and the reply of the Hundred-Hander Kottos (655–63). By this
token the performance of the *Th* would be a matter of terse diegesis, catalogic narrative
without the attention to lavish and visual detail that characterizes Homeric narrative.

But the *Th* is also the narrative whose narrator explicitly presents himself to the audience as a post-mystic-experience seer, and his account of the world to his audience is,
as we saw, interspersed with the interactive deictic pronoun *οὗτος*, which in Homer is
mostly confined to the discourse of the characters. These are features of mimesis, which
become stronger and more numerous in the *WD*. The poem revolves, as we saw, around
explicit interaction, as speech in a context that has been generated by the poem itself.
The juridical dispute between the speaker and his brother provides ample opportunities
for biographical development and hence the creation of a "role" to be played by the performer of the poem. The poem's self-presentation as *τήνδε δίκην* (or the performer's self-
presentation in the *Th* as *τόνδε*) is not attested in Homer, where the proximal deictic *ὅδε*
is used only in the speech of the characters. This applies to other features as well, such as
the speaker's famous realization, at the beginning of the harangue, that there is not one
"strife" (*ἔρις*), but two (*WD* 11–13):

οὐκ ἄρα μοῦνον ἔην Ἐρίδων γένος, ἀλλ' ἐπὶ γαῖαν
εἰσὶ δύω· τὴν μέν κεν ἐπαινήσειε νοήσας,
ἡ δ' ἐπιμωμητή· διὰ δ' ἄνδιχα θυμὸν ἔχουσιν.

<So I now see that> there is not one kind of Eris; no, upon the earth
there are two. The one you can approve of when you contemplate it,
but the other one is blameworthy; they are of an entirely different disposition.

This moment is often seen as a correction of Hesiod's earlier statement in the *Th* that there
is a single "harsh-minded" Eris/Strife (*Ἔριν . . . καρτερόθυμον*), daughter of Night and
mother of a host of grievous entities including War, Manslaughter, Conflicts, Lies, and
Disputes (*Th* 225–32). But no less important is what prompts the new insight. The bad Eris
is certainly at work in the *neîkos* between the speaker and his brother, but he now realizes
that its presence is due to the *absence* of good Eris in the lifestyle adopted by Perses, who

hangs out at the trials of others' disputes and neglects his farm and fields (in itself a recurrent element in Near Eastern wisdom poetry; cf. West 1978: 148, 1997: 309). The observation of his brother's life produces evidence on which he bases a conclusion: there must be a kind of Eris that produces the healthy strife in which Perses does not engage. In Greek the conclusion is marked by the evidential particle ἄρα, and the other part of the idiom, the imperfect (οὐκ ... ἔην), contrasts the present insight with the past lack of it (Bakker 2005: 97–98, 103). The idiom occurs frequently in the speech of the characters in Homer (e.g., *Iliad* 17.142, 20.347–48); the narrator, on the other hand, never corrects himself. The idiom (ἄρα with a verb in the imperfect tense) occurs only when the Homeric narrator, with the benefit of hindsight and in his own omniscient stance, contrasts his present understanding with a *character's* ignorance (e.g., *Iliad* 12.113; cf. Bakker 2005: 107–8).

Perses's dissolute lifestyle as basis for an adjustment of the speaker's understanding of the world is not a piece of extradiscursive reality; it is part of the poem's context and therefore of the poem. It prompts the poem's very performance, first as plea for justice (which is what the poem is itself) and then as advice for living a good farmer's life, a life driven by the good Eris. The *WD* is an extended act of mimesis—a performer impersonating Hesiod—that creates its own context. And the *Th* takes as its context nothing less than the world as the performer and his audience know it, with the former adopting the stance of being specifically authorized to explain to the latter how it works and how it came about.

Hesiod, then, is for the performer, rhapsodic or otherwise, a role to play.[10] The role, the mimesis of Hesiod, is different from the role played by the performer of Homer.[11] For "Homer" there is no "biography" as there is for Hesiod or Archilochus; nor is there in Homer a "situation" that involves him, like the quarrel between Hesiod and Perses. Homer is mere voice, mere "me," the μοι of ἄνδρα μοι ἔννεπε Μοῦσα or ἔσπετε νῦν μοι Μοῦσαι. As recipient of the Muses' immortal song, he is the mortal representation of that song.[12] The mimesis of Hesiod is also different from that of Thersites or Achilles, because it stages itself—Homer's characters cannot exist outside of the framework provided by Homer—and because the reality it deals with is the reality of the poems' audiences: the world they live in and how they ought to behave in it. Homer brings his characters to the stage, but Hesiod provides a stage for himself, being as such closer to drama, the pure mimesis that Plato envisages (*Republic* 394c1–2). Perhaps the subject matter of Hesiodic poetry, the remote past that is still everyone's present and the realities of human life after the age of heroes, is conducive to Hesiod being a persona, a personal guide who advises us to do certain things and warns us against doing others. And it is perhaps no coincidence that Hesiod, along with that other character to impersonate for rhapsodes, Archilochus, and not Homer, is the beneficiary of a hero cult (cf. Nagy 1990: 48–49; Beaulieu 2004).

The Rhapsode and the Poet

Performance is language on display, utterances looked at in the second degree: statements qua statements, experiences qua experiences. Performance is never original or spontaneous; it is always already framed. Performance is therefore always reperformance; there is never "a first time" (Schechner 1990: 43; Bauman 2004: 8–9). Nor is there ever an "original" statement. Performance is always the insertion of a statement in a context to which it did not originally belong; it is a recontextualization in which its audience in the new context can blend with earlier and purportedly more original audiences.

The Greek tradition creates the illusion of a first time and an original utterance by supplying the poems with names of authors and their experiences, sometimes even inscribing their names in the compositions, as in the case of the *Th*. But even if the *Th* goes back to the result of a genuine mystic experience of a Boeotian shepherd, and the *WD* to a real dispute between that shepherd and his derelict brother, the form in which we have the poems, and in which they were known to ancient audiences as far back as we can reconstruct, is the result of conscious self-fashioning, in which local rural Boeotian is transcended in favor of epic, metrical Greek. Or if there was indeed a primordial Boeotian form of these poems, it became superseded by the "international" epic *Kunstsprache* necessary for Panhellenic diffusion.

Performance is also competition. Hesiod says it himself in his description of the works of the good Eris (*WD* 26):

καὶ πτωχὸς πτωχῷ φθονέει καὶ ἀοιδὸς ἀοιδῷ.

And beggar envies beggar and singer singer

If singer competes with singer, then the poem's listeners in the new context in which it will be inserted will provide a critical assessment of the language on display that is the *WD*, as members of a prize-giving jury or as an audience whose positive response might contribute to the prize. The new audience potentially blends with the greedy kings who are the poem's "original" audience. It conceivably also contains fellow performers who are eager to beat the present performance: not just the performer, but also the poem and hence its poet. Rhapsode envies rhapsode, singer singer, and poet poet. Such thinking may provide a perspective on the ancient testimonia of Hesiod and Homer interacting and competing, such as the fragment quoted by the scholiast on Pindar's *Second Nemean* (Hesiod fr. 357 M-W):

ἐν Δήλωι τότε πρῶτον ἐγὼ καὶ Ὅμηρος ἀοιδοὶ
μέλπομεν, ἐν νεαροῖς ὕμνοις ῥάψαντες ἀοιδήν,
Φοῖβον Ἀπόλλωνα χρυσάορον, ὃν τέκε Λητώ

At Delos at that time for the first time I and Homer, the bards,
we both sang, stitching our performance out of new songs—
we sang of Phoibos Apollo of the golden sword, whom Leto bore.

This fragment is routinely ranked among the *spuria* or *dubia*. But instead of taking it as fake autobiographical statement, we may perhaps more fruitfully see it as the product of a thriving performance culture: the performer identifies with the poet to the point where his victory becomes the poet's. And when the poet wins, he becomes a rhapsode who stitches his songs better than others.

Notes

1. The idea of the (Homeric) rhapsode as an active force in the formation of the poem is as old as F. A. Wolf's *Prolegomena* ([1795] 1985: e.g., 111–12); cf. Nagy (1990: 40–42); Bakker (1997: 20–21).

2. Cf. Plato, *Ion* 531a1–4; for rhapsodic performance of Archilochus; cf. Heraclitus B42 DK and Clearchus fr. 92 Wehrli. On Hesiod and Archilochus (both being considered as cult heroes), see Nagy (1990: 48–51).

3. In the famous litigation scene depicted on the Shield of Achilles (*Iliad* 18.497–508), it is elders (γέροντες, 503) who do not speak themselves, but act as judges by listening to the speeches of the quarreling parties.

4. Cf. Scodel (2012: 113): "It is not easy to reconcile a Perses who comes begging for help with a Perses who is providing gifts to the *basileis* in order to win a dispute."

5. But they also seem out of place in the simple rural world of subsistence farming that the poem depicts. Their title of "kings" may be an epic equivalent for a local ruling class (West 1978: 151). Perhaps we can think of a Dark Age continuation of the Mycenaean title of *qa-si-re-u* (*γʷασιλεύς) for local magistrates under the rule of the *wanax*, e.g., PY Jn 431.6; 601.8; 845.7 (tablets pertaining to the distribution of bronze; see Hooker 1980: 115). This would mean that the "kings" of the *WD* are a notable archaism, perhaps facilitated by the conservatism of rural Boeotia. Note that Homeric communities can have many *basilēes*, e.g., *Odyssey* 1.394–95.

6. The performance of song is often presented as coming "from the god," which presents divinity both as a place of origin (the beginning of the song-path) and as a source of energy; e.g., *Odyssey* 8.499 (ὁρμηθεὶς θεοῦ ἤρχετο); *Homeric Hymn* 25.1 (Μουσάων ἄρχωμαι); Pindar, *Nemean*, 1–3.

7. The verb (imperfect) for this descent, στεῖχον (10), is sometimes seen as anomalous next to the present and aorist verbs that describe the Muses' habitual action on the summit of Helicon (West 1966: 156, 1989). But it seems best to see the verb as describing a *single* descent, thus framing the event of the encounter with the poet at 22–34. On the combination of present and aorist tense forms combined with the particle τε (a combination that typifies the Homeric similes), see Bakker (2002, 2005: 136–53).

8. Nünlist (2004: 29), without commenting on the deixis, considers this and similar "summarizing" moments signs of the presence of the Hesiodic narrator.

9. As in the self-reference of monumental literacy (τόδε μνῆμα, τόδε σῆμα, "this memorial here, this tomb here"); and Theognis 20 (τοῖσδ' ἔπεσιν) precisely refers to Theognis' *epea* as a written text (cf. Theognis 755, τῶνδ' ἐπέων μεμνημένος).

10. In narratological terms this means that the *WD* is a "pseudo-diegetic" text, i.e., a narrative with suppressed diegetic framing level; see Nünlist (2004: 32), following Genette (1972: 246–51). On "didactic" poetry as narrative with a plot, see Fowler (2000).

11. This is not to say that Homer is an entirely impersonal and objective narrator; see de Jong (1987) and Bakker (2005), each from a different perspective.

12. For Nagy (1990: 54) the opposition between an "anonymous" Homer and a personal Hesiod is a false one, since the overt presentation of a poet's persona (such as Hesiod's

Dichterweihe) typically happens in the poem's proem, the hymnic "frontpiece" that is missing in the case of Homer (conversely, the *Homeric Hymn* to *Apollo*, a detached extended *prooimion* [cf. Thucydides 3.104.4–5], does contain Homer's self-presentation, the "blind man from Chios" [*Homeric Hymn to Apollo* 172–73]). But the distinction meant here pertains to deictic and pragmatic features of the poem proper.

References

Auffahrt, C. 1991. *Der drohende Untergang: Schöpfung in Mythos und Ritual im alten Orient und in Griechenland*. Berlin.

Austin, J. L. 1975. *How to Do Things with Words*. 2nd ed. Cambridge, MA.

Bakker, E. J. 1997. *Poetry in Speech: Orality and Homeric Discourse*. Ithaca, NY.

Bakker, E. J. 1999. "Homeric $OYTO\Sigma$ and the Poetics of Deixis." *Classical Philology* 94: 1–19.

Bakker, E. J. 2002. "Remembering the God's Arrival." *Arethusa* 35: 63–81.

Bakker, E. J. 2005. *Pointing at the Past: From Formula to Performance in Homeric Poetics*. Washington, DC.

Bakker, E. J. 2010. "Pragmatics: Speech and Text." In *A Companion to the Ancient Greek Language*, edited by E. J. Bakker, 151–67. Malden, MA.

Bauman, R. 2004. *A World of Others' Words: Cross-Cultural Perspectives on Intertextuality*. Malden, MA.

Beaulieu, M.-C. 2004. "L'héroisation du poète Hésiode en Grèce ancienne." *Kernos* 17: 103–17.

Calame, C. 2004. "Deictic Ambiguity and Auto-Referentiality: Some Examples form Greek Poetics." In "The Poetics of Deixis in Alcman, Pindar, and Other Lyric," edited by N. Felson, special issue, *Arethusa* 37: 415–43.

Clay, J. S. 2003. *Hesiod's Cosmos*. Cambridge.

de Jong, I. J. F. 1987. *Narrators and Focalizers: The Presentation of the Story in the "Iliad"*. Amsterdam.

Fowler, D. 2000. "The Didactic Plot." In *Matrices of Genre: Authors, Canons, and Society*, edited by M. Depew and D. Obbink, 205–19. Cambridge, MA.

Genette, J. 1972. *Figures III*. Paris.

Herington, J. 1985. *Poetry into Drama: Early Tragedy and the Greek Poetic Tradition*. Berkeley, CA.

Hooker, J. T. 1980. *Linear B: An Introduction*. Bristol, UK.

Kirk, G. S. 1976. *Homer and the Oral Tradition*. Cambridge.

Koning, H. H. 2010. *The Other Poet: The Ancient Reception of Hesiod*. Mnemosyne Supplement 325. Leiden, Netherlands.

López-Ruiz, C. 2010. *When the Gods Were Born: Greek Cosmogonies and the Near East*. Cambridge, MA.

Martin, R. P. 1992. "Hesiod's Metanastic Poetics." *Ramus* 21: 11–33.

Nagy, G. 1990. *Greek Mythology and Poetics*. Ithaca, NY.

Nünlist, R. 2004. "Hesiod." In *Narrators, Narratees, and Narratives in Ancient Greek Literature*, edited by I. J. F. de Jong, R. Nünlist and A. Bowie, 25–34. Leiden, Netherlands.

Parry, M. 1971. *The Making of Homeric Verse: The Collected Papers of Milman Parry*. Edited by A. Parry. Oxford.

Schechner, R. 1990. "Magnitudes of Performance." In *By Means of Performance: Intercultural Studies of Theatre and Ritual*, edited by R. Schechner and W. Appel, 19–49. Cambridge.

Scodel, R. 2012. "*Works and Days* as Performance." In *Orality, Literacy and Performance in the Ancient World*, edited by E. Minchin, 111–26. Leiden, Netherlands.

West, M. L., ed. and comm. 1966. *Hesiod. Theogony.* Oxford.

West, M. L., ed. and comm. 1978. *Hesiod: Works and Days.* Oxford.

West, M. L. 1989. "An Unrecognized Injunctive Usage in Greek." *Glotta* 67: 135–38.

West, M. L. 1997. *The East Face of Helicon: West Asiatic Elements in Greek Poetry and Myth.* Oxford.

Wolf, F. A. (1795) 1985. *Prolegomena to Homer.* Translated by A. Grafton, G. W. Most, and J. E. G. Zetzel. Princeton, NJ.

CHAPTER 11

HESIOD'S RHETORIC OF EXHORTATION

JOSÉ M. GONZÁLEZ

INTRODUCTION

OF all extant Greek poetic traditions, the *Theogony* (hereafter *Th*) and the *Works and Days* (hereafter *WD*) embody the oldest one explicitly framed by a (shared) authorial persona, "Hesiod." This much is widely recognized. But few agree why this should be so and how this fact ought to shape the interpretation of the text. Not only do these two poems feature an identifiable *persona loquens* but also, at least in the case of the *WD*, explicit addressees: "Perses" and anonymous *basilēes* (not "kings" but "magistrates"). Few scholars now consider "Hesiod" and "Perses" straightforwardly historical characters, or think that actual past events motivate the references to Askra, Helikon, Aiolic Kyme, and Boiotian judges. Most would grant, with Griffith (1983), that biographical details are subservient to the poem's message and work largely within recognizable literary conventions. But I believe that this admission does not go far enough. The lingering concession of even a reduced set of genuine biographical fixed points fails to make compelling sense of central elements in "Hesiod's"[1] self-presentation—in particular, of his pre-induction pastoral occupation and of the Muses' reviling of shepherds in *Th* 26. Neither has the shifting and seemingly inconsistent characterization of Perses in the *WD* received a satisfactory biographical explanation.

A more promising approach makes the poetic tradition itself—its generic conventions, characteristic message, and social function—central to Hesiod's self-presentation. This approach considers the rhetorical shape and performance pragmatics of Hesiodic poetry traditional elements in their own right, developed over time to serve its cultural aims. The authorial voice and its addressees are thoroughgoing, deliberate constructions designed to guide the reception of the poems by their ancient audiences. This is the outlook I adopt in this study of Hesiod's rhetoric of exhortation. This exhortation, I argue, weaves together didactic content with praise and censure in a combination that was specifically tailored for, and coevolved with, the polis as the preeminent emergent sociopolitical arrangement in archaic Greece. The scope of the poetry, by its breadth and generality, ensured an enduring cultural relevance hardly to be limited to the archaic period. The *Th* highlights the collegial qualities of Zeus's leadership in his ascent to power, his embodiment of idealized aristocratic qualities that could be embraced even in a democratic milieu that prized excellence in governance. The *WD* in turn offers a Panhellenic critique of social norms and arrangements within the polis. It focuses on the *oikos* ("household") and its neighbors. It also draws attention to the proper scope and conduct of public adjudication. Three coordinate facts explain the enduring relevance of the *WD* as a reference for moral reflection, instruction, and sociopolitical contestation: first, that the *oikos* remained, ideologically and in actual fact, the basic structural unit of the classical polis, and was left by it to run largely without interference; second, that the *WD* addressed it at a high level of generality, with emphasis on the rhythms of household work and the ritual and moral propriety of its members; and finally, that the poem regarded social conflict in the universalizing context of myth and religious belief.

A CULTURE OF RECEPTION: PERFORMER AND AUDIENCE

Who is Hesiod? How, and to what ends, do the poems devise his persona? What communicative pragmatics motivates the tradition's explicit construction and management of the performer's interaction with his audience? Hesiod differs fundamentally from "Homer" in that his praise and censure ultimately regard the poem's external audience. The internal addressees allow the performer to modulate the degree of indirection with which he addresses his external audience. In the final analysis, it is the assembly of citizens listening to the rhapsode in festival performance that is to heed the advice and instruction of the poetry. Only their eager reception can secure the success of the rhapsode's speech act. This vital objective motivates the rhetoric of exhortation adopted by the authorial voice to advance the thematic concerns of his civic poetry. To this end, he adopts a range of strategies and articulates them with varying emphases, always with an overriding concern to secure the welcome of the external audience. The obstacles to this are clear. No one likes reproof, and few would readily own their need for instruction, especially in a culture that celebrated self-sufficiency. And what claim does Hesiod have to superior moral insight? What right to admonish others? In view of these obstacles, the performer's approach must be to create and foster a culture of reception or, more narrowly, to recast the festival audience as a social group that shares his moral convictions and is morally and intellectually competent to embrace his ethical worldview. The performer's explicit gestures to his audience that they share his moral convictions mix with hints that he does not intend his reproof for them. His hearers are rather invited, even expected, to join his censure.

Hesiod's authorial voice and his internal addressees serve the rhetorical functions of Hesiodic poetry. They are just as traditional as the subject matter and do not reflect the emergence of personality at the dawn of Greek civilization. Instead, they are thoroughly conventionalized framing devices that help to delimit the characteristic themes of the tradition, to clarify the rhetoric of its delivery, and to cultivate an audience that will embrace its message.

There is an ancient mode of discourse that not only features the mix of praise and blame we find in the *WD* but also makes audience construction a central aim. This mode of discourse is the *ainos* (with the related *epainos, aineō,* and *epaineō*), of which Gregory Nagy has offered the most insightful analysis to date (most recently in Nagy 2015: 270–73). Nagy defines the *ainos* as a "marked speech-act, made by and for a marked social group" (1990a: 148). I add that its defining aim is exhortation, protreptic praise and blame woven together with a range of didactic devices that include fables, exemplary narratives, proverbs, and allegory. As a mode of discourse, its pragmatics stresses the speaker's relationship to his addressees with a view to securing a favorable reception for his message. To this end, he presents himself as skilled in encoding his message and acknowledges his audience, at least implicitly, as skilled in decoding it (often applying to it adjectives like *sophos,* "skilled/wise," and *epistamenos,* "knowledgeable"). He also draws attention to his moral qualifications—he is *agathos* or *esthlos,* "good/noble"—and affirms or presumes the same of his hearers. Strictly speaking, this suggests that his audience does not actually need his admonition to adhere to the qualifying moral standards. The rhetoric is one of reaffirmation of what speaker and audience jointly champion. Finally, the speaker formalizes the bond of solidarity that creates the community of reception, typically with a reference to the sociopolitical belonging of *philia.* These three elements (intellectual, moral, and social) need not all be similarly foregrounded by every instance of ainetic discourse. Perhaps the best epic illustration of the *ainos* as a discourse modality is Phoinix's narrative of the Meleager myth in the *Iliad* (introduced at 9.524–28). Phoinix hints at the shared moral qualifications: with "thus we have learned" (οὕτω . . . ἐπευθόμεθα) he affirms that they all have been raised up on the relevant ethical *exempla.* He then states his skill: "I remember . . . how it went" (μέμνημαι . . . ὡς ἦν). And in closing he stresses the common bond of solidarity: "I will tell it among you who are all my *philoi*" (ἐν δ' ὑμῖν ἐρέω πάντεσσι φίλοισι). His rhetorical strategy is to establish correspondences between the *exemplum* and Akhilleus's anger that will urge the hero to relent and thus avoid Meleager's fortune. The persuasion of the speech depends on the cogency of the perceived correspondences. Akhilleus's interpretive involvement in the process of teasing them out—his decoding the "moral" of the story—greatly enhances their impact.

An essential characteristic of the *ainos* as a communicative modality is the variable degree of indirection it draws upon. It therefore denotes a message that has an ulterior, superficially opaque motive. It refers, for example, to a narrative whose significance is ambiguous and invites the audience to figure it out. Thus, it is applied to fables, but also by Eumaios in the *Odyssey* (14.508) to the tale with which Odysseus prompts the swineherd to honor, out of *philotēs* (505), "friendship," his beggar-guest with a cloak.

Since the goal of the *ainos* is didactic exhortation of varying explicitness, and since its admonition takes the form of praising virtue and blaming evil, *ainos* and *epainos* also denote "praise," and their use is often attended by the complementary terminology of censure. *Ainos* and *aineō* entail the speaker's appeal for a welcoming audience, and their discourse modality aims at the consensus of reception. Therefore, the verbs *aineō* and *epaineō* are also used for "to assent" (e.g., Homer, *Iliad* 8.9) and even for the "agreement" of political decision-making.

THE *WORKS AND DAYS* AS *AINOS*

Studying the *WD* as ainetic discourse represents a departure from previous scholarship. Although it contains a fable explicitly called αἶνος ("The Hawk and the Nightingale"), Nagy states that "[t]his reference [*sc. ainos*] applies to the whole discourse of the *Works and Days* only by extension" (1990a: 148n11). His opinion is understandable. After all, *ainos* draws attention to the occasionality of the discourse, whereas archaic Greek epic is thought of as deliberately non-occasional. But this is strictly true only of Homeric epic, not of the Hesiodic poems, which frame their message with the inclusion of a performance setting and occasion. This allows Hesiod to address his exhortation immediately to his internal addressees, and through them in turn to the external audience. As Maehler (1963: 47) notes, while the exhortation of Homer is subordinate to the plot and receives its function from its narrative context, in Hesiod it is immediate. Phoenix's direct *parainesis* of Akhilleus in *Iliad* 9 carries for the festival audience an implicit moral, which must be abstracted before it can be commended to their thoughtful consideration.[2] Not so with Hesiod, who directly apostrophizes Perses with explicitly didactic material and acknowledges others for whom he also intends his message.

Some, then, might dismiss the relevance of the *ainos* to the study of Hesiod because it is thought to be at odds with the non-occasionality of epic. But I submit that it is more productive to concede the occasionality of Hesiodic epic while marking its occasion as distinctly Panhellenic and conventionalized, one whose mode is mimetic. The occasion is easily stated: a public trial in the agora of an unnamed polis, in which Hesiod arraigns his brother Perses in the presence of citizens who include adjudicating magistrates. We learn that, after they had divided their father's inheritance, Perses continued to seize and carry off much else, "greatly honoring the gift-devouring judges who are minded to adjudicate this trial" (τήνδε δίκην ... δικάσσαι, 39). The deictic τήνδε points to the trial there and then ("our legal case here") as the context for Hesiod's performance, from which he expects a decisive outcome: "enough of quarrel and contention," he says (paraphrasing); and adds, "you will not get another chance to act this way, but right here and now let us have our quarrel adjudicated (διακρινώμεθα, 35) with straight judgments."[3] Although the specific polis in view is not named, one could readily imagine it to be Thespiai, in whose sphere of influence the village of Askra arguably lay. This follows naturally from *WD* 635, where Hesiod notes that his father came "this way"[4] on his journey to Askra.

The city in whose agora Hesiod speaks was therefore on the way to his father's final destination. But the anonymity of the polis is not accidental; it reflects the Panhellenic scope of the poem, which by withholding the name allows the hearers to apply to their own polis the mimesis of the performance.

The thorough conventionality of the occasion and its mimetic character help the rhapsode to constrain the interpretation of his message, to guide the audience in its reception, without compromising his ability to adopt a Panhellenic perspective and espouse Panhellenic interests: his is a performance that applies with equal cogency to any one polis at the dawn of the archaic age in its exploration of justice, of how the reign of Zeus structures and manages competition, cooperation, and conflict in the polis, both within the *oikos* and among neighbors.

THE TWO *ERIDES*

The *WD* begins with a puzzling and defining fact of social life in archaic Greece: ἔρις, "strife," is not "unique" (μούνη) in nature. The cognoscenti informed with Zeus's perspective understand the radical difference between *eris* as "destructive conflict" and *eris* as "constructive competition." The puzzle is characteristically ainetic, introduced with a verbal pun, and with it Hesiod elicits from the very start the hearer's interpretative participation. Others had wrongly assumed that *eris* was "unique in kind" (μουνογενής), but in fact the "birth" (γένος) of these two *erides* was not "single" (μοῦνον): οὐκ ἄρα μοῦνον ἔην Ἐρίδων γένος, ἀλλ' ἐπὶ γαῖαν | εἰσὶ δύω ("the birth of Strifes, you see, was not single, but on the earth there are two," 11–12). Scholars have almost universally misread this sentiment as Hesiod's admission of error in his account of *Eris* in the *Th*, where he appears to acknowledge one Strife alone. This reading impossibly conflicts with his claim to inspiration and authority at his induction by the Muses. In fact, as Bakker notes, in Homer "the narrator . . . never corrects himself," and "ἄρα with a verb in the imperfect . . . occurs only when the Homeric narrator . . . contrasts his present understanding with a *character's* ignorance" (Bakker in this volume, p. 152; his emphasis). Hesiod's rhetoric of exhortation assumes the error of others and the need for the corrective of the inspired singer. But he neither states nor requires the view that his audience actually shares the misunderstanding. They are assumed, after all, to be intellectually qualified to decode the *ainos*. The correction is authoritatively stated and discretely accessible to one and all without loss of face. Perses alone is singled out as in need of it (27–29).

As we might expect from an *ainos*, Hesiod's discourse focuses immediately on praise and its correlative blame: "the one *eris* he would praise (ἐπαινήσειε) who has taken thought of her (νοήσας);[5] the other is blameworthy (ἐπιμωμητή)" (12–13). The expression of praise and blame here is programmatic and sets the agenda for the rest of the poem. Justice is seen, on the one hand, in its close relation to conflict and its resolution, and, on the other, in the dynamics of constructive emulation, which commend the ethics of hard work and a timing for one's labor set by Zeus's design of the cosmos. The paradox of the *ainos* extends to the relationship between the two *erides*: "they are divided in heart" (13) and in competition with each other. One minds the conflict characteristic of war and internal stasis. It is inimical to *philia* and honored perforce (14–16). By contrast, the good *eris* enjoys the preeminence of an earlier birth, and Zeus has made it foundational (17–19). It leverages man's natural drive to outstrip his neighbor in a contest that on the whole redounds to the general prosperity of the polis, however fraught it may be in any one instance.[6] Even if it is not strictly cooperative, nonetheless, when put in practice by those who understand it, the good *eris* is always constructive (cf. Nagler 1992; Thalmann 2004).

Hesiod's ainetic discourse and mimetic frame challenge the audience to align itself with the right side of the dichotomy, with the good *eris*. One could envision for his trial a scene much like the one forged on the shield of Akhilleus (Homer, *Iliad* 18.497–508): the judges stand up, each in turn, to render their "sentence" ($\delta i\kappa\eta$), while a *corona* of viewers shout their assent or dissent thereto. By their particular alignment (with or against Perses), members of the audience participate in the act of adjudication. They are encouraged to demonstrate and affirm their grasp of the *ainos* and their qualifications to appropriate its moral by supporting Hesiod's claims. Those who embrace the straightest sentence (the one that best aligns with Zeus's justice) receive the prize: in the *Iliad*, two talents of gold (not a fee, as some think), and in the *WD*, the less tangible but crucial inclusion in a community of institutional *philia*, the polis.[7] This is the "law" ($\nu\acute{o}\mu os$) Zeus has assigned to mortals, so that they may not (like animals) eat each other (276–78). Passive recognition of justice ($\tau\grave{a}$ $\delta i\kappa\alpha\iota[\alpha] \ldots | \gamma\iota\nu\acute{\omega}\sigma\kappa\omega\nu$, 280–81) is not enough; one must be ready to advocate it publicly ($\epsilon\grave{\iota} \ldots \tau\acute{\iota}s$ κ' $\acute{\epsilon}\theta\acute{\epsilon}\lambda\eta \ldots \grave{a}\gamma o\rho\epsilon\hat{v}\sigma\alpha\iota$, 280), especially (as with Hesiod's appeal here and now, before the audience of his performance) in the context of judicial proceedings (282–83). This is what earns prosperity ($\acute{o}\lambda\beta o\nu$, 281) from Zeus.

The *Basilēes*

The judges whom Hesiod pronounces "gift-devouring" are outsiders to the community of reception constructed by the *ainos*; they are $\nu\acute{\eta}\pi\iota o\iota$ (40), a censure that does not regard a morally neutral deficiency of understanding. What they lack are moral qualifications to decode Hesiod's exhortation and affirm its truth with straight sentencing. Their exclusion is pointed up, in good ainetic form, with a riddling gnome: they do not know ($\acute{\iota}\sigma\alpha\sigma\iota\nu$) "how much more the half is than the whole, nor how great a benefit there is in mallow and asphodel" (40–41). The rhetoric of Hesiod's exhortation does not foresee or intend the reformation of the gift-devouring judges. They are shamed as a foil for the audience's embrace of Hesiod's claim. None of his external hearers, especially any magistrates in attendance, would think of identifying themselves with these blameworthy judges who have taken the side of the bad *eris*; none would deem themselves the target of Hesiod's censure. Reformation through instruction, while not a priori impossible, is really not the point of this poetry. But this does not prevent Hesiod from fulminating against corrupt magistrates as hypothetical members of the audience when he wants to drive home the immediate connection between unjust sentencing and divine retribution.

Gift-devouring judges have neither the intellectual nor the moral qualifications to embrace Hesiod's exhortation. Their actions threaten civic *philia*: often even the entire polis (ξύμπασα πόλις, 240) suffers because of a worthless man (κακοῦ ἀνδρός, 240), and at the instigation of maiden Dikē the demos pays the penalty for the recklessness of its unjust judges (ἀτασθαλίας βασιλέων, 261). Once again, these are branded "gift-devouring," exhorted to bear in mind Hesiod's inspired observations, to straighten their speech, and to forget crooked judgments (263–64). Two ensuing *ainoi*, a pair of proverbs marked by memorable verbal mirroring, drive home iconically the reflexive nature of retribution in Zeus's moral cosmos: the contriver of evil contrives evil for himself, and an evil plan is most evil for the planner (265–66).

The *WD* contrasts the gift-devouring judges with judges who "are *themselves* minded" (φρονέουσι καὶ αὐτοῖς, 202). The verb φρονέω embraces their attitude and intention: they are not outsiders on whom Hesiod presses his message but already regard its point without prompting. Their favorable disposition exhibits their moral qualifications to receive what is explicitly described as an *ainos* addressed to them. But φρονέω also denotes competent mental activity: the performer suggests that their prior commitment to reflect upon the theme of justice will enable them to interpret the *ainos* rightly. At a later point in the performance, once he has enunciated the moral solidarity of the polis (227, 240)—a principle that explains why magistrates[8] and people (225, 243) share prosperity or misfortune in common—Hesiod turns to them and with a pointed deictic makes application to his own ongoing legal case: "O judges, do you yourselves consider this trial here" (ὦ βασιλῆς, ὑμεῖς δὲ καταφράζεσθε καὶ αὐτοὶ | τήνδε δίκην, 248–49). Upholding his claims against Perses is one and the same with upholding the primacy of justice in the polis.

PERSES

After the opening invocation of the Muses and the inset hymn to Zeus, Hesiod directs his performance to the only named internal addressee, Perses: "I will proclaim truths to Perses" (10). To be sure, the identity of Perses as his brother will have been well known to many as a matter of tradition, but from the internal point of view of the ongoing performance it presents a puzzle to the audience. Who is this Perses? And why does the speaker ostensibly restrict his message to the narrow target of one man? Perses is not like countless Homeric characters, who are the target of another character's (or even the narrator's) words: he is addressed like any other member of the audience, but also singled out as the defendant in the ongoing trial. His very existence creates the rhetorical space the listeners need to ponder how the message of the poem concerns and applies to them. They will soon hear, if they do not already mind the fact, that they and Perses are morally solidary, held collectively responsible for upholding justice in their polis. This connection encourages them to join in censuring Perses's quarrelsomeness and to affirm Hesiod's protreptic toward justice.

In good ainetic fashion, the very name of Perses calls for thoughtful decoding. The Panhellenic shape and scope of the poetry suggest that it is not arbitrary or accidental. Πέρσης is a residual variant of Περσεύς that results from a split in declensional patterns;[9] and, as scholars have noted, Περσεύς is a hypocoristic of the τερψίμβροτος-type built on the verb πέρθω, "to sack" or "to ravage," whose characteristic direct objects in epic are πόλις, πτολίεθρον, and ἄστυ (see Nagy 1990b: 74–75, following Perpillou 1973: 239–40; cf. Morpurgo Davies 2000: 36–38). Just like the Theognidean Kyrnos, whose name "Bastard" encapsulates his debased nobility (Nagy 1985: 33, 54), Perses's onomastic connection to Perseus suggests that he belongs socially with the agathoi ("noble"), a status seemingly confirmed by the vocative Πέρση δῖον γένος at 299 (cf. West 1978). But his etymological connection to "polis-ravaging" brings us back to the bad eris as the engine of war and stasis ("discord, faction"). Perses, then, is marked by his very name as an aristocratic exponent of hubris, whose ambition and greed harm the fabric of philia that should exist within the oikos and among fellow citizens.

I adduced above the scene of adjudication on Akhilleus's shield as a parallel to the social dynamics presumed by the public exercise of justice in the WD. Of particular interest to the poem's rhetoric of exhortation are the onlookers, the corona who cheer and jeer plaintiff, defendant, and judges as they conduct the proceedings. Perses is noted as a regular member of such partisan viewers and is blamed for using his influence for the worse (29). The verb that designates this "viewing" of litigation, ὀπιπεύω, hints at voyeurism (Homer, Odyssey 19.67) and deception.[10] It is clear that, with his unhealthy fixation, Perses has joined the "evil-rejoicing eris" and has been kept from "work" (ἔργον, 28) that should provide his "livelihood" (βίος, 31). It is as if his love of strife has fed and sated Perses. There is a hint here that the WD regards unjust and excessive litigation as a form of illegitimate censure. It is blame speech, which archaic poetry often portrays as food that the insatiable stomach of eris loves to gorge upon.[11] In a rhetorical counterfactual, Hesiod states that only when one is sated with grain (κορεσσάμενος, 33) and has a sufficient store of it can he foster socially corrosive quarrels and contention. But, as Pindar shows, "satiety" (κόρος) was ideologically tied to excessive praise that does not meet with justice and to the prattling censure of gluttonous men, provoked by jealousy, which obscures, even conceals, the proper objects of praise.[12] Hesiod's counterfactual does not seriously contemplate that any circumstances could possibly legitimize the evil-rejoicing eris. Its aim is simply to connect Perses to koros.

Perses, then, is subtly assimilated to a blame speaker. As a partisan and concrete embodiment of the bad eris, words are instrumental to his promoting quarrels and contention. This in turn motivates the emphatically verbal description of his begging at 401–3: if he should still bother his neighbors after receiving their help twice or three times, "you will accomplish nothing and you [emphatic σύ] will speak (ἀγορεύσεις) much in vain, and useless will be the rangeland of your words (ἐπέων νομός)." In archaic poetry the verb ἀγορεύω regularly regards public speaking (so, e.g., at 30), while the emphatic "you" does not mark a change of grammatical speaker, and its point must be to draw an implicit contrast between Perses's public speaking and someone else's. This someone else can be none other than Hesiod, whose performance Perses's speech now inverts. Finally, the striking metaphor ἐπέων νομός, most closely paralleled by the language of *Iliad* 20.249, marks Perses's verbal activity as speech acts of blame.[13] In the *Iliad* Aineias tells Akhilleus that they both can "utter very many reproaches" (ὀνείδεα μυθήσασθαι, 246) and "great is the rangeland of words on this side and that" (249). Perses's behavior is explicitly described as "begging" (πτώσσῃς, 395), and we remember that *WD* 26, the only other passage that mentions beggars, pointedly states that "beggar envies beggar." As I noted previously, in archaic poetry verbal gluttony is a preeminent characteristic of envy,[14] and in the Indo-European tradition the beggar can serve as a stereotype for the unrighteous poet (Nagy 1979: 229–30). This suggests that behind the superficial notion of an argumentative Perses who asks for *biotos* ("substance") among his neighbors, contending with them verbally when he does not obtain his goal, lies a scheming speaker who in pursuit of unjust gain exploits his ability to reproach. He is like the performer who, disregarding the general interests of the polis, offers himself for hire to the highest bidder, ready to advance the interests of individual factions. As I note in the following section, this is what the *Th* envisions Hesiod to have done before he was inducted into his Panhellenic office.

Some scholars have wondered why Hesiod's primary addressee should be his brother. It has often been observed that this particular choice has no Near Eastern precedent. I submit that one reason has to do with the immediate thematic interests of the poetry: the moral order that should prevail in the *oikos* and the circumstances under which the institutions of the developing polis could interfere in matters traditionally within the exclusive purview of the household. Preeminent among these matters would have been property rights and rights of inheritance. If the *oikos* proved unable to manage internal disagreement, how could one ensure that magistrates would discharge their duties fairly and equitably? A mimetic speech about two brothers quarreling over their inheritance could explore precisely these issues and the moral superstructure that should govern life in the polis. A father admonishing his son could not have done so.

But even if one were to believe that the poem chiefly intended a narrow focus on abstract moral principles, without reference to a political *Sitz im Leben*—that its goal was to commend in general terms hard work and the eschewing of greed—which choice of addressee would have best served the speaker's rhetorical ends? It would be hard to imagine a suitable and naturally motivated single recipient beyond the boundaries of the household. Explicitly targeting a class—such as citizens, magistrates, or fathers— would have risked alienating its members with the corresponding presumption of ignorance or moral turpitude. The audience needs the rhetorical space to hear the exhortation, especially the rebukes, without jumping to the conclusion that the performer considers its members deficient. But I do not think that the speaker's desire to construct a "horizontal" community of learning, as opposed to a "vertical" structure of authoritative exhortation, suffices to privilege the choice of a brother as the target of the advice.

Another reason, besides the sociopolitical interests at the heart of the *WD*, further commends the choice of a brother figure. No one in the audience would be surprised to hear an older brother rebuking a younger one—the age difference naturally surmised from the direction of the exhortation, the use of *nēpios* ("childish"), and the identification of Hesiod with the elder *eris* (and Perses with the younger). It is convenient that Perses, as the defendant, must wait his turn to speak, and that Hesiod need not put up with interruptions or with a dialogue that disputes his argument. Perses's forced silence adds to the assumption of his brother's seniority. Neither would the audience take exception at the occasional harshness. A careful look at the poem reveals the expectation that brothers often do not treat each other with considerate love and respect. Proof of the moral degeneracy of the Iron Age of Hesiod's present is that "a brother will no longer be dear (*philos*), as he was before" (184), while children will "blame (μέμψονται) [their parents], uttering harsh words" (186). The characteristic Iron-Age breakdown of *philia* between brothers, in close contextual proximity to verbal reproaches, is mimetically reenacted by the poem's frame narrative. We should not be surprised that the next mention of "brother" contemplates secret adultery with a brother's wife (328–29) as one item in a list that climaxes with rebuking (νεικείη, 332) aging parents, "attacking them with harsh words" (332). Verse 371 even advises distrust of siblings in commercial dealings, urging that a witness be added to one's agreeing smile upon a brother. This background motivates Hesiod's counseling Perses not to treat companions like brothers, a statement that appears to reverse the sentiment elsewhere that a good "companion" (ἑταῖρος) is no worse than a close brother.[15] Hesiod's counsel assumes that one who treats both alike would be *more* likely to mistreat his *hetairos* in word or deed. Hence the follow-up that he must not be first to harm the companion or "lie" to him "the favor of the tongue" (ψεύδεσθαι γλώσσης χάριν, 709).[16]

Some scholars have argued that a narrative arc of Perses's moral development interpolates the mentions of his name. This arc is supposed to climax with the appellative δῖον γένος at 299, after which comes his backsliding (so Clay 1993: 30). I do not find this theory compelling, because it makes use of dubious *argumenta ex silentio* precisely where Perses allegedly takes a step forward. West's assumption of a flexible Perses figure, who comes and goes according to the rhetorical needs of the address, is more in keeping with the variegated rhetorical texture of wisdom literature. Perses stands between the audience and Hesiod; he serves to modulate the force of the argument, as a clutch that allows the necessary slippage between the crankshaft of exhortation and the gear of reception. The ability of the audience to deflect the aim of a rebuke and consider themselves not its target is essential to secure the reception of the poem's moral objectives. In the mimetic structure of the single-sided drama that is the performance, the audience members have Perses to triangulate their relationship to the speaker and his message. Just as they must consider what the hawk and the nightingale might represent, and how the fable relates to the aims of the speaker, so also can they at any one time re-evaluate the pragmatics of Hesiod's exhortation with the versatile "wild card" of Perses.

Perses also provides the speaker with a handy attention-getting vocative address that helps him to stress centerpieces of his ainetic discourse. At 286, for example, the personal pronouns σοί and ἐγώ allow Hesiod to highlight his moral, intellectual, and social qualifications: "I, minding noble thoughts (ἐσθλὰ νοέων), will tell them to you." Here ἐσθλὰ νοέων is the conceptual opposite of the *basilēes*' "minding baneful thoughts" (λυγρὰ νοεῦντες) at 261. The verb νοέω does not entail pondering and understanding, and neither does the noun νόος: its basic sense regards awareness, "to have in mind" (in the aorist, often "to take in mind"), and (like the English "to mind") it regularly implies an impact on speech and behavior. For this reason it often approaches "to intend" (and the noun denotes "intention"). Just as 261 concerns the evil intention of the magistrates, so does 286 regard the noble intention of Hesiod, the probity of his speech and behavior, his moral qualifications, which derive from his intellectual standing (i.e., his right mental activity) and undergird his social qualifications (his bearing in mind *philia* toward Perses). This explicit and emphatic rehearsal of the pragmatics of the *ainos* is motivated by the typically ainetic parable that follows, which personifies "baseness" (κακότης, 287–88) and "excellence" (ἀρετή, 289–92).

Corresponding to the vocative of Perses, a generic singular "you" sometimes serves to frame the performance. A good example is found in verses 106–7, which once again touch on the pragmatics of the discourse with an appeal to the reception of the audience ("if you will," εἰ δ᾽ ἐθέλεις, 106) and a corresponding stress on the speaker's competency ("well and knowledgeably," εὖ καὶ ἐπισταμένως, 107). The emphatic "you" in the closing appeal ("and you cast it on your heart," 107), following an equally emphatic "I" (ἐγώ), might be construed as pointing to Perses. Nothing prevents this. But the tone of deference and the anonymity of the appeal invite a broader reference that reaches beyond the immature and refractory sibling to the external audience.

One final point about Perses: at two important junctures he is encouraged with a forceful vocative address to "listen to Justice." The first one, at 213, follows the *ainos* of the hawk and the nightingale. The striking suggestion that "justice" can be heard in the birds' exchange of words underlines the necessity for interpretive engagement at the heart of Hesiod's rhetoric of exhortation. It also suggests that the *corona* of partisans in the agora ought to be listening for the voice of justice. The second, at 274–75, precedes what many think the delayed moral of the fable, viz. that Zeus has assigned the law of "force" (βίη, 275) to animals, which therefore eat each other, but not to mortals, who with their observance of justice receive the blessing of Zeus (285). If Perses can hear the voice of justice in the performance of Hesiod, this elevates the rhapsode to a position of authority as the spokesman of the goddess Dikē.[17]

HESIOD

In thinking about Hesiod's ainetic discourse, with its praise and censure, it is easy to focus on the *WD* and to forget that his sharp rebuke and instruction in song by the Muses in the *Th* lies at the heart of his performance. Predictably, the paraenetic rebuke of *Th* 26 introduces a riddling couplet that problematizes inspiration by connecting the goddesses with the telling of lies. They harshly address Hesiod and others with him as "field-dwelling shepherds, base disgraces, mere bellies" (ποιμένες ἄγραυλοι, κάκ᾽ ἐλέγχεα, γαστέρες οἶον). Building on the seminal work of Svenbro (1976) and Nagy (1990b), I have argued elsewhere that these words present Hesiod as an ideological index of specialized pastoralism, a characteristically aristocratic economic activity. This rhetorical gesture of censure points to the interest of local aristocracies in the control of poetry that, by tying them to divine and heroic genealogies, would legitimize their dominance. Local poetry for the elite is inimical to the Panhellenic project that is Hesiodic poetry, which regards instead the broader interests of the polis whose festival patronage is crucial for the performance of this poetry. I cannot here rehearse the analysis that leads me to these conclusions and must remit the reader to my earlier work (González 2016). But I would like to explore this view further with particular regard to Hesiod's ainetic rhetoric of exhortation.

The term *gastēr* ("belly") has been convincingly tied to the speaker's dependence on patronage (broadly construed) and to his subordinating the truth of his speech to the pleasure of his patrons. But a complementary implication of "mere bellies" concerns immoderate hunger and gluttony. As I noted previously, archaic poetry places "gluttony" in close connection with "envy" and "strife" and makes it typical of unjust blame poetry. While I have previously argued that *Th* 26 need not imply that Hesiod was a performer before his *Dichterweihe* (González 2016: 244–45), the details of his induction do not rule out this view, and in fact there are good reasons to adopt it as the most natural background. If so, his repertoire before his calling must have included what the Muses later qualify as unjust blame poetry (or at least its correlate, illegitimate praise poetry). Archaic Greek thought identifies φθόνος ("envy") and ἔρις ("strife") as this poetry's core motivation.

One could therefore conceptualize the induction as a turning away from the strife-fostering praise of particular local aristocratic families toward Panhellenic praise legitimized by the patronage of the polis.[18] This praise includes not only the *Th* but also the *WD*. The turn away from the socially corrosive *eris* of local poetry tied to particular aristocratic families explains the attention given by *Th* 80–92 to the *basileus* who, favored by the Muses, quickly and skillfully quells even a great quarrel, adjudicating justly with soft and persuasive words, bringing about deeds of restitution in the agora for harmed citizens. The context is emphatically public, the focus explicitly verbal, the problem strife, and the target the people (λαοί, 88) in their corporate, institutional dimension. Just as the Panhellenic performer, by instruction and vocation, turns away from the strife of illegitimate poetry, so also is the magistrate idealized not as the eager recipient of the deprecated poetry but as the champion of the social harmony and communal interests of his polity. These *basilēes* are "cherished by Zeus" (διοτρεφεῖς, 82) and "sensible" (ἐχέφρονες, 88, a functional equivalent of φρονέουσι καὶ αὐτοῖς in *WD* 202). Thus they meet the intellectual and moral qualifications of Hesiodic poetry. And their concern for the people vindicates their social qualifications.

Hesiod comes to the *WD* as the authoritatively inspired performer of the *Th*. It is often said these days that the Hesiod who addresses Perses relies on the Muses less for his performance than the Hesiod who sings Zeus's praises. Some even think his reliance in the *Th* less an emblem of authority than a sign of immaturity. And they charge his teaching on *eris* with error that the more mature farmer figure allegedly corrects. Even the words κε . . . ἐτήτυμα μυθησαίμην (*WD* 10) have been enlisted to make these points. I think all of this badly misguided (González 2013: 219–90, 2016). The ten-line proem that opens the canonical form of the poem makes a programmatic statement about the nature of the *WD* that confutes these notions. It starts with an invocation of the "Muses . . . who celebrate in song" and summons them to "come and tell of their father Zeus hymning him" (δεῦτε Δί̓ ἐννέπετε σφέτερον πατέῤ ὑμνείουσαι, 2). The emphatic deictic built into δεῦτε imports the Muses' singing into the here and now of Hesiod's performance, disallowing the opinion that the Muses' invocation is of no immediate significance to Hesiod's authority in the *WD*. The word ὑμνείουσαι need not (and here, I believe, does not) regard a hymn in its later, common acceptation of "a song of praise that relates the birth and achievements of the *laudandus*." It refers instead to a performance in its communicative integrity (including pragmatics and message). In this earlier sense, evident in *Odyssey* 8.429 (cf. González 2013: 396–98), it could well denote the performance of the *WD* as a complete unit of marked utterance. Hesiod's statement that he will proclaim truth to Perses no more prevents our appreciating his words as the Muses' (and hence carrying the Muses' authority) than the pronoun μοι and the imperative ἔννεπε in *Odyssey* 1.1 require the view that the *Odyssey* the rhapsode tells does not convey the Muses' words. In fact, by not stating the explicit object of the imperatival "listen, watching and perceiving" of verse 9, the request simultaneously looks back to the Muses' telling and forward to Hesiod's: his is one and the same with theirs, ultimately divine in origin, and with the goddesses' sanction and authority. In the *WD* the theme of their telling of Zeus is not the achievement of his ascent to power, but his ordering and structuring man's world with the principle of justice that secures communal harmony and sets the rhythms of labor. This pervasive principle gives expression to the "intention of Zeus" (νόος), whose achievements in the mortal realm are no less worthy of celebration than his political savvy in the *Th*.

These considerations explain why the proem draws attention to Zeus's supreme power to exalt and abase mortal men, irrespective of their standing. The focus is on fame and reputation, and the emphasis, from the start, is on straightening the crooked (7). When Hesiod calls on Zeus to "straighten verdicts with justice" (δίκῃ δ̓ ἴθυνε θέμιστας, 9) and follows with the emphatic juxtaposition τύνη· ἐγώ (10), he is not divorcing his ensuing discourse from the action of Zeus. Rather, he is placing himself in a subordinate, instrumental position to Zeus's oversight of adjudication in the polis, as spokesman of the Muses, who tell of Zeus's cosmic design and his establishment of justice. This design is elucidated by his locating the good Strife in the roots of the earth, as the foundation for human society. The language "straighten verdicts with justice" (9) casts Zeus's oversight as an act of adjudication, one that secures justice by potentially overriding or correcting the judgments of crooked magistrates—who are themselves enjoined to straighten their pronouncements (ἰθύνετε μύθους, 263). This is the intended effect of Hesiod's performance: that Zeus, with his active oversight—listening to, seeing, and perceiving the ongoing trial (τήνδε δίκην, 39, 249)—will uphold his claims and secure a just out-come: "The eye of Zeus, which sees and minds everything, even now beholds this, if he wills—it does not escape him[19]—what sort of trial/justice this is (τήνδε δίκην, 269) that the city encloses within" (267–69). For this reason one could say that Hesiod's perfor-mance is the performance of justice.

I noted previously that one could consider the *WD* an inspired explication of Zeus's *noos*, a poem about his cosmic plan for the world and, in particular, his design of man's social order under the rubric of "justice." But this is not the majority view. Many regard it as the reflections of a wise man who, unaided by divine inspiration, ponders his experience of the world and derives timeless principles from it.[20] The framing device of a wise but uninspired man exhorting his wayward brother, we are told, presents the speaker as a model within the reach of his addressee, who should feel encouraged to emulate him. I do not believe that this is the rhetorical setup of the poem. First, I do not think that the internal character Perses is ever the serious target of the rhapsode's *parainesis*. One could only claim so to the extent that the ex-ternal audience identifies at all with him (precisely what the rhetoric of the address inhibits), for Perses is a traditional device entirely instrumental to the aims of the poem. And second, the poem offers an unveiling of the true nature of reality—a re-ality that is otherwise confusing and inaccessible under its surface texture. This reve-lation follows from divine inspiration, without which the deep structure of the world remains inscrutable.[21] The canonical function of the proem makes this program-matic point clear, subsuming any elements of popular wisdom under the authorita-tive telling of the Muses. This is the optic that must govern our reading of Hesiod's proverbial and gnomic statements.

The poem is about revealing the mind of Zeus. The clearest proof of this claim comes at 660–62, the only passage that explicitly regards personal experience—or, rather, in-experience, in the face of which the speaker does not flinch and confidently states: "But, even so, I will tell the mind of aegis-bearing Zeus, for the Muses have taught me to sing a hymn without divinely set limits."[22] Note that, as I remarked above, Hesiod calls his per-formance (whose current focus is sailing) a hymn; he asserts its inspiration in the terms of *Th* 22, that is, as the Muses' teaching, and he ostentatiously proclaims that the scope of his hymning has no limits. Whatever our preconceived notions of the genre of the *WD*, we have to accept that it refers to itself as a hymn.

The inspired performer speaks with ultimate and all-encompassing authority to his audience, including the internal addressee Perses. Theirs is emphatically not a "hori-zontal" relationship of authority with a vocation of symmetry, intended to encourage Perses to attain to the level of his brother. As the inspired instrument of the Muses, Hesiod's standing vis-à-vis his audience can never be bridged. It is therefore an error to think of his statement about the duplicity of the *erides* as a self-correction. This would necessarily entail the intolerable imputation of deficiency against the inspiration of the *Th.* Competing local theogonies might claim so, but surely not the Panhellenic per-former himself.

CONCLUSION

In this chapter I have explored Hesiod's rhetoric of exhortation under the ancient discourse modality of the *ainos*. This approach represents a break with previous scholarship, and it is time to consider its benefits. As a mode of discourse focused on audience construction and reception, attention to Hesiod's ainetic speech reaffirms the conventionality of the biographical frame narrative, including the meaning of the name Perses. Biographical material emerges clearly as a function of the tradition, internal to it, and with a shape that is decidedly Panhellenic. The *ainos* is a marked form of communication that presumes in speaker and audience shared intellectual, moral, and social qualifications. Its felicity as a speech act both presupposes and fosters the shared commitment of sender and receiver to the values encoded by the message. The rhetoric of exhortation encourages the audience to join the performer in his praise and censure. His hearers are free to own the one and deflect the other. They too are champions of the moral values advocated by the poetry. Approaching the discourse of the *WD* as Panhellenic *ainos* explains the peculiar focus in its programmatic opening passage on praising the good *eris* and blaming the bad one. Praise and correlative blame are the fundamental agenda of the *ainos*. This discursive modality also motivates the pervasive riddling, paradoxical, and teasing quality of much of the exhortation. The oblique and enigmatic significance of Hesiod's variegated material in the *WD* elicits the interpretive engagement of the audience. The fable of the hawk and the nightingale is only the best-known example of this didactic strategy. The typical association of the *ainos* with the motif of unjust blame and the triad of envy, strife, and gluttony motivates the description of Perses as a beggar and the stress laid on his disputatiousness. Finally, focusing on the ainetic character of the discourse also offers a productive way to connect the central themes of the *WD* with the rebuke of shepherds in the *Th* as "mere bellies" and with the attention this poem gives to the ideal *basileus*, whose speech quells even great contention. In this chapter the *WD* comes clearly into view as inspired and authoritative exhortation that aims squarely at the external audience. Hesiod does not speak as a sage who has figured out on his own how the world works and who wishes to impart his gains to his wayward brother. Here, too, he is the inspired singer, whom the Muses use to reveal the justice of Zeus to the world. As their willing instrument, he daringly appeals to Zeus to maintain and safeguard the order he has established. In championing Zeus's moral cosmos, Hesiod's speech act is nothing less than a performance of justice.

NOTES

1. I henceforth forgo the use of scare quotes to make the point that in the major Hesiodic poems the ostensible historical characters and their "personal" circumstances are literary constructions. Their sole purpose is to frame for the audience the meaning and function of

the performance of the Hesiodic tradition. Any biographical reality behind them is both irrecoverable and irrelevant.

2. The abstraction of this moral consists in the audience's reapplication of Akhilleus's own moral to their circumstances. Although this real-life decoding must be built upon Akhilleus's, it goes decisively beyond it. The gap between the external audience and Akhilleus is qualitatively different from the one between them and Perses. Hence the categorically dissimilar hermeneutics called for by the reappropriation of the *Iliad* vis-à-vis the *WD*.

3. The causative middle διακρινώμεθα has been widely misread as a private settlement.

4. τῇδε, unnecessarily emended without manuscript support by Bergk (1872–1887: 1.1020n127) to τεῖδε and West (1978) to τύιδε on the arguably wrong assumption that Hesiod is performing in Askra.

5. As I observe below, νοέω does not imply an autonomous act of reflection that issues in understanding without the aid of inspired teaching.

6. Note the pointed, paradoxical use of ζηλόω ("to emulate") at 23, κοτέω ("to be angry") at 25, and φθονέω ("to begrudge") at 26.

7. The declarative sentences can be denoted by the plural δίκαι (e.g., ἰθείῃσι δίκῃς, 36); or by θέμιστες when contrasted with the single δίκη of Zeus (9).

8. The οἵ τε at 224, who seem at first quite general, are in fact the ἄνδρες ... | δωροφάγοι of 220–21, who adjudge verdicts with crooked sentences (σκολιῆς δὲ δίκῃς κρίνωσι θέμιστας, 221). They are therefore none other than the gift-devouring magistrates who elsewhere serve as a foil for Hesiod's community of reception.

9. Περσεύς, gen. Περσέος < Περσῆος < *Περσῆϝος. But gen. Περσέος ~ gen. *Πέρσεος < *Πέρσεσος, whence the nom. Πέρσης.

10. Hesykhios glosses ὀπιπᾷ with ἐξαπατᾷ.

11. "Envy" (φθόνος), "strife" (ἔρις), and the adjective "gluttonous" (μάργος) are often closely associated. See, e.g., Homer, *Odyssey* 18.1–18, which ties the beggar Iros and his "gluttonous belly" (2) to "strife" (13) and the stinginess of envy (17–18). Ibykos fr. 311a (Page) makes a "gluttonous mouth" (μάργον ... στόμα) characteristic of *Eris*. See the fundamental study by Nagy (1979: 222–42).

12. ἀλλ' αἶνον ἐπέβα κόρος | οὐ δίκᾳ συναντόμενον, ἀλλὰ μάργων ὑπ' ἀνδρῶν | τὸ λαλαγῆσαι θέλει κρυφὸν τιθέμεν ἐσλῶν καλοῖς | ἔργοις (Pindar, *Olympian* 2.95–98). I print an eclectic text. Note my emendation of the transmitted nominative συναντόμενος to the accusative (to bring it into agreement with αἶνον).

13. νομός as a metaphor for marked verbal activity can point both to blame (Homer, *Iliad* 20.249) and to praise (*Hymn to Apollo* 20).

14. Cf. Pindar, *Nemean* 8.21: "words are a dainty morsel for the envious" (ὄψον δὲ λόγοι φθονεροῖσιν).

15. Homer, *Odyssey* 8.585–86 (cf. 546–47); Theognis 97–99. Cf. [Pythagoras] *carmen aureum* 4–5; Plutarch, *de fraterno amore* (*Moralia* 478a–92d); and even Proverbs 18:24.

16. Or, with West (1978), "offer false tongue-favour." The converse is that the companion should be first to speak a word that displeases the heart (709–10).

17. There may also be a hint that Perses should listen to virgin maiden Dikē's complaints to Zeus (258–60) and to the clamor that attends her rape by gift-devouring men (220).

18. Presumably, local poetry would resort to suitably shaped theogonic and heroic material. Correlative to the praise of some would necessarily be the blame of others not so addressed.

19. Because οὐδέ ἑ λήθει (268) reiterates for emphasis τάδ[ε] ... ἐπιδέρκεται (268), the οἵην-clause at 269 should be construed *apo koinou* with both verbs. This means that the deictic τάδε anticipates τήνδε in τήνδε δίκην (269), and that all three verses 267–69 regard the here and now of Hesiod's performance.

20. A misreading of *WD* 293–97 is used to support this view. Canevaro, e.g., believes that this passage commends "intellectual autonomy" (2015: 99–100). I counter this reading in forthcoming work.

21. Many are the elements of Hesiod's performance that presuppose the revelatory insight of inspiration—to go no further, the opening passage about the two Strifes. Whatever the truths about conflict and competition one might think accessible to the uninspired man, the priority of the good *Eris* as the elder daughter of Night is not one of them. The only alternative to the view that this is a fact disclosed by the Muses is to assume that the speaker feels free to innovate theogonic material on the grounds of private insight. Once we embrace this logic, much in the *Th* too could be thought individual speculation clothed in the language of traditional religion.

22. ἀλλὰ καὶ ὧς ἐρέω Ζηνὸς νόον αἰγιόχοιο· | Μοῦσαι γάρ μ' ἐδίδαξαν ἀθέσφατον ὕμνον ἀείδειν (661–62). For the meaning of ἀθέσφατος, see Benveniste (1969: 2.140–42). Cf. also *WD* 105 and 483–84.

References

Benveniste, E. 1969. *Le Vocabulaire des institutions indo-européennes*. 2 vols. Paris.

Bergk, T. 1872–1887. *Griechische Literaturgeschichte*. Berlin.

Canevaro, L. G. 2015. *Hesiod's Works and Days: How to Teach Self-Sufficiency*. Oxford.

Clay, J. S. 1993. "The Education of Perses: From 'Mega Nepios' to 'Dion Genos' and Back." *Materiali e discussioni per l'analisi dei testi classici* 31: 23–33.

Ercolani, A. 2010. *Esiodo Opere e giorni: Introduzione, traduzione e commento*. Rome.

Fritz, K. von. 1943. "*NOOΣ* and *NOEIN* in the Homeric Poems." *Classical Philology* 38: 79–93.

González, J. M. 2013. *The Epic Rhapsode and His Craft: Homeric Performance in a Diachronic Perspective*. Hellenic Studies Series 47. Washington, DC.

González, J. M. 2016. "Hesiod and the Disgraceful Shepherds: Pastoral Politics in a Panhellenic *Dichterweihe*?" In *The Archaeology of Greece and Rome: Studies in Honour of Anthony Snodgrass*, edited by J. Bintliff and K. Rutter, 223–61. Edinburgh, UK.

Griffith, M. 1983. "Personality in Hesiod." *Classical Antiquity* 2: 37–65.

Maehler, H. 1963. *Die Auffassung des Dichterberufs im frühen Griechentum bis zur Zeit Pindars*. Göttingen, Germany.

Martin, R. P. 2004. "Hesiod and the Didactic Double." *Synthesis* 11: 31–53.

Morpurgo Davies, A. 2000. "Greek Personal Names and Linguistic Continuity." In *Greek Personal Names: Their Value as Evidence*, edited by S. Hornblower and E. Matthews, 15–40. Oxford.

Nagler, M. 1992. "Discourse and Conflict in Hesiod: *Eris* and the *Erides*." *Ramus* 21: 79–96.

Nagy, G. [1979] 1999². *The Best of the Achaeans: Concepts of the Hero in Archaic Greek Poetry*. Baltimore, MD.

Nagy, G. 1985. "Theognis and Megara: A Poet's Vision of His City." In *Theognis of Megara: Poetry and the Polis*, edited by T. J. Figueira and G. Nagy, 22–81. Baltimore, MD.

Nagy, G. 1990a. *Pindar's Homer: The Lyric Possession of an Epic Past*. Baltimore, MD.

Nagy, G. 1990b. *Greek Mythology and Poetics.* Mythology and Poetics. Ithaca, NY.

Nagy, G. 2015. "Diachrony and the Case of Aesop." In *Diachrony: Diachronic Studies of Ancient Greek Literature and Culture,* edited by J. M. González, 233–90. Berlin and Boston.

Perpillou, J.-L. 1973. *Les substantifs grecs en -ΕΥΣ.* Paris.

Schmidt, J.-U. 1973. *Adressat und Paraineseform: Zur Intention von Hesiods "Werken und Tagen".* Göttingen, Germany.

Svenbro, J. 1976. *La parole et le marbre: Aux origines de la poétique grecque.* Lund, Sweden.

Thalmann, W. G. 2004. "'The Most Divinely Approved and Political Discord': Thinking about Conflict in the Developing Polis." *Classical Antiquity* 23: 359–99.

West, M. L., ed. and comm. 1966. *Hesiod: Theogony.* Oxford.

West, M. L., ed. and comm. 1978. *Hesiod: Works and Days.* Oxford.

CHAPTER 12

GENDER IN HESIOD: A POETICS OF THE POWERLESS

SUZANNE LYE

HESIOD is famous for his perceived hatred of women.[1] In his two major works, the *Theogony* (hereafter *Th*) and *Works and Days* (hereafter *WD*), Hesiod refers to mortal women as "thievish," "doglike," and "deceitful" (*WD* 67–68, 77–79) and warns his audience to avoid them because they are a "lovely evil" (καλὸν κακὸν, *Th* 585) and a "precipitous trick, irresistible to men" (δόλον αἰπύν, ἀμήχανον ἀνθρώποισιν, *Th* 589). These adjectives appear specifically in reference to the first woman, Pandora, but they are universalized when Hesiod calls her the origin of women (*Th* 591), implying that *all* mortal women share her duplicitous nature. In other examples of women, Hesiod extrapolates female behavior in the abstract, presenting stereotypes of women and how to approach them as within his sphere of didactic expertise on proper household and lifestyle management. Immediately after introducing Pandora, Hesiod creates a dilemma out of man's relationship to women by begrudging the necessity of marriage and framing it in terms of what a wife provides to her husband, whether children to inherit or care in old age.

The poet presents marriage as a decision between negative fates, with even the happily married man subject to repeated evils (*Th* 603–12). A man's only hope is to find a woman who is "well-fitted in her thoughts" (ἀρηρυῖαν πραπίδεσσι, *Th* 608) which suggests a wife who "fits" herself to her husband's viewpoint, acting the subordinate. The poet also urges men to treat women with suspicion, giving an example of a specific type of greedy woman who fits the mold of a "lovely evil," in that she puts her body on display by "flaunting her ass" (πυγοστόλος, *WD* 373) to hide a crafty mind. In this example, he then generalizes the charge of greediness to all mortal women, essentially calling them con artists and gold-diggers by concluding that "whoever trusts a woman trusts thieves" (ὃς δὲ γυναικὶ πέποιθε, πέποιθ᾽ ὅ γε φιλήτῃσιν, *WD* 375).

Based on these negative depictions of mortal female characters and marriage, scholars have mostly taken Hesiod at his word and have designated him a misogynist. James Redfield, for example, describes Hesiod's general attitude toward women in both poems as "firmly negative—except when he rather casually says something positive on the way to saying something more negative" (Redfield 1993: 56).[2] While not denying the misogyny in Hesiod's portrayals of female characters, particularly Pandora, I would like to expand the discussion to show that his misogyny occurs within a larger framework of hierarchical power dynamics and that, through it, the poet attempts to assert his status in a system where he himself feels disenfranchised. In the examples above, the poet's main objection to women is the position in which they place men—either lonely in old age should they choose not to marry, constantly troubled even in the best of marriages, or swindled by a greedy interloper. Hesiod has framed mortal women as having too much power over the emotions and property of men. As an entity outside of man's control, woman threatens his position (Zeitlin 1996: 71).

Throughout the poems Hesiod's misogyny is inconsistent, and his vacillation between grudging respect and outright disdain suggests that women are often used as a substitute for the real objects of Hesiod's resentment: the more powerful men around him. His attacks on women mirror his attacks on men, and the vitriol he directs toward mortal women is an expression of his own insecurity within his social and economic spheres. Gendered discourse in Hesiod, therefore, is not so much a signifier of sex as a form of coded language indicating status and differentiation between those with power and those without it.

Hesiod applies traits that can be called "masculine" or "feminine" to both male and female characters, depending on the context, and places these characters in varying positions of power. Hesiod has no problem putting himself in a subordinate role if it elevates him through association. For example, when he compares himself to the Muses, he analogizes his role as a poet to their subservient role on Olympus. In the mortal sphere, however, he promotes male dominance and emphasizes his own authority as a poet, especially in the didactic epic WD. Throughout his epics, female entities are cast as negative primarily when they threaten the male hierarchy, and they are all eventually defeated, or at least contained, by stronger male elements.

This essay explores Hesiod's use of gender to define and address power dynamics existing both within and between the human and divine spheres. I propose a broader examination of the poet's descriptions of gender and of his relationship to female or male elements. I argue that Hesiod's attacks on women are narrow and reactionary, rooted in the threat females pose to masculine power, and that his treatment of gender indicates a general anxiety and frustration over his own powerlessness within existing political structures. Women become a convenient scapegoat who allow him to express frustrations with society and to display his own position of power.

In his poems Hesiod's response to situations in which he is faced with a more powerful being involves a twofold process of "assimilating" and "othering." Hesiod assimilates himself to those who are in power, whether male or female, while at the same time belittling and "othering" those whom he views as having less influence. The portrayal of male and female characters is calibrated based on how the figure can add to Hesiod's stature in his society, either by making him equal to superior beings or at least more powerful than other mortals, male or female. As a result, Hesiod's epics constitute a "poetics of the powerless," whose misogyny is a byproduct of his discontent with his society and social standing.

Gender: Beyond the Binary

According to power distance reduction tendency (PDRT) theory, individuals with less power will strive to reduce or eliminate the difference in power between themselves and the more powerful (Mulder 1979: 90). "Power distance" is a measure of the power and influence between two or more people "as perceived by the least powerful of the two" (Hofstede 1980: 98). Hesiod identifies himself as the least powerful in his relationships, for example, when he complains in the *WD* (35–41) about his situation compared to that of his brother Perses, and when he describes the low nature of his profession in the *Hymn to the Muses* in the *Th* (23–26). He tries to disrupt this narrative of his powerlessness by proclaiming himself the recipient of the Muses' poetic investiture, which aligns him to a higher sphere of power (i.e., the divine realm) and allows him to claim influence and authority in instructing society's power brokers with "true things" (*Th* 27–28; *WD* 10),[3] in keeping with his didactic program (Stoddard 2004: 88–89).

Despite asserting his connection to goddesses, the poet does not seem fully convinced of his own stature and instead acts like a person whose quest for power is only partially satisfied. In the PDRT scheme, the actors who most exhibit PDRT are those who are close to but just below a more powerful person, leading to dissatisfaction (Mulder 1979: 46). Hesiod's poetic persona has the characteristics of this category, as he continuously finds opportunities to ingratiate himself with his superiors and strike at those who remind him of his own powerlessness, whether women, inferior men, or the gods. The poet's inclusion in the *Th* of what seems to be his own name "Hesiod" in the third person is a way of marking the poet's territory and his ownership of the poetic material. Other biographical information, such as a reference to his brother and their mutual father (*WD* 633), gives vitality to the abstract notions of justice and power. This persistent personalization keeps "Hesiod the poet" firmly in mind by reinforcing the persona he creates, while his tone of grievance tries to incite a sense of shared outrage against unjust powerbrokers, like Perses. The poem suggests that Perses can redeem himself for past wrongs by taking on his proper masculine role (Zeitlin 1996: 70)—as can any person who absorbs the wisdom of the poet's words (Most 2006: vliv–vi; Nagy 2009: 309–10).

Hesiod establishes a hierarchy of gender out of resentment and as a defense against his own situation of perceived powerlessness by subtly challenging those with power, whether in the human or divine realm, and by condescending to those below him in the hierarchy, whether female or male. Gender in Hesiod, therefore, is not binary but has aspects coded as positive or negative along a spectrum based on relational factors. Hesiod's genders exist in a hierarchy, ranked from lowest to highest, as: women (mortal female), men (mortal male), goddesses (immortal female), and gods (immortal male). The existential attribute (mortal/immortal) affects how the gender attribute is treated, but both depend largely on where Hesiod places himself in the context. In the divine realm, cosmic revolution ended in a patriarchal system, but the hierarchy is not based on gender, as each god manifests multiple aspects of femininity and masculinity.[4] Indeed, Zeus seems to favor goddesses, such as Hekate and Styx, over male gods in the distribution of honors. Moreover, his "civilizing" offspring, who most counteract *eris* and *neikos*, are almost all female (Scully 2015: 48), including Themis and her daughters the Horai (Eunomia, Dikē, and Eirene), "who tend the works of mortal humankind" (*Th* 900–902). Hesiod's favorable portrayal of goddesses shows that he does not consider them a threat; they are fundamental to his vision of the cosmos and provide him with direct insights that validate his didactic. In the human realm, however, the establishment of status affects the poet directly, so he is stricter in reinforcing the roles of kings, women, and even himself as a poet and member of society. The poet bridges the mortal and immortal realms, but he must still promote himself and justify his position as a voice of authority.

In the introductory hymn to the *Th*, Hesiod analogizes himself to the Muses, suggesting that they have elevated him from his mean state as a "mere belly" and "wretched cowardly thing" (*Th* 26) to being their mouthpiece, projecting their voices. Although an imperfect receptacle, he nevertheless mimics their role on earth by singing delightful songs to audiences (*Th* 104). The poet is both the servant and "ritual substitute" for the Muses (Collins 1999: 242), and he overlooks their low estimation of him. Their divinity and superiority are more important than the fact that they are female, because they connect him to power.

The Muses' productive work is narrowly defined as singing about the other gods with their divine voice, or ὄσσα (*Th* 10), to recount the relationships and offspring of other deities, and their female reproductive function is repressed.[5] They are neither the protagonists of their own stories, nor do they take part in the reproductive genealogy, which they sing to Hesiod. Instead, they stand apart, uninvolved in the sexual congress of the gods, which populates the cosmos. They are born when Zeus has already established his position as king of the gods (*Th* 915–17), well after the "sexualizing" of the cosmos and its early female-dominated stage (Redfield 1993: 53).

Hesiod describes the Muses' charms in terms of their female qualities: "soft feet" (πόσσ' ἁπαλοῖσιν, *Th* 8), "delicate skin" (τέρενα χρόα, *Th* 5), and "beautiful dances, which excite desire" (χοροὺς ἐνεποιήσαντο καλούς, ἱμερόεντας, *Th* 7–8). By drawing attention to details of their bodies and movement, Hesiod objectifies them under the male gaze even as he tries to equate himself to them as their mortal proxy. The effect of likening himself to the Muses, whom he feminizes in his praise, is that he subsumes his masculine agency. Like the Muses, Hesiod the poet becomes an object for both scrutiny and acclaim in service to his song. In the *WD* Hesiod uses the authority he borrows from them to rebuke the mortals around him for falling short in his estimation.

Hesiod presents himself to mortals as a powerful figure equal to the "alpha males" of his society. He emphasizes that the only other mortals the Muses favor besides poets are the kings whom Zeus fosters (*Th* 80–97), suggesting by this juxtaposition that his status is equivalent to the mightiest of mortals, the kings who, like him, are supported by important goddesses. As we shall see in the next section, Hesiod's poetry is an attempt to claim status from the divine realm and transfer it into the human realm, where he has thus far been denied the power and influence that he treats as his due. The personalization of this debate on power into the figure of Hesiod and into attacks on different types of men and women clarifies the hierarchy across the mortal and immortal realms, carving out a special place for the poet.

HESIOD AND THE POWERFUL

To understand Hesiod's view of women, it is instructive first to look at how he views men and his own position in their hierarchy. In the *Th*, when Hesiod says that he is a shepherd on Mt. Helicon who endures the Muses' abuse, he identifies himself as marginal in the mortal world, both in status and location (*Th* 22–26). Hesiod shows his awareness of power differentials through his language when he refers to a singer like himself as Μουσάων θεράπων ("servant of the Muses," *Th* 100). In the *WD* Hesiod is similarly at the edge of society with a seemingly lower status than those around him. His actual power on earth among men seems limited, as the audience discovers when Hesiod bemoans his brother Perses's power grab:

> [B]ut let us settle our quarrel right away with straight
> judgments, which are from Zeus—the best ones indeed.
> For we, on the one hand, divided our inheritance already, but
> you, seizing the larger share, were carrying it off, greatly fawning on the gift-
>   devouring kings (δωροφάγους), who are very eager to pronounce this verdict.
>   (*WD* 35–39)[6]

Perses here appears to be more materially and politically successful than his brother due to bribery, even though Hesiod often labels him "foolish Perses" (νήπιε Πέρση, *WD* 286, 397, 633).[7] When admonishing Perses for being caught up in the disputes in the agora (*WD* 28–29), Hesiod locates his brother in the center of society, among those who judge disputes, including the "gift-devouring" kings who would give him a favorable judgment. This contrasts with Hesiod the shepherd-poet on the margins, giving advice—probably unsolicited—to his brother and the men in charge. The poet disdains these "gift-devouring" men (δωροφάγοι, *WD* 264), siding instead with the female deity Dikē, who will report them to Zeus for retribution (*WD* 248–73).

Hesiod's feeling of separation from his own male society is also apparent in his famous Ages of Man passage (*WD* 106–201). When he describes his tribe, the iron race, he breaks from an expository mode of narration to express his personal despair over his contemporary world, which is marked by cruel men who honor evil, commit hubris, and break their oaths (*WD* 174–94). In response, the poet offers a deeply personal invective against the men in his society, emphasizing his feelings of separation and "otherness."

This is reinforced in his myths about nature and the gods. In his famous fable of the hawk and the nightingale (*WD* 202–12), Hesiod gives a parable of the dynamic between the powerful and the powerless. In this episode, a hawk (ἴρηξ) capriciously seizes a nightingale (ἀηδόνα) in an overt display of strength to remind the songbird of its place and warn it against challenging his strength and authority. Although only the hawk speaks, the poet focalizes the nightingale's experience—it weeps as it is pierced by the hawk's strong claws and is reprimanded for its sound (*WD* 205). This perspective is reinforced by the way Hesiod positions the fable in the epic. He, the singer of the tale, tells the fable to an audience of kings (*WD* 202). The stark power difference between the hawk/king and nightingale/poet is the message of this fable, which is further emphasized by the genders of these particular birds—ἴρηξ ("hawk") is a masculine noun and ἀηδών ("nightingale") is feminine. The poet assimilates himself to the nightingale by referring to it as a "singer" (ἀοιδόν, *WD* 208), making this vivid illustration of arbitrary power exerted by the strong into a subtle rebuke directed at powerful men who act unjustly against the powerless.

This attitude extends to mighty Zeus when Hesiod casts Prometheus in a positive light, revering his trickery. Of course Hesiod's portrayal of Prometheus is partially due to the Titans' beneficence toward mankind. The sustained attention, however, to the myths of fire and sacrifice and the depiction of Prometheus as an underdog who manages to circumvent the all-powerful Zeus point to the poet's deeper resentment against those in positions of power, even among the gods.[8] When describing the divine realm, Hesiod's acrimony toward powerful male entities emerges, as Hesiod does not avoid showing Zeus's petty side. It is exposed particularly when Hesiod describes the situation leading up to the creation of Pandora as an escalating war of retaliatory gift-giving by Zeus and Prometheus (Vernant 1988: 193–97). Through this first woman, Hesiod is able to formulate two objects against which to express his anger: women and weak males.

The story of Pandora's creation occurs as part of a narrative that pits Zeus, the newly minted king of the gods, against Prometheus, a Titan who survived the Olympians' victory and acts as a protector for mortals. Prometheus challenges Zeus indirectly by carving out benefits for the human race at Zeus's expense. Although annoying, neither Prometheus nor his brother Epimetheus is a real threat to the new king of the gods, yet in a calculated maneuver, Zeus devises an insidious counterattack against these vestiges of the Titans' regime. He promises Prometheus:

> There will be great misery for you yourself and for men to come,
> and I will give to men as the price for fire an evil (κακόν), in which they all may
> delight in their spirit, while they are embracing their own downfall. (*WD* 56–58)

Zeus frames the strife as a test of wills and intelligence between himself and Prometheus (*WD* 54–55). This "evil" is, of course, Pandora: the final, devastating blow by Zeus against the rebellious Prometheus.

In both versions of Pandora's myth, from the *Th* and *WD*, Zeus orders the other Olympians to create Pandora. Surprisingly, her worst qualities—her "lies, deceitful words, and thievish character"—come not as gifts from goddesses but rather from the male god Hermes, through the contrivance of Zeus (*WD* 77–79).[9] By creating this connection between Pandora, Hermes, and Zeus, Hesiod connects the evil she brings to man with the decisions of powerful overlords against the vulnerable subjects who have no choice but to receive her. After Zeus gives her to the gullible Epimetheus, thereby instituting marriage as a gift exchange, we hear no more about the antagonistic Titan. Zeus has the final word against Prometheus, who turns out to be powerless in the face of his ruler's determination to subjugate him and mortal men.

In the myths of Prometheus, Hesiod presents the divine realm as having a male hierarchy with a distinct power structure that subsequently invades the mortal realm. Under Prometheus's patronage, mortals were living in a state "free from evils, harsh toils, and painful diseases" (*WD* 91–92), akin to the lifestyle described in the myth of the Golden Age, when "men lived just like the gods, free from pains and misery . . . outside of all evils" (*WD* 110–15). Pandora's appearance introduces strife to male society but also gives mortals an entity against which to express their displeasure with the gods, since she and her female offspring enter the mortal world at a lower status than men. Although she initially had a direct relationship with the gods by being the beneficiary of their gifts and by marrying an immortal, Pandora's objectification in the divine realm is carried over into the mortal one. In contrast with Hesiod's, Pandora's affiliation with the gods and her origins do not confer glory but rather censure. This is in part due to the patriarchal culture in which the poems are written. In addition, she is a direct rival to the poet for acclaim and attention. Like poetry, women too have beauty and cunning, and these can distract men from the lessons of Hesiod's didactic program. Through both cultural pressures and creative anxiety, therefore, the "tribe of women" is placed at the bottom of Hesiod's social ladder because of both female gender and a mortal state.

Throughout the *WD* the bitterness expressed by the poet Hesiod against his personal status in his immediate society and that of mankind as a whole is palpable, and he situates this poem as an act of defiance against those who are more powerful, whether in the human or divine realms. Just as the nightingale cannot defend herself against the more powerful hawk, the singer Hesiod has no defense against more powerful men, who could crush him or release him from his powerless position on a whim. This anger and resentment at his own impotence express themselves throughout the poem but manifest most strongly in his misogynistic descriptions of women. As a man lacking the power he wants, he in turn looks for acceptable and more vulnerable targets in his patriarchal society against which he can display dominance.

HESIOD'S TREATMENT OF THE POWERLESS

Because he has little recourse in his world besides poetry to advance his status (or regain his property from Perses), Hesiod resorts to insinuating himself into the dominant patriarchal structure by amplifying his society's views about the relationships among women, men, goddesses, and gods. He presents mixed views about the importance of women in male-dominated worlds. On the one hand, female entities have certain desirable qualities, particularly their beauty and their abilities related to producing and sustaining society, whether providing poetic inspiration as the Muses do, monitoring human society as Themis and Dikē do, or having children to inherit and support the *oikos*. On the other hand, women are reliable objects of his condescension and bitterness throughout his poems, to the point that even goddesses are fair game for judgment and scrutiny by the male gaze. His presentation of women in general, not only of Pandora, shows his ambivalence toward the "tribe of women" and their status relative to both the mortal and divine realms. His references to women tend to be generic (in contrast to his own individuation and personalization), which focuses attention on their contexts and relationships rather than their personhood.

As a product of the gods, Pandora emerges onto the scene fully formed and "perfect," in the sense that she is a complete, packaged commodity that becomes an object of exchange transferred between male entities. As an artifact manufactured through a collaboration of the gods, she exists outside the generative, genealogical cosmic system and so experiences no further development or change. She is a "secondary cultural product" separate from the natural world (Redfield 1993: 52; Loraux 1993: 36). As opposed to man, who evolves through five stages (*WD* 106–201), Pandora has a single point of origin and is "a gift, a technical invention, an artisanal product, a work of art, an artifice," whose attributes are fixed from her inception (Zeitlin 1996: 57).

In the *Th* Zeus orders his son Hephaestus to form Pandora from clay. Athena then dresses Pandora in "silvery clothing" and an "embroidered veil" (*Th* 574–75), which the poet describes as θαῦμα ἰδέσθαι ("wondrous to see," *Th* 575). Here again he situates the female as an object of the male gaze:[10]

> But when indeed he built (τεῦξε) the lovely evil as the price for the good thing,
> He led her out just where the other gods and men were,
> and she exulted in the adornment of the gray-eyed daughter of a mighty father;
> And a sense of wonder (θαῦμα) gripped both the immortal gods and mortal men,
> when they saw the precipitous trick, irresistible to men. (*Th* 585–89)

This passage frames Pandora as a commodity constructed for visual pleasure, which the poet emphasizes by repeating words related to manufacture throughout the myth, including forms of the words τεύχω, "I fashion," (*Th* 570, 581, 585); δαιδάλεος, "exquisitely ornamented" (*Th* 575, 581); and κοσμέω/κόσμος, "adorn/adornment" (*Th* 573, 587). In the *WD* Pandora is similarly produced through the gods' collaboration. Hephaestus forms her out of earth at Zeus's command (*WD* 60–61), and Athena acts as her personal stylist, adding the final touches to her "look" (Verdenius 1985: 56n76), by making sure all her goddess-given adornments suit her to produce something deeply beautiful (καλόν, *WD* 585), her loveliness masking Zeus's ulterior motive of retribution.

Zeus knows only too well that resisting Pandora is not within man's capability. Her story is another example of masculine defenselessness before creational femininity, a pattern that recurs throughout Hesiodic poetry. Against Pandora, men are literally "without contrivance" (ἀμήχανον, *WD* 589). Her arrival curtails the power of both Prometheus and mortal man. She marks a definitive moment of separation between the divine and human realms, whereas before there seemed to be none (or at least less); she makes her debut to an audience of commingled mortals and immortals who share the experience of her initial presentation in a state of wonder (*WD* 588). But while the gods enjoy her as a work of art, she creates a rift that casts mortals and immortals on separate existential trajectories. Gods align with the makers and originators of gifts (or traps), while mortals are the ensnared recipients, unable to escape the gods' deceptions. Like fire, Pandora is a gift that is dangerous to handle.

While her physical attributes please, her inner nature gives her the ominous title of a "lovely evil" (καλὸν κακόν, *Th* 585) and a "precipitous trick" (δόλον αἰπύν, *Th* 589). In addition to her physical gifts of beauty and golden jewelry (*WD* 74), Pandora also has useful skills, such as knowledge of weaving, which Athena taught her (*WD* 63–64). When the description turns from her external to her internal attributes, however, the tone turns negative, since the latter tend to be hidden, outside of male control. Aphrodite makes her an object of "troublesome longing and limb-devouring sorrow" (*WD* 66). Even worse, at Zeus's order, the trickster god Hermes gives her a "dog-like mind and thievish character" (*WD* 67–68), which can overcome might and judgment.[11] As a result of her hybrid nature, she becomes the source of evil for men, since she releases ills, such as toil and disease, into the world from her famous jar (*WD* 94–104).

Although the *Th* does not mention the jar, the poet still describes Pandora as the origin of a "deadly race and tribe of women" (*Th* 591). He then gives a litany of complaints about women that are often used by scholars as proof of Hesiod's misogyny, since he says that women are the offspring of this unnatural, manufactured creature. In the voice of the third-person narrator, Hesiod describes the tribe (φῦλον) of women as lazy, avaricious, and a "great misery for mortals" (*Th* 592). Moreover, they have been forced on men as a detrimental necessity (*Th* 603–7) and economic liability. Outside of men's control, women become specific objects of the poet's bitterness over living in an age of social and economic injustice (Pomeroy [1975] 1995: 48).

Hesiod's most striking outbreaks of spite seem to occur at moments when he expresses a sense of powerlessness before superior forces, whether Zeus, his brother, or desire.[12] Pandora represents (along with the use of fire and meat eating) man's eternal subjugation to the gods in the cosmic hierarchy (Blundell 1995: 23–24). She is the physical "signifier" and a constant reminder "who will forever inscribe man in his mortal condition" (Zeitlin 1996: 85). Through her, mortals are forever inferior to immortals because they must rely on women to procreate and because she is a constant reminder of man's vulnerability to the tricks and superiority of the gods (Zeitlin 1996: 84). Hesiod's analogy comparing women to bee drones (*Th* 594–602) focuses on the fact that their laziness, like that of the drones, *compels* others to work harder than necessary for the same result, with seemingly no gains (Lefkowitz 2007: 23). Women, like these drones, take away the autonomy and choice of the more industrious workers (who are analogized here to men), even though Hesiod must reverse genders to make this analogy, since drone (κηφήν) is a masculine noun in Greek, while worker (μέλισσα) is feminine. This may seem a dire comparison, but it is not necessarily an indicator of Hesiod's misogyny, since he elsewhere similarly compares men who do not work to bee drones (*WD* 303–6). In applying this simile to both lazy men and women, Hesiod's contention seems to be less about the gender of the individual and more about the extra work they force others to do and their lack of contribution to the community as a whole.

Further, Hesiod's unflattering description of Pandora can be ascribed to specific attributes that point to his own lack as a poet and mortal man. Pandora has a special relationship with the gods through her gifts: knowledge of weaving, golden adornments, and a beautiful face. She also, however, has characteristics unique to mortal man, such as a human voice and human strength (*WD* 61–62), making her a boundary-crossing, ambiguous creature (Blundell 1995: 23). Like poetry itself, she is a gift produced by the gods, and like the poet she is specifically given the gift of human voice (αὐδή) by the gods. Whereas the poet proclaims truth with his gifts, Pandora only uses hers to *seem* genuine, like the lies the Muses could tell as the truth (cf. *Th* 27–28; also Pucci 2009: 62). Both stand at the intersection of relations between gods and mortals, but they use their gifts to different ends (Zeitlin 1996: 62).

Hesiod's attacks on Pandora are attacks by proxy on the gods who collaborated to create her. When women appear outside of this conflict between gods and mortals, however, Hesiod is less virulent and often praises them, although mainly for their appearance and the honor they might bring to men. Women and goddesses are equivalently treated as objects of the male gaze and male judgment. Aphrodite is described as "modest and beautiful" (αἰδοίη καλή, *Th* 194); the Graces have "lovely cheeks" (καλλιπαρήους, *Th* 906); Persephone is fair-skinned, having "white arms" (λευκώλενον, *Th* 912); and Pandora is "lovely" (καλόν, *WD* 585), with the "face of a goddess" (ἀθανάτης δὲ θεῆς εἰς ὦπα, *WD* 62; cf. the Muses, *Th* 8). The poet also gives favorable descriptions of the goddesses whose honors prove positive to Zeus and the mortal realm. These include Hekate, who can be kind to mortal men (*Th* 411–52); Styx, who controls the oath and is Zeus's first ally in the war with the Titans (*Th* 389–400); and Metis, who is Zeus's first wife and the source of his cunning (*Th* 900). As Mary Lefkowitz has observed, Hesiod places goddesses such as Gaia, Rhea, and Styx at pivotal moments in his narrative[13] and "does not let us forget that without the intervention of female deities, nothing at all might have happened, or events might have come out differently" (2007: 24). All of these female "helpers," however, are eventually subjugated to male control, which may be a factor in Hesiod's positive portrayal of them. Even though they reproduce in one way or another, none has the disarming power over male gods that Pandora has over men.

Likewise, Hesiod praises mortal women who either contribute to household prosperity or are nonthreatening to men. That Hesiod sees women in economic terms is supported by his repeated use of "gold" in his description of Pandora: she wears a "golden tiara" (στεφάνην χρυσέην, *Th* 578), it was ordered that "golden Aphrodite should pour grace around her head" (χάριν ἀμφιχέαι κεφαλῇ χρυσέην Ἀφροδίτην, *WD* 65), and "the divine Graces and lady Persuasion placed golden necklaces on her skin" (ἀμφὶ δέ οἱ Χάριτές τε θεαὶ καὶ πότνια Πειθὼ / ὅρμους χρυσείους ἔθεσαν χροΐ, *WD* 73–74). She stands in for man's economic anxiety, representing, in turn, a liability, a necessity, and a means of acquiring wealth (Brown 1997: 46). She is a visible representation of her husband's brilliance and power, having an aesthetic power similar to the art of the poet. Pandora is not only the first woman but also the first mortal woman who is commodified and exchanged through marriage, with a "feminine sexuality that must be bounded by clothing lest, unrestrained, it endanger men" (Sebesta 2002: 136). Not only is mortal women's sexuality controlled by literally being "kept under wraps" with rich clothing, as Pandora's is, but it is also controlled by the necessities of childbirth and of contributing something of value to the household.

One of Hesiod's markers for a justly ruled state in which power and resources are shared equitably (*WD* 231) is that women give birth to children who resemble their parents (*WD* 235), which proves they are within their husbands' control. These child-bearing women contribute to the general sense that their society flourishes (*WD* 236), but even in this case Hesiod urges men to control female sexuality by only allowing their wives to bear a single child—a male heir (*WD* 376–77). This tenet seems tied to economic factors, particularly the ones that made Hesiod the loser against Perses over their joint inheritance. The anxieties of the Hesiodic persona about wealth and status, therefore, pervade even positive portrayals, suggesting that the poet was composing during a period of rapid population growth (Sussman 1984: 89).[14] A greater population creates stress on existing resources, and the unequal distribution of Hesiod's inheritance could indicate a larger societal problem of economic inequality.

Since women were viewed as economic objects (Brown 1997: 46), control over their bodies and activities was an overt sign of men's power. This is evident from the types of women Hesiod does praise. Besides the "devoted wife, well-fitted in her thoughts" (*Th* 608), Hesiod also praises the ἄτεκνον ἔριθον ("childless servant," *WD* 602),[15] specifically referring to this woman not by her gender but by her role, ἔριθον, which emphasizes her status as being subordinate to the men who discuss or hire her.

Hesiod reserves his most favorable description of a woman to an imagined maiden, who is completely nonthreatening:

> And [Boreas] does not blow through the soft-skinned maiden,
> who stays inside the house at the side of her dear mother,
> not yet knowing the works of golden Aphrodite,
> and after bathing her tender skin well and anointing herself richly with oil,
> she lies down in the innermost chamber inside of the house. (*WD* 519–23)

This girl is an abstract notion, a male fantasy of a complacent female, who is ensconced firmly within the boundaries of male control and removed from the deceptiveness of sexuality (Lefkowitz 2007: 23–24). The women here are in a defined female sphere, ultimately controlled by a *kyrios*. This fantasy also represents the culmination of male desire for the ideal marital commodity: isolated, sexually inexperienced, and living in some comfort (suggesting a generous dowry), she is overseen by a mother figure who acts indirectly as a future wedding planner. Meanwhile, the girl herself is a virtual bride and sexual product ready for consumption, freshly washed and anointed, already in bed at the innermost part of the *oikos*. This maiden, cloistered in her natal family, is a figure who embodies the "civil order" (Redfield 1993: 48) and does not yet threaten production (Canevaro 2015: 118). This representation of a female hidden away and held back from her own sexuality echoes the story of Metis, whose sexuality is literally bounded by Zeus's body. Both stories demonstrate isolation as a means of control over the female body in archaic Greece (Doherty 1995: 8).

In his representations of the divine and human realms, Hesiod alienates females from their own biological processes. Neuter and male gods take on female procreative and nutritive roles, which eventually lead to Zeus's consolidation of power into a patriarchal polity (Redfield 1993: 31–37; Zeitlin 1996: 79–81; Rosen 1997: 487; Scully 2015: 27). Gender roles are not tied to specific sexes or entities, but instead become a code for power differences. Just as humans sacrifice to gods to acknowledge the immortals' superior status and their existential difference from humans, the control over mortal women similarly signifies men's status—although "the wildness of woman" is a constant threat challenging man's position in the cosmic hierarchy (Redfield 1993: 44). By portraying women as "unnatural" and a punishment, Hesiod attempts to establish women's place firmly at the bottom of the hierarchy. He also tries to foster suspicion against mortal women as a group, which in turn encourages solidarity and a sense of equality among mortal men, whom he now casts as the equal victims of Zeus's "precipitous trick" (Brown 1997: 39). By the end of the *WD* Hesiod's dispute with Perses is unresolved, but the poet has found various modes of attack against others to claim status and air his grievances with the unsatisfactory honors he has received.

Conclusion

Hesiod's use of misogynistic language reflects his socioeconomic vulnerability. Indeed, his preoccupation with the status of both male and female entities, as well as how he positions himself against them, demonstrates that he interprets his own position as uncertain. His depiction of women is dominated by economic concerns (Verdenius 1985: 46n58; Pomeroy [1975] 1995: 48–49). Thus, instead of seeing women as potential partners or sources of wealth, Hesiod portrays them as direct rivals with both him and other mortals for divine favor and gifts. The first woman, Pandora, is a "byproduct of a contest between males" vying for power and only appears in the third stage of this rivalry, although she is the definitive end to the contest, fixing the hierarchy between gods and mortals (Zeitlin 1996: 82). Hesiod's poetry, particularly the *WD*, is similarly a byproduct of his own ongoing rivalry with his peers for honor and prosperity, as he tries to establish himself in a position of power through his poetry.

In both of Hesiod's major epics, gender orientations are suggestive of particular qualities and power relationships rather than fixed characteristics. Women are treated as inferior as a prerogative of the patriarchy, but Hesiod's venomous tone against them suggests he is speaking from a position on the side of the "losers" in his society's power games. In the *WD* Hesiod takes on the role of teacher and conveyor of divinely inspired wisdom as a way to mitigate the reality of his powerlessness, which he illustrates through a personalized example. Although Hesiod positions himself as a source of wisdom and knowledge in matters of justice, he presents this information from a position of personal disgruntlement with his existing position in society's hierarchy. Moreover, in both poems he moves himself from the fringes to the center of his society through his divinely inspired poetry.

By personalizing the poet with a name, the Hesiodic poems give further proof of the poet's desire to gain prestige among both his immediate and Panhellenic audiences.[16] As West argues, "the poet names himself, speaking in the third person, not to set his signature upon the poem . . . but rather out of simple pride" (1966: 161n22). By doing so, the poet brings himself out of obscurity to become an active collaborator with the female Muses in the poetic enterprise, a relationship for which he wants recognition (Stoddard 2004: 66; Tsagalis 2009: 132).

Hesiod's stance on gender and his portrayal of men and women are therefore expressions of a desire to reduce the power difference between himself and those around him in both the mortal and immortal spheres. When Hesiod feels threatened or excluded in transactions between mortals, he lashes out against both men and women, presenting himself as a valuable, legitimate voice of authority. Nevertheless, even in his didactic poetry, the poet's persona is that of an outsider who suspects he does not have his audience's full respect and must therefore continually try to convince them of his worth by juxtaposing himself against those he deems above or below him in status. For this reason, we can define Hesiod's portrayal of gender and the treatment of male and female entities in his epics as a "poetics of the powerless."[17]

NOTES

1. In this essay the name "Hesiod" refers to the persona of the poet/narrator in the *Th* and the *WD*. He is a character constructed to represent a certain type of person who existed in archaic Greek society when these poems were composed. Whether a historical figure or a construct, "Hesiod" must have accurately reflected his society's context and mores. The combination of general examples and of specific personae gives the poem added validity as protreptic (Clay 2003: 36). On the subject of Hesiod's identity, see Koning in this volume; Nagy (2009: 278); Most (2006: xvii).

2. For discussions of Hesiod's misogyny and ambivalence toward Pandora, see also Loraux (1993: 72–78); Blundell (1995: 22); Kannicht (1999: 148); Pomeroy (1975: 2 and 48); Bremmer (2008: 24); Kenaan (2008: 31–33); Canevaro (2013: passim).

3. For the difference between the two terms for "true things" (ἐτήτυμα/ἀληθέα) see Nagy (2009: 276–77).

4. For discussions on gender and the gods, see Loraux (1992); Redfield (1993).

5. Collins (1999: 243) discusses the significance of the ὄσσα of the Muses in contrast to the human voice, or αὐδή, which they give to Hesiod in *Th* 31. It should also be noted that Zeus ordered Hephaestus to construct Pandora with αὐδή (*WD* 61).

6. All translations are my own.

7. See Vernant (1989: 32–34) for a discussion of trickery and the inequitable distribution of resources as recurring themes in Hesiod.

8. Clay (2003: 108) argues that Prometheus reveals himself as a possible challenger to Zeus by trying to control the distribution of honors, which is Zeus's privilege.

9. See Bremmer (2008: 25–26), following Verdenius (1985: 53n67), on Pandora's external and internal qualities. Bremmer also observes that Hesiod points to Hermes, not the gift-giving goddesses, as responsible for "women's bad qualities."

10. Kenaan (2008: 13–14, 17–19) argues that Pandora is the first visual experience of men and humanity's first moment of self-reflection, thus acting as a temporal marker in human-divine relations.

11. The adjective "dog-like" ($\kappa\acute{\upsilon}\nu\epsilon\acute{o}\nu$) refers to selfish behavior in an economic context and can also imply sexual license (Graver 1995: 51–52). Helen describes herself as "dog-like" in both the *Iliad* (6.344, 6.356) and the *Odyssey* (4.145). Pandora and Helen are both portrayed as being irresistibly beautiful but with tricky, doglike natures, leading to destructive consequences for men.

12. Zeitlin (1996: 69) points out that both Pandora and Perses are described as "deceitful and slavish" as well as avaricious and lazy, but only the latter has the capacity for improvement.

13. See Lye (2009) for more on Styx's pivotal role in the *Th*.

14. Canevaro (2013: 188) similarly argues that the poet reflects Iron Age anxieties over social struggle and economic uncertainty. She argues that Hesiod's misogyny is based on his per-ception of an imbalance between the sexes in contributing to the *oikos*.

15. Hesiod is very specific about this woman's childbearing status, later saying $\chi\alpha\lambda\epsilon\pi\grave{\eta}$ δ' $\dot{\upsilon}\pi\acute{o}\pi\sigma\rho\tau\iota\varsigma$ $\ddot{\epsilon}\rho\iota\theta\sigma\varsigma$ ("a servant woman with a nursing child is difficult to manage," *WD* 603).

16. Nagy (2009: 309–10) and Clay (2003: 34) both argue that Hesiod's poems are "pan-Hellenic in scope" and directed "at us, his audience, both as recipients and witnesses."

17. I would like to acknowledge with gratitude the editors of this volume (Stephen Scully and Alexander Loney). Warm thanks also to Jan Bremmer, Stamatia Dova, Michael Lurie, Sarah McCallum, and Alex Purves for their helpful criticism, suggestions, and encourage-ment during our ongoing discussions about archaic poetry and gender.

REFERENCES

Blundell, S. 1995. *Women in Ancient Greece*. Cambridge, MA.

Bremmer, J. 2008. *Greek Religion and Culture, the Bible, and the Ancient Near East*. Leiden, Netherlands.

Brown, A. S. 1997. "Aphrodite and the Pandora Complex." *Classical Quarterly* 47: 26–47.

Canevaro, L. G. 2013. "The Clash of the Sexes in Hesiod's *Works and Days*." *Greece & Rome* 60: 185–202.

Canevaro, L. G. 2015. *Hesiod's Works and Days: How to Teach Self-Sufficiency*. Oxford.

Clay, J. C. 2003. *Hesiod's Cosmos*. Cambridge.

Collins, D. 1999. "Hesiod and the Divine Voice of the Muses." *Arethusa* 32: 241–62.

Doherty, L. E. 1995. *Siren Songs: Gender, Audiences, and Narrators in the Odyssey*. Ann Arbor, MI.

Graver, M. 1995. "Dog-Helen and Homeric Insult." *Classical Antiquity* 14: 41–61.

Hofstede, G. 1980. *Culture's Consequences: International Differences in Work-Related Values*. Beverly Hills, CA.

Kannicht, R. 1999. "Pandora." In *Antike Mythen in der europäischen Tradition*, edited by H. Hofmann, 127–51. Tübingen, Germany.

Kenaan, V. L. 2008. *Pandora's Senses*. Madison, WI.

Lefkowitz, M. R. 2007. *Women in Greek Myth*. 2nd ed. Baltimore, MD.

Loraux, N. 1992. "What Is a Goddess?" In *A History of Women in the West I: From Ancient Goddesses to Christian Saints*, edited by P. Schmitt Pantel, 11–44. Cambridge, MA.

Loraux, N. 1993. *The Children of Athena: Athenian Ideas about Citizenship and the Division between the Sexes*. Translated by Caroline Levine. Princeton, NJ.

Lye, S. 2009. "The Goddess Styx and the Mapping of World Order in Hesiod's *Theogony*." *Revue de philosophie ancienne* 27: 3–31.

Most, G., ed. and trans. 2006. *Hesiod: Theogony, Works and Days, Testimonia*. Cambridge, MA.

Mulder, M. 1979. *The Daily Power Game*. Leiden, Netherlands.

Nagy, G. 2009. "Hesiod and the Ancient Biographical Traditions." In *Brill's Companion to Hesiod*, edited by F. Montanari, A. Rengakos, and C. Tsagalis, 271–312. Leiden, Netherlands.

Pomeroy, S. B. (1975) 1995. *Goddesses, Whores, Wives, and Slaves: Women in Classical Antiquity*. New York.

Pucci, P. 2009. "The Poetry of the *Theogony*." In *Brill's Companion to Hesiod*, edited by F. Montanari, A. Rengakos, and C. Tsagalis, 37–70. Leiden, Netherlands.

Redfield, J. M. 1993. "The Sexes in Hesiod." *Annals of Scholarship* 10: 31–61.

Rosen, R. 1997. "Homer and Hesiod." In *A New Companion to Homer*, edited by I. Morris and B. Powell, 463–88. Leiden, Netherlands.

Scully, S. 2015. *Hesiod's Theogony: From Near Eastern Creation Myths to Paradise Lost*. Oxford.

Sebesta, J. L. 2002. "Visions of Gleaming Textiles and a Clay Core: Textiles, Greek Women, and Pandora." In *Women's Dress in the Ancient Greek World*, edited by L. Llewellyn-Jones, 125–42. London.

Stoddard, K. 2004. *The Narrative Voice in the Theogony of Hesiod*. Mnemosyne Supplement 255. Leiden, Netherlands.

Sussman, L. S. 1984. "Workers and Drones: Labor, Idleness and Gender Definition in Hesiod's Beehive." In *Women in the Ancient World: The Arethusa Papers*, edited by J. Peradotto and J. P. Sullivan, 79–93. Albany, NY.

Tsagalis, C. 2009. "Poetry and Poetics in the Hesiodic Corpus." In *Brill's Companion to Hesiod*, edited by F. Montanari, A. Rengakos, and C. Tsagalis, 131–78. Leiden, Netherlands.

Verdenius, W. J. 1985. *A Commentary on Hesiod: "Works and Days", vv. 1–382*. Mnemosyne Supplement 86. Leiden, Netherlands.

Vernant, J.-P. 1988. *Myth and Society in Ancient Greece*. Translated by J. Lloyd. New York.

Vernant, J.-P. 1989. "At Man's Table: Hesiod's Foundation Myth of Sacrifice." In *The Cuisine of Sacrifice Among the Greeks*, edited by M. Detienne and J.-P. Vernant, 21–86. Translated by P. Wissing. Chicago.

West, M. L., ed. and comm. 1966. *Hesiod: Theogony*. Oxford.

Zeitlin, F. 1996. *Playing the Other: Gender and Society in Classical Greek Literature*. Chicago.

PART III

....

HESIOD IN THE GRECO-ROMAN PERIOD

....

CHAPTER 13

SOLON'S RECEPTION OF HESIOD'S *WORKS AND DAYS*

J. A. ALMEIDA

INTRODUCTION: HESIOD, SOLON, AND POINTS OF CONTACT

HESIOD "had always occupied . . . a special place in the idea of 'ancient wisdom'" (Hunter 2014: 4) and was, along with Homer, one of the great poet-teachers of Greek culture. He achieved celebrity in his own lifetime though a victory for recital of the *Theogony* at the funeral games of Amphidamas (*Works and Days* [hereafter *WD*] 654–59; West 1966: 44–45 on *Theogony* [hereafter *Th*] 98–103), and from there interest in his poetry only increased. The *Th* and *WD* became cultural icons, and echoes of these poems are found frequently in subsequent Greek poetry from shortly after their composition (e.g., Archilochus fr. 118 ~ *Th*. 120–22; West 1966: 40n4) to the time of Solon's contemporaries (e.g., Mimnermus. fr. 6.1 ~ *WD* 91–92; Alcaeus fr. 34 ~ *WD* 582–89). By 594 BCE, the date of Solon's archonship at Athens, Hesiod was known "right across the Aegean" (West 1978: 61).

At this time Solon was experiencing events that would define his life as a politician and in large part shape his sensibilities as a poet. His career coincided with a period of extreme economic, political, and social instability at Athens. According to the *Athenaion Politeia* (hereafter *Ath.*) and Plutarch's *Life of Solon* (hereafter Plu. *Sol.*),[1] the causes of this trouble involved a combination of conflicts among aristocratic constituencies (Plu. *Sol.* 12.2), political parties (Plu. *Sol.* 13.1), and economic classes. Most acute was the wide disparity between the rich and the poor. Debt-slavery, touching both the land and the person of debtors, was everywhere oppressing the poor, and as a result many became slaves at home or were sold into slavery abroad (*Ath.* 2.2; Plu. *Sol.* 13.2). These conditions reached such a crisis that there was a clamor for the redistribution of land and fear of civil war or tyranny (Plu. *Sol.* 13.1–2). At this point the Athenians turned to Solon for a solution. By his past achievements, he had earned a high reputation for patriotism and prudent counsel (*Ath.* 5.2; Plu. *Sol.* 11.1). In addition, his middle status—impeccable birth but moderate wealth—made him acceptable to the rich and the poor alike (*Ath.* 5.3; Plu. *Sol.* 14.1–2). The Athenians therefore appointed Solon mediator, reformer of the constitution, and lawgiver with plenary power (*Ath.* 5.2; Plu. *Sol.* 14.3, 16.3). Under this authority, he enacted the *seisachtheia*, that is, a cancellation of debts, which freed the poor from oppression. He also created new classifications for participation in constitutional office, instituted a right of appeal to the popular courts, passed economic reforms including a revision of weights and measures, and enacted laws which remained influential into classical times (*Ath.* 6, 7, 9, 10.1, 11.1; Plu. *Sol.* 15.2–4, 18.1–2). In all this he acted for the common good of the city, as indicated by his refusal to make himself tyrant (*Ath.* 5.2; Plu. *Sol.* 14.7–8), a path easily within in his power at the time, and by the fact that neither the rich nor the poor were completely satisfied with the reforms, each expecting more than they got (*Ath.* 11.1, 12.5). This experience had a deep impact on Solon and became the subject of many of his poems.

In addition to this political experience, a more specific literary interest also played a role in shaping Solon's poetry. He was deeply conversant with the Ionian poetry of his day (Jaeger 1945: 139) and keenly interested in the Greek poetry of other traditions (Stobaeus 3.29.58). Such an active and knowledgeable poet would certainly have been familiar with the work of a poet as important as Hesiod, whose *Th* provided a cosmogonic knowledge of the Greek gods and *WD*, a Greek ethos of just human labor. It would be extraordinary, then, if contact with Hesiod did not affect the composition of Solon's own poetry.

Beyond the implications of interests and status, evidence of places of similarity in the poems of each poet supports the sharper notion that Solon's method of composing some of his poems included specific intentional references to Hesiod. The most significant points of contact between Solon and Hesiod involve *dikē*, that is, "justice," an idea of central importance to the work of both poets: Solon fr. 4.36 (εὐθύνει δὲ δίκας σκολιάς) ~ WD 7 (ἰθύνει σκολιόν), WD 9 (δίκῃ δ᾽ ἴθυνε θέμιστας), WD 263 (βασιλῆς ἰθύνετε μύθους); Solon fr. 13.9 ff. ~ WD 320 ff. (god-given wealth versus human wealth); and Solon 13.27 ff. ~ WD 268–69 (Zeus's inexorable punishment of injustice).[2] These points of contact indicate that Solon was predominantly interested in Hesiod's specific development of *dikē* in WD 213–326 (hereafter the "Discourse on Justice"),[3] and that Solon exploited this interest mainly in fr. 4 (the "Eunomia") and fr. 13 (the "Hymn to the Muses").

Dikē, then, is the focal point of the question of Solon's connection to Hesiod, and I explore this relationship here from a literary and a substantive perspective. The literary treatment of Solon's reception of Hesiod has received little detailed attention. Even the works of Hunter (2014) and Koning (2010) on Hesiod's general reception have treated Solon only briefly. On the other hand, there has been much scholarly work on the question of the meaning of *dikē* in the work of the two poets, and this scholarship has emphasized philosophical and political ideas more than literary concerns.

My observations are organized around this division, and I first explore the general literary relation between Solon and Hesiod on the poetry of *dikē*, then review the scholarly opinion on the meaning of *dikē* in each.

In the literary analysis I trace points of similarity between the two poets. I refer to all such similarities, from single words to entire literary tableaux, as "allusions." The greatest number of verbal allusions occur in the first part of the "Eunomia," and I argue that here Solon is incorporating into the political setting of his poem the moral force of Hesiod as a teacher of justice to validate his own condemnation of civic injustice. At the end of the poem the cities of Dusnomia and Eunomia constitute a structural allusion to the just and unjust city of Hesiod's Discourse on Justice, and I argue that through this allusion Solon transforms the Hesiodic pessimism of injustice in the first part of the poem into an optimism of hope in the possibility of civic justice for his own city. In the "Hymn to the Muses" the chief point of contact between the poets is the notion of Zeus as the punisher of injustice, and I argue that here Solon creates around this notion a sentiment of pessimism that exceeds Hesiod's own. Nothing in this discussion intends either an integral interpretation of Hesiod or of Solon or a trajectory toward a unified conclusion. Rather, it is an organized set of observations on the literary relation between the two poets from the vantage point of Solon's allusions to Hesiod.

The review of the scholarly opinion reveals a dichotomy of positions: one, that *dikē* has essentially the same meaning in Solon as it does in Hesiod; and the other, that Solon's *dikē* marks a new departure in Greek thought. Here I focus on the different governing principles of each position. The literary study and the account of the scholarly dichotomy are unified only in that the object of each is *dikē* in Solon and Hesiod.

LITERARY ANALYSIS:
SOLON'S RELATION TO HESIOD

Incorporating Hesiodic Moral Authority into a Solonian Context

In verses 4–14 of the "Eunomia" Solon signals his debt to Hesiod by choosing to articulate his own themes in noticeably Hesiodic terms. The terms are χρήμασι, ἄδικος νόος, ὕβριος, ἀδίκοις ἔργμασι, and φυλάσσονται. Individually these are ordinary words, but collectively they form a group of allusions to the Discourse on Justice, creating a chain of ideas that overlay Hesiod's moral sentiments on the problems particular to the desperate political situation in the city Solon is describing (Canevaro 2015: 16). (The "Eunomia" may reflect conditions in Solon's Athens [Noussia-Fantuzzi 2010: 219], but this issue is not essential to the analysis.)

"Eunomia" 5–14 (with lacunae):

αὐτοὶ δὲ φθείρειν μεγάλην πόλιν ἀφραδίῃσιν   5
   ἀστοὶ βούλονται **χρήμασι** πειθόμενοι,
δήμου θ᾽ ἡγεμόνων **ἄδικος νόος**, οἷσιν ἑτοῖμον
   ὕβριος ἐκ μεγάλης ἄλγεα πολλὰ παθεῖν·
οὐ γὰρ ἐπίστανται κατέχειν κόρον οὐδὲ παρούσας
   εὐφροσύνας κοσμεῖν δαιτὸς ἐν ἡσθχίῃ   10
...
   πλουτέουσιν δ᾽ **ἀδίκοις ἔργμασι** πειθόμενοι
...
   οὔθ᾽ ἱερῶν κτεάνων οὔτε τι δημοσίων
φειδόμενοι κλέπτουσιν ἀφαρπαγῇ ἄλλοθεν ἄλλος,
   οὐδὲ **φυλάσσονται** σεμνὰ Δίκης θέμεθλα.

But it is the citizens themselves who by their act of foolishness and subservience to money are willing to destroy a great city, and the mind of the people's leaders is unjust; they are certain to suffer much pain as a result of their great [hybris]. For they do not know how to restrain [koros] or to conduct in an orderly and peaceful manner the festivities of the banquet that are at hand ... they grow wealthy, yielding to unjust deeds ... sparing neither sacred nor private property, they steal with rapaciousness, one from one source, one from another, and they have no regard for [i.e., do not keep watch on] the august foundations of Justice.[4]

At 4.5–6 Solon accuses the *astoi* of his city of paying improper attention to wealth (χρήμασι πειθόμενοι) and therefore of intending the destruction of the city. Solon's use of the word χρήμασι (4.6) reflects Hesiod's precept at WD 320: χρήματα δ᾽ οὐχ ἁρπακτά· θεόσδοτα πολλὸν ἀμείνω, "Goods are not to be grabbed; much better if God / lets you have them." Hesiod's ἁρπακτά implies violent theft, wealth-grabbing, and it condemns this mode of wealth acquisition as displeasing to the gods (West 1978: 237). The minimum moral underpinning of this precept, therefore, is that wealth-grabbing is inconsistent with the divine ordinances governing human action. The allusion of Solon's χρήμασι to WD 320 thus incorporates from Hesiod's world into Solon's the moral force of a directive intended for country laborers and appropriates this moral authority to the support of Solon's own condemnation of the *astoi* in their improper desire for riches.

The allusion of χρήμασι at 4.6 to Hesiod's χρήματα at WD 320 also directs us to the words κέρδος and νόον at WD 324, and these words create a thematic link between the notions of "wealth-grabbing" and "mind," which informs Solon's next allusion to Hesiod in the phrase ἄδικος νόος at 4.7. (We translate νόος as "mind" to facilitate clarity of reference but realize that its meaning in context is closer to "intention.") WD 323–25 read εὖτ᾽ ἂν δὴ κέρδος νόον ἐξαπατήσει ἀνθρώπων ... / ῥεῖν δέ μιν μαυροῦσι θεοί, μινύθουσι δὲ οἶκον / ἀνέρι τῷ, "as so often / happens among people when [mind] is blinded / by greed / ... lightly the gods wipe out that man, and diminish the household." κέρδος or "the spectacle of wrongful gain" (West 1978: 238), debilitates the νόος or the mind of man, and this impropriety merits divine punishment. Thus, the allusion of χρήμασι to χρήματα brings with it the clarification that wealth-grabbing debilitates the mind.

At 4.7 Solon alleges that the mind of the city's leaders is unjust. Solon's ἄδικος νόος is an allusion to Hesiod's ἄδικον νόον at *WD* 260. *WD* 258–60 read: καὶ ῥ' ὁπότ' ἄν τίς μιν [Δίκην] βλάπτῃ σκολιῶς ὀνοτάζων . . . / γηρύετ' ἀνθρώπων ἄδικον νόον, "when any man uses force on [Dike] by false impeachment . . . / [she] cries out on the wicked [mind] of man." In these lines Hesiod represents the divine order anthropomorphically in the figure of Δίκη and through her words gives a practical definition of ἄδικον νόον or unjust mind. It is a mind that intends harm to Dike or, nonanthropomorphically, a mind that intends action contrary to the obligations of justice imposed by divine ordinance. We know from *WD* 320 that wealth-grabbing is contrary to the obligations of the divine order. We also know from *WD* 260 that wealth-grabbing debilitates the mind. Insofar, therefore, as wealth-grabbing is contrary to divine order, it is a particular form of ἄδικός νόος. Thus, the chain of allusions and the ideas drawn along with them from Solon's χρήμασι and ἄδικος νόος to Hesiod's χρήματα and ἄδικον νόον brings Hesiodic validation to the condemnation of wealth-grabbing as the particular form of injustice that is destroying Solon's city. Solon confirms this figuratively a little later in the poem in his image of the crumbling foundations of Dike at 4.14, which, if not strictly an allusion, evokes at least the same pathos as Hesiod's image at *WD* 258–60 of Dike crying out against the wicked minds of men.

One of the central points of Hesiod's teaching on justice is the opposition between *dikē* and *hybris* (Gagarin 1973: 90). Just one of many examples is Hesiod's instruction to Perses at *WD* 213: ὦ Πέρση, σὺ δ' ἄκουε Δίκης, μηδ' ὕβριν ὄφελλε, "Perses, listen to justice do not try to practice [*hybris*]." Thus, Solon's reference to *hybris*, in the phrase ὕβριος ἐκ μεγάλης at "Eunomia" 4.8, is another allusion in this chain of allusions to Hesiod's framework of *dikē*. The *hybris* of Solon's leaders therefore draws with it this Hesiodic opposition to *dikē* and validates Solon's attribution of *hybris* as a cause of the injustice of the city's leaders. The allusion in ὕβριος is performing a function similar to the allusions in χρήμασι and ἄδικος νόος. In this case, however, Solon adds something of his own to Hesiod's understanding of *hybris*, namely, its relation to κόρος (4.9).

The noun *koros* does not occur in *WD*, and the verbal forms that do occur all have the basic meaning "be satisfied with what one has" (*WD* 33, 368, 593; West 1978: 248.) This basic sense is extended in Solon, and *koros* comes to mean insatiability, for example, an inextinguishable desire for ever-increasing wealth (Helm 1993: 8–9). In fr. 6.3–4 Solon expounds on the relation between *koros* and *hybris* and links both to a form of debilitated mind: τίκτει γὰρ κόρος ὕβριν, ὅταν πολὺς ὄλβος ἔπηται / ἀνθρώποις ὁπόσοις μὴ νόος ἄρτιος ᾖ, "[*koros*] breeds [*hybris*] whenever great prosperity comes to men who are not of sound mind." Thus in this condition of debilitation, namely, imprudence of mind, the insatiability of *koros* guarantees *hybris*, and the relation of these three ideas in fr. 6 serves as a gloss on Solon's ἄδικος νόος in the "Eunomia." In the political context of the poem imprudence is cast as injustice, and under this form of debilitated mind Solon's leaders "do not know how to restrain their *koros*, "οὐ γὰρ ἐπίστανται κατέχειν κόρον" (4.9). These words thus link the complex of ideas, *koros, hybris,* and unjust mind to Hesiod, as Solon's οὐ γὰρ ἐπίστανται κατέχειν κόρον is a negative particularization of Hesiod's law at *WD* 217: δίκη δ' ὑπὲρ ὕβριος ἴσχει, "justice . . . [keeps restraint] over [*hybris*]." If κατέχειν ~ ἴσχει does not qualify precisely as an allusion, Solon's words nonetheless embody a specific violation of a chief Hesiodic principle, namely, that the inability to check the cause of *hybris* begets injustice, and these words with their Hesiodic overtones identify this inability as a principle concomitant of injustice in Solon's city.

In the last of these allusions, φυλάσσονται at 4.14 and ἀδίκοις ἔργμασι at 4.11, Solon's relation to Hesiod is at its most transparent because the allusions reveal on their face how Solon transfers Hesiod to his city and turns him to his own poetic purposes. At *WD* 253–54 Hesiod tells of thirty thousand immortal φύλακες or guardians, and he describes their function at *WD* 254 as follows: οἵ ῥα φυλάσσουσίν τε δίκας καὶ σχέτλια ἔργα, "they [keep a watch on] decrees given and on [wicked deeds]." Hesiod's guardians are to watch the acts of men as they impact Dike, who represents the whole divine order of justice. Through use of the word φυλάσσονται Solon conspicuously transfers this guardianship to the leaders of his city, but negatively: οὐδὲ φυλάσσονται σεμνὰ Δίκης θέμεθλα, "they have no regard for [i.e. do not keep watch on] the august foundations of Justice" (4.14). They fail in their duty of guardianship precisely because they do not acknowledge that their own wealth-grabbing is tearing at the foundations of Dike, that is, "they grow wealthy, yielding to unjust deeds," πλουτέουσιν δ' ἀδίκοις ἔργμασι πειθόμενοι (4.11). The phrase ἄδικα ἔργματα, "unjust deeds," is an allusion to Hesiod's σχέτλια ἔργα of *WD* 254 above, but one that Solon conspicuously transposes to convey his own version of Hesiod's ideas. He replaces Hesiod's σχέτλια, wicked, with his own ἄδικα, unjust, and thus emphasizes the most salient point in this section of the "Eunomia," that injustice is ruining his city.

We come now to Solon's most explicit allusion to Hesiod in the phrase at 4.36, [Εὐνομίη] εὐθύνει δὲ δίκας σκολιάς (4.36), "[Eunomia straightens] out crooked judgments." This phrase occurs in the figure of the just city that constitutes the finale of the "Eunomia" and is aligned with Hesiodic images of straightening the crooked. See, for example, *WD* 7–8, ῥεῖα δέ τ' ἰθύνει σκολιὸν καὶ ἀγήνορα κάρφει / Ζεὺς ὑψιβρεμέτης, "lightly the crooked man he straightens, / withers the proud man, / he, Zeus"; *Op* 9–10, δίκῃ δ' ἴθυνε θέμιστας / τύνη, "[you Zeus] direct [i.e., make straight] your decrees in righteousness"; and *WD* 263, βασιλῆς ἰθύνετε μύθους, "Beware, you barons . . . / Straighten your decisions." To these we may add *WD* 264, σκολιῶν δὲ δικέων ἐπὶ πάγχυ λάθεσθε, "banish from your minds the twisting of justice"; *WD* 220–21, τῆς δὲ Δίκης ῥόθος ἑλκομένης ᾗ κ' ἄνδρες ἄγωσιν / δωροφάγοι, σκολιῆς δὲ δίκης κρίνωσι θέμιστας, "there is an outcry when Justice is dragged perforce, / when bribe-eating / men pull her about, and judge their cases / with crooked decisions"; *WD* 222–24, ἥ δ' ἕπεται κλαίουσα πόλιν . . . / κακὸν ἀνθρώποισι φέρουσα / οἳ . . . οὐχ ἰθεῖαν [δίκην] ἔνειμαν, "[Dike] follows . . . weeping to the city . . . and brings a curse / upon all those / who . . . twist her in dealing"; and *WD* 225–26, οἳ δὲ δίκας ξείνοισι καὶ ἐνδήμοισι διδοῦσιν / ἰθείας . . . / τοῖσι τέθηλε πόλις, "but when men issue straight decisions / to their own people / and to strangers / . . . their city flourishes."

The action of straightening the crooked is as essential to Hesiod's poetics of *dikē* as is the opposition between *dikē* and *hybris*. This Hesiodic conception had so strong an impact on Solon that he drew upon it in fr. 36 to defend the justice of his own political reforms (*Athenaion Politeia*, 12.4; Noussia-Fantuzzi 2010: 29–32). Fr. 36.19–20 read:

θεσμοὺς δ᾽ ὁμοίως τῷ κακῷ τε κἀγαθῷ
εὐθεῖαν εἰς ἕκαστον ἁρμόσας δίκην
ἔγραψα.

I wrote laws for the lower and upper classes alike, providing straight [*dikē*] for each person.

Solon's εὐθεῖα δίκη, "straight *dikē*," reflects the same phrase at *WD* 224 in the lines from *Op* 222–24 above, and his notion of a fair distribution of justice "to the lower and upper classes alike," ὁμοίως τῷ κακῷ τε κἀγαθῷ, reflects Hesiod's ξείνοισι καὶ ἐνδήμοισι, "to strangers and to their own" at *WD* 225 from *WD* 225–26 above. While Solon's ἁρμόσας, a careful fitting together of disparates, is an idea germane to the particular nature of his political solution, the paradigmatic Hesiodic idea of straight *dikē* animates this passage and gives Hesiodic weight to Solon's attempt to justify his own actual reforms. Thus, when Solon in fr. 4 has Eunomia, whom he knew as Dike's divine sister at *Th* 901–2, straighten crooked *dikas* (4.36), he is drawing upon a central Hesiodic idea that had a wide-ranging and powerful impact on both his political and poetic sensibilities. This allusion to "straight justice" brings politics and poetry together in the mind of Solon to provide a potent Hesiodic validation of the picture of justice in the final image of fr. 4. Expressed through Eunomia's particular efficacies, Dike brings to Solon's imagined city good order (εὔκοσμα, 4.32), harmony (ἄρτια, 4.32, 39), and rationality (πινυτά, 4.39).[5]

Through these allusions and the chain of Hesiodic ideas accompanying them, Solon appropriates the moral authority of Hesiod as a teacher of justice to the condemnation of his city's ἀστοί and δήμου ἡγεμῶνες and to the affirmation of the character of his imagined city of justice in the poem's final image.

Pessimism/Optimism: The Just and Unjust Cities and the "Hymn to the Muses"

Hesiod expounds his teachings on justice in *WD* in a world of "profound pessimism" (Lesky 1966: 96). The people of his poem live in an Iron Age (*WD* 106–201; Lesky 1966: 102; West 1978: 198) in which Zeus dispenses never-ending misery for the human race (*WD* 177–78) and never fails to notice or to punish injustice (*WD* 267–69). This and more makes the age so onerous that Hesiod wishes he were never born into it. (*WD* 174–75). Yet from time to time a fragile light may pierce the darkness, and amid the burdens a little good is possible (*WD* 179; Clay 2003: 142–44). This is especially so when attention to wise precepts of justice opens a possibility for some measure of wealth and prosperity

(*WD* 279–81). This point of view, a prevailing darkness with some possibility of light, is a central element of Hesiod's poetic sensibility in the Discourse on Justice (even if perhaps not so certainly at the end of *WD* [Clay 2003: 145–46]). A poet of Solon's perception, with his keen interest in Hesiod's poetics of *dikē*, will have been sensitive to the tone of Hesiod's poetic voice. In the "Eunomia," despite his fixation on the pessimistic state of injustice in his city, Solon in the end jettisons Hesiodic pessimism for a positive faith in what his city might become under Athena's protection (Havelock 1978: 259). He does this by imitating and transposing to his own ends Hesiod's images of the just and unjust city in the Discourse on Justice. In the "Hymn to the Muses," on the other hand, Solon expands the Hesiodic idea of Zeus as the punisher of injustice and takes Hesiodic pessimism to an extreme point.

In the "Eunomia" Solon by structural allusion imitates Hesiod's vignettes of the just and unjust city. Hesiod presents his just city first at *WD* 225–37, then juxtaposes it with the image of the unjust city at *WD* 238–47. The poetic purpose of these vignettes is to support by example and counterexample the effects of compliance and noncompliance with Hesiod's precept to Perses at *WD* 213, namely, to follow *dikē* and avoid *hybris*. Hesiod's just city belongs to those who follow *dikē* (*WD* 225–27), and his unjust city to those whose concern is *hybris* (*WD* 238). The two cities therefore reflect the fundamental Hesiodic opposition between *dikē* and *hybris* (Canevaro 2016: 147). In Hesiod's just city all the people flourish as if living in an agrarian golden age (West 1978: 215). Eirene reigns throughout the land. Male births will be plentiful. Zeus will bring no wars, famine, or calamities (*Atē*). Dinners are replete with homegrown food, the trees and livestock produce without cultivation, women bear legitimate children, and there is no need to find a living in trade. In Hesiod's unjust city conditions are like those of the Iron Age, in which people perpetrate misery-bearing deeds. The reckless act of one man can infect the whole city. Zeus sets the measure of *dikē*, that is, punishment (West 1978: 216), and brings great suffering: hunger, plague, bareness in the women, and diminishment of households. Zeus destroys armies, city walls, and ships on the open sea.

In the "Eunomia" Solon's unjust city (4.17–31) is the result of the crumbling of Dike's foundations (Noussia-Fantuzzi 2010: 244–45). The elements of this image reflect the state of injustice described in verses 4–14, but here with an emphasis on the effects, not the causes, of injustice. There is incurable ulceration of the body politic, erupting from disorder among the citizens themselves. There is slavery, faction, and the awakening of dormant war, all of which threatens the future of the young. All this brings a general evil to the city, and many of the poor are sold into foreign slavery. The evil reaches even to the most personal aspects of private life. In general, the goddess Dusnomia is the source of evil in this city. Solon's just city (4.32–39), in contrast, reflects the characteristics of Dusnomia's opposite, the goddess Eunomia. She brings about good order and harmony. She incarcerates the unjust. She smooths out what is rough. She cures what were the principal causes of injustice in Solon's real city, namely, *koros* and *hybris*. She withers the bloom of *atē* (recklessness). She straightens crooked *dikas*, and this, as we have seen in the preceding section, is Hesiod's central image of justice. Eunomia tames overweening deeds. She stops faction and the troublesome anger of strife. Under her rule everything in the city is well ordered, harmonious, and rational.

The differences between Solon's and Hesiod's cites suggest the former's intentions for his structural allusion. Solon does not structure his cities around the opposition of *dikē* and *hybris*, nor does he appropriate by specific allusions the content of Hesiod's images. Rather, he transforms the Iron Age tropes of Hesiod's unjust city into more specific but generic political evils and makes Dusnomia its presiding deity. In his just city he replaces Eirene with Eunomia and transforms the golden age images of Hesiod's city into a description of Eunomia's termination of the specific political evils troubling his own city. These differences show that Solon was not interested in the content of Hesiod's construct but only in its structure, namely, the counterposing of an image of justice against that of injustice.

What Solon does with this structure is simple but transformative. He reverses the counterposition so that the image of the just city becomes the finale of his poem. In this final image the goddess Eunomia dissolves the roots of the injustice that plague the real city of verses 4–14 and represents in herself and through poetic opposition to the disorder of Dusnomia the paradigm of a just civic order. Through the image of the city of Eunomia, Solon announces to all his fellow citizens that ἡμετέρη πόλις (4.1), "our [city]," can become under the promise of Athena's perpetual protection (4.3–4) a true city of justice. Thus Solon turns away from the pessimism of condemnation to the optimism of hope.

In the "Hymn to the Muses," on the other hand, Solon takes Hesiodic pessimism to its extreme. Solon's 13:17, Ζεὺς πάντων ἐφορᾷ τέλος, "Zeus oversees every outcome," is aligned with Hesiod's *WD* 267, πάντα ἰδὼν Διὸς ὀφθαλμὸς καὶ νοήσας, "the eye of Zeus sees everything; His mind understands all," and his 13.27, αἰεὶ δὲ οὔ ἑ λέληθε διαμπερές, ὅστις ἀλιτρὸν / θυμὸν ἔχει, πάντως δ' ἐς τέλος ἐξεφάνη, "anyone who has a sinful heart never escapes his notice [and the end is shown for sure]," is aligned with *WD* 268–69, οὐδέ ἑ λήθει / οἵην δὴ καὶ τήνδε δίκην πόλις ἐντὸς ἐέργει, "nor does [Zeus] fail / to see what kind of justice this community keeps inside it." Solon takes from Hesiod the figure of Zeus, who sees and inexorably punishes all acts of injustice. In this role Zeus appears in the first part of the poem to punctuate a world of Hesiodic pessimism, but he reappears at the end to mark the transformation of this pessimism into something darker.

The first eleven verses, through allusion to Hesiod, cumulate central themes of *WD* with the addition of some uniquely Solonian elements. The opening prayer to the Muses petitions for general prosperity or ὄλβος, a thoroughly Hesiodic conception (*WD* 204, 321, 326, 379, 637), and marks Solon's acceptance of a prevalent theme in *WD*, namely, that in the end all human good is in the power of the gods. The addition of a prayer for good reputation (13.4, δόξαν ἔχειν ἀγαθήν) is Solon's own, not paralleled in Hesiod. In verses 7–13, Solon weaves into his poem ideas that are part of the central fabric of the Discourse on Justice. He desires wealth (13.7, χρήματα) but fears its unjust acquisition (13.7–8, ἀδίκως δὲ πεπᾶσθαι / οὐκ ἐθέλω), because he knows that injustice will always be punished (13.8, πάντως ὕστερον ἦλθε δίκη). Ordinary human gain is fragile, but god-given wealth is always abundant (13.9, πλοῦτον δ ὅν μὲν δῶσι θεοί). In Hesiodic fashion

Solon aligns unjust works (13.10, ἀδίκοις ἔργμασι) with *hybris* (13.11). These notions can be analyzed as allusions to Hesiod in the same manner as in the preceding section. Solon's purpose here, however, is not to treat political injustice but to recreate Hesiod's sense of the hardships of life. Solon's recreation again contains things of his own as he adds a new opposition between *hybris* and good order (κόσμον, 13.11), a term not found in this sense in Hesiod but which is the hallmark of Solon's just city in the "Eunomia." Finally, in complete agreement with Hesiod, injustice always comes mixed with *atē* (13.13 ~ WD 212–16).

With this collection of Hesiodic allusions, the "Hymn to the Muses" begins with a proper Hesiodic pessimism. Things are dark, but there is some small possibility of light, inasmuch as a prayer for ὄλβος suggests a chance of fulfillment. However, with the introduction of Zeus the punisher at verses 25–32, the pessimism becomes more severe. The inexorability of Zeus's punishment of injustice is harsh (Gagné 2013: 236) but still fundamentally Hesiodic. Solon begins the trajectory toward a more consummate darkness with the addition of Zeus's punishment of innocents: αὐτοί, μηδὲ θεῶν μοῖρ᾽ ἐπιοῦσα κίχῃ, / ἤλυθε πάντως αὖτις· ἀναίτιοι ἔργα τίνουσιν / ἢ παῖδες τούτων ἢ γένος ἐξοπίσω (13.30–31), "if [the guilty] escape . . . the pursuing destiny of the gods, it assuredly comes at another time; the innocent pay the penalty, either their children or a later progeny." In Hesiod divine punishment reaches beyond the unjust offender to the stock of the offender's household: τοῦ δέ τ᾽ ἀμαυροτέρη γενεὴ μετόπισθε λέλειπται (WD 284), "this man is left a diminished generation hereafter," but this touches riches more than persons (Gagné 2013: 244). The punishment of innocents, however, reaches beyond what can be found in Hesiod, and omniscient punishment of this sort carries with it a pessimism beyond the mere hard conditions of life.

In the litany of human pursuits that concludes the "Hymn to the Muses" (13.33–70), Solon's pessimism becomes absolute and irredeemable. Although the interpretation of these verses is debated, they certainly present a deeply troubling view of human life (Noussia-Fantuzzi, 133–39, 194). Verses 33–38 suggest that all human hope is vanity; verses 39–42 that man is so constituted as to view his present state in self-deception and his future state in delusion; and verses 43–70 that the various pursuits of human life—trading, farming, medicine—are futile, always subject either to the uncertainty of chance or to the inscrutability of divine purpose (Lattimore 1947: 167). With all of this Solon has created a pessimism of hopelessness based on man's inability to determine his own ends. Hesiod, on the other hand, believed to some degree in the possibility of achieving ends; otherwise there would be no point to his precepts of just living (Scodel 2014: 59). Even though Hesiod entertains momentary doubts, for example, when he concedes at WD 270–73 that the unjust sometimes prosper, he ultimately reverts to faith in the efficacy of good teachings (Lattimore 1947: 174). Not so Solon, for the good in fact sometimes suffer and the bad prosper (13.67–70), but Zeus does not fix it. In the last verses of the "Hymn to Muses" (13.74–76), although their relation to the poem's more confident beginning is debated, Zeus ultimately brings calamity to every human pursuit: κέρδεά τοι θνητοῖς ὤπασαν ἀθάνατοι, / ἄτη δ᾽ ἐξ αὐτῶν ἀναφαίνεται / ἣν ὁπότε Ζεὺς / πέμψῃ τεισομένην, ἄλλοτε ἄλλος ἔχει (13.74–76), "the immortals give men profit, but from [the gods] there is revealed ruin, which now one now another has, whenever Zeus sends it to punish them." This darkness is virtually absolute, and with it Solon has taken the pessimism of Hesiod to an irredeemably extreme point.

There is nothing surprising about the same poet composing different poems in different tones, especially when the subject matter warrants it. On the basis of subject matter Vlastos (1946: 76) saw a "bifurcation" of philosophic perspective in the "Eunomia" and the "Hymn to the Muses," the former concerning "political justice," in which Solon was a "great innovator," and the latter individual, "distributive justice," in which Solon remained a "traditionalist." We may understand the bifurcation of tone in the "Eunomia" and the "Hymn to the Muses" similarly: optimism in the first, which presents the just civic order as the positive hope for a presently unjust city, and pessimism in the second, which ponders the precariousness of daily human life.

SUBSTANTIVE JUSTICE IN HESIOD AND SOLON

Nothing in this literary analysis tells us what justice is in either Hesiod or Solon. As stated previously, two views divide the field: justice is the same in Solon and Hesiod; justice is an entirely new conception in Solon.

The first view is represented by, among others, Wilamowitz, Ehrenberg, and Lloyd-Jones. Their governing principle is that there is simply no lexical, linguistic, or conceptual difference between Hesiodic and Solonian *dikē* (Jaeger 1966: 40; Lloyd-Jones 1971: 44; Almeida 2003: 83n37). Solon may have transferred Hesiod's constructs from an agrarian to a political setting, but what he says about justice is simply a version of what Hesiod said. For example, when Solon condemns the leaders of his city in fr. 4 as unjust for wealth-grabbing and *hybris*, he means no more than Hesiod did in condemning Perses for similar acts (*WD* 213, 320), namely, that such behavior is a violation of the ordinances of Zeus, which are represented by the deified Dike (Lloyd-Jones 1971: 32–35). Even when Solon in fr. 36.16 says that he "[blended] together force ($\beta\ell\eta$) and justice ($\delta\ell\kappa\eta$)," in his political reforms, he has in mind the divine beings $B\ell\eta$ and $\Delta\ell\kappa\eta$, who in Hesiod reside with Zeus, and is thinking with the mind of the Archaic Age (Lloyd-Jones 1971: 44). For scholars of this bent, Solon's poetic technique is of a piece with his thinking; that is to say, as Solon adapts Hesiodic material to his own poetry but does not essentially change it, so also does he adopt without change Hesiod's conception of justice (Lloyd-Jones 1971: 45). So most recently Koning (2010: 187–88) notes that Solon's justice is not a breakthrough in thought but an updating of Hesiod to conditions in the polis.[6]

The second view comes primarily from Jaeger, whom Solmsen and Vlastos follow closely. Jaeger's governing principle is that the lexicographical history of *dikē* is unhelpful, indeed misleading, because "beneath the unchanged word-meaning lie hidden very great changes in the structure of thought" (1966, 89n2). This point of view sensitizes these scholars to passages in Solon that suggest a new sense of *dikē*. For example, in the "Eunomia" Solon counts himself as one among the citizens; speaks to them in his own voice with the authority not of the gods but of the statesman; and tells them, by allusion to the *Odyssey* (fr. 4.1, 5 ~ *Od.* 1.32–33), that they themselves and not the gods are responsible for their own evil acts (Jaeger 1966: 85–90). In the "Eunomia" punishment for injustice comes from within and affects the community itself, for example, civil faction, whereas punishment in Hesiod is sent by Zeus as unspecific requital (Jaeger 1966: 90; Solmsen 1949: 113). In Vlastos's terms (1946: 90) Hesiod's punishments belong to the "order of magic," whereas those of Solon are "consequences of the acts of citizens within the social order." The totality of the Solonian project, of which justice is a part, represents for Jaeger (1966: 90n1) "a completely new structure of man's relationship to reality." For Vlastos (1946: 67–68), Solon's justice is a naturalistic, intelligible principle tied to and comprehensible in terms of the common experience of the polis. Similarly, Solmsen (1949: 113–14) sees Solonian justice as part of "empirical laws and the regular sequence of political developments," which amounts to a "science of politics" based on an "intrinsic logic" and a "natural causality." This new natural law of justice is seen as a political analogue to Anaximander's cosmological law of reciprocating equalization in the processes of generation and corruption (Jaeger 1966: 144; Solmsen 1949: 122n76; Vlastos 1946: 80–81). Most recently Gagné (2013: 241–42) offers a version of the new natural law of justice connected to Solon's punishment of innocents, a new principle of "cosmic justice" influenced by the emergent monetary economy wherein "debts" of injustice can be paid anywhere in the course of time by a cosmic "currency" equal to the debt, for example, the innocent child has the same "value" as the guilty father.

Opposing principles lead to dichotomous views on how much Solon's *dikē* differs in substantive meaning from Hesiod's. But in each view there is recognition that Solon's poetry of *dikē* cannot be understood in isolation from its Hesiodic precedent.

Conclusion

Hunter (2014: 140) tells us somewhat summarily that the similarities between *WD* and Solon's frr. 4 and 13 "are such that an appropriation of Hesiodic themes and (in part) a Hesiodic voice may be regarded as one of Solon's principle poetic techniques." The literary analysis herein provides a set of detailed observations that fill out Hunter's claim. The review of the opinions on the meaning of *dikē* may have an independent value for the study of the philosophy of justice but, to the point here, also confirms that Solon did not compose his poetry of *dikē* in isolation from Hesiod.

Notes

1. This introductory outline of Solon's life follows the general ancient tradition. For an evaluation of the tradition on issues of the timing and the nature of Solon's political and legal

reforms and the economic and agricultural conditions of debt, e.g., hectamorage and removal of the *horoi* stones, see Almeida (2003: 23–26); Blintiff (2006: 322–23); Forsdyke (2006: 335–40); and Ober (2006: 446–48).

2. The source of these particular points of contact is the "diligent collection of ancient citations, allusions and imitations" (West 1966: 102), in Rzach (1902). Other points of similarity in Rzach, too generic to support an analyzable relation between Solon and Hesiod, follow: Solon 13.1f. ($M\nu\eta\mu o\sigma\acute\upsilon\nu\eta\varsigma$ / $Mo\hat\upsilon\sigma\alpha\iota$ $\Pi\iota\epsilon\rho\acute\iota\delta\epsilon\varsigma$) ~ *Th* 52ff. ($\dot\epsilon\nu$ $\Pi\iota\epsilon\rho\acute\iota\eta$ / $M\nu\eta\mu o\sigma\acute\upsilon\nu\eta$) ~ *WD* 1 ($Mo\hat\upsilon\sigma\alpha\iota$ $\Pi\iota\epsilon\rho\acute\iota\eta\theta\epsilon\nu$) is a generic hymnic formula (see Noussia-Fantuzi 2010: 140); there are also common tropes like the dangers on the sea: Solon 13.19 ~ *Th* 873–74, 878–79; and there are also phrases too ubiquitous to be significant to a specific reception, e.g., $\dot o\mu\hat\omega\varsigma$ $\dot\alpha\gamma\alpha\theta\acute o\varsigma$ $\tau\epsilon$ $\kappa\alpha\kappa\acute o\varsigma$ $\tau\epsilon$, Solon 13.33 ~ *WD* 669.

3. Excluding the *Th* as a significant point of contact between Solon and Hesiod requires comment. Though the motif of "straight justice" also appears at *Th* 85 ($\dot\iota\theta\epsilon\acute\iota\eta\sigma\iota$ $\delta\acute\iota\kappa\eta\sigma\iota\nu$), context argues against this passage as a source for Solon. *Th* 85 is part of *Th* 80–94, which is "a somewhat contrived transition [from the genealogy of the Olympian Muses (*Th* 53–79)] to the subject of kings" (West 1966: 181). Besides the reference to $\dot\iota\theta\epsilon\acute\iota\eta\sigma\iota$ $\delta\acute\iota\kappa\eta\sigma\iota\nu$ and its consequence of settling lawsuits at *Th* 86, nothing else in the passage is about *dikē*.

4. All quotations from Hesiod are from West (1966, 1978); those from Solon are from West (1972). Unless otherwise noted by square brackets, all translations of Hesiod are from Lattimore (1959); all of Solon are from Gerber (1999).

5. Allusion alone to Hesiod may not explain the presence of Eunomia or Dusnomia in fr. 4; these words do not occur in *WD* and occur in the *Th* only as names in divine genealogies (*Th* 230, 902). For the *Th* to be Solon's source, he would have had to attribute to these words a social/political sense within the context of Hesiod's poem. For such a perspective on Solon, see Scully (2015: 87–88).

6. Gagarin also holds that justice is the same in Hesiod and Solon but from a different governing principle. He denies that *dikē* has reached in either poet the level of a moral concept and argues etymologically that the meaning of *dikē* in both Hesiod and Solon is "straight settlement" or "legal process" (Gagarin 1973: 82, 89, 91; 1974: 190–91).

REFERENCES

Almeida, J. 2003. *Justice as an Aspect of the Polis Idea in Solon's Political Poems: A Reading of the Fragments in Light of the Researches of New Classical Archaeology*. Mnemosyne Supplement 243. Leiden, Netherlands.

Blintiff, J. 2006. "Solon's Reforms: An Archaeological Perspective." In *Solon of Athens*, edited by J. H. Blok and A. P. M. E. Lardinois, 321–33. Mnemosyne Supplement 272. Leiden, Netherlands.

Canevaro, L. G. 2015. *Hesiod's Works and Days: How to Teach Self-Sufficiency*. Oxford.

Clay, J. S. 2003. *Hesiod's Cosmos*. Cambridge.

Forsdyke, S. 2006. "Land, Labor and Economy in Solon's Athens." In *Solon of Athens*, edited by J. H. Blok and A. P. M. E. Lardinois, 334–50. Mnemosyne Supplement 272. Leiden, Netherlands.

Gagarin, M. 1973. "*Dikē* in the *Works and Days*." *Classical Philology* 68: 81–94.

Gagarin, M. 1974. "*Dikē* in Archaic Greek Thought." *Classical Philology* 69: 186–97.

Gagné, R. 2013. *Ancestral Fault in Ancient Greece*. Cambridge.

Gerber, D. E. 1999. *Greek Elegiac Poetry*. Cambridge.

Havelock, E. A. 1978. *The Greek Concept of Justice: From Its Shadow in Homer to Its Substance in Plato*. Cambridge, MA.

Helm, J. 1993. "*Koros*: From Satisfaction to Greed." *Classical World* 87: 5–11.

Hunter, R. 2014. *Hesiodic Voices: Studies in the Ancient Reception of Hesiod's Works and Days*. Cambridge.

Jaeger, W. 1945. *Paideia*. Vol. 1. 2nd ed. Translated by G. Highet. Oxford.

Jaeger, W. 1966. "Solon's Eunomia." In *Five Essays*. Translated by A. M. Fiske. Montreal, 69–85.

Koning, H. H. 2010. *Hesiod: The Other Poet; Ancient Reception of a Cultural Icon*. Mnemosyne Supplement 325. Leiden, Netherlands.

Lattimore, R. 1947. "The First Elegy of Solon." *American Journal of Philology* 68: 161–79.

Lattimore, R., trans. 1959. *Hesiod*. Ann Arbor, MI.

Lesky, A. 1966. *A History of Greek Literature*. Translated by J. Willis and C. de Heer. Indianapolis, IN.

Lloyd-Jones, H. 1971. *The Justice of Zeus*. Berkeley, CA.

Noussia-Fantuzzi, M. 2010. *Solon the Athenian, the Poetic Fragments*. Mnemosyne Supplement 326. Leiden, Netherlands.

Ober, J. 2006. "Solon and the *Horoi*: Facts on the Ground in Archaic Athens." In *Solon of Athens*, edited by J. H. Blok and A. P. M. E. Lardinois, 441–56. Mnemosyne Supplement 272. Leiden, Netherlands.

Rzach, A., ed. 1902. *Hesiodi carmina*. Leipzig, Germany.

Scodel, R. 2014. "Prophetic Hesiod." In *Between Orality and Literacy: Communication and Adaptation in Antiquity*, edited by R. Scodel, 56–76. Mnemosyne Supplement 367. Leiden, Netherlands.

Scully, S. 2015. *Hesiod's Theogony: From Near Eastern Creation Myths to Paradise Lost*. Oxford.

Solmsen, F. 1949. *Hesiod and Aeschylus*. Ithaca, NY.

Vlastos, G. 1946. "Solonian Justice." *Classical Philology* 41: 65–83.

West, M. L., ed. and comm. 1966. *Hesiod: Theogony*. Oxford.

West, M. L., ed. 1972. *Iambi et elegi Graeci ante Alexandrum cantati*. Vol. II. Oxford.

West, M. L., ed. and comm. 1978. *Hesiod: Works and Days*. Oxford.

CHAPTER 14

THE RECEPTION OF HESIOD BY THE EARLY PRE-SOCRATICS

MITCHELL MILLER

Studying the reception of Hesiod's thought by Anaximander and Xenophanes is a daunting project.[1] It is not just that we have only fragments and sketchy reports to go on; what is more, both these texts and Hesiod's reflect the development of unprecedented modes of thought. As a consequence, almost everything that one ventures to say is contestable. Let me begin by acknowledging the obscurity of the depth of each of our thinkers, as well as the inevitable danger of circularity that faces any effort to reconstruct their relations.

The project is nonetheless compelling. Anaximander and Xenophanes attempt, each in his own way, to break free from the mythopoeic tradition, and Hesiod is the most philosophical member of that tradition. In their generation of new forms of thought, Anaximander and Xenophanes develop possibilities that are arguably implicit, albeit within the mythopoeia they challenge, in Hesiod.[2] The mix of departure and return is veritably Heraclitean.

I begin with Anaximander, then turn to Xenophanes.

ANAXIMANDER AND HESIOD ON THE QUESTION OF THE *ARCHĒ*

Anaximander's *Apeiron Archē*, Justice, and the Opposites

Anaximander is best known for declaring the *archē* of the world—that is, the source of the sphere of the heavens and the earth—to be *to apeiron,* "the unlimited." He is objecting to his Milesian predecessor Thales's view that all things originate from water. He evidently agrees with Thales that the *archē* is something physical, for he holds that *to apeiron* "surrounds and embraces all things" ($\pi\epsilon\rho\iota\acute{\epsilon}\chi\epsilon\iota\nu$ $\ddot{\alpha}\pi\alpha\nu\tau\alpha$). But as the name he gives it indicates, he takes it to outstrip every given limit of place (for it lies, untraversibly vast, outside the sphere of the heavens), of time (for it is "eternal and ageless"), and of kind (for it is qualitatively indefinite, being "neither water nor any other of the so-called elements").[3]

Why does Anaximander reject Thales's identification of the *archē* as water, and why does he think it to be, instead, indefinite in kind? Our best recourse is Anaximander's one surviving fragment, in which he declares that "[the things that are] perish into the things out of which they come to be, according to necessity, for they pay penalty and retribution to each other for their injustice in accordance with the ordering of time." If we ask, for what "injustice" committed by, say, A, it would be a proportionate "penalty and retribution" for A to "perish into" B, we see that A, by coming to be, must have caused B to perish, and also that B must have perished into A; for A's "perishing" is proportionate to its having denied to B its existence, and A's perishing "into" B, that is, its letting B come to be "out of" it, restores to B what it has denied. But this restoration to B, because it costs A its existence, is also B's denial to A of A's existence. Hence Anaximander envisages an endless alternation of crime and reparation, in which each reparation is itself a new crime that calls for new reparation. And if we ask what "things that are" stand in this reciprocal relation of crime and reparation, in which the coming to be of each causes the perishing of the other and vice versa, we see that their mutual negation requires that we think of opposites—presumably, as is suggested by other reports, the hot and the cold. Anaximander discerns, in the endless alternation of the seasons, the fundamental justice that governs the basic conditions of the natural world.

These reflections show why the *archē* of the world must be "neither water nor any other of the so-called elements" but, instead, indefinite in kind. As the ultimate source of all else, the *archē* must itself have no source; hence it is "eternal" ($\dot{\alpha}\acute{\iota}\delta\iota\omicron\nu$ [Kirk et al. 1983: 107–8]). Accordingly, for it to be water would be a crime against the dry, for the dry would be forever denied coming to be, and the "penalty and retribution" for this "injustice" would be forever forestalled. More generally, just insofar as to be qualitatively definite is to be subject to having an opposite, for the *archē* to be qualitatively definite would be to make permanent the injustice of its suppressing its opposite. Justice, then, requires that the *archē* be such as to have no opposite, and this requires that it be qualitatively indefinite.

These reflections also cast light on the logic that motivates Anaximander's understanding of cosmogenesis. Insofar as the basic powers within the world are the opposites and the *apeiron* is the *archē* of the world, the coming to be of the world must involve the "separating-off of the opposites" from the *apeiron*. But this must not be understood to imply that the opposites initially exist in the *apeiron*, for this would undermine its character of being qualitatively indefinite. Accordingly, Anaximander interposes a middle term, which, in the words of Ps.-Plutarch, he characterizes only by its function: "that which is productive (γόνιμον) . . . of hot and cold." (Kirk et al. 1983: 131) In the first phase of cosmogenesis this "productive" something is "separated off" from the eternal *apeiron*, and in the second phase it somehow produces the hot and the cold and, so, the world; thus the *apeiron* itself remains unqualified by the opposites.

Hesiod's Cosmogony: The Justice of the Whole

To appreciate the way in which Anaximander's notion of the *apeiron archē* responds to Hesiod, we must first mark and interpret the key cosmogonic passage in the *Theogony* (hereafter *Th*), 116–33:[4]

116   First of all, Chaos was born (γένετ'); then next
       Broad-breasted Earth, a firm seat forever for all
       The immortals who hold the peaks of snowy Olympus,
       And misty Tartara in the depths under the wide-wayed ground,[5]

120   And Eros, handsomest among the deathless gods,
       A looser of limbs, who in all the gods and all human beings
       Overpowers in their breasts their intelligence and careful planning.
       And from Chaos were born both Erebos and dark Night,
       And from Night, in turn, were born both Aither and Day,

125   Whom she conceived and bore after joining in love with Erebos.
       But Earth first brought forth, as an equal to herself,
       Starry Sky, so that he might cover her all over,
       In order to be a firm seat forever for the blessed gods,
       And she brought forth the tall Mountains, pleasing haunts of the goddess

130   Nymphs who make their homes in the forested hills,
       And also she bore the barren main with its raging swell,
       Sea, all without any sweet act of love; then next,
       Having lain with Sky, she bore deep-swirling Ocean. . . .

Even before exploring these lines in detail, we can hardly fail to be impressed by the break in mode of thought represented by Anaximander's notion of the *apeiron*. Hesiod belongs to the mythopoeic tradition, and he proceeds by letting a series of vivid images unfold before his hearer; Anaximander, by contrast, makes inventive use of a term that, even while it brings to mind the picture of a vast expanse, also resists picture thinking itself. What is without outer bounds of place and time and qualitatively indefinite defies the individuating borders and qualitative determinateness that the constitution of a picture requires; one feels oneself challenged by Anaximander to enter unfamiliar thought space, the space of the abstract or purely conceptual. This, however, is only the beginning, not the end of the matter of Anaximander's relation to Hesiod. For in a different but analogous way, Hesiod too enters unfamiliar thought space when at *Th* 105–10 he prepares the way for his cosmogony; in the course of his appeal to the Muses to

> 105   sound out the holy stock of the everlasting immortals
>   who were born from Earth (Γῆς) and starry Sky
>   and gloomy Night, whom briny Sea brought to maturity,
>   and tell how at the first gods (θεοί) ... [,]

he makes a subtle but nonetheless sudden shift, here in the middle of line 108,[6] from straightforwardly anthropomorphic characterization of the gods to transparently cosmic characterization, shifting from the person figures of 105–8 to the sorts of structures and conditions of the natural world that these person figures represent:

>   ... and earth (καὶ γαῖα) were born
>   and rivers and boundless sea, raging in its swell,
> 110   and shining stars and wide sky above all.

What is more, some of the key structures Hesiod will introduce in the cosmogony do not belong to the *visible* natural world. Hence we must be ready to ask, before we settle on the contrasts we have begun to draw between his and Anaximander's language, whether and to what degree Hesiod too, even in the medium of vivid mythopoeic imagery, is pressing toward an abstract thought content.[7]

Let me now venture a reading of the main lines of thought in *Th* 116–33. This will put us in position to return to Anaximander and begin to mark the ways his proposal of an *apeiron archē* responds to Hesiod. I proceed in five steps:[8]

(1) *The first four: Chaos, Earth, Tartara, and Eros (116–22).* Though the first four beings are "born" (γένετ᾽, 116), Hesiod refrains from naming a parent and, indeed, from asserting any sibling relations. What he offers instead is the vision of an event that is partly topological, partly logical. His word *Chaos* derives from the root *cha-* and signifies the sort of "gap" that appears, to cite a cognate, in a "yawn" (χάσκειν, χαίνειν). The birth of Chaos is the topological event of the opening of a gap in what can only be thought of retrospectively as a hitherto undifferentiated field, and the opening brings along with it, in its immediate aftermath ("next"), the emergence of Earth and Tartaros as its two sides. The birth of Eros is, strange to say, a logical event. Eros is not to be envisaged as a thing in space but rather is the force that draws spatially distinct partners together, and its birth therefore presupposes and complements the birth of Chaos.

(2) *The character of Tartara.* To appreciate the motivation of the subsequent series of births in the cosmogony, it is important to keep in the mind's eye a vivid image of Tartaros. As the underworld, it is as far below the Earth, separated from it by Chaos (814), as the Earth is below the Sky (720–25). It is a "vast chasm" (740), and its darkness—it is associated with Erebos and filled with "murk" or "gloom" (729,

also 653, 659) and "mist" (119, 721, 729, 736 [= 807])—and its "dank, moldy" character (731, 739 [= 810]) prevent any distinct contours or shapes from appearing to sight and touch. Indeed, were a man so unlucky as to fall into it, "stormblast upon stormblast would sweep him one way and another" (742), making it impossible for him to get his bearings; as the onomatopoeia of its name suggests, it is characterized by unceasing disturbance. These vivid details help to explain the curious fact that Hesiod first names Tartaros in the plural, *Tartara*; a being so lacking in internal structure must also lack integrity.

(3) *The offspring of Chaos (123–25) and Earth (126–33): two kinds of order in interplay.* The topological event of the opening of the gap that separates Earth and Tartaros is only the first, in itself incomplete step in Hesiod's vision of cosmogenesis; Earth and Tartaros only receive their full specificities *as* Earth and *as* Tartaros through the further offspring of Chaos and Earth. These births exhibit two kinds of relation, and in their fitting together these constitute the order of the cosmos as a whole. First, already prefigured by the complementing of Chaos by Eros, there is a being's need, if it is to have its full specificity, for its opposite; thus Chaos's first-born, the spatial and temporal powers of darkness, Erebos and Night, together beget their correlative opposites, Aither and Day. By these begettings Erebos expresses his need, if he is to be the darkness of the underworld, for there also to be the brightness of the upper sky, Aither, and Night expresses her need, if she is to be the time of darkness, for there also to be the time of light, Day. Second, there is a whole's need, if it is to have genuine wholeness, for its articulation into parts. Hesiod displays this by having Earth bear, by and within herself, Mountains and Sea; thus Earth gives herself the internal differentiation essential to her *as* Earth. What is more, these two kinds of relation, each of which is itself a kind of complementarity, also complement one another. That a being's need for its opposite can complete a whole's self-differentiation is already evident in Earth's bearing of Mountains and Sea: as "tall," "forested," and the "pleasing haunts of nymphs," Mountains stand in determinate contrast with the low, "barren," and "raging swell" of Sea. More striking still is the way this self-differentiation completes Earth's acquiring of her opposite, Sky: when Earth first bears, "as an equal to herself, starry Sky," they are merely two undifferentiated masses, with Sky "covering [Earth] all over" without, however, standing in any qualitative contrast to her; by giving birth to Mountains and Sea, however, Earth makes herself into—as, now, a differentiated whole—the opposite to the undifferentiated expanse of Sky. That this achievement of qualitative contrast allows them to fit together as opposites, Hesiod lets us see in the final begetting of the cosmogony: Earth now lies with Sky and together they beget "deep swirling Ocean," the circular stream that, flowing around Earth at the farthest horizon, forms the continuous "point of contact between earth and the enclosing bowl of sky" (Kirk et al. 1983: 36n1)—thus Earth and Sky join together, constituting the upper world as a whole.

(4) *Hesiod's vision of the cosmic whole.* This constitution of the upper world of Earth and Sky is, in turn, both the analog to and the completion of the constitution of

the cosmos as a whole. If, letting ourselves "see" the process of cosmogenesis unfold, we keep vividly in the mind's eye the character of Tartaros as a "vast chasm"
without either internal structure or integrity, we will see that just as the upper
world is constituted as the whole of the internally differentiated whole of Earth,
with its Mountains and Sea, and undifferentiated Sky, so the cosmos in its entirety is constituted as the whole of the differentiated whole of the upper world
and undifferentiated Tartaros.

(5) *The cosmogony as the visible expression of the justice of Zeus.* I spoke at the outset
of the "abstract thought content" that, in the medium of his vivid imagery, Hesiod
presses toward. If we now set the cosmogony within the context of the *Th* as a
whole and, in turn, set the *Th* together with the *Works and Days* (hereafter *WD),*
we can make out this content. The main body of the *Th* tells the story of the victory of Zeus over the Titans. This victory does not consist, as did Kronos's victory
over Ouranos, merely of the violent taking of supreme power; rather, it consists of
Zeus's introduction of the rule of justice, that is, of that proper apportioning that
prevents the need for violence in the first place. Zeus's first three acts after driving
the Titans into Tartaros are to "distribute well among [the gods who fought with
him] their titles and privileges" (885, cf. 66–67 and 74); to swallow Metis and with
her inside him give birth to Athena, "the equal of her father in wise counsel and
strength"[9] (896); and with Themis (justice as established by custom) to beget
"Good Order" (Εὐνομίην), Justice, and Peace" (901–2). In the *WD*, in turn, Zeus
ordains the rule of justice for human beings. The crux of justice is to restrict one's
reach to "the half" that is one's own rather than to try to seize "the whole" for
oneself (*WD* 40); respecting boundaries, each party allows the other its due. The
cosmogony gives visible form to this idea of justice. Beginning with the birth of
Chaos, it makes central the differentiation that gives rise to Earth and Tartaros,
and at each step along its vivid way it matches part and counterpart in a nested
whole. To mark this for ourselves by tracing from the innermost parts to the
outermost whole: we are shown the pairs of Mountains and Sea, of the thereby
differentiated Earth and undifferentiated Sky, and of the *thereby* differentiated
upper world and undifferentiated Tartaros. Thus the cosmogony images the
formation of a world in which it is appropriate, because its differentiations and
pairings express the idea of justice as its ordering principle, for a just Zeus to
come to prevail.

Anaximander's Critical Response (Reconstructed) to Hesiod's Cosmogony

How does Anaximander's thought respond to Hesiod's? We have no surviving explicit
evidence—no text of Anaximander's referring to Hesiod—to guide us. What we can
do, however, is to set Anaximander's notions of the *apeiron archē* and the interplay of
the opposites against the background of *Th* 116–33; if we do, three observations present

themselves. First, while for Anaximander the coming into being of each of the opposites negates the other's existence, the requirement of justice reflects his recognition of the need that each has for the other; that each must pay reparation to the other "for [its] injustice" attests that the being of each requires the being of the other. Thus Anaximander shares the understanding that leads Hesiod to balance the being of Night with that of Day and, more generally, to structure the cosmos as a complex of counterbalancing opposites. Indeed, it is precisely because he agrees with Hesiod in letting his thought be guided by justice that Anaximander challenges Thales, rejecting the privileging of the wet over the dry. Second, this very agreement also leads Anaximander to challenge Hesiod—albeit, remarkably, in a way that Hesiod's portrayal of the birth of Chaos itself seems to invite. Just insofar as the differentiation that first begins to bring the world into being occurs as a "birth" (γένετ', *Th* 116), there would seem to need to be a parent. But what sort of being could precede the birth of Chaos and play this role? Insofar as it is only with this first differentiation, the gapping of Earth and Tartaros, that the world begins, this presupposed parent would seem to have to be an undifferentiated, indefinite, and—lacking any other to delimit it in place or time—boundless being. Thus Anaximander's conception of the *apeiron archē* in effect challenges Hesiod's beginning by making explicit the still more primal being that the birth of Chaos itself silently presupposes![10] Third, and as already noted, by giving his conception the strikingly transparent name *a-peiron*, Anaximander takes a decisive step beyond Hesiodic mythopoeia and toward the non-imagistic conceptual thinking that will eventually prevail, above all with Parmenides, in the emerging philosophic tradition; again, however, it is a step that, as the implicit conceptual order of Hesiod's cosmogony makes palpable, Hesiod's own thinking itself in effect invites.

Xenophanes and Hesiod on the Representation and Knowledge of the Divine

Xenophanes's reception of Hesiod is both indirect and critical. In our few surviving fragments, he mentions Hesiod only once, lumping him together with Homer (fr. 11.1)[11] and objecting to their attributing immoral conduct to the gods. But Hesiod is no less an implicit target in Xenophanes's critical remarks on anthropomorphism and the nature of the divine and in his declarations of the limits and source of human understanding. We shall consider each of these three concerns in turn.

Xenophanes's Moral-Political Qualms—and Hesiod's

Xenophanes claims a "wisdom" (σοφίη, 2.12) that contributes uniquely to the city's being "in good order" (ἐν εὐνομίη, 2.19) and prospering (2.22). On the basis of this "wisdom" he urges that humans "always show respect for the gods" and declares that there is nothing χρηστόν—morally right or (in Lesher's translation) "useful"—in portraying them in "battles" and "furious conflicts" such as the Titanomachy (1.21–24); similar concerns, presumably, lead him to object to "Homer['s] and Hesiod['s] attributing to the gods all the things which are matters of disgrace and censure among humans, thieving and adultery (μοιχεύειν) and deceiving one another" (11.1–3; also 12.2). Whereas the former portrayals might tempt the citizenry too easily to enter into foreign wars or even, recalling that the Titanomachy was a conflict between two generations of the same family, into internecine violence, the latter might be mistaken to legitimize violations of the proprieties of property and marriage and of the bond of trust that the unity of the city requires. Moral-political "wisdom" therefore proscribes portraying the gods as engaged in violent or immorally acquisitive comportment.

What is the bearing of this on Hesiod? First, Xenophanes's thought seems to key not from any idea of moral perfection but rather from a normative respect for what is properly another's—be this another's property or spouse or, indeed, city—and from an idea of the "good order" and prosperity that maintaining this respect enables for a community. This is strikingly Hesiodic. "Fools, all," Hesiod exclaims at *WD* 40, "who know not how much greater is the half than the whole!" Sticking to what is one's own, not trying to seize by force the "half" that is another's, but rather working on one's own land in "good strife" with one's neighbor, is the practice of the ethic of justice and work that will avoid the worst, each party's losing everything in "bad strife," and enable the best, peace and plenty for all. It is, then, a Hesiodic moral-political order that Xenophanes supports by striking from poetry and lore portrayals of the gods that fail to "show respect for [them]."

There are, of course, conspicuous cases in Hesiod's poems of various gods comporting themselves in the objectionable ways that Xenophanes decries. The "furious conflict" of the Titanomachy lies at the heart of the *Th*, and it is preceded by the tales of the violence and counter-violence of Sky and Kronos and followed by the tale of Zeus's battle against the monster Typhoeus. Attempted deception and theft are key moments in the extended tale, told once in the *Th* (521–616) and again in the *WD* (42–104), of Zeus's contest with Prometheus and the fashioning of Pandora. But a closer look at his representation of Zeus, in particular, shows that Hesiod is already guided by the moral-political scruples that motivate Xenophanes. First, the point of Zeus's violence against the Titans is to put an end to the very rule of violence that they stand for and replace it with the rule of justice; as we have already observed, Zeus's first acts after securing victory are to distribute power to the other Olympians, to beget his "equal in wise counsel and strength," and with Themis, to beget "Good Order, Justice, and Peace." Second, in the Pandora story it is not Zeus but Prometheus who is the primary thief and deceiver; Zeus's "deception" (*WD* 83) in ordering the fashioning of Pandora is a punishment that brings home the inescapability of a life of work.[12] Third, in the long catalog of Zeus's many fatherings at *Th* 886–944, there is no mention of the salacious comportment—the varieties of μοιχεύειν—attributed to him in so much of the lore that Hesiod inherited from archaic myth; especially the old tales of Zeus's beddings of Leto, Maia, Semele, and Alkmene provided rich material for portraying his variously opportunistic, shape-shifting, and exploitative philanderings, but in each case the poem forgoes this, restricting itself instead to naming the glorious offspring by which Zeus distributes his powers to later generations. Doesn't Hesiod in each of these ways morally sanitize his portrait of Zeus[13] along the lines—albeit not to the full extent—that Xenophanes later demands? Seen in this light, the notion of Xenophanes as a critic of "Homer and Hesiod" gives way to the notion of Xenophanes as extending what is already Hesiod's moral-political "wisdom" in portraying Zeus.

Xenophanes's Critique of Anthropomorphism and His Reconception of the God(s): Two Questions

Xenophanes reconceives the divine by reflections that are at once negative and positive. Exposing the tendency to project onto the gods our own ethnic looks ("snub-nosed and black," "blue-eyed and red-haired," 16.1–2), body types ("horses would draw the figures of the gods as similar to horses," etc., 15), powers ("voice," 14.2), and manners ("clothing," 14.2), he reimagines the divine as in the highest possible degree "not at all like mortals in body or in thought" (23.2). Hence he pictures the divine as having no distinct and localized organs of consciousness—rather, "all [of him] sees, all [of him] thinks, all [of him] hears" (24); he imagines the divine as "remain[ing] in the same [place], not moving at all"—for "it is not fitting for him to travel to different places at different times" (26.1–2); and, indeed, he regards the divine as having no need to move—for he is radically unlike mortals not only in his mind and in his body but also in the very relation between these: "completely without effort he shakes all things by the thought of his mind" (25).

Two sets of questions should confront any effort to interpret these declarations. The first is motivated by a seeming gap in Xenophanes's thought. Is the "showing [of] respect for the gods" that strips away morally objectionable acts compatible with the reconception of the divine that strips away anthropomorphic characters? That is, does the conception of the divine that is reached by setting aside every limiting character that critical reflection on anthropomorphic projection can discern—from particular looks and specific body type to the distinctions between faculties of consciousness and even between the powers of body and mind themselves—allow for or contradict the attribution to the divine of any distinctively moral characters of goodness and justice?

The second set of questions has motivated my use of the vague phrase, "the divine," in these last two paragraphs. Is Xenophanes a monotheist? To focus on the key fragment, 23, how should we hear the first two words, Εἷς θεὸς, as they lead into the rest of the first line, ἔν τε θεοῖσι καὶ ἀνθρώποισι μέγιστος? Is εἷς, "one," a predicate, yielding the line "god is one, greatest among both gods and humans," or is it attributive, yielding the line "one god is greatest among gods and humans"? If we take εἷς as a predicate and hear εἷς θεὸς as a declaration of monotheism, we immediately face another question: How should we understand the reference to "gods" in the very next phrase—and, multiplying the difficulty, in its appearance in at least seven other fragments: 1.24, 11.1, 14.1, 15.3, 16.1, 18.1, and

34.2? It is not implausible to hear the phrase "among both gods and humans" in 23.1 as typically Xenophanean provocative irony; as a *quasi*-Homeric and Hesiodic formula, it challenges his hearers to recognize the contrast with their anthropomorphic polytheism that Xenophanes's insight into the "greatness" of the divine, under his new conception, requires. But it is no less plausible to take the plural reference to "gods" in 23.1 and the other fragments to indicate that Xenophanes, even while he elevates his "one god" above all others, continues to affirm the reality of these others; in this view, Xenophanes is less a revolutionary who overthrows traditional polytheism than a revisionist who leaves in place the idea of a plurality of gods, whoever and however they may be, even while claiming an extraordinary primacy for his "one god."[14]

How we respond to these two sets of questions will have major implications for our understanding of Xenophanes's reception of Hesiod. If we take Xenophanes to have pushed his stripping away of anthropomorphic characters so far that he holds back from attributing not just vices but virtues as well to the divine, then we take him to abandon his own moral-political "wisdom," for such a divinity—whether one or many—would have no attributes qualifying it to serve as a source of moral-political order for human beings, much less as a moral paradigm; such a divinity would make no contribution to the establishment or maintenance of the "good order" of the city. And since, as we have argued, in his moral-political "wisdom" Xenophanes extends rather than opposes Hesiod's own, a Xenophanes whose anti-anthropomorphic theology undercuts his moral-political "wisdom" would undercut Hesiod's as well. On the other hand, turning to the second set of questions, if we take Xenophanes to be a polytheistic revisionist, then the path is open for taking his theology to remain consistent with his moral-political "wisdom" and with Hesiod's as well; a "one god" who is at once the "greatest" and yet remains situated "among both gods and men" would be an analog to Hesiod's Zeus in the exalted status Zeus achieves by his victories over the Titans and Typhoeus. And it would remain open to Xenophanes, limiting his project of de-anthropomorphization in favor of his less radical drive to purge our representations of the divine of any trace of violence or vice, to credit his "one god" with maximally virtuous relations to the other gods and to human beings; as a lordly figure comporting himself with goodness and justice, such a god would be, even if in other ways "not at all like mortals," a distillation of the essence of Hesiod's still anthropomorphic figure of the father of "Good Order, Justice, and Peace." A Xenophanes who took this course would be consistent both with his own moral-political "wisdom" and with Hesiod's.

Xenophanes—and Hesiod?—on the Limits and Means of Human Understanding

That we are reduced to outlining alternative possibilities may be the consequence of the fact that, as Aristotle famously complained, Xenophanes "made nothing clear" (*Metaphysics* 986b22–23). But Xenophanes himself might reply that it is rather a consequence of the fact that "the clear truth" ($\tau\grave{o}$ . . . $\sigma\alpha\varphi\acute{\epsilon}s$) is beyond the reach of human beings. In frs. 34 and 18, Xenophanes marks the limits and sources of human understanding:

> And the clear truth no human has seen, nor will there be anyone
> Who knows about the gods and about all the things of which I speak.
> For even if a person should happen to say most fully what is perfectly so,
> All the same he himself would not know it; for opinion ($\delta\acute{o}\kappa os$) is allotted to all.
>
> $(34.1–4)^{15}$

> By no means did the gods reveal all things to mortals from the beginning,
> But in time, by searching (or "examining," $\zeta\eta\tau o\hat{v}\nu\tau\epsilon s$), they discover better.
>
> (18.1–2)

As before, the bearing of these reflections on Hesiod is complex. On the one hand, Hesiod bases his claim to know about the gods on the "fact," as he sings in the proem to the *Th,* that the Muses visited him on Mt. Helicon and, "breath[ing] into me a divine voice, . . . commanded me to hymn the race of the blessed gods everlasting" (*Th* 31–33). If, as his shift from imperatives to the Muses in lines 104–15 to the indicative at line 116 implies we should, we take the *Th* from line 116 on as his channeling of the Muses' reply to his imperatives, then we will take Hesiod to be claiming that the *Th* is divinely in-spired and informed. Should we take Hesiod's report of the Muses' visit literally? If we do, then we make him a likely target of Xenophanes's denial in the opening clause of fr. 18: "By no means did the gods reveal all things to mortals from the beginning."

On the other hand, a variety of considerations should lead us to hesitate to take Hesiod's report at face value. West has identified six "conventional elements" in the proem, namely, that the "poet, prophet, or lawgiver who receives instructions" "on a mountain where the god lives" works there as a "shepherd" and that the god—that is, in our passage the Muses—first address him "in strongly derogatory terms," only then to give him "a visible token of [their] 'call'" and to "grant [him] eloquence."[16] That Hesiod assembles "conventional elements" in composing his song of the Muses is interpretively significant. It invites us to suspend the ascription of naiveté not only to Hesiod but also to at least some significant part of his projected audience and to wonder what different sorts of conscious activity—different, that is, than channeling the divine voices of the Muses—he was engaged in and, what is more, understood that his most sophisticated hearers would also know him to be engaged in. There is no reason to doubt that Hesiod intends his song of the Muses' visit, both in its content and in its spell-binding beauty, to constitute a claim to extraordinary insight. But the sophisticated poet and his most sophisticated hearers would recognize this insight as the result of the deliberate deploy-ment of his no less extraordinary, nonetheless *human* powers of critical and creative thought. And for those who understand Hesiod's poetry this way, Xenophanes's words are—surprisingly, on first hearing—not polemically dismissive but, quite the contrary, helpfully illuminating. For in a number of ways, Hesiod, like Xenophanes, appears to be "searching" (or "examining") the tradition he has inherited and "discover[ing] better."

Detailing all of these ways would require a full study of the *Th* and the *WD*; let it suffice here to note four. (1) *The Muses' alert at Th 27–28*. When Hesiod has the Muses declare that

> We know how to say many false things that seem like truths,
> But we also know how, when we wish, to proclaim truths,

he portrays them as at once acknowledging that they have spoken falsely to others in the past and challenging him to rise above his mundane consciousness in order to discern the truth in what they will now say. Xenophanes's words help us put this twofold point more directly: Hesiod acknowledges that he has arrived at the insight he will now utter at least in part by "examining" what others have claimed to have learned from the Muses, and he challenges his hearers, by sharing in the critical work of "examin[ing]" and "discover[ing]" that he has done, to see why what he will now claim really is "better." (2) *Finding genealogical and ethical order among the many gods*. In one massive respect that, nonetheless, is largely hidden from us, the whole of the *Th* is the result of such a "discovering better." Hesiod takes the vast aggregate of stories about the gods—stories that range from obscure and local to widely known and that tell of all manner of major and minor gods—and, selecting and reshaping them to fit within his alternating genealogical and epic narrative, integrates them within his overall account of Zeus's accession to power and establishment of justice. This extraordinary work of "examining" and "discovering better" is largely hidden, however, by its very success; whatever elements there may have been in the heterogeneous plurality of stories he inherited that resisted the requirements of his genealogical and ethical vision, he presumably revised or left out. (3) *Several such revisions and omissions, recalled*. We have just noted an extended set of such revisions and omissions. In the *Th* Hesiod treats Zeus's violence as his necessary means for replacing violence itself by the rule of justice, and in his genealogical account of Zeus's offspring Hesiod suppresses many of the details of abusive sexual aggression that we know from other sources; by "examining" the tales of Zeus that he inherited and by removing what would otherwise have presented themselves as signal inconsistencies, Hesiod clears the way for his subsequent celebration of Zeus in the *WD* as the ordainer of the ethic of justice and work for human beings. (4) *Selective de-anthropomorphizations of the representations of the gods*. We have also noted what we can now mark as a strikingly proto-Xenophanean way in which Hesiod "discovers" what is "better" than what he inherits: in order to establish the very terms needed for a genuine cosmogony, he has to partly de-anthropomorphize the figures of the great cosmic gods in *Th* 116–33. As he indicates in advance by his transition from "gods" to "earth" at *Th* 108, he shifts focus from the familiar personifications of the structures of nature to these structures themselves. Nor is this an isolated case. In at least four other sets of passages he undercuts anthropomorphism by giving as the names of gods nouns that call to mind not persons but impersonal qualities or principles: at *Th* 77–79 (to be heard against the background of 65–72), he distinguishes and names each of the nine Muses—hitherto an undifferentiated host—by picking out qualities of the experience of inspiration; at 211–25 he names as the children of Night a host of the mostly fearsome conditions that assail us as threats and worries in the darkness of night; at 226–32 he extends this doleful list by elaborating as the offspring of Discord many of its damaging consequences; and at 902, as already noted, he names as the children of Zeus and Themis "Good Order" and "Justice" and "Peace."[17]

Postscript: Heraclitus and Parmenides

If space allowed, I would extend these reflections to Heraclitus and Parmenides. As with Anaximander and Xenophanes, so here, the task of interpreting Heraclitus's and Parmenides's receptions of Hesiod is inseparable from the task of interpreting Heraclitus and Parmenides themselves. Following are some basic issues to explore.

Heraclitus and Hesiod

Unity. How much elicitative irony should we find in Heraclitus's anti-Hesiodic polemics? It is surprising enough to hear the poet who integrated cosmogony, theogony, and ethics derided as a "polymath" (40);[18] it is more than surprising to hear Heraclitus charge that Hesiod—whose unforgettable image of Night and Day exchanging a greeting as they pass each other at dawn and dusk at the edge of the underworld (*Th* 748–57) makes explicit that night's need for day, first expressed at *Th* 124–25, is reciprocal—"did not understand [that] night and day . . . are one" (57). On a straightforward reading, Heraclitus faults Hesiod for representing as separate individuals what are really phase and counterphase of a cyclical unity. But is there, in this apparent "differing" with Hesiod, a "hidden harmony" (51, 54)? Does Heraclitus seek to elicit from the hearer moved to come to Hesiod's defense the very recognition of the unity of opposites that he only ironically claims Hesiod misses?

Justice and strife. Does Heraclitus oppose the one-sidedness of Hesiod's vision of a divinely established order of "Good Order and Justice and Peace" (*Th* 902) by his tragic insight that "justice is strife" ($\delta\iota\kappa\eta\nu$ $\check{\epsilon}\rho\iota\nu$, 80) and that "war," not Zeus, "is the father . . . and the king of all" (53)? Or does $\delta\iota\kappa\eta\nu$ $\check{\epsilon}\rho\iota\nu$ mean, as well, that "strife is justice," and is the elision of "Zeus" meant to summon to mind, not banish, Hesiod's Zeus and the "Justice" he fathers as the redeeming significance of "war"? In an analogous way, does Heraclitus object to Hesiod's distinction between the two "strifes" (*WD* 11–26)—or does he, understanding their inextricability, credit Hesiod's recognition that the rule of justice is no less a mode of "strife" than is its violation?

The god. How does Heraclitus's "the god," in some sense the very unity of each pair of opposites (67, also 102), relate to Hesiod's theology? If Heraclitus takes a Xenophanean perspective in declaring that "the wise, one alone, is unwilling . . . to be called by the name of Zeus," does he at the same time counter and integrate this with a Hesiodic perspective when, seemingly contradicting himself, he also declares that "the wise . . . is willing" to be so called (32)? But why would "the wise" be "willing"? Does Heraclitus, imitating the enigmatic voice of "the lord whose oracle is at Delphi" (93), provoke us to find in "the name of Zeus"—that is, of the warrior for justice that Hesiod has portrayed Zeus to be—a "sign" (93) of that unity of opposites that, also signified by the Zeusian "thunderbolt," "steers all things" (64)?

Parmenides and Hesiod

What "is." For Parmenides's reception of Hesiod, inquiry should focus on Parmenides's appropriation of *Th* 748–57 in his image of "the gates of the ways of Night and Day" (1.11). In his proem, to reach the goddess who teaches the thought of what "is" (. . . ἔστιν, 2.3, 8.3), the traveler must arrive at and then pass through these gates; thus Parmenides grants to the insight symbolized by arriving at the gateway of opposites the status of a necessary but insufficient stage of understanding. This raises a nexus of compelling questions. Restricting ourselves first to Parmenides, what is the insight symbolized by the arrival at the gateway, and what is the process of thinking by which, upon reaching this insight, the traveler finds himself able to pass beyond it to the goddess? Second, turning to Parmenides's relation to Hesiod, does Parmenides mean to mark the limit of Hesiodic thinking and to claim to have gone beyond it—or does he, either alternatively or in addition, mean to imply that the possibility of passing beyond the gateway and on to the discovery of the thought of what "is" is already to be found, if only implicitly and without the goddess's new language, in Hesiod?[19]

Notes

1. Due to limits of space I have deferred discussion of Heraclitus and Parmenides. See the postscript for an anticipation.
2. I strongly second Clay's remark that "[it] is past time . . . to discard the antiquated notion of Hesiod's primitive simplicity and to accept the possibility that he may be fully aware of the implications of his own words" (2003: 59).
3. These characterizations of Anaximander's τὸ ἄπειρον are first reported by Aristotle and Theophrastus; see Kirk et al. (1983: 106ff., 115).
4. My translation, with help from Lattimore (1959); Athanassakis (2004); Most (2006); and the editors of this volume.
5. We face a textual uncertainty in lines 118 and 119. Both are disputed, and the stakes are high. If, following Plato at *Symposium* 178b, we excise both lines, there are only three, not four, primordial beings; Tartaros drops out. Moreover, there is a dissenting construal of the grammar that has the same consequence. On the widely accepted reading by West (1966), Τάρταρα is a nominative plural and takes the same verb γενετ' (116) that Chaos,

then Earth (117), and then Eros (120), also take; these four are the primordial beings in Hesiod's cosmogony. On the dissenting construal, recently defended by Most (2004: 175–80), τάρταρα at line 119 is an accusative and, paired with κάρη νιφόεντος Ὀλύμπου, forms a compound object of ἔχουσι at 118; hence Tartaros and the "peaks of Olympos" play the secondary role of being parts of Earth, and Tartaros is not one of the primordial powers—nor, I would note, does it have its own distinct birth. I follow West's judgment that "118 is a formula complete in itself, and unlikely to be continued [into 119]" (1966: 194). In addition, Hesiod's later characterization of Tartaros as dark, moldy, ceaselessly stormy, and hateful to the gods (739) makes it problematic to think of it as forming a part of a "firm seat forever for all the immortals." Most important, the pairing of Tartaros with Earth as the two equi-primordial "sides" of the gap formed by the birth of Chaos plays a crucial role in the order that Hesiod discerns in the cosmos at 116–33; that 119 be read to grant this status to Tartaros is essential to the balance and coherence to which every other cosmic birth in 116–33 contributes. (Thanks to Rachel Kitzinger for discussion of these issues.)

6. West (1966: 190) comments that the phrase θεοὶ καὶ γαῖα—"gods and earth"—in line 108 is "a little surprising, since Earth and the things that follow are themselves divine. To Hesiod's audience θεοί would suggest primarily the non-cosmic gods." The force of the "and," in other words, is to indicate that the terms that follow—"earth," "rivers," "boundless sea," "shining stars," "wide sky"—are to be thought of *not* in the manner of the characterizations in lines 105–7, that is, as the anthropomorphized "non-cosmic gods," but rather as structures and features of the cosmos.

7. To state explicitly what I hope is already clear, Hesiod's shift of focus from anthropomorphic person figures to what they represent introduces and is restricted to the cosmogony (116–33). That he reverts to a full personification of Earth and Sky in the rest of the poem makes his shift away from it in the cosmogony all the more conspicuous and, as an achievement in thinking, impressive.

8. For a more detailed exegesis of *Th* 116–33 together with a focused refutation of the once standard interpretation, offered by Cornford (1950), that the birth of Chaos is the splitting of Earth and Sky, see Miller (2001).

9. This complex act has a Heraclitean paradoxicality. In short, for Zeus to swallow Metis seems to represent the extreme form of the injustice of Sky and of Kronos; whereas Sky keeps all power for himself by pushing his children back into mother Earth's womb and Kronos one-ups this violence by swallowing his children, Zeus now seems to one-up Kronos by swallowing the mother before the child is born. But the upshot of his act points to a contrary significance: Zeus, who now has Metis within him to "counsel him about good and evil" (*Th* 900), gives birth to his "equal"—that is, rather than foolishly and violently hoarding all power for himself, he wisely and morally shares it.

10. Surprisingly, this may not be the last word. Two passages, Th 726–28 and 736–39, provide evidence that Hesiod himself both identified this primordial being as Tartaros and deliberately held back from giving it pride of place, subordinating it, instead, to Chaos. Could it be that Hesiod *in effect* anticipated and, well in advance, objected to Anaximander's granting τὸ ἄπειρον the status of ἀρχή? For interpretive discussion, see Miller (2001).

11. The numbers are those in Lesher (1992), following Diels-Kranz (1951).

12. What, however, of the "deception" Zeus employs in swallowing Metis (*Th* 889–90)? See note 9.

13. Scully (2015: 43–45, 47–48).

14. Cf. Lesher (1992: 98–100).
15. I follow Lesher's translation of the final clause.
16. West (1966: 159–60), citing Dornseiff (1959: 37–38, 76); Trencsényi-Waldapfel (1955: 45–76).
17. For Hesiod's naming of the Muses and the offspring of Discord, see Scully in this volume, pp. 86–88.
18. Fragment numbers for Heraclitus and Parmenides are those in Diels-Kranz (1951).
19. For discussion, see Miller (2006).

REFERENCES

Athanassakis, A., ed. and trans. 2004. *Hesiod: Theogony, Works and Days, Shield*. 2nd ed. Baltimore, MD.

Clay, J. S. 2003. *Hesiod's Cosmos*. Cambridge.

Cornford, F. M. 1950. "A Ritual Basis for Hesiod's *Theogony*." In *The Unwritten Philosophy and Other Essays*, edited by F. M. Cornford, 95–116. Cambridge.

Diels, H., and W. Kranz, eds. and comms. 1951. *Die Fragmente der Vorsokratiker*. 6th ed. 3 vols. Berlin.

Dornseiff, F. 1959. *Antike und Alter Orient*. 2nd ed. Leipzig, Germany.

Gallop, D., ed. and trans. 1984. *Parmenides of Elea: Fragments, A Text and Translation*. Toronto.

Graham, D. 2006. *Explaining the Cosmos: The Ionian Tradition of Scientific Philosophy*. Princeton, NJ.

Hyland, D. 2006. "First of All Came Chaos." In *Heidegger and the Greeks: Interpretive Essays*, edited by D. Hyland and J. Panteleimon, 9–22. Bloomington, IN.

Kahn, C. 1960. *Anaximander and the Origins of Greek Cosmology*. New York.

Kahn, C., ed., comm., and trans. 1979. *The Art and Thought of Heraclitus*. Cambridge.

Kirk, G. S., J. E. Raven, and M. Schofield, trans. and comms. 1983. *The Presocratic Philosophers*. 2nd ed. Cambridge.

Lattimore, R., trans. 1959. *Hesiod, The Works and Days, Theogony, The Shield of Herakles*. Ann Arbor, MI.

Lesher, J., ed., trans., and comm. 1992. *Xenophanes of Colophon: Fragments, A Text and Translation*. Toronto.

Miller, M. 2001. "'First of all': On the Semantics and Ethics of Hesiod's Cosmogony." *Ancient Philosophy* 21: 251–76.

Miller, M. 2006. "Ambiguity and Transport: Reflections on the Proem to Parmenides' Poem." *Oxford Studies in Ancient Philosophy* 30 (Summer): 1–47.

Most, G. W. 2004. "Two Notes on Hesiod's Theogony (116–22, 426–39)." In *Studia Humanitatis ac Litterarum Trifolio Heidelbergensi dedicate: Festschrift für Eckhard Christmann, Wilfried Edelmaier und Rudolf Ketteman*, edited by A. Hornung, C. Jaekel, and W. Schubert, 175–80. Frankfurt am Main, Germany.

Most, G. W., ed. and trans. 2006. *Hesiod I: Theogony, Works and Days, Testimonia*. Cambridge, MA.

Mourelatos, A. P. D. 2008. *The Route of Parmenides*. Las Vegas, NV.

Palmer, J. 2009. *Parmenides and Presocratic Philosophy*. Oxford.

Scully, S. 2015. *Hesiod's Theogony: From Near Eastern Creation Myths to Paradise Lost*. Oxford.

Trencsényi-Waldapfel, I. 1955. "Die orientalsche Verwandschaft des Prooimions der Hesiodischen Theogonia." *Acta Orientalia Academiae Scientiarum Hungaricae* 5: 45–76.

West, M. L., ed. and comm. 1966. *Hesiod: Theogony*. Oxford.

West, M. L., ed. and comm. 1978. *Hesiod: Works and Days*. Oxford.

....

CHAPTER 15

DEVIANT ORIGINS: HESIOD'S *THEOGONY* AND THE ORPHICA

....

RADCLIFFE G. EDMONDS III

> For all the accounts written among the Greeks about the ancient origins, although there are many others, two have pride of place, Orpheus and Hesiod.
>
> (Rufinus, *Recognitions* X.30)

WHEN the Christian apologist Rufinus looks back at the tradition of Greek cosmogonies and identifies Hesiod and Orpheus as the two most important figures to attack, he enters into the long-standing competition for authority in matters cosmological between these rival figures. Hesiod's *Theogony* (hereafter *Th*) provides one of the oldest, best known, and most widely authoritative accounts of the origin of the cosmos, but for that very reason his account has always been challenged by rivals claiming to be older, wiser, and better. While we know of cosmogonies by Epimenides, Pherekydes, and Akousilaos, the name of Orpheus has always been privileged in the evidence for ancient rivals to Hesiod.

The name of Orpheus, however, is simply a label attached to a text by someone hoping to add the authority of that most ancient of mythical poets, the name-famed hero, Orpheus, to his own account of the cosmos and its origins (cf. Edmonds 2013: esp. 3–88). Such Orphicists started forging poems in Orpheus's name in the archaic period and continued through late antiquity, borrowing verses from older poems to validate the authenticity and antiquity of their innovations. The legitimacy of such claims was doubted from early on, however, and Herodotus directly denies that any authors provided theogonies earlier than Homer and Hesiod (Herodotus 2.53). Orpheus is the foremost of these supposedly earlier poets whose accounts claim priority over Hesiod in setting out the origin of the gods, their names and forms, and the hierarchy of honor and power that exists among them in the order of the cosmos.

THE PROBLEM OF EVIDENCE

Modern scholars have a strong basis for their study of Hesiod's *Th*, since the text of Hesiod was well known and commented upon in antiquity, but the evidence for Orphic accounts of the origin of the cosmos and the gods is far more problematic, since no actual texts survive. We have only a collection of scattered fragments that must be untangled from the agendas of the authors who quote them, bits that are hard to assign to any particular era or even text. M. L. West (1983) ventures a virtuosic reconstruction of the evidence in *The Orphic Poems*, but his manuscript stemma model is too reductionistic to capture the complexity and fluidity of the hubbub of books composed under the name of Orpheus over the centuries. Later Orphicists borrowed verses from earlier Orphic poems to authenticate their new creations, and the compilers of the accounts were not always as sensitive as modern scholars like West to inconsistencies and contradictions within their accounts (cf. Betegh 2004: 151–52).

One of the most important sources for understanding the Orphic theogonies is the summary in the treatise on first principles by the fifth-century CE Neoplatonist Damascius (*de principiis* 123–24 = i.316–19 Ruelle), who refers to accounts he found in two earlier sources, the fourth-century BCE Peripatetic philosophers Eudemos and Hieronymos, as well as to the "usual" Orphic theogony of his day, found in the Orphic *Rhapsodies* (on Hieronymos, see Edmonds 2013: 18–20; Edmonds forthcoming). Damascius, however, fits all the accounts he discusses into a series of Neoplatonic ontological triads, even assuming that one element of the triad must have been present but "passed over in silence" if it was not explicitly mentioned. Similar caution must be taken in making use of Damascius's quotations from the Orphic *Rhapsodies*, which, along with those of his predecessor Proclus and his successor Olympiodorus, make up over 80 percent of the extant fragments of Orphic poetry. Damascius's Peripatetic sources, however, seem to derive their classifications of accounts of origin ultimately from the work of fifth-century BCE sophists such as Hippias (and perhaps Hellanikos), so the late Neoplatonist does preserve valuable evidence from a full millennium earlier.

The earliest quotations of Orphic poems appear in Plato, but the discovery of the fourth-century BCE Derveni papyrus provides quotations from an Orphic poem that must have been circulating even earlier. This papyrus, miraculously preserved on a Thessalian funeral pyre, preserves a text in which the author makes allegorical interpretations of a poem by Orpheus that narrates Zeus's rise to the sovereignty of the cosmos by subsuming all the earlier entities within himself. The text is full of gaps, often at the most tantalizing points, but the quotations from the Orphic poem nevertheless help fill in the fragmentary accounts of the Neoplatonists.

The most complete accounts of Orphic theogonies appear in early Christian apologists, such as the second-century CE Athenagoras or the texts under the name of Clement, preserved in the Greek *Homilies* and Rufinus's Latin version of the *Recognitions*, both of which probably date to the end of the fourth century CE. These sources provide more complete and coherent narratives than other sources, but since they were assembled to attack the perverse and shocking pagan theology of which Orpheus is the chief representative, they too must be treated with caution.

ORPHIC VARIATIONS ON A HESIODIC THEME

The fragments of other Orphic accounts, however, ranging from the Derveni papyrus to the *Rhapsodies*, make clear that shocking details and bizarre narratives were characteristic of the Orphic cosmogonies from the beginning. Advocates for the authority of Orpheus, from the Derveni Commentator to Proclus, all insist that the apparently scandalous elements indicate the profound wisdom concealed beneath the surface of the text—the most ancient wisdom of Orpheus that just so happens to coincide with their own philosophical and cosmological tenets. The creators of Orphic poems in every era include such deviant elements, creating strikingly memorable variations upon the traditional story of Hesiod to serve as markers of the special authority of their accounts.

Whether they express their ideas in theogonic myth or philosophical prose, Greek cosmological thinkers, as Cornford (1912: 71) points out, are all trying to resolve some common basic problems: "(1) the primary *physis*, (2) the disposition or structure into which this living stuff is distributed, (3) the process by which the order arose." The Orphic accounts play their variations on the Hesiodic themes at each of these points, riffing in different ways on the idea of (1) the ultimate origin of the cosmos; (2a) the processes of reproduction by which subsequent entities were generated; (2b) the conflicts between these divinities that created the changes from the original state to the current one; (2c) the way in which humans entered the story; and (3) the final resolution of the conflicts and changes that created the current, normal order of Zeus. The shocking innovations they introduce in the images of the theogonic narrative serve as rhetorical devices to bolster the authority of their often less shockingly innovative cosmological ideas. The Orphic poems tend to follow the pattern of Hesiod's cosmology, rather than creating radically different structures, and the variations they introduce in the ideas of how the cosmos came to be are often less striking than the mythic images with which they express them.

FIRST PRINCIPLES: THE ULTIMATE
ORIGIN OF THE COSMOS

Hesiod's Chaotic Beginning

In the beginning, for Hesiod, was Chaos, the yawning chasm that provides the open space for the cosmos to come into existence. Out of this gap arise the solid Earth and the airy Tartara, as well as the principles of darkness, Night and Erebos. Out of Chaos comes also one of the principles of cosmic formation, Eros. For Hesiod, then, the first beginning of the cosmos is the opening up of space in which the solid earth can appear, but this beginning takes place in darkness, without any light, and even the appearance of Tartara/Tartaros is defined as a space within the solid earth, rather than some other form of substance itself.

The absence of other elements among the primary principles in Hesiod's account worried later thinkers accustomed to seeing the cosmos begin with something less solid than Earth, and Plutarch, in his essay on the primacy of fire or water, attests to a long-standing interpretation of Hesiod's Chaos as water. "It seems to most people that he named water in this fashion [as Chaos] because of its flowing (*chysis*)" (*Aquane* 955e). Hesiod was thus grouped with Homer among those who put water first, since the line from the *Iliad* (14.201) that names Okeanos and Tethys as the origin of all the gods was interpreted to indicate a Homeric cosmogony beginning with these water principles. This grouping, as Betegh (2002) has shown, probably goes back as far as the work of the fifth-century BCE sophist Hippias, who collected and distilled the wisdom of the poets (starting with Orpheus, Musaeus, Hesiod, and Homer), but Damascius, a millennium later, nevertheless rightly categorizes Hesiod's starting principles as the indeterminate space of Chaos followed by the Earth.

Obscure Beginnings in the Orphica

While there are traces of some Orphic cosmogonies that begin with Chaos, the starting point of all creation becomes a major point of variation within the cosmogonic accounts that circulate under the name of Orpheus. Different accounts begin with water, with Night, with Chronos (Time), or even by stacking various of these primary principles in sequence. The variation of the starting point serves as a way to assert the authority and originality of the Orphic account over the traditional Hesiodic one.

The earliest Orphic cosmogonies for which evidence exists seem to start with Night; indeed, the only thing Damascius relates about the Orphic cosmogony catalogued by the fourth-century BCE Peripatetic Eudemos is that it begins with Night. Aristotle (*Metaphysics* 12.1071b) refers to the cosmologists who say everything begins from Night, and this same first principle seems to appear in the Orphic cosmogony in the Derveni papyrus (cf. Aristophanes's *Birds* 693–703). In col. 14.6, the first ruler of the cosmos is Ouranos, the first-born (Protogonos) son of Night, and his matronymic epithet, Euphronides, suggests that Night (euphemistically referred to as "Euphron," the benef-icently minded) has no male consort with whom she produces Ouranos. In this way, this first entity in the Orphic text resembles the first entity in the Hesiodic story, Gaia the Earth, who produces Ouranos by herself in the first generation. Like the Hesiodic Gaia, the Derveni Night does not rule the cosmos herself but remains around to provide help and counsel to the later generations. Just as Gaia assists both Kronos and Zeus to wrest control of the cosmos from their respective fathers, so too does Night provide the oracular advice that enables Zeus to take control of the entire cosmos in the Derveni Orphic theogony.

By contrast, Alexander of Aphrodisias, commenting on Aristotle's *Metaphysics*, claims that Orpheus begins with Chaos (*in Ar. Met.* 1091b, p. 321), and the cosmogonies ascribed to Orpheus in the *Homilies* and the *Recognitions* attributed to Clement (perhaps third century CE) also begin with Chaos just as Hesiod does, saving their variations for later stages of development. The Clementine Chaos seems to flow and swirl like the watery Chaos Plutarch describes, and the speaker, Appion, even adduces the authority of Homer (*Iliad* 7.99) to argue that the elements this primordial Chaos comprises are earth and water ([Clement] *Homilies* 6.3–4; cf. Rufinus *Recognitions* 10.17.2–4).

Other Orphic cosmogonies do begin explicitly with water, shifting both Chaos and Night to later generations. The second-century CE Christian apologist Athenagoras recounts an Orphic cosmogony in which water swirling with other "stuff" (either *hilus*, mud, or *hylê*, matter) is the first principle. Athenagoras quotes Orpheus as referring to "Okeanos, who indeed arose as the origin of all things" and describes water as the first principle (*archê*) of all things, out of which mud/matter was established (*pro Christianis* 18.4). This Orphic cosmogony resembles the one that Damascius attributes to Hieronymos (and Hellanikos), which likewise starts with water and matter (or mud), out of which comes Earth. No trace of Okeanos remains in Damascius's account, however, whereas Athenagoras claims that Homer follows Orpheus in making Okeanos the origin of the gods (citing the familiar line from *Iliad* 14.201). The demythologized elements of water and mud in both accounts suggests the intervention of an allegorical interpretation that reduced Okeanos (or Chaos?) to water and Gaia to the muddy earth that coagulates from it; it remains uncertain where this allegorical interpretation crept in—in the sophistic or Peripatetic cataloging or in the Orphic text itself. In any case, in both Athenagoras and Damascius's Hieronymos, the primordial water and earth produce another primary entity, Chronos or Time, which itself produces both Chaos and the cosmic egg.

The Orphic account that seems to have been put together the latest comes from the Orphic *Rhapsodies*, most likely stitched together in the first or second century CE from older pieces of Orphic poetry. The *Rhapsodic* account, which Damascius refers to as "the usual" Orphic account, is actually less complicated than the accounts in Athenagoras and Hieronymos. The first stage of water is not present; the first principle is Chronos, unaging Time. As in Athenagoras's account, Chronos generates Chaos and the cosmic egg, from which is born Phanes. In the *Rhapsodies*, Phanes first generates and then mates with Night to produce the succeeding generations of divine beings.

This multiplication of primary entities in both the Rhapsodic account and the accounts in Athenagoras and Hieronymos suggests an attempt to produce a cosmogony even more fundamental and authoritative than rival versions. Hesiod may think that Chaos and Earth come first, but Orpheus knows what came before these, the limitless span of Time and the egg from which both Heaven and Earth will be generated. The accounts in Athenagoras and Hieronymos take this a step further. Others (such as Pherekydes of Syros, the Persian Magoi, and the Sidonians, all mentioned in Damascius's summary of Eudemos) may think that Time was the first principle, but Orpheus knows even how

Time itself was first generated. The choice of the ultimate first principle as water, however, suggests an attempt to conform with the mass of other authoritative cosmogonies, from Homer to Thales, that put water first. All these Orphic accounts deviate from Hesiod's starting point, providing an account that goes further back to Time or that places a watery flux at the origin instead of solid Earth manifesting in the yawning gap of Chaos.

THE GENESIS OF THE COSMOS: REPRODUCTION

After Earth emerges from Chaos, much must still come into being if the world is to resemble the familiar current world of humans, and these processes of generation and change may be divided into processes of (a) (re)production, (b) conflict and conquest, and (c) the creation of humans (cf. Plato, *Sophist* 242cd). The first generates new divine entities in the cosmos, while the second creates changes in the power structure. The final stage produces mortal human beings, but Hesiod notoriously elaborates less on this phase than on the first two, providing only an allusion in the *Th* and the myth of the five successive races of mortals in the *Works and Days* (hereafter *WD*). For Hesiod, the focus in the *Th* is upon the succession of the generations of the gods, the power struggle that culminates in the reign of Zeus.

Reproductive Processes: Hesiod's Genealogies

Although Eros is among the primal forces of the cosmos, the first reproductions in Hesiod's genealogy are asexual; Earth generates first Heaven (Ouranos) and then Sea (Pontos) "without delightful love," and Chaos brings forth Erebos and Night, the powers of darkness (116–23). Since Eros is present from the first, however, sexual reproduction does begin quickly, as Night, mingling in love with her brother Erebos, produces Day and Aither, the bright shining air, while Earth takes her sons, Pontos and Ouranos, as mates (124–36). Sexual reproduction then becomes the norm for the generation of new divine entities, although it is worth noting that Night produces a brood of offspring on her own, and her daughter, Strife (Eris), likewise generates a set of personified troubles, presumably simply as a consequence of her nature. The asexual reproduction brings about these abstract horrors—Toil, Murders, Quarrels, Lies, etc.—entities that have no real personality or character (211–32).

The other lines of genealogy proceed through sexual reproduction, the children of Pontos and the children of Ouranos. The children of Ouranos who themselves reproduce, the Titans, do so through orderly brother-sister marriages, while the children of the sea form a family marked by intergenerational pairings and monstrous births (cf. Clay 2003: 151–61). The pattern of generation in the dominant forces of the cosmos moves swiftly toward the familiar mode of sexual reproduction and even, insofar as it is possible for a limited family of gods, toward exogamy, since intergenerational incest ceases in the line of Ouranos after the first generation of Earth and Heaven, and in the following generation, only Zeus mates with his sisters. The more closely the pattern of sexual reproduction resembles the current human practices, the closer the cosmos draws to the normal, current order of things.

Reproductive Processes: Orphic Perversions

In the Orphica the pattern of reproduction remains more abnormal; there are both more variations of asexual reproduction and more perverse sexual couplings throughout the entirety of the account. Intergenerational incest continues even to the generation of Zeus, and the couplings are often explicitly violent rapes, rather than the epic "mingling in love." In the earlier stages of the cosmogony, different types of asexual generation abound, from the coagulation of solid matter out of the primordial chaos of waters to the famous cosmic egg.

The Orphic account Damascius gets from Hieronymos (and Hellanikos), like that recounted by Athenagoras, makes the first generation a coagulation of matter out of the primordial maelstrom, and that matter then forms into the monstrous triformed being called by various names, Kronos or Chronos and Herakles. This dragon with the heads of a lion, a bull, and a man then produces an egg without sexual reproduction (cf. Edmonds 2013: 164–68). The Clementine Orphic cosmogonies have the egg generated directly from the primordial maelstrom, forming like a bubble in the swirling waters rather than being laid by a monstrous dragon, while the *Rhapsodies* seem to have Chronos (unaging Time, perhaps in serpentine or draconic form) produce the egg, possibly by forming it from the aither.

Out of this egg hatches an entity, called variously Eros, Metis, Erikepaios, and other names, whose epithet Phanes marks the idea that it is the first to appear (*phainein*), while the epithet Protogonos marks it as the first born.[1] In the *Rhapsodies*, as in the versions known to Hieronymos, Athenagoras, and the Clementine authors, this being is bisexual or hermaphroditic, with both male and female genitalia, which it uses to copulate with itself and produce offspring, a mode of reproduction that is neither entirely asexual nor yet quite normal sexual reproduction. In the *Rhapsodies*, Phanes does progress to sexual intercourse with Night, however, and this coupling, whether it is incest with his mother or his daughter, seems to produce Ouranos and Gaia, the Heaven and Earth that become the progenitors of the later divinities. Athenagoras, by contrast, has Chronos/Herakles coil around the egg and break it into separate pieces that become Earth and Heaven, an account that resembles the Clementine versions, in which the portions of the egg settle into three realms of earth (Pluto), sea (Poseidon), and sky (Zeus), after Phanes hatches from it. This production of material elements resembles the first principles of water and matter with which these cosmogonies begin, rather than the personified entities of Time and Night that appear in the other Orphic accounts.

Sexual reproduction continues in the later generations of all the accounts, with Ouranos and Gaia producing the Titans as well as the Cyclops and the Hundred-Handers, as in Hesiod. Presumably the Titans engage in their familiar pairings as well, but it is the sexual activities of Zeus that draw focus in the Orphic accounts, especially from the Christian commentators who recount the shocking perversions in painstaking detail. Phanes may have "robbed his own daughter of the flower of her maidenhood" (*Orphicorum Fragmenta* 148B = 98K), but Zeus rapes not only his daughter, but his sister and his mother as well. Athenagoras recounts the horrible tale:

> how he pursued his mother Rhea when she was refusing to wed him, and, when she became a she-dragon, he himself changing into a dragon, bound her up with what is called the Heraklean knot, and had intercourse with her (the rod of Hermes is a symbol of the form of this intercourse); and again, how he had intercourse with his daughter Persephone, also violating her in the form of a dragon, and from her the child Dionysus was born to him. (Athenagoras *pro Christianis* 20.3; cf. Clement *Protrepticus* 2.15)

The violence of these incestuous rapes is emphasized, as it is in his assault upon his sister, Demeter, of whom the Derveni Commentator says (Derveni papyrus col. 22.13) she is called Deio because she was torn (*edêiôthê*) in the violent sexual intercourse.

The presence of such motifs in the earliest Orphic account, the Derveni papyrus, shows that sexual violence and perversions are by no means a later variation, but a recurrent theme in Orphic cosmogonies. The Christian apologists are merely echoing the critiques of earlier Greek thinkers who see the Orphica as marked by such perversions; such strangeness often characterizes things labeled as Orphic, a sign that the Orphic material cannot be taken literally but conceals hidden wisdom beneath its surface appearance that must be read allegorically.[2] Indeed, the Derveni Commentator makes this point explicitly: "His poetry is strange and riddling for people. But Orpheus did not intend to tell captious riddles but momentous things in riddles."[3] The Orphic theogonies proliferate the strange modes of reproduction beyond the levels in the Hesiodic account to advertise the profundity they want to claim lies beneath the peculiar surface. While the Hesiodic narrative progresses from asexual reproduction to sexual relations within and then outside the family, the Orphic accounts multiply the levels of asexual reproduction and extend the perverse sexual relations beyond the first generations into the activities of Zeus himself.

THE GENESIS OF THE COSMOS: CONFLICT AND CONQUEST

War in Heaven: Hesiod's Succession Myths

Although Hesiod's *Th* focuses on the births of gods, the conflicts between them play an even more important role in the story of how the current world order came to be. The myth of the succession of the kingship of heaven forms the "backbone," as West calls it, of the *Th* (1966: 31). The offspring of Ouranos, led by Kronos, overthrow their father on the advice of their mother, Earth, leading to the permanent separation of Earth and Heaven through the castration of Ouranos. Kronos is in turn overthrown by his son Zeus, again with the assistance of the female powers of Rhea and Gaia, who conspire to save the infant Zeus from the attempts of his father to secure his own throne against any future claimants (cf. Arthur 1982). In order to secure his own power, Zeus must then engage in conflicts both with the previous generation in power, the Titans led by Kronos, and with new claimants who arise to challenge him.

Hesiod describes the Titanomachy in detail (*Th* 617–735), and he dwells on the challenge that Typhoeus brings to the new reign of Zeus (*Th* 820–80), but he only barely alludes to the other great challenge to Zeus's reign that appears in other mythological sources, the Gigantomachy. The earth-born Giants (*gêgeneis, gigantes*) spring up when the blood from the castrated Ouranos sprinkles the Earth (*Th* 183–85), and they are mentioned along with the race of men in the Muses' prologue (*Th* 50), but their great uprising against the power of Zeus is not mentioned, unless the reference to Herakles's "great labor" (*Th* 954) refers to his crucial aid to the gods in the Gigantomachy. The Titanomachy begins by Zeus tricking Kronos, with the aid of Earth, into vomiting back up the children he swallowed (*Th* 624–28), but Zeus's force and the power of his lightning provide the end to the Titanomachy, and the same power is on display in the Typhonomachy, when the lightning of Zeus destroys the last child that the Earth produces to try to topple his power. Hesiod does not mention any other children of Earth, such as the famous Gigantes, whom Earth sent against Zeus, nor is there any hint of Zeus using cunning against Typhoeus, as appears in other versions of the tale (cf. Apollodorus 1.6.1–3; Nonnus 1.481). In recounting the conflicts of the gods that shape the cosmos, Hesiod focuses on the injustices of Ouranos and Kronos that lead to their downfall and on the way Zeus recruits his allies and promises to establish a just division of the honors and authority in the cosmos.

War in Heaven: Orphic Variations

The accounts of the Orphic theogonies preserve fewer details of the ongoing conflicts that lead to the shifts of authority in the cosmos, but the same basic story of Kronos overthrowing Ouranos, to be overthrown in turn by Zeus who then establishes his rule against further uprisings, seems to occur in them all. Characteristically, however, the most shocking elements of the story in Hesiod are multiplied or elaborated in the Orphic sources; Zeus's binding of Kronos is told in more detail, and Kronos's castration of his father may be doubled in some accounts by Zeus castrating Kronos. Both the Titanomachy and the Gigantomachy appear in Orphic accounts, with the familiar slippage between the two that appears in the evidence for these battles outside the Orphica, but the Typhonomachy, the ultimate battle in the Hesiodic account, seems absent.

Athenagoras recounts (*pro Christianis* 18) that Ouranos learned (probably from the oracle of Night) that his children would overthrow him, so he imprisoned them in Tartarus; the Orphic account thus provides a motive for Ouranos's repression of his offspring, which seems in Hesiod almost an unintended consequence of Ouranos's unceasing desire to mate with Gaia. The Titans are conceived to avenge the imprisonment of their siblings, and Kronos not only castrates Ouranos but hurls him out of his seat in the sky; as in Hesiod, his bleeding genitalia generate Giants and Aphrodite in earth and sea. Kronos then proceeds to swallow his children, as in Hesiod, to prevent his own overthrow.

Whereas in Hesiod Zeus receives advice from Gaia about a drug that will make Kronos vomit back up the gods he has swallowed, in the Orphic accounts Zeus seems to receive oracular advice from Night.[4] Night advises him to ambush and bind Kronos, "when you see him beneath the high-topped oaks drunk with the works of loud-buzzing bees."[5] Taking vengeance one shocking step further than in Hesiod, Zeus castrates Kronos in his turn, so that the cutter is himself cut, and then imprisons him in Tartaros.[6]

The absence of coherent and continuous narratives in the Orphic accounts makes it difficult to determine how the story proceeded from this point, but there are sufficient allusions to Orphic accounts of a Titanomachy and Gigantomachy to conclude that at least some Orphic poems narrated these events, even if there were not continuous narratives that went from the first principles through to the end in the manner of Hesiod. Of the Typhonomachy, however, there is no real trace in the Orphica, even if various combats involving serpentine figures appear at earlier points in the narrative; the final conflict that is so important in Hesiod as the last attempt of the Earth to topple the ruler of the cosmos has no place in cosmogonies in which Earth's fundamental role is replaced by Night or some other power.[7]

Athenagoras (*pro Christianis* 20) mentions in passing that Zeus fought with the Titans for hegemony, but he has abandoned the continuous narrative by this point and is merely recounting a string of horrible things attributed to the Greek gods by Orpheus. The battles of Zeus and the Olympians as related in Hesiod seem hard to reconcile to the culminating event that appears in several of the Orphic accounts (Zeus's swallowing of Protogonos and giving birth again to the entire cosmos), yet references to Orpheus's tales of battles against the Titans and the Giants suggest that such inconsistent accounts appeared as separate tales that were probably later assembled as different parts of the *Rhapsodies* (cf. Edmonds 2013: 144–59). The similar tales of the Titanomachy and Gigantomachy were conflated and confused in many sources, and it is often difficult to tell which rebellion a particular fragment of Orphic poetry may be describing, but the proem to the *Orphic Argonautica* refers to the destructive deeds of the Earthborn as one of the previous tales of Orpheus, and the *Etymologicum Magnum*'s entry for Giant locates the tale in the eighth book of the *Rhapsodies* (Etymologicum Magnum s.v. γίγας = *Orphicorum Fragmenta* 188B = 63K). References to the generation of humans from the remains of the Giants or Titans suggest that both tales appeared in various Orphic texts and were often conflated, especially by Neoplatonists, who saw their allegorical meaning as indistinguishable.

The Genesis of the Cosmos:
Anthropogony

The Human Race: Hesiod's Absent Anthropogonies

After all the monsters spawned by Earth or the descendants of Pontos, the final inhabitants of the cosmos come into being, the humans. Hesiod, however, surprisingly provides no details about the generation of humans in the *Th*, despite the Muses' prologue that calls for the poet to sing of the race of humans and strong giants. Later scholia suggest that the Meliai, the ash-tree nymphs who are generated along with the Gigantes from the blood of Ouranos, are the ancestors of mortal men or that the Gigantes themselves are the first mortal men, born from the earth like the autochthonous Athenians or Theban Spartoi.[8] In the *WD* Hesiod provides the elaborate Myth of the Five Races (*WD* 106–80) to explain the generation of humans, how mortal men and gods sprang from the same source (108). The gods made (*poiêsan*) first a golden race in the time when Kronos ruled; these perished peacefully, to be replaced by the silver race made by the gods. These in turn were destroyed by Zeus, who created the bronze race from ash trees (like the Meliai in the *Th*) and then the race of heroes, both of whom perished in war. Finally, Zeus made the iron race, the current mortals who must work and suffer in the current order of life. All these races in the *WD* are made intentionally by the gods or by Zeus himself, in contrast to the accidentally generated humans of the *Th*, even if scholars ancient and modern try to connect the Meliai and Gigantes of the latter with the bronze race of the former (cf. Clay 2003: 81–99).

The Human Race: Orphic Anthropogonies

The same conflict of intentional artifice and accidental generation as the model for anthropogony appears in the Orphic sources, even if Orphic accounts have only three created races, instead of the Hesiodic five, and the accidental generation comes variously from the Titans or the Giants. Despite the idea among earlier scholars that the anthropogony must have been the culminating point of the Orphic cosmogonies, the event that gave meaning and purpose to the whole account, the testimonies to anthropogonies are few and far between, mostly appearing in Neoplatonic allegorical interpretations about the One and the many.

Proclus claims that Orpheus, presumably in the *Rhapsodies*, describes three races: a golden race under the reign of Phanes, a silver race ruled over by Kronos, and a Titanic race, formed from the limbs of the Titans.[9] The silver race under Kronos may have been described as living as long as the palm tree, but it is hard to imagine the life of the golden race, since it is not clear that Heaven and Earth would yet exist if Phanes were in charge, and the Orphic myth of the races may be as inconsistent with the theogonic narrative as Hesiod's five races are with his *Th*.[10] Proclus explains the golden race under Phanes as an allegory for the life of those who connect fully with the intelligibles, in contrast to the others, who either curve back (like crooked-counsel Kronos) toward the higher realms or occupy themselves with the manifold sensible world. It is unclear, however, whether the Orphic verse Proclus discusses actually concluded with a Titanic race or if it had a sequence of metallic races, ending perhaps in iron, which Proclus read as Titanic because of his allegorical interpretation of the Titans as representative of the manifold sensible world.

Most of the references to the generation of humans in Orphica appear in the context of Neoplatonic allegories of the One and many, so it is worth noting that the references mentioned above to the generation of humans from the blood of the Giants spilled in the Gigantomachy do not come from Neoplatonic contexts, whereas the Neoplatonists seem to refer to the Titanomachy instead, making use of the etymologies of Titan from *ti*, some particular thing, to connect the Titans to the manifold realm of the sensible particulars.[11] The exception is the sixth-century CE Olympiodorus, who brings together the idea of the generation of the human race from the blood of the Giants (understood as Titans) at the end of their war upon Zeus and the Olympian powers with the other tale that the Neoplatonists understood as an allegory for the division of the One into many, the Titans' dismemberment of Dionysos. Olympiodorus crafts a complex allegory of the embodiment of the soul in the human body, engaging in bricolage with all these pieces of the mythic tradition, but his narrative cannot be taken (as it too often has been) as a transparent witness to a single crucial episode of the Orphic cosmogony, one that must have been present in all the Orphic texts from the earliest instances in the sixth century BCE until the sixth century CE of Olympiodorus (cf. Edmonds 1999, 2009, 2013: 296–391). Anthropogony is hardly more important in the Orphic texts than in the Hesiodic account, despite the Neoplatonists' interest in its allegorical significance; the real emphasis in both the Hesiodic and Orphic cosmogonies lies not in how humans came into existence, but rather in the hegemony of Zeus.

The Cosmos of Zeus: The Final Structure and Order of the World

Cosmos: Zeus in Hesiod as the King Who Brings Justice

Hesiod's *Th* begins with the Muses praising Zeus, and "they sing, both in the beginning and in the end of the song, how much he is the most excellent of the gods and greatest in power" (*Th* 48–49). Zeus's excellence is made manifest through contrast with the previous rulers of the cosmos, Ouranos and Kronos, who abuse their power and treat the other deities unjustly, whereas Zeus establishes his rule as one of justice, in which all the gods receive their own fair shares of honor and authority. Hesiod's narrative of how

Zeus harnesses both force and cunning in balance to maintain his dominant place in the cosmos emphasizes the agreements that Zeus makes to obtain and retain his power.

Whereas Ouranos dominates by simple brute force as the most powerful entity in the cosmos, repressing all others, and Kronos succeeds by cunning in replacing him at the top but still keeps the rest suppressed, Zeus, as the youngest born deity, must negotiate with the older powers of the cosmos in order to win his place, promising that whoever is without power under Kronos's regime will gain their rightful honors, while anyone who holds authority under Kronos will retain that place if they fight on Zeus's behalf (*Th* 395–96). Zeus makes a deal with the underworld power of Styx, granting her new honors and thereby obtaining the support of her children, Kratos and Bie, Might personified, and he confirms the whole range of privileges in earth, heaven, and sea that Hekate had from the beginning. His treatment of these two goddesses, narrated in detail by Hesiod (*Th* 383–452), is emblematic of his method of obtaining power, just as he frees the Hundred-Handers, Obriareus, Kottys, and Gyes, from Tartarus (where they had been confined first by Ouranos and then by Kronos) and enlists their aid against Kronos, giving them nectar and ambrosia, the prerogatives of the immortal gods (*Th* 617–86), and even rewarding Obriareus after the battle with marriage to his niece (*Th* 817–19). Such promises of power to the disenfranchised, of stability to those already well off, and particularly the creation of marriage alliances to bind allies even closer, are characteristic of the kinds of strategies employed by the archaic Greek tyrants, the scions of aristocratic families who schemed their way to power through the support of some combination of those in the polis who wanted a larger share of authority and those who wanted to ensure that they were securing their own.[12]

After defeating the Titans (and Typhoeus), Zeus sets about securing his regime through a series of marriage alliances with important goddesses, both within his own family (Hera, Demeter) and among the offspring of the Titans (Themis, Eurynome, Mnemosyne, Leto). His union with Metis is particularly noteworthy because he manages to prevent her from producing a son who will overthrow him by swallowing her whole and then giving birth to her daughter Athena from his own head. This crucial short-circuiting of the succession of generations is, however, the only real deviation in Zeus's tactics from his general method of securing supporters by negotiating a redistribution of honors and authority.

Cosmos: Zeus in the Orphica as the Supreme Power

By contrast, the Zeus of the Orphic cosmogonies is the lone supreme power of the cosmos, relying on the support of no one but rather subsuming everyone and everything under his own control. This difference from the Hesiodic account of the generation of the cosmos is perhaps the most striking departure that Orphic accounts provide, and this adaptation resolves the problem with mythic cosmogonies that Aristotle (*Metaphysics* xiii.1091b) points out: the first power chronologically is not the same as the first hierarchically. Although Zeus is the last power to rise in the cosmos, in the Orphic theogonies he also becomes the first, so that he is not only the *telos* of all creation but its *archê* as well.

The Orphic poems are forged by Orphicists in each era through a process of stitching together old verses with new, and this process is most clearly demonstrated with the praise of Zeus as the supreme lord, which appears in ever-expanding versions from the earliest witnesses to the latest. Plato, our earliest source for Orphica, alludes to the idea of Zeus as first, last, and middle of all things, and the verse appears in the Derveni papyrus: "Zeus is the head, Zeus is middle, and out of Zeus all things are fashioned."[13] Later texts expand this idea, attributing to Zeus not just the opposites of beginning and end but all the pairs of opposition: male and female, fire and water, earth and air, and so forth. A version appears in the Aristotelian treatise *On the World*; it turns up in a papyrus handbook of quotes about Zeus; Plutarch refers to it; Porphyry quotes it at great length in his treatise *On Images*; and it is transformed into a paean of monotheism in the Hellenistic Jewish Testament of Orpheus, where Orpheus, having learned from his teacher Mousaios (Moses), proclaims his rejection of the many gods of the Gentiles and his adoration of the one supreme god.[14]

Zeus can encompass all these opposites because he encompasses the entirety of the cosmos; all things come into being again through him. Like the snake that swallows its own tail, Zeus consumes his own beginning, that is, the first principle that began all things—or rather, the first-born entity, since Zeus never consumes the actual first principle, be it Night or Chaos or Water, but rather the divinity designated as Protogonos, the first born (whatever its other names may be).

Although the image of Zeus swallowing Protogonos is mentioned in Athenagoras, the clearest witness to this process comes in the fragments the Neoplatonists quote from the *Rhapsodies*, since they are particularly interested in citing Orpheus's authority for the idea that all comes from one single entity who also continues to rule over all. The same motif, however, appears in the earliest theogony, the Orphic poem in the Derveni papyrus, although it is even harder to put together the precise story from the lacunose papyrus than from the fragmentary quotes of the Neoplatonists.

In the *Rhapsodies*, Zeus goes to the oracle of Night to ask how he can obtain dominion in the cosmos, inquiring, "How will all things be for me both one and each separate?" (*Orphicorum Fragmenta* 237B = 164, 165, 166 K). Following her advice, he then swallows the first-born of all creation and recreates the cosmos within himself (*Orphicorum Fragmenta* 241B = 167K). Whereas Kronos swallows his own offspring and falls because he fails to gulp down the last, Zeus swallows his own first progenitor and everything that progenitor had produced. Again, the Orphic accounts take a monstrosity in Hesiod's account and both make it greater in scope and attribute it, not to an earlier savage generation, but to the current ruler of the cosmos, Zeus himself.

This idea of Zeus swallowing the first begetter of all things in order to beget them himself seems to go back to the earliest Orphic cosmogonies, since some version of it appears in the Derveni papyrus. Many scholarly controversies hinge on how "*aidoion*" is understood in the poem; Zeus swallows either the first-born god or his generative phallos, but the idea remains the same in any reading: Zeus incorporates the originary power of generation and brings the cosmos to birth anew from himself.[15] It is perhaps a moot point whether the image of Zeus swallowing a phallos is more shocking than the image of Zeus gulping down an entire god (as his father Kronos had done with Zeus's siblings or as Zeus does with Metis), but Zeus's final act to secure his supremacy is at any rate markedly different from the kind of negotiations and alliances that the Hesiodic Zeus undertakes.

Conclusions: Weirder, Wilder, Older—Better

The writings of [Orpheus and Hesiod] are divided into two kinds of interpretation, that is, the literal and the allegorical, and indeed the literal interpretations have confused the ignorant masses. But for those interpretations, in truth, which are in accord with the allegorical, every expression is admired by the philosophical and erudite.

(Rufinus, *Recognitions* X.30)

The Zeus of the Orphic theogonies is more supreme than the Zeus of Hesiod's *Th*, more transcendent and yet more transgressive, raping and castrating his relatives with a savagery very alien to the dealmaker of the *Th*. Not only does this scandalous behavior characterize the final phase of the Orphic cosmogonies, but even from the first phases these accounts provide weirder and wilder versions of the similar stages in Hesiod. The cosmogonic process starts even earlier and more abstractly, abnormal and asexual reproduction characterizes more generations of the gods, the conflicts over succession are more violent, and the final victory is more absolute. At every step the Orphic theogonies present an account that marks itself as more extraordinary than Hesiod's, more shocking on the surface and therefore more profound in its hidden meanings (for the "extraordinary," see Edmonds 2008, 2013: 77–82). The extraordinary aspects of the narrative are meant to correlate to the extraordinary authority the account claims, just as the supposed greater antiquity of Orpheus should justify the greater authority of his accounts to the latecomer, Hesiod.

Nevertheless, it is worth noting that Hesiod's account always remains the standard from which the deviations are made—an indicator of the real authority of the Hesiodic *Th* in the face of all its competitors. The Orphic accounts' adherence to the structure of the Hesiodic model stands out when contrasted with other innovative cosmogonies, such as that in the "Eighth Book of Moses." Two versions of this same theogony appear in the midst of a magical spell for obtaining the secret name of the supreme god on a fourth-century CE Egyptian papyrus in Greek.[16] In this narrative, eight pairs of gods are produced by the seven laughs of the supreme god and an echo: Light and Radiance, Earth and Water, Mind and Wits, Generation and Procreation, Fate and Hermes, Kairos or Sun and Moon, Psyche and Python, and Fear and Iao. The primary principle, the formation of earth, sea, and heaven, the succession of generations—all of these elements are radically different from the narrative of Hesiod, showing that innovative cosmological thinkers could use other models to work out their ideas mythically. The thinkers who chose to put the name of Orpheus on their poems, however, stuck close to the traditional narrative of Hesiod, deviating ostentatiously in their efforts to outdo the authoritative *Th.*

NOTES

1. Cf. *Orphic Argonautica* 15 = *Orphicorum Fragmenta* 126B = 75K. Bernabé catalogs the various epithets in *Orphicorum Fragmenta* 138–43.

2. E.g., Isocrates *Busiris* 39 (*Orphicorum Fragmenta* 26iiB = 17K); Diogenes Laertius 1.5 (*Orphicorum Fragmenta* 1046ii, 8iiiB = OT 125K). Cf. Edmonds (2013: 80–81).

3. Derveni Papyrus 7.4–7 (*Orphicorum Fragmenta* 669iB) trans. Betegh. Cf. Plutarch fr. 157 Sandbach = Eusebius, *Praeparatio evangelica* 3.1.1 (*Orphicorum Fragmenta* 671B).

4. Derveni Papyrus 8.4; 11.1; for the account in the *Rhapsodies*, cf. Proclus, *in Platonis Cratylum Commentaria* 391 a (27.21 Pasqu.) = *Orphicorum Fragmenta* 155K.

5. Porphyry, *de Antro Nympharum*, 16. Descriptions of Kronos asleep are quoted in Proclus, *in Platonis Rem Publicam Commentaria* I 138.23 Kr. = *Orphicorum Fragmenta* 224B = 148K; Clement of Alexandria, *Stromata* VI 2.26.2 = *Orphicorum Fragmenta* 223B =149K.

6. Proclus, *in Platonis Cratylum Commentaria* 55.12, cf. Proclus, *Theologia Platonica* V.5 and Proclus, *in Platonis Timaeum Commentaria* II.208.30 (= *Orphicorum Fragmenta* 225i-iiiB = *Orphicorum Fragmenta* 137, 154, 220K).

7. Some of the Neoplatonic accounts (see *Orphicorum Fragmenta* 299–300B, along with Nonnus, *Dionysiaca*) mention a plan by Zeus to hand over the rulership to Dionysos, but the plan never comes to fruition, and Zeus remains the ruler of the cosmos.

8. With the scholia at 187, cf. scholia T at *Iliad* 22.126; Palaephatus 35, and Heschyius s.v. μελίας καρπός. Cf. Clay (2003: 95–99).

9. Proclus, *in Platonis Rem Publicam Commentaria* II.74.28–75.12 = *Orphicorum Fragmenta* 140; cf. Brisson (2002: 449).

10. Plutarch, *Quaestionum convivialum* 8.4.2 = *Orphicorum Fragmenta* 218B = *Orphicorum Fragmenta* 225K. It is worth noting that Lactantius (*Institutiones Divinae* 1.13.11 = *Orphicorum Fragmenta* 363b + 139K) claims that Kronos was the first to rule over men on earth, which is also inconsistent with either of the other versions of the anthropogony, so there must have been several accounts in different texts.

11. Olympiodorus, *in Platonis Phaedonem commentaria* 1.5.11–13. Westerink (1976: 44) compares Proclus, *in Platonis Cratylum Commentaria* 62.3 Pasquali (*Orphicorum Fragmenta* 240i B = *Orphicorum Fragmenta* 129 K), *in Platonis Rem Publicam Commentaria* 1.90.9–13 Kroll, and Damascius, *de principiis* 57 (ii.52.20–23 Westerink = i.120.1–5 Ruelle).

12. Herodotus's account of Pisistratus in Athens (I.59–64) provides a particularly apt parallel. See Clay(2003: 22) and Loney (2014: 522–28) for more on Zeus's "politics of co-optation."

13. Plato, *Laws* 715e = *Orphicorum Fragmenta* 21K, to which the scholiast quotes the Orphic lines found in the Derveni papyrus (P. Derv. 17.12).

14. [Aristotle] *de mundo* 401a25 (cf. Apuleius, *de Mundo* 37); P. Soc. Ital. xv 1476 = *Orphicorum Fragmenta* 688aB; Plutarch, *de defectu oraculorum* 48 436d; Plutarch, *de communibus*

notitiis adversus Stoicos 31 1074d; Porphyry fr. 354 = Eusebius, *Praeparatio evangelica* 3.8.2 = *Orphicorum Fragmenta* 243B; Testament of Orpheus = *Orphicorum Fragmenta* 377, 378 B.

15. The Derveni commentator quotes a line from Orpheus, Derveni Papyrus 13.3, αἰδοῖον κατέπινεν, ὃς αἰθέρα ἔκθορε πρῶτος, which either means "he gulped down the venerable one, who first sprang forth in the aither" or "he gulped down the phallus [of the one] who first sprang forth in the aither." The Derveni commentator himself explains that Orpheus likens the sun to a phallus (αἰδοῖον); Burkert (1980: 32) and, among others, Betegh (2004: 111–24) and Bernabé (2007: 107–12), understand that Zeus swallows the severed phallus of Ouranos, against the arguments of, e.g., West (1983: 84–90) and Kouremenos et al. (2006: 23–28). Santamaria (2016), however, makes a persuasive case that αἰδοῖον is a traditional epic epithet of Protogonos that the Derveni commentator reinterprets in his allegorical interpretations to signify the god in his generative capacity—the god who is swallowed is called αἰδοῖος because he is generative like an αἰδοῖον.

16. *Papyri Graecae Magicae* XIII. 161–206, 472–564. The version of the cosmogony from which these two recensions are taken must be several hundred years earlier, putting it close in time to the Orphic accounts in Athenagoras and the *Rhapsodies*. For a discussion of this text, see Smith (1996a and 1996b).

References

Arthur, M. 1982. "Cultural Strategies in Hesiod's *Theogony*: Law, Family, Society." *Arethusa* 15: 63–82.

Bernabé, A., ed. 2004, 2005, 2007. *Poetae Epici Graeci II: Orphicorum Graecorum testimonia et fragmenta*. Fasc. 1, 2, and 3. Munich, Germany.

Bernabé, A. 2007. "The Derveni Theogony: Many Questions and Some Answers." *Harvard Studies in Classical Philology* 103: 99–133.

Betegh, G. 2002. "On Eudemus Fr. 150 Wehrli." In *Eudemus,* edited by I. Bodnár and W. Fortenbaugh, 337–57. Rutgers University Studies in Classical Humanities 11. New Brunswick, NJ.

Betegh, G. 2004. *The Derveni Papyrus: Cosmology, Theology and Interpretation*. Cambridge.

Brisson, L. 2002. "La Figure Du Kronos Orphique Chez Proclus." *Revue de L'histoire Des Religions* 219 (4): 435–58.

Burkert, W. 1980. "Neue Funde zur Orphik." *Informationen zum altsprachlichen Unterricht* 2: 27–41.

Clay, J. S. 2003. *Hesiod's Cosmos*. Cambridge.

Cornford, F. M. 1912. *From Religion to Philosophy: A Study in the Origins of Western Speculation*. London.

Edmonds, R. 1999. "Tearing Apart the Zagreus Myth: A Few Disparaging Remarks on Orphism and Original Sin." *Classical Antiquity* 181: 1–24.

Edmonds, R. 2008. "Extra-ordinary People: Mystai & Magoi, Magicians & Orphics in the Derveni Papyrus." *Classical Philology* 103: 16–39.

Edmonds, R. 2009. "A Curious Concoction: Tradition and Innovation in Olympiodorus' 'Orphic' Creation of Mankind." *American Journal of Philology* 130: 511–32.

Edmonds, R. 2013. *Redefining Ancient Orphism: A Study in Greek Religion*. New York.

Edmonds, R. Forthcoming "Misleading and Unclear to the Many: Allegory in the Derveni Papyrus and the Orphic Theogony of Hieronymus." In *In the Shrine of Night. New Studies on the Derveni Papyrus*, edited by M. Santamaria. Leiden, Netherlands: Brill.

Guthrie, W. K. C. 1952. *Orpheus and Greek Religion*. Princeton, NJ.

Kern, O., ed. 1922. *Orphicorum Fragmenta*. Berlin.

Kouremenos, Th., G. Parássoglou, and K. Tsantsanoglou, eds., intro., and comms. 2006. *The Derveni Papyrus*. Firenze, Italy.

Loney, A. 2014. "Hesiod's Incorporative Poetics in the *Theogony* and the Contradictions of Prometheus." *American Journal of Philology* 135: 503–31.

Papadopoulou, I., and L. Muellner, eds. 2014. *Poetry as Initiation: The Center for Hellenic Studies Symposium on the Derveni Papyrus*. Hellenic Studies Series 63. Washington, DC.

Santamaria, M. 2016. "A Phallus Hard to Swallow: The Meaning of αἰδοῖος/-ον in the Derveni Papyrus." *Classical Philology* 111: 139–64.

Smith, M. 1996a. "The Eighth Book of Moses and How It Grew (P. Leid. J 395)." In *Studies in the Cult of Yahweh: New Testament, Early Christianity, and Magic*, edited by Shaye J.D. Cohen, 2:217–26. Leiden, New York and Köln.

Smith, M. 1996b. "P. Leid. J 395 (PGM XIII) and Its Creation Legend." In *Studies in the Cult of Yahweh: New Testament, Early Christianity, and Magic*, edited by Shaye J.D. Cohen, 2:227–34. Leiden, New York and Köln.

Vian, F., ed., 1987. *Les Argonautiques Orphiques*. Paris.

West, M. L., ed. and comm. 1966. *Hesiod: Theogony*. Oxford.

West, M. L. 1983. *The Orphic Poems*. Oxford.

Westerink, L. G. 1976. *The Greek Commentaries on Plato's Phaedo*. Amsterdam.

CHAPTER 16

···

HESIOD AND THE VISUAL ARTS

···

H. A. SHAPIRO

THE subject of Hesiod's relation to the visual arts is at the same time understudied in the scholarship on the poet and potentially so vast as to be rather daunting to anyone wishing to make a systematic study of it.[1] Of the many hundreds of divinities discussed or only mentioned in passing in the *Theogony* (hereafter *Th*), a significant number would find analogs in vase painting and sculpture from the seventh century BCE (not far in date from the composition of the poem) all the way down to the Hellenistic period. Indeed, one of the very few book-length attempts to exploit Hesiod as a source for the visual artist deals with the most famous monument of Hellenistic sculpture: Erika Simon's (1975) study of the friezes of the Great Altar of Zeus at Pergamon.

But in another sense the *Th* is not a very "visual" poem. That is, its genealogical focus and reliance on large chunks of catalog poetry mean that there is very little description of individual gods, goddesses, and forces of nature—very little for the student of iconography to go on. The *Works and Days* (hereafter *WD*) is even less promising, as its main interests in farming, justice, and everyday life in a Boeotian village are far removed from anything we are likely to find in the visual arts. It is true that here and there mention is made of objects of archaeological interest, such as the "eared tripod" (*tripod' otoenta*) that Hesiod claims to have won in the funeral games for Amphidamas of Chalkis on Euboea and later dedicated to the Muses on Mt. Helikon (*WD* 654–59). Bronze tripods with what could be described loosely as ear-like handles have indeed been found in Panhellenic sanctuaries of the eighth century BCE, as at Olympia (Valavanis 2004: 36–39). The *WD* also has the occasional mythological excursus that conjures up a visual image, especially that of the creation of Pandora (60–89); this and the version in the *Th* (570–89) comprise complementary narratives that help to illuminate the rather sparse classical iconography of the story (Shapiro 1994: 63–70).

Of the major works no longer considered to be by Hesiod himself, the *Catalogue of Women* (hereafter *Catalogue*), like the *Th*, recounts the genealogies of many mythological figures who can be found represented here and there, but the connections are apt to be fairly superficial. To take, for example, what was perhaps the best known set piece in the *Catalogue*, the contest among the suitors for the hand of Helen in marriage, it would be easy enough to find individual images of many of the suitors—Odysseus, Menelaos, even the Athenian Menestheus—but nowhere in ancient art do we find a narrative scene that can be interpreted as the courtship of Helen. The painters do occasionally show the *wedding* of Menelaos and Helen, as early as ca. 580 BCE (Bakır 1981: 69, pl. 39–45), but we do not know what their source was—probably not Hesiod, perhaps a now-lost part of the epic cycle.

The one poem in the Hesiodic corpus that can justly be described as highly visual is the *Aspis*, or *Shield of Herakles*, with the lengthy ekphasis, or poetic description, of the shield occupying almost half of the poem, and the vivid account in the framing story of Herakles's contest with the fierce son of Ares, Kyknos. Indeed, the visuality of the poem may be one argument *against* its being an authentic work of Hesiod. The conventional dating of the *Aspis* in the early years of the sixth century BCE has been arrived at primarily through comparisons with archaeologically attested realia, as well as iconographical innovations in early archaic art that seem to give a terminus post quem for the composition of the poem (Cook 1937). The topic is treated in detail in a recent monograph (Chiarini 2012), and I have myself contributed one study to the iconography of Herakles and Kyknos in relation to the *Aspis* (Shapiro 1984), so I leave consideration of the poem aside in this chapter.

A Test Case: Okeanos in Hesiod and Sophilos

The great appeal, as well as the limitations, of looking for Hesiodic figures in the visual arts may be illustrated with a single example that will lead us into an area of investigation that, as I argue here, would be especially fruitful for the larger topic at hand. Okeanos (Ocean) is a ubiquitous figure in the *Th*, receiving many mentions in a variety of contexts throughout the poem. He is the penultimate, but by no means the least, of the figures in the catalog of gods and goddesses that the poet breathlessly spills out in his initial invocation to the Muses, moving in reverse order from the generation of Zeus back to the primordial forces of nature: Earth, Ocean, and Night (20). Subsequently, Okeanos is listed as one of the dozen offspring of Gaia and Ouranos, ending with Kronos, elsewhere known as the generation of the Titans (133–38). Thereafter, Okeanos recurs periodically as the father of vast numbers of offspring, including a host of (male) rivers and an even longer list of (female) Oceanids, who include various nymphs, springs, and other minor sea goddesses (337–63). At this point the poet gives up trying to name them and simply adds that there were three thousand each of the rivers and the Oceanids, more than the most prodigious memory could master, but anyone who lived around one of these knew his or her name (369–70).

This comment is very revealing, not only of the Panhellenic scope of the *Th*, but also of the intensely local nature of Greek religion. Surely anyone who lived along the Nile (to take just one of the river gods named, 338) knew him intimately, and by the Hellenistic period artists had worked out a complex iconography to personify the Nile and his gifts to mankind (Jentel 1992). Likewise, the obscure Dione, to single out one of the Oceanids (*Th* 17; 353), would in some versions become known as the mother of Aphrodite (a relationship that seems to be familiar to Hesiod, even if he doesn't say so explicitly) and later inspire one of the most magnificent figures on the Parthenon, the seated mother goddess on the east pediment, gently caressing the voluptuous daughter in her lap (Palagia 1998: 22, fig. 42).

Elsewhere, certain children of Okeanos are singled out for special mention, such as the River Styx, his eldest daughter, whose waters constitute the dreaded oath by which the Olympians must swear, with the most dire consequences for committing perjury (*Th* 775–804). Though her craggy abode is vividly evoked (778–80), nothing is said of Styx's own appearance, and no artist ventured to try to envision her. By combing through the poem, one could also tease out many important grandchildren of Okeanos. One triad of sisters who get a special mention are the Charites (Graces), born to Zeus and Eurynome, a daughter of Okeanos (907–9). The Charites, as we shall see, did become a staple of the painters and sculptors, because of the importance of their cults, and perhaps also in part because their very name captures one of the qualities, *charis*, for which all visual artists strove (Pollitt 1974: 297–301). Another granddaughter is Thetis, a Nereid and daughter of Doris, one of the daughters of Okeanos (244), who was a favorite of poets and painters from Homer to the classical period. I return to her later in this essay.

Along with all this, Hesiod also sets many of his stories amid the eddying waters of Ocean, but gives no indication of whether he pictures the god in anthropomorphic (or theriomorphic) form, or simply as that watery realm that flows everywhere in and around the kosmos. Thus it must have come as an astonishing revelation to archaeologists and readers of Hesiod alike when, some fifty years ago, a spectacular black-figure vase entered the collections of the British Museum bearing the earliest labeled representation of Okeanos, shown in figures 16.1–16.2. The vase was made in Athens about 580 BCE and is signed by the earliest Attic painter (or potter) whose name we know, Sophilos (Williams 1983).

The long and colorful circular frieze surrounding the top register of this large *dinos*, or punch bowl, is one of two well-preserved early depictions of the procession of the gods to the house of Peleus on the occasion of his wedding to Thetis.[2] The same story was already well known from the most famous of all Greek vases, the slightly later François Vase in Florence, discussed below. The gathering of forty-three gods (and one hero, Peleus) on the *dinos* could certainly be described as "Hesiodic," since everyone present appears somewhere in the *Th*. This does not mean, however, that the poem was the painter's immediate source, since this famous and fateful wedding, the most spectacular in Greek myth, was told more than once in the years before or around the time of Sophilos, certainly in the *Kypria* and almost certainly in the *Catalogue of Women*. We cannot know whether either of those lost accounts gave more details of the appearance

FIGURE 16.1 Attic black-figure *dinos* signed by the painter Sophilos, ca. 580 BCE. London, British Museum 1971, 1101.1. Photo courtesy of the Trustees of the British Museum.

of the wedding guests, but I suspect that the striking composite creature labeled as Okeanos is more the product of Sophilos's fertile imagination than of any poetic source.

The human part of him, dressed in a short, dark red chiton, ends a little below the buttocks, where it transitions to the very long, winding fishtail of a sea monster, bordered on the underside by a band of scales and above by a brushlike rendering of fins. One large horn projects from the top of his head, up into the decorative tongue pattern around the rim of the bowl. The dolphin that he holds in his lowered right hand is fairly commonplace, often the marker of the sea on Greek vases (Vidali 1995), but the long snake in his left hand, which seems to be slithering upward, is harder to explain. Snakes are traditionally associated with the earth in Greek thought, so we may be reminded that the mother of Okeanos is Gaia, Mother Earth (*Th* 133). The bull's horn might be explained with reference to the later iconography of river gods, like Acheloös in the story of his wrestling match with Herakles (Isler 1970), and Acheloös is in fact one of the many rivers sprung from Okeanos and Gaia (*Th* 340). But this only implies that Acheloös inherited his father's horn; it does not explain why Okeanos has a horn

FIGURE 16.2 Detail of the *dinos* in figure 16.1. Okeanos and other guests at the wedding of Peleus and Thetis. Photo courtesy of the Trustees of the British Museum.

in the first place. A phrase of Hesiod's may offer a clue. In the description of the clifflike dwelling of Styx mentioned above, the poet refers to her as an *Okeanoio keras*, a branch of Ocean (*Th* 789). The primary meaning of the word *keras* is horn, usually the horn of an animal. Might the phrase "Ocean's horn" have lodged itself in the memories of Hesiod's listeners and led to the notion that Okeanos himself was marked by a horn? An object made of horn can also be referred to as a *keras*, such as the curved bow in the hand of the goddess Artemis that overlaps Okeanos's left arm on this vase (see figure 16.2).

The horn crowning Okeanos's head makes a nice complement to the fishtailed body below, an allusion to creatures of the earth and creatures of the sea. The same idea is expressed in Okeanos's two attributes, the snake and the fish. The fishtail is a tour de force of the painter as it unwinds past the god Hephaistos with his mule and eventually bumps up against the back of the house of Peleus. This building is the starting point of the scene, as the groom stands at its entrance to greet and receive the long procession of divine guests (figure 16.3). The *dinos*, a handleless bowl sitting atop a tall stand, was an especially popular shape for some of the earliest and most ambitious mythological narratives of Attic vase painting. Here, the way in which the "tail end" of the procession includes both Hephaistos's donkey's tail and Okeanos's fishtail overlapping the house where it began gives new meaning to the term "ring composition" (cf. figure 16.1). Perhaps the remarkable placement of Okeanos echoes the idea of encompassing the earth in a great circle, just as Okeanos on the Shield of Achilles constitutes the outermost band encircling the shield (*Iliad* 18.607–8; cf. Okeanos's epithet *teleentos* [genitive

FIGURE 16.3 Detail of the *dinos* in figure 16.1. Peleus receiving guests before his house. Photo courtesy of the Trustees of the British Museum.

of *teleeis*], *Th* 242, 959, which has been understood as a reference to the ever-circling nature of ocean, that which "ends in itself").

If Sophilos could not look to Hesiod for clues to the appearance of Okeanos, that does not mean that he invented the image ex nihilo for this vase. Just as every poet (and especially the oral poet, as Hesiod must have been) reworked material that he had heard from earlier poets, so too even very early painters like Sophilos had a visual tradition on which to draw. We cannot say just how far back that tradition went, with so little comparable figured ware of the seventh century BCE preserved. But we *can* say that Sophilos found inspiration for his remarkable Okeanos very close to home, in his own earlier work. We are fortunate to have a well-preserved krater, not signed but universally attributed to the hand of Sophilos (figure 16.4), that can be dated stylistically to a somewhat earlier phase of his career (Bakır 1981: 67, pl. 18). More than half of the principal scene is occupied by the massive figure of Nereus, on whose back Herakles, puny in comparison, rides as he struggles to subdue the creature. Just like Proteus in the *Odyssey* and Thetis, Nereus had a sea god's power to change shapes (Forbes Irving 1990: 173–84), hence the snake springing up from his back, to which Herakles looks back warily, and the second one in his right hand. For Hesiod, Nereus is a gentle creature (*Th* 233–36), and he does indeed ultimately surrender to Herakles.

We now understand that when Sophilos came to create our earliest representation of Okeanos, he already had a template in the figure of Nereus. The two are of course close

FIGURE 16.4   Attic black-figure column-krater attributed to Sophilos. Herakles wrestling with Nereus, ca. 590–580 BCE. Athens, National Archaeological Museum 12587. Photo by author.

kinsmen in Hesiod; Nereus is the husband of Okeanos's daughter Doris (*Th* 240–41). The snake in Okeanos's left hand does look very like the one brandished by Nereus (compare figures 16.2 and 16.4), only on the later vase it has lost its meaning as a symbol of metamorphosis (there is no evidence that Okeanos was also a shape-shifter, like his fellow sea gods), and it may have taken on other associations, as suggested previously. We see here how the imagery of Greek art is a continual reworking of older material. Unlike the stories of oral epic, whose origins are usually lost in the mists of time, every figure in the visual arts must have had a *protos heuretes*, an inventor, but the lacunose remains of the earliest mythological scenes in the seventh and early sixth centuries BCE often make it hard to identify him with certainty. In the Okeanos of Sophilos, we may have one secure example, even if some of the individual elements of this image are not entirely new.

VISUALIZING THE WEDDING OF PELEUS AND THETIS

It is furthermore of utmost importance that Sophilos is one of the earliest fully literate painters we can identify (Kilmer and Develin 2001). Not only did he sign several of his works and cover some (though by no means all) of them with identifying labels, he even titled one of his pictures *The Funeral Games for Patroklos* (PATROKLOUS ATLA: Bakır 1981: 65, pl. 6). Clearly, for these early painters literacy was not simply a tool for aiding the viewer, but rather a means of expressing pride in their work, showing off their knowledge of the epic, and embellishing the figured scene.

It is this delight in the written word that makes it possible for us to explore the relation of Sophilos to Hesiodic poetry in the first place. Without the inscriptions, only a fraction of the gods and goddesses on the London *dinos* would be immediately recognizable, for example, Dionysos, with his gift of the grapevine (cf. figure 16.8), Chiron the Centaur (cf. figures 16.7, 16.8), or Apollo with his big phorminx (cf. figure 16.5), but many more would be impossible to identify without the inscriptions. Most strikingly, the three male/female couples riding in chariots—Zeus and Hera (figure 16.6), Poseidon and Amphitrite, and Ares and Aphrodite—are indistinguishable from one another by dress or attributes.

Yet thanks to many of Sophilos's other inscriptions, we can explore further some aspects of his understanding of Hesiodic poetry. Starting from the back of the procession (cf. figures 16.1, 16.2), the two last gods, Hephaistos and Okeanos, have a family connection, since for Hesiod, Hephaistos's wife is Aglaia, one of the three Charites (*Th* 945–46), who are the daughters of Eurynome, a daughter of Okeanos,

FIGURE 16.5 Detail of the *dinos* in figure 16.1. Hermes, Apollo, and Muses. Photo courtesy of the Trustees of the British Museum.

FIGURE 16.6 Detail of the Dinos in figure 16.1. Chariot of Zeus and Hera.

FIGURE 16.7 Detail of the *dinos* in figure 16.1. Three Nymphs, Themis, and Chiron. Photo courtesy of the Trustees of the British Museum.

FIGURE 16.8 Detail of the *dinos* in figure 16.1. Chiron, Hebe, and Dionysos. Photo courtesy of the trustees of the British Museum.

by Zeus (*Th* 907–9). The relationship is even closer than it looks, for we learn in the *Iliad* (18.398–405) that after Hera threw the child Hephaistos out of Olympos in disgust at his lameness and he landed on the island of Lemnos, it was Eurynome who brought him up, along with Thetis. Now here he is—whether lame or not we cannot tell, since his lower legs and feet are lost—just behind the father of that same Eurynome, celebrating the marriage of Thetis, his other benefactress. His wife is here too, but she remains with her sister Charites further ahead in the procession, alongside the chariot of Poseidon and Amphitrite (Williams 1983: 25, fig. 30). In fact Sophilos is very fond of the divine triads who originate in the *Th*; in addition to the Charites, he includes a threesome of Nymphs (cf. figure 16.7), the three Moirai (Fates: *Th* 904–5; Williams 1983: 27, figure 16.33), three unnamed Muses, looking very much like the triads (figure 16.5), and one more triad, alongside the chariot of Zeus and Hera, whose inscription is lost (figure 16.6). They are most likely to be the Horai (Seasons: *Th* 900–1), who are also present on the François Vase (Shapiro, Iozzo and Lezzi-Hafter 2013: pl. 25). Both the Horai and the Moirai are Zeus's daughters by Themis, who has a place of honor near the head of Sophilos's procession and holds a scepter with a flowering tip (figure 16.7). Though a consort of Zeus toward the end of the *Th* (901–6), Themis (whose name means justice or righteousness) is a revered goddess (*Th* 16: *aidoiê*) of the generation that preceded Zeus, that of the Titans, and her siblings present here include Okeanos and his wife Tethys (cf. figure 16.2).

Tethys is a good example of a figure who, to a modern reader of Hesiod, makes sense here beside her husband Okeanos, but we could not have been sure without the inscription, especially since this image is the only secure depiction of Tethys before the Roman Empire (Jentel 1997). Yet another big surprise on the Sophilos *dinos* is the goddess who shares Tethys's mantle, Eileithyia (cf. figure 16.2). She is the goddess who assists in childbirth, best known in the visual tradition for her presence at the birth of Athena, a particularly complicated birth, as it entailed Hephaistos splitting open the head of Zeus with an axe (Pingiatoglou 1981).

Eileithyia's presence here, if not her exact placement, can best be understood by turning once again to the *Th*. Toward the end of the poem, once the dominion of Zeus has been established he takes seven wives in succession to father children on them all. The first is Metis, mother of Athena, and the last is his sister Hera (*Th* 921–24), who then remains his consort and queen of Olympus, as also in Homer. But they have only three children together, a somewhat unlikely mix: Hebe, Ares, and Eileithyia (*Th* 922). It cannot be coincidental that all three of these siblings are present on the Sophilos *dinos*, even if scattered through the scene and nowhere near the chariot that bears their parents (figure 16.6). Hebe, the personification of youth and the favorite of Hera's children, is among the group on foot near the head of the procession (figure 16.8). Sophilos and his audience surely knew that Hebe would one day marry the hero Herakles, when he had completed his mortal life amid much suffering and undergone an apotheosis (*Th* 950–54). It was to be a wedding almost as opulent as the one shown here. But that day has not yet arrived, and Hebe remains single, almost lost in the crowd.

The third of Zeus and Hera's children, Ares, is often shunned by the other gods in the *Iliad* for his angry, warlike demeanor. In the *Odyssey* we see a very different side of Ares, when the blind bard Demodokos at the Phaeacian court sings of the illicit love affair of Aphrodite and Ares, caught in the act by her cuckolded husband Hephaistos and held up to the ridicule of the other gods (8.266–366). Surely such an adulterous couple would not be so brazen as to show up together at a wedding, in the same vehicle, as they are depicted here (figure 16.9). But the bard's story is nothing like Hesiod's authoritative account. Hephaistos is, as we saw, married to one of the Graces, Aglaia, and before that Homer had given him yet a different wife, Charis (*Iliad* 18.382–83). Ares and Aphrodite are indeed a couple (their marital status is unclear in Hesiod; *Th* 933–37) and the parents of three children, two frightful and one just the opposite. The two boys, perhaps twins, are Phobos and Deimos, Fear and Terror, who stalk the battlefield together with their father (cf. *Shield of Herakles* 465), and their sister is Harmonia. Like Thetis and Hebe, she is a goddess fated to marry a mortal hero, Kadmos of Thebes (*Th* 937), in a glittering wedding attended by the Olympian gods. But that too lies in the future, even after the wedding of Hebe and Herakles.

HESIOD'S MUSES AND THE VASE PAINTERS

Among the various female triads on Sophilos's *dinos* we have noticed yet another, a group of three Muses alongside the chariot of Apollo (figure 16.5). Their close proximity to the god with his big lyre makes good sense for those who know Apollo as "Leader of the Muses" (*Mousagetês*: Pindar, Fr. 94c Race). Curiously, the *Th* never places Apollo in the company of the Muses. But where are the rest of Sophilos's Muses? He has given us five more, arranged ingeniously in a semicircle, with Kalliope in the middle, facing front and playing the syrinx, or Pan pipes (figure 16.9). Though the inscription is the same—MOSAI (with O for OU, as in many archaic inscriptions)—we know she must be Kalliope, because the identical figure appears, named, on the François Vase (figure 16.10). No doubt both painters have singled out Kalliope for special treatment, because she is named last of the Muses by Hesiod and is the "greatest of them all" (*Th* 79). This raises the question: If Sophilos knew his Hesiod so well, why did he not give each of the Muses her own name, as Kleitas would do a few years later, and why are there only eight and not the canonical nine (*Th* 76)? It must first be said that, as enthusiastic as Sophilos was about writing on some of his vases, no painter before or since has approached Kleitias in his obsessive use of inscriptions (Giuliani 2003: 140): more than 130 on the François

FIGURE 16.9   Detail of the *dinos* in figure 16.1. Ares, Aphrodite, and five Muses. Photo courtesy of the Trustees of the British Museum.

FIGURE 16.10 Attic black-figure volute-krater (François Vase), signed by Kleitias as painter and Ergotimos as potter. Detail of the wedding of Peleus and Thetis: chariot of Zeus and Hera, with Muses. Florence, Museo Archeologico Nazionale 4209. Photo courtesy of the National Archaeological Museum of Florence.

Vase alone, including two double signatures (potter and painter). He has divided his nine Muses into groups of two, four, and three, extending from the chariot of Zeus back to the area beneath one handle (figures 16.10, 16.11). Reading them from left to right, that is, in the direction of the procession, the first of the nine is Stesichore, literally "she-who-sets-up-the-chorus" (in place of Hesiod's Terpsichore). For Sophilos it was enough to include the Muses under their collective name, as for the Charites, the Moirai, and (perhaps) the Horai, and, with none singled out but Kalliope, it mattered little that he was one short.

DEPICTING HESIODIC GENEALOGIES

Let us look finally at the grouping at the head of the procession and at their destination, the house of Peleus, on the *dinos* by Sophilos (cf. figure 16.3). Dionysos is not as extraordinary as on the François Vase (Shapiro, Iozzo, and Lezzi-Hafter 2013: pl. 25), where he lurches forward, his demonic face turned to us, the viewers, staggering under the weight of a heavy amphora. Sophilos's Dionysos is, rather, an integral part of the stately procession, a small vine with clusters of grapes hinting discreetly at his identity and his contribution to the festivities (cf. figure 16.8).

FIGURE 16.11 Detail of the krater in figure 16.10. Muses. Photo courtesy of the the National Archaeological Museum of Florence.

The densely packed group of five divinities who are the first to arrive are all female and at first sight an unexpected gathering (cf. figure 16.3). The very first is the divine messenger Iris, who, in her accustomed role from Homer onward announces the arrival of the gods and mediates between the divine and mortal realms (cf. *Th* 780; 784). Her short chiton, winged boots, and long herald's staff establish her iconography for the remainder of classical art. The distinctive double-curved tip of the scepter, which she shares with the messenger god Hermes, has been obscured by the kantharos (an elaborate drinking cup) that Peleus holds out, as if to greet the guests with a toast (Williams 1983: 22). On the François Vase we get the feeling that Iris was expecting to play the same role, but Chiron has suddenly elbowed her out of the way, in order to be the first to congratulate Peleus with a handshake (figure 16.12). We shall return to the special relationship of Peleus and Chiron.

Behind Iris follow two pairs of goddesses, led by Demeter and Hestia (cf. figures 16.3, 16.8). Both daughters of Kronos and Rhea, their names stand side by side in the *Th* (454), just as the goddesses themselves do here. In the context of this wedding, their roles complement each other well. Demeter, aside from providing the harvest of grain that is essential to all mankind, became early on the prototype of the devoted mother in Greek myth, when her daughter by Zeus, Persephone, was abducted by her uncle Hades, who made her queen of the Underworld (*Th* 767–69). We know this story best from the splendid Homeric *Hymn to Demeter*, whose composition cannot be far from the date

FIGURE 16.12   Detail of the krater in figure 16.10: Peleus greeting guests at the wedding. Photo courtesy of the National Archaeological Museum of Florence.

of that of Sophilos's vase (Foley 1994: 29–30). The wedding scene looks ahead to Thetis's future, which will be defined by her role as mother of the greatest of the heroes at Troy, Achilles (*Th* 1006–7). Demeter's sister Hestia, though she remained a virgin, has a special role here of a different sort. As goddess of the hearth, who protects the household and by extension the family dwelling in it, she is among the first to bless the new household that has just been created.

The theme of motherhood is picked up by another goddess, one whose entire role in Greek tradition is defined by the children she gave birth to, the divine twins Apollo and Artemis. Leto, the daughter of two of the Titans, Koios and Phoibe (*Th* 134–36), is characterized by Hesiod twice in the space of three lines (*Th* 406–408) as gentle (*meilichos*), a good attribute for a mother. Her children are elsewhere in the scene, though not together. Instead, Artemis joins her sister Athena in one car, and Apollo his younger brother Hermes in another (figure 16.5). As none of the four has a steady "partner" like their elders (Zeus and Hera, Poseidon and Amphitrite), and the girls are both virgins, they are more comfortable in the company of their own sex.

Finally, the goddess alongside Leto is labeled as Chariklo, another revelation thanks to an inscription (figure 16.3). The *Th* does not know of Chariklo at all, but the *Catalogue of Women*, on the evidence of a Scholiast to Pindar, did record that Chiron was married to a Naiad (sea nymph) named Chariklo (Fr. 42MW). Her appearance on our *dinos*, not far from her husband Chiron (figures 16.3, 16.8), confirms the antiquity of this tradition.

In a story apparently told in the *Catalogue of Women*, the kindly Chiron had once saved Peleus from savage centaurs (March 1987: 4–5). Akastos, king of Iolkos in Thessaly, suspected Peleus of attempting to seduce his wife and lured him to a hunt on Mt. Pelion, where he hid Peleus's weapon, leaving him defenseless against the wild centaurs. Chiron (the one benevolent centaur) intervened and found the sword, and Peleus escaped unscathed. This created a bond between the two that resonates clearly in their handshake on the François Vase (figure 16.12).

Kleitias also knows of Chariklo, who joins with Demeter and Hestia, beside her husband (figure 16.12), much as on the *dinos* by Sophilos (figure 16.3). This should lead us to re-evaluate the image of the lone Chiron receiving the toddler Achilles from Peleus, which we see on countless Greek vases, even one of the mid-seventh century BCE and perhaps inspired by the *Kypria* (Morris 1984: pl. 12). If Chiron was renowned for being a mentor and foster father to heroes—not only Achilles, but also Jason and an obscure son of Jason, Medeus, whom Hesiod knows *(Th* 1001–2)—it seems unlikely he could have done so alone. His mother, Philyra, is known to Hesiod (*Th* 1002, a daughter of Okeanos), even if his wife is not. Raising a little boy requires a mother's touch, and it seems that Chiron and Chariklo became surrogate parents to Achilles, with a grandmother around the cave for good measure. We see Philyra on a much later vase, a red-figure depiction of the wedding of Peleus and Thetis (Shapiro 1994: 102–3). She is not at the gatherings of Sophilos or Kleitias, but the presence of the future foster parents of Achilles, Chiron and Chariklo, may help explain why Peleus acts as the host of the celebration. His real parents, the hero Aiakos of Aegina and Endeis, are long gone from his life by this time.

The last and perhaps most intriguing element of both the Sophilos *dinos* and the François Vase is the house before which Peleus proudly stands (figures 16.3 and 16.12). Architecturally, the two buildings are quite similar, though Kleitias, with typical bravado, has made his bigger and more ornate, with a gabled roof and better articulated triglyph-and-metope frieze (Pedley 1987: 70). More to the point, he has put the bride, who is entirely absent from Sophilos's composition, inside, seated demurely as she holds out her large veil (Shapiro, Iozzo, and Lezzi-Hafter 2013: pl. 26). But where are we exactly? Most early sources tell us that the wedding took place at Chiron's cave on Mount Pelion (March 1987: 7), and this hardly looks like our idea of a mountain cave. The ancients, however, might have thought differently. In the Homeric *Hymn to Hermes*, the cave where Hermes and his mother Maia live is several times described in language that evokes a palace (Vergados 2011). The word *megaron* (pl. *megara*) is used of the cave, which elsewhere describes the main room of a royal palace (e.g., *Odyssey* 17. 604). Similarly, a fragment of the *Catalogue of Women* says of Peleus, "he who in these halls (*megarois*) going up into the holy marriage-bed" (fr. 211MW, line 10).

Sophilos is very Hesiodic indeed, in the sense that the selection and placement of the forty-four figures on the *dinos* are marked by the very same kinds of genealogical connections and familial groupings that are at the heart of the *Th*. The same can be said of the François Vase, which works its own variations on the earlier version but is no less Hesiodic in spirit. It is hard to understand why no subsequent artist even attempted a composition on this scale. And it would be fascinating to know how, where, and on what occasions our *dinos* and krater were used—questions that form the basis of much archaeological research but have so far yielded few answers (Reusser 2002). They may belong to the latest period in which Hesiodic epic was still being transmitted in oral form and as such provide precious evidence for the way that archaic poets and painters alike continually reshaped traditional material.

Notes

1. I thank the editors for their invitation to contribute to this volume and their perceptive comments, and David Sider (NYU) for bibliographical advice.
2. A third, fragmentary version of the same story on a vase that is close in date has been published in Iozzo (2009).

References

Bakır, G. 1981. *Sophilos: Ein Beitrag zu seinem Stil*. Mainz, Germany.

Boardman, J. 1990. "Herakles." *Lexicon Iconographicum Mythologiae Classicae* IV. 728–838. V 1–192. Zurich.

Chiarini, S. 2012. *L'archeologia dello Scutum Herculis*. Rome.

Cook, R. M. 1937. "The Date of the Hesiodic Shield." *Classical Quarterly* 31: 204–14.

Cristofani, M. 1981. *Materiali per servire alla storia del vaso François*. BdA Seria special 1.

Euphronios der Maler. 1991. Exhibition catalogue, Antikenmuseum Berlin. Berlin, Germany.

Foley, H. P. 1994. *The Homeric Hymn to Demeter*. Princeton, NJ.

Forbes Irving, P. M. C. 1990. *Metamorphosis in Greek Myths*. Oxford.

Giuliani, L. 2003. *Bild und Mythos*. Munich, Germany.

Iozzo, M. 2009. "Un nuovo *dinos* da Chiusi con le nozze di Peleus e Thetis." In *Shapes and Images: Studies on Attic Black Figure and Related Topics in Honour of Herman A. G. Brijder*, edited by E. M. Moormann and V. V. Stissi, 63–85. Leuven, Belgium.

Isler, H. P. 1970. *Acheloos*. Bern, Switzerland.

Jentel, M.-O. 1992. "Neilos." *Lexicon Iconographicum Mythologiae Classicae* VI 720–26.

Jentel, M.-O. 1997. "Tethys I." *Lexicon Iconographicum Mythologiae Classicae* VIII (supp.): 1193–95.

Kilmer, M. F., and R. Develin. 2001. "Sophilos' Vase Inscriptions and Cultural Literacy in Archaic Athens." *Phoenix* 55: 9–43.

March, J. 1987. *The Creative Poet: Studies on the Treatment of Myths in Greek Poetry*. London.

Moore, M. B. 2010. "Hephaistos Goes Home: An Attic Black-figured Column-krater in the Metropolitan Museum." *Metropolitan Museum Journal* 45: 21–54.

Morris, S. P. 1984. *The Black and White Style*. New Haven, CT.

Nagy, G. 1996. *Homeric Questions*. Austin, TX.

Oakley, J. H., and R. H. Sinos. 1993. *The Wedding in Ancient Athens*. Madison, WI.

Palagia, O. 1998. *The Pediments of the Parthenon*. 2nd ed. Leiden, Netherlands.

Pedley, J. 1987. "Reflections of Architecture in Sixth Century Attic Vase-Painting." In *The Amasis Painter and his World*, edited by M. True, 63–80, Malibu, CA.

Pingiatoglou, S. 1981. *Eileithyia*. Würzburg, Germany.

Pollitt, J. J. 1974. *The Ancient View of Greek Art: Criticism, History, and Terminology*. New Haven, CT.

Pollitt, J. J. 1990. *The Art of Ancient Greece: Sources and Documents*. Cambridge.

Reusser, C. 2002. *Vasen für Etrurien: Verbreitung und Funktionen attischer Keramik in Etrurien des 6. und 5. Jahrhunderts vor Christus*. Kilchberg, Switzerland.

Shapiro, H. A. 1984. "Herakles and Kyknos." *American Journal of Archaelogy* 88: 523–29.

Shapiro, H. A. 1994. *Myth into Art: Poet and Painter in Classical Greece*. London.

Shapiro, H. A., M. Iozzo, and A. Lezzi-Hafter 2013. *The François Vase. New Perspectives*. Kilchberg, Switzerland.

Simon, E. 1975. *Pergamon und Hesiod*. Mainz, Germany.

Stewart, A. F. 1983. "Stesichoros and the François Vase." In *Ancient Greek Art and Iconography*, edited by W. G. Moon, 53–78. Madison, WI.

Stewart, A. 2014. *Art in the Hellenistic World*. New York.

Valavanis, P. 2004. *Games and Sanctuaries in Ancient Greece: Olympia, Delphi, Isthmia, Nemea, Athens*. Translated by D. Hardy. Athens, Greece.

Vergados, A. 2011. "Shifting Focalization in the Homeric Hymn to Hermes: The Case of Hermes' Cave." *Greek, Roman and Byzantine Studies* 51: 1–25.

Vidali, S. 1995. *Archaische Delphindarstellungen*. Würzburg, Germany.

Williams, D. 1983. "Sophilos in the British Museum." In *Greek Vases in the J. Paul Getty Museum* 1, 9–34. Malibu, CA.

CHAPTER 17

HESIOD AND PINDAR

TOM PHILLIPS

THREE snapshots of Pindar's dialogue with Hesiod are examined in this chapter. I begin and end with Pindar's accounts of Zeus's marriage (the "First Hymn") and Typhon's imprisonment (*Pythian* 1) in relation to their antecedents in the *Theogony* (hereafter *Th*), readings that flank a section on the use made by Pindar of the famous passage in the *Works and Days* (hereafter *WD*) that pictures the "path to ἀρετή." The textual relationships explored here take various forms. In the "First Hymn," divergences from Hesiod accentuate a boldly original account of poetry's origins. Allusions to Hesiod's "path to ἀρετή" activate wider Hesiodic associations, which remind listeners of mortal limitations. In *Pythian* 1, local rewritings of Hesiod combine with larger shifts in emphasis to produce an ekphrasis that both enacts and complicates the containment of violent forces. Running through these readings is the basic claim that intertextual dialogues heighten meaning at the level of phrases and individual words, as well as deepening the significance of larger sequences.

Although my second section also considers receptions of Pindar's Hesiodic engagements as reflected in the scholia, my main concern is to explore the poems in the context of public performance. Discussion of intertextuality against this background has to wrestle with the question of how well audiences might be expected to grasp the subtleties of meaning and implication that intertextual connections produce for readers. Skepticism about such capacities has begun to give way to approaches that see intertextuality at the level of both lexis and theme as crucial to Pindar's and Bacchylides's poetics (see Silk 2007: 184; Fearn 2007: 267–87; Pavlou 2008; Phillips 2016: 241–44), and there are good reasons to think that the complexity of textual relationships that modern scholars (and at least some ancient readers) detect(ed) would have been manifest to early audiences. This is the case even if we posit, as most scholars would, limited availability of physical texts, with performance being the dominant mode through which listeners encountered poetry (see Pavlou 2008: 536–41).

There is an obvious correlation between the sense-making capacities that a competent language user brings to bear on everyday usage and the capacities needed to see one text in relation to another. Like any other set of words, "literary" language, words marked with "literary" usages, and their accompanying associations would have been part of listeners' mental furniture. The same basic cognitive mechanisms are employed when listening and when reading; the time available to process one's responses is the chief differentiating factor. This is of course not an insignificant difference, but it does not call for an absolute distinction between modes of response. A listener's "real-time" response to an intertextually suggestive word or phrase might be more fleeting and less elaborately considered than that of a reader, but it does not follow that the felt connection will be less effective. What readers linger over, and what modern scholars attempt to capture with detailed analyses, might well resonate for a listener as an intuitively sensed significance or an implicitness of meaning to be recalled and pondered.

Nor should variations in receptive environments be discounted; some of Pindar's early listeners will have had access to texts of the poems, and sympotic reperformances will have offered ample opportunity for the sort of critical discussion we see represented in Plato's *Protagoras* and elsewhere, some of which would doubtless have dwelled on intertextual relationships. With these considerations in mind, the following readings sketch out the kinds of textual relationships to which listeners might have responded and the intuitions they might have formed about meanings. Needless to say, not all listeners will have reacted in the same ways or responded to all the details I suggest are at work (cf. the helpful remarks of Budelmann 2001: 8–14; Matzner 2016: 22–23 on audiences); rather, my readings elaborate the intertextual frames by which a range of possible responses is shaped.

PINDAR'S "FIRST HYMN"

Pindar's appropriations of Hesiodic language and narratives were part of a tradition that stretched back a century or more. Solon's political poetry utilizes Hesiodic concepts for contextually specific ends, while on a smaller scale, Alcaeus's picture of sympotic wine drinking (fr. 347 V) both pays tribute to and ironizes Hesiodic authority (Hunter 2014: 123–26). Stesichorus's well-known poem (or poems) about Helen, in which he asserts that a "phantom" went to Troy in her place, might have included explicit engagement with Hesiod (see Davies and Finglass 2014: 311–17 for discussion), and scholars have detected echoes of Hesiod's lines about seafaring (*WD* 646–62) in Ibycus's poem for Polycrates (*Poetae Melici Graeci* 282: see Hunter 2014: 54n37). Cosmological accounts such as those of Epimenides of Crete and the Derveni papyrus are likely to be engaging, more or less agonistically and obviously, with the framework of Hesiod's *Th*, while the criticisms directed by Xenophanes and Heraclitus at Hesiod's representations of the gods testify to the ongoing importance of Hesiod's works as a body of thought to be contested and departed from (see Scully 2015: 70–78 with further references, and Miller in this volume, pp. 213–20).

Pindar's departures from or "corrections" of Hesiod are often less agonistic than those of the early philosophers but are still important components of larger poetic strategies. Two representative examples might be useful. In *Isthmian* 6, composed for Phylacidas of Aegina, Pindar modifies the narrative in the Hesiodic *Megalae Ehoeae* to include Telamon in Heracles's expedition against Troy, a move designed to underscore Aegina's historical significance (Indergaard 2011: 306–21). At *Pythian* 3.27–30 Apollo's "all-knowing mind" enables him to detect Coronis's adultery, whereas in Hesiod he was told of the event by a crow (fr. 60 M–W = *Σ Pythian* 3.52a: see Phillips 2016: 175–78). Correcting the version with which listeners were familiar makes them aware of their implication in the false story and their vulnerability to deception (by contrast with Apollo at *Pythian* 3.29), even as the necessity of correcting Hesiod testifies to the power and endurance of his story. Intertextuality here brings home both the inventiveness of the human mind in constructing explicatory narratives and its openness to deception, and is hence crucial to the way in which the poem seeks to shape the conditions of its reception.

Intertextual relationships are similarly vital to Pindar's "First Hymn," a poem that was clearly felt by the ancients to be one of his most important and distinctive achievements, as indicated by its position at the beginning of the Alexandrian edition and references made to it in later literature.[1] Both at the level of phrase and of narrative structure, Pindar's poem elicits a set of responses the distinctiveness of which is framed by departures from Hesiod. One of the longest fragments (fr. 30 S–M) is an account of Zeus's marriage to Themis, a union that produces the Horae:

πρῶτον μὲν εὔβουλον Θέμιν οὐρανίαν
χρυσέαισιν ἵπποις Ὠκεανοῦ παρὰ παγᾶν
Μοῖραι ποτὶ κλίμακα σεμνὰν
    ἆγον Οὐλύμπου λιπαρὰν καθ᾽ ὁδόν
σωτῆρος ἀρχαίαν ἄλοχον Διὸς ἔμμεν·   5
    ἁ δὲ τὰς χρυσάμπυκας ἀγλαοκάρ-
    πους τίκτεν ἀλαθέας Ὥρας.

First the Moirae brought wise-counselling, heavenly Themis with golden horses from Ocean's springs towards Olympus' sacred stair, along a shining road, to be the first wife of Savior Zeus: she it was who bore the gold-filleted bearers of shining fruit, the constant Horae. (All translations are my own.)

Pindar's account seems to differ deliberately from Hesiod's, in which Themis is Zeus's second wife after his marriage to Metis (*Th* 886–900) and gives birth to both the Moirae and the Horae (*Th* 901–4). Making Themis Zeus's first wife emphasizes the importance of intellectual order (εὔβουλον) to the new cosmic dispensation (thus Snell 1953: 75–76; cf. Scully 2015: 98). Although there has been some debate about whether Pindar was deliberately rejecting Hesiod's mythography or the differences are simply the result of him not knowing it, the passage's combination of mythographical differentiation and lexical echoing makes the former scenario much more likely.[2]

Pindar invites listeners to register a series of departures from Hesiod, which constitute a cumulative progression in complexity of form and implication. Verse initial πρῶτον answers Hesiod's verse initial δεύτερον (*Th* 901), before the focal emphasis on Themis as "wise-counselling" (εὔβουλον) distinguishes her from both the Metis and indeed the Zeus of the *Th*, especially the latter's employing deceit to give birth to Athena (*Th* 888–900). More complex is λιπαρὰν καθ᾽ ὁδόν ("along a shining road"), a reference to the "Milky Way" with parallels in Pythagoreanism and later philosophy. Whether this phrase was intended to signal allegiance to a particular form of cosmology or mystery cult is difficult to say (see Hardie 2000: 25–26), but what is clear is its redirection of Hesiodic language. The transfer of the adjective from Themis's appearance (δεύτερον ἠγάγετο λιπαρὴν Θέμιν, *Th* 901) crystallizes the larger shift from Hesiod's emphasis on beauty being instantiated by individual figures to Pindar's on its inscription within the material structures of the cosmos. Capping this sequence, the phrasing of ἀρχαίαν ἄλοχον substitutes the qualitative "primordial" (Race 1997) or "original" for Hesiod's "second," verbally reinforcing genealogical difference (cf. Scully 2015: 98).

In hearing Pindar's account against Hesiod's, therefore, listeners are involved in a deepened and more detailed understanding of Themis's and the Horae's cosmic role and a concomitant responsiveness to the greater pregnancy and polyvalence of Pindar's language. This process occurs again in τὰς χρυσάμπυκας ἀγλαοκάρπους τίκτεν ἀλαθέας, which expands on Hesiod's τεθαλυῖαν, / αἵ τ᾽ ἔργ᾽ ὠρεύουσι ("flourishing [Peace], who superintend deeds [for mortals]," *Th* 902–3). The word order of the adjectives χρυσάμπυκας ἀγλαοκάρπους . . . ἀλαθέας iconizes a series of focalizations, creating a run of images and ideas through which the listener moves. The line projects an imaginary "viewer" who moves from a view of the goddesses in physical form (χρυσάμπυκας, which hints at the formal properties of cult statues and hence at a theoric encounter), to an apprehension of the goddesses' agricultural role (ἀγλαοκάρπους), to a conception of their "truthfulness." The final adjective might have a number of meanings, including the "truthfulness" or "honesty" of the goddesses (cf. Pindar's use of the adjective of his "mind" at *Olympian* 2.92; Race (1997) translates the adjective in the present passage as "ever-true"), and "consistent" (referencing the regularity of the seasons). Whatever the precise force of ἀλαθέας, however, the adjectives articulate a move from concrete to abstract that encourages an increasingly conceptual understanding, while also promoting an interaction that lends ἀλαθέας heightened affective force by association with the former terms (on association in Pindar see Silk 2012: 363–64, quoted in note 6 in this chapter). By allowing listeners to inhabit multiple relations to the Horae, this line demands a greater imaginative engagement than Hesiod's lines and is thrown into sharper relief by recall of them.

A rather different version of the intertextual dynamic in which departure from Hesiod accentuates a feature of Pindar's poem and helps to foreground the particularity of its demands occurs in the account of the Muses being created by Zeus. We owe our knowledge of this episode to descriptions of it in Aelius Aristides and Choricius of Gaza, but Bruno Snell was probably right to claim that "if we had this episode in Pindar's own language . . . it would surely be among the most famous in Greek literature" (1953: 78). Its extraordinariness can be glimpsed even in Aristides's synopsis: "Pindar says that when [Zeus] asked the gods themselves if they needed anything, they requested that he create for himself some gods [the Muses] who would adorn with words and music (κατακοσμήσουσι λόγοις καὶ μουσικῇ) those great works and all his arrangements" (Pindar fr. 31 S-M = Aelius Aristides, *Orations* 45.106 = 1.277 Lenz-Behr). It appears from Choricius's account that this event took place just after Zeus had completed his "adornment" of the cosmos (τὸ πᾶν ἄρτι κοσμήσας, 13.2).

Even in the absence of Pindar's words, we can see how different this account would have appeared from Hesiod's canonical narrative. In the *Th*, Zeus fathers the Muses with Mnemosyne "apart from the other gods" (57), and while their genealogy symbolizes their associations with authorized speech and cultural memory, no specific rationale is given for their "creation." In Pindar the creation is not merely a communal act, but rather the result of a conversation that dramatizes the gods' intuition about the importance of song to the new cosmos. This account performs a remarkable piece of poetic archaeology, explaining the Muses (and by implication all subsequent poetry) as the aftereffect and reflection of the shared understanding that underpins the gods' request.[3] While caution is necessary in attempting to grasp the sequence's wider significance, it seems clear that the intuition about song's value and the receptive attitude toward it that the Muses were created to reflect approximates, and is programmatic for, that which historical songs aim to produce in audiences. Crucially, the episode also enables a closer imaginative encounter with the "minds" of the gods than that which Hesiod's mythography makes available.

Insofar as this episode stages a moment of contact that is context transcendent not only in bridging temporal frames but also in being able to reoccur in any iteration of the poem regardless of its context of performance or reading, its psychological structure mirrors the effects created by Pindar's intertextually inflected language. Hesiodic recollections position the poem within a poetic tradition, but they also project the poem's performative self-constitution into the future. As long as Hesiod continues to be performed (and read) in the way Pindar's appropriations presuppose, the hymn's intertexts will continue to resonate, guaranteeing the inventiveness through which the hymn makes its claims on listeners (and readers). Understood in these terms, the Hesiodic intertextuality of the "First Hymn" is more than literary positioning or the adornment of ritual discourse, comprising instead a formalization of the poem's bid for transcontextual assertiveness, its attempt to constitute a mode of thinking that will continue to make its claims on listeners (and readers) beyond the "original" context of performance. The frequency with which later authors and readers were drawn to the poem testifies to its success.

ETHICS AT WORK

The assertion that athletic success requires hard work as well as native skill is a Pindaric signature. In what follows I focus on three occurrences of this topos in which Hesiodic undertones resonate and were picked up on by ancient commentators. Although the precise effects of the three passages vary considerably, common to each is a congruity between theme and intertextual dynamics. In each passage Hesiodic intertexts import associations of menial labor and human vulnerability (cf. Hunter 2014: 125–26 on the more lightheartedly ironical effect created by Alcaeus's "citation" of Hesiod in fr. 347 V). These associations are partially transcended by the sublime trajectories of Pindar's rhetoric but also serve to reinforce injunctions to respect mortal limitations. Moreover, by resituating Hesiodic precepts about human conduct in contexts very different from those in which those ideas are employed in the *WD*, Pindar impels his listeners to consider their self-constitution as ethical agents.

At *Olympian* 6.9–11 we find the claim "achievements without danger are no honors, neither among men nor in hollow ships" (ἀκίνδυνοι δ' ἀρεταί / οὔτε παρ' ἀνδράσιν οὔτ' ἐν ναυσὶ κοίλαις / τίμιαι). One scholium on this passage (Σ *Olympian* 6.14f) glosses ἀκίνδυνοι δ' ἀρεταί by quoting, without additional contextualizing comment, *WD* 289 (τῆς δ' ἀρετῆς ἱδρῶτα θεοὶ προπάροιθεν ἔθηκαν, "the gods set sweat before [the path to] achievement"; this line is also quoted at Σ *Olympian* 5.34c), before giving a paraphrastic analysis of Pindar's lines. Juxtaposing the two passages draws attention to a semantic shift: Hesiod's ἀρετή names a "superior standing in society . . . determined principally by material prosperity" (West 1974: 229) and is therefore more limited in scope than Pindar's ἀρεταί, which refers explicitly to athletic, and implicitly to military, achievement. The social consequences of such achievements help to define them. Pindar develops the claim about achievements by saying that "many men remember if a fair thing is accomplished with toil" (πολλοὶ δὲ μέμνανται, καλὸν εἴ τι ποναθῇ, 11), but such fame also requires the kind of self-limitation adumbrated by the speaker's insistence that the *laudandus* is "neither quarrelsome nor excessively fond of victory" (οὔτε δύσηρις ἐὼν οὔτ' ὢν φιλόνικος ἄγαν, 19).

The abrupt abstraction of ἀκίνδυνοι δ' ἀρεταί contrasts with Hesiod's earthily concrete and more fully visualized image (ἱδρῶτα, προπάροιθεν), while the scholiast's citation gives impetus to a reading of ἀκίνδυνοι δ' ἀρεταί as a compression of Hesiod's whole passage about the steep path to ἀρετή.[4] But Pindar's phrase also transplants its antecedent. In addition to the ethical and social complexity of the ἀκίνδυνοι δ' ἀρεταί just discussed, the Homeric tone of ἐν ναυσὶ κοίλαις (for which see Hutchinson 2001: 380) adds a more "heroic" register to the Hesiodic ἀκίνδυνοι δ' ἀρεταί. By subjecting the Hesiod intertext to verbal reconfiguration and contextual transposition, the phrasing of ἀκίνδυνοι δ' ἀρεταί . . . τίμιαι stages, and prompts listeners to reflect on, the "emergence of new conceptual possibilities" (Payne 2007: 12) that occurs as the Hesiodic language of ἀρεταί is expanded and complicated in the encomiastic context.

A similar "emergence" occurs in the phrase σοφίαι μὲν / αἰπειναί at *Olympian* 9.107–8. The Hesiodic character of this phrase was registered by a scholium, which gives the explanation that "having virtue is elevated and is set on high," before quoting *WD* 289 (ὑψηλόν ἐστι καὶ ἐν μετεώρῳ κείμενον τὸ ἀρετὴν ἔχειν. ὡς Ἡσίοδος . . .), and a similar reading is given by Σ 161b: "that is, wise acts lie on high and ahead, so that the road to them is difficult" (τουτέστιν ἐφ' ὑψηλοῦ καὶ προβάσεως κεῖνται αἱ σοφίαι, ὥστε εἶναι τὴν ἐπ᾽ αὐτὰς ὁδὸν δυσχερῆ). The interpretation of σοφίαι μὲν αἰπειναί in the light of Hesiod may well also have been impelled by the preceding lines: "for some paths are longer than others, and no single training will nurture all of us" (ἐντὶ γὰρ ἄλλαι / ὁδῶν ὁδοὶ περαίτεραι, / μία δ᾽ οὐχ ἅπαντας ἄμμε θρέψει / μελέτα, 104–7). The imagery of ὁδοὶ περαίτεραι is redolent of the "path to ἀρετή," and (as explored further below in relation to *Isthmian* 6.66–69) μελέτη is replete with Hesiodic associations.

When we look at the whole Hesiodic passage, we can see the extent of its influence on both Pindar and the scholia:

σοὶ δ᾽ ἐγὼ ἐσθλὰ νοέων ἐρέω, μέγα νήπιε Πέρση·
τὴν μέν τοι κακότητα καὶ ἱλαδὸν ἔστιν ἑλέσθαι
ῥηιδίως· λείη μὲν ὁδός, μάλα δ᾽ ἐγγύθι ναίει·
τῆς δ᾽ ἀρετῆς ἱδρῶτα θεοὶ προπάροιθεν ἔθηκαν
ἀθάνατοι· μακρὸς δὲ καὶ ὄρθιος οἶμος ἐς αὐτὴν   290
καὶ τρηχὺς τὸ πρῶτον· ἐπὴν δ᾽ εἰς ἄκρον ἵκηται,
ῥηιδίη δὴ ἔπειτα πέλει, χαλεπή περ ἐοῦσα.

And I shall speak to you, foolish Perses, with good things in mind. Badness is grasped by many and easily: smooth is the road and it lies close at hand. But before the path of achievement the immortal gods set sweat. Long and sheer is the way that leads to it and rough at first, but when one reaches the summit, then it is easy, though difficult before.

Pindar's αἰπειναί, and the scholia's ἐφ᾽ ὑψηλοῦ and δυσχερῆ, approximate Hesiod's μακρὸς δὲ καὶ ὄρθιος . . . / καὶ τρηχὺς τὸ πρῶτον and χαλεπή. It seems likely that the scholiast(s) responsible for this analysis were influenced, consciously or not, by the Hesiodic passage (an influence quite possibly mediated by its extensive *Nachleben*, for which see Hunter 2014: 93–100, 141–45, 269–75), an influence felt especially strongly in the use of τὸ ἀρετὴν ἔχειν to gloss σοφίαι. The paraphrases that the scholia elaborate reflect the difficulties of Pindar's phrasing: σοφίαι μὲν αἰπειναί is highly compressed, the plural σοφίαι conveying a meaning such as "acts" or "ways" of wisdom (Race 1997 translates this as "the ways of wisdom are steep").

As with ἀκίνδυνοι δ᾽ ἀρεταί, the phrase allows the Hesiodically attuned listener or reader to hear it as condensing Hesiod's lines and implying a process of response to those lines on the part of the *persona loquens*. As in that passage, the onerous associations of the Hesiodic "path to ἀρετή" provide a subtextual counterweight to encomiastic celebration. Unlike in *Olympian* 6, however, the Hesiodic reminiscence σοφίαι μὲν αἰπειναί leads immediately into an exhortation to celebrate the *laudandus*'s physical qualities and "courage" (*Olympian* 9.107–12):

σοφίαι μέν
αἰπειναί· τοῦτο δὲ προσφέρων ἄεθλον,
ὄρθιον ὤρυσαι θαρσέων,

> τόνδ' ἀνέρα δαιμονίᾳ γεγάμεν   110
> εὔχειρα, δεξιόγυιον, ὁρῶντ' ἀλκάν,
> Αἴαν, τεόν τ' ἐν δαιτί, Ἰλιάδα,
> νικῶν ἐπεστεφάνωσε βωμόν.

The ways of wisdom are steep. In bestowing this prize, cry out boldly and loud that this man was born by fate with strong hands, nimble of limb, of bold look; and at your banquet, Ajax son of Ileus, the victor garlanded your altar.

Given the connection between σοφία and poetry, and the fact that Pindar often uses the imagery of height to conceptualize his poetry's affective force, σοφίαι μὲν αἰπειναί can be understood as adumbrating the heightened apprehension of meaning that takes place in the act of listening.[5] The metaphor anticipates the emotive power the closing image will have when channeled through the voice of the imagined respondent, and it is answered by the undertone of height imagery in ὄρθιον ὤρυσαι. Its compression elicits interpretation, challenging the reader or listener to expand on the phrase's implicit possibilities (a challenge answered by the scholia's paraphrases). More concretely, it also metaphorically enacts ethical comportment, the adjective (usually used of landscapes such as cliffs) connoting both elevation and the constraints placed on men by their physical environments.[6] This combination of enactment and self-description focuses attention on the ethical charge of the form, as well as the propositional content, of Pindar's language, the distinctiveness of which is thrown into further relief by its difference from Hesiodic precedent.

In moving beyond Hesiodic physical labor into the brighter, more abstract world of athletic achievement and simultaneously activating reminiscences of men's environmental limitations, the Hesiodic intertextuality of these passages enacts ethical comportment by balancing celebration and restraint and calls on listeners to reproduce this balance in their responses. This synergy of ethics and intertexts is most explicitly realized in Pindar's most salient engagement with Hesiod, the passage in the final triad of *Isthmian* 6 in which Lampon, the *laudandus*'s father, is described as "honoring" a Hesiodic maxim and quoting it to his sons (*Isthmian* 6.66–69):

> Λάμπων δὲ μελέταν
> ἔργοις ὀπάζων Ἡσιόδου μάλα τιμᾷ τοῦτ' ἔπος,
> υἱοῖσί τε φράζων παραινεῖ,
> ξυνὸν ἄστει κόσμον ἑῷ προσάγων ...

Lampon, bestowing care on his deeds, especially honors this saying of Hesiod's, and quoting it commends it to his sons, bringing to his town an adornment experienced in common ...

The reference is to *WD* 412, where "industry fosters work" (μελέτη δέ τοι ἔργον ὀφέλλει), one of a series of maxims about good husbandry. This is the only passage in the epinicians where Hesiod is mentioned by name, and the explicitness of the reference calls attention both to the content of the maxim and its interaction with the context into which it is transposed.

The basic point is that, like Hesiod's good farmer, Lampon works hard and is rewarded, an equation made clear by the scholium that glosses the phrase μελέταν / ἔργοις (Σ Isthmian 6.97):

ὁ δὲ Λάμπων, φησί, διηνεκῶς τοῖς ἔργοις τὴν μελέτην διδοὺς τὸν τοῦ Ἡσιόδου τιμᾷ καὶ ἀποδέχεται λόγον, καὶ τοῖς ἑαυτοῦ παισὶ λέγων τὸν στίχον παραινεῖ ἄθλων καὶ εὐδοξίας ἀντέχεσθαι, κοινὴν εὐδοξίαν τῇ ἑαυτοῦ πατρίδι προσάπτων.

And Lampon, he says, continually giving care to his labors honors and accepts Hesiod's statement, and in speaking the line to his sons advises them to cleave to labors and good repute, bestowing public good repute on his country.

As well as demonstrating a familiarity with the Hesiodic text that affirms his status as an educated καλὸς κἀγαθός, in repeating the phrase to his sons and instantiating its advice through his own conduct Lampon also exercises an independent agency and ethical self-awareness that anticipates and embodies the "pursuit of measure in his thoughts" attributed to him at 71 (μέτρα μὲν γνώμᾳ διώκων, μέτρα δὲ καὶ κατέχων).

The idiomatic aspect of Lampon's agency is made clear by the contextual transplantation to which Hesiod's dictum is subject. Hesiod's μελέτη takes place in the context of tough, unglamorous physical labor on the farm, but while the athletic activity for which Lampon and his sons are celebrated is dependent on physical exertion, and while the present poem commemorates a victory in an event, the pancration, which placed particular demands on the body, both the act of athletic success and its recuperation by the poem bathe the athlete in a radiance remote from Hesiod's quotidian realities: ἀγλαοὶ παῖδές τε καὶ μάτρως. ἀνὰ δ' ἄγαγον ἐς φάος οἵαν μοῖραν ὕμνων ("[these] radiant boys and their uncle. They brought into the light such a great share of songs," 62). Athletic κλέος is also more socially complex than the success of Hesiod's farmer, bringing a ξυνὸν κόσμον to the town as opposed to prosperity to an individual. This differentiation between applications of Hesiod's ἔπος is implicit in the passage as a whole and may be hinted at in Pindar's substitution of ἔργοις for Hesiod's ἔργον, where the plural can be understood as referencing Lampon's commitment (indicating that he engages in the same activity repeatedly, as in the scholium's reading), but also suggests a greater range of actions; unlike Perses, Lampon is not tied to the farm.

The Hesiodic reminiscence reinforces Lampon's socially elevated status, but in suggesting recall of the farmer's difficulties, it also acts as an implicit reminder of the mortal limitations against which athletes must strive and of which listeners should take account in responding to athletic success. The intertextual associations of 66–68 thus parallel and reinforce the double emphasis on glorifying the city and the importance of "due measure" in the lines that follow. In this sense, Lampon's role as a listener to and purveyor of Hesiod's works partially anticipates the ethically inflected listening that Pindar's poem itself demands. Like Lampon, the Pindaric listener appreciates the importance of μελέτη, but what makes listening to epinician distinctive as a "pursuit of measure" is that it also requires the listener to reflect on the difference between how Hesiod's advice operates in the (narrative) situation to which it was originally directed and its potential application to contemporary circumstances. In rewriting Hesiod's paraenesis, Pindar opens up a space for listeners to reflect on their own agency.

A Volcano's Voice

Composed in 470 BCE to celebrate both a chariot victory and Hiero's foundation of the city of Aetna, *Pythian* 1 begins with a famous invocation of the "golden *phorminx*" and an account of music's power, channeled through the Muses' choral dancing, to lull even violent elements of the Olympian community such as Ares and Zeus's eagle into quiescence (1–12). There follows an ekphrasis of the monster Typhon, imprisoned under Etna (18–20), who is responsible for the volcano's eruptions. As critics have long recognized, the passage instantiates a cosmic order sanctioned and imposed by Zeus that parallels the political order brought about by Hiero's rule and contains numerous reminiscences of Hesiod's account of Typhoeus's fall in the *Th* (for clarity, I use "Typhon" for Pindar's character and "Typhoeus" for Hesiod's).[7] As with the passages examined in the previous section, listeners' familiarity with the *Th* would have enabled them to detect connections between microtextual elements of Pindar's poem and its Hesiodic predecessor, as well as to sense larger differences between the two accounts. The following reading explores the dynamic of connection and contrast that Pindar creates and situates it in relation to *Pythian* 1 as a whole.

In Hesiod, Typhoeus is conspicuous for the many noises he produces, the multiplicity of which indexes his disruptive power (*Th* 829–35):[8]

> φωναὶ δ' ἐν πάσῃσιν ἔσαν δεινῆς κεφαλῇσι,
> παντοίην ὄπ' ἰεῖσαι ἀθέσφατον· ἄλλοτε μὲν γὰρ   830
> φθέγγονθ' ὥς τε θεοῖσι συνιέμεν, ἄλλοτε δ' αὖτε
> ταύρου ἐριβρύχεω μένος ἀσχέτου ὄσσαν ἀγαύρου,
> ἄλλοτε δ' αὖτε λέοντος ἀναιδέα θυμὸν ἔχοντος,
> ἄλλοτε δ' αὖ σκυλάκεσσιν ἐοικότα, θαύματ' ἀκοῦσαι,
> ἄλλοτε δ' αὖ ῥοίζεσχ', ὑπὸ δ' ἤχεεν οὔρεα μακρά.

Voices there were in all of his terrible heads, sending forth all manner of unspeakable utterance. Sometimes he spoke as if to be understood by the gods, and other times his voices was the might of a bellowing, majestic bull, uncontainable in its power, and sometimes having a lion's reckless spirit, and sometimes like to whelps, a wonder to hear, and sometimes he hissed, and the great mountains echoed under him.

By contrast, although he stresses the sounds associated with Typhon, Pindar focuses just as much on how the monster's subterranean presence is registered through light, the "blazing stream of smoke" and the "rolling red flame" offset by the darkness, an emphasis driven home by the paired senses of 26 (προσιδέσθαι ... ἀκοῦσαι):

τᾶς ἐρεύγονται μὲν ἀπλάτου πυρὸς ἁγνόταται
ἐκ μυχῶν παγαί· ποταμοὶ δ' ἀμέραισιν
    μὲν προχέοντι ῥόον καπνοῦ
αἴθων· ἀλλ' ἐν ὄρφναισιν πέτρας
φοίνισσα κυλινδομένα φλὸξ ἐς βαθεῖ-
    αν φέρει πόντου πλάκα σὺν πατάγῳ
κεῖνο δ' Ἀφαίστοιο κρουνοὺς ἑρπετόν   25
δεινοτάτους ἀναπέμπει· τέρας μὲν
    θαυμάσιον προσιδέσθαι,
    θαῦμα δὲ καὶ παρεόντων ἀκοῦσαι . . .

from whose [sc. Etna's] depths holiest springs of unapproachable fire are belched
forth. In the day lava streams pour forth a blazing stream of smoke, but in the
darkness a rolling red flame carries rocks into the deep expanse of the sea with a
crash. That creature sends up most terrible springs of Hephaestus' fire, a portent
wondrous to behold, and a wonder even to hear of from those present . . .

In comparison to Hesiod's description, the ekphrasis confronts listeners with an atten-
uated soundscape, substituting the multiple φωναί of Typhoeus for the "crash" made
as the rocks reach the sea (σὺν πατάγῳ). For all its awesome power, this sound is not
generated by the monster himself, but is a secondary outcome of his situation: Hesiod's
catalog of sounds registers the agency Typhoeus is able to exercise by projecting himself
through different vocal identities, while Pindar's crashing rocks are a symptom of the
monster's captivity as much as an expression of his vestigial power. This auditory diminution is matched by geographical localization, the eruptions' effects being limited to
the mountain's immediate environs, while Zeus's defeat of Typhoeus causes "the earth
[to] sound terribly round about and the broad heaven above and the sea, and Ocean's
streams, and the deep places of the earth" (Th 839–41). Hesiod's whole cosmos becomes
a vessel through which the noise made by Zeus and Typhoeus is transmitted; Pindar's
topography (ἐς βαθεῖαν φέρει πόντου πλάκα) emphasizes the boundaries imposed on
Typhon's generation of physical disorder.[9]

Pindar keeps Zeus and Typhon firmly separate: picking up where Hesiod's
narrative ends (ὅς τ' ἐν αἰνᾷ Ταρτάρῳ κεῖται, 15, recalling ῥῖψε δέ μιν θυμῷ ἀκαχὼν
ἐς τάρταρον εὐρύν, Th 868) and moving directly from the monster's "rearing" to
his present situation (τόν ποτε / Κιλίκιον θρέψεν πολυώνυμον ἄντρον· νῦν γε μάν,
16–17), he avoids the Hesiodic picture of entangled protagonists, even as his elision
invites listeners to recall Hesiod's account, which in depicting the moment of conflict fuses the antagonists' noisemaking together in a minimally differentiated din
(Th 844–49):

καῦμα δ' ὑπ' ἀμφοτέρων κάτεχεν ἰοειδέα πόντον
βροντῆς τε στεροπῆς τε πυρός τ' ἀπὸ τοῖο πελώρου   845
πρηστήρων ἀνέμων τε κεραυνοῦ τε φλεγέθοντος·

ἔζεε δὲ χθὼν πᾶσα καὶ οὐρανὸς ἠδὲ θάλασσα·
θυῖε δ' ἄρ' ἀμφ' ἀκτὰς περί τ' ἀμφί τε κύματα μακρὰ
ῥιπῇ ὑπ' ἀθανάτων, ἔνοσις δ' ἄσβεστος ὀρώρει·

Burning gripped the violet-hued sea, both from thunder and lightning and from
the monster's fire, and from tornados and winds, and the flaming thunderbolt.
The whole earth and heaven and sea seethed, and the great waves raged around the
headlands and back and forth from the onrush of the immortals, and an uncontrollable quaking arose.

Hesiod gives us a sonic snapshot that encapsulates the supernatural conflict and focuses
on the sounds that Typhoeus and Zeus generate; Pindar focuses on stable, temporally extended modes of response and relationships to sound. Exemplifying these relationships
are the Olympian deities lulled and bewitched by the Muses' song in the poem's first
two stanzas to Typhon, who belongs among "those whom Zeus does not love" who are
"terrified on hearing the cry of the Pierians" (ὅσσα δὲ μὴ πεφίληκε Ζεύς, ἀτύζονται βοάν
/ Πιερίδων ἀΐοντα, 13–14). These structural contrasts slant recollection by emphasizing
those aspects of the Hesiodic narrative, the battle and the confusion of sound, that are
absent from Pindar, and so encourage the poems to be related to each other not just
as a unified teleological narrative in which *Pythian* 1 acts as a sequel to the *Th* and
emphasizes containment over conflict, but also in terms of the different experiences of
their subjects they afford.

Yet even as Pindar presents a Typhon whose sound-generating capacities and environmental effects are diminished by comparison with his Hesiodic forebear and
shows him more definitively separated from the Olympian order that he threatens
than in Hesiod's narrative, he also confronts listeners with an unsettlingly ambivalent sonic experience. The vividly mimetic alliteration and dactylic rhythm of
φοίνισσα κυλινδομένα φλὸξ ἐς βαθεῖαν φέρει πόντου πλάκα σὺν πατάγῳ, the ugliness
of ἐρεύγονται, and the mimetic dactylic movement of δεινοτάτους ἀναπέμπει make
for an expressively threatening sonority that unsettles any simple distinction between
sound and sense. The urgent immediacy with which these phrases resonate in the ear
of the listener underscores Typhon's threateningly proximate presence, even as poetic
stylization transforms its referents into an enchanting artifact (for discussion of the
link between Etna as a θαῦμα and the effect of the poem itself see Morrison 2012: 131
and Phillips 2016: 151–52).

A similar tension can be seen at work in other elements of *Pythian* 1 that look back to
Zeus's conquest of Typhoeus (*Th* 853–68):

Ζεὺς δ' ἐπεὶ οὖν κόρθυνεν ἑὸν μένος, εἵλετο δ' ὅπλα,
βροντήν τε στεροπήν τε καὶ αἰθαλόεντα κεραυνόν,
πλῆξεν ἀπ' Οὐλύμποιο ἐπάλμενος· ἀμφὶ δὲ πάσας   855
ἔπρεσε θεσπεσίας κεφαλὰς δεινοῖο πελώρου.
αὐτὰρ ἐπεὶ δή μιν δάμασε πληγῇσιν ἱμάσσας,

ἤριπε γυιωθείς, στονάχιζε δὲ γαῖα πελώρη·
φλὸξ δὲ κεραυνωθέντος ἀπέσσυτο τοῖο ἄνακτος
οὔρεος ἐν βήσσῃσιν † ἀιδνῆς παιπαλοέσσης   860
πληγέντος, πολλὴ δὲ πελώρη καίετο γαῖα
αὐτμῇ θεσπεσίῃ ...

So when Zeus had gathered his might and seized his arms, the thunder and lightning and the blazing thunderbolt, he leapt from Olympus and struck, and he
scorched all the fell monster's terrible heads on every side. But when he had overcome him, scourging him with blows, the monster fell crippled, and the vast earth
groaned. Flame rushed from the thunderstruck lord as he was struck down in the
mountain glades of rocky Aidna, and the vast earth was singed with the awful
blast ...

While in narrative terms Pindar's ekphrasis provides a sequel to Hesiod, stressing
that Typhon no longer threatens the Olympian order, listeners are also invited to hear
Pindar's language as expanding on Hesiodic antecedents. Formally, these may be
compared to the description of the Horae in the "First Hymn," but whereas that passage
mapped linguistic onto generative abundance, here verbal animation and descriptive
exorbitance induce an imaginative involvement that complicates the poem's narrative of
containment.

This dynamic is evident in numerous phrases. Pindar's κυλινδομένα φλὸξ ... (24)
expands φλὸξ δὲ κεραυνωθέντος ἀπέσσυτο, with φέρει πόντου πλάκα σὺν πατάγῳ
enacting through sound and rhythmical movement a phenomenon that parallels that
denoted by ἀπέσσυτο (although there the "flame" is created by the thunderbolt with
which Typhoeus is struck). Hesiod's οὔρεος ἐν βήσσῃσιν are answered by the more pic-
torial "dark-leaved peaks" by which Typhon is held down (ἐν μελαμφύλλοις δέδεται
κορυφαῖς, 27), while Pindar's picture of Typhon's "couch scratching the whole of his
back as he lies on it" (στρωμνὰ δὲ χαράσσοισ' ἄπαν νῶτον ποτικεκλιμένον κεντεῖ, 28),
focusing on the monster's physical incapacity and suffering, continues the Hesiodic detailing of ἤριπε γυιωθείς. This line takes us down under the earth more vividly than
Hesiod does (the transplantation of στρωμνά out of its normal use is lexically emblematic of this effect) and may prompt a fleeting sympathy with the creature's suffering.
Somewhat paradoxically, Pindar emphasizes Typhon's captivity while affording
listeners an intense imaginative and sensuous access to his present condition, which
overflows the demarcation between geographical regions achieved at the level of
narrative.[10]

What is at stake in the different modes of listening the two poems project can be
brought into further focus by comparing endings. Hesiod closes with a simile which,
employing a vehicle that miniaturizes its tenor and evokes processes of craftsmanship
at odds with Typhoeus's disordering effervescence, achieves an effect of diminution that
parallels Zeus's conquest of the monster. The simile also hints at a metapoetic parallelism between the shaping of material "violence" (δαμαζόμενος πυρὶ κηλέῳ) for cultural

ends, which in turn acts a synecdoche for the function of the poem itself in sublimating its dark materials (for readings of the simile see Goslin 2010: 367):

> καὶ ἐτήκετο κασσίτερος ὣς
> τέχνῃ ὑπ' αἰζηῶν ἐν ἐυτρήτοις χοάνοισι
> θαλφθείς, ἠὲ σίδηρος, ὅ περ κρατερώτατός ἐστιν,
> οὔρεος ἐν βήσσῃσι δαμαζόμενος πυρὶ κηλέῳ   865
> τήκεται ἐν χθονὶ δίῃ ὑφ' Ἡφαίστου παλάμῃσιν·
> ὣς ἄρα τήκετο γαῖα σέλαι πυρὸς αἰθομένοιο.
> ῥῖψε δέ μιν θυμῷ ἀκαχὼν ἐς τάρταρον εὐρύν.

and [the earth] was melted as when tin is heated by the craft of skilled men in crucibles with well-bored holes, or iron, the strongest of metals, melts in mountain glades when overcome by burning fire in the divine earth under Hephaestus' hands. So then did the earth melt at the blast of blazing flame. And Zeus, angered in his heart, flung Typhoeus into broad Tartarus.

More important for comparison with *Pythian* 1, however, is the simile's positioning of listeners, who are distanced from the mythological fabula by being reminded of the smaller experiential scale in which their grasp of that fabula is grounded. Pindar's framing of the ekphrasis (τέρας μὲν θαυμάσιον προσιδέσθαι, θαῦμα δὲ καὶ παρεόντων ἀκοῦσαι) emphasizes more direct forms of perceptual contact through which Etna (itself) can be seen and "heard about from those present." Just as the textures of Pindar's poem foreground the way sound invades and inhabits us as we listen, the "cry" of the Muses hinting at the irreducibly unmeaningful sonority out of which poetry is made, as well as at the focalization of the Muses' utterance by Typhon, so the formulation προσιδέσθαι ... ἀκοῦσαι intimates Typhon's capacity to spill out (or rather, to create effects that spill out) into the inhabited world, straining against Zeus's ordering power. This intimation is driven home by the succeeding lines picturing Typhon under the earth (27–28); iconically, "seeing and hearing" is framed within the ekphrasis itself.

The Hesiodic intertextuality of the ekphrasis can thus be understood in two contradictory but also complementary senses. The passage continues the *Th*'s narrative, but its recall of the *Th*'s language also encourages listeners to hear the texts alongside each other. The former relation accentuates the completion and endurance of Zeus's cosmic order, while the latter compels an imaginative engagement that compromises any sense of secure progression; even as Pindar's narrative positions Zeus's battle with Typhon in the past, echoes of the *Th* replay it. This relationship inscribes within the structure of poem a tension that enacts the poem's wider struggle to impose order on its subject matter. *Pythian* 1 opens out into a violent and unstable world: the threats posed by the Carthaginians and the Etruscans have been overcome, but linger (71–75); the ruler must guard not only against envious subjects, but also against his own potential for excess (85–98); and the compositional act itself is figured as balancing achievement and restraint (45–46). Understood in terms of their directedness toward a receptive listening, the tensions at work in ekphrasis foreshadow the ways in which listeners are asked to position themselves in relation to the problems these passages adumbrate.

Conclusions

Although these readings inevitably give a provisional picture of a complex literary relationship, they illustrate the variety and sophistication with which Pindar responds to Hesiod and the corresponding complexities of response that his poems demand. Pindar's mythographic and verbal departures from Hesiod in the "First Hymn" frame a more direct "psychological" encounter with the gods as well as affording listeners a heightened and more detailed imaginative access to material realities. The appropriations of Hesiod's "path to ἀρετή" activate associations of mortal limitations and the importance of hard work, even as they are transcended by the act of victory and its commemoration in the poem. In *Pythian* 1, Pindar presents a picture of Typhon that stresses the monster's containment within the cosmic order, but the immediacy with which the poem realizes its subject through sound and rhythm drives home the monster's ever-present threat. Again, departures from Hesiod at the level of both structure and phrase accentuate this dynamic.

As approximations of the responsive environment inhabited by Pindar's audiences, these readings are necessarily to an extent deformative. During performances the effects I have elaborated through readings of individual words and phrases will have appeared for listeners as momentary hints and suggestions rather than fully realized structures of argument. Similarly, the dynamics of containment and musical affectivity in *Pythian* 1 will have been sensuously experienced more than reflectively analyzed. The variety of response evidenced by the scholia, as well as by modern interpretations of these and other connections, is likely to have been paralleled in the reactions of Pindar's early listeners, who will have identified more and fewer intertextual connections and responded to them in different ways. These qualifications, however, do not lessen the importance that such intertextual dialogues have in creating effects and drawing listeners into reflection on their own role in making sense of the poems. Pindar's mastery in "maxims, figures, and wealth of subjects and language" (*sententiis, figuris . . . rerum uerborumque copia*, Quintilian, *Institutio Oratoria* 10.1.61) has long been recognized, and on this reading the sophistication of his intertextual poetics deserves equal recognition.[11]

Notes

1. Following Snell (1946), the hymn is commonly referred to as the "Hymn to Zeus," but while this reconstruction is plausible, there is no compelling evidence to suggest that Zeus was the original dedicatee, and several recent articles have made a strong case for regarding it as composed for Apollo; see D'Alessio (2005, 2009).

2. For this view see D'Alessio (2009: 140), who calls it "a rewriting of Hesiod," and Scully (2015: 98); thus also West (1966: 406) with older bibliography. An intertextual connection between the two texts may be suggested by their pairing at Lucian 24.27, for which reference I am indebted to Oliver Thomas.

3. It may be significant that at *Th* 60, the Muses are "of one mind' (ὁμόφρονας); Pindar's emphasis on the gods' collective agreement (a kind of ὁμοφροσύνη) may repurpose this detail, although of course we do not know whether Pindar employed this vocabulary. Another

difference of emphasis occurs in relation to *Th* 73–75, where the Muses sing about Zeus's dispensation of cosmic order apparently unmediated by the other gods; in emphasizing such mediation, Pindar's handling of the Muses seems to have stressed the other gods' active assent to this dispensation. The hymn's scenario also develops *Th* 881–85; whereas Hesiod has Zeus "dispensing honors" to the gods (ἐὺ διεδάσσατο τιμάς), Pindar has the gods participating in the celebration of the order that results from this dispensation.

4. The dramatic condensation of Pindar's phrase is also indexed by the plurality of interpretations to which it is subject. The scholia offer a selection of views, according to which ἀκίνδυνοι δ' ἀρεταί refers to the fact that the victor's house was encompassed by dangers or that the victor won with toil (Σ 14e); the phrase can also be interpreted specifically as consoling the victor for his sufferings in winning his victory (παραμυθεῖται δὲ αὐτόν, Σ 14f). Modern commentators have detected a connection with the victor's skill in battle, which is explicitly referenced at 17–18 (see Hutchinson 2001: 380–81, who suggests for ἐν ναυσὶ κοίλαις, "an oblique reference to the battle of Cumae," and Adorjáni 2014: 131–33 for further discussion).

5. For σοφία and/as poetry see *Olympian* 1.116, *Pythian* 1.12. For Pindar's imagery of height, its connection with the discourse of "sublimity," and its critical reception in antiquity see Porter (2016: 350–60).

6. With this effect may be compared Ὀγχηστίαισίν τ' ἀϊόνεσσιν περιστέλλων ἀοιδάν (*Isthmian* 1.33), with the comments of Silk (2012: 363–64): "the several uses of the verb [sc. 'cover with a shroud,' 'wrap up,' and 'conserve'] are made available, without decisive articulation of any one, in an associative co-presence which serves to bring together positive and negative, celebration and loss . . . achievement in time and celebration that defies time."

7. On the political dynamics of the passage see Athanassaki (2009); Currie (2012: 297–99); and Morgan (2015: 308–20 with further references). Hesiodic elements are discussed by Morrison (2012: 131); Morgan (2015: 314–16); and Fearn (2017) 177–84, 200–2, whose readings coincide with those advanced here at several points.

8. See Goslin (2010: 360–62) and Gurd (2016: 32–33).

9. Goslin (2010: 365) stresses the difference between Zeus's thunder and Typhoeus's noise, the former "reflect[ing] the god's power in a clear and immediate way."

10. Pindar may imply that Typhon is physically closer to the surface of the earth than Typhoeus, of whom Hesiod says simply ῥῖψε δέ μιν θυμῷ ἀκαχὼν ἐς τάρταρον εὐρύν; on the text of *Th* 860 and the possible location to which it refers see West (1966: 393), who argues that it is unlikely to be Etna. For further discussion of the geography of *Pythian* 1 and its political significance see Currie (2012: 297–99).

11. I would like to thank the editors and Tim Rood for their comments.

References

Adorjáni, Z., ed. and comm. 2014. *Pindars sechste Olympsiche Ode: Text, Einleitung und Kommentar*. Leiden, Netherlands.

Athanassaki, L. 2009. "Narratology, Deixis, and the Performance of Choral Lyric: On Pindar's First Pythian Ode." In *Narratology and Interpretation*, edited by J. Grethlein, and A. Rengakos, 241–73. Berlin.

Budelmann, F. 2001. *The Language of Sophocles: Communality, Communication and Involvement*. Cambridge.

Currie, B. 2012. "Pindar and Bacchylides." In *Space in Ancient Greek Literature*, edited by I. de Jong, 285–303. Leiden, Netherlands.

D'Alessio, G.-B. 2005. "Il primo *Inno* di Pindaro." In *Lirica e teatro in Grecia: Il testo e la sua recezione; II Incontro di Studi (Perugia, 23–24 gennaio 2003)*, edited by S. Grandolini, 113–49. Naples, Italy.

D'Alessio, G.-B. 2009. "Re-Constructing Pindar's First Hymn: The Theban 'Theogony' and the Birth of Apollo." In *Apolline Politics and Poetics: International Symposium*, edited by L. Athanassaki, R. Martin, and J. Miller, 129–47. Athens, Greece.

Davies, M., and P. Finglass, eds. and comms. 2014. *Stesichorus: The Poems*. Cambridge.

Fearn, D. 2007. *Bacchylides: Politics, Performance, Poetic Tradition*. Oxford.

Fearn, D. 2017 *Pindar's Eyes*. Oxford.

Goslin, O. 2010. "Hesiod's Typhonomachy and the Ordering of Sound." *TAPA* 140: 351–73.

Gurd, S. 2016. *Dissonance: Auditory Aesthetics in Ancient Greece*. New York.

Hardie, A. 2000. "Pindar's 'Theban' Cosmogony (the First Hymn)." *Bulletin of the Institute of Classical Studies* 44: 19–40.

Hunter, R. 2014. *Hesiodic Voices*. Cambridge.

Hutchinson, G., ed. 2001. *Greek Lyric Poetry*. Oxford.

Indergaard, H. 2011. "Thebes, Aegina, and the Temple of Aphaia." In *Aegina: Contexts for Choral Lyric Poetry*, edited by D. Fearn, 294–322. Oxford.

Matzner, S. 2016. *Rethinking Metonymy*. Oxford.

Morgan, K. 2015. *Pindar and the Construction of Syracusan Monarchy in the Fifth Century BC*. Oxford.

Morrison, A. 2012. "Performance, Re-Performance, and Pindar's Audiences." In *Reading the Victory Ode*, edited by P. Agócs, C. Carey, and R. Rawles, 111–33. Cambridge.

Pavlou, M. 2008. "Metapoetics, Poetic Tradition, and Praise in Pindar *Olympian* 9." *Mnemosyne* 61: 533–67.

Payne, M. 2007. "Ideas in Lyric Communication: Pindar and Paul Celan." *Modern Philology* 105: 5–20.

Phillips, T. 2016. *Pindar's Library: Performance Poetry and Material Texts*. Oxford.

Porter, J. 2016. *The Sublime in Antiquity*. Cambridge.

Race, W. J. 1997. *Pindar*. Cambridge, MA.

Scully, S. 2015. *Hesiod's Theogony: From Near Eastern Creation Myths to Paradise Lost*. Oxford.

Silk, M. 2007. "Pindar's Poetry as Poetry: A Literary Commentary on *Olympian* 12." In *Pindar's Poetry, Patrons, and Festivals: From Archaic Greece to the Roman Empire*, edited by S. Hornblower and C. Morgan, 177–97. Oxford.

Silk, M. 2012. "Reading Pindar." In *Reading the Victory Ode*, edited by P. Agócs, C. Carey, and R. Rawles, 347–64. Cambridge.

Snell, B. 1946. "Pindars Hymnus auf Zeus." *Antike und Ahendland* 2: 180–92.

Snell, B. 1953. *The Discovery of the Mind*. Oxford.

West, M., ed. and comm. 1966. *Hesiod: Theogony*. Oxford.

West, M., ed. and comm. 1974. *Hesiod: Works and Days*. Oxford.

CHAPTER 18

......

HESIOD AND TRAGEDY

......

ALAN H. SOMMERSTEIN

INTRODUCTION

......

IN this chapter I use the term "Hesiod" to mean the *Theogony* (hereafter *Th*) and *Works and Days* (hereafter *WD*) (or their author), and "tragedy" is taken to include satyr-drama, which was composed by tragic poets and performed by tragic actors and choruses as part of the tragic competition at the Athenian Dionysia. Satyr-drama accounted for a significant part of tragic poets' interaction with Hesiod. This chapter deals with three tragic poets: Aeschylus (ca. 525–456 BCE), Sophocles (ca. 496–406 BCE), and the unknown poet (possibly Aeschylus's son Euphorion) who, most likely in the 430s (Sommerstein 2010: 231–32), composed the sequence of plays about Prometheus, of which only the *Prometheus Bound* (hereafter *PB*) survives in full.

HESIODIC MYTH IN TRAGEDY 1: PROMETHEUS, PANDORA, AND THE SATYRS

......

Greek tragedy was primarily a drama of human suffering, and the myths recounted in Hesiod's narratives, being almost entirely concerned with the interactions of gods with other gods, were not well adapted to it. Indeed, so far as we know, only one Hesiodic myth, or rather two myths that Hesiod blends into one story, were dramatized by fifth-century tragic poets: the myth of Prometheus, associated with the bringing of fire to mortals and with the creation of the first woman.

This story is told both in the *Th* (507–616) and the *WD* (42–105). In the *Th*, Prometheus is the son of Iapetus, a brother of Cronus, and the Oceanid Clymene, and the story begins with a feast held at Mecone and attended by men and gods (535–36). Prometheus attempts to trick Zeus into taking the less desirable portion of the sacrificial beast (bones wrapped in fat) so that men can have the meat and offal (536–41); Zeus sees through the deception, but pretends to be taken in, apparently out of malice toward humanity (550–52). Mortals thus acquire the right to eat the sacrificial meat (cf. 556–57), but they suffer for it, as Zeus deprives them of fire (562–64). Prometheus, however, steals fire and brings it to men in a fennel stalk (565–67), so Zeus contrives a fresh punishment for men by causing Hephaestus and Athena to create the first woman (570–89). Prometheus's own punishment has already been described (521–25): Zeus confined him in bonds and sent an eagle to eat daily of his liver, which then grew back during the night for the eagle to eat again next day. Our text of the *Th*, and undoubtedly also the text known to the fifth-century tragedians, has, prima facie, two accounts of Prometheus's final fate. According to one (615–16) he is still in bonds; according to the other (526–34) Zeus, in order to enhance the glory of his son Heracles, "ceased from his anger" against Prometheus and permitted Heracles to kill the eagle and "release the son of Iapetus from his distress" (we are not told explicitly that he released Prometheus from his *bonds*, so the two passages are not technically contradictory).

The *WD* tells essentially the same story and draws from it the same conclusion: that it is impossible to outwit Zeus (*WD* 105 ~ *Th* 613). This time Hesiod passes rapidly over the first half of the story (*WD* 47–52 corresponds to *Th* 535–68) and omits entirely the punishment of Prometheus, to focus on the creation of the woman and its sequel. The woman's body, mind, and adornments are fashioned by all the gods in collaboration, whence she is named Pandora, and she is sent to Prometheus's brother Epimetheus ("Afterthought"), who accepts her, forgetting Prometheus's warning that he should reject any gift offered to him by Zeus (86–88); in his house, she opens the famous jar of evils, and that is why human life is full of miseries. (Epimetheus had been mentioned as a brother of Prometheus in *Th* 511–14 and was said to have been responsible for bringing evil on men by accepting Zeus's gift of "the manufactured virgin woman," but he is entirely ignored in the ensuing narrative about Zeus, Prometheus, and the creation of woman, and in 590–612 the impression is given that men's miseries stem directly from the existence of women and the necessity of marriage.)

The theft of fire by a clever god could be a suitable subject for the lighthearted genre of satyr-drama; this was all the more true because "marvellous inventions and creations" were a common theme of satyr-plays (Seaford 1984: 36–37). And in 472 BCE Aeschylus made a satyr-play out of it. We know from the ancient headnote (Hypothesis) to his *Persians* that in that year he produced a *Prometheus* as the fourth play of a tetralogy, after *Phineus, Persians*, and *Glaucus of Potniae*. As this was not the only play about Prometheus attributed to Aeschylus, it was later given an epithet to distinguish it from the others; according to Pollux (9.156, 10.64) this epithet was *Pyrkaeus* ("the Fire-Kindler"), but Brown (1990; see also Sommerstein 2010: 227–28) has made a good case for identifying this play with the *Prometheus Pyrphoros* ("the Fire-Bearer" or "the Fire-Bringer") known from other sources. We possess one quotation from *Pyrkaeus* (Aeschylus fr. 205); one quotation (fr. 208) and one paraphrase (fr. 208a) from *Pyrphoros*; several quotations cited simply from *Prometheus* (and one wrongly from the surviving *PB*), which might or might not belong to the satyr-play (fr. 187a Radt 1985 = 206 Sommerstein 2008; fr. 188,

188a, 189); a few quotations or testimonies for which no play title is given at all but which look as though they belong to it (fr. 207, 207a, and 369 Radt = 207b Sommerstein); and a papyrus fragment (fr. 204a–d), which certainly comes from a satyr-drama and which celebrates Prometheus's gift of fire.

In this play as in *PB* (see below), it seems to be assumed that when Prometheus stole fire and brought it to earth, this was the first time that mortals (or satyrs) had ever seen it (whereas in Hesiod men had possessed fire before Zeus denied it to them in revenge for Prometheus's attempt to cheat him). Certainly the satyrs have no idea that fire can hurt them. One of them, we learn (Plutarch, *Moralia* 86e–f = Aeschylus fr. 207), seeing a flame for the first time, was about to embrace and kiss it when Prometheus told him, "Then you'll be mourning for your beard like a billygoat!" In another quotation (fr. 187a Radt = 206 Sommerstein) a satyr, perhaps the same one, is apparently watching a pot boiling and is warned not to let the water touch his lips; it is possible that a reference to "linen plugs and long strips of raw flax" (fr. 205) indicates that someone needed treatment for a burn. In general, however, the satyrs are delighted with the new discovery, not least because they expect it will make them irresistibly attractive to nymphs (fr. 204b).

If the *Pyrphoros* was the satyr-drama of 472, then Prometheus's binding was mentioned in it and said to have lasted thirty thousand years (fr. 208a); if so, it was mentioned by way of prophecy, since the satyrs could hardly have been imagined as making the acquaintance of fire for the first time in the days of Heracles.

There are also some indications that the story of Pandora was brought into the play. A scholium on the *WD* (89 = Aeschylus fr. 207a), mutilated at the beginning, states:

> <   > says that Prometheus received the jar of evils from the satyrs and deposited it with Epimetheus, warning him not to accept anything from Zeus, but that Epimetheus ignored the warning and accepted Pandora.

The reference to the satyrs shows that the scholiast's source must be a satyr-play, and Aeschylus's play is the only one we know of in which the satyrs met Prometheus. Aeschylus seems to have noticed that Hesiod does not say how the jar of evils came to be in Epimetheus's house, and he invented the idea that the satyrs gave it to Prometheus, presumably in gratitude for his gift of fire—for, like Pandora herself, they would not have known what the jar contained.

In another Hesiodic scholium (on *WD* 157) we are told that Aeschylus described Pandora as "a mortal woman created by the fashioning of clay" (lit. "from clay-fashioned seed") (Aeschylus fr. 369 Radt = 207b Sommerstein). This line, quoted without a play title, has often been ascribed to one of the lost Prometheus plays, and in view of fr. 207a, it might well belong to our satyr-drama. But how exactly could the Pandora-Epimetheus story be accommodated in the play? It is unlikely that Epimetheus, let alone Pandora, appeared on stage. Prometheus may have announced his *intention* of leaving the jar with his brother, predicted that Zeus would try to take revenge for the theft of fire (and perhaps that he would do so by creating the first human female), and said that he would therefore warn his brother not to accept any gift from Zeus. The scholiast on *WD* 89 seems to say that Epimetheus acquired his name because he only realized when it was too late what a curse he had brought into his house; perhaps then the Aeschylean Prometheus did not use the name but merely called him "my brother." Awareness of the coming disaster would have cast a shadow over the conclusion of the satyr-play, but this would not be unique. The only satyr-play whose conclusion survives, Euripides's *Cyclops*, ends with a correct prediction by the blinded Cyclops (from an oracle once given to him) that Odysseus will pay a penalty for what he has done, "being tossed on the sea for a long time" (698–700); Odysseus replies that he will now set sail "for the Sicilian sea, and my homeland" (702–3), but we know that he will not reach home for nearly ten years.

Prometheus Pyrkaeus (or *Pyrphoros*) does not seem to have engaged with the issues concerning the human condition that are explicit or implicit in Hesiod; indeed, it probably contained no human characters. Its focus was rather on the naiveté of the satyrs, to whom fire is a delightful toy and seduction aid, and secondarily on the folly of Epimetheus (who disregarded Prometheus's warning) and the more surprising un-wisdom of Prometheus (who knew less well than Zeus that there was at least one gift that his brother would be incapable of rejecting).

The first three plays of the 472 tetralogy, unlike most tragic programs of their time, did not present episodes of a single story, but they were probably linked together by the theme of the recent Persian war, which was the subject of the second play and may have been foretold in the first and third (Sommerstein 2012). It is not clear whether the satyr-play also reflected this theme.

Sophocles wrote a play called *Pandora or The Hammerers* (*Sphyrokopoi*), about which very little is known for certain, though there can be little doubt, given some of its vocabulary, that it was a satyr-drama. In one of the few quotations (fr. 482) someone (Hephaestus?; cf. *Th* 571–72, *WD* 70–71) is instructed to "first start kneading clay with your hands." The "hammerers" are no doubt satyrs who, as so often in the genre, have become slaves to a new master (instead of their true master, Dionysus) and are working in Hephaestus's smithy. The verb *blimazein* (fr. 484), which can mean "grope" (a woman), suggests that the satyrs responded to the appearance of Pandora in typically lustful fashion. There is nothing to indicate that Prometheus appeared in this play.

HESIODIC MYTH IN TRAGEDY 2: PROMETHEUS, ZEUS, AND HERACLES

The only known serious tragic dramas based on a Hesiodic myth are the Prometheus plays attributed to Aeschylus—the surviving *Prometheus Bound* (*Prometheus Desmotes*), its lost sequel *Prometheus Unbound* (*Prometheus Lyomenos*), and *Prometheus the Fire-Bearer* (*Prometheus Pyrphoros*), if that was a distinct play rather than a name for the satyr-play of 472 (see above). The attribution of these plays to Aeschylus was not questioned in ancient times, but since the nineteenth century it has been increasingly disputed, often on somewhat question-begging theological grounds, but in recent decades mainly on more convincing grounds of style and technique (Griffith 1977; West 1990: 51–72; Sommerstein 2010: 228–32), though their authenticity continues to find defenders (e.g., Lloyd-Jones 2003; Podlecki 2005: 195–200). Aeschylus's son Euphorion is reported to have won four victories with (what he said were) previously unperformed plays by his father (*Suda* ε3800); it is possible that he was the author of the Prometheus plays but produced them in his father's name (so West 1990: 67–72), perhaps in 431 BCE when he defeated both Sophocles and Euripides (Euripides's production included *Medea*). At any rate we can be sure that we are dealing with fifth-century BCE Athenian tragedies: *Prometheus Unbound* was extensively imitated in the *Ploutoi (Wealth-Gods)* of the comic poet Cratinus, probably in 429 BCE (Cratinus fr. 171), and in 424 BCE Aristophanes in his *Knights* (836) virtually quoted a line of *PB* (613).

The tragedian has focused entirely on the binding of Prometheus as punishment for his theft of fire and his subsequent release through the action of Heracles; the two other leading features of the Hesiodic story—Prometheus's attempt to trick Zeus in the matter of the sacrificial meat, and the creation of Pandora—are entirely discarded (indeed it is taken for granted, without explanation, that the two human sexes already exist, and a woman, Io, is the only human character in *PB*). On the other hand, the story of Prometheus is brought into relation with several other myths, only one of which is Hesiodic:

(1) *The succession myth, in particular the conflict between the Olympians and the Titans (Th 617–720).* In Hesiod the Olympians win this war with the aid of the three Hundred-Handers, whom they enlist as allies after receiving a prophecy from Gaea (624–28); Prometheus, who is not a Titan but the son of a Titan, plays no part. In *PB* he is a son of Ge/Gaea (209–10; cf. 90, 1091), and another passage (163–65) implies that he is also a son of Uranus and therefore himself one of the Titans. His mother had revealed to him—not to the Olympians—how the war would be decided, not (as in Hesiod) by brute force, but by guile (209–13); he explained this to the Titans, but they completely ignored him (214–15), and he then decided to go over to the other camp, together with his mother; by his counsels (no details are given) the Titans were defeated (216–21). This story elevates Prometheus's status, making him both a senior figure in the older generation of gods and the architect of Zeus's victory. It also makes him a turncoat, which may well seem morally dubious, but once the Titans had rejected his advice, they would never have been able to achieve anything beyond prolonging the war indefinitely and making the establishment of a stable world order forever impossible. The most powerful effect of the change, however, is to make Zeus's treatment of Prometheus an act of monstrous ingratitude, since but for Prometheus he would never have gained supreme power. By the time *Prometheus Unbound* begins, however, Zeus has already mellowed somewhat: Prometheus is

still in his bonds (and tormented by the eagle, until Heracles shoots it), but the other Titans, who formed the chorus of the play, have been released from their prison in Tartarus. The release of the Titans is mentioned by Pindar (*Pythian* 4.291) as if already familiar to his hearers, and that of Cronus in what appears to be a late interpolation in some papyrus copies of the *WD* (173a–c); on the other hand, Aeschylus (*Eumenides* 644–46) makes Apollo tell the Erinyes that Zeus *might* release his father, when he would have had a much stronger argument if he had been able to say that Zeus *had* done so.

(2) *The Flood.* Prometheus tells the chorus that after his victory Zeus had planned to destroy the human race and create another, but he, Prometheus, prevented this (*PB* 231–36). The only known myth to which this can allude is the Greek version of the Flood story, which had Prometheus advising Deucalion and Pyrrha to build their ark; the story was dramatized by the Sicilian comic poet Epicharmus (early fifth century BCE) in his *Prometheus or Pyrrha* (Epicharmus fr. 113, 120), but in some form it must have been considerably older, for according to the pseudo-Hesiodic *Catalogue of Women* (fr. 2 M–W = 3 Most), Deucalion was actually the son of Prometheus. It is possible, however, that the destruction from which Prometheus saved humanity was not always supposed to have taken the form of a flood; in *PB* he says that he prevented mortals "being shattered and going to Hades," which suggests thunderbolts or the like rather than drowning. There may also be an evocation of *WD* 180–201 where it is predicted that Zeus *will* in due course destroy the present human race; we can be fairly sure that by the end of *Prometheus Unbound*, contrariwise, humanity's permanent survival was secure, since otherwise all Prometheus's endeavors and endurance would have been for nothing.

(3) *Io.* Io was an Argive maiden loved by Zeus, who incurred the jealousy of Hera and was transformed (wholly or partly) into a cow, tormented by a gadfly, and driven to distant lands, eventually reaching Egypt, where she gave birth to Epaphus; after five generations her descendants, Danaus and his daughters, returned to Argos (the subject of Aeschylus's *Suppliants* and its companion plays, recalled in *PB* 853–69). In *PB* her itinerary has to be drastically revised and extended to bring her to the place where Prometheus is bound at the northern extremity of Europe (*PB* 1–2), about as far from Egypt as it was possible to get in the world as contemporary Greeks imagined it. She has no connection with Prometheus, except that both are victims of Zeus and she is the ancestress, thirteen generations distant, of Heracles (*PB* 771–74, 871–73).

(4) *Thetis.* In the *Th* (886–900) Zeus is warned by Gaea and Uranus that his first wife, Metis, already pregnant with Athena, will bear as her second child a new "king of gods and men"; he therefore forestalls a fourth round of the divine succession by swallowing Metis and giving "birth" to Athena himself. In the Prometheus plays, too, Zeus is threatened with being overthrown by a son. Prometheus tells Io (755–70) that Zeus will fall from power when he makes "a marriage that he will come to regret" with a female who is destined to "bear a son superior to his

father." This alludes to a story for which the earliest surviving witness is Pindar (*Isthmian* 8.27–53): Zeus and Poseidon were rivals for Thetis's hand until Themis prophesied that Thetis would bear a son superior to his father and possessing more powerful weapons, and he recommended that she should be married to a mortal, Peleus. Prometheus is put in possession of this prophecy by the device of identifying his mother, Gaea, with Themis (*PB* 209–10; in *Th* 135 Themis had been a *daughter* of Gaea) and having her confide the prophecy to her son (*PB* 873–74). Prometheus must eventually have revealed the secret as part of the reconciliation with Zeus, which he predicts in *PB* 190–92, so that *Prometheus Unbound*, like the *Th*, ended with Zeus firmly and permanently installed in power.

(5) *Cheiron*. In *PB* 1026–29 Hermes tells Prometheus that his torment by the eagle will never end until "some god appears to be your successor in suffering and is willing to go down to rayless Hades." This condition may well be designed by Hermes (or Zeus, for whom he speaks) to be impossible of fulfillment, but the Athenian audience probably recognized an allusion to a story we now know only from later sources (e.g., [Apollodorus], *Library* 2.5.4, 2.5.11). The (immortal) centaur Cheiron, having been painfully and incurably wounded by Heracles's arrow, longed to die but could not do so until "Prometheus gave to Zeus one who would become immortal in exchange for him" (probably meaning Heracles; Robertson 1951).

By combining and modifying the myths in these ways, the dramatist has created a powerful new tale in which a god who has performed one great service to Zeus, and two to humanity, on account of the latter endures terrible suffering at the hands of a tyrannical Zeus, until he is saved from the worst of it by Zeus's son and finally pardoned by Zeus himself after performing yet another great service for him. The brutal young tyrant (*PB* 35) has become a mature and responsible god, and both he and the human race are safe. And—clearly contrary to the conclusion of both Hesiod's versions of the Prometheus-Pandora story—it *has* proved possible to defy Zeus and finish unbowed, though only at the cost of enduring, for several centuries, such pain as no human being can imagine because none could survive it.

PB begins with Prometheus being brought by two servants of Zeus, Kratos and Bia (Power and Force)—their names and natures come from *Th* 385–401—to the ravine where he is to be bound, "at the furthest limits of earth" in northern Scythia; they are accompanied by Hephaestus (the god most directly affected by the theft of fire), who is to carry out the binding. He does so reluctantly, hectored and threatened by Kratos; the bonds include a wedge driven right through Prometheus's chest (64–65). Prometheus is then left alone, calling on the elements (sky, winds, rivers, sea, earth) to witness his sufferings (88–92), until the chorus, daughters of Ocean, arrive and try to console him, with little success; he tells them the history of his relations with Zeus and his services to humanity, which include the planting of "blind hopes" in men's minds so that they have no foreknowledge of the time of their death (248–50; a transformation of *WD* 96–99?), and the gift of fire, which will enable them to acquire many skills (252–54; cf.

110–11, 442–506). His next visitor is Ocean himself (who does not notice his daughters' presence, nor they his, perhaps because they are temporarily offstage); he offers to intercede with Zeus on Prometheus's behalf, but Prometheus tells him that any such effort will be wasted and reminds him of the fate of Atlas and Typhoeus (347–72; cf. *Th* 517–20, 746–48, 853–68). With Ocean gone, he tells the chorus more fully how, thanks to him, mortals have acquired all the techniques of civilization, and hints (515–25) that he knows a secret that may lead to the fall of Zeus.

In Hesiod Prometheus gave humans two gifts only, though important ones: fire and the right to eat almost all the edible parts of sacrificial animals. In *PB* he is portrayed as having given them almost every aspect of their culture. At 254 the acquisition of "many skills" is treated as a spin-off from the gift of fire; but in the fuller account in 442–506 most of the skills listed have little or no connection with fire: the seasonal calendar (456–58); arithmetic (459–60); writing (460–61); the domestication of oxen, asses, and horses (462–66); ships (467–68); medicine (478–83); and most forms of divination (484–95). Only at the end do we hear of the burning of parts of sacrificial animals on the altar (496–99)—not here as part of a scheme to cheat Zeus, but as a method of gaining information for the benefit of mortals—and of the extraction and use of metals (500–503), for which fire to melt them is, of course, essential. Prometheus here has been given a role as all-round culture hero reminiscent of, but even more extensive than, that ascribed in other fifth-century BCE texts to Palamedes, a participant in the Trojan War (e.g., Aeschylus fr. 181a, 182; Sophocles fr. 432, 479).

Enter now Io; her appearance is that of a woman with a cow's horns (588, 674), and she is intermittently harassed by the invisible gadfly. She tells her history to Prometheus and the chorus (640–86), and Prometheus then reveals her future destinies and those of her descendants, down to the one who will be his liberator (700–876); in the course of this exposition he says a little more about Zeus's possible overthrow and, to prove that he has genuine prophetic knowledge, describes some of her past wanderings, which she had not mentioned in her own account (824–43). Hereabouts Zeus appears in a somewhat better light than hitherto; through the speaking oaks of Dodona he hails Io as his future "glorious spouse" (824–25), and he will procreate Epaphus with a mere touch (848–49).

After Io's departure (driven off by the gadfly) Prometheus exults in the coming overthrow of Zeus (907–40), but now Zeus's messenger Hermes arrives, to demand that he reveal the secret of which he has been boasting. Prometheus refuses, and Hermes tells him that the ravine will collapse and bury him underground for a vast length of time, until he is restored to the light to become the prey of the eagle. Prometheus remains defiant. Hermes, before he leaves, warns the chorus to get out of the way; they insist that they will never desert Prometheus, but in the elemental catastrophe that ends the play (with Prometheus again appealing to earth and sky to witness how unjustly he is suffering) they probably scatter in terror.

From *Prometheus Unbound* we have fragments (one in a Latin translation by Cicero) totalling more than sixty lines, as well as Cratinus's imitation and various other statements about the play. Prometheus's subterranean detention is now at an end, but he is being savaged every day by the eagle, as he tells the chorus of released Titans who have come to visit him (fr. 193). Heracles appears, en route (or rather badly off his route) to the far west in quest of the apples of the Hesperides (his eleventh labour) (Strabo 4.1.7). He shoots the eagle (fr. 200) but apparently does not release Prometheus from his bonds; Prometheus describes him as "dearest son of a father who is my enemy" (fr. 201). An ancient commentator (pseudo-Probus) on Virgil's *Eclogues* (6.42), in a summary of the story manifestly based on the tragic version, says that Heracles killed the bird "but was afraid to liberate Prometheus, lest he might offend his father"; Prometheus, he says, was liberated later by Zeus/Jupiter himself when he revealed the secret of the fatal mating that Zeus must avoid. The mythographer Pherecydes (fr. 17 Fowler 2000), writing in the first half of the fifth century BCE, also has Heracles visit Prometheus on his way to the Hesperides (though at a different point of the journey) and speaks of his shooting the eagle but not of his releasing Prometheus, so it appears that in these two matters the dramatist was following an existing tradition. At any rate he is significantly departing from Hesiod (*Th* 526–32), who has Heracles shoot the eagle "in accordance with the will of Zeus," who desired to increase his son's glory.

The list of dramatis personae for *PB*, transmitted in several manuscripts, includes the names of Ge and Heracles. Since Heracles appeared in *Prometheus Unbound*, it is a reasonable conjecture that Ge (alias Themis), the mother of Prometheus, did so too, and that by some confusion both names got into the wrong cast list; it has often been suggested (e.g., Wecklein 1891: 11; Winnington-Ingram 1983: 186–87) that Ge visited her son and encouraged him to reveal his secret. A scholium on *PB* (168–77) seems to indicate what happened next:

> He is talking about the passion Zeus had for Thetis. Having become enamoured of her, he was pursuing her through the Caucasus mountains to have intercourse with her, but was prevented by Prometheus, who told him that the son who would be born to her would be far stronger than his father. So Zeus, afraid for his kingship, refrained from intercourse with Thetis.

There is no reason to doubt the prima facie implication of this scholium that Zeus and Thetis appeared on stage in *Prometheus Unbound*, and that Prometheus revealed his secret directly to Zeus (cf. Fitton Brown 1959: 57). He had said in the previous play (175–77) that he would do so only if he were released and given compensation for his sufferings; clearly he was indeed released, as we are explicitly informed by another scholium (on *PB* 511), and compensated by being given a garland or crown to wear (fr. 202)—which could also be regarded as a symbolic continuation of his binding (so pseudo-Probus)—and perhaps also (though no source actually mentions this) by the creation of an Athenian cult in his honor. Zeus also seems to have been an onstage character in another play attributed to Aeschylus, *Psychostasia* (*The Weighing of Souls*), which West (2000: 345–47) thought might be by the same author (Euphorion) as the Prometheus plays.

If, as we can safely assume, the matter of Cheiron (see above) was also cleared up at the conclusion of *Prometheus Unbound*, it will have ended with thoughts turning to three humans of exceptional qualities, as the most powerful of mortals (Heracles) was promised divinity, while the most righteous of mortals (Peleus; cf. Pindar, *Isthmian* 8.44) was promised a marriage with a goddess whose offspring would be the most valiant of mortals (Achilles).

The author of these plays knew Hesiod's poems intimately and took from them not only his basic story but many other details. Yet he has taken a myth told to demonstrate the irresistible supremacy of Zeus and the impotence and misery of men and turned it into a tale of how humans were saved from destruction at the hands of Zeus and endowed with the arts of civilized life, how one of them was later able to help save their savior, and how he and others were finally exalted to divine or near-divine status; he has taken a punished trickster and thief and turned him into a god who has twice had the power to decide the future of the universe, and has twice, in defiance of Zeus, ensured that the human race shall not perish from the earth.

HESIODIC IDEAS IN TRAGEDY

Of the three great tragic dramatists, only Aeschylus shows any significant intellectual influence from Hesiod. This influence is evident above all in his last Athenian production, the *Oresteia*, mainly in reflections of Hesiod's presentation in the *WD* of the power, inscrutability, and especially the justice, of Zeus (see Solmsen 1949: esp. 163–65, 178–224). The other main theme of that poem—the necessity of work and the folly of idleness—makes little impact: the main characters of tragedies are usually members of ruling families, and for humbler people like the Watchman in *Agamemnon* or the Nurse in *Libation Bearers* work is something to grumble about (*Agamemnon* 1–21; *Libation Bearers* 750–62).

In the undisputed works of Aeschylus, reflections can be perceived of three aspects of the *Th*. Two passages of the *Oresteia* recall the succession myth. In the so-called Hymn to Zeus (*Agamemnon* 160–83), Zeus is presented as beyond compare (163–67), and his two predecessors, though clearly identified, are not so much as named (168–72), being called merely "the one who was formerly great" and "he who was born later": the wise man will sing a song of victory to Zeus (173–75). It is Zeus, sing the chorus (176–78), who established the law *pathei mathos* ("learning by suffering"). In Hesiod (*WD* 218) it is only the fool who has to learn by suffering; here, seemingly, everyone has to. But the two statements are not inconsistent. Hesiod is speaking of the man who learns from *his own* suffering (*pathōn*, "having suffered"), but one may also learn by observing the suffering of others—or, as Hesiod urges Perses to do, by listening to an inspired poet telling him about it (a privilege also available to the spectator of tragedy). In the time of Zeus's predecessor, Cronus, there was no suffering (*WD* 109–19), but there was also no learning (Sommerstein 1993): the rule of Zeus has brought many misfortunes to humanity but has also enabled it to become intellectually and morally adult. In the *Oresteia*, arguably, a learning process of this kind can be traced from the likes of Thyestes, Atreus, Agamemnon, and Clytaemestra, through Orestes and Electra, to the Athenians of

Eumenides (or is it the Athenians of Aeschylus's own day?), in whom humanity has become "wise at last" (*Eumenides* 1000) and knows that (as Hesiod puts it) in the end justice has the upper hand over *hybris* (*WD* 217–18). The overthrow of Cronus by Zeus is mentioned again, as we have seen, in the trial scene of *Eumenides* (640–48).

Two of the other divine powers who are given prominence in the *Th* are prominent also in certain plays of Aeschylus, and in both cases there are signs that Aeschylus had the Hesiodic passages in mind. The description of the birth of Aphrodite (*Th* 190–206) ends by speaking of the powers and phenomena associated with her:

> Eros accompanied her, and beautiful Longing (*Himeros*) followed her, when she was first born and when she joined the family of the gods; and this is the portion (*moira*) and honour (*timē*) which has been allotted to her and which she has possessed from the beginning among men and immortal gods, the whispering of maidens, and smiles, and deceptions, and sweet delight, and love-making, and gentleness. (*Th* 201–6)

At the end of Aeschylus's *Suppliants*, the daughters of Danaus, who have fled from Egypt to Argos to avoid marriage with their cousins, and in whose defense Argos has just accepted an Egyptian declaration of war, proclaim their gratitude to Argos and its gods (*Suppliants* 1018–29), ask the virgin goddess Artemis to show them favor (1030–31), and apparently wish to die rather than have "Cytherea's consummation" come to them by compulsion (1031–33; the text is uncertain, but the following lines show that it must have been interpretable as a rejection of Aphrodite and her works). Then another voice or set of voices (most probably, it is now thought, the Argive soldiers who have been assigned to escort the family into the city) declare (1034–42) that "it is a wise rule not to ignore Cypris" and describe her sphere of influence in terms very reminiscent of the Hesiodic passage:

> For she holds power very close to Zeus, together with Hera,
> a goddess of *cunning wiles*
> who is *honoured* (*tietai*) for awesome deeds;
> partners and associates with their dear mother
> are Desire (*Pothos*) and the charmer Persuasion . . .
> and also given to Aphrodite as her *portion* (*moira*) are Union
> and the *whispering* paths of the Erotes.

There may well have been echoes of this passage in the final play of the Danaid trilogy, where Aphrodite herself made an appearance. In the seven lines of her speech that have survived (Aeschylus fr. 44), however, she claims to be the cause of a sexual union between Heaven and Earth whose physical expression is the rain that "makes Earth conceive" and bring forth grain for men, grass for their beasts, and the fruit of trees—very different offspring of Earth and Heaven from those we hear of in the *Th* (132–87)—the Titans, the Cyclopes, the Hundred-Handers, the Erinyes, and the Giants—issue of a relationship that ended when Heaven was castrated by his son Cronus at the instance of Earth, an act that led to the generation of Aphrodite herself.

The Erinyes are the other power (besides Zeus) that is prominent both in the *Th* and in Aeschylus. The latter's Erinyes are in fact an amalgam of two Hesiodic powers. Hesiod's Erinyes are children of Earth and Heaven (*Th* 185); elsewhere (*WD* 802–4) we hear that they were present at the birth of Horkos, the god of oaths, which probably identifies them with the self-curse implicit in every oath; in Homer their name can be almost synonymous with *ara* "curse" (e.g., *Iliad* 21.412), and in Aeschylus *Arai* is an alternative name for them (*Seven* 70; *Eumenides* 417). But Aeschylus's Erinyes, being daughters of Night (*Eumenides* 322, 416, 745, 792, 844, 1033) and sisters of the Moirai (961–62), also owe some of their characteristics to another group of Hesiodic divinities, the Kêres (*Th* 217–24)—a fact that was perceived by the poet (not Aeschylus) who wrote the extant conclusion of *Seven against Thebes*, in which the chorus apostrophize the *Kêres Erinyes* who have destroyed the family of Oedipus (*Seven* 1055). In Homer the Kêres are spirits of death (e.g., *Iliad* 12.326–27), whose name is often coupled with death (*thanatos*) itself (e.g., *Iliad* 21.565; *Odyssey* 2.352). In Hesiod they are "merciless punishers . . . who pursue the transgressions of men and gods, and never cease from their terrible wrath until they have visited evil on whoever has done wrong," which precisely describes the Aeschylean Erinyes (their power over gods as well as men is affirmed by Athena; *Eumenides* 951–52). Like many other powers (evil powers for the most part), they are children of Night, and like most of Night's other offspring they were born parthenogenetically (*Th* 213). Aeschylus's Erinyes refer frequently to Night as their mother but never mention any father, making it appropriate that they should champion the cause of a mother (Clytaemestra) who is killed by her son in revenge for his father; but we never quite forget that they also have a wider sphere of interest, the punishment of "whoever has done wrong," as they themselves emphasize in *Eumenides* 490–565, and likewise Athena later (930–37, 990–95) when she has recruited them to help in fostering the virtue and the greatness of Athens. In addition to their crucial role in the *Oresteia*, the Erinyes also figure prominently in *Seven against Thebes*, where they appear to be thought of as the embodiments of Oedipus's curse on his sons (*Seven* 70, 723, 886–87) and are responsible, in parallel with Apollo, for their slaying of each other (791, 977, 988).

The theme of the power and justice of Zeus is as ubiquitous in the *Oresteia* as it is in the *WD*—though in the *Oresteia* Zeus's justice seems for a long time to be seriously flawed, inasmuch as the punishment of one crime regularly involves the committing of another, which then itself requires to be punished (see Sommerstein 2010: 193–203, 274–79). At certain moments the intertextual presence of the *WD* is particularly evident:

(1) At the very outset of Hesiod's poem Zeus is spoken of, with a pun on his name (accusative case *Dia*), as "him *through* (*dia*) whom mortal men are famous or obscure, spoken of or not spoken of" (*WD* 3–4). Toward the end of *Agamemnon* (1485–88) the chorus face the horrifying fact that all the terrible things that have happened to the royal house of Argos have happened "through Zeus" (*diai Dios*), because Zeus is

the Cause of all things, the Effector of all effects;
for what comes to pass for mortals, except by Zeus's doing?

(2) *WD* 225–85 contains perhaps the strongest statement in the poem of the principle
that Zeus rewards justice (225–37, 280–81, 285) and punishes injustice; Hesiod
recognizes (270–72) that as things stand, the unjust often seem to fare better than
the just, but adds (273) that he does not expect Zeus to let this situation endure.
In tragedy, as one might expect, attention is focused mainly on the punishment,
which is held to be inescapable though it may be delayed to a later generation (as
for example in the case of Atreus, whose murder of the children of Thyestes was
punished only long after his own death by the murder of Agamemnon), but we
hear about the rewards of virtue, too (cf. Hunter 2014: 156–57):

> A house *that keeps the straight path of justice*
> breeds a fortune that is always fair (*Agamemnon* 761–62).

> He will *be righteous without painful compulsion,*
> will not fail to enjoy prosperity,
> and will never come to utter destruction (*Eumenides* 550–52).

> [I bid you invoke blessings upon this land] such as are appropriate to an
> honourable victory, coming moreover both from the earth, and from the
> waters of the sea, and from the heavens; and for the gales of wind to come
> over the land breathing the air of bright sunshine; and for the fruitfulness of
> the citizens' land and livestock to thrive in abundance, and not to fail with the
> passage of time; and for the preservation of human seed. But may you *give
> greater fertility to those who are pious*; for like a shepherd of plants, I cherish
> the race to which *these righteous men* belong, and wish it free of all grief
> (*Eumenides* 903–12).

> From these fearsome faces [of the Erinyes]
> I see great benefit coming to these citizens;
> for by always kindly giving great honour
> to these kindly powers, *you will keep your land and city
> on the straight road of justice*
> and be glorious in every way (*Eumenides* 990–95)

This theme is also expressed in a papyrus fragment of a play, which is certainly by
Aeschylus (fr. 281a) but has never been securely identified and is usually referred to
as "the Dike play." A divine being, speaking apparently to the chorus, says that she
sits on (or beside) the throne of Zeus (line 10, cf. *WD* 259), who sends her to those
to whom he is friendly (11–12); presently she identifies herself as Dike (Justice), who
prolongs the life of the righteous (15, 17) and ensures the punishment of the wicked
(19–23); the next two, badly mutilated, lines (24–25) can be tentatively restored to
say that great blessings will come to those who receive Dike with goodwill.

In the surviving fragments of the "Dike play," Dike says nothing of her parentage, but in *Seven* 662 and *Libation Bearers* 949–51 she is called the maiden

daughter of Zeus, as in *WD* 256 and in *Th* 902, where Themis is named as her mother.

(3) A form of wrongdoing particularly singled out in the *WD* (320–26) is the unjust acquisition of wealth by violence or fraud; such prosperity will be of short duration. This note is struck several times in the *Oresteia*, notably in *Agamemnon* 462–66 (where the rare word *amauron*, "feeble," seems to echo *maurousi*, "they enfeeble," in *WD* 325) and in *Eumenides* 553–65 (which, like the *WD* passage, contains the word *olbos*, "prosperity," in its first and last sentences).

(4) When discussing the best time for ploughing, Hesiod remarks (*WD* 483–84) that "the mind of aegis-bearing Zeus is different at different times, and hard for mortal men to perceive." He is no doubt thinking of the unpredictability of the weather (cf. 474, 488), but his words can readily be given a more general application. In Aeschylus the theme of the capriciousness and inscrutability of Zeus tends to be used with an ironic twist; the audience can sometimes see that Zeus is less inscrutable than those within the drama suppose. The Danaids (*Suppliants* 87 + 93–95) sing that

> the desire of Zeus is not easy to hunt out:
> the paths of his mind
> stretch tangled and shadowy,
> impossible to perceive or see clearly—

but they are still perfectly confident that Zeus, their ancestor, will protect them against their cousins (who are, of course, equally his descendants). At the end of the play their attitude is the same. The secondary chorus warn them that they may not be able to avoid the threatened marriage, for "the great, unfathomable mind of Zeus cannot be eluded" (1048–49; cf. *Th* 613, *WD* 105), and they agree that they cannot be expected to "see into the mind of Zeus, gazing into its bottomless depths" (1057–58), but though they are then warned "not to ask too much of the gods" (1061), they repeat the same prayer to Zeus that they have made many times before, that he may succor them as he once succored their (and their cousins') ancestress, Io (1062–73). The audience know that the Danaids' prayers will be in vain, and that Zeus's mind is not as they think and hope it is; they will indeed be forced to marry their cousins—and will then murder them.

The *WD* passage is again echoed in *Eumenides* (530–31), but here the assertion that divine power "manages different things in different ways" is all but contradicted before it is made. In one respect at least the ways of god are consistent: "in everything [he] gives pre-eminence to the mean" over either of the opposite extremes (preferring, for example, in the political field, constitutional government over anarchy and despotism, 526–28).

In various smaller matters, too, Aeschylus shows that he has drunk deeply of Hesiod. The *WD* begins, after its proem, with an elaborate passage (11–36) arguing that Strife (*eris*) is not one thing, as the poet had previously thought, but two, one evil (unproductive quarrelling) and one good (emulation and competition in effort and achievement). In tragedy, including Aeschylus, the evil Strife is usually more prominent; thus in *Libation Bearers* 471–75 the chorus sing that the cure for the ills of Agamemnon's family can only come from its own members, "through raw, bloody (*haimatēran*) strife." But that phrase is echoed a play and a half later: when Athena has conciliated the Erinyes and persuaded them to reside in Athens, she praises the power of Persuasion and "Zeus of Assemblies" (patron of the art of public speaking, at which Athena has just shown outstanding skill) and says in conclusion that

> our (*hēmetera*) strife for good
> has won a victory that will last for ever. (*Eumenides* 974–75)

We cannot tell, and perhaps were not meant to be able to tell, whether "our strife" really means "my strife," that is, Athena's strenuous and successful efforts at persuasion, or whether her first person plural includes the Erinyes and the reference is to the way in which she and they have competed, since 902, in bestowing blessings on Athens. At any rate, "raw, bloody strife" has become "our strife for good"—similar-sounding Greek, but almost the opposite meaning.

Further Reading

For further reading, see Desclos (2011), Gantz (1993: 154–66), and Lloyd-Jones (1983).

References

Brown, A. L. 1990. "Prometheus Pyrphoros." *Bulletin of Institute of Classical Studies* 37: 50–56.

Desclos, M. L. 2011. "D'Hésiode à Eschyle: 'Prométhée', un mythe de souveraineté entre rupture et continuité." In *Figures de la rupture, figures de la continuité chez les Anciens*, edited by M. L. Desclos, 65–78. Grenoble, France.

Fitton Brown, A. D. 1959. "Prometheia." *Journal of Hellenic Studies* 79: 52–60.

Fowler, R. L., ed. 2000. *Early Greek Mythography*. Vol. 1, *Text and Introduction*. Oxford.

Gantz, T. N. 1993. *Early Greek Myth: A Guide to Literary and Artistic Sources*. Baltimore. MD.

Griffith, M. 1977. *The Authenticity of Prometheus Bound*. Cambridge.

Hunter, R. L. 2014. *Hesiodic Voices: Studies in the Ancient Reception of Hesiod's Works and Days*. Cambridge.

Kitto, H. D. F. 1961. *Greek Tragedy: A Literary Study*. 3rd ed. London.

Lloyd-Jones, H. 1983. *The Justice of Zeus*. 2nd ed. Berkeley, CA.

Lloyd-Jones, H. 2003. "Zeus, Prometheus and Greek Ethics." *Harvard Studies in Classical Philology* 101: 49–72.

Podlecki, A. J. 2005. *Aeschylus: Prometheus Bound*. Oxford.

Radt, S. L., ed. 1985. *Tragicorum Graecorum Fragmenta*. Vol. 3, *Aeschylus*. Göttingen, West Germany.

Robertson, D. S. 1951. "Prometheus and Chiron." *Journal of Hellenic Studies* 71: 150–55.

Seaford, R. A. S., ed. 1984. *Euripides: Cyclops*. Oxford.

Solmsen, F. 1949. *Hesiod and Aeschylus*. Ithaca, NY.

Sommerstein, A. H. 1993. "*Pathos* and *Mathos* before Zeus." In *Tria Lustra: Essays and Notes Presented to John Pinsent*, edited by H. D. Jocelyn, 109–14. Liverpool, UK: Liverpool Classical Monthly. Reprinted with updates in A. H. Sommerstein, *The Tangled Ways of Zeus and Other Studies in and around Greek Tragedy* (Oxford, 2010), 178–88.

Sommerstein, A. H., ed. and trans. 2008. *Aeschylus: Fragments*. Cambridge.

Sommerstein, A. H. 2010. *Aeschylean Tragedy*. 2nd ed. London.

Sommerstein, A. H. 2012. "The Persian War Tetralogy of Aeschylus." In *Greek Drama IV: Texts, Contexts, Performance*, edited by D. Rosenbloom and J. Davidson, 95–107. Oxford.

Wecklein, N., ed. 1891. *The "Prometheus Bound" of Aeschylus, and the Fragments of the "Prometheus Unbound"*. Translated by F. D. Allen. Boston.

West, M. L. 1990. *Studies in Aeschylus*. Stuttgart, Germany.

West, M. L. 2000. "*Iliad* and *Aethiopis* on the Stage: Aeschylus and Son." *Classical Quarterly* 50: 338–52.

Winnington-Ingram, R. P. 1983. *Studies in Aeschylus*. Cambridge.

CHAPTER 19

HESIOD AND COMEDY

JEFFREY HENDERSON

COMIC dramas, attested for public performance as early as the later sixth century BCE in Sicily and from ca. 486 BCE in Attica, reflect familiarity with Hesiodic poetry from the time our actual documentation begins, in the 470s for Sicily and 430s for Attica.[1] Comedy engages not only at the level of specific allusion or echo but also (and more frequently) in a general way, with Hesiodic stories, thought, themes, ideas, and style, now common cultural currency, and with Hesiod as a poet, whether bracketed with Homer as a great cultural authority or distinguished as the anti-Homer in subjects and style, or showcased as an emblematic persona of poet and sage. As in their engagement with other poetic genres, the comic poets incorporated the Hesiodic along a spectrum from mere parody (ridicule of particular features) to paradidactic and paramythic adaptation (borrowing ideas or narrative or channeling them for novel tonal or thematic effects). At least one poet, Aristophanes, also imbued his own competitive and didactic persona with Hesiodic elements.

Hesiodic influence on comedy may indeed have been greater than we can now see. It clearly figured in such popular but poorly attested types of comedy as those featuring mythical plots, versions of the golden age/race, and a utopia/dystopia (Henderson 2015). Poetry and poetics were also popular comic subjects, but the centrality of (especially Euripidean) tragedy in Aristophanes—other than Menander, the only Greek comic poet from whom complete plays survive—obscures the attention paid by his rivals to other genres and poets, including Hesiod (Bakola et al. 2013); there is reason to think that epic/didactic resonances were especially prominent in the generations of comic poets preceding that of Aristophanes, notably Epicharmus, Cratinus, Hermippus, and Teleicleides.

After the fifth century BCE, resonances of Hesiodic and other nondramatic poetry in comedy seem to dwindle. Poets developed, and their audiences increasingly favored domestic plots peopled by fictional types speaking in more natural fashion; and poets abandoned their overt rivalries, didactic postures, and patterns of topical engagement to suit a new post-populist era that was more acquiescent in elite domination satisfactorily refereed by the democratic judicial system and therefore less amenable to complaints about unjust authority that might evoke Hesiodic typologies. But again, the picture might be different if we had more information; after all, myth comedy (including the birth of gods as a popular subject) did persist as a prominent subgenre into the 350s BCE, and attested in this period are a *Hesiod* by Nicostratus and a *Theogony* by Antiphanes.

MYTH, MYTHIC PARADIGM, THEOGONY

For comic and tragic/satyric dramatists alike, Hesiodic poetry was an important source both for myth proper—genealogies and traditional stories of gods and heroes—and (especially in comedy) for mythical patterns and paradigms of thinking about the world. These were its origins, the births and relationships of gods, the races of mankind, the succession and primacy (for good or ill) of the Olympian order, archetypal or transformative figures like Prometheus and Pandora, and (particularly Hesiodic) ubiquitous and frequently staged personifications of abstract nouns and allegorical figures like Peace and her attendants Harvest and Holiday (*Peace*), Reconciliation (*Acharnians* and *Lysistrata*), and Wealth and Poverty (*Wealth*). The key sources were *Theogony* (hereafter *Th*), *Catalogue of Women*, and the non-almanac section of *Works and Days* (hereafter *WD*) (rare are references like *Adespota* 1086.9–10 ~ *WD* 765–828 to Hesiod as an authority on a particular day). Myth comedy was often reactive, making fun of familiar traditions through parody and burlesque, but it could also be creative, introducing novel versions and variants or treating subjects inappropriate for serious poetry, for example Zeus's adulteries (actually staged, unlike in tragedy; Dixon 2015: 154–231), so that ancient mythologists cite comic poets as authorities alongside poets like Hesiod (Dixon 2015: 22–33). In this mode comic poets exploited for their own purposes a mythographic tradition that they shared with other poets.

An early example is Epicharmus's *Hebe's Wedding* (revised as *Muses*), whose fragments (e.g., 47 and 57) parallel the typical structure of an epic-didactic catalog and contain specific Hesiodic reference: fr. 39 (= Tzetzes on *WD* 6) parodies *Th* 338–63—the catalog of rivers (boys) and springs (girls "who work with Apollo") whom Tethys bore to Ocean—in naming the seven Muses who attend the wedding (whose banquet apparently featured seafood): "daughters of Pieros [Mr. Fat] and Pimpleis [Mrs. Full]: Neilo, Tritone, Asopo, Heptapore, Achelois, †Titoplo†, and Rhodia." Phrynichus's *Cronus* (Stama 2014: 84–104) seems to have featured the eating of children with Hesiodic inspiration (e.g., fr. 14 καταπί[νει τέκνα); similarly (and perhaps from this play) *Adespota* 1062, adapted from *Th* 453–67, has Cronus being overthrown in a naturalized, domestic setting. Hermippus's *Moirai* of ca. 430 BCE (also the title of a tragedy by Achaeus of which no fragments remain) seems to have involved Hesiod's bestowers of good and evil to mortals (cf. fr. 49, 50) and a complacent Zeus (fr. 42) in an attack on Pericles (cf. Gkaras 2008: 79–103), the thundering Olympian (Aristophanes, *Acharnians* 530–35) comic poets frequently assimilated to Zeus, as in the Hesiodic-style theogony in Cratinus's *Cheirons*: "Faction (*Stasis*) and venerable Time (*Chronos*, var. Cronus) commingled in love (ἀλλήλοισι μιγέντε) and bore the greatest of all tyrants, whom the immortals call the Head Gatherer . . . and Shameful Lust (*Katapygosyne*) bore him a heart-pleasing (*aspasian*) Hera, a bitch-faced concubine" (fr. 258, 259).

Much as Aristophanes's preferred mode for creatively repurposing myth is paratragedy, for example using Euripides's *Telephus* as his model for *Acharnians*, so the theogony in *Birds*—much too elaborate, heterogeneous, and thematically integral to be regarded as mere Hesiodic parody—serves similar purposes in the paratheogonic mode, at once parodying and creatively rivaling its models. The plot of the play amounts to a succession myth: Peisetaerus has convinced the birds to follow him in a plan to use their position between earth and sky to depose the Olympian gods and install him in Zeus's place. This is no mere gigantomachic coup but also a challenge to the primacy and thus the legitimacy of Zeus's rule, for Peisetaerus claims that the birds were the original kings of creation (465–538). As formal justification only a revisionist theogony will do, and it is duly presented by the chorus leader in the parabasis speech (685–736), together with a catalog of the birds' benefactions to mankind (superior to those from the Olympians) that revises the practical didacticism of *WD* and thus keeps the spectators attuned to the Hesiodic ambience (e.g., the crane, shipowner, kite, and augury in lines 708–18 specifically recall *WD* 448–51, 619–29, 568–69, and 800–801). For its dense interaction with conventional theogonies, the speech is worth quoting in full:

> Ye men by nature just faintly alive, like the race of leaves,   685
> ye do-littles, artefacts of clay, tribes shadowy and feeble,
> ye wingless ephemerals, suffering mortals, dreamlike people:
> now pay ye attention to us, the immortals, the gods everlasting,
> the etherial, the ageless, whose counsels are imperishable;
> once you hear from us the truth about all celestial phenomena,   690
> and the true nature of birds, the genesis of gods, rivers, Erebus, and Chaos,
> then you'll be able to tell Prodicus from me to go to hell!
>   In the beginning were Chaos and Night and black Erebus and broad Tartarus,
> no Earth, no Air nor Sky. But in the boundless bosom of Erebus
> did black-winged Night at the very start bring forth a wind-egg,   695
> from which as the seasons revolved came forth Eros the seductive,
> like a swift-wheeling whirlwind, his back aglitter with wings of gold.
> And mating by night with winged Chaos in broad Tartarus
> he hatched our very own race and first brought us up to the daylight.
> No race of immortal gods till Eros commingled (ξυνέμειξεν) everything;   700
> then, this commingling with that, Sky came to be, and Ocean
> and Earth, and the whole imperishable race of blessed gods.
> Thus *we're* far older than the blessed gods; it's abundantly clear
> that we're Eros' offspring: we fly and consort with lovers. Yes,
> many fair boys swear they won't, and almost make it to the end   705
> of their bloom, but thanks to *our* power their lovers do spread their thighs,
> one presenting a quail, another a porphyrion, a goose, or a Persian bird.
>   And from us, the birds, do mortals get all their greatest blessings.
> To start with, we reveal the seasons of spring, winter, and autumn.

It's time to sow when the crane whoops off to Africa;   710
that's when it tells the shipowner to hang up his rudder and rest,
and Orestes to weave a cloak so he won't catch cold as he mugs you.
And then it's the kite's turn to appear and reveal a new season,
when it's time to shear the sheep's spring wool. And then there's the swallow,
and now you ought to sell your coat and buy a jacket.   715
And we're your Ammon, Delphi, Dodona, and Phoebus Apollo,
for you embark on nothing without first consulting the birds,
whether it's business, or making a living, or a man who's getting married.
Whatever's decisive in prophecy you deem a bird:
to you, an ominous word's a bird, a sneeze is a bird,   720
a chance meeting, a sound, a good-luck servant, a donkey: all birds.
So isn't it obvious that we're your prophetic Apollo?
    Well then, if you treat us as gods,
you'll have your prophets, muses,
breezes, seasons, winter,   725
mild summer, stifling heat. And we won't run off
and sit up there preening
among the clouds, like Zeus,
but ever at hand we'll bestow on you,
your children, and your children's children   730
healthy wealthiness,
happiness, prosperity, peace,
youth, hilarity, dances, festivities,
and birds' milk. Why, you're liable
to knock yourself out from good living,   735
that's how rich you'll all be!

The echoes of the Hesiodic *Theogony* are plain, but spectator appreciation of their retooling to suit the primacy of birds required some detailed familiarity with the text. This is unsurprising, since already Epicharmus could have a character arguing against the primacy of Chaos (fr. 275.4 ~ *Th* 116). Thus for example the birds' initial claim to authority (685–92) is programmatic, like *Th* 104–11 (also echoing the poet's initiation at *Th* 26–34), but leaves out the Muses, since Olympians are disqualified; the appropriation by the birds of "the ageless, whose counsels are imperishable" (689) ironically reverses its application in *Th* to Zeus's superiority over Prometheus, who like our birds was plotting to deceive him and who indeed will appear later in the play to advise Peisetaerus (521–616). In addition, at the beginning the birds allow, and thus claim for their own, Chaos (portrayed as empty air and thus winged), Night (also traditionally winged, e.g., Homer, *Iliad* 24.366), Erebus ("sire of Air" 1193), Tartarus (traditionally windy, e.g., *Th* 742–44), and of course winged Eros, but not Earth, who as Peisetaerus had claimed (469–78) was younger than the birds. But the birds' theogony does not restrict itself to the Hesiodic version; it incorporates elements from subsequent traditions, so long as they were mythic and poetic (the birds explicitly reject the alternative accounts of materialists and rationalists like Prodicus; 692). Thus Air as a cosmogonic figure, the wind-egg, and humans as "artifacts of clay" (unless this is an inference from *WD* 61–82, of Pandora) evidently invoke traditions attached to Orpheus (cf. Euripides's *Hypsipyle* fr. 758ab) and Epimenides, perhaps also to Musaeus and Aristeas, and 700 seems to allude to Empedocles's poem *On Nature* (cf. F 35 D–K). (For this texturing see the commentary of Dunbar 1995.)

Whether Peisetaerus's success should be viewed straightforwardly as a triumph for both birds and humanity (utopia restored) or with Orwellian irony (dystopia achieved) is debated by scholars and was a choice that the original spectators were left free to make according to their attitude on political questions that were very divisive at the time, in particular how far to trust the ascendant Alcibiades (cf. Henderson 1998). But in either view the point of Aristophanes's theogony was not to ridicule or discredit theogonies— as "sophists" or philosophers like Prodicus were doing, to the alarm of Aristophanes in *Clouds* and elsewhere—but rather to claim theogonic authority for his comic hero's plan. A crucial element of the birds' claim to power—not unlike the Athenians' appeal to autochthony to justify their right to empire—was their primogeniture vis-à-vis the Olympians, and theogony was the traditional model for such claims on the cosmic scale. Whether we view their claim as dishonest sophistry or beguilingly logical, the question of primogeniture was a relevant factor, and the theogonic argument, traditionally casting Zeus as a usurper, was the natural recourse.

Ironic or dystopian readings see such a challenge to Zeus's authority as self-evidently impious ("self-evidently" because there is no explicit warrant for it in the play) and therefore as misguided, but it can also suit a utopian reading; both are at home in comedy. In a play like *Clouds*, in which the Olympians safeguard a wholesome traditional order of society that is being challenged by wicked sophists, the primacy of Zeus is portrayed positively (even if sophistic members of the audience might scoff). But elsewhere defiance of Zeus (see generally Yasumura 2011) is portrayed sympathetically. It is indeed a recurrent motif in Old Comedy—after all, an essentially antiauthoritarian genre—always justified by complaints about the world under his reign—our world— that were both plausible (fueling satire) and voiced in hope of producing or restoring a more just world. Chremylus, the hero of *Wealth* who travels to Delphi to learn whether "in this day and age" (50; ἐν τῶι νῦν γένει, echoing Hesiod's Myth of the Races, *WD* 109– 201) the best way to assure success for his son is to raise him as a criminal (32–38), is not far from the Hesiodic pessimism of *WD* 270–73: "In this time (νῦν δή) I myself wouldn't want to be a just man among human beings, neither I nor a son of mine, since it is bad for a man to be just if the more unjust man will receive greater justice." The difference is that in comedy Zeus can be righteously taken to task for the injustice (he resents humanity; 87–92), and a Chremylus can repair it, in this case by restoring Wealth's eyesight. In comedy, as in Hesiod, rebellious humans are aided by a divine ally—in *Birds* by Prometheus, in *Peace* by Hermes, in *Wealth* by Apollo—but in comedy the rebels can justifiably succeed. Certainly in *Birds* a strong case is voiced against Zeus's rule, and his ambassadors (Poseidon, Heracles, and the Triballian) are laughable incompetents. This antiauthoritarian attitude suits the more progressive aspect of fifth-century BCE Athens, where Zeus could be seen as tyrannical and Prometheus's theft of fire as a means of liberation from unjust hardship and a symbol of progress (cf. Plato, *Protagoras* 320c–23a), as in tragedy in Aeschylus's Prometheus trilogy, an important intertext (along with the *Oresteia*) for Cratinus's *Wealth Gods* (Bakola 2013), which like *Prometheus Unbound* featured a chorus of Titans.

Aristophanes had already adopted the succession myth of *Theogony* ten years earlier (424 BCE) as the pattern for *Knights*, for both its allegorical plot and his own poetic self-presentation. As in *Birds* (with a nod to Hesiod's Myth of the Races), the goal was elimination of an unjust regime in order to restore an earlier utopia; such had perhaps also been the pattern in Cratinus's attack on the regime of Pericles as Zeus in *Cheirons* and *Wealth Gods* (below). But the political environment in 424 required a different orientation of the myth; the Olympian caricature of Pericles suited a leader whose control of the demos and ascendancy over fellow aristocrats amounted to tyranny, but it did not suit the populist politicians who emerged after his death in 429. These were the first leaders from the commercial rather than the landed elite, in the eyes of traditionalists like the comic poets "sellers" of dubious pedigree who had disrupted the traditional order from below. In *Knights* a new-bought, barbaric, and villainous slave, Paphlagon (transparently representing the populist politician Cleon), has gained control of the House of the senile and gullible Demos, following a rapid, pseudo-dynastic/theogonic succession of "sellers," each one baser than the last, from Eucrates (hemp), to Lysicles (sheep), to Cleon (leather); Thucydides 2.65 presents a similar narrative of decline. But Demos's loyal household slaves, representing traditional politicians, discover an oracle predicting Paphlagon's overthrow at the hands of an even baser seller (sausages). The slaves recruit Sausage Seller, who beats Paphlagon using his own demagogic techniques in a series of violent contests, rescuing Demos from enthrallment to Paphlagon and then magically rejuvenating him, returning Athens to its golden age of Miltiades and Marathon.

Sausage Seller, among comic heroes anomalously youthful, is assimilated with Hesiod's young Zeus as the champion of justice and order, fighting off a challenge from the monstrous Typhoeus (*Th* 820–85; for the many close structural similarities see Bowie 1993: 58–66); his helpers are the Knights ("fine gentlemen a thousand strong, who detest him") together with "all fine and upstanding citizens, and every smart spectator, and myself (Slave A) along with them, and the god will lend a hand too" (225–29). Sausage Seller's initial similarity to Paphlagon suits the play's satire—politics is no longer a job for decent people, so that Paphlagon can only be bested by someone even worse—but at the same time aligns with myth, where gigantomachic opponents are often similar. Like Zeus, who transforms from a lightning-bolt-wielding battle-god to a just god with a stable reign, Sausage Seller transforms from a vulgar battler to Demos's honest adviser; figures allegorizing peace and prosperity mark both transitions. And like the chthonic Typhoeus hurled into Tartarus (*Th* 868), the vanquished Paphlagon is cast outside the city gates, freeing Athens from hardship and injustice and (the play suggests) thus enabling a better future.

In addition, the young poet explicitly assimilates Sausage Seller's battle against Paphlagon to his own battle against Cleon, who had prosecuted him after the production of *Babylonians* two years earlier. In the parabasis the Knights say that Aristophanes has earned their appearance as his chorus because "he hates the same people we do, and dares to say what's right, and nobly strides forth against Typhos and the whirlwind" (510–11; cf. also *Wasps* 1033). And for good measure Aristophanes includes his own poetic succession over his elderly rival Cratinus, once an elemental force, too, but now spent like a worn-out lyre (520–50).

Clearly the theogonic tradition that Hesiod was credited with launching was familiar in detail to a broad popular audience in the fifth century BCE and thus available to comic poets for interactive repurposing in both novel accounts of the past and hopeful constructions of the future.

SOCIETY

Visions of the world as it should be, intrinsic to all satire and variously thematized in Greek comedy, took center stage in a strain of plays with utopian or dystopian main themes and set in the past or imminent future, in the underworld, in the exotic east or west, or (like *Birds*) in a vague not-here or neverland. Paradigmatic of these types of play were Hesiod's Islands of the Blest (*WD* 156–73; cf. also Homer, *Odyssey* 4.561–69) and the metallic Races (especially the golden one; *WD* 109–20), along with their didactic context of labor and justice as laid out in *WD* and in light of the myth of divine succession from *Th* (Ruffell 2000, 2011: 386–93). Comedy elaborates Hesiod's original scenario while rejecting the model of irreversible decline (which Hesiod had hedged by inserting an age of heroes), so that utopias could be used as topical lenses and vantage points for social critiques in the new contexts of democratic culture. Athenaeus 6.267e–270a singles out eight such plays to illustrate the theme of automatism (*WD* 116–18), that is, the spontaneous provision of goods by the gods and/or the earth to mankind without the need for work or slaves. Athenaeus quotes six of the plays chronologically to illustrate how the poets tried to outdo one another: to Hesiod's original provisions are added plenty of food, wine, playtime, and (what is either absent or evil in a Hesiodic or biblical paradise) sex, all with surprising new implications.

Earliest in Athenaeus's sequence is Cratinus's *Wealth Gods* (*Ploutoi*), in which Hesiod's "wealth-giving spirits," once the golden race, are refashioned as Titans imprisoned under the tyranny of Zeus but ultimately freed to restore utopian blessings to the people; the play seems to allegorize the circle of Pericles (among them Hagnon) as unjustly enriched—descendants of Hesiod's gift-eating nobles—and Pericles's loss of his generalship in 430 BCE (fr. 171; cf. Thucydides 2.59–65; Plutarch, *Pericles* 35.3–4). Such notions of fairness in the availability of life's blessings as well as a redistributive ideology are pervasive in comedy. Crates's *Beasts*, contrasting utopias of food and luxury, and Telecleides's *Amphictyon and Company*, conflating Hesiod's golden age with Athens under King Amphictyon (fr. 1; these extravagant blessings included abundant peace), seem to blend or update Hesiodic themes with parody of contemporary thinkers, specifically Pythagoras and Empedocles. Pherecrates's *Miners* and Aristophanes's *Fry Cooks* (*Tagenistai*) locate utopia in the underworld, the latter detailing the superiority of Plutus's realm to Zeus's and perhaps satirizing the elite institution and exclusive luxury of the symposium, thus making utopian luxuries a satirical target. This critical stance probably informed such plays as Pherecrates's *Persians*, Metagenes's *Thuriopersians*, and Nicophon's *Sirens*, which are set in places already legendary for luxury (Dicaeopolis in *Acharnians* 61–90 represents the common man's indignant contempt) and anticipate the preoccupation in fourth-century comedy with the lifestyles of the rich and famous not only in Athens but also abroad, in what would soon become the Hellenistic world.

Dystopian comedies, like Hesiod's iron race, conversely focus on how bad society has become by generalizing its worst features, often (but not inevitably) in a scenario of decline from a (recoverable) better past. Aristophanes's *Knights* incorporates this pattern, while Eupolis's sarcastically titled *Golden Race* (also mid-420s BCE) is set in a remote and barbaric city (perhaps Mariandynia near Paphlagonia on the Black Sea; fr. 302) where the social inversions of demagogic Athens under Cleon are native. If there was a rescue, as in *Knights* or Cratinus's *Wealth Gods*, it is unclear how it would have been realized in such a place. The scenario of *Birds*, in which two Athenians simply walk away from the hopelessly litigious world that Athens has become and create an ideal world among the birds (at least for themselves), also operated in plays like Phrynichus's *Hermit* (*Monotropos*) and Pherecrates's *Savages*, which was read by Plato as engaging Protagoras's socioeconomic interpretation of Hesiod's golden race (*Protagoras* 327c–d).

Elements of Hesiodic utopianism could be used as ingredients in other types of comedy too, in which ideals of justice reminiscent of *WD* are the norm. Justice is conceived as valid across all classes and hierarchies and serves the best interests of both individual and society, and its model is the honest, practical, and hard-working farmer, though comedy prefers to dwell on the rural pleasures of leisure and festivity. The idealized countryside of Aristophanes's *Peace*, including this time the virtues of honest labor, richly recalls Hesiod both specifically and in general flavor (Hunter 2014: 151–56), as does the Hesiodic tradition of a Panhellenic culture. The rescue of the goddess Peace, hidden by Zeus out of disappointment in humankind, reverses the Pandora pattern and restores an antebellum state of grace for all of Greece, which, in *Acharnians*, the hero restores by obtaining a peace treaty and a return to the countryside for himself and his family alone—and for a bridesmaid, "since as a woman she isn't responsible for the war" (1062). The redistributive ideology of *Wealth* similarly relies on the notion of an earlier deprivation or depravation by Zeus, and Poverty echoes Hesiod when she argues against Wealth that the need to work is morally beneficial, while too much leisure is detrimental; the hero may laugh this off but does not offer a convincing counterargument. In *Assemblywomen* the new regime will leave nothing for men to do but don their new clothes, eat, drink, and copulate; in effect, they will live a life of carefree boyhood with women doing all the chores, much like the time of Hesiod's golden race, when men "lived like gods, with carefree heart, free and apart from trouble and pain" (*WD* 112–13), and the silver race, when "a boy was raised by his dear mother for a hundred years, a large infant playing in his house" (130–31)—except for the inclusion of sex (and women, if Hesiod's golden race under Cronus lacked them), for which comedy departs from the negative and puritanical Hesiodic model.

In comedy sex is not a punishment inflicted by Zeus upon mankind but for the most part an unalloyed good that figures in any catalog of blessings and rewards, and while the comic portrayal of women often exploits the same stereotypes found in Hesiodic, iambic, and sympotic poetry, Pandora is not women's archetype, and women are not simply a necessary evil. The foibles and schemes of horny housewives, the vulgarity of market women, and the rapacity of courtesans are colorfully depicted, but for the comic poets marriage, family, and household are the traditional bulwarks and anchor of society, and women's management of the private sphere is often very favorably contrasted with men's (mis)management of the public spheres. The utopia of *Assemblywomen* indeed amounts to the conversion of the entire polis into a single large household managed by its women.

A COMIC *CERTAMEN*? POET, POETIC PERSONA, COMPETITION

Comic poets took an interest not only in Hesiodic poetry but also in the poet and poetic persona behind it, either bracketed with Homer as a great cultural authority, distinguished as the anti-Homer in subjects or style, or showcased as an emblematic persona of poet and (didactic) sage. Aristophanes, for one, also adopted elements of the Hesiodic persona in fashioning his own.

Literary-critical themes and the portrayal of famous poets, living or dead, not uncommon in comedy, could have an agonistic setting, pitting one poet against another, like Aeschylus and Euripides in our one extant example, Aristophanes's *Frogs* of 405. In that play the poets are portrayed less as individuals than as poetic personae, and they represent not only contrasting styles of tragedy but also the ethos of their respective eras. The contest programmatically channels the poet's own aesthetic tenets and moral orientation, which are explicitly offered didactically (like the *Certamen*), as useful to the community. Similar fragmentary plays doubtless had much the same character, though *Frogs* was exceptionally successful: Aristophanes won not only the first prize but also a civic crown and the unique honor of a reperformance of the play for his advice to the Athenians in its parabasis.

Such comedies participate in a tradition that is first attested in Hesiod's programmatic and evidently archetypal victory at Chalcis (*WD* 650–59), which was carried on in the archaic period in such contests as between the cyclic poets Lesches and Arctinus (Phaenias F 33 Wehrli) and the seers Calchas and Mopsus ([Hesiod], *Melampodia* F 278). The contest between Homer and Hesiod known as the *Certamen*, in which Hesiod is the victor, must belong to this tradition as well—that its inspiration was Hesiod himself is signaled by its identifying the victory over Homer with the dedication at Chalcis—though it is first attested in a version by Alcidamas dating from the early fourth century BCE. It circulated in various versions (Koning 2010: 239–68; Bassino 2013: 11–52), but its core elements are stable: opposition between warfare and farming and a judge awarding the prize not to Homer, the crowd favorite by virtue of his grand and exciting style, but to the plainer and simpler Hesiod, on moral grounds, because "it was right for the poet who encouraged people towards farming and peace to win, not the one who rehearsed battle and carnage" (*Certamen* 13).

The *Certamen* can hardly have originated with Alcidamas; "sophists" are typically compilers and interpreters, not inventors, and the basic terms and pattern of the *Certamen*—the competitive recitation of one's own distinctive poetry; the association of aesthetic quality with socially, morally, or politically useful content either practical or moral; and a judge's choice of winner that is surprising because it is based on the latter criterion rather than mere popularity—are found not only in *Frogs* but also with specific reference to Hesiod in earlier fifth-century BCE comedies, so that is not impossible that the *Certamen* originated in comedy. One example, the miniature song contest in Aristophanes's *Peace* of 421 (1265–1304) between the general's warlike son and the shield-thrower's son, who is declared the victor by Trygaeus as judge, may serve as a *terminus ante quem* in that it also contains evidence for prior circulation of the *Certamen*, quoting two of the verses (1270, 1282–83) that appear at a similar juncture in the extant *Certamen* (107–8, 259) and thus calling attention to the episode's specifically Hesiodic character in the most Hesiodic movement of the play.

The earlier instances are very fragmentary but not uninformative. Telecleides's *Hesiods* (*Hesiodoi*), probably earlier than 429 BCE (Pericles is again assimilated to Zeus), seems à la *Frogs* to involve an anabasis from the underworld in order to reinvigorate contemporary poetry, with Hesiod (and/or poets like Hesiod? or partisans of Hesiod?) probably representing traditional values, perhaps in a contest, since the play contained literary polemic. In fr. 15 a female speaker expresses a positive opinion of Aeschylus and a negative one of his nephew Philocles, perhaps Poetry or Tragedy or a muse acting as the judge? Reference to Olympian Pericles (fr. 18; this time he is in love with Chrysilla of Corinth) points to the alignment of literary with political themes—perhaps a choice of war or peace, in which case Hesiod would doubtless be invoked in support of the latter— and/or the unprecedented power that the Athenians have surrendered to Pericles (if fr. 45, from a parabasis, belongs to this play). (For discussion see Bagordo 2013: 116–38; Ornaghi 2012.) Of the only other comedy with Hesiod in the title, the much later *Hesiod* by Nicostratus (fl. ca. 350), only the title remains.

The similarity in title of Cratinus's *Archilochus and Company* (*Archilochoi*) to *Hesiod and Company* suggests similarity in content and even an intertextual relationship, though which play came first is unknown. Cratinus's play does seem to feature a literary contest, one that includes Hesiod; compare fr. 2, "what a swarm (*smenos*) of sophists you people have stirred up," with Diogenes Laertius 1.12: "Sophist was another title for wise men (*sophoi*), and not only for them but also for poets, just as when Cratinus in *Archilochus and Company* gives the followers of Homer and the followers of Hesiod this title as a compliment." Given Cratinus's consistent self-identification with the iambic poetics of abuse in general and Archilochus in particular (in antiquity already recognized as a hallmark of Cratinus's persona, e.g., T 17 = Platonius, *Diff. Char.* 1, p. 6 Koster), it is likely that in the play (poets like? partisans of?) Archilochus won the day against Homer and Hesiod, perhaps (as suggested by Bakola 2010: 65–80) by demonstrating the greater value of the iambic (blame) poet and his poetry to the polis than the epic praise poetry of Homer or the agrarian didactic of Hesiod; the connection of personal abuse with the interests of the community is in fact a distinctive dimension of Archilochean iambus. The outcome for the hierarchy of the epic and didactic genres is unclear (Biles 2011: 140–45), but Cratinus elsewhere orients himself (in contrast with Aristophanes) to the martial, mythic, and epic worlds of Aeschylus and Homer (see Telò 2014).

In other respects, too, Cratinus's self-presentation is decidedly un- or anti-Hesiodic. Like Archilochus he claims inspiration from wine (countering Aristophanes, who had portrayed Cratinus as a washed-up alcoholic; *Knights* 400, 526–36), for intoxication produces bold, forceful, manly, and therefore good poetry, while "a water drinker will produce nothing good (*sophos*)" (fr. 203, from his last play, *Wine Flask*, whose main character was Cratinus himself). This association of wine with frenzied artistic inspiration (e.g., *Frogs* 356–57; Euripides, *Bacchae* 298–301; Plato, *Ion* 534a–b; cf. O'Sullivan 1992: 118–19), natural genius, and a grand style, and of water with craft, learning, and a plain style, was already current in the fifth century BCE (see O'Sullivan 1992); it is explicitly aligned respectively with Homer and Hesiod first in Hellenistic times (Koning 2010: 337–39), but no doubt the alignment had already figured in such fifth-century comic contexts.

Cratinus's programmatic, critical, political, and personal self-alignment with a past poet and his poetics is hardly unique in or to fifth-century BCE comedy. Aristophanes and other leading playwrights such as Eupolis and Plato each fashioned a special poetic persona for asserting and certifying his own excellence and superiority over rivals and predecessors, a persona that could include actual personal elements (e.g., Aristophanes's confrontations with Cleon) and merge with the themes, characters, and moral or civic/political ambitions of a play (for the various criteria see Sommerstein 2009). In this the comic poets were following a form of competitive poetics already familiar in the archaic period and perhaps originating with its earliest attested expression: the hymn to the Muses that opens *Th.* There Hesiod proclaims in his own name and fictive (poetic) identity (which as in comedy may or may not correspond in every respect with reality) a uniquely favored relationship with the Muses, as certified by their advice, their gift of a scepter, and the song that they inspire in him. When in *WD* (654–59) he wins a contest at Chalcis (with *Th*?), he dedicates his tripod to the Muses on Helicon, where they first inspired him (Biles 2011: 22–27). The assertion of excellence is linked with another important ingredient in the comic persona first exemplified by Hesiod: the posture of the lone moralizer, admonisher, and adviser, often beleaguered, angry, self-righteous, and in despair of his benighted community, which "prefigures some of the central themes and postures of satiric literature" (Telò 2013: 135). Noteworthy in this regard is the broad portfolio of Hesiod's Muses: his senior Muse Calliope bestows eloquence upon princes

(*Th* 81–93), remarkably extending the Muses' functions beyond poetry into council and rhetoric (persuasion), both important heroic assets already in epic and claimed also by poets like Cratinus and Aristophanes.

Aristophanes, bracketed by Cratinus with Euripides as "an oh-so subtle wordsmith and chaser of conceits" (fr. 342), did in fact contrast himself with the old master in more Hesiodic directions: championing the joys of peace and the virtues of the countryside; prizing originality, intellectual sophistication, and truth-telling; enjoying divine patronage and protection (especially Athena and Dionysus) as well as a familiar relationship with the Muses (e.g., *Wasps* 1022, 1028; *Peace* 775–817; *Frogs* 356, 674, 686, F 348); priding himself not only on *dexiotes* (technical skill) but also (uniquely among comic poets) on *nouthesia*, the ability to improve the community by giving it good advice (not only criticism and abuse); and fighting as selflessly and courageously as Heracles against the community's greatest (never its trivial) threats. Like Hesiod, Aristophanes thus asserts his poesis as "a skill divinely bestowed on a member of the community, to be used for the community's good as well as his own" (Sommerstein 2009: 132). Cleon's prosecutions after *Babylonians* and *Knights*, and the civic honors recognizing *Frogs*, prove that this was not mere posturing.

Aristophanes naturally had his own iambic affiliations as well, but these he tempers with various alignments, including the Hesiodic. This he does rather programatically in the miniature song contest near the end of *Peace* discussed above as exemplifying the *Certamen* pattern, where Trygaeus plays the role of judge between two boys who are practicing their preludes for performance at his wedding feast (1265–1304). One is the son of the general Lamachus, the other the son of the politician Cleonymus, notorious (uniquely) in comedy as a shield thrower. The first offers epic quotations, which Trygaeus vainly attempts to reorient from fighting to feasting (apparently composing the alternative verses himself), and is dismissed in favor of the second son, who offers the song by Archilochus about the abandoned shield (fr. 5). Trygaeus thus identifies as well as exemplifies (in mocking Cleonymus) a particular iambic ethos that suits the Hesiodic environment of the play—swords are literally turned into ploughshares— which has become increasingly tangible since the parabasis (729–818) and continued in the "second parabasis" at 1127–90, recapitulating Hesiod's linkage in *WD* between peace and plenty (228–30) and war and hunger (242–47). (See further on this scene Compton-Engle 1999; Hunter 2014: 154–56; Telò 2013; and for the poetry of peace versus the poetry of war, Koning 2010: 269–84.)

Contributing to the Hesiodic persona in comedy was Hesiod's reputation as a didactic poet, a teacher of practical wisdom, and a sage who produced wise sayings. The Hesiodic *Precepts of Cheiron* is identified as a comic intertext in plays of the 430s and 420s BCE; the mission of Cratinus's *Cheirons* (430s) included delivering such precepts (fr. 253), which are quoted or parodied also in Pherecrates's *Cheiron* (fr. 162 is a pastiche of the Hesiodic and the Theognidean) and in Aristophanes's *Banqueters* (fr. 239), which contrasted traditional with sophistic education. And Hesiod's stature as a didactic poet is programmatic in setting the terms for the poetic contest in *Frogs*, where both Aeschylus and Euripides agree that poets should "make men better members of their communities" (1009–10), stressing a poetic function exemplified by a quartet of predecessors who are named in the order that seems to have become standard (1030–36; cf. Hippias of Elis 86 B 6):

> Just consider   1030
> how beneficial (ὠφέλιμοι) the noble poets have been from the earliest times:
> Orpheus revealed mystic rites to us, and taught us to abstain from killings;
> Musaeus gave us oracles and cures for diseases; Hesiod agriculture,
> the seasons for crops, and ploughing; and where did the godlike Homer
> get respect and renown if not by giving good/useful instruction (χρήστ᾽ἐδίδαξεν)   1035
> in the tactics, virtues, and weaponry of men?

Throughout the contest the poet's didactic function is understood, as in Hesiod, as embracing both information (for guidance) and inspiration (to right action), so that Aeschylus's depiction of "the tactics, virtues, and weaponry" of heroes inspired the Athenians of his day to be great fighters, while Euripides's emphasis on mundane matters (οἰκεῖα πράγματα, 959) has turned his contemporaries into duty-shirking pettifoggers and rascals. The resurrection of Aeschylus might thus reverse both the decline of tragedy and the decline of Athens.

The similarities between the contest of *Frogs* and the *Certamen* are salient (Rosen 2004), but so are the differences. This time the crowd favorite and ultimate loser is not the Homeric Aeschylus but the antiheroic and didactic Euripides, whose practical wisdom, everyday expertise, stylistic simplicity, and egalitarianism align him with Hesiod. This time the surprise set up by the narrative typology of the *Certamen* is that Homer defeats Hesiod. For Rosen, this "strongly implies that the wrong person was chosen" (2004: 309). But the choice of Aeschylus can hardly have been a real surprise; Dionysus's initial desire to rescue Euripides exemplified the current misdirection and bad taste of the majority of the public, as the heroic Heracles immediately understood (98–107), but by the end there is little doubt about who deserves to win. That Aristophanes, the inveterate champion of peace, would consider Homer the right choice this time is a mark of how desperate he considered the Athenian situation to be.

Further Reading

If "the pursuit of Hesiodic themes and ideas through antiquity" is "at least as important a task for the understanding of ancient culture as . . . the tracking of verbal echoes of Hesiod's poems" (Hunter 2014: 34), then the pursuit in comedy—barely begun—should include not only the extant plays of Aristophanes but also his and the other poets' fragmentary plays, a task made considerably easier by the production of new editions, translations, and commentaries in the wake of Kassel and Austin (1980), notably the *Fragmenta Comica* (*FrC*) series being published by Verlag Antike (Heidelberg); Harvey and Wilkins (2000); Henderson (2007); Olson (2007); Rusten et al. (2011); and Storey (2011).

NOTE

1. Comic fragments are cited from Kassel and Austin (1980); all translations are my own.

REFERENCES

Bagordo, A., ed. and comm. 2013. *Telekleides: Einleitung, Übersetzung, Kommentar*. Freiburg, Germany.

Bakola, E. 2010. *Cratinus and the Art of Comedy*. Oxford.

Bakola, E. 2013. "Crime and Punishment. Cratinus, Aeschylus' *Oresteia*, and the Metaphysics and Politics of Wealth." In *Greek Comedy and the Discourse of Genres*, edited by E. Bakola, L. Prauscello, and M. Telo, 226–55. Cambridge.

Bakola, E., L. Prauscello, and M. Telò, eds. 2013. *Greek Comedy and the Discourse of Genres*. Cambridge.

Bassino, P., ed. and comm. 2013. "*Certamen Homeri et Hesiodi*: Introduction, Critical Edition and Commentary." PhD diss., Durham University.

Biles, Z. 2011. *Aristophanes and the Poetics of Competition*. Cambridge.

Bowie, A. M. 1993. *Aristophanes: Myth, Ritual and Comedy*. Cambridge.

Castaldo, D., A. Barker, B. Gentili, P. Giannini, and A. Manieri, eds. 2012. *Poesia, Musica e Agoni Nella Grecia Antica*. Galatina, Italy.

Compton-Engle, G. 1999. "Aristophanes *Peace* 1265–1304: Food, Poetry, and the Comic Genre." *Classical Philology* 94: 324–29.

Dixon, D. W. 2015. "Myth-Making in Greek and Roman Comedy." PhD diss., Boston University.

Dobrov, G. 1998. *The City as Comedy: Society and Representation in Athenian Drama*. Chapel Hill, NC.

Dunbar, N. V., ed. and comm. 1995. *Aristophanes Birds*. Edited with Introduction and Commentary. Oxford.

Gkaras, C., ed. and comm. 2008. "Hermippos: Die Fragmente; Ein Kommentar." PhD diss., Freiburg University.

Harvey, D., and W. John. 2000. *The Rivals of Aristophanes: Studies in Athenian Old Comedy*. London.

Henderson, J. 1998. "Mass versus Elite and the Comic Heroism of Peisetairos." In *The City as Comedy: Society and Representation in Athenian Drama*, edited by G. Dobrov, 135–48. Chapel Hill, NC.

Henderson, J., ed. 2007. *Aristophanes: Fragments*. Cambridge.

Henderson, J. 2015. "Types and Styles of Comedy Between 450 and 420." In *Fragmente einer Geschichte der griechischen Komödie*, edited by S. Chronopoulos and C. Orth, 146–58. Studia Comica 5. Verlag Antike:

Hunter, R. 2014. *Hesiodic Voices: Studies in the Ancient Reception of Hesiod's Works and Days*. Cambridge.

Kassel, R., and C. Austin, eds. 1980. *Poetae Comici Graeci*. New York.

Koning, H. H. 2010. *Hesiod: The Other Poet; Ancient Reception of a Cultural Icon*. Mnemosyne Supplement 325. Leiden, Netherlands.

Montanari, F., A. Rengakos, and C. Tsagalis, eds. 2009. *Brill's Companion to Hesiod*. Leiden, Netherlands.

Olson, S. D., comm. and trans. 2007. *Broken Laughter: Select Fragments of Greek Comedy.* Oxford.

Ornaghi, M. 2012. "Gli *Esiodi* di Teleclide e le Variazione Comiche del Modello Agonale." In *Poesia, Musica e Agoni Nella Grecia Antica*, edited by D. Castaldo, A. Barker, B. Gentili, P. Giannini, and A. Manieri, 385–414. Galatina, Italy.

O'Sullivan, N. 1992. *Alcidamas, Aristophanes and the Beginnings of Greek Stylistic Theory.* Hermes Einzelschriften 60. Stuttgart, Germany.

Rosen, R. 2004. "Aristophanes' *Frogs* and the *Contest of Homer and Hesiod*." *TAPA* 134: 295–322.

Ruffell, I. 2000. "The World Turned Upside Down: Utopia and Utopianism in the Fragments of Old Comedy." In *The Rivals of Aristophanes. Studies in Athenian Old Comedy*, edited by D. Harvey and J. Wilkins, 473–506. London.

Ruffell, I. 2011. *Politics and Anti-Realism in Athenian Old Comedy: The Art of the Impossible.* Oxford.

Rusten, J., ed. 2011. *The Birth of Comedy: Texts, Documents, and Art from Athenian Comic Competitions, 486–280.* Baltimore, MD.

Sommerstein, A. H. 2009. "Old Comedians on Old Comedy." In *Talking About Laughter and Other Studies in Greek Comedy*, edited by A. H. Sommerstein, 116–35. Oxford.

Stama, F., ed., comm., and trans. 2014. *Frinico: Introduzione, Traduzione e Commento.* Freiburg, Germany.

Storey, I., ed. and trand. 2011. *Fragments of Old Comedy.* Cambridge.

Telò, M. 2013. "Epic, *Nostos* and Generic Genealogy in Aristophanes' *Peace*." In *Greek Comedy and the Discourse of Genres*, edited by E. Bakola, L. Prauscello, and M. Telo, 129–52. Cambridge.

Telò, M. 2014. "On the Sauce: Cratinus, Cyclopean Poetics, and the Roiling Sea of Epic." *Arethusa* 47: 303–20.

Yasumura, N. 2011. *Challenges to the Power of Zeus in Early Greek Poetry.* London.

CHAPTER 20

....

PLATO'S HESIODS

....

MARCUS FOLCH

THE reception of Hesiod in the fourth century BCE is so variegated in nature that it is difficult to synthesize within a single essay. As they did in the fifth century BCE, rhapsodes in the fourth performed *Theogony* (hereafter *Th*) and *Works and Days* (hereafter *WD*) throughout the Greek-speaking Mediterranean (Plato, *Ion* 531a–d; Athenaeus 14.620), and dramatists turned to Hesiodic myth for the settings and themes of their comedic and tragic works (Olson 2007: 125, 318–20). Just as English speakers quote Shakespeare—sometimes unknowingly—adapting what at the time of composition were idiosyncratic poetic coinages within the texture of everyday conversation, Hesiodic language and imagery resurface in the ways fourth-century Athenians spoke and wrote. Orators occasionally cite Hesiod in support of their legal cases (Aeschines 1.129, 2.144–45; Demosthenes 19.243), as do philosophers, relying directly and indirectly on *WD* and *Th* when developing ethical and cosmological theories. Schools appear to have played a crucial role in determining Hesiod's position in fourth-century culture; although Hesiodic poetry had long been part of elite education, by the fourth century aphoristic expressions appear to have been excerpted especially from *WD* and circulated in textbooks, providing educated ancient readers a shared canon of ethical commonplaces to quote and adapt within an array of contexts (Isocrates 2.42–44; Plato, *Protagoras* 325e–326a, discussed below). Reception of a different variety is on display in the cult of the Muses on Mt. Helicon, in which Hesiod occupied an honorific position and which remained vibrant into the third century BCE (*Certamen* 13.210–23; Pausanias 9.30.3).

Any attempt to treat so vast and heterogeneous a field of reception necessarily involves a degree of eclecticism and simplification. Rather than survey contexts in which Hesiod reappears in the years 399–300 BCE, this essay approaches Hesiodic reception through the lens of one author and text: Plato's *Laws*. The selection of author needs little explanation; Plato's sustained and often critical engagement with the poetic tradition will be familiar to most readers. His dependence on Hesiod in particular is evident in many of the dialogues.[1] Hesiod formed part of an authoritative intellectual tradition, literary canon, and cultural system, which Plato and his contemporaries inherited; language and imagery from *Th* and *WD* therefore often lurk not far beneath the surface of Plato's own language and imagery. Solmsen (1962: 179) describes Hesiod and Plato as two of the "great organizers of the realities of the Greek world." Perhaps it would be more accurate to say that Plato was a *reorganizer* of a reality whose contours Hesiodic poetry had shaped; for Plato Hesiod was both a source and a rival. Precisely in the areas of human experience, literature, and knowledge in which Hesiod was regarded as an authority, Plato presented philosophy as a more coherent, aesthetically compelling, and rigorously argued alternative. Plato's encounter with Hesiod is thus one of the most nuanced chapters in the history of Hesiodic reception, and there is no better author on whom to ground a study of the fourth-century BCE afterlife of Hesiodic poetry.

The choice of text requires more extensive justification. Plato's last and longest work, the *Laws*, is also the only Platonic dialogue in which Socrates makes no appearance. Instead, it records the conversation of three elderly interlocutors—the Spartan Megillos, the Cretan Kleinias, and an unnamed Athenian Stranger—who undertake a journey through the hinterlands of Crete. Although it was once conventional to disparage Plato's final dialogue for its perceived paucity of artistic embellishments and dialectical argumentation, the *Laws* is now regarded as an ambitious work of literature and philosophy; it contains elevated passages both sweeping in vision and poetic in style, and it presents a novel philosophical approach to the soul and cosmology. Much of the dialogue consists of detailed analysis of the political institutions and law code (whence its title) for an ideal city named Magnesia. The result is one of the most extensive and detailed surviving explorations of the civic and social institutions that structured life in the ancient Greek city-state. In no small part because of its literary aspirations and wide-ranging discussion of ancient institutions, the *Laws* provides a uniquely comprehensive overview of Plato's Hesiodic entanglements. Like many of Plato's earlier works, the *Laws* draws on language, ideas, and styles of thought that originate in Hesiod's poetry. Plato alludes to Hesiod in the *Laws* more so than he does in any work except the *Republic* and *Timaeus*.[2] Unlike the *Republic*, moreover, which seeks to banish mimetic poetry from the ideal city, the performance and reading of epic are regular—and carefully regulated—occurrences in the city envisaged in the *Laws*. What the *Laws* gives is a window into the ways in which Hesiod was *thought* to operate and *did* operate in the fourth century BCE, and it is therefore an ideal starting point for a discussion of fourth-century Hesiodic reception. Although the *Laws* has garnered much scholarly attention of late, its indebtedness to Hesiod is often overlooked.[3] This essay thus provides a general survey of fourth-century Hesiodic reception and by doing so addresses the need for an assessment of Plato's dialogue with Hesiod in his final work.

Each of the following sections begins from a single episode or passage in the *Laws*, illustrating a particular dimension of Plato's engagement with Hesiod's poetry. Using these episodes to explore the broader historical scene in which the Hesiodic poems circulated, this essay shows that Hesiod continued to supply a significant conceptual framework within which ancient audiences, readers, and authors made sense of their reality. Prose writers treat Hesiod as a contemporary, with whom to engage and from whom to draw inspiration, and in the particular context of the *Laws*, Hesiod informs the fundamental philosophical and political projects of Plato's final work. At the same time, each of Hesiod's poems was read, quoted, and adapted within distinct literary, social, and political environments. Hence the title of this essay—Plato's *Hesiods*—which stresses the multiplicity of avenues of transmission and reception along which the Hesiodic poems entered the fourth century BCE.

PERFORMANCE, EDUCATION, TEXT

The first reference to Hesiod in the *Laws* appears in a discussion in which the Athenian Stranger invites his interlocutors to imagine a Panhellenic competition in which the victory prize is awarded to the contestant who provides the greatest amount of pleasure to the audience (*Laws* 2.658d–e). Performers of all varieties would enter, but the Athenian Stranger insists that the outcome would be predictable: young children would vote in favor of the contestant who offers puppet shows; older boys would choose the comedian; and among educated women, young men, and the majority of the population, tragedy would take first prize. If the elderly were to choose, however, the performer of epic poetry would be victorious:

> The rhapsode, who gave a beautiful recital of the *Iliad* or the *Odyssey* or something from the Hesiodic poems (τι τῶν Ἡσιοδείων), would probably please us old men listeners most and be proclaimed the winner by far. (2.658d5–7)[4]

Rhapsodic performance remained the principal scenario in which ancient audiences encountered Hesiod's poetry, and thus the type of festival here envisaged would have been familiar to Plato's readers (Perlman 1965: 154; Graziosi 2010: 111–12). At the same time, this passage forces us to confront numerous intractable difficulties in mapping fourth-century BCE Hesiodic reception, the first of which is that evidence for Hesiod is often entangled with and inferred from evidence for Homer (Koning 2010a: 25–51). As a result, boundaries between what each poet may have been thought to communicate are not always carefully delineated.

A second difficulty is the possibility of a hierarchy in the relationship between the two poets. Some scholars have taken 2.658d5–7 as evidence that Hesiod may have been overshadowed by Homer (Graziosi 2010: 112–13; Yamagata 2010: 71–72). It is perhaps telling in this respect that Plato mentions Homer's works by title in contrast to the generic τι τῶν Ἡσιοδείων, and that elsewhere in the *Laws* (2.358b8) Homer is treated as emblematic of the genre of epic as a whole.[5] If 2.658d5–7 points to an implicit prioritization of Homer over Hesiod, Plato's usage would appear to reflect ancient practice. For on those occasions in which it is possible to differentiate performance venues for each poet, Homer consistently is given pride of place; the Great Panathenaea, for instance, which remained the premier musical and poetical venue in fourth-century BCE Athens, effectively prohibited performance of Hesiod (Lycurgus 1.102). The law limiting rhapsodic performance at the Great Panathenaea to Homer is perhaps an *exceptio probat regulam*; rhapsody of poets in addition to Homer was likely the rule at other festivals (West 2010: 3–7). Yet as Plato's *Ion* (531a) reveals, some rhapsodes restricted their repertory to the *Iliad* and *Odyssey*—all of which suggests that however closely associated the two poets may have been, Hesiod might have played, as Yamagata (2010: 72) argues, "second fiddle to Homer."

Whatever we make of Hesiod's relationship to Homer, *Laws* 2.658d5–7 also sheds light on the *perception* of Hesiodic performances in Plato's day. More precisely, *Laws* 2.658d suggests that rhapsodic performance was regarded as out of vogue (West 2010: 5). Rhapsody remained central in Athenian cultural mythology, so much so that Athenians attributed the establishment of rhapsodic contests to legendary, foundational figures, such as Solon and the Pisistratids ([Plato] *Hipparchus*; Lycurgus 1.102; Diogenes Laertius 1.57). But epic had ceased to be the epicenter of poetic innovation in the fourth century BCE. That (in Plato's mind, dubious) distinction belongs to choral genres such as comedy, dithyramb, and tragedy, performed in accompaniment with the *aulos* and associated with the "New Music" that was all the rage in Plato's day. Hesiod and Homer, by contrast, had become classics, members of canon. As I observe in subsequent sections, the aura of canonicity defines the way that Plato and his contemporaries read and deployed Hesiod in conversation and literature.

Rhapsodic performance is only one context in which ancient audiences encountered Hesiodic poetry in the fourth century. What distinguishes the fourth-century reception of Hesiod from its sixth- and fifth-century BCE antecedents is the degree to which Hesiodic poetry found its way into the textual record. Of the poems attributed to Hesiod in antiquity, *WD* is by far the most frequently and directly cited in the *Laws* and the Platonic corpus. This much is consistent with the relative popularity of the poems and the institutions in which they circulated in the fourth century; *WD* was by far the more read of the two poems in the fifth and fourth centuries, and, importantly, it appears to have been a seminal text in elite education (Koning 2010a: 21). Rhapsodes, who often moonlighted as tutors for the children of aristocratic families, may have owned complete copies of Homer (Xenophon, *Memorabilia* 4.2.10), and we may speculate that the same might have held true of Hesiod. Less speculative is evidence that excerpts of the Hesiodic poems were published together with Theognis and Phocylides in anthologies, which were read and memorized in schools—to the students' great dismay, if Isocrates is to be believed (Isocrates 2.42–44; cf. Plato, *Protagoras* 325e–326a). The contents of such compendia of moral precepts are difficult to discern with precision, but Hesiod's gnomic expressions, principally drawn from *WD*, appear especially to have been susceptible to excerpting and memorization (Ford 2010: 146–48). How significant Hesiodic education was felt to be in the fourth century BCE is evident in a remarkable passage in the *Laws* (7.811c–d), in which the Athenian Stranger argues that education in the ideal city ought to be modeled on education in Hesiod and other gnomic poets.[6]

Although many spurious works passed under Hesiod's name in the fourth century, Plato refers to no Hesiodic poems other than *Th* and *WD*, suggesting that Hesiod's oeuvre as he understood it consisted entirely of these two works (Most 2010: 57–62). Some scholars have taken this as a sign of Plato's acute poetic sensibility; Most (2010: 62), for instance, concludes that "Plato had developed so fine a sensitivity to the specific individual nature of Hesiod's poetry that he was able . . . to identify as Hesiod's his own poems and to separate them out from the others bearing Hesiod's name that circulated in his culture." There is a more pedestrian explanation for Plato's circumscribed knowledge of the Hesiodic corpus: the existence of a manuscript containing only *Th, WD*, and possibly the spurious *Catalogue of Women*—such as the Alexandrian and Pergamese scholars are known to have possessed by the third century BCE (West 1966: 50).[7]

Quoting Hesiod

In part because Hesiodic poetry was an integral element within the educational curriculum, the ability to quote Hesiod in everyday conversation was a source of pride and a sign of elite distinction—so much so that Plato's interlocutors are shown repeatedly to cite Hesiod (esp. *WD*) in support of their claims.[8] Here we focus on two such instances. The first—the longest direct quotation of Hesiod in the *Laws*—appears in a passage from Book 4, in which the interlocutors discuss a theory of law. According to the Athenian Stranger, laws must consist of two parts: an injunction that describes the crime and penalty for infraction, and a preamble (or "prelude," *prooimion*), which appears before the injunction and is designed to educate the citizens in virtue. Hesiod (*WD* 289–92), the Athenian Stranger insists, tells us why we must preface every law with a prelude:

> Now it seems to me that the things that were just said [i.e., the prelude to the laws], if they took hold a soul that was not entirely savage, would contribute something to making the hearer listen in a more tame and agreeable mood to the advice. So even if these words [i.e., the prelude] have no great effect, but only a small one, still, insofar as they make the one who listens to what was said more agreeable and a better learner, that is in every way desirable. For there is no great plenty or abundance of persons who are eager in spirit to become as good as possible in the shortest possible time; indeed, the many (οἱ πολλοί) show that Hesiod is wise (σοφόν) when he says that the road to vice is smooth to travel and without sweat, since it is very short, but "before virtue," he asserts,
> "the immortal gods have put sweat,
> And a path to it that is long and steep,
> And rough at first. When you arrive at the top,
> Then it is easy to endure; but the ascent is hard." (4.718d1–719a2)

WD 289–92 is especially popular among Plato's (near) contemporaries. Xenophon's *Memorabilia* (2.1.20) cites the same lines to demonstrate that in life and athletics, excellence (*aretē*) requires sustained effort. In *Protagoras* 338c–340d Plato portrays Socrates and Prodicus debating variant interpretations of a poem by Simonides by reference to *WD* 289–92. The historical Prodicus appears to have based his theory of semantic distinctions on study of *WD* 289–92 (Wolfsdorf 2008: 3–5, 8–9). In *Republic* 364d,

Glaucon gives the verses a subversive twist, suggesting that the gods have made vice easy. Socrates in *Phaedrus* 272c invokes the passage without any mention of virtue or vice when considering the easiest path by which to present his argument. Obviously, *WD* played an important role in fourth-century BCE philosophical debates, but we ought not to conclude that ancient readers would have been familiar with the poem in its entirety. It is more likely that Hesiod's discussion of the hard path to virtue appeared in one of the textbooks discussed above. What quotations of *WD* 289–92 show is that citing poetry in conversation served as an argumentative strategy—a form of persuasion. What is true of casual conversation appears to have been characteristic of Athenian courtrooms as well. Aristotle (*Rhetoric* 1.15.13) argues that poetry might be called on as a "witness," and orators often cite poetry to make their cases and attack opponents, the assumption being that the presence—real or imagined—of an idea in a venerated ancient poet constituted a kind of proof (Perlman 1965: 155–58, 161–72).

Another style of quotation is in evidence in *Laws* 8.838c8–d2, the shortest quotation of Hesiod in the dialogue.[9] The Athenian Stranger argues that reproductive behavior may be controlled by consistent, programmatic messaging; to support his claim, he observes that the taboo against incest, universally endorsed in tragedy and myth, has exerted a profound influence on sexual norms. Megillos replies:

> You are quite correct to this extent: rumor (φήμης) has an amazing power (θαυμαστήν τινα δύναμιν), when no one ever even tries to breathe against the law in any way. (8.838c8–d2)

Compare *WD* 763–64:

> Rumor (φήμη) is never entirely destroyed, whom (ἥν τινα) the many
> people voice; for she too is in some way a god (θεός νύ τίς).

Again, Hesiodic citation caps or confirms an argument, but in contrast to the direct quotation at 4.718d1–719a2, nothing in *Laws* 8.838c8–d2 betrays conscious awareness of the Hesiodic subtext on the interlocutors' (or even Plato's) part. Indeed, we are told elsewhere that, unlike Athenian elites, who, we have observed, were familiar with *Th* and *WD* from rhapsodic performances and school textbooks, Megillos and Kleinias are ignorant of Hesiodic poetry (*Laws* 10.886b, discussed below). The text at 8.838c8–d2 thus suggests that one need not quote Hesiod with knowledge or precision to quote Hesiod. Instead, Hesiodic voices resonate throughout fourth-century BCE language and literature, a discursive register to which speakers might switch, consciously or unconsciously, with or without attribution.

As mimetic representations of how people thought and spoke in the fourth century, *Laws* 4.718d1–719a2 and 8.838c8–d2 reveal the degree to which (at least in Plato's mind) Hesiodic poetry permeated everyday language, supplying an implicit conceptual framework for making and justifying ethically complicated decisions. But there appears to have been no agreement regarding what any particular passage might or might not signify. Indeed, one of the most striking features of Hesiod's poetry in the fourth century BCE (and antiquity in general) is its malleability. As we observed with respect to *WD* 289–92, various authors—and sometimes even the same author—might discover wildly divergent meanings in the very same lines (Ford 2010: 150–51). The same is true of *WD* 763–64, which played an especially conspicuous role in the fourth century. Aristotle (*Nicomachean Ethics* 7.13.5, 1153b27–28) quotes the lines to acknowledge that pleasure is in some sense "the supreme good" (τὸ ἄριστον). Aeschines (1.129) quotes the same verses to accuse his opponent, Timarchus, of having engaged in male prostitution, a rumor that was widely spread but for which there was no hard evidence. In response, Demosthenes (19.243) turns *WD* 763–64 against Aeschines, reading the lines as proof that Aeschines profited from an embassy to Philip II of Macedon, another widespread rumor. Aeschines (2.144–45) rejoins by reinterpreting the lines yet again, writing off Demosthenes's reading of Hesiod not as "rumor" (φήμη) but as "slander" (συκοφαντία): the former, a goddess on whose altar Athenians offer annual sacrifices; the latter, a prosecutable crime.

That *WD* figures in such disparate scenarios to support unrelated and occasionally antithetical claims has led some scholars to conclude that Hesiodic poetry in the fourth century BCE had become an empty signifier, conveniently rewritten with modified meanings as each new situation demanded (Solmsen 1962: 176). Yet, the points of continuity between Hesiod and passages in which he is cited are often more sustained than passing references and turns of phrase might seem to suggest. For Plato's Hesiodic quotations underscore a principle that frequently informs the manner in which ancient authors made use of Hesiod: as Hunter (2014: 14) has argued, the general context within which a quotation or reference appears is often appreciably consonant with the general context in Hesiod from which the lines have been excerpted. Thus, the citation of Hesiod at 4.718d1–719a2 appears as part of a larger discussion in which the Athenian Stranger urges the would-be citizens of Magnesia to honor gods and parents (*Laws* 4.718a3–6), and that exhortation recalls Hesiod's advice to Perses to remember the rewards of upholding Zeus's justice at *WD* 274–85. It is notable in this respect, moreover, that both Plato (*Laws* 718a–719a) and Hesiod (*WD* 293–95) emphasize the value of reasoning for oneself and of being persuaded by those who speak well. The key observation here is that there is more of Hesiod being cited in *Laws* 4.718d1–719a2 than six lines of *WD*. It is as though by quoting Hesiod the *Laws* has assumed a Hesiodic voice and persona. The citizens of Magnesia are, as it were, so many Perseis listening to the advice of their didactic poet—the legislator.

Similar contextual consonance is on display in the allusions to *WD* 763–64. Despite differences of genre and argument, Plato, Aristotle, and the orators share with Hesiod an underlying anxiety over the normative role of pleasure. Hedonic anxiety in Hesiod, Plato, and the orators centers on activities that might threaten sexual purity: bathing in menstrual waters (*WD* 753–55), incestuous and unsanctioned sexual liaisons (*Laws* 8.837e–840e), and male prostitution (Aeschines 1.122–24; Demosthenes 19.240–41); in Aristotle (*Nicomachean Ethics* 7.13.5, 1153b27–28), the concern for pleasure is self-evident. Once again, the original context in which the lines appear remains relevant to the fourth-century BCE reception.

HESIOD: SOPHIST AND PHILOSOPHER

All of the quotations of Hesiod in the *Laws* discussed thus far originate in *WD*. The poem's gnomic form, we have observed, made it especially amenable to excerpting and adaptation. *Th* appears to have been subject to a different sort of appropriation. A lengthy passage from the cosmology of Book 10 suggests that ancient audiences viewed the poet of *Th* as making distinct ethical and metaphysical arguments:

> Among us [in Athens] there are accounts found in writings, which are not among you [in Crete and Sparta] because of the virtue of your constitutions, as I understand. These are discussions of the gods, some with certain meters and others without meters. The most ancient (παλαιότατοι) discuss how the first nature of heaven (πρώτη φύσις οὐρανοῦ) and other things came into existence, and then, proceeding on to a point not much after the beginning (τῆς ἀρχῆς), they go through how the gods came into being (θεογονίαν) and how they mingled one with another once they had come into being. It is not easy to pass judgment, in the case of writings so ancient, as to whether they have some other sort of noble or ignoble effect (καλῶς ἢ μὴ καλῶς) on the audience, but as regards services and honors toward parents (εἰς μέντοι γονέων τε θεραπείας καὶ τιμάς), I at least would never speak of them in praise (ἐπαινῶν), either as beneficial (ὠφέλιμα) or as spoken entirely in accordance with reality (ὡς τὸ παράπαν ὄντως εἴρηται). What pertains to ancient writings should be left alone and bid good-bye (μεθείσθω καὶ χαιρέτω), and spoken of in whatever way is pleasing to the gods; but what pertains to the works of our new and wise men (τὰ δὲ τῶν νέων ἡμῖν καὶ σοφῶν) must be accused, insofar as it is responsible for bad things. Now the following is what is done by the arguments of such men: when I and you adduce evidence that the gods exist, bringing forward these very things—sun and moon and stars and earth—as being gods and divine things (ὡς θεοὺς καὶ θεῖα ὄντα), those who are convinced by these wise men (τῶν σοφῶν) would say that these things are earth and stone, and incapable of thinking anything about human affairs, however well decked-out they may somehow be, with arguments that make them plausible. (*Laws* 10.886b10–e2).

The Athenian Stranger's misgivings regarding the deleterious effects of Hesiod's theogonic myths recall an episode from the *Euthyphro* (5d-6a), in which the eponymous interlocutor invokes the castration of Ouranos as justification for prosecuting his own father. It is also reminiscent of *Republic* 2.377d–378b, in which Socrates argues that the youth must be shielded from "the greatest lie about the things of greatest concerns" (τὸ μέγιστον καὶ περὶ τῶν μεγίστων ψεῦδος, 378e6–7): the stories Hesiod tells of Ouranos, Kronos, and Zeus. To a modern audience Plato's concerns may seem tendentious, for there certainly is nothing in *Th* to suggest that Hesiod *recommends* that sons mimic Kronos's behavior. Nevertheless, these passages illuminate an important dimension of ancient reading strategies, which informs virtually every context in which Hesiodic themes emerge in Plato: the tendency to view literary art through an ethicizing lens.

Criticism of Hesiod in Plato and elsewhere often assumes that narrative, particularly when concerned with gods and heroes, establishes normative models of behavior (cf. Aeschylus, *Eumenides* 640–44; Aristophanes, *Nubes* 905; and Plato, *Respublica* 364c–e with Koning 2010b: 95–98).

Laws 10.886b10–e2 also underscores the propensity among Plato and his contemporaries to read *Th* as metaphysics, that is, as an account of the first principles of nature (πρώτη φύσις οὐρανοῦ, ἀρχῆς). In Plato's mind Hesiod got nature wrong; in the *Laws, Th* represents an antiquated (παλαιότατοι) and erroneous approach to the inherent causes and structures of the cosmos. To be sure, Hesiod had not lost his identity as a poet first and foremost; his name often appears alongside Orpheus, Musaeus, and Homer as one of the archetypal inventors of poetic art (Plato, *Apology* 41a). It is not Hesiod, moreover, whom Plato singles out as the most dangerous metaphysician; more harmful are sophists and natural philosophers—the "new and wise men"— whose materialist philosophy was perceived in antiquity as compatible with moral relativism or, worse, immoralism. But Hesiod appears listed among sophists and materialist philosophers elsewhere in fourth-century BCE literature, representing one of two competing explanations—traditional animism and newfangled atheism—for the origins and organizing principles underlying reality (cf. Plato, *Symposium* 178b; [Plato], *Epinomis* 990a with Koning 2010a: 191; Yamagata 2010: 75–76).

All of this underscores a tradition very much in the making in the fourth century BCE, in which Hesiod appears as an "intellectual," with interests in linguistics, etymology, genealogy, astronomy, theories of separation and categorization, and education (Koning 2010b: 100–110). If "intellectual" Hesiod sounds too much like a fourth-century philosopher and a sophist and too little like an epic poet, it is because his prestige was called into the service of the many schools and teachers of philosophy and rhetoric popular in fourth-century Athens. It is telling in this respect that Plato's Protagoras claims Hesiod as one of the earliest sophists (*Protagoras* 316d). In Hunter's (2014: 9) memorable expression, " 'Hesiod'. . . acted as a wind-mill against which any would-be σοφός could try his lance." By virtue of being adapted to the historical environment of fourth-century Athens, Hesiod took the form that Plato and his contemporaries needed him to take and answered questions they needed him to address.

ALLUSION AND INSPIRATION

The critical posture displayed toward *Th* in *Laws* 10.886b10–e2 is only one level on which Plato engages that poem, and it is belied by the ubiquitous role both *Th* and *WD* play as reservoirs of motifs, metaphors, and imagery throughout the Platonic corpus. Hesiod's influence may be felt in Aristophanes's epideictic speech on erotic desire (*Symposium* 188c–193d), Protagoras's lecture on the origins of divine and political justice (*Protagoras* 320c–323c), the history of political and psychological constitutions in Books 8 and 9 of the *Republic*, the cosmological myths of the *Statesman* (268–74e) and *Timaeus*

(40e–41a), and the story of Atlantis (*Timaeus* 21e–26d; *Critias* 108e–121c). Plato's debt to Hesiod is discernible in his penchant for hypostasis and personification—for instance, in the distinction drawn between celestial and pandemic Aphrodites (*Symposium* 180c–185c; cf. Xenophon, *Symposium* 8.6–42) and the primordial figures who populate the cosmology of the *Timaeus* (29d–92c). Although such sophisticated and often structural Hesiodic resonances resist generalization, we cannot but conclude that—on the microscopic level of word choice and the macroscopic scale of conceptual organization— Plato found in Hesiod a symbolically significant vocabulary to define and expand the horizons of philosophy. Two examples illustrate the point.

The first appears in a passage from Book One, in which the Athenian Stranger compares the soul to a puppet drawn in contradictory directions by opposing strings. The analogy, intended to explain what it means for an individual to be "self-superior," that is, in control of one's irrational impulses, presents in visual terms what Plato regards as the inherently conflicted structure of the human psyche:

> Now our argument asserts that each person would always follow one of the cords, never letting go of it and pulling with it against the others; this cord is the gold and sacred pull of calculation (τὴν τοῦ λογισμοῦ ἀγωγὴν χρυσῆν καὶ ἱεράν), and is called the common law of the city; the other cords are hard and iron (σκληρὰς καὶ σιδηρᾶς), while this one is soft, inasmuch as it is golden (μαλακὴν ἄτε χρυσῆν); the others resemble a multitude of variegated forms (παντοδαποῖς εἴδεσιν). It is necessary always to assist this most noble pull of law because calculation (λογισμοῦ), while noble, is gentle rather than violent, and its pull is in need of helpers so that within us (ἐν ἡμῖν) the race of gold might have victory over the other races (τὸ χρυσοῦν γένος νικᾷ τὰ ἄλλα γένη). Thus, the myth of virtue (ὁ μῦθος ἀρετῆς), the myth about us being puppets, would be preserved, and what was intended by the notion of being superior to oneself or inferior (τὸ κρείττω ἑαυτοῦ καὶ ἥττω εἶναι) would be somewhat clearer. Moreover, as regards a city and private individual, it will be clearer that the latter should acquire within himself a true, rational account concerning these cords and live according to it, while a city should acquire for itself a rational account (λόγον) either from one of the gods or from one who knows these things, and then set up that account as the law for itself (νόμον θεμένην) and for its relations with other cities. (1.644e4–645b8)

In this passage, conspicuously flagged as "myth" (μῦθος), Hesiodic resonances may be detected in the imagery of metals, succession, and conflict; the gold and iron cords and the language of noble and baser races, which harken back to the Hesiodic Myth of the Races; and the struggle to establish reason as law, which recalls Zeus's ordering of the cosmos.

The second passage is a well-known account of the origins of democracy in *Laws* 3.700a–701c. The Athenian Stranger claims that the theater in Athens was carefully regulated and permitted the performance of a delimited number of genres, each defined in contradistinction to the other. Athenian theater culture began to evolve (or devolve) when poets mingled dirges with hymns, paeans, and dithyrambs, replicating the sounds of the *aulos* on the lyre and promoting a general sense of artistic confusion. Poets convinced spectators that music has no absolute standard of "correctness" (ὀρθότητα), and that poetry may be judged by the "pleasure" (ἡδονῇ) it affords the audience. Spectators began believing themselves competent to judge every melody and song, and there arose a "base rule of the spectator" (θεατροκρατία τις πονηρά), which replaced what had erstwhile been an "aristocracy" (ἀριστοκρατίας) in poetic art. Democracy in the theater spread to other institutions, and "political liberty" (ἐλευθερία) followed. To my knowledge, Plato's reliance on Hesiod in 3.700a–701c has gone unnoticed in the secondary literature, but the subtext is clear in the Athenian Stranger's pessimistic prediction:

> Next after this freedom would come the sort that involves the loss of the willing-ness to be enslaved (δουλεύειν) to the rulers; following upon this is rejection of the enslavement to and guidance (δουλείαν καὶ νουθέτησιν) by one's father and mother and elders; the next to the last stage involves seeking not to have to obey laws; in their final stage they are contemners of oaths, and pledges, and everything sacred and di-vine, and they present the spectacle of the Titanic nature of which the old stories tell (τὴν λεγομένην παλαιὰν Τιτανικὴν φύσιν ἐπιδεικνῦσι καὶ μιμουμένοις)—arriving back again at those same conditions, and introducing a harsh epoch (χαλεπὸν αἰῶνα διάγοντας) in which there is never a cessation of evils (λῆξαί ποτε κακῶν). (3.701b5–c4)[10]

Plato's prediction of complete dissolution of familial and social bonds as a result of Athenian democracy is a paraphrase of WD 176–201. Compare lines 176–79:

> For now indeed is the race of iron; neither by day do they cease from toil and sorrow (παύονται καμάτου καὶ ὀιζύος), nor ever at night from perishing. Rather, the gods have laid grievous cares (χαλεπὰς . . . μερίμνας) upon them; but nevertheless even for them goods are mixed with evils (κακοῖσιν).

The verbal resonances—χαλεπὸν αἰῶνα διάγοντας, χαλεπὰς . . . μερίμνας; λῆξαί ποτε κακῶν, παύονται καμάτου—are unmistakable. Moreover, if, as some commentators have argued, "Titanic nature" refers to the Hesiodic motif of sons overthrowing fa-thers, the passage also contains an allusion to the castration of Ouranos in Th 176–82.[11] We have in Laws 3.701b–c a translation of WD and Th into the idiomatic vernacular of Athenian prose.

What this suggests is that Hesiodic poetry was subject to creative compression and expansion. A single passage or phrase (e.g., Titanic nature) might direct readers to long stretches of either poem or both. Conversely, Hesiod might form a substructure spanning and unifying several books at once. Thus, the concerns of the first several books of the Laws—the nature of a just society, the origins of law and social order, the connections between forms of governance and forms of poetic art, the basic patterns of human history—all have precursors in Hesiod's poetry. Overt Hesiodic allusions at 1.644e–645b and 3.700a–701c are, as it were, bookends to a series of arguments and inquiries that have been construed implicitly in Hesiodic terms. The astute reader of the Laws will have picked up that the first four books are a retelling of Hesiodic myth, presenting a historical narrative that appropriates features of, and supplants, both poems.

This brings us to what may be the most striking feature of Hesiod in the *Laws*: the manner in which Hesiodic poetry addresses fourth-century BCE Athenian concerns. Plato's Hesiod is no mythologist of prehistoric times; he is rather a contemporary, providing an interpretive prism through which Plato's readers may see their souls and their city from a new—and not always flattering—perspective. We are all, as it were, susceptible to experiencing stages of decline and Titanomachy within our souls and our cities. For a fourth-century audience, Plato's retelling of Hesiod as allegory of the soul and of Athenian constitutional history might have had decidedly political undertones. The claim that calculation ought to occupy a supervisory role over the soul's competing passions contains implicit criticism of Athenian and Doric political values, the former excessively prioritizing pleasure, the latter celebrating militaristic asceticism and valor to the exclusion of other virtues. Political connotations are even more apparent in 3.700a–701c; the end of Athens's aristocratic constitution, the rise of democracy, its impending anarchy, and final dissolution—all of this may be understood as a Hesiodic Myth of Races. Plato has rewritten Athens's most celebrated cultural and political institutions—theater and democracy—as Hesiodic epochal decline. Readers who proceed to Books 4–12 will see that Magnesia, whose laws and institutions the interlocutors turn to in these later books, offers an alternative to the psychological and political decline Plato has cast in Hesiodic terms.

CONCLUSIONS

What are we to make of the many levels on which Plato and his contemporaries engage with Hesiodic poetry? On the one hand, we find Plato infinitely rewriting Hesiod, casting philosophy in Hesiodic vocabulary, figures, and mythology. Although (or perhaps because) Plato discovered in Hesiod an authoritative rival artist, theorist, and mythologist, whose works presented a model with which to vie and from which to borrow language and images, Platonic dialogues preserve Hesiodic poetry, reformed and remade in the image of philosophy. On the other hand, we have not identified a single, unified Hesiod or Hesiodic tradition, but many Hesiods and many ways of interacting with, inheriting, and redeploying Hesiodic poetry. Fourth-century readers—like twenty-first-century readers—encountered Hesiod, mediated through a maze of interpretations and hermeneutic strategies. They made sense of Hesiod within the categories in which others had made sense of Hesiod before them. It is useful to recall Ford's warning not to read Plato's dialogue with Hesiod "as a timeless conversation between Olympians but as part of the processes by which the meaning of an old corpus of poetry was shaped and circumscribed by the social institutions that preserved it" (2010: 135). Rhapsodic performance, education in schools, literature, and the literate communities in which texts were quoted, read, and contested—all are social institutions of one kind or another in which the Hesiodic corpus was preserved, reshaped, and circumscribed. What emerges is a spectrum of interconnected Hesiodic responses and appropriations, which depend to a large extent on who is reading (or hearing) Hesiod, in which context (or contexts), and to what end. We must speak, therefore, not of Hesiodic reception but *receptions*, for there often appear to be as many Hesiods in the fourth century BCE as there are institutions and media in which the poems are transmitted. Regardless of the medium through which Hesiod entered the fourth century, however, Plato and writers like him treat Hesiod as a contemporary, a dynamic site for the production of the philosophical, literary, and political debates which animated that century.

NOTES

1. The principal points of Hesiodic engagement in the Platonic corpus are surveyed below, but for illuminating discussion, see the contributions in Boys-Stones and Haubold (2010) and Scully (2015: 111–21).
2. See Most (2010: 59); Yamagata (2010: 70). I count the following references to Hesiod in the *Laws*, defined capaciously as instances in which Plato mentions or attributes information to Hesiod, quotes or misquotes lines of Hesiodic poetry, emulates Hesiod's poetic register, or refers to identifiably Hesiodic mythology: 2.658d–e, 3.677c–e, 3.690d–e, 3.700a–701c, 4.713b–714a, 4.718d–719a, 7.795c, 8.838c–d, 10.886c–e, 10.901a, 12.943d–e, 12.944d, 12.948b.
3. For recent treatments of the *Laws*, see Peponi (2013); Folch (2015).
4. Unless otherwise indicated, translations of the *Laws* are Pangle's (1980) with modifications.
5. An alternative reading renders τι τῶν Ἡσιοδείων more narrowly, as referring to selections of *Th*. As (Ford 2010: 136, 153) observes, the Hesiod performed by rhapsodes and most frequently paired with Homer in the fourth century BCE is the poet of the *Th*.
6. See Folch (2015: 299–313), whose claims pertain principally to Homer, but, *mutatis mutandis*, are apropos to Hesiod as well.
7. That the pseudo-Platonic authors cite the *Astronomy, Catalogue of Women*, and other, unidentifiable Hesiodic works points to the possibility of at least two fourth-century BCE manuscript traditions (Most 2010: 61–62).
8. For a survey of contexts in which Hesiod is quoted, see Koning (2010b: 89–91).
9. *Laws* 12.943e1–3 may in fact be a shorter reference; its poeticized language, genealogy, and hypostasis of abstract concepts as divinities are felt to have Hesiodic resonances, but commentators have struggled to identify the poem Plato appears to quote. *WD* 256–57 is the most likely candidate. See Solmsen (1962: 192–93); Most (2010: 59); Hunter (2014: 268n9).
10. The translation follows closely Pangle's (1980) and England (1921: 1:411).
11. Other commentators suggest that "Titanic nature" refers to a tradition according to which humans were born from the blood of Titans. See Pangle (1980: 524); England (1921: 1:411).

REFERENCES

Boys-Stones, G. R., and J. Haubold, eds. 2010. *Plato and Hesiod*. Oxford.
England, E. B., ed. and comm. 1921. *The Laws of Plato*. 2 vols. Manchester.

Folch, M. 2015. *The City and the Stage: Genre, Gender, and Performance in Plato's Laws*. Oxford.

Ford, A. 2010. "Plato's Two Hesiods." In *Plato and Hesiod*, edited by G. R. Boys-Stones and J. Haubold, 133–54. Oxford.

Graziosi, B. 2010. "Hesiod in Classical Athens: Rhapsodes, Orators, and Platonic Discourse." In *Plato and Hesiod*, edited by G. R. Boys-Stones and J. Haubold, 111–32. Oxford.

Hunter, R. 2014. *Hesiodic Voices: Studies in the Reception of Hesiod's Works and Days*. Cambridge.

Koning, H. H. 2010a. *Hesiod: The Other Poet; Ancient Reception of a Cultural Icon*. Mnemosyne Supplement 325. Leiden, Netherlands.

Koning, H. H. 2010b. "Plato's Hesiod: Not Plato's Alone." In *Plato and Hesiod*, edited by G. R. Boys-Stones and J. Haubold, 89–110. Oxford.

Most, G. W. 2010. "Plato's Hesiod: An Acquired Taste?" In *Plato and Hesiod*, edited by G. R. Boys-Stones and J. Haubold, 52–67. Oxford.

Olson, S. D., ed., trans., and comm. 2007. *Broken Laughter: Select Fragments of Greek Comedy*. Oxford.

Pangle, T. L., trans. and comm. 1980. *The Laws of Plato: Translated, with Notes and an Interpretive Essay*. New York.

Peponi, A., ed. 2013. *Performance and Culture in Plato's Laws*. Cambridge.

Perlman, S. 1965. "Quotations from Poetry in Attic Orators of the Fourth Century BC." *American Journal of Philology* 85: 155–72.

Scully, S. 2015. *Hesiod's Theogony: From Near Eastern Creation Myths to Paradise Lost*. Oxford.

Solmsen, F. 1962. "Hesiodic Motifs in Plato." In *Hésiode et son influence*, edited by 171–211. *Entretiens sur l'antiquité classique* 7. Geneva.

West, M. L., ed. and comm. 1966. *Hesiod: Theogony*. Oxford.

West, M. L. 2010. "Rhapsodes at Festivals." *Zeitschrift für Papyrologie und Epigraphik* 173: 1–13.

Wolfsdorf, D. 2008. "Hesiod, Prodicus, and the Socratics on Work and Pleasure." *Oxford Studies in Ancient Philosophy* 35: 1–18.

Yamagata, N. 2010. "Hesiod in Plato: Second Fiddle to Homer?" In *Plato and Hesiod*, edited by G. R. Boys-Stones and J. Haubold, 68–88. Oxford.

CHAPTER 21

....

HELLENISTIC HESIOD

....

LILAH GRACE CANEVARO

INTRODUCTION

....

CALLIMACHUS as the "New Hesiod" (Fantuzzi and Hunter 2004). Aratus as the "Hellenistic Hesiod" (Fakas 2001). Apollonius, Theocritus, and Nicander: all have been shown to owe some kind of debt to the archaic Greek poet. In this chapter I survey a broad range of interactions with Hesiodic poetry in the Hellenistic period. Many of the issues explored in the 2011 *Brill's Companion to Callimachus* in relation to Hesiod, such as the role of the Muses, didactic language, polyphony, and poetic voices, are relevant beyond the Callimachean corpus, and it is this reach of the Hesiodic legacy that this chapter seeks to convey. The editors of that volume note that "we do not include chapters on Callimachus' relationship to individual Greek precursors like Homer or Hesiod or Pindar" (Stephens 2011: 15), and yet in her chapter "Callimachus on Kings and Kingship," for example, Silvia Barbantani cannot avoid the admission that "Hesiod is Callimachus' most important Greek model in constructing an image of the just king from whom wealth, prosperity and peace flow" (Barbantani 2011: 178). In *Brill's Companion to Hesiod*, Evina Sistakou (2009) dedicates a chapter to "Callimachus Hesiodicus Revisited," updating Hannelore Reinsch-Werner's 1976 study "Callimachus Hesiodicus" in light of modern theoretical approaches and with the aim of re-evaluating common misconceptions. Sistakou's focus on one Hellenistic poet is indicative of the wealth of material to be discussed and of the fact that a full-scale treatment of the reception of Hesiod in the Hellenistic period is necessarily beyond the scope of a single chapter. Yet leaving questions of breadth aside, Sistakou's chapter needs in its turn to be revisited and updated in light of a recent wave of interest in the ancient reception of Hesiod.

In his *Hesiod: The Other Poet*, Hugo Koning (2010) considers Hesiodic reception in literary sources over one millennium (from the seventh century BCE to 300 CE), consulting works of some two hundred ancient writers as well as epigraphic material and papyri and collating around twelve hundred references. The primary concern of this book is how Homer defines the way in which Hesiod is received: "Homer's omnipresence was strongly felt, however, and in the Hellenistic age the only way to oppose it was by reviving the traditional image of Hesiod as a counter-force to Homer" (Koning 2010: 295). George Boys-Stones and Johannes Haubold's *Plato and Hesiod* (2010) and Ioannis Ziogas's *Ovid and Hesiod* (2013) each focuses on a particular author and his interaction with the Hesiodic corpus (the latter is specifically concerned with the *Theogony* [hereafter *Th*] and the *Catalogue of Women*). Helen Van Noorden's *Playing Hesiod* (2015) takes Hesiod's Myth of the Races, told at *Works and Days* (hereafter *WD*) 106–201, as a starting point, and traces later engagements with and appropriations of this myth. Richard Hunter's *Hesiodic Voices* provides a number of case studies of ancient reception of the *WD*, in an attempt "to build a more general picture of how the Hesiod of the *Works and Days* acted as a creative stimulus throughout the literature of antiquity" (2014: 32).

Sistakou begins her chapter with a discussion of "the three faces of Hesiodic poetry, the theogonic, the didactic and the genealogical" (2009: 219) and notes that "it would be a misconception to speak of the 'Hesiodic voice' as a unified, homogeneous whole; one should rather consider the diverse voices as emerging from the different styles dominating each poem of the Hesiodic corpus, mainly the autobiographical/authoritative of the *Theogony* and the moralizing/gnomic of the *Works and Days*" (222). Van Noorden picks up on this idea when she establishes some principles for her analysis— "The first is the formation of different 'Hesiods' from selected elements of his poetry" (2015: 10)—and Hunter's title, *Hesiodic Voices*, with its use of the plural, makes the point clearly. In my *Hesiod's "Works and Days": How to Teach Self-Sufficiency* (2015) I discuss the "Hesiod stamp": a strong guiding hand on the diverse material in the Hesiodic corpus, which influences the way the poetry is experienced and read and as such sows the seeds of its own reception. It is from this polyphonic yet coherent poetic persona that the current chapter takes its structure, drawing out the variegated voices that constitute the multifaceted appeal of the poems comprising the Hesiodic corpus. This chapter, then, is a study of the Hellenistic reception of Hesiod, but it begins from the invitations for that reception embedded in Hesiodic poetry itself.

At the beginning of his book Koning presents quantitative information about the reception of Hesiod's poetry over time. The table reproduced here as Table 21.1 is of particular interest.

Table 21.1 Distribution of references to Hesiod through time, from Koning (2010: 21)

	Archaic	Classical	Hellenistic	2nd Sophistic
Works and Days	37 (8%)	97 (18%)	48 (9%)	344 (65%)
Theogony	5 (2%)	26 (11%)	49 (21%)	158 (66%)

In this table the first figures are the number of references to each poem in a particular period (within Koning's parameters of citation), and the percentages show the distribution through time of references to the *WD* and *Th*, respectively. To give an example: the *WD* is referred to thirty-seven times in the Archaic period, and this makes up eight percent of the total number of references to the *WD* that fall within Koning's study. From these figures we can observe that something unique happened during the Hellenistic period: references to the *WD* took a dip in both percentual and finite terms, whilst the *Th* continued on an upward trajectory. The result is that this is the only period in which both Hesiodic poems were referenced with more or less equal frequency (Koning 2010: 22). The key question I ask in this chapter is: Why might this be the case? To phrase it in one way, what is it about the *Th* and the *WD* that made them equally appealing at this time; considered from another angle, what is it about the Hellenistic period that balanced out the reception of these two poems?[1] The reception of Hesiodic poetry in other eras is explored in other chapters in this *Handbook*, but I hope to show that something special happened to Hellenistic Hesiod.

THE HELLENISTIC HESIODIC EXPERIENCE

Koning's table charts explicit references to Hesiod and the Hesiodic poems, and for this reason, though it is a useful starting point, it shows us just the tip of the iceberg. In the Hellenistic period in particular, the allusive nature of the poetry in vogue meant that references would more often than not be implicit: a nuanced alignment with Hesiodic poetics, a scholarly appropriation of Hesiodic diction, or an insertion of new poetry into a tradition shaped by that of Hesiod. This subtle and sophisticated response to poetic predecessors was due in large part to the ways in which Hesiod was experienced in the Hellenistic period. By the fourth century BCE Hesiod's poetry featured in the school curriculum,[2] and it may have been used as training for the *progymnasmata* (Canevaro 2015: 18). Egyptian papyri of the Hellenistic and Roman periods confirm Hesiod's canonical status in education at that time, and in particular extant school texts verify the presence of the *Catalogue of Women* in the classroom (Cribiore 2001: 141, 197; on education in the Hellenistic period see Wissmann 2010). Hesiod's presence in schools, then, is one element of continuity in the reception of his poetry. However, the Hellenistic period saw one major development: the library (for an overview of the impact of the library on Hellenistic poets see Harder 2013). This propelled Hesiodic poetry from study by the student to study by the scholar, making it not just part of rhetorical education but a constant reference point for the scholar-poet. Rather than relying on memory, education, and experience, poets immersed in the Alexandrian library such as Callimachus and Apollonius could return again and again to texts, engaging with them at the level of minute detail. This had implications for the treatment, analysis, and critique of earlier poetry, as well as for the production and again, critique, of new poems.

A common element of stylistic critique in the Hellenistic period was an assessment of a poem's χαρακτήρ (lit. "character"): the way it is written, the stylistic category into which it falls, and the stamp of its author. To offer just one example (for others see Hunter 2014: 298–99), a report of Apollonius's defense of Hesiodic authorship of the *Shield of Heracles* (Hesiod T 52 Most) gives as one of the reasons the poem's χαρακτήρ. The argument goes that since it is Hesiod-like, it must be by Hesiod. This kind of assessment is on the one hand built on minutiae like word choice, theme and myth, and gnomic formulations, but on the other hand it encompasses all of these minutiae simultaneously, and so much more. The Hesiod stamp (Canevaro 2015), a χαρακτήρ generated by the corpus itself, had by the Hellenistic period been internalized through easy familiarity with Hesiod's poetic oeuvre and could in turn be used as a critical tool with other poetry.

Most notable in Koning's table is that the number of explicit references to the *WD* falls during the Hellenistic period. Whereas the *Th* sees a steady increase in references over time, the *WD* experiences a marked Hellenistic dip in both finite and percentual terms. One reason for this may be the prevalence of *new* didactic poetry at this time. The genre, or "mode" of the *WD* has been much discussed (see Heath 1985; Fowler 2003; Canevaro 2014; Sider 2014). Particularly relevant here is the argument that the genre of didactic poetry was essentially created in the Hellenistic period and retrojected back onto earlier texts (Sider 2014; see also Koning 2010: 343). The Hellenistic period is therefore important in the history of the reception of the Hesiodic corpus and the *WD* in particular, as it is the time during which genres began to be clearly defined (though the didactic genre remains nebulous to this day, as we can see from the various attempts to delineate criteria for it; see, e.g., Effe 1977; Toohey 1996; Volk 2002), and poets began consciously to operate within their parameters, producing new material. The new wave of didactic poetry in the Hellenistic period is often attributed to Aratus, the first poet to show the kind of awareness of a genre that can be specifically defined (Effe 2005: 30–31).[3]

In operating within this genre, however we define it, Hellenistic poets were creating an affiliation with the poet of the *WD*. This can be seen not only in general generic terms but also at the level of detail: allusions of the sort that would not register in Koning's analysis of explicit references, such as the use of kennings. This particular mode of expression, common in the *WD* and probably originating in folkloric or popular language, found its way into the writings of Callimachus and Aratus, but most notably into that of Nicander, who uses it in deliberate imitation of Hesiod (Overduin 2015: 79). Yet looking back to the Hesiodic model, Hellenistic didaxis also branched out in terms of the material on which the poets were drawing. Take, for instance, the work of Nicander (for an overview see Magnelli 2010). The *Alexipharmaca* covers poisons and their antidotes, and the *Theriaca* teaches about venomous creatures. This is a technical, pharmacological poetic corpus, and it has been argued that Nicander drew on several prose treatises for his information, most of all the toxicological work of Apollodorus of Alexandria.[4] It has been argued, too, that it is probable Nicander also wrote prose (Overduin 2015: 5), just like Callimachus, whose prose works seem even to have outweighed his poetic output. Another example of new didactic enterprises is that of Aratus and his *Phaenomena*, a didactic poem much of which (at least according to Aratus's second-century BCE commentator Hipparchus) may have been derived from Eudoxus's prose treatise on stars and star signs.[5] As Harder (2013: 106) summarizes, "the availability of so much material in the library may to a certain extent account for the increasing popularity of the genre of didactic poetry in the Hellenistic period, because poets *could* now find a great deal of accumulated knowledge in prose texts which they could 'transfer' to poetry." Yet the examples of Nicander and Callimachus show that there was not always a divide between those producing poetry and those producing prose. We can say that this was not only a case of poetic appropriation of others' knowledge; rather, these Hellenistic poets were true scholars, generating, sharing, accumulating, and transmitting knowledge through a cohesive body of work including catalogs (such as Callimachus's monumental *Pinakes*), prose treatises, *and* poetry. We can also say that this Alexandrian moment of intense didaxis did not operate in splendid isolation; it was a culmination of the preceding centuries of prose as a way of recording knowledge. Historiography, philosophical dialogue, and scholarly treatises all came together in the Hellenistic libraries and spurred their recipients on to a new phase of poetic production in a Hesiodic vein, yet informed by their prose predecessors. The fact that the preceding centuries *had* seen such a proliferation of scientific writings in prose, however, highlights the striking achievements of Hellenistic didactic poets. They *chose* to revert to an archaic mode of knowledge transmission, showing themselves to be not only scholars, but scholar-*poets*.

Something else had changed drastically since the time of Hesiod: writing. Wherever we place Hesiod chronologically and at whatever point on an oral to literate continuum (for discussion, see the introduction to this volume), what we can say is that the Hesiodic corpus, like the Homeric, is rooted in a tradition of oral composition and dissemination. Hellenistic poetry, on the other hand, is not only written, but it prizes, reflects on, and plays with its written status. Hellenistic poets were avid readers, but they were also committed writers. With the archaic wisdom tradition is integrated not only knowledge gleaned from other writings, but also new features possible exclusively in the written medium. Such features include visual techniques like acrostics (see Gale forthcoming), which both Aratus in his *Phaenomena* and Nicander in his *Theriaca* incorporate.[6] Hesiod's penchant for riddling and for hiding meaning (on which see Canevaro 2015: 166–79; one prominent example is the fable of the hawk and the nightingale at *WD* 202–12) is perpetuated in new ways in this period of markedly *literary* innovation.

A CHORUS OF HESIODIC VOICES

Hesiod's *Th* starts "from the beginning" (ἐξ ἀρχῆς, 115), from first things (πρώτιστα, 116). It tells of how the gods came to be, how the Olympian pantheon was established, and the spheres of influence of each of the gods within it. The poem thus has a strong aetiological impetus (see Loney in this volume, pp. 112–13), which becomes key in the Hellenistic period. Selden (1998) begins his article "Alibis" with the statement: "Callimachus of Cyrene wrote for a society of displaced persons," and indeed this reality goes a long way toward explaining the prevalence of *aetia* in Hellenistic poetry. Callimachus himself composed his *Aetia* in an estimated six thousand lines comprising four books. Callimachus's *Aetia* constitutes a kind of sequel to the *Th*, as it provides a complete human history to match Hesiod's divine history and takes the story to the next stage by narrating the *aetia* of the interactions (cults, rites) between men and gods (Hunter 2004a: 54–55; Sistakou 2009: 226). In many ways, then, the *Aetia* looks beyond the *Th* to the Hesiodic corpus as a whole. The *Catalogue of Women*, too, provides the next chapter in the story begun in the *Th*, and the *WD* can also be thought of as a human history, taking us as it does up to the present Iron Age (176–201).

Within the didactic genre, Hesiod's *WD* has a strong catalogic element, and the *Th* and *Catalogue of Women* take this even further. Indeed, the catalog came to be considered a Hesiodic form, to the extent that Aristarchus called the embedded catalogs in the *Iliad* and the *Odyssey* "un-Homeric" because they showed a Ἡσιόδειος χαρακτήρ (see Pfeiffer 1968: 220). There was a proliferation of this type of poetry in the proto-Hellenistic age, with some even encroaching on Hesiodic themes such as the *Catalogue of Women* by one Nicaenetus (sadly nothing of this poem survives but its title). Of Hellenistic didactic poetry we can say that "when stripped of its dramatic framing the *Theriaca*, like the *Alexipharmaca* and Aratus' *Phaenomena*, can be characterized as a catalogue" (Overduin 2015: 29). Callimachus summarizes the charge against him:

>]ι μοι Τελχῖνες ἐπιτρύζουσιν ἀοιδῇ,
> νήιδες οἳ Μούσης οὐκ ἐγένοντο φίλοι,
> εἵνεκεν οὐχ ἓν ἄεισμα διηνεκὲς ἢ βασιλ[η
> ...]ας ἐν πολλαῖς ἤνυσα χιλιάσιν
> ἢ ...]ους ἥρωας, ἔπος δ'ἐπὶ τυτθὸν ἑλ[ίσσω
> παῖς ἅτε, τῶν δ'ἐτέων ἡ δεκὰς οὐκ ὀλίγη.

> ... the Telchines mutter against my song,
> fools who are not friends of the Muse,
> because I did not accomplish one continuous poem
> in many thousands of lines on kings
> or heroes, but like a child I turn out a short story,
> though the decades of my years are not few.

> *Aetia* 1.1–6

Callimachus did not complete one continuous song in many thousands of lines on the glory of kings and heroes. The emphasis, however, is necessarily on the first part of the statement, that focused on structure and length. Callimachus cannot be claiming that he will not tell of kings and heroes, since the *Aetia* include stories of both; what he is suggesting, rather, is that he will narrate stories about kings and heroes, but from an alternative perspective (Sistakou 2009: 241). In this respect, then, the *Aetia* takes its cue from Hesiod's *Catalogue of Women*, a poem that tells of the heroes resulting from amorous encounters between gods and mortal women. Its catalogic structure and its focus on the particular theme of women takes it far from repeating the structure of Homeric epic and shows the poet adopting an alternative perspective to treat heroic subject matter. Callimachus picks up on these catalogic elements and transfers them to an Alexandrian milieu by taking care not to thunder and to keep his Muse slender.

Sistakou (2009: 227) observes that one feature tying Callimachus's *Aetia* to Hesiod's *Th* is "the positive outlook on the notion of progress as a development from a chaotic past towards a civilized present," and she suggests that this "should be perhaps contrasted with the *Works and Days*, when it expresses e.g. a pessimistic view on the decline of mankind in the myth of the five ages." However, the Myth of the Races in the *WD* is importantly *not* a story of steady decline, as the race of heroes provides the calm before the Iron Age storm, and through Hesiod's didaxis even the race of iron is offered ways of turning their dire situation around. The civilized present to which Callimachus's *Aetia* directs us can be found in the glimmers of hope Hesiod presents in the *WD* too, a potentiality most fully worked out in the vignette of the Just City (*WD* 225–37). Sistakou also notes that "Callimachus, in his catalogue-structured *Aetia*, proceeds from one story to another rather randomly." Such randomness is a charge that has frequently been leveled at the *WD* (though for counterarguments, see Hamilton 1989; Clay 2003, 2009; Canevaro 2015), and the catalogic element inevitably recalls the *Catalogue of Women*.[7] Callimachus's *Aetia*, then, combines multiple Hesiodic voices in its structure and ordering, its content and tone.

In Book 3 of the *Aetia* Callimachus offers no fewer than three explanations for why women having difficulty in childbirth call upon the virgin goddess Artemis.[8] This has, first of all, a *WD* parallel in the Prometheus and Pandora myth and Myth of the Races as two competing (or complementary) *aetia* for work (Hunter 2004a: 58)—or, more appropriate to the comparison, labor. Callimachus, like Hesiod, uses multiple *aetia* to display his comprehensive knowledge and to present a challenge to the reader, who has to choose between and put together different strands of myth and explanation. Further, the Prometheus and Pandora myth is an *aetion* that straddles the Hesiodic corpus, with the account in the *Th* differing in detail and focus from that in the *WD* (Fraser 2011). Callimachus's multiple *aetia*, then, recall not only the complexity of the *WD*'s structure but also the aetiological dialogue between *Th* and *WD*. Just as Callimachus's *Aetia* cannot be compared strictly with the *Th*, so can it not be limited to the *WD*: it incorporates elements from both, as well as from the *Catalogue of Women*, and puts them all together in a Hellenistic framework for "a society of displaced persons."

A similar example is the relationship Callimachus establishes with the Muses in his *Aetia*. Rather than beginning by invoking the Muses and asking them for knowledge of genealogies in the divine realm, Callimachus *tells* the Muses that he knows of at least three genealogies of the Graces. The genealogical armature of the *Th* is thus combined with the poetic independence marked out by Hesiod in the proem to his *WD*, when he asks the Muses to sing of Zeus but proclaims that he himself will tell "true things" (*WD* 10 ἐτήτυμα) to Perses. Whereas in the *Th* (and in Homeric epic) the poet and the Muses sing in unison (Graziosi/Haubold 2010: 1–8), the *WD* seems polyphonic: the Muses are invited to sing a song tangential to Hesiod's own (Clay

2003: 72–78; Haubold 2010: 21; Canevaro 2015: 100–102). In parading his knowledge in front of the Muses, then, Callimachus is combining different Hesiodic voices—or, more accurately, different stages in the development of the Hesiodic voice as he grows from ignorant shepherd to self-sufficient didactic poet—*and* he is incorporating a model that is itself polyphonic.

Immersed in contemporary library culture, the Hellenistic poets could draw on a wealth of accumulated knowledge, a range of collected sources, and thus "the aetiological impulse here grows not from ignorance, but from knowledge" (Hunter 2004a: 58). Hesiod's poetry therefore begins in this period to be treated more holistically, with the multifaceted Hesiodic stamp triumphing over individuated Hesiodic voices. This is another possible explanation for the statistics that show a more balanced reception of the *Th* and *WD* in the Hellenistic age. Callimachus's *Aetia* is a case in point: its aetiological thrust is not simply modeled on or a sequel to the *Th*, its most obvious comparandum, but a chorus of Hesiodic voices drawn from across a varied yet essentially coherent poetic corpus and epic cosmos (on the epic cosmos see especially Clay 2003).

Hesiodic Inspirations

Ἡσιόδου τό τ᾽ ἄεισμα καὶ ὁ τρόπος· οὐ τὸν ἀοιδῶν
ἔσχατον, ἀλλ᾽ ὀκνέω μὴ τὸ μελιχρότατον
τῶν ἐπέων ὁ Σολεὺς ἀπεμάξατο· χαίρετε λεπταί
ῥήσιες, Ἀρήτου σύμβολον ἀγρυπνίης.

The matter and manner are those of Hesiod: not the ultimate of songs,
    but it may be that the man of Soli has caught
the sweetest of the verses. Hail slender sayings,
symbol of Aratus' sleepless nights.

Callimachus, *Epigram* 27

This is Callimachus's review of Aratus's poetry, which aligns it with Hesiod's work in terms of subject and style. Although the poem is not named, we assume it is referring to the *Phaenomena*, as λεπταί in the third line is thought to be an acknowledgment of the λεπτή acrostic of *Phaenomena* 783–87. It is a difficult epigram to translate and interpret, and it seems to evade consensus (Stewart 2008). In my translation I bring out a potential contrast between Homeric (the ultimate) and Hesiodic (the sweetest) poetry (as Hunter 2014: 292–94). Koning 2010 has shown much of Hesiod's reception to be inextricably linked with that of Homer, and this antithesis fits with his analysis. For another interpretation, namely that these lines indicate that Aratus did not follow Hesiod in everything, see Volk (2010: 199).[9] Whatever its stylistic relationship to its predecessors, it is clear that Aratus's poetry meets the contemporary Alexandrian aesthetic of "slender" verses, just as Callimachus in his *Aetia* claims to have been told by Apollo to keep the Muse "slender" (τὴν Μοῦσαν ... λεπταλέην, 1.24).

Aratus is presented as a hard-working poet, one who has spent many a sleepless night honing his craft (and condensing his verses). This in itself has its roots in Hesiod's *WD*, which both advocates hard work on the part of its audience and gives the impression of a teacher practicing what he preaches. For instance, though at *WD* 597–98 Hesiod sets up a didactic hierarchy in which the poet instructs the farmer, who must in turn instruct his workers, at 459 the hierarchy is blurred when the farmer is advised to pitch in (ὁμῶς δμῶές τε καὶ αὐτός, "your slaves and yourself alike"). And the practical and intellectual self-sufficiency Hesiod advocates throughout the *WD* (Canevaro 2015) is put into practice on a poetological level in terms of Hesiod's own independent didactic persona in the poem. Hesiod's concern for hard work (among other characteristics) makes him in the Hellenistic period a symbol of the learned and laboring poets of a new, markedly un-Homeric, kind (Koning 2010: 378). These scholar-poets do not attribute their achievements solely to inspiration, but also to their own hard graft.

Callimachus joins Hesiodic hard work with Hesiodic inspiration, thus fusing the *Th* and the *WD*. In his *Aetia* he reworks Hesiod's inspiration, told in the *Th* as a dream experience; importantly, he does not reject the Hesiodic model but appropriates it and adapts it to his own purpose, employing new techniques to shape his own story.[10] He replaces what is presented in the *Th* as a real-world encounter with a dream sequence, putting his own twist on the event, notably one that is simultaneously more indirect and more credible. As Fantuzzi (2004: 1) writes, "Hellenistic poets turned to their advantage the distinction between inspiration by the poetic divinities, on the one hand, and the primacy of 'craft', *technē*, on the other; the two now formed a powerful unit, no longer a pair of opposed possibilities." What must be noted, however, is that the bridge between the *Th* Muse-inspired voice and the blended voice of Hellenistic "technical" poetics is that of Hesiod in his *WD*. In differentiating his voice from that of the Muses yet keeping them on side to help with difficult topics such as seafaring (Canevaro 2015: 130), Hesiod was edging toward this model by combining inspiration with experience, divine guidance with intellectual independence.

Nicander moves even further away from the Hesiodic model in his *Theriaca*, dispensing with an appeal to the Muses altogether:

ἀλλ᾽ ἤτοι κακοεργὰ φαλάγγια, σὺν καὶ ἀνιγροὺς
ἑρπηστὰς ἔχιάς τε καὶ ἄχθεα μυρία γαίης
Τιτήνων ἐνέπουσιν ἀφ᾽ αἵματος, εἰ ἐτεόν περ
Ἀσκραῖος μυχάτοιο Μελισσήεντος ἐπ᾽ ὄχθαις
Ἡσίοδος κατέλεξε παρ᾽ ὕδασι Περμησσοῖο.
τὸν δὲ χαλαζήεντα κόρη Τιτηνὶς ἀνῆκε
σκορπίον, ἐκ κέντροιο τεθηγμένον, ἧμος ἐπέχρα
Βοιωτῷ τεύχουσα κακὸν μόρον Ὠαρίωνι,
ἀχράντων ὅτε χερσὶ θεῆς ἐδράξατο πέπλων·
αὐτὰρ ὅγε στιβαροῖο κατὰ σφυρὸν ἤλασεν ἴχνευς
σκορπίος ἀπροϊδὴς ὀλίγῳ ὑπὸ λᾶι λοχήσας·
τοῦ δὲ τέρας περίσημον ὑπ᾽ ἀστέρας ἀπλανὲς αὔτως
οἷα κυνηλατέοντος ἀείδελον ἐστήρικται.

> They say that evil-working spiders, along with
> grievous reptiles and vipers and countless burdens on the earth,
> came from the blood of the Titans, if indeed
> the Ascraean on the slopes of furthest Melisseis,
> Hesiod, by the waters of the Permessos, narrated true.
> The Titan maiden sent forth the chilling scorpion
> with its sharpened sting, when in her anger
> she planned an evil fate for Boeotian Orion,
> because he grabbed the undefiled garments of the goddess with his hands.
> But the scorpion, lurking unseen under a small stone,
> struck him on the ankle of his strong foot.
> His famous sign is fixed unmoving among the stars,
> as of a hunter, impossible to look at.

Theriaca 8–20

The reference at lines 10–12 to Hesiod at the Permessos River recalls the archaic poet's encounter with the Muses, recounted at *Th* 22–34 (and the Muses are bathing in the waters of the Permessos at *Th* 5). This reference shows Nicander's awareness of the Hesiodic model—away from which he then makes a conscious shift. Interestingly, at times he actually replaces the Muses with Hesiod himself as a source of information. In this passage Nicander gives us two mythological notes: first, that according to Hesiod all deadly beasts come from the blood of the Titans, and second, that Orion was killed by a scorpion sent by Artemis as a punishment. The first reference situates Nicander within a dense Hesiodic tradition (Hunter 2014: 26), even though there is a problem with it: it references something not in our texts of Hesiod and already unknown to the scholiasts on Nicander. The second reference bears striking similarities to Aratus's treatment of the same myth at *Phaenomena* 637–46 (Overduin 2015: 47). Already in the proem, then, it is clear that Nicander is drawing on both Hesiod and Aratus as models. It is worth noting, too, that the story of Orion becomes an *aetion* for his constellation. Myth becomes *aetion*: a narrative direction that, as we have seen, is characteristically Hellenistic. A similar instance of the synthesis of models occurs at the beginning of the second part of the *Theriaca* (715–16):

Ἔργα δέ τοι σίνταο περιφράζοιο φάλαγγος
σήματά τ' ἐν βρυχμοῖσιν·

Guard against the works of the grievous spider,
and the signs of its bites.

Here Hesiodic ἔργα start the first line, and Aratean σήματα the second (Overduin 2015: 51–52). The Muses take a back seat to Nicander's two didactic models, which become bedfellows across a substantial temporal gap. With the creation of new didactic poetry in the Hellenistic period, allusions within the genre become layered as archaic and contemporary reference points intertwine.

The first word of the *Theriaca* is ῥεῖα, "easily." The importance of the first word of a poem is well rehearsed in discussions of the *Iliad*'s μῆνιν and the *Odyssey*'s ἄνδρα, both thematic openings—the other traditional possibility being an appeal to a particular source of inspiration (e.g., Μοῦσαι, *WD* 1; Μουσάων, *Th* 1; ἐκ Διός, *Phaenomena* 1). Nicander takes another route, yet one keyed into Hesiod's *WD* (Fakas 2001: 63n190; Overduin 2015: 47–48). The opening word of the *Theriaca* picks up on the anaphora at lines 5–7 of the *WD*, in which Zeus easily accomplishes opposites:

ῥέα μὲν γὰρ βριάει, ῥέα δὲ βριάοντα χαλέπτει,
ῥεῖα δ' ἀρίζηλον μινύθει καὶ ἄδηλον ἀέξει,
ῥεῖα δέ τ' ἰθύνει σκολιὸν καὶ ἀγήνορα κάρφει

For easily he strengthens, and easily oppresses the strong,
easily he diminishes the conspicuous and raises up the inconspicuous,
easily he straightens the crooked and withers the arrogant

WD 5–7

We might take this point further and note that the theme of ease persists throughout the *WD*; at line 325, for example, the gods easily diminish the household of the profit-grabbing, shameless man, and at line 288 ῥηιδίως is indicative of the Iron Age human condition as, while Zeus can change our fortunes easily, all we mortals can do easily is grab misery.[11] With this choice of opening word, then, Nicander presents himself not only as operating independently, but as doing so with ease. It is relevant, too, that his work and that of other Hellenistic didactic poets lacks the strong ethical dimension of Zeus's "reversals" in the *WD*. Hesiod is concerned with the difficulty of restoring a mortal moral balance, whereas Hellenistic poets are more interested in aesthetic display and delight. Nicander picks up on the *WD* voice of didactic autonomy and authority but pushes it even further (if in a different direction): he professes that he is having no Aratean sleepless nights. Indeed, Aratus provides a midpoint on this spectrum of ease. Though according to Callimachus he works hard at his poetry, what comes more easily is the meaning of the stars:

πάντα γὰρ οὔπω
ἐκ Διὸς ἄνθρωποι γινώσκομεν, ἀλλ' ἔτι πολλὰ
κέκρυπται, τῶν αἴ κε θέλῃ καὶ ἐσαυτίκα δώσει
Ζεύς· ὁ γὰρ οὖν γενεὴν ἀνδρῶν ἀναφανδὸν ὀφέλλει
πάντοθεν εἰδόμενος, πάντῃ δ' ὅ γε σήματα φαίνων.

For not yet do men find out everything
from Zeus, but many things are still hidden—
things which Zeus will grant us presently, if he wishes.
For he openly helps the race of men, appearing from everywhere,
and everywhere revealing his signs.

Phaenomena 768–72

Hesiod in his *Th* concludes that "so it is not possible to deceive the mind of Zeus" (ὡς οὐκ ἔστι Διὸς κλέψαι νόον οὐδὲ παρελθεῖν, 613). In the *WD* also he professes that the mind of Zeus is difficult for mortals to know (483–84), even though *he* can speak of it because the Muses have taught him a boundless song (661–62). Aratus picks up these cues but depicts a more open situation in which not only can the inspired poet understand Zeus, but also anyone who learns how to read σήματα. A lot is still hidden, and we remain dependent on Zeus's goodwill, yet the situation seems to be more promising than that presented by Hesiod (Hunter 2004b: 230). We still have to interpret Zeus's signs, and (Aratus advertises) we need a "handbook" like the *Phaenomena* to do so, but with the right guidance we may stand a chance. Van Noorden (2015: 170) sees a nuanced integration of Hesiodic didaxis: "It may be seen that for Aratus, Hesiod's poetry has become itself part of the 'mind of Zeus', a world of material to be interpreted and appropriated, written in the sky, and hence susceptible to new meaning." The σήματα of the stars stand in for the polysemy of didactic poetry, something integral to Hesiod's *WD* with its myths, fables, riddles, and kennings, all of which require interpretation.

However easily poetry has supposedly come to him, Nicander envisages an ideal audience who are alert, attentive, and sharp, who know not only Hesiod but also Aratus, Callimachus, Theocritus, and Apollonius well enough to appreciate Nicander's allusions (Clauss and Cuypers 2010: 5–6). Aratus, too, expects input from his reader. For instance, the story of the Maiden leaving the earth (one of the passages of dense dialogue with the *WD*) "can be read as an *aetion* of the need, not only for economic activity such as trade, but also for the individual observation that characterizes the present" (Van Noorden 2015: 176). This may create a contemporary reference point, but as we have seen throughout this chapter, that does not preclude an engagement with an archaic *aetion* of its own. In the *WD* Hesiod also models an ideal audience, through the intellectual ideal of the πανάριστος, the very best kind of man, who thinks of everything for himself:

> οὗτος μὲν πανάριστος, ὃς αὐτῷ πάντα νοήσει
> [φρασσάμενος τά κ' ἔπειτα καὶ ἐς τέλος ᾖσιν ἀμείνω]·
> ἐσθλὸς δ' αὖ κἀκεῖνος ὃς εὖ εἰπόντι πίθηται·
> ὃς δέ κε μήτ' αὐτῷ νοέῃ μήτ' ἄλλου ἀκούων
> ἐν θυμῷ βάλληται, ὃ δ' αὖτ' ἀχρήιος ἀνήρ.

> That man is altogether the best, he who thinks of everything himself,
> considering the things which are then better in the end.
> He too is good, who listens to one who speaks well.
> But he who does not think nor, listening to another,
> considers in his heart, this man is useless.

WD 293–97

This takes us back to the importance of the library to Hellenistic poetics. As Harder (2013: 107) has argued, "the poets seem to refer their readers back to the library. The *Aetia* and *Argonautica* are products of the library, but the relevance of the library does not stop there. Readers are invited to think about the different points of view in scholarly discussions or to complete the picture with other information, for which they in their turn must consult the library." This ongoing analytical, evaluative, and dialogic process picks up on a key aspect of Hesiod's didaxis and propagates it in a very real setting of scholarly poetics.

Conclusion

To return to the questions with which I started: What is it about the *Th* and the *WD* that made them equally appealing at this time, and what is it about the Hellenistic period that balanced out the reception of these two poems? First, I hope to have shown that the Hellenistic poets treated the Hesiodic corpus as polyphonic but coherent, and thus though allusions may favor one poem in a particular context, the other poem was never far away. I took Callimachus's *Aetia* as a case study, but we might draw similar conclusions from the *Phaenomena*; for example, Aratus's Maiden can be interpreted as combining different Hesiodic resonances in that in the golden age she evokes the Just King of Hesiod's *Th* (81–93) and in the silver age her warnings resemble those of Hesiod himself to the iron race in the *WD* (Hunter 2004b: 241)—and her presentation in both is reminiscent of that of Hesiod's Muses (Van Noorden 2015: 195).

The particular contexts in which we find affiliations with or responses to Hesiod in the Hellenistic period are often marked by genre, which can be considered a relatively new departure in formal terms. This does not always make things more straightforward; as Rossi (1971) so neatly put it, in the archaic period generic laws were unwritten but respected; in the classical period they were both written and respected; and in the Hellenistic period they were written but not respected. Didactic poetry has throughout this chapter been a case in point, as one of the reasons the *WD* became less explicitly referenced in the Hellenistic age (the key shift we can extrapolate from Koning's figures) is that new didactic poetry was being produced that alluded to the archaic poem in much more complex and nuanced ways. Such "learned" poetry, sidelining the Muses in favor of *technē*, was a culmination of an accumulation of knowledge in the Hellenistic library culture and a further step along the road from archaic poetry, through classical prose treatises, to a resurgence of didactic verse. In this age of information, the Hellenistic poets sought to open things up once again: "Whereas systematic philosophy and the technical handbook seek to close down options, didactic poetry can offer multiple readings which draw on diverse traditions and emphasize the role of the reader, rather than that of the omniscient teacher" (Hunter 2004b: 234–35). Hesiod's *WD* champions an audience who work hard not only in the fields but also at the site of meaning, and Hellenistic didaxis reiterates this requirement. Further, it does so in a specifically and emphatically *literary* milieu: "Aratus' poem not only encourages viewers to read and reread the sky but also prompts readers to view and re-view his poem, regrouping its elements to form new signs" (Van Noorden 2015: 191). The visual aspect, the idea of returning again and again to a "stored" didactic poem without fluctuations, is something newly Hellenistic, yet the attention to detail, in terms of both contents and semantics, is familiarly Hesiodic.

As Hunter (2014: 20) puts it, "Homer and Hesiod are always as modern as one wants them to be." The Hellenistic age, with its "society of displaced persons," was a time of intense interest in *aetia*. The *Th*'s genealogical armature, the *Catalogue of Women*'s structure, the *WD*'s multiple origin myths: all could be mobilized in support of this preoccupation. Nicander repeatedly presents us with *protoi heuretai* (Overduin 2015: 109–12), and the label of *protos heuretes* of didactic poetry can convincingly (if not necessarily accurately) be applied to Hesiod himself. In the Hellenistic period, therefore, Hesiod became the *aetion* not only for the *Aetia* but for an entire genre of didactic poetry, sometimes reworked almost beyond recognition but always there as a constant reference point.

NOTES

1. Koning's table provides information for the *Th* and the *WD* only. In this chapter I also consider the *Catalogue of Women*, treating it as part of the Hesiodic corpus. I am guided in this not by our modern scholarly views on the authorship of the poem, but by the ancient reception of the Hesiodic corpus, which was thought to be broader than we now treat it.
2. Though Ford (2010: 146–7) argues that only the *WD*, not the *Th*, was taught in schools. He gives as evidence the observation by Plato's Protagoras (*Protagoras* 325e–26a) that letter-teachers "set before their students on their benches works of good poets and compel them to learn them by heart, in which there are many admonitions and detailed narratives, panegyrics, and eulogies of the good men of the past."
3. As Overduin (2015: 26) notes, "It is this literary awareness that separates him and Nicander from Empedocles and Parmenides, who clearly wrote in the epic tradition, but less evidently in a Hesiodic-didactic vein."
4. On Nicander's other sources see Overduin (2015: 7–23). On the pharmacological didactic "heirs" of Nicander, a small corpus of poetry written between the late Hellenistic and early Imperial age, see Overduin (forthcoming).
5. In the case of both Nicander and Aratus, the technical nature of the teachings might lure us into supposing firsthand knowledge of the subject matter (e.g., hypothesizing that Nicander must have been a physician). However, such conclusions would be simply extrapolations from intratextual evidence in these figures' poetry, as we have no external verification. Such autobiographical readings are rife also in Hesiodic scholarship; on their risks see, e.g., Canevaro (2015: 41–43).
6. Nicander chooses to include an acrostic of his own name (*Theriaca* 345–53). Aratus includes a number of literary (*ΛΕΠΤΗ*) and contextual (*ΠΑΣΑ*, *ΜΕΣΗ*) acrostics. Overduin (2015: 60–61) suggests that "Nicander's 'hidden' signature seems to play on Aratus' concealed name, viz. the self-reference contained in the word ἄρρητον (*Phaen.* 2)." We have in Nicander, then, an example of layered references in Hellenistic poetry, combining Hesiod's riddling approach to didactic with Aratus's visual codification.
7. Sistakou (2009: 238): "Callimachus (at least partly) conceived his *Aitia* not only as a 'sequel to the *Theogony*' but also as a neoteric version of the Hesiodic *Catalogue*, in terms of arrangement, content and story-patterning." See further Hunter (2005).

8. We know this not from the surviving fragments of the poem itself, but from a summary: *Diegesis* 1.27–36.

9. See Volk's chapter also for a clear overview of the relationship between Aratus and Hesiodic poetry. As Volk (2010: 200) notes, the clearest examples of Aratus in his *Phaenomena* engaging closely with sections of Hesiod's *WD* are "the proem with its hymn to Zeus (1–8), which harks back to the beginning of the *Works and Days* (1–10), and the myth of Dike (96–136), an amalgam of Hesiod's account of the races of men (*WD* 109–201) and his description of the 'maiden Dike' as a guardian of justice (*WD* 220–62)." For detailed discussion, see Van Noorden (2015: 168–203).

10. Hunter (2014: 21): "This reworking calls attention to the crucial relationship between the subject-matter of the *Aitia* and that of Hesiod's *Theogony*, as well perhaps as to that between the form of the *Aitia* and that of Hesiod's *Catalogue of Women*, but it is also true that the *Aitia* goes very far beyond the subject-range of these invoked archaic models. The past, then, is appropriated and made appropriate to new forms, not rejected." Fantuzzi (2004: 7) suggests that the dream form creates a parallel also with the experience of another theogonic poet, Epimenides, who wrote about receiving the contents of his works from the gods in a didactic dream.

11. See also *WD* 43; in the time before Prometheus and his epoch-changing encounter with Zeus, a man would "easily" ($\acute{\rho}\eta\iota\delta\acute{\iota}\omega\varsigma$) have been able to work enough in one day to last him through an idle year.

References

Acosta-Hughes, B., L. Lehnus, and S. Stephens, eds. 2011. *Brill's Companion to Callimachus*. Leiden, Netherlands.

Barbantani, S. 2011. "Callimachus on Kings and Kingship." In *Brill's Companion to Callimachus*, edited by B. Acosta-Hughes, L. Lehnus, and S. Stephens, 178–200. Leiden, Netherlands.

Boys-Stones, G. R., and J. H. Haubold, eds. 2010. *Plato and Hesiod*. Oxford.

Canevaro, L. G. 2014. "Genre and Authority in Hesiod's *Works and Days*." In *Gêneros Poéticos na Grécia Antiga: Confluências e Fronteiras*, edited by C. Werner, B. B. Sebastiani, and A. Dourado-Lopes, 23–48. São Paulo.

Canevaro, L. G. 2015. *Hesiod's Works and Days: How to Teach Self-Sufficiency*. Oxford.

Clauss, J., and M. Cuypers, eds. 2010. *A Companion to Hellenistic Literature*. Malden, MA.

Clay, J. S. 2003. *Hesiod's Cosmos*. Cambridge.

Clay, J. S. 2009. "*Works and Days*: Tracing the Path to *Arête*." In *Brill's Companion to Hesiod*, edited by F. Montanari, A. Rengakos, and Chi. Tsagalis, 71–90. Leiden, Netherlands.

Cribiore, R. 2001. *Gymnastics of the Mind: Greek Education in Hellenistic and Roman Egypt*. Princeton, NJ.

Effe, B. 1977. *Dichtung und Lehre: Untersuchungen zur Typologie des antiken Lehrgedichts*. Zetemata 69. Munich, Germany.

Effe, B. 2005. "Typologie und literarhistorischer Kontext." In *Wissensvermittlung in dichterischer Gestalt*, edited by M. Horster and C. Reitz, 27–44. Stuttgart, Germany.

Fakas, C. 2001. *Der hellenistiche Hesiod: Arats Phainomena und die Tradition der antiken Lehrepik*. Wiesdbaden, Germany.

Fantuzzi, M. 2004. "Performance and Genre." In *Tradition and Innovation in Hellenistic Poetry*, edited by M. Fantuzzi and R. L. Hunter, 1–41. Cambridge.

Fantuzzi, M., and R. L. Hunter. 2004. *Tradition and Innovation in Hellenistic Poetry*. Cambridge.

Ford, A. 2010. "Plato's two Hesiods." In *Plato and Hesiod*, edited by G. R. Boys-Stones and J. H. Haubold, 133–56. Oxford.

Fowler, A. 2003. "The Formation of Genres in the Renaissance and After." *New Literary History* 34: 185–200.

Fraser, L. G. 2011. "A Woman of Consequence: Pandora in Hesiod's *Works and Days*." *Cambridge Classical Journal* 57: 9–28.

Gale, M. R. Forthcoming. "Name Puns and Acrostics in Didactic Poetry: Reading the Universe." In *Didactic Poetry: Knowledge, Power, Tradition*, edited by L. G. Canevaro and D. O'Rourke. Swansea, UK.

Graziosi, B., and J. H. Haubold, eds. and comms. 2010. *Homer Iliad VI*. Cambridge.

Hamilton, E. 1989. *The Architecture of Hesiodic Poetry*. Baltimore, MD.

Harder, A. 2013. "From Text to Text: The Impact of the Alexandrian Library on the Work of Hellenistic Poets." In *Ancient Libraries*, edited by J. König, K. Oikonomopoulou, and G. Woolf, 96–108. Cambridge.

Haubold, J. H. 2010. "Shepherd, Farmer, Poet, Sophist: Hesiod on His Own Reception." In *Plato and Hesiod*, edited by G. R. Boys-Stones and J. H. Haubold, 11–30. Oxford.

Heath, M. 1985. "Hesiod's Didactic Poetry." *Classical Quarterly* 35 (2): 245–63.

Hunter, R. L. 2004a. "The Aetiology of Callimachus' *Aitia*." In *Tradition and Innovation in Hellenistic Poetry*, edited by M. Fantuzzi and R. L. Hunter, 42–88. Cambridge.

Hunter, R. L. 2004b. "Epic in a Minor Key." In *Tradition and Innovation in Hellenistic Poetry*, edited by M. Fantuzzi and R. L. Hunter, 191–245. Cambridge.

Hunter, R. L., ed. 2005. *The Hesiodic Catalogue of Women: Constructions and Reconstructions*. Cambridge.

Hunter, R. L. 2014. *Hesiodic Voices: Studies in the Ancient Reception of Hesiod's Works and Days*. Cambridge.

Koning, H. H. 2010. *Hesiod: The Other Poet; Ancient Reception of a Cultural Icon*. Mnemosyne Supplement 325. Leiden, Netherlands.

Magnelli, E. 2010. "Nicander." In *A Companion to Hellenistic Literature*, edited by J. Clauss and M. Cuypers, 211–23. Malden. MA.

Montanari, F., A. Rengakos, and C. Tsagalis, eds. 2009. *Brill's Companion to Hesiod*. Leiden, Netherlands.

Overduin, F. 2015. *Nicander of Colophon's Theriaca: A Literary Commentary*. Mnemosyne Supplement 374. Leiden, Netherlands.

Overduin, F. Forthcoming. "Elegiac Pharmacology: The Didactic Heirs of Nicander?" In *Didactic Poetry: Knowledge, Power, Tradition*, edited by L. G. Canevaro and D. O'Rourke . Swansea, UK.

Papanghelis, T. D., and A. Rengakos, eds. 2008. *Brill's Companion to Apollonius*. Leiden, Netherlands.

Pfeiffer, R. 1968. *History of Classical Scholarship from the Beginnings to the End of the Hellenistic Age*. Oxford.

Reinsch-Werner, H. 1976. *Callimachus Hesiodicus: Die Rezeption der hesiodischen Dichtung durch Kallimachos von Kyrene*. Berlin.

Rossi, L. E. 1971. "I generi letterari e le loro leggi scritte e non scritte nelle letterature classiche." *Bulletin of the Institute of Classical Studies* 18 (1): 69–94.

Schroeder, C. 2007. "Hesiod in the Hellenistic Imagination." PhD thesis, University of Michigan.

Selden, D. L. 1998. "Alibis." *Classical Antiquities* 17: 289–412.

Sider, D. 2014. "Didactic Poetry: The Hellenistic Invention of a Pre-Existing Genre." In *Hellenistic Studies at a Crossroads: Exploring Texts, Contexts and Metatexts*, edited by R. Hunter, A. Rengakos, and E. Sistakou, 13–29. Berlin.

Sistakou, E. 2009. "Callimachus Hesiodicus Revisited." In *Brill's Companion to Hesiod*, edited by F. Montanari, A. Rengakos, and C. Tsagalis, 219–52. Leiden, Netherlands.

Stephens, S. 2011. "Introduction." In *Brill's Companion to Callimachus*, edited by B. Acosta-Hughes, L. Lehnus, and S. Stephens, 1–19. Leiden, Netherlands.

Stewart, S. 2008. "Emending Aratus' Insomnia: Callimachus *Epigr.* 27." *Mnemosyne* 61: 586–600.

Toohey, P. 1996. *Epic Lessons: An Introduction to Ancient Didactic Poetry*. London.

Van Noorden, H. 2015. *Playing Hesiod: The "Myth of the Races" in Classical Antiquity*. Cambridge.

Volk, K. 2010. "Aratus." In *A Companion to Hellenistic Literature*, edited by J. Clauss and M. Cuypers, 197–210. Malden, MA.

Volk, K. 2002. *The Poetics of Latin Didactic: Lucretius, Vergil, Ovid, Manilius*. Oxford.

Wissmann, J. 2010. "Education." In *A Companion to Hellenistic Literature*, edited by J. Clauss and M. Cuypers, 62–78. Malden, MA.

Ziogas, I. 2013. *Ovid and Hesiod: The Metamorphosis of the Catalogue of Women*. Cambridge.

CHAPTER 22

HESIOD FROM ARISTOTLE TO POSIDONIUS

DAVID CONAN WOLFSDORF

πολλὰ ψεύδονται ἀοιδοί

INTRODUCTION

THIS chapter examines the reception of Hesiod among the Peripatetics, Epicureans, and Stoics, from Aristotle to the end of the Hellenistic Period.[1]

Two Hesiodic passages above all seem to have captured the attention of these philosophers: the genesis of the primordial divinities in *Theogony* (hereafter *Th*) and the Myth of Ages, especially the golden age in *Works and Days* (hereafter *WD*). Both pertain to origins, cosmic-divine and human, respectively. Broadly speaking, their attraction is easily explained: gods and humans are of central interest in Greek culture, and *archai* are a quintessential concern of ancient philosophy.

Granted the importance of these passages and their provision of one unifying thread within this particular history, philosophical interest in and use of Hesiod over the three centuries in question was diverse and complex. The reception is in fact not tightly unified at all.

One factor contributing to the disunity is the state of the evidence. This is extremely limited, disparate, and elusive. Often we know little about the central philosophical contributions of the philosophers, let alone the loci or aims of their remarks about or treatments of Hesiod. A second factor is the diversity of interests and attitudes among, as well as within, the schools. The poverty of evidence surely bears some responsibility for the way this extant content appears, but in many cases the two factors seem to bear independent responsibility for the lack of unity.

Consider one obvious point of entry into the reception history: the topics of poetry and Hesiod as poet. Take the Peripatetics first. Despite the value Aristotle accorded to poetry, he did not treat Hesiod's works as worthy of poetic theoretical attention. Instead, Aristotle appears to have been interested in Hesiod principally as a *theologos*. Some of Aristotle's prominent successors, for example Theophrastus and Eudemus, seem to have regarded Hesiod likewise. In contrast, and although in this case the evidence is extremely scanty, other second- and third-generation Peripatetics integrated Hesiod into the important advances they made in literary criticism. The lack of evidence impedes our ability to explain this divergence among the Peripatetics, but there is no reason to believe that the lack merely makes the divergence apparent as opposed to real.

In the case of the Epicureans, we have relatively clear evidence for striking disparities among their views toward poetry and poetic theory. Epicurus himself was largely uninterested in poetry and apparently hostile toward poetic form as a vehicle of philosophical expression. Philodemus, by contrast, composed both poems and, like a number of Epicurus's successors, philosophical works on poetry. Lucretius broke still more radically with his master and predecessors when he versified the central ideas of Epicurus's *On Nature*.

For their part, the Stoics were interested in poetry, and for various reasons. The dearth of evidence limits our appreciation of this variety. But we know that one of the distinctive and remarkable ways the Stoics viewed poetry, in particular archaic poetry, was as a kind of repository of the cosmological and theological ideas of early humans. Insofar as these ideas were not apparent to the poets themselves—for example, because they were embedded in the etymologies of divine names—such Stoic interpretations of the poetic texts have been described as allegorical. I prefer to call them archaeological. And insofar as the Stoics employed the texts in this way, they engaged them not as poetry per se, but again as records of ideas that happened to be transmitted in poetic form. Consequently in this case at least, the Stoics were not interested in Hesiod as poet or even in Hesiod per se, although they were very much interested in Hesiod's texts.

Archaeological excavation constitutes a significant part of the Stoic evidence on Hesiod, but there were numerous other things that they, as well as the Epicureans and Peripatetics, said and made of Hesiod, whether in the guise of poet, *theologos*, cultural icon, or even *philosophos*. We have tantalizing traces of these sayings and doings, but often little more.

Throughout my discussion I refer to many of these traces as well as the broader themes and forms of engagement mentioned previously. Doing so introduces many loose ends and provocative but dangling questions into the account. I have preferred to render such an untidy picture precisely because it is a more faithful one.

THE PERIPATOS

Aristotle

Hesiod is not mentioned in the surviving portions of Aristotle's *Poetics*. Nor is there a good reason to believe he was mentioned in the lost portions.[2] Given the popularity of Hesiod in fourth-century BCE Athens, Aristotle's silence requires explanation.

Central to Aristotle's theory of poetry is imitation of human action and unified plot structure (*muthos*). As Stephen Halliwell writes, "even human themes will not provide suitable substance for a . . . *muthos* unless they are organized into a single structure of action" (1986: 282). Hesiod's *WD* and *Th* arguably depart from these conditions to such an extent that unless Aristotle sought to highlight these poems as paradigms of failure, he would have little motivation to discuss them.

Although Hesiod is not a subject of interest in *Poetics*, Aristotle was interested in Hesiod. The *Vita Menangiana* lists among Aristotle's writings a *Hesiodic Problems* in one book. Compare Aristotle's *Homeric Problems* and *Problems in Archilochus, Euripides, and Choerilus*. No fragments from the *Hesiodic Problems* survive, but some idea of its content might be gained by considering the numerous fragments of the *Homeric Problems*. Some fragments concern Homer's biography; most engage specific passages or verses and discuss pertinent heroic behavior, customs, and society, including textual inconsistencies and narrower philological issues.

"Problems in *X*" does not however designate a well-defined category, and it is noteworthy that Aristotle and his contemporaries lack a term for this type of inquiry. For convenience I refer to it as "literary critical" (Blum 1991: 46–47, 86; Richardson 1994: 26). But we should acknowledge that "literary criticism" does not designate a particularly well-defined theoretical domain. Both "literature" and "criticism" are vague terms.

Aristotle makes about ten references to Hesiod in his surviving corpus and fragments.[3] Most are of a metaphysical and cosmological nature. For example, at *Metaphysics* 984b28 Aristotle cites *Th* 116–20 to illustrate that Hesiod was the first to adumbrate the *aitia* of motion and change. At *Physics* 208b29–31 he cites *Th* 116 to suggest how Hesiod would be justified in committing to the view that space is distinct from body. And at *On the Heavens* 298b28 and *Metaphysics* 1000a9 Aristotle refers to Hesiod's general commitments in *Th* apropos of the question of whether the principles of perishables and imperishables are the same or different.

Aristotle's first three references express no disparagement, but the one at *Metaphysics* 1000a9 does. There, Aristotle insists on turning from those such as Hesiod, who do not use proof (*apodeixis*), to those who do. An explanation for this disparagement is that Aristotle is primarily concerned with the epistemic value of the content of Hesiod's contribution, whereas in the three other cases he is interested in locating Hesiod's contribution within a teleological history of philosophy.

The evidence suggests the following tentative conclusions. Aristotle did not appreciate Hesiod as a poet. However, he did recognize the cultural historical importance of Hesiod's poetic contributions. Aristotle was principally interested in Hesiod as a *theologos* (cp. *Metaphysics* 1000a9) and so as a proto-philosopher.[4] Accordingly, Aristotle did not esteem Hesiod's intellectual contribution for its own sake, but he appreciated its importance for the development of philosophical thought.

Several of Aristotle's prominent successors appear to have regarded Hesiod in the same terms.

Theophrastus

Theophrastus cites Hesiod four times, all in the *History of Plants* (3.7.6, 7.13.3, 8.1.2, 9.19.2) and in each case it is a passage from *WD*. Each citation is in passing. Sometimes Theophrastus simply adduces Hesiod in agreement, sometimes in disagreement.

From Aristotle to Posidonius numerous Hesiodic citations are of this kind. A default interpretation of such en passant citations, as I call them here, is that they serve to demonstrate or merely express the philosopher's *paideia* or to give to some thought a veneer of archaic precedence. Consider a comment by Tony Long on Chrysippus's citations from Homer: "Like all educated Greeks, of course, the Stoics had lines of Homer and other poets in their heads which they could use to make an ethical point and to show that their philosophy accorded with 'the common conceptions' of people" (1992: 49).

The philosophers' attitudes toward traditional culture are diverse and complex. Various reasons may motivate an en passant citation. Sorting out the explanation in a given instance requires attention to the Hesiodic content of the citation, the philosopher's broader philosophical commitments, and the philosophical context in which the citation is made. For example, if a citation is ethical and the author is a Peripatetic, then possibly the citation is being employed endoxically. Observe that in Long's remark "common conception" (*koina ennoia*) is a technical Stoic epistemological term. Space constraints here do not permit much scrutiny of en passant Hesiodic citations. But I underscore that their meanings may not be transparent and are worthy of consideration.

Given the relatively large number of Theophrastus's surviving works, the dearth of references to Hesiod is suggestive. Consider further that there is no reference, in particular to *WD*, in Theophrastus's *On Signs*. Again, one might expect a number of citations from *WD* in the Peripatetic *Economics*, a text some, including some ancients, attribute to Theophrastus. In this case there are two citations (1343a20, 1344a16), and in each instance the author agrees with Hesiod. But both, like those in the *History of Plants*, are en passant.

Like Aristotle, Theophrastus took a theoretical interest in poetry. He also wrote on rhetoric and specifically encouraged the study of poetry for rhetoric (fr. 666.1–16, 24, 707 Fortenbaugh, Huby, Sharples, and Gutas [= FHS&G]). If more than scraps of works such as Theophrastus's *On Poetry* and *On Style* had survived (fr. 681–709 FHS&G), we might have more to say about his reception of Hesiod. On the other hand, what does survive does not indicate that Theophrastus drew Hesiod into the poetic-theoretical discussion.

In sum, the dearth of Hesiodic citations in Theophrastus suggests that he found little in Hesiod worthy of theoretical engagement and probably even so with respect to the domain of literary criticism.

Eudemus

A fragment from Eudemus includes Hesiod among other Greek and "barbarian" prephilosophical *theologoi*, listing their various claims about the primordial divinities (fr. 150 Wehrli). In Hesiod's case these divinities include Chaos, Earth, and Tartarus and hence derive from *Th* 116–20. The original source of the fragment is contested, but one plausible view is a *History of Theology*, which Gábor Betegh describes as "a synoptic collection of the theologians' 'genealogical narratives'" (2002: 354). As Betegh also emphasizes, one of Eudemus's central and original contributions in this work is the "application and institutionalization" of Aristotle's distinction between *theologoi* and *philosophoi* (355). That is, the figures whose views of the primordial divinities Eudemus includes belong to a category that Aristotle had defined, but whose "demarcation was not usually observed outside the Peripatos" (355).

Eudemus's interest in Hesiod as a prephilosophical *theologos* is a notable exception that underscores the generalization that evidence of Peripatetic interest in Hesiod during the Hellenistic period is literary critical. Before turning to this evidence, I consider one further possible exception, in this case from Dicaearchus.

Dicaearchus

Dicaearchus composed a work of historical anthropology, *On the Life of Greece*. Evidence of its content is slim. But the work apparently began with a description of the first humans. In this portion Dicaearchus appears to have engaged with Hesiod's Myth of Ages, specifically with the golden age. Under Trevor Saunder's interpretation (2001), in both Hesiod's and Dicaearchus's accounts early human life is autarkic and free of labor. But Dicaearchus seems to have departed from Hesiod's idyllic view of the period, maintaining that the quality of nourishment available to the first humans was poor and that in subsequent ages technical developments such as hunting and agriculture brought certain qualitative improvements.

Granting some engagement with Hesiod's golden age, Dicaearchus's theoretical view of Hesiod's contribution remains obscure. Was Dicaearchus's aim doxographical: to provide a (critical) record of his predecessors' historical anthropologies and in particular Hesiod's prominent treatment? Or did he have a different objective?

Praxiphanes, Chamaeleon, Megacleides, Hieronymus

Despite its extremely fragmentary and elusive nature, there is important evidence that a number of Hellenistic Peripatetics made significant advances in literary criticism and in doing so integrated Hesiod into their studies.

Praxiphanes of Mytilene is mentioned among those who athetize the proem of Hesiod's *WD* (fr. 28A–B Matelli). No work on Hesiod is attributed to him. However, a work *On Poems* and a dialogue *On Poets* are. The discussion of Hesiod's proem might have occurred in one of these.

The athetization may also be significant insofar as Praxiphanes was, at least within one literary critical tradition, considered the first *grammatikos*—"as we use the word now," Clement of Alexandria remarks (fr. 9A Matelli). Regarding this and related testimonies, Elisabetta Matelli comments: "Praxiphanes was considered the founder of a new kind of [literary study] that dealt with critical exegesis of texts" (2012: 55–56n5).

Chamaeleon of Heraclea composed works on a number of poets, including Homer, Anacreon, Sappho, Simonides, Stesichorus, and Aeschylus. No title *On Hesiod* is attributed to him. However, testimonies report that he accused Heraclides Pontus of plagiarizing his view of the relative chronologies of Homer and Hesiod (Diogenes Laertius 5.92). Chamaeleon must therefore have devoted some work or portion of a work to this aspect of Hesiod's life. The testimonies are also significant in indicating the biographical dimensions of Peripatetic literary criticism and the development of chronography more broadly. The latter is a subject Aristotle and his successors variously fostered, for example through their research and composition of lists of athletic and dramatic victories.

Chamaeleon's contemporary Megacleides (Janko 2000: 138–43) composed a work *On Homer*, which among other things compared Homer's treatment of Heracles with those of other poets. Megacleides apparently criticized the treatment of Heracles in the Hesiodic *Shield*.

The third-generation Peripatetic Hieronymus of Rhodes also discussed the *Shield*. The *Gudian Lexicon* reports that Epaphroditus, in his *Commentary on the Shield*, cited Hieronymus's explanation of the word "*alkaia*" (at line 430) as principally referring to the lion's tail because it rouses the animal's strength (*alkē*) (fr. 45 White). The same explanation occurs in Hieronymus's contemporaries Callimachus and Apollonius of Rhodes. Apollonius expressly defended Hesiod's authorship of *The Shield*, and it is noteworthy that with the exception of Aristophanes of Byzantium's athetization, *The Shield* "remained with [*Th*] and [*WD*] in every ancient text of Hesiod" (Pfeiffer 1968: 178).

Andrea Martano observes that Hieronymus's explanation of "*alkaia*" does not occur in Peripatetic zoological works (2004: 458–63). This supports the possibility that it was introduced in a literary critical context. More precisely, Martano argues that Hieronymus cited the explanation in a *hypothesis* (465–70).

Conclusion to the Peripatos

In his oration on Homer, Dio Chrysostom speaks of Aristotle as he "from whom, as they say, *kritikē* and *grammatikē* began" (53.1). Dio's claim may be defended to this extent. The literary critical work of Aristotle and his successors appears to have harnessed the general methodological and theoretical interests and advances of the Peripatos to traditions of literary criticism extending back through the sophists and rhapsodes. Contra Plato, Aristotle invigorated these traditions, and in doing so he and his successors prepared and informed the work of the Alexandrians.

Granted this, one fundamental question to be considered is on what grounds those Hellenistic Peripatetics who made literary criticism one of their central preoccupations departed from Aristotle in making Hesiod an important object of study. Above all it would be valuable to know whether and how they explicitly responded to the absence of Hesiod from their master's *Poetics*.

A more general philosophical question that the Peripatetics' literary critical activity raises is why they recognized and then embraced poetry as a legitimate object of inquiry. The basic answer seems to be that poetry is a central contribution of culture and that culture is a legitimate object of inquiry. But why? Relative to Aristotle's scheme of theoretical, practical, and productive knowledge, poetry exemplifies productive knowledge. So the answer requires not simply clarifying that poetry has value as a human achievement, but how its value, apparently diminutive relative to other objects of inquiry, qualifies it for sustained theoretical attention. Consider the familiar, loosely analogous question of how in Aristotle's ethics the choice between theoretical and practical lives is to be adjudicated. Our question concerns the choice between different sorts of theoretical pursuits.

The Garden

Epicurus

A central feature of Epicurus's ethics, including the epistemology and physics that serve it, is criticism of traditional mythology and mythological poetry, especially for their portrayals of the gods, divine involvement in human affairs, and post-mortem existence. Epicurus is notoriously hostile toward conventional *paideia*. In an often-cited fragment, he encourages Pythocles to avoid it; in another, he praises his student Apelles for having done so to that point (fr. 89, 43 Arrighetti). Consequently, we would expect Epicurus either to have engaged with Hesiod in a hostile manner or to have deliberately ignored him altogether.

There is no explicit reference to Hesiod in Epicurus's extant texts, and there is just one testimony explicitly associating Epicurus and Hesiod. This is ostensibly a biographical remark, although probably fictional, from Apollodorus, scholarch of the Garden in the second century BCE, which claims that Epicurus turned to philosophy because he despised his schoolmasters for their inability to explain to him Hesiod's primordial Chaos (Diogenes Laertius 10.2).

Granted this there is some, admittedly speculative reason to think that in *On Nature* Epicurus criticized Hesiod among a number of early sources of misguided theology. The grounds derive from the Epicurean Velleius's criticism of Homer and Hesiod in

Cicero's *On the Gods* and topically related sections of Philodemus's *On Piety* (cf. Obbink 1995: 201–2). These treatments have a common source, although its identity is disputed (cf. Heinrichs 1975; Asmis 1990a:35). But given Lucretius's dependence on Epicurus and account of the origins of religion in *On the Nature of Things* (5.1161–240), I speculate that all three authors depend, directly or indirectly, on portions of Epicurus's *On Nature* (probably book 12 or 13) that discussed these topics.

Beyond this there is little to say about Epicurus directly on Hesiod. There is, however, something to be added regarding Epicurus's and his successors' attitudes toward poetry. Given that Epicurean ethics is hedonistic and that a traditional and central function of poetry is to be pleasing, the enjoyment or even composition of poetry might be thought to have some role in the Epicurean life. For example, Epicurus might have admitted traditional poetry within symposiastic contexts for purposes of entertainment rather than instruction.

In fact, the topic of poetry in the Epicurean philosophical tradition is complex and controversial. Philodemus composed well over a hundred epigrammatic poems, some of which were intended to celebrate the *Eikas*, the monthly festival Epicureans held in honor of their master. But Lucretius's epic versification of the central ideas of Epicurus's *On Nature* is intended to be instructive as well as to charm. And Philodemus's *On the Good King according to Homer* in fact employs Homeric epic didactically.

Diogenes Laertius lists the titles *Symposium* and *On Music* within his catalog of Epicurus's writings (10.27), and he attributes to Epicurus this *doxa*: "It is only the wise man who can converse properly about music and poetry" (10.121). On the other hand, Diogenes also attributes to Epicurus this *doxa*: "The wise man would not be actively engaged in the composition of poems" (10.121). Moreover, we know of a number of Epicurean theoretical works on poetry and poems. Metrodorus, Demetrius Lacon, and Philodemus each wrote treatises *On Poems*, and Zeno of Sidon wrote a work *On the Utility of Poems*.

However determinate Epicurus's own views were, they evidently left theoretical space for development and disagreement among his successors. For example, the *doxa* against the composition of poetry could be interpreted as entailing only that poetic composition should not be an Epicurean's central or professional occupation. And the *doxa* supporting the wise man's reception of poetry could be interpreted to mean that he is intellectually fortified against the harmful potential of traditional poetry and therefore equipped to enjoy as well as to discourse on it. Granted this, we have no explicit evidence that Epicurus himself included, let alone admired, Hesiod's poems qua poems.

Philodemus

Philodemus's theory of poetry survives in the fragments of his treatise *On Poems*. Hesiod is mentioned there once (book 4, col. 103.7). The context is Philodemus's statement that Hesiod is a better poetic craftsman than Stesichorus. Philodemus's intriguing claim may constitute a criticism of Aristotle who, in his dialogue *On Poets*, arguably stated the contrary (Janko 2011: 263, 411). However, the grounds for the contradictory claims are obscure (cf. Janko 2011: 222–38).

David Sider has suggested that the rare use of an inflected form of "*triēkonta*" in Philodemus's seventeenth epigram, which concerns marriage, alludes to Hesiod's use of this word in the genitive at *WD* 695–97, where the context is the appropriate age for a man to marry (1995: 54). Some support for Sider's position may be gained from Philodemus's explicit citation of *WD* 405–6 in his *On Economics* (col. 8.25–40), a treatise concerning marriage and the household. The context is a discussion of Theophrastus's citation of the same Hesiodic verses in his *On Economics* (1343a20)—assuming Theophrastus is the author, as Philodemus does—in which Theophrastus is concerned with the essential components of a household and subsequently addresses the appropriate qualities of a wife and how a husband should treat her. In this latter case, Theophrastus once again cites Hesiod, in this instance *WD* 696, with approval (1344a16).

Philodemus treats Theophrastus critically, among other reasons because the Epicurean rejects the Peripatetic's idea that a wife is indispensable to a well-functioning household. But the interpretation of Philodemus's criticism is complicated by the question of whether *WD* 406 was absent from Philodemus's text or whether his text contained a variant reading (cf. Tsouna 2012: 90).

Philodemus mentions Hesiod a number of additional times. One instance occurs in *On Piety* (B 9970–80 Obbink). In addition, Dirk Obbink has convincingly argued that in another fragment from this treatise Philodemus refers to the Hesiodic *Catalogue of Women* (2004: 188–90). The broader context of these references is traditional mythological representation of the gods' unethical behavior, especially Poseidon's sexual exploits.

Overall, Philodemus's engagements with Hesiod are minimal. His references to Hesiod in *On Piety* are representative of Epicurean hostility to traditional mythographic poetry. Those in *On Economics* indicate a willingness to address other aspects of Hesiod's thought. But with the exception of the claim in *On Poems* and the possible and indeed tenuous allusion to Hesiod in one of his epigrams, Philodemus evinces little appreciation for or interest in Hesiod as a poet.[5]

Lucretius

The evidence from Lucretius suggests the same conclusion. As an epic poet, Lucretius views himself as heir to Homer and Ennius, and as a didactic poet as heir to Empedocles. But Lucretius never refers to Hesiod, and it is difficult to find in *On the Nature of Things* clear and specific allusions to Hesiod.

Monica Gale has argued that Lucretius's engagement with Hesiod, specifically *WD*, is to be found less in "close verbal correspondences" than in "wide-ranging thematic and symbolic interaction" (2013: n6). In particular, through his treatments of piety, labor, and justice Lucretius creates "a kind of anti-Hesiod . . . holding up an Epicurean mirror to the Hesiodic world view." Lucretius rejects Hesiod's view that the gods involve themselves in human affairs and that toil, in particular physical labor, is required for well-being. In contrast to Hesiod's view of the theistic grounds of justice, the Epicurean views justice as arising out of social agreement.

It may be objected, however, that Lucretius's handling of these three themes does not constitute a direct response to Hesiod, but rather to broadly accepted traditional views. More compelling is Gale's argument that Lucretius engages with Hesiod's Myth of Ages in his own history of civilization in book 5 (2013: 42–50). Most strikingly, Lucretius reproduces the metallic stages of gold, silver, bronze, and iron, yet in an account of the history of metallurgy (5.1241–96). Within this discussion, in particular in the transition from the Bronze to Iron Ages, Lucretius clearly alludes to Hesiod's language at *WD* 150–51 (5.1289–91).

Conclusion to the Garden

I have suggested that some indeterminacy in Epicurus's own views about poetry may have enabled his successors' more accommodating and eventually welcoming developments. But this is hardly a satisfactory explanation for what occurred. The history of Epicureanism might instead have followed a course of increasing hostility.

The basic explanation for Lucretius's decision and justification for versifying Epicurean philosophy seems to be that he was the first to appeal to a Roman audience in their own language. As he emphasizes in a much-discussed passage, the sweetness of the verse serves to attract the patient so that the difficult content will be more easily digested (1.933–42, 4.8–25).

But this answer cannot straightforwardly be applied to explain Philodemus's poetic theorizing and composition. Philodemus did spend most of his life in Rome and Herculaneum and had a significant influence on a number of the most prominent Augustan poets. But he first studied in Athens under Zeno of Sidon, who was already interested in the utility of poems. Philodemus's poetic and aesthetic contributions are therefore likely to be understood as a function of various factors: his personal interests and the interests of his Roman students and hosts, but also the aesthetic theoretical interests of the Athenian Garden in the late second and early first centuries BCE.

Despite their poetic theories and compositions, neither Philodemus nor Lucretius took much of an interest in Hesiod. The reasons for that may be drawn from Gale's discussion: Hesiod's theology and emphasis on the value of labor are antithetical to the relevant aspects of Epicurean philosophy.

THE STOICS

Zeno

On the basis of several testimonies pertaining to Zeno's interpretations of select passages in Hesiod's *Th* (*Stoicorum Veterum Fragmenta* [hereafter *SVF*] 1.103–5, 100, 118,

276) Hans von Arnim attributed to the founder of Stoicism a commentary on Hesiod's *Th* (*SVF Fragments relating to Zeno's titles* 1.71–72, nr. VI). But Diogenes Laertius lists no such title in his catalog of Zeno's works (7.4). And while Diogenes's catalogs are not always complete or reliable, Keimpe Algra has forcefully argued that von Arnim's attribution is misguided (2001).

All of the testimonies concern the names of mythical divinities, and all appear to derive from cosmological or cosmogonic contexts. Most significantly among them, Zeno interprets Hesiod's primal cosmogonic sequence of Chaos, Earth, and Eros at *Th* 116–20 as largely in agreement with his own view of the genesis of the cosmic elements. Consequently, Algra plausibly suggests that the likeliest source for the Zenonian testimonies is Zeno's physical treatise *On the Whole*.

Following Algra's interpretation, two basic questions arise: What general theoretical grounds support Zeno's interpretation of the *Th* passages? And why was Zeno motivated to engage Hesiod at all? Consideration of these questions leads to a particularly vexed set of issues. I address the first question here and the second in the conclusion.

Allegory and Etymology

Discussions of the Stoics' treatments of poetry have been bound up with the topic of allegory. The basic claim is that the Stoics' interpretations of the poets are allegorical; hence Zeno's interpretations of passages in Hesiod's *Th* are. The basic claim should, however, be qualified. Although most of what they wrote on the topic has perished, we know that the Stoics had much to say about poetry. Zeno composed a *Homeric Problems* in five books and a work *On Listening to Poems* (*SVF* 1.41); Cleanthes composed a work *On Homer* (Diogenes Laertius 7.175); and Chrysippus composed books *On Poems* and *On How One Should Listen to Poems* (*SVF* 2.16). Additionally, in fragments from book 5 of Philodemus's *On Poems* the poetic theory of a Stoic, perhaps Aristo of Chios, is discussed and criticized. Not all of this poetic theoretical and exegetical work is limited to allegorical theory and interpretation, and not all of the Stoics' references to or citations from Hesiod are allegorical—although the bulk of those that survive are (cf. Asmis n.d.; Blank 2011).

Granted the qualification, interpretation of Stoic allegorical interpretation is variously complicated. One fundamental problem concerns the uses of "allegory." In a paper on the Stoics' readings of Homer, Tony Long proposes a distinction between so-called weak and strong allegory (1992). Assume that mythological poetry such as Hesiod's preserves certain cosmological and theological ideas that, unbeknown to the poets themselves, were conceived by primitive humans. In the transmission of these ideas through cultural shifts and turns, the original meanings became obscured and distorted. Interpretation of poetry whose aim is to recover these primitive ideas may be called "allegorical" in the sense that the interpreter gleans information from the text, but not as the poet himself intended his work to be received. Long distinguishes this as "weak" allegory (1992: 43). Contrast this with poets who deliberately compose their works to be interpreted in ways that "go beyond" their literal meanings. Corresponding interpretations are allegorical in a strong sense.

The ideas motivating Long's distinction are helpful. But it may be questioned whether weak allegory deserves the name "allegory" at all. Note that the Old Stoics themselves never characterize their reading as "*allēgoria*," a word that only came to prominence centuries later.

Insofar as the Old Stoics were attempting to exhume early thought embedded in later poetic forms, they were engaged in a kind of textual archaeology. Consequently, it should also be emphasized that their interests in archaic poetry—whatever other interests in poetry the Stoics had—are not interests in poetry per se. In fact, the Stoics' archaeological exegetical practices extend to other forms of mythological representation, including painting, statuary, and cult ritual.

Granted this, the key premise of the interpretive practice—that certain poetry and other mythological artifacts preserve primitive cosmological and theological ideas—requires justification. I note the point, but cannot discuss the Stoics' justification for it here.

In the specific case of linguistic archaeological interpretation, etymological interpretation plays a prominent role (cf. Allen 2008)—although, it must be stressed, not an exclusive one. For example, Zeno interprets Hesiod's Chaos as water on the (dubious) grounds that the word "*chaos*" derives from "*chusis*" or "*cheësthai*" (*SVF* 1.103, 104). Observe further that the theoretical significance of etymology vis-à-vis the practice of textual archaeology is consonant with the broader theory of the gradual development and departure of human thought from a primordial conceptual clarity and core.

At the origin of language lies a set of semantic primitives (*prōta onomata*) (*SVF* 2.146). All other words derive from these by various phonetic and semantic transformations. These linguistic transformations accordingly encode a record of conceptual development, corruption, and obscuration. Etymological techniques thus serve to recover the ideas and meanings of the first speakers. For example—to return to the Zenonian testimonies on *Th*—a central corruption has involved the personalization and anthropomorphization of the primordial elements, key features of Hesiod's *Th*.

Generalizing from the case of proper and common nouns, similar transformations and corruptions have occurred in early accounts of cosmic or natural events. In view of such cases, textual archaeology may be applied not merely to the names of mythological divinities or to natural kinds, but to historical processes. Even in the case of the Zenonian testimonies, Hesiod's divinities are not merely identified with cosmic elements; their genetic sequence is identified with the cosmogenesis of the elements.

Observe finally that while the Stoics' textual archaeological and etymological theories and practices clearly rest on large and controversial ideas, in certain respects they echo a common philosophical theme running from the Pythagoreans to Plato to the Cynics to Epicurus: traditional culture manifests psychological corruptions; philosophy endeavors to purify the mind and to redirect motivation and action.

Cleanthes

Cleanthes engaged with many archaic poets and in fact maintained that poetry is the most appropriate form of theological expression (*SVF* 1.486, 487; Thom 2005: 5–6). Hence it is implausible that he ignored Hesiod. One testimony reports that, like Chrysippus, Cleanthes tried to accommodate (*sunoikeioun*) Hesiod's account of the gods and his own beliefs (*SVF* I.123.13). However, there is no testimony regarding any specific reading Cleanthes made of Hesiod.

There are, however, several echoes of Hesiod in Cleanthes's *Hymn to Zeus*. For instance, verses 18–19, which characterize Zeus as knowing how to "make the uneven even" and "to put into order the disorderly," are comparable to Hesiod's description of Zeus's administration of justice at *WD* 5–9. Likewise at verse 12—"you guide straight universal reason"—Cleanthes's use of the verb *kateuthneis* echoes Hesiod's use of *ithunei*, also applied to Zeus, at *WD* 7 (cf. Asmis 2007: 416). Generally speaking, as Johan Thom remarks, "Zeus' ability to level out differences is . . . an ancient motif . . . found in authors like Hesiod and Solon" (2005: 23).

Chrysippus

The evidence for Chrysippus is better. We have about twelve or thirteen testimonies or fragments in which Chrysippus refers to Hesiod's *Th* and *WD*.[6] Most of these derive from Galen's lengthy discussion of Chrysippus's *On the Soul*, in which the doctor remarks that Chrysippus filled his book with verses from Homer, Hesiod, and Stesichorus, among other poets (*SVF* 2.907.31–34).

In the lengthy fragment from *On the Soul*, Chrysippus cites Hesiod about five times in support of the thesis that the heart is the locus of the mind (*hēgemonikon*) (*SVF* 2.906). Setting aside what Galen regards as the dubious evidential worth of such poetic citations, he treats three of these critically on the grounds that Chrysippus appeals to emotions such as anger "in the breast" (*eni stēthessi*). In this case, the Platonist objects that since the soul is tripartite, the location of the emotions, but not the mind, is the chest or heart. In other words, Chrysippus is simply begging the question. Accordingly, Galen argues that Chrysippus should have limited his citations to those in which Hesiod mentions mind, intelligence, thought, or reason in the heart.

In considering Chrysippus's citations that do appeal in this way, Galen cites and discusses a long passage in which the Stoic interprets Hesiodic verses concerning the birth of Athena.[7] Note that while the portion of Chrysippus's interpretation that survives is allegorical in the weak sense, it does not explicitly employ etymological interpretation.

Prima facie, the passage actually provides support against Chrysippus's thesis, for the birth of Athena, here explicitly identified with wisdom, is from the head of Zeus. However, Chrysippus interprets the text in defense of his thesis as follows: Zeus first swallowed Metis, here identified as a sort of practical wisdom and craft of living (*SVF*

2.909). This description is treated as symbolic (*sumbolou*) of the idea that the crafts must be "swallowed and stored up within us." Following this acquisition, intelligent speech is produced "through the mouth by way of the head." In other words, the birth of Athena is symbolic of the generation of intelligent speech. In short, Chrysippus appeals to Hesiod here in defense of a certain psychophysiological thesis.

Most of Chrysippus's remaining references derive from Plutarch. In *On the Principle of Cold*, Plutarch cites Chrysippus as a proponent of the view that air is the source of cold, hence with regard to a cosmological and specifically elemental thesis. An argument Chrysippus advances for the thesis is that since fire is warm and bright, its opposite must be cold and dark. In support of his claim, he cites passages from both *WD* and *Th* (*SVF* 2.430; cf. 2.429). The latter also makes an etymological appeal: "to shake and shiver with cold is to 'tartarize' (*tartarizein*)" (cf. *SVF* 2.563).

In all of his remaining citations from Hesiod, Chrysippus cites from Hesiod's *WD*. For example, Stobaeus preserves a maxim from Chrysippus in which verses 410 and 413 are cited in support of the view that the wise man does not procrastinate (*SVF* 3.163.29–36). And in *On Stoic Contradictions*, Plutarch has Chrysippus in book 1 of his treatise *On Justice* citing *WD* 242–43 in support of the thesis that Zeus punishes misdeeds in order to warn and dissuade people from committing future infractions (*SVF* 2.337.35–41). Broadly speaking, the contexts of these and all remaining citations (*SVF* 2.31.37–43, 3.33.32) are ethical, even if the details of their original contexts and hence Chrysippus's intentions are obscure.

The Middle Stoics

Like the Old Stoics, most if not all of the Middle Stoics engaged with the poets. But there is little evidence among them of engagement with Hesiod. For instance, there is nothing in Zeno of Tarsus, Antipater of Tarsus, or Panaetius, let alone even more fragmentary members of the school. Diogenes of Babylon and perhaps Posidonius are exceptions.

In his discussion of Chrysippus's interpretation of Hesiod's account of the birth of Athena, Galen mentions that some (*tines*) objectors locate the mind in the head (*SVF* 2.908). Galen does not identify these others. But a passage from Philodemus's *On Piety* cites a passage from Diogenes of Babylon's work *On Athena* in which Chrysippus's interpretation is contrasted with that of other Stoics who locate the mind in the head (*SVF* 3. 33 Diogenes Babylon).

A direct reference to Hesiod by Diogenes occurs in book 4 of Philodemus's *On Music*, in which Diogenes's theory of music is Philodemus's central target of criticism. The context of the reference is a discussion of the value or disvalue of traditional poetry as an accompaniment to music. Philodemus cites Diogenes in favor of the value: "Even the ignorant have professional musicians at their banquets . . . but they fail in their purpose because they do not have Homer, Hesiod and other epic and lyric poets. One should recognize the superiority of those banquets which call on the ornaments of these poets" (131.4–13 Delattre).

The fragments of Posidonius contain a more speculative case. Sextus Empiricus reports that "some of the more recent (*neōterōn*) Stoics say that the first, earth-born humans far exceeded humans of the present day in intelligence . . . and that those heroes, whose mental acuity was like a prodigious sense organ, apprehended the divine nature and grasped certain powers of the gods" (*Against the Mathematicians* 9.28). This testimony appears to raise serious problems for the account offered above regarding the Old Stoics' justification for their textual archaeology, for it appears to attribute crucial grounds for this practice only to later, that is Middle, Stoics. I note the problem, but do not pursue it here. Instead, I briefly discuss the referent of Sextus's "more recent Stoics."

In *Epistle* 90 Seneca attributes to Posidonius a view akin to that expressed in Sextus (fr. 254 Edelstein-Kidd). The context in Seneca's letter is the role of philosophy in the development of culture. Seneca discusses Posidonius's view that philosophy existed at the inception of humanity, rejecting this for the view that philosophy arose in response to and as therapy for cultural decline following an initial harmonious period. Observe that for Seneca, as presumably for the Old Stoics, humans of this initial period did not possess, let alone pursue, *sophia* in the strict sense. Instead, true belief governed their lives. In contrast, Posidonius holds that some humans possessed wisdom and that all required philosophy from the beginning. George Boys-Stones, whose account of the development of Stoicism and ancient allegory crucially relies on an interpretation of Posidonius's influence, stresses the role of Posidonius's rejection of Chrysippus's (monistic) psychological theory and with it the idea that "mankind, in its natural, created state, would have no impulse to vice" (2003).

Whether or not we accept Boys-Stones's interpretation, Posidonius's view evidently derives from a historical anthropological context and specifically concerns the golden age. As Seneca writes: "In the era that people call 'golden' (*aureum*) Posidonius holds that sovereignty was in the power of wise men" (*Epistle* 90.5). Hesiod is not explicitly referred to or cited within Seneca's discussion. But given the context, there is some reason to think that Posidonius touched upon, if not engaged, Hesiod's Myth of Ages.

Conclusion to the Stoics

Recall our deferred question above: Why was Zeno—and, we may now add, why were his successors—motivated to engage Hesiod and other poets at all? There cannot be a simple answer to this question, for the Stoics' engagements with the poets were not uniformly motivated. Even so, we can narrow the question: to the extent that they did, why did the Stoics spend time excavating, that is, performing textual archaeology on, certain mythographic poetry?

Various answers have been proposed, and I confess I cannot find compelling evidence in favor of one. The most common view is that the Stoics were seeking support for their doctrines (cf. van Sijl 2010: 135). Assuming this was so, such support might be construed as authoritative insofar as it was understood ultimately to derive from the pure insights of primitive humanity. Alternatively, it might be construed as merely persuasive (*pithanon*), that is, corroborating independent philosophical arguments the Stoics adduced.

Ilaria Ramelli grants that this sort of explanation might have been important for the founder of Stoicism, but she argues that if it were the sole justification for Stoic exegesis, the practice should have declined as the school established itself. In fact, the practice of textual archaeology increased (2011: 340). Consequently, Ramelli suggests the following alternative: Chrysippus in particular, and also later Stoics, were attempting to construct a broad cultural synthesis based on the unity of the Logos that providentially governs and orders the cosmos. In support of her proposal, Ramelli cites a passage from book 2 of Chrysippus *On Gods*, which is preserved in a section of Aëtius's *Placita* devoted to the question whence humans derive their conception of gods. Chrysippus claims that the beauty and order of the stars and the cosmos inspired humans with the idea of gods; he continues: "Those who have handed down the worship of the gods have presented it to us in three forms: first in the physical form, second in the mythical form, and third in the form to which laws bear witness. Now the physical form is taught by the philosophers, the mythical by the poets, and the legislative is always established by each city" (*SVF* 2.1009).

To be sure, Chrysippus here states how divinity is variously represented in diverse facets of culture; given the unity of the Logos, these various representations ought to be unified in some way. But Chrysippus does not indicate why philosophers ought to busy themselves with nonphilosophical representations, let alone seek to clarify their consistency with philosophical views.

The basic problem is that while we have some evidence of the Stoics' exegetical practice, we lack anything like direct or explicit evidence regarding the motivation for it. That said, Ramelli's appeal to the unity of the Logos, the synthesis of culture, and—it should be added—the historical anthropology connecting them constitute an attractive explanatory point of departure.

CONCLUSION

The preceding account of the philosophical reception of Hesiod from Aristotle to Posidonius is as much one of reception as of anti-reception and non-reception. I have tried to show how and why the philosophers received Hesiod as well as why they rejected or ignored him.

In the introduction I emphasized the disunity of the account and its specific grounds: evidential and philosophical theoretical. In the wake of the discussion, the degree and character of this disunity should be clear. Such a result may not be aesthetically pleasing or in some respects intellectually satisfying, but insofar as it is a faithful record, it is intellectually responsible.

This is the first study devoted to the philosophical reception of Hesiod from Aristotle to the end of the Hellenistic period. The issues raised here are wide-ranging and complicated. Almost every paragraph, often each sentence, could be developed into an article or more. Among the loose threads and dangling questions, I hope to have provided some framework or orientation from which further inquiry may fruitfully proceed.

Notes

1. For Liz Asmis, whose papers on Hellenistic aesthetics (1990a, 1990b, 1991, 1995, 2007, 2017, unpublished manuscript) provided some of the central scaffolding for the present work.

2. Some, e.g., Janko (1987), have thought that book 2 discussed didactic poetry, but cf. Volk (2002: 26–34).

3. *Physics* 208b29, 31; *On the Heavens* 298b28; *Metaphysics* 984b28, 989a10, 1000a9; *Nicomachean Ethics* 1095b9; *Politics* 1252b10, 1312b4; *Rhetoric* 1388a17. The reference at *History of Animals* 601b2 is probably a corruption of "Ἡρόδοτος." In his *Constitution of the Orchomenians* (fr. 8.44.565 Rose), Aristotle discusses Hesiod's exhumation and reburial.

4. I understand Aristotle's distinctions among *theologos, physiologos, philosophos*, and poet basically as follows. A *theologos* presents accounts of the traditional Greek gods and their roles in nature and cosmology in traditional (i.e., in anthropomorphic terms). Aristotle principally identifies *theologoi* with archaic poets and explicitly includes Homer and Hesiod among them (*Metaphysics* 983b28–32, 1000a9). A *physiologos* presents natural and cosmological accounts without appealing to traditional Greek gods in anthropomorphic terms. For example, Aristotle explicitly refers to the following as *physiologoi*: Anaximander (*Physics* 203b15), Empedocles (*Eudemian Ethics* 1235a10–11), Anaxagoras (*On the Generation of Animals* 763b31), Democritus, and Leucippus (*Physics* 213b1). Aristotle clearly distinguishes Hesiod from *physiologoi* at *On the Heavens* 298b29. A *philosophos* presents theoretical and practical theses, which he buttresses using proofs and advances for the sake of knowledge and its exercise. A poet presents mimetic accounts, which are typically both in verse and in nonphysiological terms. For example, Aristotle claims that Empedocles, although he versifies, is a *physiologos*, not a poet (*Poetics* 1447b18–20).

5. I note two additional occurrences, in Philodemus's *On Music*, book 4, fr. 31.39 and fr. 131.10, one of which I discuss below.

6. *SVF* 2.1175 (re *WD* 242), 2.430 (re *WD* 255), 2.100 (re *WD* 348), 2.430 (re *Th* 119), 2.908 (re *Th* 641), 2.908 (re fr. 317, 318 Merkelbach-West, fr. dub. 69 Merkelbach-West), 2.908 (re *Th* 886–929).

7. It is questionable whether the verses were in fact composed by Hesiod or are a later adaptation. Cf. *Th* 886–929.

References

Algra, K. 2001. "Comments or Commentary? Zeno of Citium and Hesiod's *Theogonia*." *Mnemosyne* 54: 562–81.

Allen, J. 2008. "The Stoics on the Origin of Language and the Foundations of Etymology." In *Language and Learning: Philosophy of Language in the Hellenistic Age*, edited by D. Frede and B. Inwood, 14–35. Cambridge.

Asmis, E. 1990a. "The Poetic Theory of the Stoic 'Aristo." *Apeiron* 23: 147–202.

Asmis, E. 1990b. "Philodemus' Epicureanism." *Aufstieg und Niedergang der römischen Welt II* 36 (4): 2369–2406.

Asmis, E. 1991. "Philodemus' Poetic Theory and *On the Good King According to Homer*." *Classical Antiquity* 10: 1–45.

Asmis, E. 1995. "Epicurean Poetics." In *Philodemus and Poetry: Poetic Theory and Practice in Lucretius, Philodemus, and Horace*, edited by D. Obbink, 15–34. Oxford.

Asmis, E. 2007. "Myth and Philosophy in Cleanthes' *Hymn to Zeus*." *Greek Roman and Byzantine Studies* 47: 413–29.

Asmis, E. 2017. "Lucretius' Reception of Epicurus: *De Rerum Natura* as a Conversion Narrative." *Hermes* 144: 439–61.

Asmis, E. n.d. "The Stoics on the Craft of Poetry." Unpublished manuscript.

Betegh, G. 2002. "On Eudemus Fr. 150 (Wehrli)." In *Eudemus of Rhodes*, edited by I. Bodnár and W. W. Fortenbaugh, 337–57. New Brunswick, NJ.

Blank, D. L. 2011. "Reading between the Lies: Plutarch and Chrysippus on the Uses of Poetry." *Oxford Studies in Ancient Philosophy* 40: 237–64.

Blum, R. 1991. *Kallimachos: The Alexandrian Library and the Origins of Bibliography*. Translated by H. A. Wellisch. Madison, WI.

Boys-Stones, R. 2003. "The Stoics' Two Types of Allegory." In *Metaphor, Allegory, and the Classical Tradition*, edited by G. R. Boys-Stones, 189–216. Oxford.

Gale, M. 2013. "Piety, Labor, and Justice in Lucretius and Hesiod." In *Lucretius: Poetry, Philosophy, Science*, edited by D. Lehox, A. D. Morrison, and A. Sharrok, 25–50. Oxford.

Halliwell, S. 1986. *Aristotle's Poetics*. London.

Henrichs, A. 1975. "Philodems De Pietate als mythographische Quelle." *Cronache Ercolanesi* 5: 5–38.

Janko, R., trans. and comm. 1987. *Aristotle Poetics*. Indianapolis, IN.

Janko, R., ed., trans., and comm. 2000. *Philodemus: On Poems*. Book 1. Oxford.

Janko, R., ed., trans., and comm. 2011. *Philodemus: On Poems*. Books 3–4. Oxford.

Long, A. A. 1992. "Stoic Readings of Homer." In *Homer's Ancient Readers*, edited by R. Lamberton and J. J. Keaney, 41–66. Princeton, NJ.

Martano, A. 2004. "Hieronymus ἐν ὑπομνήματι Ἀσπίπος Ἡσιόδου." In *Lyco of Troas and Hieronymus of Rhodes*, edited by W. W. Fortenbaugh and S. White, 457–74. New Brunswick, NJ.

Matelli, E. 2012. "Praxiphanes, Who Is He?" In *Praxiphanes of Mytilene and Chameleon of Heraclea*, edited by A. Martano, E. Matelli, and D. Mirhady, 525–78. New Brunswick, NJ.

Obbink, D. 1995. "How to Read Poetry about the Gods." In *Philodemus and Poetry: Poetic Theory and Practice in Lucretius, Philodemus, and Horace*, edited by D. Obbink, 189–209. Oxford.

Obbink, D. 2004. "Vergil's *De pietate*: From *Ehoiae* to Allegory in Vergil, Philodemus, and Ovid." In *Vergil, Philodemus, and the Augustans*, edited by D. Armstrong, J. Fish, P. A. Johnston, and M. B. Skinner, 175–209. Austin, TX.

Pfeiffer, R. 1968. *History of Classical Scholarship*. Oxford.

Ramelli, I. 2011. "The Philosophical Stance of Allegory in Stoicism and Its Receptions in Platonism, Pagan and Christian: Origen in Dialogue with the Stoics and Plato." *International Journal of the Classical Tradition* 18: 335–71.

Richardson, N. J. 1994. "Aristotle and Hellenistic Scholarship." In *La philologie grecque à l'époque hellénistique et romaine*, edited by F. Montanari, 7–28. Geneva.

Saunders, T. J. 2001. "Dicaearchus' Historical Anthropology." In *Dicaearchus of Messana*, edited by W. W. Fortenbaugh and E. Schütrumpf, 237–54. New Brunswick, NJ.

Sider, D. 1995. "The Epicurean Philosopher as Hellenistic Poet." In *Philodemus and Poetry: Poetic Theory and Practice in Lucretius, Philodemus, and Horace*, edited by D. Obbink, 42–57. Oxford.

Thom, J., ed., trans., and comm. 2005. *Cleanthes' Hymn to Zeus*. Tübingen, Germany.

Tsouna, V., trans. and comm. 2012. *Philodemus, On Property Management*. Atlanta, GA.

van Sijl, C. 2010. "Stoic Philosophy and the Interpretation of Myth." PhD diss., University of Utrecht.

Volk, K. 2002. "'Improbable Art': The Theory and Practice of Ancient Didactic Poetry." In *The Poetics of Latin Didactic: Lucretius, Vergil, Ovid, Manilius*, edited by K. Volk, 25–68. Oxford.

CHAPTER 23

HESIOD, VIRGIL, AND THE GEORGIC TRADITION

STEPHANIE NELSON

ALTHOUGH it is arguably through the tradition of the georgic that Hesiod has had his greatest influence on English poetry, that influence was almost entirely filtered through the very different vision of Virgil. By 1790 Dryden's 1697 translation of the *Georgics* had gone through ten editions (Gillespie 2011: 11), and as Joseph Addison wrote in his enormously influential introduction, "all are unanimous in giving [Virgil] the precedence to Hesiod in his Georgics" (Chalker 1969: 17). In contrast, only three English translations of Hesiod had appeared by 1850, and all referred pointedly to Virgil. George Chapman's 1618 translation, rather defensively, draws attention to passages in which Virgil "even to a word almost recites" out of Hesiod (note to Greek line 289). Nearly half of Thomas Cooke's "A View of the *Works and Days*," appended to his 1728 translation, considers Hesiod's ability to compete with Virgil (pp. 100–110 of 94–115), a topic Charles Elton, in his 1815 translation, treats vehemently: "Addison, with that squeamish artificial taste which distinguishes the age of Anne, as compared with that of Elizabeth, underrates, as might have been expected, the vigorous simplicity of Hesiod. But the strong though simple sketches of the old Ascraean bard are often more striking than the finished paintings of the Mantuan" (lvii). Nonetheless, it is Virgil, and the division he depicts between nature and the human, that later georgics followed.

Although Virgil's *Georgics* works with a great number of sources, from Aratus and Nicophron to Lucretius (Thomas 1988: 4–11; Farrell 1991; Gale 2000), his declaration, "I sing the song of Ascra through Roman towns" (2.176), cited by each of his early English translators, puts Hesiod in a different category. The aim appears to be contrast.[1] Just as the *Aeneid*'s allusions to Homer reveal a very different view of the gods and human society, the concerns of the *Georgics*—questions of peace and war, empire, and force, and doubts about the efficacy of poetry, precisely the concerns that lived on in the English georgic tradition—are marked as particularly Roman in that they do not arise in the *Works and Days* (hereafter *WD*).

For all these differences, however, there are also deep commonalities between the poems. Hesiod's focus on the centralizing power of Zeus is notably absent in Virgil, but the sense that some centralizing force is essential (as well as deeply dangerous) is acute. Similarly, the bleakness and terror of a world without social order and justice appears, if anything, more vividly in the *Georgics* than in the *WD*, and all the more so since the poem lacks Hesiod's sense of a natural conjunction between a cosmic and a human order. And although Virgil does not have Hesiod's tendency to move between elements of the cosmos personified as gods and these same elements embodied in the human world, his poetry, like Hesiod's, is infused with a sense of dynamic powers informing all aspects of human life, particularly the countryside.

It would thus be a mistake to take the *Georgics'* use of either Hesiod or the countryside as merely symbolic, although the Hellenistic view of Hesiod does certainly color Virgil's reference to him (Hunter 2014: 20–25). It would also be mistaken, however, to attempt a literal biographical reading; stories about Virgil's farm and its restoration by Augustus, largely read back from the *Eclogues* into Virgil's "biography," remain only stories, an element of the poetry and not its explanation. And finally, neither poem, as has long been understood, teaches one how to farm. This does not mean that the poems are not actually about farming. Both are deeply about farming, because in both farming reveals the place of the human within a greater whole. Where the poems differ is in what that place is. For Virgil, the human relation to nature is deeply problematic. For Hesiod, as in the joke about the fish who asks what water is, humans are so firmly part of nature that it hardly exists as a separate entity.

Hesiod's sense of both farming and nature appears immediately in his poetics of naming. As has been noted in this volume (see the Introduction, p. 4 and chapter 6, pp. 84–92), Hesiodic poetry is marked by an extensive use of personification, amplified by the use of personified words as common nouns and in their verbal and adjectival forms. Earth, the mother of the gods, is also for Hesiod the earth he plows; *Dikē* or Justice, the goddess who sits beside her father, Zeus, imbues all that is *dikaios* or "just" and is also the particular *dikē*, or "lawsuit" that Perses perverted to get the family farm. The technique extends even to the Olympian gods. Wine is the gift of Dionysus (*WD* 614) and grain that of Demeter (*WD* 32, 466, 597, etc.); the carpenter is the "servant of Athena," whose realm is wisdom and craft (430); and Aphrodite is the destiny of the young girl still at her mother's side (*WD* 521). Farming is for Hesiod the distinctive way that Zeus has set out for human beings to interact with the world, and it is a world shot through with the divine.

The *WD* takes not farming, but rather justice and Zeus, as its subject. Farming comes in as the background, marked as all the more crucial because it is simply assumed. By line 33 Hesiod has declared that when you have enough in the barn for a year (and good luck with that), you can waste your time in the agora. Until then stick to your proper concern, "the grain of Demeter" (*WD* 32). As he points out, with withering logic, if Zeus had meant us not to work, he could have arranged things so that we would work for a day and have enough for a year (*WD* 43–44). But he didn't. He hid *bios*, and he and the gods hold it close (WD 42). To "let the works of the oxen go hang, and of the laboring mules" (*WD* 46) is not, it turns out, an option for men.

Even before we get here, however, farming has already entered the picture, in the description of the good Eris, which Zeus placed "in the roots of the earth" (WD 18–19) and in the envied, wealthy neighbor "who hastens to plow and to plant" (WD 22). Farming underlies Hesiod's puns on *bios*, "life" and "livelihood," and *erga*, both the "works" of men (and oxen) and the "fields" that are their locus, and it informs the "hiding" (*WD* 42, 47, 50) that recalls seed "hidden" in the earth.[2] In Hesiod's just city prosperity stems from the "well cared for fields (*erga*)" (*WD* 231). Even in his golden age, before Zeus was running things, when the ideal of a life without work was realized, Hesiod's imagination does not run to honey dripping from the leaves or rivers flowing with wine, as Virgil's does (*Georgics* 1.131–32)—or even to clear-flowing brooks and fruit dropping off the branches. For Hesiod, the men of the golden age were "rich in sheep" (*WD* 120) and "at leisure tended their *erga*," which produced grain all on their own (*WD* 117–18; see West 1978: 181). There was still farming. The difference is that back then it was effortless.

The assumption that farming is the essential condition of human life continues throughout the poem, intertwined with all its topics. In the section on right behavior we learn that "if one's neighbor was not bad, not even a cattle-beast would be lost" (*WD* 348), and that one should be wary of a cajoling woman—she is after your barn (*WD* 374). The list of best days include when to shear sheep, castrate cattle, or winnow the grain (*WD* 775, 790–91, 805–7). And as the sections on right behavior assume farming, so the section on the farmer's year includes the right way to treat one's neighbor, servants, and oxen and the need to be prepared, to rise early, to avoid wasting time, to be sparing, and even, occasionally, to rest. It includes the lust of women (and the fatigue of men) (*WD* 585), the servant with a child of her own (*WD* 402), the slave boy just old enough to hoe (*WD* 469), the idlers in the blacksmith's shop (*WD* 493), the young plowman hankering after his mates (*WD* 447), and the voyager on the road (*WD* 580). Each must be treated in the proper way, and farming presupposes them all.

Nor is the world of farming limited to the world of men. The structure of the farming section, from the setting of the Pleiades and the need to plow (*WD* 383), through the seasons and the seasons' tasks, to the next year's setting of the Pleiades (*WD* 615), creates a whole that integrates the yearly passage of stars, seasons, birds, beasts, and plants with the yearly cycle of the farmer's tasks. The elements of the cycle range from the enormous to the minute, from the beasts of the wild (*WD* 529–33) to the "house-carrier" (the snail, *WD* 571), from the octopus "in his sunless home and dismal haunts" (*WD* 525) to the cranes (*WD* 448), from the golden thistle (*WD* 581) to Orion (*WD* 598), and from the jagged-toothed dog (*WD* 604) to Boreas (*WD* 506).

As I have argued elsewhere, Hesiod has his audience imaginatively re-experience this cycle in order to reveal, at its center, the will of Zeus (Nelson 1998; see Beall 2004). The role of the gods here also reveals the connection of the *WD* to the *Theogony* (hereafter *Th*) and the importance of Hesiod's poetics of personification. Boreas, Orion, the Pleiades, Ouranos (or Sky), Demeter, the rainfall of Zeus, the skill of Athena's handyman, and most fundamental of all, Earth herself, each play a defining role in the fundamental rhythm. Nor, in Hesiod's regular method of personification, are Dikē and Hybris absent, or Eris, Give and Grab, Rumor, or, behind all, the Horae or Seasons of the *Th*, that "look over (*horeousi*) the *erga* for mortals" (*Th* 903). And at the center of the order, as at the center of the order of divine *timae* ("honors") that constitutes the cosmos, is Zeus (Clay 2003: 140–49). Perses can tend to the farm, and so adapt to this order, or he can try to defy it. The choice is his, although if he chooses the latter, the poet does not think much of his chances.

While Virgil's *Georgics* clearly signals its connection to Hesiod, it also makes a point of the differences. Hesiod opens with his attack on the "gift-gobbling kings" (*WD* 39); Virgil introduces the relation of poet and ruler by systematically dedicating each book to Maecenas (1.2, 2.41, 3.41, 4.2) and by addressing Augustus (then Octavian) with the attitude that such a dedication implies. Hesiod depicts a contemporary world and a contemporary farm. Exactly by adopting that same farm, Virgil distances himself from the *latifundia* of his own times, huge slave-run agricultural estates owned by patricians legally disbarred from investing in business (Perkell 1989: 29; Mynors 1990: v; Thibodeau 2011: 5–6). And where Hesiod brings in farming as the background for his poem on justice, Virgil introduces his poem as being about "what makes the crops happy, with which star to turn / the earth, and when it suits to join / the vines to elms . . ." (1.1–2) and brings in questions of justice through the back door.

The pattern appears also in the relation of the poet and the poem. Like Hesiod (*Th* 22), Virgil names himself at the end of the *Georgics* (4.463), the only time he does so in his poetry. And as Hesiod linked the *WD* and *Th* by recalling how the Muses made him a poet (*Th* 22–34; *WD* 654–59), Virgil ends the *Georgics* with the first line of his earlier poem, the *Eclogues* (4.566). Moreover, just as the *Eclogues* flirted with including the poet's life in the poem, the *Georgics*' first-person narrator, like Hesiod, acknowledges himself to be a poet (3.1–48, 4.559–66) and claims a direct, personal involvement in what he describes: "Often I myself, while the farmer was leading the reaper / into his yellow fields, and even now stripping the barley from the brittle stalk, / I have seen all the winds rush together in battle . . ." (1.316–18; see 1.451, 1.193, etc.); "For I remember, under the towers of Oebalia's stronghold, / where the black Galaesus waters its golden fields, / I saw an old Corycian . . ." (4.125–27). Hesiod, however, united the roles of farmer and poet, depicting his poetry, grounded as it is in Zeus's order, as more effective than the crooked words of the kings (*WD* 258–64, etc.). Virgil instead contrasts himself, the singer, to "great Caesar," the man of action (4.559–66), and depicts himself as an observer rather than a participant, distant from the objects of his observation. And so he follows his famous image of the "happy husbandman" (2.458–74) with a reflection—"But for me, first of all may the sweet Muses / whose rites I bear, struck by great love, / accept me . . ." (2.475–77)—that explicitly opposes himself to the farmers he is idealizing.

But the most extreme difference between the *WD* and the *Georgics* lies in Virgil's many different images of farming. Although the *WD* can appear haphazard, its disparate elements all point to the single will of Zeus, just as the contrasting depictions of cold and heat, labor and relaxation, haste and leisure reveal the farmer's year, progressing in the regular order of Zeus's Seasons. In contrast, behind the *Georgics*' regular and programmatic sequence of topics—crops (Bk. 1); trees (Bk. 2); cattle and horses, then sheep and goats (Bk. 3); and finally bees (Bk. 4)—lies a wild and apparently erratic variation in the way farming, and with it, human life, is viewed. In Book 1, which ends with Virgil's despairing view of the civil wars, the work of the farmer, fighting against constant degeneration, is like that of a man struggling to row upstream against the tide (1.199–203). In Book 2, in contrast, "the most just earth herself, far from discordant arms, / pours from her soil an easy livelihood" (2.458–60). In Book 3, which ends with an apocalyptic vision of plague, farming varies from African herdsmen contending with the heat to Scythians buried in ice and snow, and from the ruthless elimination of an aging stallion (3.95–96), to the tender care of young foals (3.174–78), to muzzling kids to keep them from their mother's milk (3.398–99). Finally, in Book 4 Virgil's bees themselves become tiny farmers, now in peace and harmony (4.51–66), now abandoning their work in rage for battle (4.67–85), now dire enemies of the farmer (4.228–38), now allies (4.239–50), and now with their mini-civilization in ruins (4.251–63).

The difference lies not in the farm, which Virgil adopts from the WD, but in what the farm is asked to convey. For Hesiod, the farm is part of a continuous whole. In the *Georgics*, where nature and man have become divided, the farm is part of a radically split vision that ranges from a pastoral world of peace and harmony to a violent realm of war. In both cases, the contrast to Hesiod stands out.

In the case of the pastoral, Virgil incorporates a major shift in poetry itself. As we saw above, the *Georgics'* last lines remind us of the *Eclogues*, recalling the relation of the *Th* and *WD*. The difference is that Hesiod moves from the *Th* to the *WD* without any change in genre. For Virgil, in contrast, the shepherding of the *Eclogues* is part of a poetic genre, the pastoral, which implies an ideal of harmony opposed to the politics, warfare, suffering, and labor, including the labor of the farm, of the *Georgics* (Coleman 1977: 1–14; Halperin 1983). For Hesiod, shepherding is another kind of farm work; in the *Georgics*, the closer the farm gets to the pastoral, the further it gets from itself.

And likewise with war: Virgil again fractures his Hesiodic model. Although the bad Eris who opens the *WD* "fosters evil war and conflict" (*WD* 14), Hesiod's focus soon shifts to the agora, lawsuits, and cheating, and war fades into the mythic past as the livelihood of the bronze race and the heroes. In the *Georgics*, in contrast, war is real and immediate. And, as in the pastoral, poet and farmer are both opposed to war and identified with it. Virgil's description of himself "singing the song of Ascra through Roman towns" (2.176) follows a Hesiodic catalog of names—but they are the names of Roman warriors and generals, culminating with Caesar (2.166–73). Virgil's promise that his next poem will describe Caesar's triumphs (3.16–41) brings the poet closer to war, but also sets himself, as a poet of nature, against Caesar, who "thunders in war beside the deep Euphrates" (4.560–61). The images of pruning hooks beaten into swords, of plowmen unearthing the bones of Romans (1.493–97), and of farmers made into soldiers as their land lies abandoned and desolate oppose the farm to war. But farming is also itself a form of warfare, with its own arms, enemies, and battalions (1.160; 2.279–84), and while Virgil's farmer can appear as a pastoral figure, enjoying "the fruits that trees, that the willing fields themselves / bear of their own accord" (2.501–2), he is also a warrior, "at his post to discipline the ground, and give his orders to the fields" (1.97–99, trans. Fairclough).[3]

Virgil is nothing if not attuned to the nuance of language. It is inconceivable, for example, that he replaced Hesiod's Horkos, "Oath," with the far more sinister Orcus, a Roman god of the Underworld, without noticing (1.277–78). Nor is it a chance of vocabulary that Virgil's *labor* implies not fields and industry, as *erga* does, but struggle, suffering, and pain. This sort of difference, the parallel that, when pushed, opens into something critically out of sync, characterizes the *Georgics*. It appears in Virgil's gods, peaceful deities, "the rural gods, / Pan, old Silvanus and the sisterhood of Nymphs" (2.493–94), juxtaposed to the underlying violence of Bacchus (2.454–57); in Justice, leaving her last footsteps amid pious farmers, but still gone (2.473–74); and in Virgil's invocation of a golden age, recalling as well Saturn's expulsion by Jove (4.536–40).[4] This is also the world of Virgil's farm. On the one hand Virgil's is a world as far-reaching as Hesiod's, and often even more charming. His "tiny mouse / under the earth sets up his home and makes his storehouse" (1.181–82); his ant fears "an impoverished old age" (1.186); sea birds play in the waves like carefree children (1.383–85); one must spare the vines' tenderness "while they grow up, their first youth budding with new leaves" (2.362–63); and the serpent "fresh, with old skin sloughed off, gleaming and young / rolls on" (3.437–78). But for all this, the creatures of Virgil's farm are not, as Hesiod's, pursuing their seasonal course as the farmer pursues his. Rather, they are plundering the farm, threatening the farmer, furthering a harsh opposition of interests, or reveling in the conditions that may annihilate the farm.

Virgil's divided vision may be summed up in his account of how farming began. The *WD* offers no reason why human life degenerated after the golden age. Hesiod sees that Zeus means life to be hard, and that is all he needs to know. Virgil's account seems at first more hopeful. Here the hardship of life is due not to divine whim, but to Jupiter's realization that work is needed to sharpen men's wits (1.121–24). But as Virgil's account of the golden age focuses on peace and harmony rather than on ease, as Hesiod's does, the change involves not just hardship, but imbalance, distance, distrust, and violence. The result is captured in the famous line, and its equally famous (if often omitted) enjambment, that sums up this section: *labor omnia vicit / improbus* ("work conquered all / dire work," 1.145–46). The line implies a potential division between human beings and nature unknown to Hesiod.[5] It is in this direction that English georgic poetry went.

The first three translations of the *WD* into English appeared, quite neatly, at the rate of one per century, all in heroic couplets (for which see Wolfe in this volume, on Hesiod in the Renaissance). In 1618 Chapman, who had moved from the fourteeners of his *Iliad* to pentameters in the *Odyssey*, completed the trio of Homer, Musaeus, and Hesiod (MacLure 1963: 174) with a translation of the *WD*, notably entitled "The Georgicks of Hesiod." Translations of the *WD* and *Th* by Thomas Cooke followed in 1715 (2nd ed. 1728), and Charles Elton published the *WD*, *Th*, and *Shield of Heracles* in 1815 (doing the *Th* and *Shield* in blank verse, but the *WD* in couplets).

Significantly, all three of Hesiod's translators are interested less in nature or farming than in the ethical and the divine, interests that will finally place all three outside of the

English georgic tradition. Chapman does not mention either farming or nature in his introductory "Of Hesiodos," but rather classes Hesiod with the philosophers, describing his "*Axioms* or *Oracles*" (italics in original) as "all teaching good life, and humanitie. . . . Here beeing no dwelling on any one subject; but of all humane affaires instructively concluded." Cooke sees the farming section as included so that Perses "may not be tired with his precepts, because of a too much sameness" (liv), while Elton's summary of the "Argument" ("The poem comprehends the general economy of industry and morals") devotes 44 lines to *WD* 1–380 and 11 to the remaining 450 lines, including "the Georgical part of his subject."

Chapman in particular, although he came to the translation as a follow-up to Homer, suited Hesiod perfectly, largely due to his own general pessimism and Stoic vision (Low 1985: 114; MacLure 1963: 172–82; Presson 1969: 44–50). While Hesiod might have been surprised at some of Chapman's Christianizing interpretations, his epigram to the *WD*—*Nec caret umbra Deo* ("It does not lack the shadow of God," Statius 4.425; capitalization Chapman's)—points to his sympathy with Hesiod's view of the world. As Gary Wills puts it: "The 'cosmologizing' of man in the Renaissance made the easy communication between Homer's gods and his heroes something that Chapman could take with entire seriousness." And the conjunction between man and the universe that the Elizabethan "mix of science, magic, astronomy and theology" gave rise to worked just as well with the *WD* as it did with Homer (Wills 1998: vii–viii).[6]

That Chapman thought Hesiod theologically relevant is already clear from his epigram and title, which describes the "Days" as "not superstitious, but necessarie (as farre as naturall causes compell) for all men to observe." The same interest also appears in his expansions of Hesiod's Greek. For Hesiod's initial lines (*WD* 1–3):

> Μοῦσαι Πιερίηθεν ἀοιδῇσι κλείουσαι,
> δεῦτε Δί᾽ ἐννέπετε, σφέτερον πατέρ᾽ ὑμνείουσαι.
> ὅν τε διὰ βροτοὶ ἄνδρες ὁμῶς ἄφατοί τε φατοί τε . . .

> Muses, from Pieria, glorifying in songs
> come here, tell of Zeus, your father, hymning [him]
> through whom mortal men are both not-spoken and spoken of . . .

Chapman gives us (with additions underlined):

> Muses! That out of your Pierean state,
> All worth, in sacred Numbers celebrate;
> Use here your faculties so much renownd,
> To sing your sire; And him in hymns resound;
> By whom, All humanes, that to death are bound,
> Are bound together: Both the Great in fame;
> And Men, whose Poore Fates fitt them, with no Name . . . [.]

Similarly, in a transmutation that is beyond underlining, Hesiod's injunction to Zeus at *WD* 9–10—

κλῦθι ἰδὼν ἀίων τε, δίκη δ᾽ ἴθυνε θέμιστας
τύνη· ἐγὼ δέ κε Πέρσῃ ἐτήτυμα μυθησαίμην.

Hear, seeing and listening, and with justice straighten the decrees,
on your part; and for me, I will declare to Perses the very truth.

—becomes in Chapman:

> Heare then, O *Ioue,* that dost both see and heare;
> And, for thy Justice sake, Be Orderer,
> To these just Praecepts; that in Prophecy;
> I use; to teach my Brother Pietie[.]

Where the original Hesiod aims at truth, Chapman's teaches piety. Both would agree, however, that the two are fundamentally linked, which may be the most important point.[7]

All of Hesiod's early translators are, like Chapman, interested in the theological and moral, although they express this interest very differently. Chapman, in good Neoplatonic fashion, works through allegory. Cooke, in 1728, rationalizes (his five ages, for example, are not created by the gods but simply "appear") and points regularly to biblical parallels. Elton, in 1815, has an anthropological interest in the relation of the Greek and Hebrew traditions.[8] The three also use these various approaches to address theological difficulties. Elton, for example, points out, "It would appear extraordinary that the crime of Prometheus, who was a god, should be visited on man." He concludes that Prometheus was rather "a deified mortal" and suggests that this mortal, "the maker of man according to Ovid, and his divine benefactor according to Hesiod," may "be in reality Noah" (xciii). Cooke, in contrast, takes Prometheus as signifying a period of time when men, grown "*more cunning, more apt to contrive,*" "departed from their primitive temperance, and consequently their serenity" (n69; emphasis in original). But for Chapman, Prometheus simply stands for man's overweening pride; Epimetheus for "Mans corporeall part" that refuses to obey reason; and Woman for appetite, which strives to get the better of reason and lead it into sin (n29).[9]

There remains, however, a fundamental distinction between Chapman on the one hand and Cooke and Elton on the other. Unlike Cooke and Elton, for whom parts of the *WD* are simply superstitious, for Chapman even Hesiod's "Days" reveal the conjunction of man and nature, "for it were madnesse, not to ascribe Reason to Nature; or to make that Reason so farre above us, that we cannot know by it, what is daily in use with us; all beeing for our cause created of God" (note to Greek line 765). Chapman Christianizes Hesiod as a matter of course, regularly using a general "God" (avoided by both Cooke and Elton) for Hesiod's divinities, and, suggestively, repeating the word "love," which bears a strong iconographic similarity to his spelling of Jove as "Ioue." And although his supreme god creates Earth, rather than being descended from her, Chapman no more divides the "natural" from the "man-made" than Hesiod does.

After Chapman, however, the link between farming and civilization that would come to be assumed by English georgic poetry, and that is as basic as the words "culture" or "cultivation" (Low 1985: 8–9), would also set that tradition off from Hesiod. For Hesiod, living at a time when the Greek polis was in its infancy, farming is simply the way human beings live, the *nomos* determined by Zeus. Although the coming money economy appears in his inducement to respect the gods, "so that you might buy the farm of another, and not he yours" (*WD* 341), and although his section on sailing is informed by the (dangerous) potential of commerce, for Hesiod human *bios* still comes, finally and necessarily, from the earth. While Chapman can share the sense of integration this understanding implies, along with the religious certitude that accompanies it, the age that gave rise to georgic poetry in Britain was to find meaning less in the gods and the earth, and more in human labor and the empire (Low 1985: 354–57).

For while translations of the *WD* focused on the theological, the English georgic was heading in a different direction, toward an interest in work and national identity. In Chapman's case, most of the trends that were to build into English georgic poetry had not yet occurred. As Low notes: "Even given Chapman's interest in Greek, it seems significant that he chose to translate Hesiod's *WD* rather than Virgil's *Georgics*, for Hesiod has none of Virgil's sense that labor may contribute to national progress" (1985: 114). Cooke, in contrast, wrote during the Augustan heyday of English georgic poetry, which included Philip's "Cyder" (1708), Gay's "Rural Sports" (1720), Pope's "Windsor Forest" (1717), Thomson's "The Seasons" (1730), and Dyer's "The Fleece" (1757), while Elton, who was friendly with both Coleridge and Charles Lamb, was closer to the Romantic than the Augustan age.[10] But while both comment on the power of Hesiod's vignettes of nature, with Elton choosing passages such as Chapman's depictions of plowing (*WD* 465–78), of winter (*WD* 504–35), and of a summer picnic (*WD* 588–608) to include in an appendix to his translation, neither translator seems particularly interested in labor or politics, the two hallmarks of English georgic poetry.

Virgil, in contrast, was interested in both. He was also extremely popular. While Chapman's editor, Richard Hooper, comments in 1888 on the "extreme rarity" of his translation of the *WD* (xi–ii), Gillespie notes that between 1550 and 1800 there were over 103 translations of Virgil, and some 15 or 16 of the *Georgics* alone (2011: 4).[11] There are various reasons for Virgil's precedence over Hesiod. As Latin was more commonly studied, the skill of a translation from Latin was more easily appreciated (see Gillespie 2011: 11–12). The English Augustan Age also identified itself with Rome rather than Greece and with ideals of judgment and adaptation rather than of originality. But most importantly, English georgic poetry had a strong interest in empire (Williams 1973; O'Brien 1999; Rogers 2005; Irvine 2009) and in civil war (Chalker 1969: 10, 109, 208; Low 1985: 10–12, 124, 294–95; Fowler 1986; Schoenberg 2015). Prepared by a seventeenth-century "georgic revolution," in which a move from aristocratic to commercial power placed a new value on labor (Low 1985), the union of England and Scotland in 1701 and the resulting emergence of "Great Britain" as a nation, exhibiting its economic and military power on a world stage, found in Virgil a natural model (Crawford 2002: 93; Wilkinson 1969: 299–301). Pastoral and georgic poetry had played out a long history centered on the importance of labor, which had landed firmly on the side of the georgic (Pellicer in Hopkins and Martindale 2012: 287–322). That focus now had very new associations. As Irvine argues, Locke's association of labor with the basic right of property and with the benefit that comes from the use of property connected the georgic tradition first to commerce and then to nationhood and empire (2009: 971).

In addition, the English georgic tradition shares with Virgil an interest in nature as such and therefore in the possibility of a division between nature and man (Pellicer 2007). This appears even in an aspect of georgic poetry that seems initially closer to Hesiod, the tendency, from Edmund Spenser's 1579 "The Shepherd's Calendar," to Alexander Pope's "Pastorals" (1709), to James Thomson's "The Seasons" (1730), to James Grahame's "British Georgics" (1809), to Vita Sackville-West's "The Land" (1926), to organize by the season, a tendency also influenced by the medieval "Book of Hours," which invariably opened with a calendar. As in the *WD*, the structure grounds nature in a fundamental order, but now one also associated with the Bible's "seedtime and harvest, and cold and heat, and summer and winter" (Gen. 8.22; Eccles. 3.1–2) and with human labor as the mark of our division from nature in Eden. As in Virgil, nature varies, as do human concerns, but it also is separated from the human. Hesiod, in contrast, would recognize Thomson's vision of a nature separate from the human neither in his sense of crisis—

> At last, extinct each social feeling, fell
> And joyless Inhumanity pervades,
> And petrifies the Heart. Nature disturb'd
> Is deem'd, vindictive, to have chang'd her course! (Spring, 305–8)

—nor in his appreciation of nature's sublimity:

> Nature! great Parent! whose directing Hand
> Rolls round the Seasons of the changeful Year,
> How Mighty! how majestic are thy Works!
> With what a pleasing Dread they swell the Soul,
> That sees, astonish'd! and, astonish'd sings! (Winter, 106–10)

The division between Hesiod and the English georgic tradition was to grow only greater. Although Cooke (1703–1756), in the prime age of English georgic poetry, earned a place in both Robert Anderson's 1795 *Works of the British Poets* and in Pope's *Dunciad* (Gillespie 2011: 92) (although not necessarily for his translation of Hesiod), the dominance of Virgil over Hesiod was only to be expected in an age that generally valued Rome over Greece. Nor did the Romantic age's preference for Greece, despite John Keats's famous lines on Chapman or Elton's scathing remarks about Addison and Cooke (Gillespie 2011: 14–16), favor Hesiod, as the age turned to the rebel Prometheus, not Zeus, for its values, and to the wild cliffs of the Caucasus, not the modest farm in Ascra, for its model of nature.

Still, Hesiod persisted, and in a poem such as Sackville-West's "The Garden" (1946), less grounded in national place than "The Land" of 1926 and more determined to deny that war and politics can have any ultimate power over a universal cycle of the seasons, one might claim that he even prevailed.[12] As in the sentence from Edgar Quinet that became a leitmotif for *Finnegans Wake*, on the wildflowers that survive the rise and fall of civilizations (*FW*, 281), Sackville-West's "The Garden" echoes not Virgil, but Hesiod's assurance of the transience of all that attempts to oppose Zeus's great order: "How temporary, War, with all its grief! / Permanence only lay in sap and seed." (Sackville-West, "Summer," *The Garden*).

Notes

1. As most of the direct references to Hesiod appear in *Georgics* 1, it may be that Virgil marks his poem as "Ascraean" exactly because he is beginning to diverge from Hesiod. As with Joyce's much later use of Homer, which appears only in the title, *Ulysses*, one reference is all it takes, if it is explicitly programmatic.

2. Hesiod in particular is very much thinking of men, specifically, in considering the human condition, a focus not unconnected to the centrality of farming in the poem.

3. Irvine (2009: 974) misses the subtlety of Virgil's poem but indicates how the military side of the *Georgics* was taken in later English poetry: "In Virgilian georgic, labor naturalizes and legitimates imperial expansion, because the military flowing-out of the roman nation into heroic conquest is imagined as similar to the rich superfluity of its agriculture. The farmer subduing the soil with the plow and the soldier subduing the rebellious border provinces with the sword, provide metaphors for each other."

4. Virgil's *Aeneid* goes further, marking a possibility of divine unreason and malevolence ("Can such fury be in celestial hearts?," 1.11) unknown to Hesiod, and which, perhaps because of its extremity, went largely unremarked until the twentieth century (Thomas 2001; Harrison 1990; in contrast Morgan 1999; and overall Nappa 2005).

5. See Thomas's edition of the *Georgics* (1988: 1:192–93). Modern eco-criticism has taken this position even further. See Fairer (2011) for an account of this view and a response.

6. Chapman's Christianizing is also derived in part from his sources: the text of Jean de Sponde, with Latin translation and commentary (whose folio of Homer he had used earlier), the Melanchthon text, and Scapula's Greek Lexicon (MacLure 1963: 177). MacLure (1963: 178) cites the "Old Testament ring" of Chapman's "The Gods forewarnings, and pursuits of Men, / Of impious lives, with unavoided paine; / Their sight, their rule of all, their love, their feare, / Watching, and sitting up, give all thy care" for *WD* 706 ("Take care to avoid the anger of the deathless gods").

7. The position is not accidental, as Steiner and Langer (1970: 50) note: "In England, between 1598 and 1611 George Chapman developed his theory stressing empathy with the original poet and the role of poetic creativity in translation, a theory which went far beyond the slender legacy of ideas left by the classical rhetoricians to modern translators; and his contemporaries, even when they were more traditional, echoed some of his statements."

8. "There is not one of the ten commandments of *Moses*, which relates to our moral duty to each other, that is not strongly recommended by our poet" (Cooke 1728: 96). Cooke solves the difficulty that Hesiod has the people, who are innocent, pay for the sins of the

ruler, by emending the line (n. on 1.341, pp. 30–32); concludes that Hesiod advises sparing at the middle of the cask not out of frugality ("If so, all his former rules of liberality are destroyed"), but to avoid drunkenness (n. on 1.498, pp. 40–41); and analyzes the question of whether or not Hesiod's cicada is a grasshopper (n. on 2.269). Elton, who pours scorn on the idea that Hesiod's beliefs are those of a proper English gentleman (1815: xxiv–xxx), recommends an analytic system in which "the affinities in the pagan sister-mythologies are explained by the general dissemination of these idolatrous mysteries, and the traditions which they were designed to commemorate, through the dispersion of a peculiar people in the early ages" (Dissertation on the Mythology of Hesiod, lxxv).

9. In contrast see Cooke (1728: n. to 1,140, p. 15): "*Pandora*'s box may properly be took in the same mystical sense with the apple in the book of *Genesis*; and in that light the moral will appear without any difficulty."

10. Low (1985: 74) includes John Evans's "The Bees" (1806–1813) and James Grahame's "British Georgics" (1809); Blyth (2009: 21) includes Bloomfield's "The Farmer's Boy" (1800) and Clare's "The Shepherd's Calendar" (1827); and see Goodman (2004: 142) for Wordsworth's *Excursion* as within the georgic tradition.

11. Mustard (1908: 31) lists Abraham Fleming (1589), May (1628), Ogilby (c. 1647), Lord Lauderdale (1694–1737), Dryden (1696), Trapp (1731), Warton (1753), Andrews (1766), Sotheby (1800), Sewell (1846), Singleton (1855), Kennedy (1861), Blackmore (1871), Rhoades (1881), Lord Burghclere (1904), and six partial translations, along with Tennyson's "testimonial" that he "often looked at his Virgil, more than ever delighting in what he called 'that splendid end of the second Georgic'" (Memoir, ii. 348).

12. Sackville-West replaced her first Hesiodic epigraph for "The Land" ("work is no disgrace; not working is the disgrace," *WD* 311) with *Nec sum animi dubius, verbis ea vincere magnum / quam sit et angustis hunc addere rebus honorem* ("Nor am I ignorant of how great a task it is / to conquer these things in words, and bring this honor to tiny things," *Georgics*, 3.289–90) (Blyth 2009: 22; Pomeroy 1982: 274, and see 278–81; Pellicer 2007: 110).

REFERENCES

Alpers, P. 1996. *What Is a Pastoral?* Chicago.

Beall, E. F. 2004. "The Plow That Broke the Plain Epic Tradition: Hesiod *Works and Days*, vv. 414–503." *Classical Antiquity* 23: 1–31.

Blyth, I. 2009. "A Sort of English Georgics: Vita Sackville-West's the Land." *Forum for Modern Language Studies* 45: 19–31.

Chalker, J. 1969. *The English Georgic: A Study in the Development of a Form*. Baltimore, MD.

Chapman, G., trans. and comm. 1618. *The Georgicks of Hesiod, by George Chapman; Translated Elaborately out of the Greek*. London. Early English Books Online reprint.

Clay, J. S. 2003. *Hesiod's Cosmos*. Cambridge.

Coleman, R., ed. and comm. 1977. *Vergil: Eclogues*. Cambridge.

Cooke, T., trans. 1728. *The Works of Hesiod*. London.

Crawford, R. 2002. *Poetry, Enclosure and the Vernacular Landscape, 1700–1830*. Cambridge.

Dalzell, A. 1996. *The Criticism of Didactic Poetry: Essays on Lucretius, Virgil, and Ovid*. Toronto.

Dryden, J., trans. 1697. *The Works of Virgil: Containing his Pastorals, Georgics, and Aeneis. Translated into English Verse; by Mr. Dryden. Adorn'd with a Hundred Sculptures*. London.

Elton, C., trans. 1815. *The Remains of Hesiod the Ascraean, Including the Shield of Heracles.* London.

Fairclough, H. R., trans. 1916. *Eclogues, Georgics, Aeneid I–VI.* Cambridge.

Fairer, D. 2011. "'Where Fuming Trees Refresh the Thirsty Air': The World of Eco-Georgic." *Studies in Eighteenth Century Culture* 40: 201–18.

Farrell, J. P. 1991. *Vergil's Georgics and the Tradition of Ancient Epic: The Art of Allusion in Literary History.* Oxford.

Fowler, A. 1986. "The Beginnings of English Georgic." In *Renaissance Genres: Essays on Theory, History, and Interpretation,* edited by B. K. Lewalski, 105–25. Cambridge.

Gale, M. R. 2000. *Virgil on the Nature of Things: The Georgics, Lucretius, and the Didactic Tradition.* Cambridge.

Gillespie, S. 2011. *English Translation and Classical Reception: Towards a New Literary History.* Chichester.

Goodman, K. 2004. *Georgic Modernity and British Romanticism.* Cambridge.

Halperin, D. 1983. *Before Pastoral: Theocritus and the Ancient Tradition of Bucolic Poetry.* New Haven, CT.

Harrison, S. J. 1990. "Some Views of the *Aeneid* in the Twentieth Century." In *Oxford Readings in Vergil's Aeneid,* edited by S. J. Harrison, 1–20. Oxford.

Heinzelman, K. 1971. "Roman Georgic in the Georgian Age: A Theory of Romantic Genre." *Texas Studies in Literature and Language* 33: 182–214.

Hooper, R., ed. and intro. 1888. *George Chapman: Homer's Batrachomyomachia, Hymns and Epigrams.* London.

Hopkins, D., and C. Martindale, eds. 2012. *The Oxford History of Classical Reception in English Literature.* Vol. 3, *1660–1790.* Oxford.

Hunter, R. 2014. *Hesiodic Voices: Studies in the Ancient Reception of Hesiod's Works and Days.* Cambridge.

Irvine, R. P. 2009. "Labor and Commerce in Locke and Early Eighteenth-Century English Georgic." *English Literary History* 76: 963–88.

Low, A. 1985. *The Georgic Revolution.* Princeton, NJ.

Lyne, R. O. A. M. 1990. "Vergil and the Politics of War." In *Oxford Readings in Vergil's Aeneid,* edited by S. J. Harrison, 316–38. Oxford.

MacLure, M. 1963. "The Minor Translations of George Chapman." *Modern Philology* 60: 172–182.

Morgan, L. 1999. *Patterns of Redemption in Virgil's Georgics.* Cambridge.

Mynors, R. A. B., ed. and comm. 1990. *Virgil: Georgics.* Preface by R. G. M. Nisbet. Oxford.

Nappa, C. 2005. *Reading after Actium: Vergil's "Georgics", Octavian, and Rome.* Ann Arbor, MI.

Nelson, S. 1996. "The Drama of Hesiod's Farm." *Classical Philology* 91: 45–53.

Nelson, S. 1998. *God and the Land: The Metaphysics of Farming in Hesiod and Virgil.* Oxford.

Mustard, W. P. 1908. "Virgil's Georgics and the British Poets." *American Journal of Philology* 29: 1–32.

O'Brien, K. 1999. "Imperial Georgic, 1660–1789." In *The Country and the City Revisited: England and the Politics of Culture, 1550–1850,* edited by G. MacLean, D. Landry, and J. P Ward, 160–79. Cambridge.

Patterson, A. 1986. "Pastoral versus Georgic: The Politics of Virgilian Quotation." In *Renaissance Genres: Essays on Theory, History, and Interpretation,* edited by B. K. Lewalski, 241–67. Cambridge.

Pellicer, J. C. 2007. "Reception, Wit, and the Unity of Virgil's *Georgics*." *Symbolae Osloenses* 82: 90–115.

Perkell, C. G. 1989. *The Poet's Truth: A Study of the Poet in Virgil's "Georgics"*. Berkeley, CA.

Perkell, C. G. 2001 "Pastoral Value in Vergil." In *Poets and Critics Read Vergil*, edited by S. Spence, 26–43. New Haven, CT.

Pomeroy, E. W. 1982. "Within Living Memory: Vita Sackville-West's Poems of Land and Garden." *Twentieth Century Literature* 28: 269–89.

Presson, R. K. 1969. "Wrestling with This World: A View of George Chapman." *Publications of the Modern Language Association of America* 84: 44–50.

Rogers, P. 2005. "John Philips, Pope, and Political Georgic." *Modern Language Quarterly* 64: 414–15.

Sackville-West, V. 1946. *The Garden*. London.

Schoenberger, M. 2015. "Cultivating the Arts Of Peace: English Georgic Poetry from Marvell to Thomson." PhD diss., Boston University.

Spurr, M. S. 1986. "Agriculture and the Georgics." *Greece and Rome* 33: 164–87.

Steiner, T. R., and S. Langer. 1970. "Precursors to Dryden: English and French Theories of Translation in the Seventeenth Century." *Comparative Literature Studies* 7: 50–81.

Thibodeau, P. 2011. *Playing the Farmer: Representations of Rural Life in Vergil's "Georgics"*. Berkeley, CA.

Thomas, R. F., ed. 1988. *Virgil, Georgics*. Cambridge.

Thomas, R. F. 1999. *Reading Virgil and His Texts: Studies in Intertextuality*. Ann Arbor. MI.

Thomas, R. F. 2001. "The 'Georgics' of Resistance: From Virgil to Heaney." *Vergilius* 47: 117–47.

Volk, K. 2002. *The Poetics of Latin Didactic: Lucretius, Vergil, Ovid, Manilius*. Oxford.

Volk, K., ed. 2008. *Vergil's "Georgics"*. Oxford Readings in Classical Studies. Oxford.

West, M., ed. and comm. 1978. *Hesiod: Works and Days*. Oxford.

Wilkinson, L. P. 1969. *The "Georgics" of Virgil: A Critical Survey*. Cambridge.

Williams, R. 1973. *The Country and the City*. Oxford.

Wills, G. 1998. Preface to *Chapman's Homer: "The Iliad"*, edited by A. Nicoll, vii–xiii. Princeton, NJ.

CHAPTER 24

OVID'S HESIODIC VOICES

IOANNIS ZIOGAS

INTRODUCTION

WHY does Hesiod appeal to Ovid? A common answer is that Ovid views the archaic poet through the lens of Hellenistic reception. A figure emblematic for Alexandrian poetics, Hesiod symbolizes the poet of peaceful pursuits and artistic refinement as opposed to the pompousness of martial epic. This approach can be useful, provided that we acknowledge that for Ovid the Hellenistic Hesiod functions as a "window"[1] on Hesiod's poetry, which itself anticipates its own reception (cf. Haubold 2010; Hunter 2014; Canevaro 2015). The antagonism between Homeric and Hesiodic poetry, for instance, is already suggested in the *Works and Days* (hereafter *WD*) and is developed in the tradition of the competition (*certamen*) of Homer and Hesiod, which Ovid appropriates. Ovid is also aware of trends in Hesiodic reception other than Hellenistic poetry, such as the philosophy of Empedocles and Plato or the criticism of Xenophanes and Philodemus. Some of these philosophical analyses of Hesiodic poetry are related to main preoccupations of Ovidian poetics, such as the issue of gods' morality, the controversy about truth and falsity in mythology, and the interplay between fabulous tales and their scientific interpretations.

The Hesiodic voice, which is variously pitched but invariably recognizable, fascinated Ovid. Distinctive traits of Hesiodic poetics must have attracted Ovid; personified abstractions, etymological wordplay, and sylleptic puns[2] feature prominently in Hesiod and Ovid. The thematic diversity of Hesiodic poetry was equally appealing to Ovid's genius. Hesiod's interests range from the creation of the world to mundane things of everyday life and combine a universal worldview with a deep concern about his times. As the ultimate authority on didactic poetry, poetic cosmogonies, and affairs between mortals and immortals, he provides a model for Ovid's simultaneously diverse and unified works. The variety and unity of the Hesiodic corpus, an interpretative approach that Hesiodic poetry itself invites (Clay 2003; Haubold 2010; Canevaro 2015), appealed to

Ovid. Hesiod and Ovid assume different voices and personas in different works, which are nonetheless self-consciously interconnected (cf. Van Noorden 2014: 204–60).

HOMER AND HESIOD

The first explicit reference to Hesiod in Ovid is in *Amores* (hereafter *Am.*) 1.15. The poet from Ascra appears right after Homer:

> uiuet Maeonides, Tenedos dum stabit et Ide,
>   dum rapidas Simois in mare uoluet aquas;
> uiuet et Ascraeus, dum mustis uua tumebit,
>   dum cadet incurua falce resecta Ceres. (*Am.* 1.15.9–12)

> Maeonian Homer will live, as long as Tenedos and Ida will stand, as long as Simois will roll his waters rushing into the sea, the Ascraean Hesiod will live too, as long as the grape will swell for must, as long as Ceres will fall beneath the stroke of the curving sickle.[3]

The mention of key geographical locations in the Trojan War (the island Tenedos, Mount Ida, and the river Simois) celebrates Homer as the poet of the *Iliad* before Ovid commemorates Hesiod as the poet of the *WD* by associating him with viticulture and agriculture. This juxtaposition alludes to the tradition of the *certamen Homeri et Hesiodi*, which pits the warlike poetry of the *Iliad* against the peaceful agenda of the *WD*.[4] The *Theogony* (hereafter *Th*) is not evoked, an indication that Hesiod was identified primarily, though certainly not exclusively, as the poet of the *WD*, and the *WD* as a poem about agriculture.

The reference to the rushing waters of Simois further evokes Callimachus's muddy river (*Hymn* 2.108–9), a symbol of epic poetry to be avoided. Ovid's response to Envy (*Liuor*, see *Am.* 1.15.1–6) invites us to read *Am.* 1.15 against the background of Apollo's retort to Envy (Φθόνος, Callimachus, *Hymn* 2.108–9).[5] Apollo contrasts the dirty streams of epic with the pure water that the bees fetch for Demeter (*Hymn* 2.110–12). Ovid appropriates the Callimachean imagery by juxtaposing the rushing river of martial epic with Hesiod's Ceres. Thus, the Roman poet alludes to the tradition of the *certamen* and views it through the "window" of Alexandrian poetics. While both Homer and Hesiod are praised for their immortal poetry, Ovid implies the long-standing antagonism between Homeric/martial and Hesiodic/didactic poetry.

ARS AMATORIA

Homer and Hesiod appear together in passages that evoke the tradition of the *certamen*. A case in point is the beginning of *Ars Amatoria* (hereafter *Ars*) 2:

Laetus amans donat uiridi mea carmina palma,
    praelata *Ascraeo Maeonioque* seni.
Talis ab armiferis Priameïus hospes Amyclis
    candida cum rapta coniuge uela dedit;
talis erat qui te curru uictore ferebat,
    uecta peregrinis Hippodamia rotis. (*Ars* 2.3–8)

The happy lover crowns my poem with green palm-leaves and prefers it to the Ascraean and Maeonian old men. Such was the guest, Priam's son, who spread his gleaming sails from belligerent Amyclae in the company of his stolen bride; such was he who bore you in victorious chariot, Hippodamia, conveyed upon his foreign wheels.

In the *Certamen* (205–10), the Greeks support Homer, but King Panedes crowns Hesiod with the victory wreath because he prefers the poet of peace and agriculture to the poet of wars and slaughters. Ovid inserts himself into the tradition of the *certamen* and beats both Homer and Hesiod. In this revisionist version, the judge is not a king concerned with peace, but a lover who conquered the object of his desire thanks to Ovid's instructions. *Ars* 2.5–8 advertises the subordination of Greek epic to Ovid's didactic agenda. The abductions of Helen and Hippodamia suggest that Homeric and Hesiodic poetry alike are incorporated into Ovid's work. The lines that mention Helen and the epic compound *armiferis* anticipate the Trojan War; however, at the same time, Ovid repeats *talis* in a way that evokes Hesiod's formula of *ehoie* ("or such as") in the *Catalogue of Women* (aka *Ehoiai*). The examples of Helen and Hippodamia further resonate with the contents of the *Catalogue of Women* (hereafter *CW*), which included the stemma of the Pelopids (in Book 4) and concluded with the wooing of Helen (fr. 196–204 M–W).[6] But the female-oriented tradition of the *Ehoiai* is focalized through the eyes of Ovid's male lovers. This is suggested by the gender shift from the feminine *ehoie* to the masculine *talis*.

The beginning of *Ars* 2 anticipates the importance of Hesiod in the shift to the female-oriented contents of *Ars* 3. Ovid gives his own twist to the playful Alexandrian versions of Hesiodic *Kataloggedicht*, but also evokes the motifs, formulae, and contents of the *Ehoiai* directly.[7] As he moves from the first to the second book, he emphasizes that conquering a girl is not everything, but just the first step (Book 1). The second and equally important task is to learn how to keep the vanquished woman (Book 2). In this context, the evocation of the *CW* suggests its status as a sequel to the *Th*; the progression from *Ars* 1 to 2 parallels a transition in the Hesiodic corpus. Likewise, in the unexpected transition from *Ars* 2 to 3, Ovid evokes the shift from the end of the *Iliad* to the beginning of the *Aithiopis*, but also from the end of the *Th* to the beginning of the *CW* (see Gibson 2003: 86). The mention of Penthesilea (*Ars* 3.1–2) replays the seamless transition from the last line of the *Iliad* (24.804, Ὣς οἵ γ᾽ ἀμφίεπον τάφον Ἕκτορος ἱπποδάμοιο, "thus they took care of the burial of Hector, tamer of horses") to the beginning of the *Aithiopis* (fr. 1.1–3 Bernabé, ὣς οἵ γ᾽ ἀμφίεπον τάφον Ἕκτορος· ἦλθε δ᾽ Ἀμαζών,/ . . . ἐνειδὴς Πενθεσί〈λ〈ε〉ια, "thus they took care of Hector's burial; and the Amazon came . . . beautiful Penthesileia"). Moreover, the last couplet of *Ars* 2, in which

Ovid announces his plan to move on to the subject of women, evokes the last two lines of the *Th*, which are also the first two lines of the *CW* and in which Hesiod invokes the Muses to sing of the tribe of women. Two catalogues of women at the beginning of *Ars* 3 (3.11–22, 33–42) further suggest the transition to the *Ehoiai*. The first contrasts vile with virtuous heroines, while the second focuses on heroines who were betrayed by men. Ovid praises women, touching upon the very program of Hesiod's *Ehoiai*. As he does not give just a list but an exemplary catalogue of virtuous heroines, his work is aligned with the program of the *Ehoiai*.

The *praeceptor* also imagines that he answers an objection that equipping his Amazons with the art of love is like entrusting a sheepfold to a hungry she-wolf (*Ars* 3.7–8). This recalls the misogynistic aspect of Hesiodic poetry, in particular the *WD*, in which we read that "whoever trusts a woman, trusts swindlers" (375). From that perspective, *Ars* 3 signals another transition within the Hesiodic corpus: from the male-oriented *WD*, whose didactic focus on work and profit often views women as rapacious and thus undermining men's hard work, to the female-oriented *CW*, which revolves around the praise of famous heroines who are a great asset to their families. Hesiod, as the male-oriented instructor of the *WD* and the author of poetry in praise of female virtue, provides Ovid with the model for his transition to *Ars* 3. At the same time, the idea of teaching women is found in Hesiod, who instructs his addressee to marry a virgin, so that he can teach (διδάξῃς) her good habits (*WD* 699). Teaching one's bride carries sexual connotations, as she is to be taught the works of Aphrodite (cf. Canevaro 2015: 120n119), the very aim of *Ars* 3. By teaching women love, Ovid both fulfills and subverts Hesiod's advice. Far from teaching morality and marital sex to a virgin he married, Ovid instructs his female students to enjoy extramarital affairs.

Hesiod himself draws attention to the progression from the *Th* to the *WD*. The temporality of these works corresponds to Hesiod's career. A poem on the creation of the universe (*Th*) is composed by a young shepherd, while the contemporary world of the *WD* is the work of a mature farmer. In the *WD* Hesiod's autobiographical representation of his personal development appears in the form of a sequenced intertextuality (see Most 1993: 76–80), what Haubold (2010: 21) calls the biographical hermeneutics of the Hesiodic corpus. This provides a model for Ovid, who incorporates biographical information about his poetic career in the literary progression of his works.[8] The expert teacher of the *Ars*, for instance, who learned from the mistakes of his youthful *Am.*, corresponds to the experienced narrator of the *WD*, who sets out to revise or complement his earlier *Th*.

At the beginning of the *Ars*, Ovid denies an encounter with the Muses and declares that his work is the product of experience rather than divine inspiration. This very disavowal aligns him with the narrator of the *WD*:

> Nec mihi sunt uisae Clio Cliusque sorores
>   seruanti pecudes uallibus, Ascra, tuis:
> usus opus mouet hoc: uati parete perito;
>   uera canam . . . (*Ars* 1.27–30)

Neither did Clio and Clio's sisters appear to me while I kept flocks in your vale, Ascra: experience sets this work in motion: obey an experienced bard; I shall sing of true things...

Ovid is referring to the famous initiation in *Th* 22–35 (cf. Callimachus, *Aetia* fr. 2.1–2 Pf.). While denying this divine epiphany, he echoes the program of the *WD* (cf. *WD* 10, ἐτήτυμα μυθησαίμην, "I should tell the truth," with *uera canam*), which is itself a revision of the *Th*. Experience as the basis of his *opus*/ἔργον suggests the practical program of the *WD* ("Ἔργα καὶ Ἡμέραι), not the divinely inspired, and thus potentially false, poetry of the *Th* (see Rosati 2009: 349–51; Canevaro 2015: 42–43). Thus, Ovid's renunciation of the Muses' epiphany reproduces Hesiod's personal development and throws into sharper relief the tension between the *Th* and the *WD*.

Yet the dichotomy between the divinely inspired *Th* and the practical *WD* is not clear-cut (cf. Canevaro in this volume). The Muses in the *Th*, not unlike Hesiod in the *WD*, declare that they can sing the truth (28), and Hesiod's didactic persona proclaims that he can instruct Perses in seafaring, even though he has no expertise in the subject (*WD* 646–49). Hesiod gained knowledge without experience thanks to the Muses (*WD* 662, "For the Muses taught [ἐδίδαξαν] me to sing an inconceivable hymn," which clearly echoes *Th* 22, "they taught [ἐδίδαξαν] Hesiod a beautiful song"). Likewise, Ovid invokes the Muse Erato to favor his work (*Ars* 2.16), and his dismissal of Apollo is undercut by the god's epiphany (*Ars* 2.493–510). These inconsistencies reiterate the tension and continuity between the mythological *Th* and the didactic *WD*.

The *Ars* includes a scientific cosmogony that resonates with Hesiod's *Th* but downplays the mythological and anthropomorphic origins of Hesiod's cosmos (cf. *Met.* 1.5–7 with Ziogas 2013: 57–59). The beginning of Ovid's cosmogony opens a dialogue with Hesiod and the reception of his poetry:

> *Prima* fuit rerum confusa sine ordine moles,
>   unaque erat facies sidera, terra, fretum;
> mox *caelum impositum terris, humus aequore cincta est*
>   inque suas partes cessit inane *chaos* ... (*Ars* 2.467–70)

First there was a confused mass of things without order, and stars and earth and sea had but one appearance; presently the sky was set over the earth, the land was ringed by the sea, and empty chaos retired to its own place.

To begin with Chaos is to begin with Hesiod's *Th*, and *prima* alludes to πρώτιστα Χάος γένετ' (116, "first Chaos came to being"). The image of the sky as set over the earth recalls Ouranos's oppressive union with Gaia (cf. *Th* 177–78, "and he [Ouranos] spread himself around her [Gaia]"), while the encircling of the land by sea refers to the river Oceanus. Ovid's cosmogony has its origins in the *Th* but follows a trend in Hesiodic reception that sees the archaic poet as a pioneer in philosophical and scientific thought, not as the author of false myths. Within the *Ars*, Ovid's cosmogonic digression aims to instruct his students that *eros* ("love") is the solution to *eris* ("strife"), thus giving a further twist to

Empedocles's philosophy, which is in turn influenced by Hesiod.[9] In the *Th*, *eros* leads to sexual violence and results in generational and gendered discord. For the *praeceptor*, love is the origin and dissolution of conflict, a subtle revision of the Hesiodic worldview. Thus, Ovid incorporates a scientific lesson about the origins of the world in the didactic agenda of the *Ars*.

The dialectic between Ovid's *Ars* and Hesiod's *WD* revolves around the reprocessing of agricultural themes and language as amatory metaphors. Ovid calls Hesiod *praeceptor arandi* (*Fasti* 6.13, "teacher of plowing"), echoing *praeceptor amandi* (*Ars* 2.161, "teacher of lovemaking"). The parallel is not only intentionally antonymic (Rosati 2009: 359n48), but further draws attention to the similarities between plowing and lovemaking. Ovid's *opus*, for instance (e.g., at *Ars* 1.29), not only points to the *Ars* as an ἔργον of didactic poetry but also suggests sex as an agricultural metaphor.[10] Ovid uses *opus* in the sense of "sexual intercourse" several times (see *Am*. 1.4.48, 2.10.36, 3.7.68, 3.14.28; *Ars* 2.480, 3.770), and this meaning is actually a metaphor from agriculture (see Adams 1982, 157; cf. Plautus, *Asinaria* 873–74). Ovid eroticizes Hesiodic poetry, but it should also be noted that the sexual connotations of ἔργον are already attested in Hesiod (see *WD* 521, οὔπω ἔργα ἰδυῖα πολυχρύσου Ἀφροδίτης, "still ignorant of the works of golden Aphrodite"). The seeds of the Ovidian interplay between the works of sex and agriculture were sown by Hesiod.[11]

The *WD* contains other material that is relevant to the *praeceptor amoris*. Hesiod advises about the right age of marriage: late twenties to early thirties for a man and five years after she reaches puberty for a woman (*WD* 695–98). One should marry a virgin who lives nearby lest he be a laughingstock of the neighborhood (*WD* 699–701). While the recommendation about marrying a woman who lives nearby corresponds to Ovid's claim that men do not need to search beyond Rome to find attractive women (*Ars* 1.55–59), Hesiod's advice about marriage contrasts with Ovid's instructions about extramarital love. Ovid responds to the strict age limits for the appropriate woman with his more relaxed instructions; the right age depends entirely on his students' tastes (*Ars* 1.61–66).

Ovid introduces his reworking of Hesiod's "Days" (*Ars* 1.399–436 echoes *WD* 765–828; cf. Vergil, *Georgics* 1.268–96) by announcing that not only farmers and sailors but also lovers should be concerned with time and timing:

> *Tempora* qui solis *operosa* colentibus arua,
>   fallitur, et nautis aspicienda putat . . . (*Ars* 1.399–400)

> He errs who thinks that seasons are to be marked by sailors alone, and by those who till the toilsome fields . . .

Tempora operosa glosses over Ἔργα καὶ Ἡμέραι (cf. *Ars* 1.415, *die*). Ovid's statement is not necessarily a denial of Hesiod, but may remind us that even in Hesiod's "Days" we find advice that is directed neither to farmers nor to sailors. Hesiod marks the right day for getting married (*WD* 784, 800) and the appropriate days for the birth of male and female offspring (*WD* 783–800). Issues of marriage and procreation are grafted into the right time for sowing and taming animals. Hesiod himself provides Ovid with the basis for combining the works of farming with the works of love.

The Hesiodic instructions about avoiding greedy women inform Ovid's "Days." The *praeceptor* marks the days on which the shops are closed and advises his students to avoid big festivals and to brand their beloved's birthday a "black day," since a gift to her cannot be avoided then (1.417–18). The literal reference to the rising of the Pleiades in Hesiod becomes a metaphor for financial loss in Ovid:

> *Differ opus*: tunc tristis hiems, tunc *Pliades* instant,
>   tunc tener aequorea mergitur Haedus aqua . . . (*Ars* 1.409–10)

> Put off work: the storm is lowering then, and the Pleiades loom over, the tender Kid is merged in the watery waves . . .

By instructing his students to put off the task of courting when the days invite spending, Ovid appropriates Hesiod, who advises avoiding certain tasks on certain days (e.g., *WD* 780–81), but also brings up a tension between working hard and procrastinating. Hesiod warned against procrastination (*WD* 410–12, "Do not postpone [μηδ' ἀναβάλλεσθαι] until tomorrow and the next day: for the futilely working man does not fill his granary, nor does the procrastinator [ἀναβαλλόμενος]; industry fosters work [ἔργον]"), and Ovid's *differ opus* not only contrasts with Hesiod's "don't put off work" but also pits the serious agricultural pursuits of Hesiodic didactic against the playful task of courting. Yet it is not accurate to think of the *Ars* as simply undermining or mocking the *WD*. The playfulness of Ovid's work should not distract us from noticing the continuity between Ovidian and Hesiodic didactic. The *praeceptor* is a true heir of Hesiodic tradition. Hesiod's warning about avoiding parasitic women who charm men's minds while poking into their granary (*WD* 373–74) is in tune with the economy of wooing in the *Ars* (see 1.419–20). Resisting the mercenary habits of charming *puellae* is the *praeceptor*'s markedly Hesiodic preoccupation.[12]

The winter rise of the Pleiades is associated with stormy weather at *WD* 619–22 (cf. Vergil, *Georgics* 4.232–35), in which Hesiod advises to put off sailing. Ovid may link the wintry rise of the Pleiades and the Kid (cf. Aratus, *Phaenomena* 158–59) with the Saturnalia (Hollis 1977 on 408), a big festival in December that involved gift exchanges, thus combining the dangers of winter storms for sailors with the financial hazards of the Saturnalia for lovers. The metaphor of a lover as a sailor buffeted in stormy weather (e.g. Horace, *Ode* 1.5; cf. Ovid, *Remedia Amoris* 13–14) is in play here. But Ovid gives an unexpected twist to the metaphor of loving as sailing. The storms that threaten the lover do not arise from uncontrollable passion but from loss of income. The lover resembles a ship that may lose its cargo due to inclement weather, a distinctly Hesiodic concern. The *praeceptor* appropriates the traditional association of the Pleiades and the Kid with the dangers of seafaring and transforms the themes and diction of traditional didactic into novel metaphors.

The deceitful and mercenary nature of the *puellae* calls for elaborate instructions about the reciprocity of gifts. Hesiod's straightforward advice, "give to one who gives and do not give to one who does not give: for one gives to a giver, but no one gives to a non-giver" (*WD* 354–55, καὶ δόμεν ὅς κεν δῷ καὶ μὴ δόμεν ὅς κεν μὴ δῷ·/δώτῃ μέν τις ἔδωκεν, ἀδώτῃ δ᾽ οὔ τις ἔδωκεν) is updated and applied to the exchange of gifts and favors in elegiac love. Ovid complicates Hesiod's instructions by warning that women like to receive without giving back (*Ars* 1.433, *Multa rogant utenda* dari, data *reddere nolunt*, "They ask to be given many things to borrow, but, once given, they do not want to give them back") and suggesting that his students should promise gifts without giving them. A man should always give the impression that he is about to give without actually giving (*Ars* 1.449, *At quod non* dederis, semper uideare daturus, "But what you have not given you may seem always on the point of giving"; cf. *Ars* 1.454). The polyptota (*dari, data; dederis, daturus*) evoke Hesiod (δόμεν, δῷ, δώτῃ, ἔδωκεν, ἀδώτῃ, ἔδωκεν). Ovid casts the economy of reciprocity in gendered terms, adjusting Hesiod to the world of Latin love elegy. Elegiac women prefer snatching to giving, and Ovid's male students should match female wiles with equal cunning. Such a negative view of women is a characteristic of the *WD*. Ovid combines Hesiod's advice about gift exchange with his warnings about greedy females.

Women who appreciate expensive gifts more than good poetry give the *praeceptor* the opportunity to literalize and thus ironize the golden age:

> *Aurea* sunt uere nunc *saecula*: plurimus *auro*
> uenit honos: *auro* conciliatur amor. (*Ars* 2.277–78)

Truly now our age is golden: the greatest honor comes with gold: love is gained with gold.

The Hesiodic myth of ages (*WD* 109–201) becomes *the* great Roman myth (see Feeney 2007: 112), thanks to Augustus, who claimed that he had restored the golden age in Rome.[13] The imperial appropriation of the Hesiodic myth relies on Augustus's claims that he had established peace and justice and restored good old Roman morality. Wealth is the enemy of the Roman virtues of *paupertas* and *frugalitas*, and the "gold" of the golden age is metaphorical, not literal (cf. Plato, *Cratylus* 398a; *Am.* 3.8.35–36; *Metamorphoses* 1.89–112). But in the *Ars*, the voice of the elegiac lover who suffers from the greed of desirable women literalizes Hesiod's gold.[14] It should be added, however, that the interplay between the figurative and literal meanings of the metallic races features already in Hesiod (see Van Noorden 2015: 33, 77–78). The bronze race, for instance, had bronze weapons, lived in bronze houses, and worked with bronze (*WD* 150–51).[15] Thus, Ovid's literalization of the golden age can be interpreted as simultaneously undermining and Hesiodizing Hesiod.

While the condemnation of gold suits the imperial appropriation of Hesiodic morality, the power of gold in Augustan Rome lays bare the paradox of a wealthy society entertaining nostalgic dreams of returning to the simplicity of idealized ancestors. Ovid distances himself from this nostalgia in a way that complements and contrasts with Hesiod's voice. While Hesiod bemoans the fact that he was born in the iron age, Ovid fully enjoys Roman modernity:

Prisca iuuent alios: ego me nunc denique natum
  gratulor: haec aetas moribus apta meis. (*Ars* 3.121–22)

Let ancient times delight others: I congratulate myself that I was not born till now;
this age fits my character well.

Ovid responds to Hesiod's wish that he had lived in an age different from his own (see La
Penna 1979: 195; cf. *Fasti* 1.225–26); *alios* should include Hesiod, who would have been
pleased had he lived in a previous or later era (*WD* 174–76). Ovid not only contradicts
Hesiod's statement (La Penna 1979: 195; Barchiesi 1997: 235), but also fulfills his desire
to have lived in a future era. As a *Hesiodus rediuiuus*, Ovid does not regret living in
his times. Yet the golden age that suits his character (*moribus*) is at odds with Hesiod's
ideal age of morality. Ovid enjoys the sophistication and refinement of the city, not the
strict morality and hard work of the countryside. The Hesiodic background to the *Ars*
highlights the contrast between the country as the setting of Hesiod's *WD* and the city as
the playground for Ovid's games of love.

METAMORPHOSES

The continuity of Hesiod's works features prominently in the *Metamorphoses* (hereafter *Met.*). After a short proem, Ovid begins with Chaos (*Met.* 1.7), a poetic and cosmic
opening of Hesiodic origins. The myth of the four ages (Ovid omits the heroic age)
follows Ovid's scientific cosmogony and the creation of man (1.89–150).[16] From the *Th*
we move to the *WD*; Ovid's *ultima* (1.127), which introduces the iron age, teases us to
think that we have already reached Ovid's times (see Van Noorden 2014: 219–20). Yet
after the myth of the races we are back to the theogonic material of Gigantomachies
(1.151–62). The shift from the anthropocentric perspective of the *WD* to the *Th*'s battles of
gods and Giants is indicative of the complex temporal progression of the *Met.*, which is
more intricate than the linear move from the beginning of the world to Ovid's times that
is promised in the proem (*Met.* 1.3–4). The world is on the verge of returning to Chaos
several times in the *Met.*; after the flood, for instance, or during Phaethon's doomed ride.
Phaethon's demise resonates with Zeus's battle with Typhoeus and the god's decision to
put an end to the age of heroes in the *CW* (see Ziogas 2013: 69–73). The heroic race may
not feature in Ovid's version of human races, but the poet compensates for this omission by dealing with heroes in the greatest part of his work. In Hesiodic terms, the *Met.*
covers the age of gods (*Th*), heroes (*CW*), and mortals (*WD*), and repeatedly combines
and shifts between these works. The narrative and temporal progression of the *Met.*
within the Hesiodic corpus is both linear and circular.

The transition from the *Th* to the *CW* is replayed several times. The *CW* is a sequel
to the *Th*, since the last two lines of the *Th* overlap with the first two of the *CW* (*Th*
1021–22 = *CW* fr. 1.1–2 M–W). We move from the affairs of goddesses with men, the

last section of the *Th* (963–1020), to heroines who slept with gods, the *leitmotif* of the *CW*. Narrative sequences in the *Met.* reproduce the continuity of these two Hesiodic works. The entrance of Apollo (*Met.* 1.437–52) replicates this transition, since the god is transformed from an Olympian who fights with a primordial monster (Python) into an immortal who falls in love with a beautiful nymph (Daphne). In this programmatic episode, Amor's victory over Apollo recalls the powers of Hesiod's primordial Eros, who conquers all gods and mortals (*Th* 120–22; see Scully 2015: 147). The narrative continuity from the *Th* to the *CW* is reiterated in the shift from Phaethon's cosmic conflagration to Jupiter's passion for Callisto (*Met.* 1.401–10), as well as in the internal narratives of the Muses (*Met.* 5) and Orpheus (*Met.* 10; see Ziogas 2013: 66–68, 73–75, 86–94, 149–50).

The *WD* is woven into Ovid's Hesiodic trajectory from the *Th* to the *CW*. The victorious song of the Muse, for instance, in the competition with the Emathides, praises Ceres and agriculture, thus evoking Hesiod's victory in the *certamen* due to the peaceful agenda of the *WD* (see Bilinski 1959). At the same time, the Muse reiterates a transition from the Typhonomachy to the loves of the gods (*Met.* 5.356–84). In this episode, Venus's address to Amor clearly refers to Hesiod's Eros.[17] While the *CW* comes to an end after the wooing of Helen, Ovid continues until he reaches his own times, thus including the contemporary perspective of the *WD*. As a whole, the *Met.* moves from Chaos to divine loves and from the race of heroes to the age of mortals, covering the entire spectrum of the Hesiodic worldview.

Stephen Scully (2015: 146) brilliantly observes that the end of the *Met.* signals the establishment of Augustus's peace in Hesiodic terms. The emperor resolves the primordial strife that opened the poem. Yet the sphragis (*Met.* 15.871–79) upsets the omnipotence of a Jovian regime by declaring Jupiter's/Augustus's fires incapable of silencing Ovid. Zeus's lightning bolt puts an end to the discordant rebellion of Typhoeus at the end of the *Th*, while the *Met.* ends with the failure of Jupiter's weapons to erase Ovid's defiant voice from memory. Unlike Hesiod, Ovid is not the mouthpiece of the Muses that celebrate a Jovian cosmos, but echoes the rebellious voices of Jupiter's last enemy.[18] The *Met.* ends with a hint that the universe can revert to chaos, back to the beginning of Ovid's work. The poet, not the prince, has the power to shift from chaos to cosmos and vice versa.

The *Met.* has structural, thematic, verbal, and stylistic similarities with Hesiod. Etymological wordplay and personifications of abstract ideas are distinctive aspects of Hesiod (e.g., Ζῆλος, Φήμη, Λιμός) and Ovid (e.g., *Inuidia, Fama, Fames*). Metamorphosis is a recurring motif in the *CW* (see Hirschberger 2008). Transformation was associated with the Hesiodic character in ancient criticism and was related to implausible and thus false myths. The problematic truth of the poets, the lies of mythological tales, and the simultaneous appeals to readers' disbelief and gullibility are central to the magical realism of the *Met.* (cf. Feeney 1991: 229–35; Wheeler 1999: 162–93). This crucial aspect of Ovid's poetry originates in the initiation scene of the *Th*, in which the Muses enigmatically proclaim that they can either speak the truth or tell lies similar to the truth. Metamorphosis is also reflected in poetic language. An interplay between the figurative and literal meaning, recognized as key to Ovidian poetics (see Tissol 1997), also features prominently in Hesiod (Ziogas 2013: 16–17, 105–6, 142–43, 174–78). Formulas of Homeric epic appear transformed in amatory contexts. The eroticization of epic diction and the juxtaposition of martial and marital narratives feature prominently in Hesiod and Ovid.[19]

Ovid evokes Hesiod not only to signal his adherence to the themes and poetics of the archaic Greek bard, but also to stress his departure from Hesiod's world. As Conte (1986: 81) notes, "[r]eference to the norm obviously does not mean submission to the norm; rather it delimits the common space within which the new poetry can both emulate tradition and speak with a fresh voice." Ovid's scientific cosmogony contrasts with Hesiod's anthropomorphic *Th*. While the *Ehoiai* praises the sexual affairs of gods with mortal women and focuses on their offspring, Ovid problematizes the violence of divine rapes and plays down the *CW*'s genealogies.

Transformations may be a recurring motif in Hesiod, but in Ovid they often replace the genealogical contents of the *CW*. A telling case is Pyrrha and Deucalion's puzzlement about how they should repopulate the earth after the annihilation of mankind in the flood. Curiously, sex as a means of procreation does not occur to the married couple (cf. Ahl 1985: 107), and they resort to metamorphosis from stones. In the *CW*, Pyrrha and Deucalion have biological children *and* create men and women out of stones. Deucalion's daughters have children with Zeus, and the genealogy of his son Hellen defines Hellenism. But Ovid distances himself from the *CW*'s genealogical progression and edits out the very origins of the Greek race. That is not to say that genealogy is not important in the *Met*. Genealogical links and associations may ostensibly be suppressed, but they are still crucial (see Cole 2004; 2008; Ziogas 2013: 75–81, 133–35).

Ovid's revival of Hesiodic poetry does not occur in an intellectual or literary vacuum. The tales of Coronis and Mestra, for instance, open a dialogue with Callimachus's reception of Hesiod, while Ovid restores these myths to the narrative structure of the *Ehoiai* (Ziogas 2013: 112–47). In Book 10, the tales of Orpheus begin with allusions to Phanocles's *Erotes* (Segal 1972: 477; Gärtner 2008: 31–32), an elegiac catalogue of homoerotic affairs, and move on to heterosexual affairs with clear references to the *Ehoiai* (Ziogas 2013: 151–64). Ovid is fully aware of the philosophical arguments that revolve around Hesiodic poetry. The song of Calliope (*Met*. 5) engages with Empedocles's philosophy (Trencsényi-Waldapfel 1969). Arachne, who gives an obscene version of the *CW* as she depicts the deceptive transformations and sexual violence of the Olympians, is from Colophon (*Met*. 6.8), the fatherland of Xenophanes, who criticized Hesiod for attributing all sorts of blameworthy deeds to the gods, such as deception and adultery (fr. 21 B 11 D–K; cf. Rosati 2009: 364–65). Achelous evokes the structural and thematic dynamics of a Mestra-*ehoie*, while answering Pirithous's objection about the power of gods to change shapes. The episode is set against the background of Philodemus's critique of Hesiodic theology (Ziogas 2013: 144–45; cf. Obbink 2004). A study of Ovid's Hesiod requires knowledge of Hesiodic reception in antiquity, not only in Hellenistic poetry but also in ancient philosophy.

FASTI

Ovid casts the transition from the *Met.* to the *Fasti* as a progression within the Hesiodic corpus. The proem invokes the gods to inspire the poet to spin a song from the beginning of the world to his own times (*Met.* 1.3–4, *ab origine mundi / ad mea . . . tempora*). Beginning with Chaos (*Met.* 1.7) refers to the beginning of the *Th*, while ending with *mea tempora* suggests the *WD*, which deals with Hesiod's times and the right time for different tasks. *Tempora* is the first word of the *Fasti*, and thus the proem to the *Met.* already anticipates the *Fasti* as the sequel to Ovid's epic (Barchiesi 1991: 6–7). The unified reading of the Hesiodic corpus provides Ovid with the model for transitioning from the *Met.* to the *Fasti*. The first word (*tempora*) and thus the alternative title of the *Fasti* casts Ovid's work as a version and elaboration of Hesiod's "Days"; the *Fasti* follows the Roman calendar, which prescribes which days are suitable for work and which for festivals. To some extent the *Fasti*, with its emphasis on holidays, contrasts with Hesiod's focus on work.

Just as the *Met.* includes the entire spectrum of the Hesiodic worldview and is chronologically arranged, thus reproducing the move from the creation of gods (*Th*) to the birth of the demigods (*CW*) and from the demise of the heroes to Hesiod's times (*WD*), the *Fasti* replays the continuity and progression within the main three Hesiodic works. The god Janus is emblematic of the simultaneously unified and multifaceted nature of Hesiod's works. Janus's epiphany echoes the programmatic appearance of Apollo in Callimachus's *Aetia* (cf. *Fasti* 1.93–94 with *Aetia* fr. 1.21–22 Pf.), which is in turn a reworking of Hesiod's encounter with the Muses in the *Th*. In his address to Ovid, the god reveals his original identity as Chaos, the primordial beginning of the *Th*, while associating the poet of the *Fasti* with Hesiodic didacticism:

> "*disce* metu posito, uates *operose dierum*,
>   quod petis, et uoces percipe mente meas.
> me *Chaos antiqui* (nam sum res prisca) uocabant:
>   aspice quam longi temporis acta canam." (*Fasti* 1.101–4)

> "Set aside fear and learn, laborious bard of the days, what you seek, and bear my words in mind. The ancients used to call me Chaos (for I am old matter): notice the deeds of very old times of which I am singing."

Janus's imperative *disce* is a marker of didactic poetry (cf. *Fasti* 2.584, 4.140, 145, 6.639; cf. *WD* 213, ἄκουε, 275 ἐπάκουε) that echoes the Muses' instructions to Hesiod (*Th* 22, Ἡσίοδον καλὴν ἐδίδαξαν ἀοιδήν, "they taught Hesiod a beautiful song"; cf. *WD* 662); *operose dierum* paraphrases *Opera et Dies*.[20] Janus exemplifies the combination of the lessons of the *WD* with the cosmogony of the *Th*. In this context, the mention of the *antiqui* can be read as a reference to the ancient authority of Hesiod.

In his reminiscence of Saturn's arrival in Latium, Janus briefly mentions the succession myth of the *Th*; Saturn found refuge in Latium after Jupiter drove him away from the kingdom of the sky (1.235–36). Janus was ruling over the Ianiculum in an era of agricultural simplicity, when gods and humans were mingling on earth:

> tunc ego regnabam, *patiens* cum terra deorum
>   esset, et *humanis numina mixta locis.*
> nondum *Iustitiam facinus mortale fugarat*
>   (ultima de superis illa reliquit humum),
> proque metu populum sine ui *pudor* ipse regebat;
>   nullus erat iustis reddere iura labor.
> nil mihi cum bello: *pacem* postesque tuebar. (*Fasti* 1.247–53)

> I was ruling then, when earth was enduring gods and deities mingled in human places. Mortal crime had not yet put Justice to flight (she was the last of the gods above to leave the ground) and instead of fear and without violence shame itself guided the people; it was no toil to give back justice to the just. I had nothing to do with war: I was the guardian of peace and doorposts.

The society of gods and humans recalls the joint feast at Mekone (*Th* 535) and the beginning of the *CW* (fr. 1.5–7 M–W); *mixta*, in particular, implies the affairs of gods with mortal women (see fr. 1.5 M–W, μισγόμεναι θεοῖσ[ιν, "mingling with gods"; cf. fr. 5.4, 253.3 M–W, μιχθεῖσ᾽ ἐν φιλότητι, "having mingled in love"). The offspring of these liaisons are the race of heroes, who eventually become a burden on the earth. The *CW* opens with the common feasts of gods and men and ends with Zeus's plan to decimate mankind by causing the Trojan War, which relieves Earth of the human burden and finalizes the gap between mortals and immortals (see Clay 2005). Ovid's *patiens . . . terra* suggests the anthropomorphic suffering of Hesiod's Gaia (cf. *Th* 159, 843, 848), implying that Earth is oppressed by the presence of the gods and their mingling with mortals. The proclaimed flight of Justice combines the departure of Αἰδώς, "Reverence" (cf. *pudor*), and Νέμεσις, "Retribution," from the earth (*WD* 197–200) with the maltreatment of Δίκη, "Justice" (*WD* 220–27), at the hands of greedy mortals, who drag and drive her away (*WD* 224, οἵ τέ μιν ἐξελάσωσι; cf. *Iustitiam facinus mortale fugarat*). The transition from Justice to peace reproduces the sequence in the *WD* (Δίκη, 219–27; εἰρήνη, 228–37), adding a Greek layer to the association of Janus with the closing of the gates of War. The interplay between abstract nouns and their personifications is characteristically Hesiodic. Besides *Iustitia*, it is tempting to capitalize *patiens . . . Terra, Pudor*, and *Pacem*. The use of an abstract noun as subject of *regere* is peculiar (see Green 2004: 119), inviting us to take *Pudor* as the personified Shame, while the syllepsis *pacem postesque tuebar* suggests that Janus was the physical guardian of Peace in his temple (contra Green 2004: 119–20). Her escape would result in a disaster tantamount to the opening of Pandora's jar.[21]

In *Fasti* 1, Janus shows that the *Th* and the *WD* are the two faces of the same coin. But the god makes another, rather surprising, appearance in *Fasti* 6.100–30. Janus returns and rapes the nymph Cranae. This peculiar story evokes a tale from the Hesiodic *Ehoiai*. The beginning of Ovid's etiology with the introduction of Cranae recalls the typical opening of an *ehoie* with the presentation of the heroine. Cranae is wooed by many suitors, a salient motif of the *CW* (see fr. 22.5–6, 75, 196–204 M–W; cf. Homer, *Odyssey* 11.288), but refuses to marry (108). While she can deceive men by escaping as they are leading the way, she cannot deceive two-faced Janus. The god rapes her and then announces that she will control the hinges of the doors as a recompense for her lost virginity (127–28). The narrative sequence and direct speech recall the speech of Poseidon to Tyro, whom the god seduced and then comforted by promising the birth of glorious children (see *CW* fr. 31 M–W; cf. Homer, *Odyssey* 11.248–52). The *CW*'s promise of heroic offspring is replaced with the *Fasti*'s etiological conclusion, a common Ovidian twist. Thus the presence of Janus in the *Fasti* marks a progression within the Hesiodic corpus: from the *Th* and the *WD* to the *CW*.

CONCLUDING REMARKS

Helen van Noorden (2014: 216) notes that while we might think of the *Met.* and the *Fasti* as a pair to rival the *Th* and the *WD*, a more accurate view is that both recall both. To some extent the Hesiodic corpus already suggests this interplay between progression and inclusion. The *Th* and the *WD* present a trajectory from mythological to didactic epic, two different worldviews, each of which contains aspects from the other. There are didactic elements in the *Th* and theogonic elements in the *WD*. Reading the *Th* and the *WD* as two poems that complement and at times contradict each other has been the focus of modern scholarship (see Clay 2003). The *CW*, a sequel to the *Th* in ancient manuscripts, has recently attracted more attention as a work offering a heroic and thus intermediate perspective between the divine (*Th*) and the human (*WD*), both chronologically and conceptually (see Clay 2005). This approach has at times been criticized as a modern interpretation of Hesiod through the lens of a preconceived master narrative (Kerr Prince 2005). Yet this master narrative is not a modern invention, but is suggested in the Hesiodic corpus. The polyphony and coherence of Hesiod's many voices features prominently in the poet's Hellenistic reception (see Canevaro in this volume). In his holistic view of the Hesiodic corpus, Ovid follows in the footsteps of Hesiod's Hellenistic reception. He seems to have been very much interested in perceiving Hesiod's cosmos through the lens of a comprehensive narrative as he repeatedly points to the harmony and conflict between and within Hesiod's works. Ovid is himself obsessed with the continuities and disruptions, the unities and contradictions, the evolution and circularity of his career. In Hesiod, he found an archetype for reflecting on his poetic and personal development.

NOTES

1. On "window reference," defined as the adaptation of a model, noticeably interrupted in order to allow reference back to the source of that model, see Thomas (1986: 188–89, 197).

2. "Syllepsis" is the simultaneous employment of the literal and metaphorical meaning of words, which results in a combination of physical and linguistic transformations.

3. All translations are adapted from the Loeb editions (Showerman 1914; Frazer 1931; Most 2006, 2007).

4. On the tradition of the *certamen*, see Koning (2010: 239–68); and Hunter (2014: 302–15). On Hesiod's reception as inextricably linked with that of Homer, see Koning (2010); and Canevaro in this volume.

5. On the Hellenistic reception of Hesiod, see Canevaro in this volume.

6. On Ovid and the Hesiodic *CW*, see Fletcher (2005); Hardie (2005); and Ziogas (2013). On the structure of the *CW*, see West (1985).

7. Like Ovid's *talis*, Sosicrates or Sostratos's Ἠοῖοι suggests a similarly peculiar masculine version of the Hesiodic formula. But a gendered play with the *ehoie* formula may be as old as Homer; see *Iliad* 1.262–64 with Ziogas (2013: 190–92). On the *CW* and Hellenistic poetry, see Hunter (2005).

8. See Farrell (2004) on Ovid modeling his career on Vergil. Yet Hesiod is the archetype for both Vergil and Ovid. Vergil connects and contrasts the *Eclogues* with the *Georgics* in a way that evokes Hesiod's cross references between *Th* and *WD*. The autobiographical aspects of Vergil's *Georgics* follow in the footsteps of Hesiod's *Th* and *WD*; see Nelson in this volume.

9. In *Th* 224–25, Φιλότης ("Sexual Intercourse") is the sister of Ἔρις. Cf. the contrast between *lites* and *amor* at *Ars* 2.151–52. See also Scully (2015: 145).

10. On ἔργα meaning "fields" in Hesiod, see Nelson pp. 365–68 in this volume.

11. Cf. Canevaro (2015: 122–23) on procreation in the *WD*, which is seen in terms of productivity, analogous to planting or rearing animals.

12. Alexander Loney points out to me that at *Th* 594–612, work, sex, offspring, production, consumption, and greedy women are all tied together.

13. The return to the golden age is predicted by Anchises in Vergil, *Aeneid* 6.792–94. Cf. *Eclogue* 4, which predicts the return of a second heroic age and another golden era. On the golden age and Augustan ideology, see Wallace-Hadrill (1982).

14. Cf. Feeney (2007: 134–36). See Barker (1996) for the inherent ambiguity of the golden race as morally superior due to its lack of greed and as corrupt due to its literal goldenness.

15. The interplay between metals and metallic ages is in play in Janus's speech (*Fasti* 1.192–226). The copper coins of olden days have been replaced with gold. See below on Ovid's Janus and Hesiod.

16. On Ovid and the Hesiodic myth of races, see Van Noorden (2014: 204–60).

17. Cf. *Met.* 5.366, *superas omnes*; 369–70, *superos. . . domas* with *Th* 121–22, πάντων τε θεῶν . . . δάμναται . . . νόον.

18. On Typhoeus as a foil for the Muses, see Goslin (2010).

19. See, e.g., Atalanta in the *CW* and *Met.* 10 with Ziogas (2013: 164–74); Ormand (2014: 119–51).

20. Barchiesi (1997: 223); Green (2004: 74–75). On Janus and Hesiod, see Barchiesi (1997: 230–36).

21. Labate (2005: 190–91) argues that Janus's opening and closing of the gates of war recalls the opening of Pandora's jar (*WD* 20–105).

References

Adams, J. N. 1982. *The Latin Sexual Vocabulary*. Baltimore, MD.

Ahl, F. 1985. *Metaformations: Soundplay and Wordplay in Ovid and Other Classical Poets*. Ithaca, NY.

Barchiesi, A. 1991. "Discordant Muses." *Proceedings of the Cambridge Philological Society* 37: 1–21.

Barchiesi, A. 1997. *The Poet and the Prince*. Berkeley, CA.

Barker, D. 1996. "'The Golden Age Is Proclaimed': The *Carmen Saeculare* and the Renascence of the Golden Race." *Classical Quarterly* 46: 434–46.

Bilinski, B. 1959. "Elementi Esiodei nelle 'Metamorfosi' di Ovidio." In *Atti del Convegno Internazionale Ovidiano, II*, 101–23. Rome.

Canevaro, L. G. 2015. *Hesiod's Works and Days: How to Teach Self-Sufficiency*. Oxford.

Clay, J. 2003. *Hesiod's Cosmos*. Cambridge.

Clay, J. 2005. "The Beginning and End of the *Catalogue of Women* and Its Relation to Hesiod." In *The Hesiodic Catalogue of Women: Constructions and Reconstructions*, edited by R. Hunter, 25–34. Cambridge.

Cole, T. 2004. "Ovid, Varro, and Castor of Rhodes." *Harvard Studies in Classical Philology* 102: 355–422.

Cole, T. 2008. *Ovidius Mythistoricus: Legendary Time in the Metamorphoses*. Frankfurt am Main.

Conte, G. B. 1986. *The Rhetoric of Imitation: Genre and Poetic Memory in Virgil and Other Latin Poets*. Ithaca, NY.

Farrell, J. 2004. "Ovid's Virgilian Career." *Materiali e Discussioni per l'analisi dei testi classici* 52: 41–55.

Feeney, D. C. 1991. *The Gods in Epic: Poets and Critics of the Classical Tradition*. Oxford.

Feeney, D. C. 2007. *Caesar's Calendar: Ancient Time and the Beginnings of History*. Berkeley, CA.

Fletcher, R. 2005. "Or Such as Ovid's *Metamorphoses*. . . ." In *The Hesiodic Catalogue of Women: Constructions and Reconstructions*, edited by R. Hunter, 299–319. Cambridge.

Frazer J. G., ed. and trans. 1931. *Ovid: Fasti*, revised by G. P. Goold. Cambridge, MA.

Gärtner, T. 2008. "Die hellenistische Katalogdichtung des Phanokles über homosexuelle Liebesbeziehungen: Untersuchungen zur tendenziellen Gestaltung und zum literarischen Nachleben." *Mnemosyne* 61: 18–44.

Gibson, R., ed. and comm. 2003. *Ovid, Ars Amatoria*. Book 3. Cambridge.

Goslin, O. 2010. "Hesiod's Typhonomachy and the Ordering of Sound." *TAPA* 140: 351–73.

Green. S. J., ed. and comm. 2004. *Ovid, Fasti I: A Commentary*. Leiden.

Hardie, P. 2005. "The Hesiodic *Catalogue of Women* and Latin Poetry." In *The Hesiodic Catalogue of Women: Constructions and Reconstructions*, edited by R. Hunter, 287–98. Cambridge.

Haubold, J. H. 2010. "Shepherd, Farmer, Poet, Sophist: Hesiod on His Own Reception." In *Plato and Hesiod*, edited by G. R. Boys-Stones and J. H. Haubold, 11–30. Oxford.

Hirschberger, M. 2008. "Il tema della metamorfosi nel *Catalogo* esiodeo delle donne." In *Esiodo: Cent'anni di papiri: Atti del convegno internazionale di studi, Firenze, 7–8 Giugno 2007*, edited by G. Bastianini and A. Casanova, 113–27. Florence.

Hollis, A. 1977. *Ovid: Ars Amatoria*. Book 1. Oxford.

Hunter, R. 2005. "The Hesiodic *Catalogue* and Hellenistic Poetry." In *The Hesiodic Catalogue of Women: Constructions and Reconstructions*, edited by R. Hunter, 239–65. Cambridge.

Hunter, R. 2014. *Hesiodic Voices: Studies in the Ancient Reception of Hesiod's Works and Days*. Cambridge.

Kerr Prince, C. 2005. "Review of Clay (2003)." *Bryn Mawr Classical Review* 4: 23.

Koning, H. H. 2010. *Hesiod: The Other Poet; Ancient Reception of a Cultural Icon*. Mnemosyne Supplement 325. Leiden..

La Penna, A. 1979. "L' *usus* contro Apollo e le Muse." *Annali della Scuola Normale di Pisa* 9: 985–97.

Labate, M., 2005. "Tempo delle origini e tempo della storia in Ovidio." In *La représentation du temps dans la poésie augustéenne—Zur Poetik der Zeit in augusteischer Dichtung*, edited by J. P. Schwindt, 177–201. Heidelberg.

Most, G. 1993. "Hesiod and the Textualization of Personal Temporality." In *La componente autobiografica nella poesia Greca e Latina fra realtà e artificio letterario*, edited by G. Arrighetti and F. Montanari, 73–92. Pisa.

Most, G., ed. and trans. 2006. *Hesiod: Theogony, Works and Days, Testimonia*. Cambridge, MA.

Most, G., ed. and trans. 2007. *Hesiod: The Shield, Catalogue of Women, Other Fragments*. Cambridge, MA.

Obbink, D. 2004. "Vergil's *De pietate*: From *Ehoiae* to Allegory in Vergil, Philodemus and Ovid." In *Vergil, Philodemus and the Augustans*, edited by D. Armstrong, J. Fish, P. Johnston, and M. Skinner, 175–209. Austin, TX.

Ormand, K. 2014. *The Hesiodic Catalogue of Women and Archaic Greece*. Cambridge.

Rosati, G. 2009. "The Latin Reception of Hesiod." In *Brill's Companion to Hesiod*, edited by F. Montanari, A. Rengakos, C. Tsagalis, 343–74. Leiden.

Scully, S. 2015. *Hesiod's Theogony: From Near Eastern Creation Myths to Paradise Lost*. Oxford.

Segal, C. 1972. "Ovid's Orpheus and Augustan Ideology." *Transactions of the American Philological Association* 103: 473–94.

Showerman, G., ed. and trans. 1914. *Ovid: Heroides, Amores*. Revised by G. P. Goold. Cambridge, MA.

Thomas, R. F. 1986. "Vergil's *Georgics* and the Art of Reference." *Harvard Studies in Classical Philology* 90: 171–98.

Tissol, G. 1997. *The Face of Nature: Wit, Narrative, and Cosmic Origins in Ovid's "Metamorphoses"*. Princeton, NJ.

Trencsényi-Waldapfel, I. 1969. "Eine Invektive gegen Hesiod bei Ovid." *Collection Latomus* 101: 728–50.

Van Noorden, H. 2014. *Playing Hesiod: The "Myth of Races" in Classical Antiquity*. Cambridge.

Wallace-Hadrill, A. 1982. "The Golden Age and Sin in Augustan Ideology." *Past and Present* 95: 19–36.

West, M. L. 1985. *The Hesiodic Catalogue of Women: Its Nature, Structure, and Origins*. Oxford.

Wheeler, S. 1999. *A Discourse of Wonders: Audience and Performance in Ovid's "Metamorphoses"*. Philadelphia, PA.

Ziogas, I. 2013. *Ovid and Hesiod. The Metamorphosis of the Catalogue of Women*. Cambridge.

CHAPTER 25

HESIOD TRANSFORMED, PARODIED, AND ASSAULTED

Hesiod in the Second Sophistic and Early Christian Thought

HELEN VAN NOORDEN

INTRODUCTION

WHAT do pagan and early Christian authors of the period 50–250 CE have to offer the story of Hesiod's reception in antiquity? Hugo Koning has found that 65% of the surviving quotations of Hesiod's text come from authors of this period (2010: 21), a period defined by Philostratus's characterization of its orators as those of a "second sophistic" (*Lives of the Sophists* 1.481). The quantity of citations may not, however, point to a vastly increased interest in Hesiod as much as to a milieu that encourages this form of reference, a mode of using archaic poets that privileges rhetorical interests (see, e.g., Whitmarsh 2005). Koning argues that interest in Hesiod per se in fact fades by comparison with interest in Homer, since Homer increasingly takes over functions and identities formerly associated with Hesiod (Koning 2010: 294, 378–79).

Yet Koning's own survey and recent overviews by Richard Hunter (2014) and Stephen Scully (2015) of (respectively) the receptions of Hesiod's *Works and Days* (hereafter *WD*) and *Theogony* (hereafter *Th*) have revealed plenty to be said about authors such as Plutarch and Lucian. Moreover, one of the most famous pieces of Hesiodic reception, the extant *Contest of Homer and Hesiod*, dates from the second century CE. Study of this text, the first focus of the first section below ("Hesiod Transformed"), yields insights into contemporary notions of "essential" or "core" Hesiod, biographical traditions about him, and his value for communities. Testimonia from Athenaeus and Plutarch in Most (2006: T85–86) indicate continued performance of Hesiod's poems at the theater and at dinner; other comments in these authors aid our sense not only of how Hesiod was used in the symposium but also of contemporary forms of scholarship on the Hesiodic poems, especially concerning their authenticity.

Some of this chapter's basic questions about attitudes to Hesiod continue from earlier periods: Do we find more sympathy or aggression toward Hesiod? Were Hesiodic verses read in isolation or in (what) context? On a first impression, the *WD*, praised by Plutarch for its social wisdom, in this period garnered more sympathy than the *Th*, which was condemned (both in jest by Lucian and in earnest by Christian apologists) for its tall stories. However, this impression will be qualified, and the second section below, "Hesiod Parodied," presses the question of how far the tracks of reception of the two major Hesiodic texts overlap. Here I focus primarily on Lucian to demonstrate ways in which Hesiodic poetry was both subverted and exploited in this period, particularly for Hesiod's claimed relation to the Muses, a feature that enables cross-referencing from one Hesiodic work to another. I also point out the dominance of certain passages, such as the Two Roads and the Myth of the Races, sometimes at a structural level, in the tradition of appropriating Hesiod for new (especially rhetorical) projects.

Finally (in the third section below), I focus on the Christian apologists, especially Clement of Alexandria and Theophilus, to consider ways in which their references and allusions to Hesiod both follow and diverge from their pagan contemporaries. Inconsistency or incompatibility between details forms a major prong of attack on Hesiod in both the Christian writers and Lucian, yet also discernible is a stake in harmonizing different traditions; this is not a surprising discovery given that the majority of writers in this period were operating as educators (Koning 2010: 96–100).

HESIOD TRANSFORMED: REFASHIONING "HESIOD" IN THE *CERTAMEN* AND BEYOND

Traditionally, the sense that Hesiod was for antiquity the main contender to Homer stems from arguments over their chronological priority, as a means of asserting their relative importance (see Koning in this volume, p. 18). Although authors of the imperial period refer to the evidence for this question as inconclusive (e.g., Clement of Alexandria, *Miscellanies* 1.21.117.4) or too contentious to go into (Pausanias, *Description of Greece* 9.30.3), interest in the larger stakes of the question are evident; the first two centuries CE yield several accounts of a poetic competition between Homer and Hesiod, which, assuming their contemporaneity, focus more directly on their respective merits and popularity.

The fullest and most famous of these accounts is the anonymous compilation known since the Renaissance as the *Certamen*; its Greek title more fully describes its contents as "concerning Homer and Hesiod and their descent and contest" (see in general Koning 2010: 248–59). In this text, whose core account of a poetic contest is thought to go back at least to the fourth century BCE (Richardson 1981), accounts of the birth and death of

Homer and Hesiod, "the most inspired of all poets" (1.1), frame a story of their rivalry in funeral games for King Amphidamas at Chalcis in Euboea. This is best understood as creatively building on the claim in *WD* 650–59 that "Hesiod," favored as he was by the Muses, won a poetic competition at these funeral games on the only (short) sea voyage he ever took out of Ascra; Nagy (1982: 66) is one of those who see in the Hesiodic passage implicit polemic against heroic epic, of which Homer is the primary representative. In the *Certamen,* Hesiod challenges Homer to answer a series of riddles (unlike Plutarch's briefer account in *Symposium of the Seven Sages* 153f–4a, in which Hesiod is challenged by Homer/Lesches [on the variant manuscripts, see Stamatopoulou 2014: 541–42]). Hesiod's first and last questions for Homer consist of requests for classic poetic wisdom, such as "What is the best thing for mortals?"; the body of the competition consists of his setting Homer a verse "conundrum" (τὴν τῶν ἀπόρων ὥρμησεν ἐπερώτησιν, §8 in West 2003) and a series of "ambivalent propositions" (ἐπὶ τὰς ἀμφιβόλους γνώμας ὥρμησεν, §9 West), that is, nonsense verses that Homer's responses must turn into sense. At a basic level, Hesiod's taking the initiative in this, the fullest surviving account of the contest, surely reflects his status as an authority on the very notion of competition, as suggested by the fact that Dio's *Oration 77/78, On Envy,* begins from a discussion of *WD* 25 on "Good Strife" (see further Hunter 2014: 1–7); moreover, within the *Certamen* Hesiod's characterization as φθονῶν (§11 West) is, as Koning notes, a reference to *WD* 26 on bardic jealousy of bards.

In the *Certamen,* following these exercises in capping verses, King Panedes, brother of the deceased, invites each poet to recite his best verses, to which Hesiod responds with *WD* 383–92, the start of the farmer's calendar, and Homer with a virtual "aestheticization of war" comprising two extracts from *Iliad* 13 (see further comment on these lines in Hunter 2014: 303–5). The audience of "the Greeks" cheer for Homer, but King Panedes adjudicates Hesiod the winner on the grounds that Hesiod promotes peace and not war.

The choice of Hesiodic passage points to a notion of "core" Hesiodic poetry based on the *WD* only. Barbara Graziosi has demonstrated that in contexts of contrast with Homer, both in this period and in earlier antiquity, the popular sense of Hesiod's oeuvre narrows to the *WD* (and equally Homer's oeuvre is narrowed to the *Iliad*; for use of the *Certamen* in this argument, see Graziosi 2002: 168–76). This kind of "essentialism" may be traced in other forms as well; in the late second century CE, Pausanias 9.31.4–5 writes that the Boeotians on Mt. Helicon regarded the *WD* (minus its proem) as the only genuine Hesiodic work (on which see Scully 2015: 153).

When read with an eye to its second-century CE context, the second point of interest in the *Certamen* is its summary of accounts of Homer's and Hesiod's births and deaths. According to the *Certamen* (§14 West), Hesiod was murdered by his hosts on suspicion of having seduced their sister, after which his body was cast out to sea but recovered by dolphins, and his bones were transported by order of an oracle to Orchomenus. The full version of the title, which highlights this frame, identifies the *Certamen* as itself a Hesiodic *Life* narrative, part of the "marked biographical trend" of literature under the Roman Empire (Whitmarsh 2005: 75–79), of which Plutarch's *Parallel Lives* is only the most famous example; indeed, Plutarch and Pausanias predominate in the ancient "testimonia" about Hesiod's life and death (Most 2006: T31–35). These biographical fictions of violent death and divine favor, evidently drawing in part on autobiographical elements of the *WD* and the narrative in the *Th* of inspiration by the Muses, elevate Hesiod to the status of a hero (Koning 2010: 133–38); similar structures have been noted in ancient "Lives" of Orpheus (Scodel 1980) and Aesop (Hunter 2014: 257–64).

Hesiod beats Homer in all ancient versions of their poetic encounter, but there is significant variation in *how* he wins. The point on which Hesiod's victory turns in the *Certamen*, King Panedes's judgment in favor of Hesiod, is the third aspect of the text worthy of remark in the context of second sophistic concerns. James Uden notes that since the *Certamen* narrative has presented Homer as successful in all the challenges and more popular than Hesiod throughout, King Panedes's decision comes across as a reversal. Noting the repeated emphasis on "all Greeks" in the audience, Uden suggests that this reflects the philhellenic Hadrian's establishment of the Pan-Hellenia at Athens and argues that Panedes is a figure for Hadrian; Panedes's "gaffe" recalls the opening of the *Certamen*, an unflattering anecdote of Hadrian consulting the Delphic Oracle about Homer's parentage (Uden 2010: 130–32). While such an agenda does much to explain the shape of this particular contest narrative, it is striking that the majority of other, briefer contemporary references to the *Certamen* tradition, in Dio Chrysostom (*Oration* 2.12), Lucian (*True Histories* 2.22), and Philostratus (*Heroicus* 43.9–10), likewise opine that Hesiod's victory was unfair, although only Philostratus refers to it explicitly as Panedes's decision. In Dio's *Second Oration on Kingship*, a dialogue between Alexander the Great and his father Philip, Alexander blames the result on the judgement of "rustics" before whom the poets were performing. The king's judgment in the *Certamen* marks a temporary exception in the tendency of ancient sources to associate "Hesiod" more often with ordinary people and Homer with kings, generals, and aristocrats—a function of the point mentioned above, that Hesiod is primarily associated with the *WD* (which is markedly critical of "kings") when presented in contrast with Homer (Koning 2010: 284–90). The issue of how the two main Hesiodic works are brought together is revisited below.

Hesiod's traditional expertise in farming, emphasized whenever he is presented in opposition to Homer, is turned to a novel argumentative agenda in Maximus of Tyre's paired *Orations* 23 and 24 (late second century CE), arguments respectively for soldiery and farming. At 23.6, the proponent of soldiery is arguing that farming leads to war rather than peace, because well-farmed land actually provokes the desire for territorial expansion: "Desires wander everywhere over the whole earth . . . and everything is full of armies." Hunter (2014: 73–75) observes that the speaker appropriates the language of *WD* 100–1, the conclusion to the story of Pandora ("countless other miseries roam among men; / full is the earth of evils"), which in the *WD* functioned as the etiology of the modern need to work/farm the land. An earlier example of "updating" Hesiodic wisdom on farming, however, follows Hesiod's self-identification in the *WD* as the poet of the *Th*; what survives of Discourse 11 of the Stoic Musonius Rufus (first century CE), on farming as a way of life for the philosopher, cites Hesiod as an example of someone whose shepherding did not prevent him from becoming "loved by the gods," proceeding to reconfigure in terms of Stoic education Hesiod's lessons of self-sufficiency from the *WD* (Hunter 2014: 71–73). A third creative adaptation of Hesiod on farming, this time in tandem with a reworking of Homer, is found in the *Euboean Oration* of Dio Chrysostom (late first/early second century CE). Here, an urgent diatribe, reminiscent of the tone of the *WD*, about the self-sufficiency of the poor outside the city and the work they should do within it, is framed by a narrative of shipwreck reminiscent of the *Odyssey*, while the body of the discussion includes citation and discussion of verses from both Hesiod and Homer (Hunter 2014: 17–20).

Such extensive rhetorical reworkings of Hesiod's *WD* are, however, less frequently found in second sophistic literature than citations of Hesiodic wisdom, whose quotability is brought out above all in the contemporary profusion of miscellanies. A "compilatory aesthetic," which embraces discontinuities (Uden 2010: 123), may be adduced to explain why Hesiod's *WD*, in particular, finds new life as a repository of sympotic wisdom. Notably, Hesiod is discussed by the wise men and their friends pictured in Plutarch's *Symposium of the Seven Sages*, and Hesiod's *WD* is cited numerous times, along with the works of Homer, in the third-century CE work of Athenaeus, *The Learned Banqueters*. The latter contains discussions which, over fifteen books, range from food and wine, through contemporary mores, to philology. For example, *WD* 596, advising when to make a libation to the gods, is twice recycled in Athenaeus (10.426c and 11.782a) as an expert's opinion on how to mix wine and water at a symposium. Hesiodic tags are also applied in good humor to trivial matters—Athenaeus 14.653d cites *WD* 410, advice not to procrastinate, as assurance that the speaker will promptly answer his interlocutor's recherché challenge about words for dried figs. However, not all the participants in the series of banquets Athenaeus portrays consider Hesiod a sympotic expert. During a discussion of friendship as one benefit of a symposium, *WD* 342–43, "invite your friend to the feast, but let your enemy be; / and above all invite those near to you," is judged parochial (Βοιωτικῆς ἀναισθησίας, "of Boeotian insensibility") by comparison with Homer, who (in the person of Agamemnon at *Iliad* 2.404) instructs us simply to invite the best people (Athenaeus 5.186f).

This raises the wider issue of support or otherwise for Hesiod among authors writing in Greek under the Roman Empire. We should expect some nuancing of his legacy, given the parallel engagement with Homer as a contestable authority on the story of the Trojan War (on which see Kim 2010). One form of defense construes Hesiod as speaking to elite audiences who have the ability to apply particular illustrations more widely. Dio follows the Stoic Chrysippus in citing *WD* 348 ("not even an ox would be lost, if the neighbor were not wicked") as an example of a statement not to be restricted literally to this animal; rather, Hesiod is speaking "to intelligent people" (πρὸς συνιέντας, *Oration* 77.5) (Hunter 2014: 2–3). We may find this a reasonable presumption in the light of Hesiod's introduction to his story of the hawk and nightingale, as an αἶνος for "kings who understand" (*WD* 202).

Other forms of charitable interpretation of Hesiodic verses are found in Plutarch, who stands out as one writer invested in Hesiod (citing him 207 times, according to the table of citations at Morgan 1998: 318). Plutarch tends, at least in the fragments traceable to his lost four-book commentary on the *WD*, to defend Hesiod against detractors (e.g., fr. 48 in the numeration of Sandbach 1969: 104–227 on the above-quoted *WD* 342–43; it is in fact very sensible advice to focus on inviting friends rather than enemies to a feast, since one faces a dilemma if those enemies invite you back).[1] Plutarch also reinforces the truth of Hesiodic verses with reference to his own scientific interests; for example, fr. 29 Sandbach explains as "tarnishing" the fact that Hesiod's "silver race" of men fall into hubris on leaving the homes of their extended childhoods (*WD* 216–17).

Plutarch's sympathy for Hesiod seems to inform his brief account of the contest between Homer and Hesiod in *Symposium of the Seven Sages* 153e–54a (following several other imagined encounters between legendary figures), which, unlike other versions that present Hesiod's victory as unfair, records the poets as "evenly matched" in reciting their poetry, until Hesiod wins outright with a brilliant piece of improvisation to make sense of an ἀπορία (nonsense verse/riddle). The framing "Life" narrative in this account also exonerates Hesiod, attributing to a travel companion the seduction for which Hesiod was condemned to death (162c–e). However, Stamatopoulou (2014) finds Plutarch renegotiating Hesiod's legacy, arguing that the value of Hesiod's wisdom is in various ways downgraded in the community of sages; for example, an assertion of Hesiod's medical knowledge, based on interpreting *WD* 41 (the value of mallow and asphodel) as the origin of Epimenides's miraculous "no-hunger" drug, is replaced with an image of Hesiod as the inventor of the fable developed by Aesop (*Symposium of the Seven Sages* 158b).

In relation to Hesiodic myths, Plutarch selectively appropriates material for his own moralizing agenda; in both *On How to Study Poetry* 23e–24a and *On Chance* 99e–f, Plutarch refers to Pandora, thoughtlessly welcomed by Epimetheus at *WD* 85–89, as an example of how "Zeus" is synonymous with Fortune, whose gifts should not be accepted if one cannot make good use of them (similarly interpreted in Dio's *Oration On Fortune* [64.8] in relation to *WD* 6–7). Again, *WD* 101, from the gloomy etiology concluding that text's version of the Pandora story, is cited along with other literary sources on mankind's ephemeral condition, in order to console Plutarch's bereaved friend Apollonius ([ps. Plutarchan] *Consolation to Apollonius* 105e and 115a). Plutarch also contributes substantially to the tradition, implied already in Empedocles, that Hesiod, based on his account of golden and silver men becoming *daimones* (*WD* 121–26, 140–42), is an expert on demonology and the afterlife (Plutarch, *On the Obsolescence of Oracles* 415b and often elsewhere; see Koning 2010: 170–71).[2]

Such selective acceptance of Hesiodic wisdom is found also in Plutarch's scholarship on the poem. He sometimes quietly adjusts Hesiodic wisdom to fit his theme (*WD* 25 becomes "potter must *not* envy potter"; *How to Profit from One's Enemies* 92a) and elsewhere openly corrects it (Hesiod was not right to assert [with "potter envies potter"] that people are envious only of those like themselves [see Morgan 2007: 19]). That correction of Hesiod is of course found already in Plato (see, e.g., *Lysis* 215c); likewise in the wake of Plato and others, Plutarch picks up a Hesiodic verse long found morally problematic (*WD* 311, "No work is a disgrace") but explains it in a manner far more sympathetic to Hesiod (Plutarch, *Solon* 2.3–4; contrast Dio Chrysostom *Oration* 7.110–11, qualifying Hesiod's assertion in order to rail against prostitutes as part of a denunciation of city life—on both these engagements with Hesiod, see Hunter 2014: 17, 208–15). Plutarch is also ready to excise lines of the *WD* that he considers "unworthy" of Hesiod, such as *WD* 267–73, the famous complaint that it is not worth being just, since (Plutarch says, in Platonic spirit) justice is choice-worthy whatever the circumstances (fr. 38 Sandbach); *WD* 353–54, on giving only to one who gives (fr. 51 Sandbach); and *WD* 757–59, on not urinating in the rivers (fr. 98 Sandbach). However, Plutarch seems to have had no problem with *WD* 727–32 on the right way to urinate, probably because these lines would hold appeal in view of the second sophistic concern with εὐσχημοσύνη (the right way to perform actions) (Hunter 2014: 183, discussing Plutarch's deletions). Plutarch's atheteses may be construed as kinder reflections of, and solutions to, accusations of "inconsistency" leveled at Hesiod by Lucian and the early Christian apologists (see second and third sections below).

Traces of broader discussions of Hesiodic authenticity, as well as scholarly interest in Hesiod's vocabulary, are found in authors of this period. I have mentioned the claim, found in Pausanias, that the Boeotians considered only the *WD* as genuine Hesiod. However, Athenaeus cites from several works as "attributed to Hesiod" (*Great Ehoiai, Aegimus, The Marriage of Ceyx, Melampodia* and [although not consistently] *Astronomy* [cf. T66, T68, T75, T79 Most]). Athenaeus's learned banqueters show off their extensive knowledge of Hesiod also through discussion of recherché vocabulary from Hesiodic works, such as ἔνηφι for "the day after tomorrow" (Athenaeus 3.100b), specialist vocabulary for types of drinking cup (11.498a–b, 503d), or Hesiod's use of the mysterious word ἀμολγαίη apparently for "barley cake" (3.115a–b). Hesiod's kenning vocabulary also attracts comment (2.63a on "house-carrier" for snail), and he is characterized at 3.101f. as speaking γνωμικῶς, "gnomically" or "proverbially"; we may therefore connect the riddling Hesiod of the *Certamen* with wider contemporary recognition of such discursive modes in the *WD*.

A different form of scholarship on Hesiod may be closely linked to second sophistic interests in rhetoric—that is, analyses of his style, which, while attracting unfavorable comparison with Homer, was praised for its "sweetness" and "smoothness" by writers on oratory such as Quintilian (*Institutes* 10.1.52, 12.10.58; see Scully in this volume, pp. 91–92). Richard Hunter (2014: 282–83) has noted the importance of the *Th* and *Catalogue of Women*, rather than the *WD*, for imperial ideas of Hesiod's style (beyond the fact that, as Quintilian says, "a great part of his work is taken up by names"), along with the suggestion that an ancient rhetorician would have interpreted as programmatic for Hesiod's own work the famous evocation of Muse-gifted "sweetness" flowing from the mouths of kings (*Th* 81–98, esp. 96–97). In this respect, comments on the "flow" of Hesiodic verses seem to diverge from the mainstream of contexts of comparison and contrast with Homer, not least the *Certamen* tradition, in which the *WD* is uppermost. When they wish, however, authors of the second sophistic, especially Lucian (ca. 125–180 CE), are ready to bring together the three major Hesiodic poems.

Hesiod Parodied: Subversions and Exploitations of Hesiod-as-a-whole in Lucian and Others

Lucian's *Conversation with Hesiod*, which cross-references Hesiodic works, exhibits a mixture of admiration and criticism of Hesiod, and resituates Hesiod in the world of the rhetorical self-defense, may be used to showcase these aspects of the Lucianic reception of Hesiod evident in other works such as the *Dream, Saturnalia, Teacher of Rhetoricians*, and *Prometheus*. In *Conversation with Hesiod*, Lycinus (Lucian's literary alter ego) declares that Hesiod's poetry proves his claim to be inspired by the Muses' gift of a laurel branch; Lycinus's sole complaint is that while the Muses reportedly promised to enable Hesiod to hymn the past and prophesy the future, Lycinus finds only the former task fulfilled in the poems (1). Hesiod reacts as if on trial, first declaring that the Muses, not he, are to be held to account (4). He then has recourse to the argument of ἐξουσία, poetic license (5, "it is not proper . . . to criticize bitterly any unconscious oversight in the flow of composition"; Koning [2010: 95] with reference to Sluiter [2005] links Hesiod's shifting grounds for his defense to contemporary legal-rhetorical theory). Hesiod then points to his "prophetic" predictions in the *WD* regarding the consequences of right action and penalties for neglect (6, citing *WD* 482, warning of a bad harvest). Lycinus, disregarding such examples, eventually concludes that Hesiod himself knows nothing, so he was indeed inspired, but unreliably so, since the Muses have given only part of what they promised.

A different form of the defense of "poetic license," referring to the demands of poetry over strict truth, had been made on behalf of Homer and Hesiod together by the geographer Strabo (1.2.35). In Lucian's *Conversation with Hesiod*, however, we find again Hesiod in contrast with Homer, albeit implicitly, in that Lycinus does not accept Hesiod's warnings to farmers as prophecies of "what is not at all evident" and points rather to Calchas's prediction that Troy will be captured in the tenth year (*Conversation with Hesiod* 8). A contrast between Hesiod and Homer on these grounds is explicitly drawn by the orator Aelius Aristides (117–181 CE) in *On Rome* (26 Keil §106), faulting Hesiod for not being μαντικός ("oracular") like Homer. It seems surprising that in such a judgment, neither Lucian nor Aristides appears to take into account Hesiod's memorable forecast of doom for the iron age concluding his "Myth of the Races" (*WD* 180–201).

Lucian's dialogue illustrates well the centrality of Hesiod's encounter with the Muses (*Th* 22–34) to the wider image of Hesiod for authors of the second sophistic. In Lucian's oeuvre, the initiation scene is the most cited passage of Hesiod's poem; for example, an ignorant book collector is rated less likely than the shepherd Hesiod to have attained "knowledge without instruction" (*Against an Ignorant Book-Collector* 3). Again, a professor of rhetoric advocates a quick route to success, citing Hesiod's sudden transformation from shepherd to poet, as preferable to the arduous road of education (*Teacher of Rhetoric* 4). At a structural level, the professedly autobiographical *Dream, or Lucian's Career*, which presents the speaker's dream of a choice between Sculpture and Culture, follows the long tradition of literary initiations, from Archilochus through Callimachus and Theocritus to Virgil and others, that stem ultimately from this same Hesiodic passage (on other ironic recollections of the Muses' voices within Lucian's *Dream*, see Hopkinson 2008: 93–104).

Particularly worth noting from the *Conversation with Hesiod* is the fact that the poet under duress is made to turn to his *WD* to substantiate a claim made in his *Th*. We could read this as Lucian's mocking acknowledgment of that "interconnected" aspect of Hesiodic poetry (Nelson 2005: 333) that encourages the cross-referencing and fusion of his works in reception. This practice goes back at least to Plato (see, e.g., Van Noorden 2014: 106–41), flourishes in Hellenistic and Roman poetry (see Ziogas in this volume, pp. 377–78, 385, 390), and emerges through other unusual examples in the literature of the second sophistic (see Hunter 2014: 36–38 on Theocritus, Callimachus, and Dio 2.8). The sense that Lucian "sees Hesiod whole" is supported by Lycinus's opening summary of the contents of, in order, Hesiod's *Th* ("Hesiod has recounted the birth of the most ancient gods"), *Catalogue of Women* ("told of virtuous women"), and *WD* ("gave advice to farmers"; *Conversation with Hesiod* 1). Maximus of Tyre in *Oration* 26.4.89–93 also summarizes the contents of the Hesiodic "big three," but places the *Catalogue of Women* in pole position, perhaps due to its contemporary popularity (Scully 2015: 152n104), as revealed by the circulation of papyri.

Equally significant is the double-edged tone of the allusion to Hesiod's *Th* in Lucian's *Conversation with Hesiod*; Hesiod's inspiration elicits both admiration and (in the end) blame for his ignorance. This is a feature common to several Lucianic dialogues referring to the proem or main storyline of the *Th*. Hesiod's world history is employed as evidence, for example, for the history of dance (*On Pantomime* 7, 24, 37, 61) or for knowledge of heaven (*On Sacrifices* 8), but tales of warring and misbehaving gods are equated with "lies," seductive but dangerous for young people to take as gospel (*Menippus* 3; *Icaromennippus*; *Lover of Lies* 2; *On Grief* 2). In Lucian's *Saturnalia*, which features Cronus in debate about the origins of his festival, the character Cronus denies the Hesiodic version of events, rather emphasizing his voluntary abdication and consequent decision to take up the kingdom again for seven days each year to remind mortals of the fabulous, toil-free life they enjoyed under his rule (another instance of Lucian's cross-referencing material from the *Th* with a story from the *WD*).

A subset of this trend in Lucian's references to Hesiod's *Th* is criticism of Zeus as out of touch with the philosophical know-how and urbanity of contemporary (second sophistic) elites. The two main Lucianic dialogues featuring Zeus as protagonist mock his leadership skills by portraying him caught between mutually incompatible poetic traditions about the power of Fate over the gods (*Zeus Catechized*) and unable to defend the gods' existence in the face of Epicurean doubts (*Tragic Zeus* 4). The dialogue *Timon* begins (1–6) with the eponymous misanthrope's extended attack on Zeus, in which it is suggested that Zeus, by not punishing contemporary wrongdoing, is turning into a "Cronus" (the name here is synonymous with "old fool"), because he is being usurped without realizing it. Finally, the eponymous Titan of Lucian's *Prometheus* argues that Zeus's reaction to being tricked into eating the bone-filled portion of the sacrifice at Mecone was out of proportion to the joke.

Lucian's designation of the contents of the *WD* as "advice to farmers" in the *Conversation with Hesiod* pinpoints a wider contemporary idea that this Hesiodic work targets farmers above all. When it comes to citations of this poem, however, farming is not to the fore; by far the front runner, for Lucian and for other imperial authors, is the motif of the "Two Roads" (*WD* 287–92), of which one is the steep path to ἀρετή (virtue), applied metaphorically to philosophical or rhetorical training. The variety of ways in which the Hesiodic lines could be adjusted to new didactic purposes has been showcased in a study of Plutarch's essay *Progress in Virtue* (*Moralia* 77d), which creatively fuses the "smoothness" of the path to wickedness with the ease of the final section of the path to Virtue (Hunter 2014: 93–94). The importance of this image for the Stoic tradition in particular is reflected, for example, in the Homerizing epic of Quintus of Smyrna (third century CE), who adds the image of the mountain of Arete to others on the Shield of Achilles (*Posthomerica* 5.49–56; see Maciver 2012: 68–73). In Lucian's dialogues, the Stoics are a particular target of satire in connection with Hesiod's "Two Roads" image; for example, the narrator transported around the known and mythical world in *True Histories* notes (2.18) that the Stoics had not yet reached the Isles of the Blessed because they were still on the steep path to Virtue. Lucian's *Philosophies for Sale*, presenting various philosophies as if in a slave market, likewise envisages (23) the Stoics stuck *within* the image that was so important to their philosophy.

In *Teacher of Rhetoricians*, Lucian's exploitation of these Hesiodic lines reaches a structural level and is combined with material from the "Myth of the Races" in the *WD* and (again) the initiation scene of the *Th.* A young man is advised with explicit reference to Hesiod that there are two roads to Rhetoric (7); the speaker himself recommends one involving "no sweat" (3), such that the young man could imitate both Hesiod's own swift progress to knowledge in moving instantly from shepherd to poet (4) and the easy life of the golden race (8). A figure reminiscent of Hesiod's ever-toiling farmer is invoked to recommend the tougher path (9–10), but much more space is given to a verbatim presentation of a seductive invitation to the easy route (11–25). The irony of this "extensive inversion of Hesiod" (Hunter 2014: 98, within discussion spanning 97–100) is given a new twist in the ending of the work, in which the original speaker notes that the pupil has already overtaken him by an easy path downhill; his own teaching is now redundant.

The second sophistic interest in rhetoric takes a different form in Lucian's two *Prometheus* dialogues, in which elements of Hesiod's two accounts of Prometheus are blended with their transformations in the Aeschylean *Prometheus Bound* and Plato's *Protagoras*. In *Prometheus* the eponymous Titan, bound on the Caucasus mountain, enters into a debate with his captors Hermes and Hephaestus to defend himself against the charges of theft from the gods and the creation of mankind.[3] The subject of *To One Who Said "You're a Prometheus in Words"* is a defense of Lucian's own style. It includes (7) a "reminiscence" (so classified in Householder [1941]) of *Th* 540–41 (Prometheus's setting before Zeus at Mecone a portion of bones covered in fat) as a figure for the potential disappointment of Lucian's audience upon discovering that his serious-looking dialogue form contains no meaty philosophy (Hopkinson 2008: 116).

Scholars hoping for real depth of engagement with Hesiod in Lucian may likewise find the banquet disappointing, but Lucian's Hesiodic foci, although uniquely sardonic, are shared by several second sophistic authors and display strong continuity with the Hesiodic interests both of the Augustan poets and of earlier Greek authors. One example is furnished by Lucian's various exploitations of Hesiod's "Myth of the Races" (*WD* 106–201). When Cronus in Lucian's *Saturnalia* asserts that he abdicated voluntarily in favor of Zeus, Lucian is effectively probing a gap in Hesiod's text concerning the reason for the transition from the golden race "in the time of Cronus" to that of the silver, whose generation was forcibly ended by Zeus, then in charge. This crux had already been picked up by Ovid in his *Metamorphoses*, who explained the transition through allusive reference to the Hesiodic succession myth (1.113–14; see Van Noorden 2014: 245). In Lucian's *Tragic Zeus*, an extended fuss about the hierarchy of the gods' seating in council based on the metal of their statues (7) gains new humorous point in the wake of Virgilian and Ovidian innovations in the ordering and relative value of the metals in the narrative of races (Van Noorden 2014: 29).

Lucian's satires of Zeus and Cronus follow in the longer wake of Plato's challenges to the traditional ideas of the "golden age." Especially notable is the story of a reversing cosmos in Plato's *Statesman* 269–74, which re-presents the periods of both Zeus's and Cronus's rule as running into trouble. The influence of this Platonic account is even clearer in an odd revision of elements from Hesiod's races narrative found in the Greek miscellany of Aelian (175–235 CE); in a tale attributed to the fourth-century BCE historian Theopompus, far-off, peace-loving, and warlike communities are envisaged as bordering a land of no return, where the afterlife options for humans are forgetfulness or growing backward (*Historical Miscellany* 3.18). Framed as a narration by the old satyr Silenus to King Midas, the chapter is found in Aelian within a run of stories about philosophers and drunkenness (Aelian, *Historical Miscellany* 3.9–23); this may reflect contemporary applications of both Platonic and Hesiodic wisdom to the symposium.

The outline of Hesiod's metallic myth was also appropriated in this period as the premise of the fable. Babrius (perhaps second century CE) introduces his verse collection of Aesopic fables by remarking that in the golden age, when everything grew spontaneously, animals had articulate speech, and the sailor and the farmer could talk with (and so learn from) fish and birds (Babrius, *Proem* 1; text as in Perry [1965] 2). From here Babrius builds on a Callimachean construction of the didactic Hesiod as the first "fabulist," based on the notorious story of the "hawk and the nightingale" (*WD* 202–12; cf. Callimachus, *Iambus* 2). It is Babrius who brings out the potential for other stories and motifs from the *WD* to be viewed as fables; note, for example, Babrius 58 (312 Perry), an account of Zeus's depositing a closed jar of goods among mankind, apparently as a test of man's control over curiosity, which he fails, such that only Hope is left readily available (see further Hunter 2014: 227–51).

In Greek literature under the Roman empire, however, the most extended structural employment of Hesiod's "Myth of the Races" alongside elements of the *WD* is found in the extant collection of *Sibylline Oracles*, in books probably written by Christians in the late first century CE (perhaps working partly from Jewish oracles) but attributed to the pagan prophetess Sibyl. *Sibylline Oracles* 1–2 present a world history divided into ten generations, based on material from Genesis, Jewish and Christian apocryphal material, as well as features of Hesiod's races myth (out of order) and of the *Th*'s creation myth (details in Lightfoot 2007). The combination of historical, oracular, and ethical authorities in the *WD* is also imitated in this construction of Sibylline prophecy, for inserted into the *Sibylline Oracles* (2.56–148) is a segment of Hellenistic Jewish ethical teaching attributed to the sixth-century BCE philosopher Phocylides, whose gnomic style is strongly reminiscent of the ethical instructions of the *WD*. The *Sibylline Oracles* were much cited (as a pagan witness to Christian wisdom) by church fathers such as Athenagoras, Theophilus, Clement, and Lactantius, to whom we now turn.

HESIOD ASSAULTED: THE CHRISTIAN APOLOGISTS

Early Christian bishops had in common with Hesiod interests in the beginning of the cosmos, divine character, and human destiny. In the context of defending Christian faith to Greek audiences, Hesiod's *Th* was still the account to answer to, despite the prevalence of Orphic theogonies in this period (see Edmonds in this volume). Both Hesiod's *Th* and his *WD* were selectively cited and appropriated for anti-pagan projects; other Hesiodic works are cited very occasionally (Grant 1993: 21).

Hesiod was still on the school curriculum in this period, but from the limited range of Hesiodic material cited by most of the Christian apologists, it is thought that they were citing from memory or perhaps making use of anthologies. Zeegers-Vander Vorst (1972: 114) has argued, however, that the bishop Theophilus, writing to his pagan friend Autolycus (after 180 CE), had a copy of Hesiod's *Th* before him when composing, since he cites extensively, with paraphrases of intervening content.

More commonly, however, early Christian bishops followed the example of the great "citers" of Greek literature, such as Plutarch (Zeegers-Vander Vorst 1972: 23), in briefly quoting or echoing famous lines from the Hesiodic poems, especially the *WD*, although not often with the name of Hesiod attached. In particular, although attacking Hesiod's place in the history of religion (see below), the trilogy of works by Clement of Alexandria (ca. 150–211 CE)—in particular *The Instructor* and *Miscellanies*, but already also the *Exhortation to the Greeks*—displays an apparent "predilection" for Hesiod's *WD* as a source of moral advice for daily life (Zeegers-Vander Vorst 1972: 39 and 165). For example, Clement cites *WD* 218 ("having suffered the fool learns") to urge heathens to abandon superstitious customs (*Exhortation* 10.90.3) and *WD* 373–74 ("do not let a woman deceive you") to warn against the pursuit of Pleasure (*Exhortation* 12.118.3). Particularly popular Hesiodic lines include those on the two kinds of strife (*WD* 11–24) and the "Two Roads" to virtue and vice (*WD* 289–92). The latter is cited, for example, by Clement at *Miscellanies* 4.2, encouraging his readers to persevere in other researches once he has pointed the way,[4] and by the Christian scholar Lactantius (250–325 CE) (*Divine Institutes* 6.3.1), reglossed as paths to heaven and hell. Irenaeus, *Against Heresies* (ca. 180 CE) 2.14.5, criticizes as not particularly novel the Valentinian (Gnostic) appropriation of "the Pandora of Hesiod" (specifically the pun on her name as "given by all," which is found in the *WD*, as a way of talking about Jesus the Savior; Irenaeus also cites directly from this version of the story at 2.21.2). Several early church fathers exploit or adapt *WD* 276–80, in which Hesiod contrasts humans, to whom Zeus gave justice, with fish and birds, who eat each other. Clement cites the passage twice (*Miscellanies* 1.29 and 1.181), but in one instance changes "fish" to "animal." Theophilus, *To Autolycus* 2.16, describes transgressors as resembling fish and birds, while the righteous keep God's laws and live in justice. Irenaeus, *Against Heresies* 5.24.2, recalls the same passage in extolling human political authority as preventing men from consuming one another like fish (see Grant 1988: 142 on this "more subtle" use of Hesiod).

Early Christian reference to Hesiod's *Th* is, as a rule, likewise focused on its "highlights," particularly from the proem, but the level of creative engagement with this text is perhaps higher than with the *WD*. A primary focus of interest is Hesiod's famous account of his inspiration by the Muses. The Athenian convert Athenagoras, in *Embassy on Behalf of the Christians* (176/177 CE), mischievously cites *Th* 27 (the Muses' teasing declaration that "we know how to utter many lies resembling truths") so as to imply Greek poets' awareness of their own lies, as part of asserting an essential distinction between pagan/worldly wisdom and Christian/heavenly wisdom, even if they appear to share reference points (24.6; in this citation, he terms Hesiod τὸν ἄρχοντα τῆς ὕλης, "the originator/prince of the matter"). Theophilus refers to the claim of inspiration by the Muses and asserts that Homer and Hesiod in fact spoke out of "imagination and error"; ancient poets were "inspired by demons" (*To Autolycus* 2.8). This assertion may exploit Hesiod's own reputation as an expert on demonology, stemming from the few lines on the δαίμονες in the *WD* (discussed, e.g., by Lactantius, *Divine Institutes* 2.14.7, and critically by Clement at *Exhortation* 10.90.2 and 2.41.1). Theophilus continues, however, with an echo of the next lines in Hesiod's text, as *To Autolycus* 2.9 presents the prophets inspired by truth in speaking of what had happened, was happening, and was being fulfilled in the present (cf. *Th* 32 on Hesiod's Muse-given power to sing of the future and the past). Appropriations of the proem of Hesiod's *Th* to further a "new hymn" are found also in Clement's *Exhortation to the Greeks* 1.3; Scully (2015: 155–56), arguing that Clement knew the poem intimately, highlights ways in which Clement "cannibalizes" the *Th*'s vision, even as he follows a long tradition of attacking its immoral gods.

Targeting Hesiod for immorality and false claims to inspiration was a practice long familiar from earlier philosophers, from the pre-Socratics and Plato to the Stoics and skeptics. The early church fathers, like the pagan authors of the second sophistic, appeal to their readers' love of learning (Grant 1988: 148). In common with Lucian, in particular, they bring against Hesiod the charges of inconsistency (e.g., Theophilus, *To Autolycus* 2.8, on Hesiod's accounts of the world's origins) and illogicality in presentation.

Hesiod is criticized for philosophical lacunae, such as not declaring his hypotheses before launching in (Zeegers-Vander Vorst 1972: 114). For Christians, however, the consequences of such irresponsible exposition are more serious. Branham (1989: 162–63) regards the Christian apologists' lack of amusement, in contrast with Lucian's parodic spirit, as indicating their position outside the cultural tradition that assumes the authority and status of Hesiod. Yet Lucian too was long beyond believing in Hesiodic divinities; it is rather that stories about gods, which were for Lucian merely old-fashioned, were for Christian evangelists the most important discourse.

It is striking, therefore, to see how early Christian theologians, deeply read in classical texts, match Lucian in co-opting Hesiodic narratives for anti-Hesiodic projects (while exposing other pagan stories to ridicule in the quest to convert pagans). Canevaro (2015: 53–54) points to Christian citations of WD 42 ("for the gods have hidden the means of life [βίον] from human beings") and 60–62 ("and [Zeus] ordered renowned Hephaestus with all speed / to mix earth with water and to put the voice and / strength [σθένος] of a human within it"), which change "life" and "strength" to "mind" (νόον) in order to further arguments for a form of Christian Platonism (Eusebius, *Preparation for the Gospel* 14.4.15, and Clement, *Miscellanies* 5.14.100.3, respectively). Theophilus appropriates Hesiod in other ways; as has long been noted (Curry 1988), he creates his own theogony in part by drawing on Hesiodic stories (divine generation of the Logos as "vomiting forth" in *To Autolycus* 2.10) and of a Stoic version of them (Logos in the inward parts [σπλάγχνοις] of God [*To Autolycus* 2.10] tracks Chrysippus's allegorical reading of Zeus's swallowing Metis and begetting Athena).

The moralizing trend in reading Hesiod practiced by Stoics may be cited as a particularly influential background to the Christian use of Hesiod. However, a Jewish source has been mooted as the effective "anthology" from which these early theologians drew their pagan quotations (Zeegers-Vander Vorst 1972: 187). We might posit a collection of *Sibylline Oracles* as a likely candidate, given that these first expositions of Christianity extensively cite "the Sibyl" as a pagan witness to Christian truths.

Conclusion

Several aspects of Hesiodic reception in the second sophistic are not unique to this period, above all the appropriation of Hesiod for non-Hesiodic projects. However, we may highlight Hesiodic inconsistency as a particular concern, even as these second-century CE authors are invested in harmonizing different traditions. Further, while Greek culture was always agonistic, new contexts for ambition in this period (Whitmarsh 2005: 37–40) may have fueled interest in Hesiod in connection with the notion of competition. A striking degree of attention given to Hesiod's riddling and fable-like discursive modes, exhibited in the *Certamen* and elsewhere, may perhaps be influenced by the climate of imperial rule, in which consideration of how to speak to power gained a new urgency (Van Noorden 2014: 267). The sheer quotability of Hesiod for rhetorical discourse results in a plethora of citations, apparently out of context in genres such as miscellanies, but as Hunter (2014: 14–20) has emphasized, for the second sophistic as for earlier periods of Greek literature, even when verses of the *WD* are cited in apparent isolation, we can detect larger "ideas" of Hesiod in operation.

NOTES

1. Quite a few fragments of the scholia to the *WD* are assigned by Sandbach and earlier editors to Plutarch's lost commentary on the WD, based on parallel lines of thought in Plutarch's other extant work; for discussion of methods of "finding Plutarch" in these scholia, see Hunter (2014: 167–226).
2. The same Hesiodic passages, fused with Hesiod's account of the heroes' afterlife, enable Philostratus *Heroicus* 43.3 to envisage a "daemon" of the Trojan War hero Protesilaus speaking to a vine-dresser.
3. Prometheus in Hesiod brings fire to mankind but is not their creator; Lucian's Prometheus recounts his creation (13) using the phrase "mix of clay" from Hephaestus's creation of Pandora in Hesiod (*WD* 61). The idea of Prometheus as creator of mankind is reflected also in the fable tradition as represented by Babrius (240, 430, and 535 Perry).
4. Clement's interpretation of these lines makes the thought match Jesus's sermon ("strait is the gate") in Matthew 7:14.

REFERENCES

Branham, R. B. 1989. *Unruly Eloquence: Lucian and the Comedy of Traditions*. Cambridge, MA.

Canevaro, L. G. 2015. *Hesiod's Works and Days: How to Teach Self-Sufficiency*. Oxford.

Curry, C. 1988. "The Theogony of Theophilus." *Vigiliae Christianae* 42: 318–26.

Grant, R. M. 1988. *Greek Apologists of the Second Century*. Philadelphia, PA.

Grant, R. M. 1993. *Heresy and Criticism: The Search for Authenticity in Early Christian Literature*. Louisville, KY.

Graziosi, B. 2002. *Inventing Homer: The Early Reception of Epic*. Cambridge.

Hopkinson, N., ed. and comm. 2008. *Lucian: A Selection*. Cambridge.

Householder, F. W. 1941. *Literary Quotation and Allusion in Lucian*. New York.

Hunter, R. L. 2014. *Hesiodic Voices: Studies in the Ancient Reception of Hesiod's Works and Days*. Cambridge.

Kim, L. 2010. *Homer between History and Fiction in Imperial Greek Literature*. Cambridge.

Koning, H. H. 2010. *Hesiod: The Other Poet; Ancient Reception of a Cultural Icon*. Mnemosyne Supplement 325. Leiden, Netherlands.

Lightfoot, J. L., trans. and comm. 2007. *The Sibylline Oracles: With Introduction, Translation, & Commentary on the First and Second Books*. Oxford.

Maciver, C. 2012. *Quintus Smyrnaeus' Posthomerica: Engaging Homer in Late Antiquity*. Leiden, Netherlands.

Morgan, T. 1998. *Literate Education in the Hellenistic and Roman Worlds*. Cambridge.

Morgan, T. 2007. *Popular Morality in the Early Roman Empire*. Cambridge.

Most, G., ed. and trans. 2006. *Hesiod: Theogony, Works and Days, Testimonia*. Cambridge, MA.

Nagy, G. 1982. "Hesiod." In *Ancient Writers*, edited by T. W. Luce, 43–73. New York.

Nelson, S. 2005. "Hesiod." In *A Companion to Ancient Epic*, edited by J. M. Foley, 330–34. Oxford.

Perry, B. E. 1965. *Babrius and Phaedrus*. Cambridge, MA.

Richardson, N. 1981. "The Contest of Homer and Hesiod and Alcidamas' *Mouseion*." *Classical Quarterly* 31: 1–10.

Sandbach, F. H., ed. and trans. 1969. *Plutarch Moralia: Fragments from Other Named Works*. Cambridge, MA.

Scodel, R. 1980. "Hesiod Redivivus." *Greek, Roman and Byzantine Studies* 21: 301–20.

Scully, S. 2015. *Hesiod's Theogony: From Near Eastern Creation Myths to Paradise Lost*. Oxford.

Sluiter, I. 2005. "Homer in the Dining Room: An Ancient Rhetorical Interpretation of the Duel between Paris and Menelaus (Plut. *Quaest. Conv.* 9.13)." *Classical World* 98: 379–96.

Stamatopoulou, Z. 2014. "Hesiodic Poetry and Wisdom in Plutarch's *Symposium of the Seven Sages*." *American Journal of Philology* 135: 533–58.

Uden, J. 2010. "The Contest of Homer and Hesiod and the Ambitions of Hadrian." *Journal of Hellenic Studies* 130: 121–35.

Van Noorden, H. 2014. *Playing Hesiod: The "Myth of the Races" in Classical Antiquity*. Cambridge.

West, M. L., ed. and trans. 2003. *Homeric Hymns, Homeric Apocrypha, Lives of Homer*. Cambridge, MA.

Whitmarsh, T. 2005. *The Second Sophistic*. Cambridge.

Zeegers-Vander Vorst, N. 1972. *Les citations des poètes grecs chez les apologistes chrétiens du IIe siècle*. Louvain, Belgium.

PART IV

··

HESIOD FROM
BYZANTIUM TO
MODERN TIMES

··

CHAPTER 26

....

HESIOD IN THE BYZANTINE AND EARLY RENAISSANCE PERIODS

....

NICCOLÒ ZORZI

INTRODUCTION

....

IN this chapter I focus on the three works attributed to Hesiod that have been transmitted in full by medieval manuscripts: the *Theogony* (hereafter *Th*), *Works and Days* (hereafter *WD*), and *Shield of Herakles*. The Byzantine reception of Hesiod remains a largely unexplored topic.[1] Here I limit myself to providing an overview of the insights attained so far and suggesting some possible research perspectives. The reference list is limited to essential texts.

BYZANTIUM AND THE CLASSICAL TRADITION

....

Whereas in the West the knowledge of Greek was almost completely lost in the Middle Ages, and scholars no longer had any direct access to the masterpieces of ancient literature until the Renaissance, in the East the classical tradition survived throughout the Byzantine period. The first centuries of the Christian era witnessed a rejection of Hellenic culture as something foreign and contrary to Revelation, followed by a progressive and partial acceptance of this cultural heritage. Basil of Caesarea, a leading Greek Church father (ca. 330–380), in his writings acknowledges the moral value of the *WD* and accepts the idea that this work, along with the Homeric poems and other masterpieces of Classical Antiquity, may serve as the foundation of the educational system (*Address to Young Men* I 4, V 3). On the other hand, drawing on Plato's criticism, Basil (IV 5) does not hesitate to criticize the polytheistic conception of the divinity presented by unnamed ancient poets (see Wilson 1975: 47; Naldini 1984: 163). Throughout the following millennium, Byzantium embraced the heritage of antiquity within the limits set by the fourth-century CE Church fathers and, especially from the ninth century onward, cultivated more or less intensely the study of pagan authors. The latter were primarily read for their exemplary language and style, but also for their moral, philosophical, and scientific value, across all educational levels—from the elementary to the advanced.[2]

It is difficult to ascertain just to what extent Hesiod's poetic works were read as part of the school curriculum, and no studies have been devoted to this issue, particularly in relation to the "Dark Ages" (seventh–eighth centuries), when the opportunities to enjoy the *enkyklios paideia* dwindled greatly.[3] Be that as it may, from the dawn of the Macedonian renaissance in the ninth century to the late Palaeologan age, Hesiod enjoyed an established place in school education (Markopoulos 2006: 89).

Over the course of the Byzantine millennium, secular culture—referred to as $\dot{\eta}$ $\ddot{\epsilon}\xi\omega$ $\sigma o\phi i\alpha$ ("the external wisdom") in contrast to Christian culture, $\dot{\eta}$ $\dot{\eta}\mu\epsilon\tau\dot{\epsilon}\rho\alpha$ $\sigma o\phi i\alpha$ ("our wisdom")—was at times made a target for attacks, directed in particular against the authors of the school curriculum. The charge of "Hellenism," a byword for paganism, is almost invariably—and more or less explicitly—connected to polemical contexts.

In the ninth century Leo the Philosopher—one of the leading figures of the so-called pre-Macedonian renaissance, bishop of Thessaloniki (840–843), and professor at the Magnaura School established by Caesar Bardas in Constantinople—was charged, after his death, with paganism and apostasy by his former pupil, Constantine of Sicily. In a poem the latter accused Leo of having renounced Christ for the gods of Greece and expressed the hope that the bishop might rot in hell with many philosophers and with the poets Homer, Hesiod, and Aratus (Spadaro 1971; Valerio 2016: 294–300).

Radical rejection of secular wisdom is voiced now and then in various periods of the Byzantine millennium within the monastic milieu and, more often, within the framework of religious polemics, which also provide an occasion to address the question of the role of classical works in Christian education. One telling example is the beginning of the *Defence of the Holy Hesychasts*, written by Gregory Palamas, a saint of the Orthodox Church (ca. 1296–1359): "Definition of the rules and limits within which it is useful to devote oneself to [secular] studies." Palamas argues that the wisdom made foolish by God, according to St. Paul (cf. Rom. 1:22), is not only unnecessary for monks but even harmful, since it contributes neither to genuine spiritual knowledge nor to the knowledge of God. In a passage criticizing ancient philosophers and wise men (*Triads* I, 1, 15), Palamas claims that they are possessed by demons, and after criticizing Plato, Socrates, and Homer, he mocks Hesiod's proem of the *Th*, saying that the Muses filled him with "all wisdom" as he pastured his *pigs* (v. 23 has *lambs*), eating the laurel of Mt. Helicon (Meyendorff 1959: I:45–47).

The Hesiod of the *Th*—the poem of polytheism—was an easy target, and it is possible to detect polemical references to the poem in many different works from the same period, such as, for example, in the second refutation (*Antirrhetikos*), which Gregory Akindynos (ca. 1342–1343) addresses to Gregory Palamas (*Ref.* II 4, 24, lines 32–36; Nadal Cañellas 1995: 89). Later in that century, even an opponent of Palamism and later convert to Catholicism, Demetrius Cydones (ca. 1324–ca. 1398), evokes the "absurd theology of Hesiod and Orpheus," including a quote from *Shield* 390, followed by *WD* 101 (Mercati 1931: 327–28 and 334, respectively).

These were rhetorical disputes within the context of late Byzantine Christian polemics. The case of John Italos illustrates the problems that could arise from a too-serious adherence to ancient Greek philosophical thought: Italos, who was the head of the school of philosophy in Constantinople, was condemned in 1082, and a series of articles against his philosophical-theological arguments was added to the *Synodikon of Orthodoxy*, a liturgical document that celebrates the victory over iconoclasm in 843 and has been recited ever since on the first Sunday of Lent (Kaldellis 2007: 191–224).

A paradoxical case of "censorship" concerns quotations of Homer and Hesiod (*Th*) within Plato's dialogues: in three Platonic codices, some of these quotes were materially erased. According to Pagani (2009), this censorship is the work of the last Platonist philosopher of Byzantium, George Gemistos or Pletho (ca. 1360–1452). Its purpose would be to eliminate passages pertaining to the genealogy of the gods that contrast with the new theogony, which Gemistos himself had developed as part of his philosophical system, as best it can be reconstructed on the basis of the surviving passages from his work, the *Laws*, later destroyed by orders of the patriarch of Constantinople, George/Gennadius Scholarios.

The Testimony of the Manuscripts

The manuscript tradition of Hesiod's three works is an extensive one, which bears witness to the popularity enjoyed by Hesiod's poems, and especially by the *WD*, in the Byzantine age, even though manuscripts from the middle Byzantine period (ninth–twelfth centuries) are rare, as is the case for many other classical authors.[4]

The most ancient Hesiodean codex of the Byzantine age, Parisinus graecus 2771 (see figure 26.1), recording the *WD*, dates from the second half of the tenth century, that is, the period in which the so-called Macedonian renaissance was in full swing (ninth–tenth centuries), and an increasing number of ancient authors were being copied, in the minuscule script that had become popular over the course of the ninth century. The most ancient complete testimony of the *Th* dates from the late thirteenth century (West 1964: 165); however, two parchment folios in ms. Parisinus supplementum graecum 663 have been dated to the late eleventh century or earlier (West 1974: 166; see also Corrales Pérez 1994: 54, 66–67).

West's pioneering yet strictly philological approach is not enough to provide a complete picture of the value and historical significance of Hesiod's manuscripts from the Byzantine age. As a work of craftsmanship with unique features, each manuscript bears witness not only to the (ancient) text it records but also to the age that produced it, through its palaeographical and codicological characteristics and the very choice of texts it reflects. Hence, in recent decades scholars have focused their attention

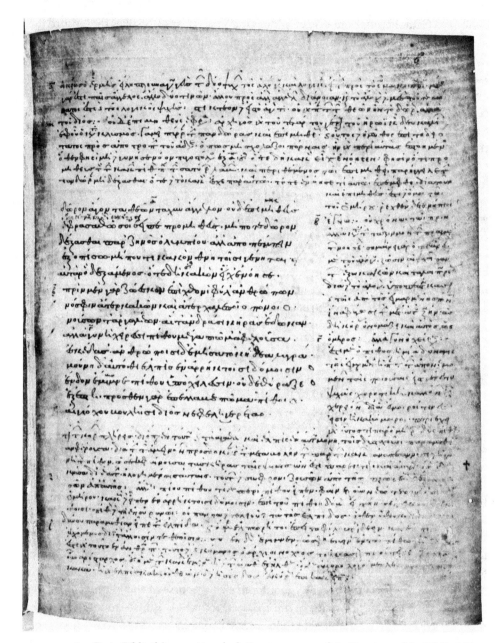

FIGURE 26.1   Paris, Bibliothèque nationale de France, gr. 2771, f. 6r. Courtesy of the Bibliothèque nationale de France. The oldest manuscript of *WD* (tenth century).

not just on the history of the text, but also on that of individual manuscripts; the circumstances in which they were copied, their circulation and use; and the known or unknown people who commissioned, copied, and annotated them, whether lay or ecclesiastical scholars, who were active in the cultural milieu of Constantinople and, especially in the Palaeologan age, of Thessaloniki and other Greek-speaking areas (e.g., southern Italy).

Within the context of such a vast and complex tradition, it is not unusual for individual codices to be assigned a new date or be attributed to known copyists upon more accurate analysis. For instance, manuscript Ambros. C 222 inf., formerly assigned to the thirteenth or fourteenth century, has been newly dated to the late twelfth century, and is thus one of the oldest copies of the *WD* (Mazzucchi 2003–2004, 2007). Parisinus graecus 425 includes a section with *WD* 1–201, probably to be dated to the early fourteenth century, which is especially interesting because of the presence of an otherwise unattested redaction of the *Vita Hesiodi* (Janz 2002: 5–19). Vaticanus graecus 1825, already known to editors in relation to the *WD*, had completely escaped their attention in relation to the *Th* and *Shield* (Galán Vioque 2009: 1–10).

It is worth mentioning a few examples of the manuscripts associated with famous representatives of late Byzantine culture, whose importance for the Hesiodic tradition will become evident in the section devoted to the Byzantine exegesis of the poems. Ms. Laurentianus 32.16 (dated to 1280–1283), which includes Hesiod's three poems, was produced within Maximus Planudes's circle.[5] Ms. Laurentianus 32.2, with the *WD*, is likewise associated with Planudes; it was later corrected by Demetrius Triclinius[6] and eventually fell into the hands of Simon Atumanus (fourteenth century), a monk and learned bishop (Weiss 1977: 41, 208; Fedalto 2007). Ms. Laurentianus Conv. Soppr. 158, a fourteenth-century paper manuscript recording Hesiod's three poems, as well as other texts, belonged to the cleric of Hagia Sophia Nikephoros Kallistou Xanthopoulos (ca. 1256–ca. 1335), an ecclesiastical historian and teacher of rhetoric (Kolovou 2001; Martano 2008: 551). Ms. Parisinus graecus 2578, with the *WD*, has recently been ascribed to a leading fourteenth-century scholar, Isaak Argyros, a pupil of Nikephoros Gregoras (Mondrain 2007: 169).

One further chapter in the history of the Byzantine manuscript tradition of Hesiod and Byzantine reception of his works is the inclusion of Hesiodean verses in gnomologies, from the *Anthologion* by John Stobaeus (fifth century) to later Byzantine gnomologies, mixing the sacred and the profane (see Richard 1962; Van Deun and Macé 2011), such as the Ῥοδωνιαί (*Rose Gardens*) by Macarius Chrysocephalus (early fourteenth century–1382). This organized anthology, designed as a collection of ethical and moral quotes, includes (ff. 243v–244v) around eighty verses from Hesiod's *WD* with suggestions about what forms of conduct and choices man is to adopt or avoid in order to escape misfortune (Mioni 1985: 231; Mazzon 2016: 257).

BYZANTINE EXEGESIS

Ancient exegesis on Hesiod's poems survived, albeit in a partial and redeveloped form, in medieval scholia. Byzantine scholars expanded this older exegetical corpus during periods of classical revival in the twelfth, mid-thirteenth, and early fourteenth centuries (succinct overview in Dickey 2007: 40–42; Ciccolella 2012: 145–46).

The *Scholia Vetera* and Proclus's Scholia on the *Works and Days*

The *scholia vetera* on the *WD* were first published by Vittore Trincavelli in 1537. After the Heinsius (1603) and Gaisford (2nd ed. 1823) editions, today the reference edition is Pertusi (1955; Italian translation by Cassanmagnago 2009: 593–885). Within the *scholia vetera* published by Pertusi it is possible to distinguish two different corpora. On the one hand, we have the actual *scholia vetera*, which are anonymous and bring together an extensive corpus of Hesiodic scholarship, ranging from Aristotle to the first century CE (West 1978: 68–69; Montanari 2009: 313–42). On the other hand, we have the scholia from the commentary on the *WD* composed by the Neoplatonist philosopher Proclus of Constantinople (ca. 410–483). This commentary (Marzillo 2010) was written for Proclus's students—and in particular for an audience unacquainted with the more technical and complex aspects of philosophical speculation, but with a more general interest in *paideia*—possibly "to convey Platonic messages through content known to everyone" (Marzillo 2012; see also Faraggiana di Sarzana 1987). For his commentary, Proclus drew upon the lost commentary by Plutarch of Cheronea, "arguably Hesiod's greatest fan in antiquity" (Koning 2010: 186; Sandbach 1969, fr. 25–112). The issue of the extent to which he did so still remains open (Hunter 2014: 167–215).

Commentaries on the *Works and Days* and *Theogony* from the Twelfth to Fourteenth Centuries

Works and Days

After Proclus, the exegesis of the *WD* was resumed by John Tzeztes (ca. 1110–1180/1185), probably about 1135–1140.[7] Only Gaisford's edition includes Tzetzes's commentary, although Aristide Colonna established solid foundations for the *recensio*, and new critical contributions have recently been published (Ponzio 2003: 129–47; Cardin 2009: 237–49). As West notes, "it is actually the text of his lectures, delivered to an audience to whom he had supplied a text equipped with interlinear glosses" (1974: 173, 1978: 69). The oral nature of this teaching is evoked by Tzetzes himself in different passages: ἄκουε, "listen"; τοὺς ἀκροωμένους, "the listeners" (Gaisford 1823: 28, line 22 and 80, line 17); at times he mentions the fact that he does not wish to dwell on a given topic, for fear that "my text becomes unprofitably long" (Gaisford 1823: 80).

The scholia, which are often very long, are preceded by an introduction about Hesiod.[8] This introduction begins with some verses in which Tzetzes openly criticizes his predecessor, Proclus (a polemic that spills over into the scholia themselves). The introduction comes across as the opening lecture of a course or the presentation of the topic to a class of students, in which the teacher is keen to display his great erudition. Despite his criticism, Tzetzes makes use of Proclus's scholia and of the *scholia vetera*, which may have been available to him in a more extended version than the surviving one; occasionally he also adds material of his own (Dahlen 1933: 55–83).

In the scholia Tzetzes from time to time makes room for personal observations, which offer contemporary philologists an opportunity to make their ancient colleague the butt of some sharp criticism, but are also a welcome anchorage in the impersonal sea of Byzantine exegesis.[9]

Tzetzes is also the author of a theogony, consisting of 855 decapentasyllabic verses. This work, composed for the *sebastokratorissa* Irene Komnene around 1143, weaves a tale of gods and heroes in the footsteps of Hesiod, Homer, and especially Apollodorus. It constitutes a chapter of Tzetzes's exegesis of Homer more than it does of the reception of Hesiod.[10]

In the late thirteenth century some scholia described as being "of Maximus" (Μαξίμου) reveal that Maximus Planudes (ca. 1255–ca. 1305), a monk, scholar, and teacher, also engaged with the *WD* (Pertusi 1951: 342–52; West 1974: 174). This small group of scholia (twelve certain and eighteen probable ones) was published by Pertusi on the basis of ms. Neap. II F 9, a fourteenth-century miscellany with the incomplete *WD*, accompanied by various exegetical texts, including Moschopoulos's commentary and fragments from the *scholia vetera* (with Proclus) and Tzetzes.

Manuel Moschopoulos (b. ca. 1265, fl. ca. 1300), an influential teacher and scholar and a pupil of Planudes, composed his extensive commentary (entitled *Exegesis* in the manuscripts) post ca. 1290 and ante 1310. The work is available through the critical edition produced by Grandolini (1991). Moschopoulos's commentary underwent several stages of composition and rewriting: the first stage is represented by Laurentianus 32.2 (early fourteenth century), later owned by Demetrius Triclinius, and the final one by Marcianus graecus 464 (completed on August 20, 1316), in which Moschopoulos's commentary is in Triclinius's hand.

Moschopoulos's work is clearly a school commentary, similar to the one he composed on Pindar's *Olympians* and that on the first two books of the *Iliad*. First of all, Moschopoulos provides an almost word-by-word explanation of each passage of the whole work; he then adds some notes on grammar. The negative verdict of some classical philologists should not overshadow the educational value of commentaries of this sort, which proved very popular in Byzantine schools of the Palaeologan age (Canart 2011).[11]

As in the case of other authors, the work on Hesiod carried out by Demetrius Triclinius (fl. ca. 1300–1325) takes the form of an edition of the text accompanied by many commentaries, which the Byzantine scholar copied in ms. Marcianus graecus 464, his autograph manuscript of *the whole* of Hesiod (see figure 26.2).[12] Triclinius did not compose scholia of his own to the *WD*.

Two numerological commentaries on the "Days" (vv. 765 ff.) feature symbolical interpretations rooted in the Pythagorean tradition. One, entitled Ἐξήγησις φυσικὴ τῶν Ἡμερῶν, is attributed to a certain John Protospatharios (*PLP* 8731), and was printed by Gaisford;[13] the other is an anonymous commentary from Vaticanus graecus 915 published by Schultz (1910: 34–40).

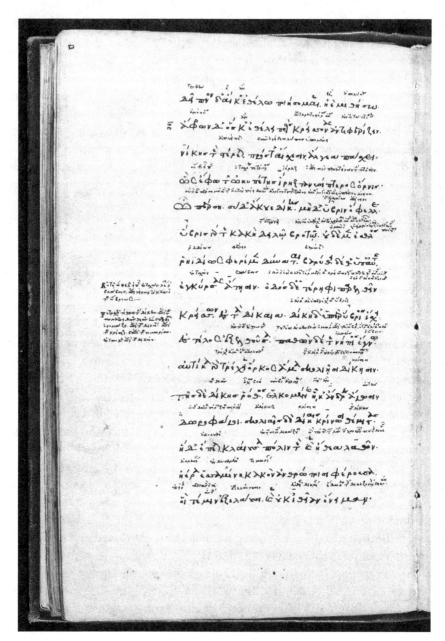

FIGURE 26.2 Venice, Biblioteca Nazionale Marciana, gr. 464, f. 26v. Courtesy of the Ministero dei Beni e delle Attività Culturali e del Turismo, Biblioteca Nazionale Marciana. Demetrius Triclinius's manuscript of Hesiod (fourteenth century).

Theogony

The exegetical work on the *Th* is less extensive and less well-documented than that on the *WD*. The *scholia vetera* on the *Th*—a pre-Byzantine corpus whose *editio princeps* we owe to Vittore Trincavelli (1537)—may be found in the critical edition by Di Gregorio

(1975; Italian translation of the scholia by Cassanmagnago 2009: 467–591), which has superseded the old editions by Gaisford (1823) and Flach (1876) and was preceded by the publication of some studies shedding light on the manuscript tradition of these scholia (Di Gregorio 1971, 1972). Di Gregorio's edition is based on fourteen manuscripts selected among the forty-eight (partly fragmentary) witnesses of the scholia, dating between the twelfth (but mostly fourteenth) and sixteenth centuries. Only one folio survives of the most ancient codex (Parisinus supplementum graecum 679), dating from the twelfth century.

The so-called *Anonymous Exegesis* edited by Flach (1876: 369–413) is best dated not to the eleventh–twelfth centuries, but to the thirteenth–fourteenth. Less extensive and accurate than the *scholia vetera*, it represents a running commentary that was largely compiled from other sources, but nonetheless presents certain original features (Capone Ciollaro 1981, 1996).

John Diaconus Galenus (*PLP* 3521)—not to be confused with John Pediasimos Pothos, the author of scholia on the *Shield* (see infra)—composed an allegorical exposition (*Allegoriai*) on the *Th* (as well as on *Iliad* 4.1–4), which was published by Gaisford (1823: 544–608) and Flach (1876: 295–365). The dating of the *Allegoriai* is disputed, but the late twelfth century, an age rife with allegorical interpretations, seems plausible (Roilos 2014: 231–46). The work serves an educational purpose: it is dedicated to the author's "son John" (Gaisford 1823: 607, line 32; Flach 1876: 365, lines 3–4)—where *teknon* may not mean "son" in a literal sense. It is prefaced by a proem in which the author, following a widespread topos, mentions the dangers to which young people expose themselves by reading pagan writings, while voicing his appreciation for the work of Plotinus and Socrates, which turned their minds to loftier matters.[14]

Roilos has emphasized the relationship between the kind of allegorical interpretation practiced by John Diaconus and that of Michael Psellus; alongside the traditional type of physical allegoresis (whereby mythological figures are explained in terms of natural forces and phenomena) and psychological/moral interpretations (only historical allegoresis is missing), John Diaconus—like Psellus—adopts a Christianizing reading ("theological allegoresis") of specific elements of the *Th*, in particular the myth of Prometheus and those of Briareos, Gyges, and Kottos (Roilos 2014: 239–44). Tzetzes, by contrast, distanced himself from the Christian interpretation of myths.

Demetrius Triclinius appended some scholia of his own to the *Th* in his ms. Marcianus graecus 464; they are only distinguished from the others in the Flach (1876) edition, which however does not make direct use of the autograph manuscript. The relationship between Triclinius's scholia and the other scholia on the *Th* has never been critically examined (see Di Gregorio 1971: 1–24, 1972: 7).

Shield

The *scholia vetera* on the *Shield*, first published in Basel in 1542, are currently only available in outdated editions by Gaisford (1823) and Ranke (1840: 19–65).[15] Martano (2005) is working on an edition of the scholia based on a new *recensio*, which expands Schultz's (1910). This exegetical material has proven to be of ancient origin, since it may be traced back to a commentary (*hypomnema*) drafted in the first century CE by the grammarian

Epaphroditus, known from the *Etymologicum Gudianum*. Four witnesses record a better and more extensive text than the one previously known, with numerous new notes, as well as longer versions of the ones already known.

Martano (2002) also published a different redaction of scholia and glosses on the *Shield*, based on the already mentioned ms. Ambros. C 222 inf., possibly connected with John Tzetzes.

The scholia on the *Shield* (labeled *paraphrastika* in the manuscripts) by John Pediasimos Pothos (ca. 1240–1310/1314; see *PLP* 22235) may be found in Gaisford (1823: 609–54), where they are interspersed with those incorrectly attributed to Tzetzes. Pediasimos was a pupil of George Acropolites and a correspondent of George/Gregory of Cyprus and was assigned the role of *hypatos ton philosophon*, probably in the 1270s (see Constantinides 1982: 116–25). According to Wilson (1996: 242), his "scholia on the pseudo-Hesiodic *Shield of Heracles* are linguistic notes of the most humdrum kind imaginable." Pediasimos is also credited with a work on the labors of Hercules, which was based on Apollodorus and circulated as part of several school anthologies (Canart 2010: 461). Despite their unremarkable quality, his commentaries—like those by Moschopoulos—enjoyed considerable success in schools during the Palaeologan age.

THE PRESENCE OF HESIOD
IN BYZANTINE AUTHORS

As is widely known, learned Byzantine literature is often built on a dense web of intertextual references, with quotes and allusions to classical, Christian, and Byzantine authors (see Rhoby-Schiffer 2010). A search for the keyword Ἡσιοδ- in the *Thesaurus Linguae Graecae*, including all the authors of the corpus from the fifth century onward, yields more than twenty-three hundred occurrences. As one would expect, Hesiod's name occurs most frequently in the scholia on various ancient authors, in grammatical and rhetorical treatises, in etymological works and lexica, in philosophical commentaries, and in collections of proverbs. With a lower frequency, Hesiod's name also crops up in actual works of literature (belles lettres), especially those exemplifying literary genres in which the mimesis of ancient authors is practiced to the highest degree: letters, orations, and historiographical works. In this context, the tendency to quote verses or expressions from Hesiod explicitly would appear to have begun in the eleventh century with Michael Psellus, gained momentum in the twelfth century, and continued throughout the Palaeologan age. Quotations from the *WD* are far more common than ones from the *Th*.

It is particularly important to examine the occurrences of Hesiod's name in the literature of the "Dark Ages" and early Macedonian age (ninth century), so as to ascertain to what extent the reception of Hesiod may be seen to reflect the rift between the late antique period and the Macedonian renaissance. In the latter period, the *Bibliotheca* of Photius (ca. 810–890) has little to contribute on Hesiod; after all, the work does not include any chapter on poetry. Hesiod is mentioned in several chapters (Schamp 1991: 149), but the only direct quote—*WD* 122–23—along with two detailed references to Hesiod' s text occur within extracts from Aelius Aristides (Schamp 1991: 483). Likewise, in the index of Photius's *Epistolae et Amphilochia* the only quote recorded is a generic reference to the Prometheus myth (Westerink 1983, *Ep.* 83, 3–4; see Vichos 1993: 273). In the *Lexicon* also (ed. Ch. Theodoridis, 3 vols., down to letter φ), Hesiod is very inconspicuous.

One generation after Photius, Arethas (ca. 850–post 932)—who was appointed bishop of Caesarea in 902/903—quotes a famous verse of Hesiod's *WD* (295) in his brief intro-duction to Dio of Prusa (Wilson 1996: 126). Arethas also alludes to the crow from *WD* 746–47 in the speech delivered in honor of Emperor Leo VI on July 20, 902 (Westerink 1972: 24, line 17).[16] Still, there is nothing to suggest an interest in the poet deep enough to support Pertusi's hypothesis that Arethas was responsible for assembling the corpus of scholia on the *WD*, later incorporated into Parisinus graecus 2771.

Even in later periods, quotes from Hesiod are always far less common than ones from the Homeric poems. In some cases, Hesiodic quotes are intertwined with biblical ones, according to the common procedure of combining the words of ancient authors (gener-ally Homer) with ones from the Bible.

We can pick an example from the erudite historical work of Nicetas Choniates (ca. 1155–1217), a high-ranking official under the Angelos dynasty (late twelfth century). Nicetas (van Dieten 1975: 364, 33–34) writes: τρύφος ἄρτου διαθρύπτειν ὀκτάβλωμον ("break an eight-part chunk of bread"), which draws upon *WD* 442 ἄρτον δειπνήσας τετράτρυφον ὀκτάβλωμον ("after he has breakfasted on a four-piece, eight-part loaf," trans. Most 2006: 123)[17] and Isaiah 58:7, διάθρυπτε πεινῶντι τὸν ἄρτον ("break your bread for the hungry"). The quotation of this difficult Hesiodean passage is made even more striking by the fact that the text is combined with a biblical passage in which the prophet Isaiah exhorts one not to fast in vain, but rather to feed the hungry. This double quote occurs within the context of criticism leveled by the king of Sicily against Emperor Isaac II Angelos, who is accused of starving Norman prisoners to death (ca. 1185).

At the end of the twelfth century, a quote from Hesiod was included in the proem of an official letter by Alexios III Angelos (or, rather, by his "ghostwriter") to the Republic of Genoa, dated March 1199. It begins with a famous verse (*WD* 240): "The dicta and sayings of the wise men of pagan antiquity are not false but hit the mark regularly; for example their wise poet Hesiod declared that *a whole city reaps the benefit of an evil man*" (the translation is Wilson's; cf. 1996: 3).

Hesiod's name crops up much less often in religious or theological literature. In his *Encomium of the Martyr Saint Procopius*, Nicetas David Paphlagon (late ninth–early tenth centuries) paraphrases *WD* 293–97, although we cannot tell whether he knew the Hesiodean passage firsthand or from a *florilegium* (see Crimi 2003: 125–30). The cruel judge who questions Procopius asks him to sacrifice to the gods, arguing (Halkin 1962: 188–89): "As you do not happen to belong to the first rank, since *you have not un-derstood on your own* what you needed to do, join the second one and, as the poet says (κατὰ τὴν ποιητήν), *heed he who speaks well* (τῷ εὖ εἰπόντι πείσθητι)." The judge goes on to say that the emperor, the senate, and he himself advise Procopius to behave wisely; if he insists on refusing to sacrifice, he will be sentenced to death like "a good-for-nothing man" (ἀχρεῖον ἄνδρα). Only a portion of each of Hesiod's verses is quoted word for word (vv. 295, 297), but Nicetas David was clearly familiar with the entire passage, which enjoyed considerable success in the ancient Greek, Patristic, and Byzantine literary traditions on account of its gnomic value and was quoted in particular by Basil of Caesarea at the beginning of his *Address to Young Men* (I 4).

ITALIAN HUMANISM

Men of letters in the Western Middle Ages did not have any particular interest in that area of Greek classical literature encapsulated by the name of the greatest Greek poet: Homer (see Berschin 1980). For centuries, Hesiod too was little more than a name in the Latin West.

Petrarch's attitude marked a turning point in this respect. Hesiod—along with Homer—was among the authors whom the Italian poet wished to read. In a famous letter addressed to the Byzantine ambassador and scholar Nicholas Sigeros (*PLP* 25282) on January 10, 1354, to thank him for the gift of a Greek manuscript of Homer, Petrarch also requests manuscripts of Hesiod and Euripides (*Epistolae Familiares* XVIII 2, 13). But despite having been taught some Greek by Barlaam (who died in 1348), Petrarch did not acquire any firsthand knowledge of Hesiod, although he had access to Hesiodean quotes via Latin authors such as Macrobius.[18]

Boccaccio too acquired a rudimentary command of Greek thanks to his Greek teacher, Leonzio Pilato. His Italian and Latin works occasionally mention Hesiod, alongside Homer, as an example of a lofty poet.[19] Most significantly, Boccaccio could draw upon the accurate references to Hesiod's works in Leonzio's commentary; in the *Genealogie deorum gentilium* (VII 3, 2), for example, we read that Hesiod referred to Persa, the daughter of Oceanus, by the name *Hecathe* (Zaccaria 1998: I:721; see Pertusi 1964: 315).

The end of the century marked a real watershed, as for three years (1397–1400) the teaching of Greek in Florence was taken up by the Byzantine ambassador, aristocrat, and scholar Manuel Chrysoloras. Through him a small yet eager group of Italian humanists was able to acquire firsthand knowledge of Greek. Chrysoloras's private library included the aforementioned ms. Laurentianus 32.16, with Hesiod's three poems (Rollo 2002: 95, 97), brought to Italy from Constantinople by Francesco Filelfo in 1427 (Sabbadini 1967: I:48).

Hesiod's writings entered the humanistic school curriculum at an early date and came to be used as teaching material by both Western and Byzantine humanists, both in secondary schools and at university (Ciccolella 2008: 135; Botley 2010: 101).

Latin translations of Hesiod's works were produced and issued in print in the second half of the fifteenth century. Niccolò Della Valle (Rome 1444–1473) translated the *WD* at the age of eighteen and died an untimely death at the age of twenty-eight (*DBI* 37, 1969: 759–62). His translation was preserved in a handful of manuscripts and published by C. Sweynheym and A. Pannartz in Rome around 1471 as an appendix to Silius Italicus's *Punica*, in a volume edited by Giovanni Andrea Bussi; it was later reprinted a number of times (Cortesi-Fiaschi 2008: I:595–602).

The first translation of the *Th* was produced by the Milanese humanist Bonino Mombrizio (1424–1478/1482), who studied in Ferrara—probably under Guarino Veronese—before moving on to become professor of Latin and Greek in Milan (*DBI* 75, 2011: 471–75). It was published in Ferrara in 1474, with a dedication to Borso d'Este, and was later reprinted by various publishers (Cortesi-Fiaschi 2008: I:602–5). Pietro Bembo, a pupil of Constantine Lascaris in Messina, translated a few lines of *Th* (861–67) in his *De Aetna*, possibly competing with Mombrizio's translation (Williams 2017: 255–59).

The *editio princeps* of the Greek text of the *WD* was published in Milan around 1480 and also included Theocritus's *Idylls* 1–18. The publisher, Bonaccorso da Pisa, was a friend of Francesco Filelfo's who played an active role in Milan in the editing and publishing of Latin and especially Greek works—chiefly grammar books and basic textbooks (*DBI* 11, 1969: 464–65; Botley 2010: 102).

Hesiod's three works, in the order *Th, Shield*, and *WD*, were published—in the case of the first two texts as an *editio princeps*—by Aldus Manutius in Venice in February 1496, at the end of a miscellany containing Theocritus's *Idylls* and other texts.[20] Aldus dedicated the volume to Battista Guarini, who had been his teacher in Ferrara around 1480. The preface makes it quite clear that the texts, and especially the *Th*, were expected to be used in schools (Wilson 2016: 23). Commentaries on Hesiod were issued as part of a volume edited by the physician and philosopher Vittore Trincavelli (1491–1563), published by Bartolomeo Zanetti in Venice, in 1537 (see Sicherl 1993: 68–73, 87–88; Corrales Pérez 1994: 229). The volume, serving as the *editio princeps* of the scholia and commentaries, represents a considerable innovation.

Notes

1. On reception in Greek patristic literature, see Rzach (1899: 198–215); Wolbergs (1988: 1199–1205); Scully (2015: 150–57, 161–62); Cardin and Pontani (2017: 245–88).
2. Wilson (1996: 1–27); Speck (2003: 166–68); Kaldellis (2007: 120–72).
3. Lemerle (1971: 74–108); Wilson (1996: 61–78); Kaldellis (2007: 173–87); Reinsch (2000: 29–46).
4. West (1965, 1966, 1974, 1978); Corrales Pérez (1994).
5. Turyn (1972: 28–39 and pl. 16–23); Montana (2011: 53–54 and tab. 6).
6. West (1964: 175–77); Turyn (1972: 209–14 and pl. 170, 255d); Wilson (1978, 1996: 236); Montana (2011: 51–52).
7. West (1974: 173, see also 1978: 69–70); Pontani (2015: 380–81).
8. Gaisford 91823: 9–22); critical edition of this introduction (up to Gaisford 1823: 19, line 16), which includes the so-called *Vita Hesiodi*, in Colonna (1953: 27–39); partial translation by Most (2006: 156–61 [T2]).

9. Gaisford (1823: 264, line 18–265, line 2). See West (1978: 69); Wilson (1996: 191).

10. See Hunger (1978: II:59); Rhoby (2010–2012: 166–67); Scully (2015: 162).

11. Wilson (1996: 245) describes the work as an "unpretentious paraphrase," although West (1978: 70) regards its author as "far better equipped to understand Hesiod than either Proclus or Tzetzes."

12. Turyn (1972: 123–27 and pl. 96–99); Mioni (1985: 248–51).

13. Gaisford (1823: 448–59, from Vaticanus graecus 216, dated 1342); see Schultz (1910: 25).

14. Similar considerations introduce John's interpretation of *Iliad* 1.1–4 (translation in Roilos 2014: 235).

15. See Corrales Pérez (1994: 140).

16. Wilson (1996: 131). Arethas also mentions Hesiod in his scholia on Dio Chrysostom (Sonny 1896: 97, 110).

17. While their meaning remains uncertain, "these words presumably indicate that the loaf is of a decent size" (West 1978: 270–71; for a different interpretation, see Ercolani 2010: 304–5).

18. See, e.g., his notes to the Ambrosian Virgil in Baglio, Nebuloni Testa, and Petoletti (2006: 375–76, 866). See also Scully (2015: 161).

19. See, e.g., *Amorosa visione*, IV 71–72 (Branca 1974: 36, 160 and 579); *Genealogie deorum gentilium* XIV 4, 25 (Zaccaria 1998: II:1384); etc.

20. Wilson (1992: 135); on the translation of the *Shield*, see Corrales Pérez (1994: 221–29).

References

DBI = Dizionario biografico degli Italiani. 1960–. Vols. 1–. Rome. http://www.treccani.it/biografico/.

PLP = Trapp, E., ed. 1976–1995. *Prosopographisches Lexikon der Palaiologenzeit.* 22 vols and *Addenda.* Vienna.

Baglio, M., A. Nebuloni Testa, and M. Petoletti, eds. 2006. *Francesco Petrarca, Le postille del Virgilio ambrosiano.* 2 vols. Rome.

Berschin, W. 1980. *Griechisch-lateinisches Mittelalter: Von Hieronymus zu Nikolaus von Kues.* Bern, Switzerland.

Botley, P. 2010. *Learning Greek in Western Europe, 1396–1529: Grammars, Lexica, and Classroom Texts.* Philadelphia, PA.

Branca, V., ed. 1974. "Amorosa visione." In *Tutte le opere di Giovanni Boccaccio*, edited by V. Branca, 3: 1–272. Milan, Italy.

Canart, P. 2010. "Pour un répertoire des anthologies scolaires commentées de la période des Paléologues." In *The Legacy of Bernard de Montfaucon: Three Hundred Years of Studies on Greek Handwriting*, edited by A. Bravo García and I. Pérez Martín, 1:449–62. Turnhout, Belgium.

Canart, P. 2011. "Les anthologies scolaires commentées de la période des Paléologues, à l'école de Maxime Planude et de Manuel Moschopoulos." In *Encyclopedic Trends in Byzantium? Proceedings of the International Conference Held in Leuven, 6–8 May 2009*, edited by P. van Deun and C. Macé, 297–331. Leuven, Belgium.

Capone Ciollaro, M. 1981. "L'Esegesi anonima alla Teogonia di Esiodo in due codici napoletani." *Atti della Accademia Pontaniana* 30: 113–28.

Capone Ciollaro, M. 1996. "Forme e funzioni dell'Esegesi anonima alla Teogonia di Esiodo." In *Byzantina Mediolanensia. V Congresso Nazionale di Studi Bizantini, Atti*, edited by F. Conca, 79–86. Soveria Mannelli, Catanzaro, Italy.

Cardin, M. 2009. "Heroogonia. Il catalogo delle donne di Giovanni Tzetze." *Philologus* 153: 237–49.

Cardin, M. and F. Pontani, 2017. "Hesiod's Fragments in Byzantium." In *Poetry in Fragments: Studies on the Hesiodic Corpus and its Afterlife*, edited by Ch. Tsagalis, 245–88. Berlin.

Cassanmagnago, C., ed. and trans. 2009. *Esiodo: Tutte le opere e i frammenti con la prima traduzione degli scolii*. Milan, Italy.

Ciccolella, F. 2008. *Donati Graeci: Learning Greek in the Renaissance*. Leiden, Netherlands.

Ciccolella, F. 2012. "Hesiod (Hesiodus)." In *Brill's New Pauly. The Reception of Classical Literature*, edited by C. Walde and B. Egger, 142–54. Leiden, Netherlands.

Colonna, A. 1953. "I prolegomeni ad Esiodo e la Vita Esiodea di Giovanni Tzetzes." *Bollettino del Comitato per la preparazione dell'edizione nazionale dei classici greci e latini* 2: 27–39.

Constantinides, C. N. 1982. *Higher Education in Byzantium in the Thirteenth and Early Fourteenth Centuries (1204–ca. 1310)*. Nicosia, Cyprus.

Corrales Pérez, Y. 1994. "Überlieferungsgeschichte des pseudohesiodischen Scutum Herculis." PhD diss., Hamburg University.

Cortesi, M., and S. Fiaschi. 2008. *Repertorio delle traduzioni umanistiche a stampa, secoli XV–XVI*. 2 vols. Florence, Italy.

Crimi, C. 2003. "Esiodo in un passo di Niceta David Paflagone." In *Munera amicitiae. Studi di storia e cultura sulla Tarda Antichità offerti a Salvatore Pricoco*, edited by R. Barcellona and T. Sardella, 125–30. Soveria Mannelli, Catanzaro, Italy.

Dahlen, C. 1933. "Zu Johannes Tzetzes Exegesis der Hesiodeischen Erga." PhD diss., Uppsala University.

Di Gregorio, L. 1971. "Sulla tradizione manoscritta degli scholia vetera alla Teogonia di Esiodo." Parts I–III. *Aevum* 45: 1–24, 187–207, 383–408.

Di Gregorio, L. 1972. "Sulla tradizione manoscritta degli scholia vetera alla Teogonia di Esiodo." Part IV. *Aevum* 46: 1–15.

Di Gregorio, L., ed. 1975. *Scholia vetera in Hesiodi Theogoniam*. Milan, Italy.

Dickey, E. 2007. *Ancient Greek Scholarship*. Oxford.

Ercolani, A., comm. and trans. 2010. *Esiodo, Opere e giorni*. Rome.

Faraggiana di Sarzana, C. 1987. "Le commentaire à Hésiod et la *paideia* encyclopédique de Proclos." In *Proclus lecteur et interprète des anciens*, edited by J. Pépin and H. D. Saffrey, 21–41. Paris.

Fedalto, G. 2007. *Simone Atumano: Monaco di Studio, arcivescovo latino di Tebe, Secolo XIV*. Brescia, Italy.

Flach, H., ed. 1876. *Glossen und Scholien zur hesiodischen Theogonie mit Prolegomena*. Leipzig, Germany. (Reprint, Osnabrück, Germany, 1970).

Gaisford, T., ed. 1823. *Scholia ad Hesiodum e codd. mss.* 2nd ed. Leipzig, Germany.

Galán Vioque, G. 2009. "Notes on a Forgotten Manuscript of Hesiod's *Theogony*." *Mnemosyne* 62: 1–10.

Grandolini, S., ed. 1991. *Manuelis Moschopuli Commentarium in Hesiodi Opera et Dies*. Rome.

Halkin, F. 1962. "Le panégyrique du martyr Procope de Palestine par Nicétas le Paphlagonien." *Analecta Bollandiana* 80: 174–93.

Heinsius D., ed., 1603. *Hesiodi Ascraei quae extant (. . .)*. Leida.

Hunger, H. 1978. *Die hochsprachliche profane Literatur der Byzantiner*. 2 vols. Munich, West Germany.

Hunter, R. 2014. *Hesiodic Voices: Studies in the Ancient Reception of Hesiod's Works and Days*. Cambridge.

Janz, T. 2002. "Un manuscrit méconnu d'Hésiode et son histoire: Le Paris. gr. 425." *Scriptorium* 56: 5–19.

Kaldellis, A. 2007. *Hellenism in Byzantium: The Transformation of Greek Identity and the Reception of the Classical Tradition.* Cambridge.

Kolovou, F. 2001. "Der Codex Hamburgensis 31 in scrinio (Fragm. 2, ff. 1r–2v): Iambische Synaxarverse des Nikephoros Kallistos Xanthopoulos." *Jahrbuch der Österreichischen Byzantinistik* 51: 337–41.

Koning, H. H. 2010. *Hesiod: The Other Poet; Ancient Reception of a Cultural Icon.* Leiden, Netherlands.

Lemerle, P. 1971. *Le premier humanisme byzantin: Notes et remarques sur enseignement et culture à Byzance des origines au Xe siècle.* Paris. [*Byzantine Humanism, the First Phase: Notes and Remarks on Education and Culture in Byzantium from Its Origins to the 10th Century.* Translated by H. Lindsay and A. Moffatt. Canberra, Australia, 1986.]

Markopoulos, A. 2006. "De la structure de l'école byzantine: Le maître, les livres et le processus éducatif." In *Lire et écrire à Byzance*, edited by B. Mondrain, 85–96. Paris.

Martano, A. 2002. "Scolii e glosse alla *Scudo di Eracle* dal manoscritto ambrosiano C 222 inf." *Aevum* 76: 151–200.

Martano, A. 2005. "La tradizione manoscritta dell'esegesi antica allo *Scudo di Eracle* esiodeo: La famiglia del Vat. Gr. 1332 (sec. XIII–XV)." *Aevum* 79: 461–89.

Martano, A. 2008. "La tradizione manoscritta dell'esegesi antica allo *Scudo di Eracle* esiodeo: Due gruppi di codici (sec. XIV–XVI)." *Aevum* 82: 543–80.

Marzillo, P., ed., comm., and trans. 2010. *Der Kommentar des Proklos zu Hesiods Werken und Tagen: Edition, Übersetzung und Erläuterung der Fragmente.* Tübingen, Germany.

Marzillo, P. 2012. "Performing an Academic Talk: Proclus on Hesiod's *Works and Days.*" In *Orality, Literacy and Performance in the Ancient World*, edited by E. Minchin, 183–200. Leiden, Netherlands.

Matranga, P., ed. 1850. *Anecdota graeca e mss. bibliothecis Vaticana, Angelica, Barberiniana, Vallicelliana, Medicea, Vindobonensi deprompta.* 2 vols. Rome.

Mazzon, O. 2016. "Manuale di sopravvivenza per un giovane monaco: Macario Crisocefalo e il Marc. gr. Z 452." *Segno e testo* 4: 203–68.

Mazzucchi, C. M. 2003–2004. "Ambrosianus C 222 inf. (Graecus 886): Il codice e il suo autore." *Aevum* 77: 263–75 and 78: 411–40.

Mazzucchi, C. M. 2007. "Per la storia del codice ambrosiano C 222 inf. in età umanistica." In *L'antiche e le moderne carte: Studi in memoria di Giuseppe Billanovich*, edited by A. Manfredi and C. M. Monti, 419–31. Rome.

Mercati, G. 1931. *Notizie di Procoro e Demetrio Cidone, Manuele Caleca e Teodoro Meliteniota ed altri appunti per la storia della teologia e della letteratura bizantina del secolo XIV.* Vatican City.

Meyendorff, J., ed., comm., and trans. 1959. *Grégoire Palamas, Défense des saints hésychastes: Introduction, texte critique, traduction et notes.* 2 vols. Leuven, Belgium.

Mioni, E. 1985. *Bibliothecae Divi Marci Venetiarum codices Graeci manuscripti.* Vol. II, *Thesaurus antiquus: Codices 300–625.* Rome.

Mondrain, B. 2007. "Les écritures dans les manuscrits byzantins du XIVe siècle." *Rivista di studi bizantini e neoellenici* 44: 157–96.

Montana, F. 2011. "Dallo scaffale mediceo della poesia greca antica." In *Voci dell'Oriente. Miniature e testi classici da Bisanzio alla Biblioteca Medicea Laurenziana*, edited by M. Bernabò, 37–54. Florence, Italy.

Montanari, F. 2009. "Ancient Scholarship on Hesiod." In *Brill's Companion to Hesiod*, edited by F. Montanari, A. Rengakos and C. Tsagalis, 313–42. Leiden, Netherlands.

Most, G., ed. and trans. 2006. *Hesiod I: Theogony, Works and Days, Testimonia*. Cambridge, MA.

Nadal Cañellas, J., ed. 1995. *Gregorii Acindyni Refutationes duo operis Gregorii Palamae cui titulus Dialogus inter orthodoxum et Barlaamitam*. Turnhout, Belgium.

Naldini, M., ed. 1984. *Basilio di Cesarea, Discorso ai giovani: Oratio ad adolescentes, con la versione latina di Leonardo Bruni*. Florence, Italy.

Pagani, F. 2009. "Damnata verba: censure di Pletone in alcuni codici platonici." *Byzantinische Zeitschrift* 102: 167–202.

Pertusi, A. 1951. "Intorno alla tradizione manoscritta degli scolii di Proclo ad Esiodo, V: Scolii planudei e bizantini alle Opere." *Aevum* 25: 342–52.

Pertusi, A., ed. 1955. *Scholia vetera in Hesiodi Opera et Dies*. Milan, Italy.

Pertusi, A. 1964. *Leonzio Pilato fra Petrarca e Boccaccio: Le sue versioni omeriche negli autografi di Venezia e la cultura greca del primo Umanesimo*. Venice, Italy.

Pontani, F. 2015. "Scholarship in the Byzantine Empire (529–1453)." In *Brill's Companion to Ancient Greek Scholarship*, edited by F. Montanari, S. Matthaios and A. Rengakos, 297–455. Leiden, Netherlands.

Ponzio, A. 2003. "Gli scoli di Tzetze agli *Erga* di Esiodo: Elementi per la costituzione del testo e rapporti con il commentario plutarcheo." In *L'erudizione scolastico-grammaticale a Bisanzio: Atti della VII Giornata di studi bizantini*, edited by P. Volpe Cacciatore, 129–47. Naples, Italy.

Ranke, F. 1840. *Hesiodi quod fertur Scutum Herculis ex recognitione et cum animadversionibus F. A. Wolfii*. Quedlinburg, Germany.

Reinsch, D. R. 2000. "Literarische Bildung in Konstantinopel im 7. und 8. Jahrhundert. Das Zeugnis der Homiletik." In *I manoscritti greci tra riflessione e dibattito: Atti del V colloquio internazionale di paleografia greca*, edited by G. Prato, I: 29–46. Florence, Italy.

Rhoby, A. 2010–2012. "Ioannes Tzetzes als Auftragsdichter." *Graeco-Latina Brunensia* 15: 155–70.

Rhoby, A. and E. Schiffer, eds. 2010. *Imitatio—Aemulatio—Variatio: Akten des internationalen wissenschaftlichen Symposions zur byzantinischen Sprache und Literatur (Wien, 22.–25. Oktober 2008)*. Vienna.

Richard, M. 1962. "Florilèges spirituels grecs." In *Dictionnaire de spiritualité ascetique et mystique, doctrine et histoire*, fasc. 33–34, 475–512. Paris. Reprinted in M. Richard, ed., *Opera minora*, vol. I, no. 1 (Turnhout, 1976).

Roilos, P. 2014 "Unshapely Bodies and Beautifying Embellishments: The Ancient Epics in Byzantium, Allegorical Hermeneutics, ant the Case of Ioannes Diakonos Galenos." *Jahrbuch der Österreichischen Byzantinistik* 64: 231–46.

Rollo, A. 2002. "Titoli bilingui e la biblioteca di Manuele Crisolora." *Byzantinische Zeitschrift* 95: 91–101.

Rzach, A. 1899. "Zu den Nachklängen hesiodischer Poesie." *Wiener Studien* 21: 198–215.

Sabbadini, R. 1967. *Le scoperte dei codici latini e greci ne' secoli XIV e XV*. Rev. ed. 2 vols. Florence, Italy.

Sandbach, F. H., ed. and trans. 1969. *Plutarch's Moralia*. Vol. XV, *Fragments*. Cambridge, MA.

Schamp, J. 1991. *Photius, Bibliothèque*. Vol. 9, *Index*. Paris.

Schultz, H. 1910. *Die handschriftliche Überlieferung der Hesiod-Scholien*. Berlin.

Scully, S. 2015. *Hesiod's Theogony: From Near Eastern Creation Myths to Paradise Lost*. Oxford.

Sicherl, M. 1993. *Die griechische Erstausgaben des Vettore Trincavelli*. Paderborn, Germany.

Sonny, A., ed. 1896. *Ad Dionem Chrysostomum analecta*. Kiev, Ukraine.

Spadaro, M. D. 1971. "Sulle composizioni di Costantino il Filosofo del Vaticano 915." *Siculorum Gymnasium* 4: 175–201.

Speck, P. 2003. "A More Charitable Verdict: Review of N.G. Wilson, *Scholars of Byzantium*" in Id., *Understanding Byzantium: Studies in Byzantine Historical Sources*, edited by S. Takács, 163–78. Aldershot, UK (original German version in *Klio* 68, 1986: 615–25).

Turyn, A. 1972. *Dated Greek Manuscripts of the Thirteenth and Fourteenth Centuries in the Libraries of Italy*. 2 vols. Urbana, IL.

Valerio, F. 2016. "Analecta Byzantina." *Medioevo greco* 16: 255–302.

Van Deun, P., and C. Macé, eds. 2011. *Encyclopedic Trends in Byzantium? Proceedings of the International Conference Held in Leuven, 6–8 May 2009*. Leuven, Belgium.

van Dieten, I. A., ed. 1975. *Nicetae Choniatae Historia*. 2 vols. Berlin.

Vichos, A. 1993. "Antike Dichtung in den Briefen des Patriarchen Photios." In *Symbolae Berolinenses für Dieter Harlfinger*, edited by F. Berger et al., ii, 271–77. Amsterdam.

Weiss, R. 1977. *Medieval and Humanistic Greek: Collected Essays*. Padua, Italy.

West, M. L. 1964. "The Medieval and Renaissance Manuscripts of Hesiod's *Theogony*." *Classical Quaterly* 14: 165–89.

West, M. L. 1965. "Review of A. Livadaras, Ἱστορία τῆς παραδόσεως τοῦ κειμένου τοῦ Ἡσιόδου." *Gnomon* 37: 650–55.

West, M. L., ed. and comm. 1966. *Hesiod: Theogony*. Oxford.

West, M. L. 1974. "The Medieval Manuscripts of Hesiod's *Works and Days*." *Classical Quarterly* 24: 161–85.

West, M. L., ed. and comm. 1978. *Hesiod: Works and Days*. Oxford.

Westerink, L. G., ed. 1968–1972. *Arethae archiepiscopi Caesariensis Scripta minora*. 2 vols. Leipzig, East Germany.

Westerink, L. G., ed. 1983–1988. *Photii patriarchae Constantinopolitani Epistulae et Amphilochia*. 6 vols. Leipzig, East Germany.

Williams, G. D. 2017. *Pietro Bembo on Etna: The Ascent of a Venetian Humanist*. Oxford.

Wilson, N. G. 1975. *Saint Basil on the Value of Greek Literature*. London.

Wilson, N. G. 1978. "Planudes and Triclinius." *Greek Roman and Byzantine Studies* 19: 389–95.

Wilson, N. G. 1992. *From Byzantium to Italy: Greek Studies in the Italian Renaissance*. London.

Wilson, N. G. 1996. *Scholars of Byzantium*. Rev. ed. London.

Wilson, N. G., ed. and trans. 2016. *Aldus Manutius: The Greek Classics*. Cambridge, MA.

Wolbergs, Th. 1988. "Hesiod." In *Reallexikon für Antike und Christentum*, edited by E. Dassmann and others, 14 (Lieferung 111/112): 1191–1205. Stuttgart.

Zaccaria, V., ed. 1998. "Genealogie deorum gentilium." In *Tutte le opere di Giovanni Boccaccio*, edited by V. Branca, vols. 7–8: 1–1813. Milan, Italy.

CHAPTER 27

HESIOD AND CHRISTIAN HUMANISM, 1471–1667

JESSICA WOLFE

Textual History: Editions and Translations

SIXTEENTH-CENTURY printers often printed Hesiod's works alongside those of kindred Greek poets, particularly those, such as Orpheus and Musaeus, sometimes understood to be Hesiod's ancestors. A 1515 Strasbourg imprint of the *Dicta Catonis* by Ottmar Luscinus includes the Greek texts of three works by Hesiod (*Works and Days* [hereafter *WD*], *Theogony* [hereafter *Th*], and *Shield*) alongside Cebes's *Table* and works by Pythagoras and Phocylides, while a pair of 1543 imprints place Hesiod alongside Musaeus Grammaticus's *Hero and Leander*—a sixth-century CE work whose author was conflated during the Renaissance with the much earlier Greek prophet and poet of the same name—and the *Hymns* and *Argonautica*, the latter work commonly misattributed to Orpheus. The scholia of Tzetzes was first printed in Venice in a 1537 edition of Hesiod by Bartholomeo Zanetti and Giovanni Francesco Trincavelli, while Johann Birckmann's edition of Hesiod (Basel: Oporinus, 1542) includes a fuller range of commentary and biographical testimonia, including Tzetzes's scholia and two vitae, one from the *Suda* (Kivlio 2010).

The two most important Renaissance editions of Hesiod, those of the German reformer Philip Melanchthon (1532) and the Flemish scholar Daniel Heinsius (1603), are discussed below. Also worthy of mention is Henri Estienne's 1566 *Poetae Graeci Principes Heroici Carminis*, an influential anthology containing poems, many never before printed, by Hesiod, Theocritus, Moschus, Aratus, Nicander, Bion, Colluthus, and Tryphiodorus, all prefaced by an introduction distinguished for its philologically and historically precise treatment of Greek lyric. While some printed editions of Hesiod place him alongside other Greek lyric poets, others present Hesiod as Virgil's model for the *Georgics*: the 1492 and 1497 Deventer imprints of Della Valle's Latin translation of *WD* are entitled *Georgicorum Liber*, while Josse Bade's 1503 edition goes one step further: *Hesiodi Ascraei Opera & Dies: Quod in Georgicis imitatus est Virgilius* (*Hesiod of Ascraea's Works and Days, which Virgil imitated in his Georgics*).

Particularly in the earlier Renaissance, as measured by the relative numbers of both printed editions and manuscripts, *WD* was by far Hesiod's most widely read work, although *Th* aroused the serious interest of poets and philosophers from Ficino to Milton (West 1964, 1978: 78; Scully 2015: 163–83). Hesiod was widely regarded as one of several early Greek custodians of the *prisca theologia*, or pristine theology (Allen 1963; Seznec 1953). Along with Homer, Orpheus, Hermes Trismegistus, and Pythagoras, Hesiod was linked to Moses, and less frequently to Abraham, and he was held to "hid[e] the principles of [his] wisdom under a veil of obscurity," much like the scriptures themselves (Bodin 1975: 91). Yet as church fathers such as Clement of Alexandria, Origen, and Tertullian were quick to point out, Hesiod's supposed genealogical and intellectual sympathies with the Old Testament did not automatically earn him the title of honorary Christian. Clement proposes that Moses transmitted his wisdom to Hesiod but also calls Mount Helicon, from whose heights the Muses descend to inspire Greek poets, a "temple of initiation into error," while Tertullian represents the cosmogonic myths of the earliest Greek poets, Hesiod included, as deceptive perversions of Christian theology.[1] Especially in England and northern Europe, the profound ethical and theological inconsistencies between *WD* and *Th* tend to produce a double-edged view of Hesiod as both "truly, religious and right Christian"—to cite George Chapman's assessment in the first English translation of *WD* (1618)—and yet also a poet whose mythographic imagination deviates perilously from Christian ethics and cosmology (Chapman 1618: 13). This is nowhere truer than in Renaissance responses to the popular Hesiodic myths of Prometheus and Pandora, the latter often interpreted as a mirror image of Eve but also as a pagan distortion of Judeo-Christian truth (Panofsky 1956: 11–13).

ITALIAN NEOPLATONISM AND THE MYTHOGRAPHIC TRADITION

Although the poems of Hesiod began to make their way back to Western Europe sometime after the middle of the fourteenth century, it would take another century for Italian humanists, particularly those active in the Florentine circle of Lorenzo de' Medici, to initiate a more robust program of construing Hesiod's poems. Interpreting the myths recounted in *Th* through the lens of the Medici circle's prevailing interest in Platonic and Orphic philosophy, late fifteenth-century philosophers, poets, and painters, including Ficino, Cristoforo Landino, Angelo Poliziano, and Sandro Botticelli, display a keen attraction to Hesiod's accounts of Eros, the birth of Aphrodite, and the Graces, often interpreting these and other figures as Christian allegories. In his commentary on Dante's *Commedia*, Landino explains that *Aglaia*, or Splendour, one of the three Graces, represents the workings of divine grace through us, because "it is certainly divine grace alone that makes our soul splendid by illuminating it" (*certo solo la divina gratia fa l'anima nostra splendida perche l'illumina*), while Ficino interprets the Graces as a model for the Trinity or for the Neoplatonic pattern of procession, rapture, and return (Landino 1497: 14v; Ficino 1985: 5.2; Allen 1984).

Such allegories served the Italian humanists as a means of defending and rationalizing some of the more perplexing or disturbing moments in *Th*, for instance, the birth of Aphrodite out of the foam generated when Cronus castrates his father Ouranos and tosses his testicles into the ocean. In his commentary on Plato's *Philebus*, Ficino interprets this scene cosmogonically as referring to the "first principle" that is "needed for creating all things," an interpretation echoed by Poliziano's account of the birth of Venus in his *Stanze* (Ficino 1975: 138; Poliziano 1993: 8–9, lines 97–104; Scully 2015: 163–67). This habit of interpreting Hesiodic myths as allegories of the natural world, and especially of the processes of generation and decay, in turn shapes the popular mythographic texts of the sixteenth and early seventeenth centuries. Interpreting Hesiod's *Th* alongside later classical accounts by Plato, Cicero, and Horace, works such as Lillio Giraldi's *De Deis Gentium* (Basel, 1548) and Natale Conti's *Mythologiae* (Venice, 1567) explain that Night (*Nyx*) is the "oldest goddess" because "no light existed before the sun and Heaven were created," and Cronus's dismembering of his father symbolizes how the "Sun brings on both birth and decay in the things of nature, and nothing at all occurs without the intervention of Time" (Conti 2006: 193, 104). As Ernst Gombrich has noted, Conti turns the most "outlandish" myths into the "ultimate esoteric wisdom," interpreting the intricate genealogies of *Th* as scientific allegories that confirm both biblical accounts of the Creation and contemporary natural philosophical beliefs (1972: 120).

HESIOD AND THE REFORMATION: ERASMUS AND MELANCHTHON

Hesiod's reputation as a purveyor of hidden wisdom begins to change as his texts travel north of the Alps around the beginning of the sixteenth century. The Dutch and German scholars of the Reformation era tend to prefer *WD* over *Th* and to regard Hesiod not as an inspired source of esoteric mysteries so much as a stern moralist, often one with a Hebraizing bent, whose poems are filled with "honest precepts" (*honesta praecepta*) about political and familial conflict, greed and moderation, and the workings of justice in both divine and human spheres (Melanchthon 1543: sig. A2r).

Often appreciated during the Renaissance for the gnomic quality of his verse, Hesiod's *WD* figures prominently in the *Adages* (1500–1533) of Desiderius Erasmus, an encyclopedic, repeatedly revised collection of classical maxims that helped to introduce Hesiodic wisdom into the lingua franca of northern Renaissance humanism. Erasmus is attentive to the "riddling" quality of certain Hesiodic verses, in particular the para-doxical maxim that "the half is more than the whole" (*WD* 40, ἴσασιν ὅσῳ πλέον ἥμισυ παντός), which Erasmus adapts into an adage, "Dimidium plus toto," interpreting the proverb variously as a lesson about the value of taking "fair shares" or as a means of dissuading someone from inflicting an injury (Erasmus, Adage 1.9.95, *CWE* 32: 228–30).

Erasmus admired Hesiod in particular for his concern about the perils of rivalry and conflict. In the adages *Figulus figulo invidet, faber fabro* (Potter envies potter, and smith envies smith) and *Inimicus et invidus vicinorum oculus* (Unfriendly and spiteful is the neighbor's eye), Erasmus interprets Hesiod's analysis of good and bad strife, or *Eris*, in the opening lines of *WD* in an even more negative light than Hesiod seems to have in-tended, omitting Hesiod's observation that envy between men of the same profession fosters healthy competition and thus demonstrates the kind of "strife [which] is good for mortals" (ἀγαθὴ δ' ῎Ερις ἥδε βροτοῖσιν, *WD* 21–26; Erasmus, Adage 1.2.25, *CWE* 31:170–71, Adage 3.1.22, *CWE* 34: 190). Yet Erasmus also perceives ways in which Hesiod anticipates Christian ethics. In his adage *Qui Quae Vult Dicit, Quae Non Vult Audiet*, which is based on *WD* 721, "if you say evil, soon you yourself will hear it more" (εἰ δὲ κακὸν εἴπῃς, τάχα κ' αὐτὸς μεῖζον ἀκούσαις), Erasmus observes that the verse echoes similar sentiments about wayward tongues in Homer (*Iliad* 20.250) as well as in Jerome and the New Testament, especially James 3.5–6 (Erasmus, Adage 1.1.27, *CWE* 31:75).

Although a careful translator into Latin of Hesiod's Greek, Erasmus also introduces some errors into his account of the myth of Pandora, errors subsequently disseminated throughout later Renaissance emblem books and mythographies. In a series of alterations traced by Erwin Panofsky, Erasmus transforms Pandora's *pithos* (Lat. *dolium*, or urn) into a *pyxis*, or box, and he makes Epimetheus, rather than Pandora herself, the opener of it (Panofsky 1956: 17–18). Erasmus's mistake may stem from his conflation of Pandora's urn with the "two jars" of Homer's Zeus (*Iliad* 24.527–30), scenes often asso-ciated with each other by classical and Renaissance readers. Jean Jacques Boissard, in his 1588 *Emblematum Liber*, depicts "Jove arbitrating Justice" (*Iusti Iovis Arbitratu*) by showing the god with two *pithoi*, or jars, marked *kalon* and *kakon*, an allusion to Hesiod's description of Pandora as a "beautiful evil" (καλὸν κακόν) at *Th* 585 (Boissard 1588: 30–31; Panofsky 1956: 50–51). Hesiodic myths feature prominently in many sixteenth-century emblem books, in particular Andrea Alciato's *Emblematum Liber* (1531 et al.), a work in-debted to Erasmus's *Adages* that contains inventive verbal and visual allegories inspired by Hesiodic myths. In *In Simulacrum Spes* (A picture of hope), Alciato depicts *Spes bona*, a beneficent counterpart to Pandora who sits atop a jar, flanked by two friends, *bonus Eventus* and *praeceps Cupido* (Happy Ending and Eager Desire), yet though the emblem's motto and subsequent commentary both mention the "reverend old muse" (*musa verenda senis*) of Hesiod, Alciato's mythography is original and possesses a dis-tinctly Christian cast (Alciato 1556: 129–30).

Both Erasmus and Melanchthon extract philosophical and spiritual lessons out of Hesiod's contempt for human folly, especially as reflected in his two accounts of the intertwined myths of Prometheus, Epimetheus, and Pandora. In *Malo accepto stultus sapit* (Trouble experienced makes a fool wise), Erasmus derives the adage from *WD*

218, "the fool only knows after he has suffered" ($\pi\alpha\theta\grave{\omega}\nu$ $\delta\acute{\epsilon}$ $\tau\epsilon$ $\nu\acute{\eta}\pi\iota\sigma\varsigma$ $\acute{\epsilon}\gamma\nu\omega$), and observes that the same moral is encapsulated in "that very old story about the two brethren, Prometheus and Epimetheus" as related at *WD* 47–89, in which the latter brother "began to be wise . . . too late," only after he opens Pandora's box (Erasmus, Adage 1.1.31, *CWE* 31:78–80). Similarly, Melanchthon admires Hesiod's disdain for the "sloth and stupidity of humankind" at *WD* 40–41, "saying that stupid mortals do not even known the uses of the mallow and the asphodel." Melanchthon appreciates Hesiod's intermittently ironic tone (1543: 11a), and he appears to take even more seriously than Erasmus the moral sympathies between Hesiod and the Old Testament, even comparing a verse in Hesiod to one in Ecclesiastes (18a), a strategy typical of a scholar who did not "observe the distinction between secular and sacred texts" (Melanchthon 1988: 4). In the essay prefacing his edition of *WD*, Melanchthon describes how Hesiod teaches obedience to natural laws as "the tablets of Moses" (*Mosi tabulis*) do, and he later interprets a phrase at *WD* 284 ($\dot{\alpha}\mu\alpha\nu\rho\sigma\tau\acute{\epsilon}\rho\eta$ $\gamma\epsilon\nu\epsilon\acute{\eta}$) as reflecting a concept similar to the ancient Hebrew idea of corporate responsibility, in which an individual's actions and mistakes affect his family and community (1532: sig. b2v).

HESIOD IN THE FRENCH RENAISSANCE

The poems of Hesiod fared well in sixteenth-century France, particularly after mid-century, a period when Hellenic poetry and philosophy flourished under the influence of the *Pléiade* poets. Three translations of Hesiod appeared between 1547 and 1574: *Les Livres d'Hésiode*, translated into French verse by Richard Le Blanc (Lyon: Jean de Tournes); a translation of *WD* (as *Les Oeuvres et les Jours*) by the Calvinist theologian and jurist Lambert Daneau, printed in Geneva in 1571; and finally Jean-Antoine de Baïf's *Les Bezognes è Jours d'Èziode*, printed in a verse miscellany entitled *Ètrènes de poézie fransoèze an vers mezurés* (Paris, 1574) that also contains Baïf's translations of Pythogoras's Golden Verses. Although Parisian printers produced Greek and Greek-Latin editions of Hesiod at regular intervals, including a 1543 printing of Melanchthon's edition and the 1544–1546 edition by Jacques Bogard and Martin Le Jeune, Geneva was the more important site for classical scholarship in the latter half of the century, as evidenced by the editions of Henri Estienne: a 1566 collection of Greek poetry that includes the works of Hesiod and, in 1573, the first printed edition of the *Contest of Homer and Hesiod* (*Homērou Kai Hēsiodou Agōn*), with a Latin translation and commentary of this ancient legend of Hesiod's triumph over his poetic contemporary and rival, repeated with variations by Plutarch, Pausanias, and others. This latter text was one of the chief focal points for the many Renaissance debates concerning the relative ages of Homer and Hesiod, a subject of scholarly controversy well into the seventeenth century (Vossius 1654: 9–10).

This wave of vernacular translations of Hesiod in France was preceded and accompanied by a surge of interest in early Greek poetry on the part of lyric poets including Pierre de Ronsard, Joachim Du Bellay, and Baïf. United by their shared desire to resuscitate lesser-known Greek and Roman poetic forms in the vernacular; a common interest in ideas of poetic inspiration; and their shared habits of personification, complex mythological allusion, and reliance on compound epithets, the poets of the *Pléiade* often incorporate stylistic and thematic elements from Hesiod's poems into their works. In sonnet 42 of his *Amours de Cassandre*, for instance, Ronsard reworks the Hesiodic theogony in his account of how Amour (Love) is born out of Chaos (Ronsard 4.45), an allegory that imitates the Hesiodic pattern of narrating generational progression as an alternation between contraries, much like his later and more ambitious *Hymne de l'Eternité* (Ronsard 8.246–54). In his *Ode à Michel de L'Hospital* (Ode 5.8, 1552), Ronsard divides classical poets into three categories and groups Hesiod with other "divine poets" such as Musaeus, Orpheus, and Homer, a status that demonstrates Hesiod's "*fureur*," or poetic enthusiasm; his capacity to search into the "secrets of the gods" (*secretz des Dieux*); and his "*nayve escripture*" or stylistic artlessness (Ronsard 3.149–50, lines 560, 549–52). In his own poems Ronsard emulates the Hesiodic model of prophetic fervor, explaining in his 1563 *Hymne de l'Hyver* that he models Homer and Hesiod in creating texts that appear to be covered with "a subtle veil" (*un voile bien subtile*) so as to prompt the reader to "search for the concealed beauty that they dare not approach" (*chercher / La couverte beauté dont il n'ose approcher*; Ronsard 12.71–72, lines 73–80).

Counter to the tendency of the *Pléiade* poets to view Hesiod as a divinely inspired poet who trafficked in Orphic mysteries, the two most significant editions of Hesiod to appear in print in the later Renaissance, those of the Béarnaise poet and translator Jean de Sponde (Johannes Spondanus) and the Flemish scholar Daniel Heinsius, push back against the radical allegorism of the *Pléiade* and instead approach Hesiod's texts from a predominantly ethical and philological framework that owes much to Melanchthon. In his Greek-Latin edition of *WD*, printed at La Rochelle in 1592, Sponde labors to position Hesiod's moral and political observations about strife, envy, and *pleonexia*, or the insatiable desire to possess more than one's fair share, with respect to later Greek moral philosophers, especially Aristotle and Plato. Of particular concern to Sponde, writing his commentary in the wake of the French religious wars, is the question of whether and how conflict might ever be productive or beneficial. He struggles throughout his commentary with the problem that while Hesiod seems to praise *Eris* and other deities of discord, Plato strikes an extremely condemnatory attitude toward *Eris* across his writings, often condemning Hesiod's praiseworthy competition between experts as a form of sophistry or eristic disputation (Sponde 1592: 7–9).[2]

Heinsius's Greek-Latin edition of Hesiod, first printed by the Plantijn press in Antwerp in 1603, appeared the same year as that scholar's edition of Theocritus, Bion of Smyrna, and Moschus. In addition to containing all the major scholia on the poet (Proclus, Tzetzes, and the thirteenth-century Byzantine scholar Manuel Moschopoulos), Heinsius's edition includes—unusually, for the period—the *Shield of Herakles* and the Fragments. In a long Prolegomenon that elaborates on an oration ("*De Poetis et eorum interpretibus*") he delivered that same year, Heinsius celebrates Hesiod's observance of both ethical and stylistic norms, in particular the "natural and genuine simplicity of his diction" (*dictionum nativa genuinaque simplicitas*), the characteristic that made the earliest Greek poets superior, for Heinsius, to later masters of ornate elegance such as Virgil (1603: sig. Ar). Although he shies away from the elaborate allegories of Hesiod's late antique and Byzantine scholiasts, Heinsius does endorse the idea of a pristine theology in his Prolegomenon, representing Hesiod, along with Homer, as the "first herald of human wisdom" and praising him for a natural talent that Heinsius prizes over technical skill and also uses to advance a narrative of cultural and literary decline sympathetic to Hesiod's own account of the five ages of humankind (Meter 1984: 58).

Like Sponde, Heinsius emphasizes Hesiod's ethical teachings over his cosmographical and theological wisdom but also seeks out correspondences between these two aspects of Hesiod's poems, rationalizing the most outlandish fables of *Th* and insisting on the structural unity of *WD*, despite the oddly disconnected nature of the poem's two parts. One prominent motif of *WD*, for Heinsius, is the relationship between divine providence and "human provision," a theme he interprets by way of Plato's *Statesman*, which argues that the gods formerly cared for humankind but then gradually ceased to, leaving humans to live under the sway of fortune (Meter 1984: 64–66). Heinsius discerns sympathies with this argument both in Hesiod's account of the degeneration from the golden age to the iron age and also in the myth of Pandora, interpreted as a fable about the necessity of labor that also illustrates how the gods abandon humankind to chance.

HESIOD IN THE ENGLISH RENAISSANCE

Hesiod was first printed on English soil in 1590 by Richard Field, an edition of *WD* that includes Melanchthon's annotations on the "Works" and a commentary by Johannes Frisius Tigurino on the "Days". In 1635 the Cambridge printer Roger Daniel brought out a new edition of Estienne's 1566 *Poetae Minores Graeci* with a new commentary by the physician and scholar Ralph Winterton, entitled *Observationes . . . in Hesiodum* and dedicated to William Laud, archbishop of Canterbury. In between these two Greek printings of Hesiod appeared the first English translation of *WD*, George Chapman's *The Georgicks of Hesiod* (London, 1618), also discussed by Stephanie Nelson in this volume (pp. 368–73). The work's full title boasts that Chapman translated Hesiod "elaborately out of the Greek," a comment that reflects the translator's efforts to render Hesiod in iambic pentameter rhyming couples (with the odd triplet) as well as his attempt to provide creative renditions of Hesiod's epithets and periphrases such as "swarth-check't Hunger" (translating *WD* 363, αἴθοπα λιμόν) and "The Day-sleep-wake-Night Man," the latter translating ἡμερόκοιτος ἀνήρ (*WD* 605) and glossed in Chapman's commentary as the "Periphrasis of a Theefe" (Chapman 1618: 17; 28). In a prefatory biographical essay entitled *Of Hesiodus*, mostly pilfered from classical paratexts, Chapman observes of Hesiod that "his verses were commonly learned, as *Axioms* or *Oracles*," a practice whose survival through the Renaissance is confirmed by Chapman's own referencing of Erasmus's Hesiodic adages in his annotations (Chapman 1618: 3). Chapman also praises

Hesiod for the encyclopedic range of his knowledge; he is not a poet who dwells on "any one subject; but of all humane affaires instructively concluded," a claim that is likewise commonly made of Homer during the Renaissance (Chapman 1618: sig. A3v).

Much of Chapman's commentary is deeply indebted to Hesiod's earlier Renaissance annotators, especially Melanchthon and Sponde, from whose commentary on Homer Chapman had previously borrowed heavily for his translations of the *Iliad* and *Odyssey* (printed in 1611 and 1616, respectively). Yet in other portions of his commentary, Chapman introduces some strikingly original interpretations of *WD*, as he sustains a particular focus on Hesiod's representation of divine and human justice and on the parallels between Hesiod's ethics and those of the scriptures. Glossing the epithet "wisdome-wresting Prometheus" (*WD* 48, Προμηθεὺς ἀγκυλομήτης), Chapman explains that the fire stolen by Prometheus represents "learned Mens over-subtile abuse of divine knowledge; wresting it in false expositions to their own objects," an interpretation in turn indebted to Francis Bacon, to whom Chapman dedicated his translation on account of Bacon's efforts to renew "Antient wisedome" in his 1609 *De Sapientia Veterum* (Chapman 1618: dedication, sig. A2r). Bacon's essay *Prometheus, Or the State of Man* in his *De Sapientia Veterum* interprets the fire-stealing hero as a fable about Providence but also as a cautionary tale about how the "wise and fore-thoughtful class of men . . . torment and wear themselves away with cares and solicitude and inward fears" until their "innumerable thoughts . . . prick and gnaw" at them like the eagle who punishes Prometheus (Chapman 1618: 3; Bacon [1609] 2011: 751–52; Lamberton 1986: 103). Another of Chapman's glosses likewise focuses on Hesiod's opposition between Zeus, who "straightens the crooked" (τ'ἰθύνει σκολιόν), and the "crooked Justice" (σκολιῆς δὲ δίκης) meted out by human judges, the latter metaphor explicated by Chapman as representing the way things may be "wrapt together like brambles; that catch and keep with them whatsoever touches them" (*WD* 7, 221; Chapman 1618: 11). At times Chapman's annotations miss the mark in fascinating ways. Translating and glossing a passage in which Hesiod explains how winter's long nights may be a help to the farmer as well as a hindrance (*WD* 2.560–63), Chapman concocts an epithet, "ingenious Night," and then explains that this is the time most "fit for Mentall painetakers" to pursue their "studies and labours of the soule," an interpretation that enlists Renaissance conceptions of melancholy genius to explain a passage that instead concerns ancient agricultural practice (Chapman 1618: 27n31).

Like Heinsius before him, Chapman's interpretations of Hesiod reflect the translator's pessimism, his sense that his own culture suffers from the litigiousness, discord, and moral decay represented in Hesiod's poem. Chapman accentuates the misogyny of the fable of Pandora, noting that she is given the voice of Hermes, the messenger god, because "All faire women, affecting, to be furthest heard, as well as most seen" (Chapman 1618: 5). He also voices the belief that he inhabits the fifth and final age, described at *WD* 174–200 as a prophecy of a future era. If Hesiod anticipates for Chapman the moral degeneracy of Jacobean England, he also anticipates certain Christian doctrines, such as the belief in "guardian angels" (*custodes hominum*) that Chapman discerns in Hesiod's discussion of the "spirits" (δαίμονές) appointed as "guardians over mortal beings" (φύλακες θνητῶν ἀνθρώπων) at the end of the golden age, a passage that prompts the translator to assert that Hesiod "could not, but have some light of our Parents lives in Paradise" (WD 122–23; Chapman 1618: 6–7n32). Chapman's desire to align Hesiod with Christian theology is also reflected in his defense of the poet from charges of superstition, especially in the "Days," a calendar of auspicious and inauspicious days in each month that Chapman's full title declares is "Not superstitious, but necessarie (as farre as naturall Causes compell) for all Men to observe."[3]

Both Chapman and the epic poets of the English Renaissance are influenced in their interpretations of Hesiod by the mythographic traditions of the earlier Renaissance. Chapman's interpretations of Hesiodic episodes at times echo Edmund Spenser's adaptations in his *Faerie Queene* (1590–1596), infused with a similarly allegorical spirit. Chapman's gloss on Epimetheus, for example, asserts that because he is "deceived with a false shadow of pleasure" he symbolizes "Mans corporeall part . . . signifying the inconsiderate and headlong force of affections, not obeying his reasonable part, or soule" (1618: 5). Spenser cleaves to a similar interpretation in his rather comic rendition of the myth of Pandora (Spenser, *Faerie Queene* [hereafter *FQ*] 3.8.5–10): a witch creates a "snowy lady" for her son, a false version of the maiden Florimell who then entertains the son "with shadows" in an episode that dramatizes, allegorically, the delusions of pleasure or sexual appetite.

The *FQ* draws liberally and eclectically from *Th* in its depiction of various deities and giants. Spenser's preoccupation with Hesiodic genealogy tends to rework Hesiodic material in order to launch distinctly Protestant arguments about the origins of sin, error, and pride; the etiology of strife in the world; and the dynamic coincidence of opposites, such as concord and discord, that animates Spenser's cosmos. In Book 1 Spenser creates a variant heritage for Hesiod's Night; whereas Hesiod makes Night the daughter of Chaos and the progenitor of the Destinies and Fates (Μοίρας καὶ Κῆρας) and of Deception (Ἀπάτην) and Strife (Ἔριν), Spenser's Night is the "most auncient Grandmother of all" and the mother of falsehood, a figure whose affinity with the fates is converted by Spenser into an erroneous "chayne of strong necessitee," a falsification of the Calvinist doctrine of predestination (*Th* 216, 224–25; *FQ* 1.5.22, 27, 25). The giants and monsters that populate the *FQ* often possess Hesiodic lineages even as Spenser transforms these genealogies into allegories of contemporary religious and political conflict; the physical descriptions of Gerioneo and Echidna (*FQ* 5.11.20–26) are derived from *Th* 979–83 and 295–322, respectively, yet in Spenser's retelling of their defeat at the hands of King Arthur, they represent the Catholic threat posed by Philip II of Spain, whose correspondence to triple-headed Geryon symbolizes that monarch's vast imperial reach. So too, Spenser transforms Hesiodic agents of righteousness and concord into figures who exemplify markedly Protestant, and Elizabethan, virtues; his three Graces (*FQ* 6.10.21–23), spied as a fleeting vision by Calidore, the knight of courtesy, possess little of the sexual allure exhibited by Hesiod's Χάριτας, or Graces, whose eyes melt limbs with desire (*Th* 907–10, ἀπὸ βλεφάρων ἔρος). Similarly, Spenser's *Litae*, or Prayers, who flank Mercilla at *FQ* 5.9–31–32, are derived principally from the Horai (Hours or Seasons) of *Th* 901–3 and play a similar role, "often [entreating] for pardon and remission / To suppliants," and yet Spenser invokes them to celebrate not the justice of Zeus their father, but rather the "peace and clemencie" of Queen Elizabeth I, thus explaining why Spenser's triadic goddesses of justice appear as "Virgins clad in white" (*FQ* 5.9.29).

It can be difficult to ascertain when Spenser is working directly from Hesiod's poems and when he instead has in mind later classical accounts of familiar myths by writers such as Apollodorus, Diodorus Siculus, or Hyginus. This is especially the case because the *FQ*'s allusions to Hesiod are so inventively intermingled with allusions to other classical texts, for instance the three-way conflation of Typhoeus, Typhon, and Tityus at *FQ* 1.5.35.6–7, where Spenser is clearly following not *Th* (306, 820–35, 869) but rather Ovid (*Metamorphoses* 5.319–20) and Vergil (*Georgics* 1.276–79). Even when imitating Hesiod directly, Spenser appears to follow the Latin translation of Mombritius rather than the Greek text, especially in his adaptation of the catalog of the Nereids, or daughters of Nereus (*FQ* 4.11.48–51, following *Th* 240–64; Bennett 1931). Hesiod's influence on Spenser is often felt most powerfully not in detailed allusions but rather in the poem's grand cosmic designs: in Spenser's allegorical marriage of Thames and Medway that concludes Book 4 and offers a vision of cosmological harmony rooted in Hesiod's representation of Oceanus, Tethys, and their lineage (*Th* 337–70); in Book 5's repeated scenes of Titanomachy and Gigantomachy as a means of narrating the moral and political deterioration of his own age; and finally in the *Cantos of Mutabilitie*, where Spenser constructs his own theogony, staging a juridical war in heaven to narrate the origins of change and decay in the sublunary world.

MILTON'S HESIOD

John Milton was arguably Hesiod's most sophisticated Renaissance imitator. He was steeped in the poet's works from an early age, referring to Hesiod by name in two of his *Prolusions* and listing him in *Of Education* among classical authors to be studied (Milton, *Complete Prose Works* 1:223, 289 and 2:394). The many allusions to Hesiod in *Paradise Lost* (1667, 1674) reveal a poet eager to expose the fallacies of pagan myth in contradistinction to Christian truth; the pagan gods, for Milton, "rul'd the middle Air" on the "Snowy top / Of cold Olympus," never reaching the higher heaven of his own God (Milton, *Paradise Lost* [hereafter *PL*] 1.515–17; Gallagher 1979: 128). Likewise, Milton's imitation of Hesiod's Titanomachy, as P. Gallagher (1979: 121–22, 129–30) has argued, is a "diabolically inspired distortion of the War in Heaven" that underscores the profound disparity between Hesiod's Zeus and Milton's God, the latter fully omnipotent but also unwilling to deploy all his *biē*, or force, as does Zeus when combating the Titans at *Th* 687–89. By contrast, Milton's God uses less than "half his strength" to defeat the rebel angels at *PL* 6.853–54, and "checked / His thunder," verses that illustrate Milton's eagerness to prove, despite Satan's arguments to the contrary, that God does not merely retain his throne by virtue of his superior force. Like Hesiod's Titanomachy, Milton's war in Heaven long remains a stalemate—"long time in even scale / The battle hung," the angel

Raphael explains, echoing *Th* 638 ("the outcome of the war was evenly balanced," ἶσον δὲ τέλος τέτατο πτολέμοιο)—but he does so to make a rather different point about divine justice: Milton's God postpones victory in order to give the rebel angels ample opportunity to surrender (*PL* 6.245–46).

Milton's allusions to Hesiod often illustrate how his poems anticipate a vision of divine justice fulfilled, or perfected, by Christianity. Milton's choice of the word "justify" in the opening lines of *PL* hints at the Hesiodic roots of his own theodicy, for Hesiod, much like the opening scene of Homer's *Odyssey*, justifies Zeus by emphasizing the disparity between the actual rectitude of divine judgments and the apparent crookedness of those judgments when viewed from a limited mortal perspective. As Milton argues in the *Doctrine and Discipline of Divorce*, God's judgments are "constant and most harmonious" but they often appear "variable and contrarious" to us (*Complete Prose Works* 2: 321). Milton's most definitive articulation of his poetic project in *PL*—to "justify the ways of God to men" (*PL* 1.26)—stakes its claim with a distinctly Hesiodic vocabulary: *WD* begins by asking its audience to "make judgments straight with righteousness" (δίκῃ δ᾽ἴθυνε θέμιστας), phrasing also common to Homer's depiction of Zeus as a god who makes *themistas*—judgments or decrees—straight (*WD* 9).[4] When Adam, in the final book of *PL*, repeats the archangel Michael's lesson that God "by small / Accomplish[es] great things, by things deemed weak / Subverting worldly strong, and worldly wise / By simply meek," he echoes the opening lines of *WD*, in which Zeus "humbles the proud and raises the obscure, and easily he straightens the crooked (δέ τ᾽ἰθύνει σκολιόν) and blasts the proud" (*PL* 12.566–69; *WD* 5–8). As Milton recognizes, these verses bear a close resemblance to the leveling and justifying God of Isaiah 40.4 and Luke 3.5, parallel verses whose similarities to Hesiod are even more striking in the Greek of the Septuagint: "[T]he crooked (*skolia*) will be made straight (*eutheian*), and the rough ways will be made smooth."

Paradise Lost contains a number of unconventional adaptations of Hesiodic myths in which Milton reshapes ancient fables to accommodate his own political or theological arguments. It is worth examining four of these in detail: Milton's adaptation of the myth of Zeus and Mētis, his reworking of the Horai, his retelling of the fable of Pandora, and his representation of Chaos.

Milton's depiction of the birth of Sin out of Satan transforms the Hesiodic myth of Zeus and Mētis, as well as the subsequent birth of Athena. The myth was routinely interpreted as a myth of *eubolia*, or good counsel (ἐπίφρονα βουλήν), by Renaissance poets and mythographers (*Th* 896). According to Bacon, the myth of Zeus and Mētis illustrates how rulers must create the illusion that "decision[s] come out of their own head" as if "shaped in the womb" rather than hammered out through debate in council (Bacon [1609] 2011: 761–62). Milton's revisionary interpretation of the myth is fueled by his concern that efforts at establishing Republicanism in England have been compromised by the rapacious tyranny of popular opinion during the Protectorate (Milton, *Complete Works* 6:123, 6:114). In Milton's version of the myth, Sin is born "a goddess armed / Out of [Satan's] head" at the assembly of the empyreal host in Heaven, the very assembly at which God anoints the Son. Satan and his daughter then copulate "in secret," in turn spawning Death, a genealogy that imitates the monstrous birth of Athena even as it also echoes James 1.15: "Then when lust hath conceived, it bringeth forth sin: and sin, when it is finished, bringeth forth death" (*PL* 2.757–66; Scully 2015: 177–78).

In *Th*, as well as in Homer's *Iliad*, the union of Themis and Zeus yields the Horai, three sisters—Eunomia (Order), Dikē (Justice), and Eirene (Peace)—who safeguard the timely and orderly interchange of the hours and seasons (Harrison 1927: 485). The temporal seams of noon and twilight that embellish *PL*'s most decisive moments are complexly indebted to the Horai, who provide a macrocosmic counterpoint to Milton's representation of the deliberative process of the umpire conscience, their motions replicating the turn and counter-turn of revolving minds. Milton's Pandemonium lacks this diurnal alternation; outside the realm of the Horai, there is no "grateful vicissitude" of night and day, whereas in Heaven, as in Eden, Milton calls upon the Horai to ensure that day and night revolve "in perpetual round" and "[l]odge and dislodge by turns" (*PL* 6.6–8), symbolizing a reciprocity that proves fragile in the poem. Milton adapts for his own Christian ethics Hesiod's account of Night and Day greeting each other as they pass in opposite directions over the bronze threshold of the House of Night (*Th* 748–50). In so doing, he transforms the theological and moral significance of the Horai, and of Night and Day, by accentuating the sense of spiritual urgency that accompanies their appearance, such that the revolution of the seasons or hours in Milton's poem comes to signify the sharp edge between mutually exclusive values or the decisive moment at which one must choose between them, an interpretation that reveals Milton's perception of an affinity between the mythological Horai and the scriptural emphasis, particularly in the Psalms, upon the *eukairos* or *horaios*—the seasonable or ripe time to perform spiritual actions.

Milton also complicates the commonplace Renaissance analogy between Eve and Pandora, invoking Hesiod's fable to provide an ironic prolepsis of the fall of humankind. When we first meet Eve, she is described as "more lovely than Pandora, whom the gods / Endowed with all their gifts" (*PL* 4.714–15), an ominous anticipation of Eve's error that also implicitly casts Adam as Epimetheus, a parallel that Milton makes explicit in his *Doctrine and Discipline of Divorce* (*Complete Prose Works* 2:293). The allusion sets into motion an investigation into the uses and perils of hope that dominates the final books of *PL*. In Hesiod's fable, the preservation of *Elpis*—hope, or anticipation—is a blessing, an act of divine beneficence that spares humankind the agony of anticipating future pain, instead allowing "evil to come to mortals in silence" (κακὰ θνητοῖσι φέρουσαι σιγῇ, *WD* 100–104). Yet Milton infuses the myth with ambivalence about the virtue of hope, an affection at once pervasive and damaging in Milton's hell, where the rebel angels suffer under the delusion of a "fallacious hope" (*PL* 2.568).

Finally, Milton's imitation of Hesiod's account of Chaos and of "sable-vested Night, eldest of things" at *PL* 2.959–67 reveals a creative reworking of *Th* 116–23 that aims to bring the Greek poet's cosmogony in line with Milton's own views about the relationship between good and evil and about the nature of matter (Northrup 1981; Porter 1983: 44–54; Adams 1975). Whereas Hesiod's Night is an active source of evil, her offspring all malignant, Milton's Night is "unoriginal" (*PL* 10.477), and his Chaos contains the potential for both good and evil, both light and darkness, a space of confusedly warring elements but also the origin of all fertility. Milton's transformation of Hesiod's cosmogony signals his struggle to make sense, within a Christian framework, of the ancient Greek view that qualities could only be conceived if their opposing qualities could be conceived, a position that Milton alters so as to demonstrate that evil and disorder, perversions of the good and the orderly, cannot exist without goodness and order (Northrup 1981: 313).

NOTES

1. See Clement, *Exhortation to the Greeks* 1.3; Origen, *Contra Celsum* 4, in Migne, *Patrologia Graeca* 11:1086–87; Tertullian, *De Corona Militis* 7, in Migne, *Patrologia Latina* 2:84.
2. See, for example, *Republic* 349b–350b; *Philebus* 17a; *Sophist* 225c–226a.
3. Compare Melanchthon (1543: 42a), also discussing whether Hesiod's treatment of lucky and inauspicious days is superstitious or may be explained by natural causes.
4. Compare Homer, *Odyssey* 4.691, 11.569–70, 12.439–40, 14.83–88 and the discussion by Cook (1995: 97–100). On the ancient Greek understanding of Themis, see Rudhardt (1989).

REFERENCES

Adams, R. M. 1975. "A Little Look into Chaos." In *Illustrious Evidence: Approaches to English Literature of the Early Seventeenth Century*, edited by E. Miner, 71–89. Berkeley, CA.

Alciato, A. 1556. *Emblematum libri II*. Lyon, France.

Allen, D. C. 1963. *Mysteriously Meant: The Rediscovery of Pagan Symbolism and Allegorical Interpretation in the Renaissance*. Baltimore, MD.

Allen, M. J. B. 1984. "Marsilio Ficino on Plato, the Neoplatonists, and the Christian Doctrine of the Trinity." *Renaissance Quarterly* 37: 555–84.

Bacon, F. (1609) 2011. *De Sapientia Veterum: The Wisdom of the Ancients*. Vol. 6 of *The Works of Francis Bacon*. Edited by J. Spedding, R. L. Ellis, and D. D. Heath. Cambridge, MA. (Reprint).

Bennett, J. W. 1931. "Spenser's Hesiod." *American Journal of Philology* 52: 176–81.

Bodin, J. 1975. *Colloquium of the Seven about Secrets of the Sublime*. Translated by M. Kuntz. Princeton, NJ.

Boissard, J.-J. 1588. *Emblematum Liber*. Metz, France.

Butler, G. F. 2005. "Milton's Pandora: Eve, Sin, and the Mythographic Tradition." *Milton Studies* 44: 153–78.

Chapman, G., trans. and comm. 1618. *The Georgicks of Hesiod*. London.

Conti, N. 2006. *Mythologiae*. 2 vols. Edited and translated by J. Mulryan and S. Brown. Tempe, AZ.

Cook, E. F. 1995. *The Odyssey in Athens: Myths of Cultural Origins*. Ithaca, NY.

Erasmus, D. 1974–. *Collected Works of Erasmus*. Toronto.

Ficino, M. 1959. *Opera Omnia*. 4 vols. Edited by P. O. Kristeller. Torino, Italy.

Ficino, M. 1975. *The Philebus Commentary*. Edited and translated by M. J. B. Allen. Berkeley, CA.

Ficino, M. 1985. *Commentary on Plato's Symposium on Love*. Translated by S. Jayne. Dallas, TX.

Gallagher, P. 1979. "Paradise Lost and the Greek Theogony." *English Literary Renaissance* 9: 121–48.

Gombrich, E. H. 1972. "The Subject of Poussin's Orion." In *Symbolic Images: Studies in the Art of the Renaissance II*, 119–22. London.

Harrison, J. E. 1927. *Themis: A Study of the Social Origins of Greek Religion*. 2nd ed. Cambridge.

Heinsius, D., ed. and comm. 1603. *Hesiodou Askraiou . . . quae extant, Cum Graecis Scholiis, Procli, Moschopuli, Tzetzae*. Antwerp, Belgium.

Kivlio, M. 2010. *Early Greek Poets' Lives: The Shaping of the Tradition*. Leiden, Netherlands.

Lamberton, R. 1986. *Homer the Theologian: Neoplatonist Allegorical Reading and the Growth of the Epic Tradition*. Berkeley, CA.

Landino, C., ed. and comm. 1497. *Commento . . . sopra la Commedia do Dante Alighieri*. Venice, Italy.

Melanchthon, P., ed. and comm. 1532. *Hesiodou tou Askraiou Erga kai Hêmerai: Opera et Dies*. Hagenau.

Melanchthon, P. (1540) 1999. *Oration on the Life of Galen*. In *Orations on Philosophy and Education*, edited by S. Kusukawa and translated by C. F. Salazar, 212–19. Cambridge.

Melanchthon, P., ed. and comm. 1543. *In Hesiodi libros De Opere et Die*. Paris.

Melanchthon, P. 1988. *A Melanchthon Reader*. Translated by R. Keen. New York.

Menager, D. 2005. *La Renaissance et la nuit*. Geneva.

Meter, J. H. 1984. *The Literary Theories of Daniel Heinsius*. Assen, Netherlands.

Milton, J. 1931–1938. *Complete Works*. 18 vols. in 21. Edited by F. A. Patterson. New York.

Milton, J. 1953–1982. *Complete Prose Works*. 8 vols. Edited by D. M. Wolfe. New Haven, CT.

Milton, J. 1971. *Paradise Lost*. Edited by A. Fowler. London.

Northrup, M. D. 1981. "Milton's Hesiodic Cosmology." *Comparative Literature* 33: 305–20.

Panofsky, D., and E. Panofsky. 1956. *Pandora's Box: The Changing Aspects of a Mythical Symbol*. New York.

Petrarch, F. 1985. *Letters on Familiar Matters: Rerum Familiarum*. 3 vols. Translated by A. Bernardo. Baltimore, MD.

Poliziano, A. 1993. *The Stanze of Angelo Poliziano*. 2nd ed. Translated by D. Quint. University Park, PA.

Porter, W. M. 1983. *Reading the Classics and Paradise Lost*. Lincoln, Nebraska.

Reynolds, H. 1632. *Mythomystes: Wherein a short survay is taken of the nature and value of true poesy and depth of the ancients above our moderne poets*. London.

Ronsard, P. 1914–1975. *Œuvres Complètes*. 20 vols. Edited by P. Laumonier. Paris.

Rudhardt, J. 1989. *Themis et les Hôrai*. Geneva.

Scully, S. 2015. *Hesiod's Theogony: From Babylonian Creation Myths to Paradise Lost*. Oxford.

Seznec, J. 1953. *The Survival of the Pagan Gods: The Mythological Tradition and Its Place in Renaissance Humanism and Art*. Translated by B. Sessions. Princeton, NJ.

Spenser, E. 1978. *The Faerie Queene*. Edited by T. P. Roche Jr. New York.

Sponde, J., ed. and comm. 1592. *Hesiodou tou Askraiou Erga kai Hêmerai*. La Rochelle, France.

Vossius, G., ed. and comm. 1654. *De Veterum Poetarum Temporibus Libri Duo*. Amsterdam.

West, M. L. 1964. "The Medieval and Renaissance Manuscripts of Hesiod's Theogony." *Classical Quarterly* 14: 165–89.

West, M. L., ed. and comm. 1978. *Hesiod: Works and Days*. Oxford.

CHAPTER 28

HESIOD IN THE EIGHTEENTH AND NINETEENTH CENTURIES

ADAM LECZNAR

THE traces of Hesiod in the eighteenth and nineteenth centuries are faint, but two fleeting examples of his reception will give some sense of what we can understand about his significance. The first comes from August 11, 1832, when the Romantic poet Samuel Taylor Coleridge (1772–1834) turned to Hesiod during his "table talk": "I like reading Hesiod, meaning the Works and Days. If every verse is not poetry, it is, at least, good sense, which is a great deal to say" (1835: 46). Coleridge goes on to use Hesiod's *epea* on rustic life to dismiss Virgil's *Georgics*: "There is nothing real in the *Georgics*, except, to be sure, the verse. Mere didactics of practice, unless seasoned with the personal interests of the time or author, are inexpressibly dull to me. Such didactic poetry as that of the *Works and Days* followed naturally upon legislation, and the first ordering of municipalities." Coleridge appreciates the way that Hesiod wrote "good sense," compared to the superficial versification of Virgil, and believes that the *Works and Days* (hereafter *WD*) brought together a concern for poetic form with a desire to preserve the conditions of rural life in a context of great historical change accompanying the birth of the polis.

Another brief encounter with the ancient Greek poet took place twenty years later, when the French novelist Gustave Flaubert (1821–1880) was on a ten-day expedition to visit Thermopylae in January 1851 (see Brown 2006: 267–68 for the following account). Flaubert had already visited Egypt and Carthage on his travels and was keen to explore the landscape of the classical world when he reached Greece. But bad weather struck during his journey, and he and his companions were left fearing for their lives on Mount Cithaeron in a freezing blizzard. Fortunately the sound of a barking dog directed them to a nearby inn, and Flaubert would later recount the strange rustic customs of the Greeks that he encountered while he was recuperating: "Whenever someone arrived a cry of 'Khandi! Nadji!' was heard, the door would open, a man and his steamy horse would enter, the horse would settle at the feeding trough and the man at the fireplace. . . .

I thought of the age of Saturn as Hesiod describes it! This is how people traveled for centuries . . ." (cited in Brown 2006: 268). This experience put Flaubert immediately in mind of Hesiod, and in particular the section of the *WD* (109–20) where the ancient Greek poet described the inhabitants of the golden age. Hesiod's account of prelapsarian humanity, with its simple existence and archaic religion, reminds Flaubert that outside the metropolitan centers of the nineteenth century, there still exist untouched ways of life.

The responses of Coleridge and Flaubert are representative of some of the possible attitudes and approaches to Hesiod in this period. He is an author who requires positioning in relation to his more famous classical counterparts (Virgil for Coleridge, but more frequently Homer), one who offers a window onto ways of life, in *WD*, and forms of religious belief, in *Theogony* (hereafter *Th*), that were utterly alien to the educated urban elite who could call his poetry to mind. As such, he and his works became symbolic in this period for the strangeness of antiquity rather than its familiarity. In an age gripped by the increasingly vocal demands of Christianity, reason, and the Enlightenment, Hesiod stood as a reminder of the persistent appeal of pagan myth and of the need to grapple with the primitive past that still lurked beneath the neoclassical architecture of European civilization. By exploring examples of Hesiod's reception in France, England, and Germany, this chapter focuses on some of the dark flashes of insight that Hesiod could offer into the intellectual and literary debates of the era.

France: Voltaire

The first author I examine is the French philosopher, poet, novelist, and historian François-Marie Arouet, better known as Voltaire (1694–1778). Voltaire's passion for classical antiquity was ignited while he was learning Latin and Greek at the Jesuit college Louis-le-Grand in Paris between 1704 and 1711, and he went on to explore the modern resonance of both tragedy, in his adaptation of Sophocles's *Oedipus* as his debut play *Œdipe* in 1718, and epic, in his 1727 essay "An Essay on Epick Poetry of European Nations, From Homer down to Milton" (see Voltaire 1728: 37–130 for the original version, written in English; for its later revision, see Voltaire 1733). None of his early reflections on epic mention Hesiod, and it was not until Voltaire compiled his *Questions sur l'Encyclopédie* in the 1770s that the ancient author made an appearance in Voltaire's writing. In the entry on "Epic Poetry," Hesiod is the first poet to be discussed, and Voltaire begins by listing the different topics covered by Hesiod's *WD*, including Prometheus and the Myth of the Ages, in a way that brings the poem directly in line with contemporary experience:

> Hesiod afterwards describes the four famous ages, of which he is the first who has spoken, at least among the ancient authors who remain to us. The first age is that which preceded Pandora—the time in which men lived with the gods. The iron age

is that of the siege of Thebes and Troy. "I live in the fifth," says he, "and I would I had never been born." How many men, oppressed by envy, fanaticism, and tyranny, since Hesiod, have said the same! (Voltaire 1824: 97–98)

Voltaire's account of the Hesiodic myth is strange, in that it includes five ages while also equating the age of heroes with the age of iron; he has perhaps assumed the age of heroes to be that of iron (following on from the age of bronze), and taken the fifth age to be an unnamed era of persecution and tyranny that has stretched on into modernity. Voltaire then lists some of the moral and agricultural maxims that are to be found in Hesiod's *WD* and comments that "[there] are also very fine passages in his Theogony," including the images of "Love, who disentangles chaos" and "Venus, born of the sea from the genital parts of a god" (98). These examples build to a question: "Why, then, has Hesiod had less reputation than Homer?," to which Voltaire responds: "They seem to me of equal merit, but Homer has been preferred by the Greeks because he sang their exploits and victories over the Asiatics, their eternal enemies. He celebrated all the families, which, in his time, reigned in Achaia and Peloponnesus; he wrote the most memorable war of the first people in Europe against the most flourishing nation, which was then known in Asia. His poem was almost the only monument of that great epoch" (Voltaire 1824: 98–99). Voltaire attributes the preference for Homer over Hesiod to the nationalism of the former's poetry and its influence on Hellenic cultural identity. But despite this rationalizing explanation, Voltaire's comments nevertheless suggest that he believes Hesiod's poetry and maxims speak more clearly to the everyday life of his readers. While Homer can help to explain the fundamental nationalistic purpose of epic poetry, Hesiod helps to elucidate the basic similarities among human beings across history.

ENGLAND: COOKE AND POPE, ELTON AND SHELLEY

The two main English translations of Hesiod of this era can also help us to understand the possible roles that this poet could play in contemporary debates. Before Thomas Cooke (1703–1756) published his translation of the *Th* and the *WD* in 1728, the only English translation of Hesiod was the 1618 English version by George Chapman, which contained only the *WD*. (On Hesiod's reception in England before 1900, see also the chapters by Wolfe and Nelson in this volume) Alongside Hesiod, Cooke also translated the pastoral poetry of Moschus and Bion, Cicero's *De Natura Deorum*, the plays of Terence, and Plautus's *Amphitryon*, though it was on account of his translation of Hesiod that he came to be known among his contemporaries, positively it seems, as "Hesiod Cooke" (see Lee and Sherbo 2004). Cooke is also famous for his conflict with the poet Alexander Pope (1688–1744). In 1725 Cooke launched two attacks on Pope, one in a satirical poem, *The Battle of the Poets*, which responded to *The*

Battle of the Books (1704) by Pope's ally Jonathan Swift, and the other in a letter to the *Daily Journal* that criticized Pope's translation of the Thersites section of the *Iliad* (both included in Cooke 1729). Cooke later tried to defuse the row by sending Pope a copy of his Hesiod translation, but Pope responded by making Cooke one of the dunces in his *Dunciad*, published in 1728, the same year as Cooke's Hesiod translation (see Book II.130 and Pope's notes to this line). The *Dunciad* itself displays some affinities with Hesiodic epic, via Pope's deep poetic debt to John Milton, through its account of a kind of reverse *Th*, as the world slips from cosmos into chaos (see Weinbrot 2007; Robertson 2009).

The context for their conflict was the "Quarrel of the Ancients and the Moderns," the debate that took place in France and England in the late seventeenth century about the competing values of the ancient and modern worlds. While the Moderns believed that the unprecedented amount of knowledge, scientific and otherwise, available to modern people enabled them to surpass the skill and intelligence of their ancient predecessors, the Ancients believed that classical authors would forever serve as unsurpassable models. Although Pope had an ambivalent attitude toward classical authors throughout his career, in this debate he came closer to the belief that the ancient past formed a high point of cultural achievement, while Cooke was more optimistic about the value of his contemporary world. This position is legible in his introduction to the translation (see Cooke [1728] 1740: xiii–xlix), which is almost entirely devoted to collating modern sources for the dating of Hesiod's life. Cooke's reliance on accounts like that of the sixteenth-century Danish astronomer Christen Sørensen Longomontanus and Isaac Newton's *The Chronology of Ancient Kingdoms Amended* (published posthumously in 1728) demonstrates a desire to affirm how modern knowledge can provide more insight into ancient authors than is available from ancient testimony alone (see Cooke [1728] 1740: xvii, xxxi).

The second English translation, by Charles Abraham Elton (1778–1853), was published eighty years later, in 1809 (with a second edition in 1815) and enjoyed greater success. After serving as an officer in the British Army, Elton became involved in literary circles and was friends with both Samuel Taylor Coleridge and Charles Lamb. Elton's translation of Hesiod, which included *The Shield of Hercules*, began with an introductory preface (along with four essays on Hesiod's biography, historical dating, poetry, and mythology) that was critical of Cooke's translation:

> With respect to Hesiod, either Cooke's knowledge of Greek was in reality superficial, or his indolence counteracted his abilities; for his blunders are inexcusably frequent and unaccountably gross: not in matters of mere verbal nicety, but in several important particulars: nor are these instances, which tend so perpetually to mislead the reader, compensated by the force or beauty of his style; which, notwithstanding some few unaffected and emphatical lines, is, in its general effect, tame and grovelling. (Elton 1815: v–vi)

At the beginning of this essay, Elton made a strong case for the literary worth of Hesiod's poetry as a whole (without identifying any specific poems):

The remains of Hesiod are not alone interesting to the antiquary, as tracing a picture of the rude arts and manners of the ancient Greeks. His sublime philosophic allegories; his elevated views of a retributive Providence; and the romantic elegance, or daring grandeur, with which he has invested the legends of his mythology, offer more solid reasons than the accident of coeval existence for the traditional association of his name with that of Homer. (1815: iii)

Elsewhere he praises both *Th* and *WD*, describing "the bold and simple majesty" of the former poem (xlviii) and offering the following account of the latter, focusing in turn on lines 220–24, 197–201, and 122–23 of the work:

In the mental or moral sublime I consider Hesiod as superior to Homer. The personification of Prayers in the latter is almost the only allegory that can be compared with the awful prosopopoeia of Justice, weeping her wrongs at the feet of the Eternal: while Justice and Modesty, described as virgins in white raiment, ascending out of the sight of men into heaven, and the Holy Dæmons, after having animated the bodies of just men, hovering round the earth, and keeping watch over human actions, are equalled by no conception in the Iliad or Odyssey. (1815: lvii)

While Voltaire confessed himself surprised by, but ultimately understanding of, Homer's superior reputation, Elton argues that Hesiod surpasses his epic counterpart through his "sublime philosophical allegories" and his treatment of ancient Greek mythology.

This positive reading of Hesiod's qualities compared to Homer, and particularly the praise of his allegorical potential, seems to have been transmitted to readers of his translation, and it sparked off some of the nineteenth century's most interesting engagements with the ancient poet. One of these was in the work of Mary Shelley (1797–1851). Alongside her appropriation of the Prometheus myth as a major motif in *Frankenstein, or the Modern Prometheus* (1817), particularly in its relation to the creation of Pandora as present in both Hesiod's *WD* and *Th*, Shelley also incorporated four quotations from Elton's translation into her apocalyptic novel *The Last Man* (1826), which describes a plague that has swept across the globe, destroying almost all of humankind (see Shelley 1994: 162, 229, 315 and 400; these references correspond respectively to *Th* 89–90, *WD* 245–47, 101–4, and *The Shield of Hercules* 152–53). One possible source for Shelley's interest in Hesiod could be her father, William Godwin (1756–1836), who published an introductory handbook to ancient mythology in 1806 under the pseudonym Edward Baldwin, entitled *The Pantheon: Or Ancient History of the Gods of Greece and Rome for the Use of Schools and Young Persons of Both Sexes*, that used Hesiod as a major source (see Baldwin 1809 for second edition). Godwin was keen to downplay the more violent scenes from the *Th*, describing the castration of Ouranos by Kronos (*Th* 174–92) as follows:

When Saturn deposed his father Cœlus from the government of heaven, in the scuffle he gave Cœlus a wound, and cut away part of his flesh: the part which was separated Saturn threw into the sea, and from it, as from a seed, sprung the Goddess

Venus: the drops of blood from the wound, fell on the earth, and were the parent source of the Giants. (Baldwin 1809: 69)

Another intriguing collaboration that made use of Elton's translation of Hesiod took place between the sculptor and artist John Flaxman (1755–1826) and the poet William Blake (1757–1826). In 1817 they published a set of engravings of scenes from both of Hesiod's major poems, beginning with the *WD*, based on drawings by Flaxman that Blake copied out onto copper plates. The printed edition of these compositions (Flaxman 1817) repeated a particular form of composition throughout, with each page using a tripartite structure of a title (e.g., "Hesiod admonishing Perses" or "Pandora gifted"), a line-drawn image, and a short quotation from Elton's translation. Their collaboration is not immediately surprising: at this late stage of their careers (both were around the age of sixty) Flaxman regularly helped Blake financially by securing him commissions for engraving. One possible intellectual context for their choice of Hesiod as a subject was Flaxman's interest, shared with Blake, in the religious movement of Swedenborgianism, also known as the New Church.

This movement had been inspired by the Swedish scientist and engineer turned prophet Emanuel Swedenborg (1688–1772), who had gained fame after he experienced a series of divine visions in the early 1740s. In 1758 Swedenborg published a book written in Latin called *Heaven and its Wonders and Hell from Things Heard and Seen* (*De Caelo et Eius Mirabilibus et de Inferno, ex Auditis et Visis*), which declared that the Last Judgment had begun the previous year and that he had seen it taking place in visions of heaven and hell. The doctrine of Swedenborg became popular among dissenters from the Church of England due to its emphasis on the spiritual element of Christianity and on human love as a manifestation of divinity, but he also gained public popularity for his descriptions of these revelations, some of which demonstrated clear parallels with Hesiod's *WD*. For example, Swedenborg describes the inhabitants of the golden age thus:

> They told me in heaven that the thoughts of the most ancient people on our planet, who were heaven-life people, were composed of correspondences themselves, and that all the natural components and phenomena of the world which were before their eyes enabled them to think in this way. And as this was their nature, they associated with angels and spoke with them, and it was thus, through them, that heaven was joined with the world. That is why this period was called the Golden Age. (Swedenborg 2010: 77–78)

"Correspondences" was a term developed by Swedenborg to describe similarities between distinct spheres of existence, such as the divine, the natural, and the human; the suggestion that the inhabitants of the golden age were "correspondences themselves" means that they embodied a prelapsarian harmony among these different spheres. Swedenborg continues to describe the following ages of silver, bronze, and iron as representing the gradual loosening of these bonds between humans and divinity (see also Swedenborg 2010: 163); in a later work from 1768 entitled *The Delights of Wisdom*

FIGURE 28.1 "Good Daemons." John Flaxman, *Compositions from the "Works and Days" and "Theogony" of Hesiod* (London, 1817), plate 10. ©Trustees of the British Museum.

Concerning Conjugial Love after Which Follows The Pleasures of Insanity Concerning Scortatory Love he describes further what he saw when angels showed him the inhabitants of these different ages (Swedenborg 1794: 79–91). This resonance between Hesiod and Swedenborg was made explicit in the engravings of Flaxman and Blake, in particular in one entitled "Good Daemons" (see figure 28.1). This design quoted the description to be found in Hesiod's *WD* of the afterlife of the race of the golden age and incorporated an image of these "daemons" that made them look exactly like winged angels: "Earth-wandering daemons they their charge began / Ministers of good, and guards of men" (see Elton 1815: 19; *WD* 122–23). It is possible that Flaxman was aware of the links between Hesiod's account of ancient Greek religious belief and mythology and the details of Swedenborg's visions of the golden age (see Lamberton 1988: 156–58 for possible resonances of Hesiod in Blake's poetry).

GERMANY: CREUZER AND NIETZSCHE

The German reception of Hesiod in this period tended to revolve around two poles, philology and philosophy. One of the main events of the philological response to the poet came in 1818, when Hesiod played an integral role in one of the foundational debates of the burgeoning discipline of German classical scholarship. His name appeared in the title of the collection of letters exchanged between two classical scholars, Georg Friedrich Creuzer (1771–1858) and Johann Gottfried Hermann (1772–1848), *Briefe über Homer und Hesiodus, vorzüglich über die Theogonie*. Earlier in the decade Creuzer had published his controversial work *Symbolik und Mythologie der alten Völker, besonders der Griechen* (1810–1812), which offered a vision of ancient Greek religion permeated with darkness and violence that ran counter to the neoclassical idea of ancient Greece to be found in the work of figures like Winckelmann that took the Greeks as direct ancestors of the European Enlightenment (see Creuzer 1837: 68–73 for a discussion of Hesiod's *Th*). The debate between Hermann and Creuzer was about whether the ancient Greek poets, and in particular Homer and Hesiod, wrote poems that were consciously symbolic and allegorical or believed the events and ideas that their poems recount to be factual and historical. In the first letter of this exchange, Hermann declared:

> My opinion is that to be able to come to a satisfying resolution, first the question must be answered whether the poet spoke symbolically or if the symbolism lay in the matter itself. I absolutely deny the first answer. Homer and Hesiod, under which names I understand everything that these names entail, certainly did not know anything at all about symbolism and mysticism, but everything that they narrated they narrated in full belief as fact, without questioning after reasons and causes or other meanings. This is so much the character of ancient epic poetry that no exception at all can be made. (Hermann and Creuzer 1818: 1–2; my translation)

Creuzer responded that Hermann's idea about Homer and Hesiod, "whereby they should have narrated everything 'in full belief', seems to me to invite difficulties" (5). He continued:

> As you will remark from everything that I write, the relationship of Homer and Hesiod (to use these names once more) to the older religious belief and to the priest-caste of Greek still provides me with a riddle that is hard to unravel, and more than anything I would like to see more lucidly into what Herodotus II.53 says about them: οὗτοί εἰσι οἱ ποιήσαντες θεογονίην Ἕλλησι. (Hermann and Creuzer 1818: 10)

In response, Hermann accused Creuzer of believing too strongly that writers like Hesiod and Homer wrote symbolically in their discussions of ancient Greek religious belief; in this way, he tried to distance himself from the idea that Hesiod's writing could demonstrate the parallels between ancient Greek religion and foreign belief systems such as the Egyptian or the Phoenician. The sense that Hesiodic texts could put their readers in touch with an archaic and avowedly unclassical worldview that was closer to the structures of premodern religious belief than to the institutions and understandings of the present day fueled the popularity of Creuzer's work among his readers. Though his *Symbolik* has never been completely translated into English, his ideas came to the attention of Coleridge and George Eliot (see Louis 2009: 6–13); the comprehensive

French translation of J. D. Guigniaut, published between 1825 and 1851, made Creuzer much better known among French readers, where he influenced authors including Flaubert, Jules Michelet, and Ernest Renan (see Sohnle 1972).

In terms of the philosophical response, one of the most striking invocations of Hesiod from this period was by Friedrich Nietzsche (1844–1900). Nietzsche began his professional life as a professor of classical philology at the University of Basle and turned increasingly to philosophical writing after he resigned his post in 1879. A crucial part of his philosophical project was to interrogate the received morality of the late-nineteenth century; drawing on his philological past, Nietzsche often turned to classical literature to comment on the elements of the ancient world that demonstrated how different its inhabitants were from those of modernity and to bring to light the contingency of what could seem like natural nineteenth-century beliefs. One influential example of this occurred in his 1872 work *The Birth of Tragedy, out of the Spirit of Music* (*Die Geburt der Tragödie, aus dem Geiste der Musik*), in which Nietzsche used the ancient Greek god Dionysus to advance the idea that the ancient Greeks were much more aware of the irrational forces at work in their lives and their art (for Nietzsche's predecessors in this irrationalist tradition, including Creuzer, see Bambach 2012). If we look at some of Nietzsche's writings on Hesiod, it becomes clear that the ancient Greek poet represented an alternative cipher for Nietzsche's belief in the profound strangeness of the ancient world.

Nietzsche included many glancing references to Hesiod in his published works and unpublished notes, including a parody of Hesiod's account in the *Th* (535–60) of what happened when Prometheus tricked Zeus with a sacrifice at Mekone (Nietzsche 1978: 461–63), and allusions to the Myth of Ages in the first essay of *On the Genealogy of Morality* (*Zur Genealogie der Moral*) and in *Daybreak* (*Morgenröte*) (see Nietzsche 2010: 24, 1997: 110–11). A review of an edition of Hesiod's *Th* (Schoeman 1868) also formed one of his few philological publications (see Latacz 2014: 10). But by far Nietzsche's most extended treatment of Hesiod was in his writings on the *Certamen*, "The Contest between Homer and Hesiod." One of Nietzsche's responses to this piece was philological, as he published a new scholarly edition that traced the text's manuscript tradition back to the *Mouseion* of the fourth-century BCE poet Alcidamas (see Nietzsche 1870 and 1873; Latacz 2014: 12–19), but his other response was much more philosophical. This was an unpublished essay, written in 1872, entitled "Homer's Contest" ("Homers Wettkampf"); a translation of this essay is included in Nietzsche 2010: 174–81 as a text that helps to explain *On the Genealogy of Morality*; see also Vogt 1962). Nietzsche begins with a provocation to the Enlightenment credentials of his imagined readers: "If we speak of *humanity*, it is on the basic assumption that it should be that which *separates* man from nature and is his mark of distinction. But in reality there is no such separation: 'natural' characteristics and those called specifically 'human' have grown together inextricably. Man, at the finest height of his powers, is all nature and carries nature's uncanny dual character in himself" (2010: 174). Nietzsche suggests that the abstract concept of "humanity" obscures the fundamental combination of human and natural, or animal, qualities, and he immediately turns to classical antiquity to suggest that the integral role of barbaric wildness in the ancient Greek understanding of human activity is too often ignored. From the ancient Greek literary corpus, Nietzsche immediately invokes Homer as representative of this procedure, asking, "Why did the whole Greek world rejoice over the pictures of battle in the Iliad? I fear we have not understood these in a sufficiently 'Greek' way, and even that we would shudder if we ever did understand them in a Greek way" (2010: 175).

To answer this question, and to seek out this particular "Greek" way of understanding antiquity, Nietzsche believes that we have to search out "what lies *behind* the world of Homer, as the womb of everything Hellenic"; it is here that he turns to Hesiod, as the main surviving evidence of the barbaric, Dionysiac world that is occluded by a focus on the gleaming, Apolline forms of Homeric epic:

> Let us imagine the air of Hesiod's poems, difficult to breathe as it is, still thicker and darker and without any of the things to alleviate and cleanse it which poured over Hellas from Delphi and numerous seats of the gods: let us mix this thickened Boeotian air with the dark voluptuousness of the Etruscans; such a reality would then *extort* from us a world of myths in which Uranus, Kronos and Zeus and the struggles of the Titans would seem like a relief; in this brooding atmosphere, combat is salvation and deliverance, the cruelty of the victory is the pinnacle of life's jubilation. (Nietzsche 2010: 175).

For Nietzsche, Hesiod's poetry contains the most accurate representation that the Dionysiac ancient Greece has to offer of the dark message suppressed by Homeric poetry, which Nietzsche describes as follows: "Combat and the pleasure of victory were acknowledged: and nothing severs the Greek world so sharply from ours as the resultant coloring of individual ethical concepts, for example *Eris* and *envy*" (2010: 176). The invocation of "Eris," the ancient Greek word for "strife," leads Nietzsche to quote from the beginning of Hesiod's *WD*: "There are *two* Eris-goddesses on earth"; he glosses this as "one of the most remarkable of Hellenic ideas" and says that it "deserves to be impressed upon newcomers right at the gate of entry to Hellenic ethics," before quoting the entirety of lines 12–26 of the *WD*. Here, Hesiod differentiates between two good and bad forms of "Eris," the former created by Zeus as a constructive way of making human beings desire to better themselves through competition with others and the latter a destructive principle that "promotes wicked war and feuding, the cruel thing!" (2010: 176). Nietzsche suggests that the idea of this good form of strife is impossible for modern culture to understand, and that it takes us closer to the truly agonistic nature of ancient Greek existence.

Though the essay is called "Homer's Contest," it is Hesiod who is more important in elucidating the significance of the contest itself, and Nietzsche proceeds to construe this ethical imperative throughout all of Hellenic culture. He concludes by suggesting that the decline of ancient Greek civilization commenced when the internal competition ceased and was turned outward in its more destructive form, without envy, jealousy and ambition in the contest, the Hellenic state, like Hellenic man, deteriorates. It becomes evil and cruel, it becomes vengeful and godless, in short, it becomes "pre-Homeric"—it then only takes a panicky fright to make it fall and shatter. Sparta and Athens surrender to the Persians like Themistocles and Alcibiades did; they betray the Hellenic after they have given up the finest Hellenic principle, the contest: and Alexander, the rough copy and abbreviation of Greek history, now invents the standard-issue Hellene and so-called "Hellenism." (Nietzsche 2010: 181)

In *The Birth of Tragedy* Nietzsche had attributed the fall of Hellenic culture to the diminishing influence of Dionysus and the growing power of Platonic idealism; here, he suggests that this took place because the Greeks, and in particular powerful and complex figures like Themistocles, Alcibiades, and Alexander, lost touch with the teachings of Hesiod and allowed the encroachment of external, more barbaric, cultural influences. In this account, Nietzsche was perhaps thinking of Plutarch's account of Themistocles's flight from Athens to the court of the Persian king Artaxerxes, as well as of Alcibiades's close relationship with the satrap Tissaphernes and Alexander's controversial adoption of Persian dress and customs during his campaigns; in each account, this engagement with the Persians operates as part of their downfall (see, e.g., Plutarch, *Themistocles* 27–31, *Alcibiades* 24–27, *Alexander* 45; see also Ingenkamp 1998 for Nietzsche's reception of Plutarch). Although Hesiod becomes less prominent in the essay as it progresses, by the end it is clear that for Nietzsche the poet offers a particularly powerful expression of one of Greek antiquity's essential doctrines, and he is keen to point out the destruction of Hellenism that took place when this doctrine was forgotten.

CONCLUSION

I want to conclude with a rather more personal engagement with Hesiod's poetry by Thomas Babington Macaulay (1800–1859), a British civil servant who was stationed in India between 1834 and 1838 and who is best known as the author of the notorious "Minute on Indian Education," published on February 2, 1835. Here, Macaulay encouraged the widespread teaching of English in Indian schools, claiming that "a single shelf of a good European library [is] worth the whole native literature of India and Arabia" (Macaulay 1999: 165). This "Minute" has come to represent one of the central statements of nineteenth-century British ideas of imperial superiority. Macaulay also became an avid reader of Greek and Latin literature during his time in India; Phiroze Vasunia (2015: 146) has argued that he pursued this reading because "to be a 'classicist' in India was, for Macaulay, also a way of being British and of asserting his European identity among what he perceived as trying local conditions."

In the same week as the publication of his infamous "Minute" Macaulay received the belated news from England of the death of his beloved sister Margaret the previous August, and in a letter to his one of oldest friends, Thomas Flower Ellis, there is a striking reference to Hesiod:

> Even now, when time has begun to do its healing office, I cannot write about her without being altogether unmanned. That I have not utterly sunk under this blow I owe chiefly to literature. What a blessing it is to love books as I love them,—to be able to converse with the dead and to live amidst the unreal. Many times during the last few weeks I have repeated to myself those fine lines of Hesiod. (Macaulay 1976: 129)

Following this, written in Greek without accents, come six lines of Hesiod's *Th* (98–103):

> For though a man have sorrow and grief in his newly-troubled soul and live in dread because his heart is distressed, yet, when a singer, the servant of the Muses, chants the glorious deeds of men of old and the blessed gods who inhabit Olympus, at once he forgets his heaviness and remembers not his sorrows at all; but the gifts of the goddesses soon turn him away from these. (Evelyn-White [1914] 1926: 85)

In December 1835 Macaulay wrote again to Ellis to explain how in the aftermath of the shocking news, "Literature has saved my life and my reason. Even now I dare not, in the intervals of business, remain alone for a minute without a book in my hand" (1976: 159). Macaulay turned to Hesiod in those first moments of anguish not just to affirm his European identity, but also to ensure his emotional survival.

The examples of Hesiod's reception in this chapter speak to some of the fundamental elements of the poet's significance during the eighteenth and nineteenth centuries. While Voltaire used Hesiod's *WD* to consider the nature of epic poetry, Flaxman and Blake turned to vivid scenes from across Hesiodic poetry to create a set of images that resonated with contemporary discourses of religious mysticism. At the same time, in Germany Creuzer and Nietzsche were using Hesiod to make a case for the otherness of ancient Greek religious and ethical belief. In all these instances, and especially in the brief examples that have book-ended the chapter, Hesiod's writings represented parts of contemporary experience that could not be understood according to the abstract conceptual apparatus of the Enlightenment. He was a poet who sang of strange beliefs and alien lifestyles in the *WD*, and of cosmic and divine mythologies in the *Th*, and in both of these guises he presented a Romantic version of ancient Greece that posed difficult questions for attempts to narrate a clear and unbroken descent from antiquity to modernity and to the ideologies of neoclassicism that were so important in this period. This chapter serves as an introduction to the different roles that Hesiod played during the eighteenth and nineteenth centuries; it is to be hoped that others will delve deeper into the appeal that this poet held for some of the greatest thinkers and writers of the age.

FURTHER READING

Few works focus on the reception history of Hesiod in this period, and all the areas discussed in this chapter merit further study. For the English tradition, see Gillespie (2000 and 2008), Davis (2005), and Priestman (2012). Studies do exist for the reception of myths found in Hesiod, such as Panofsky and Panofsky (1962) for Pandora and Kerenyi (1997) for Prometheus. Robertson (2009: 130–57) treats Voltaire's attitude to epic poetry. See Morrison and Stone (2003) for Mary Shelley's use of Hesiod in *Frankenstein* and *The Last Man*, and Stafford (1994) for her ideas about apocalypse. On William Blake's attitude toward antiquity see Raine (1979); for his Hesiod engravings see Essick (1991); and see further Irwin (1979) on Flaxman and Rix (2007) on his and Blake's interest in Swedenborg. Howald (1984), Marchand (1996), and Williamson (2004) introduce the scholarly and cultural context to the controversy surrounding Creuzer's *Symbolik*; Porter (2000) and Jensen and Heit (2014) are the best places to start for Nietzsche's philological writings.

REFERENCES

Baldwin, E. 1809. *The Pantheon: Or Ancient History of the Gods of Greece and Rome for the Use of Schools and Young Persons of Both Sexes*. 2nd ed. London.

Bambach, C. 2012. "The Idea of the Archaic in German Thought: Creuzer, Bachofen, Nietzsche, Heidegger." In *The Archaic: The Past in the Present*, edited by P. Bishop, 147–68. London.

Brown, F. 2006. *Flaubert: A Biography*. London.

Coleridge, S. T. 1835. *Specimens of the Table Talk of the Late Samuel Taylor Coleridge, In Two Volumes*. New York.

Cooke, T. (1728) 1740. *The Works of Hesiod, Translated from the Greek by Mr. Cooke*. London.

Cooke, T. 1729. *Tales, Epistles, Odes, Fables, etc., With Translations from Homer and Other Antient Authors: To Which Are Added Proposals for Perfecting the English Language*. London.

Creuzer, F. 1837. *Symbolik und Mythologie der alten Völker, besonders der Griechen: Erster Theil*. 3rd ed. Leipzig and Darmstadt, Germany.

Davis, P. 2005. "Didactic Poetry." In *The Oxford History of Literary Translation in English*, Vol. 3, *1660–1790*, edited by S. Gillespie and D. Hopkins, 191–203. Oxford.

Elton, C. A. 1815. *The Remains of Hesiod the Ascraean Including The Shield of Hercules, Translated into English Rhyme and Blank-Verse; With a Dissertation on the Life and Aera, The Poems and Mythology, of Hesiod, and Copious Notes*. 2nd ed. London.

Essick, R. N. 1991. *William Blake's Commercial Book Illustrations: A Catalogue and Study of the Plates Engraved by Blake after Designs by Other Artists*. Oxford.

Evelyn-White, H. G., trans. (1914) 1926. *Hesiod, the Homeric Hymns and Homerica with an English Translation*. London.

Flaxman, J. 1817. *Compositions from the Works and Days and Theogony of Hesiod, Designed by John Flaxman, Engraved by William Blake*. London.

Gillespie, S. 2000. "Hesiod." In *Encyclopedia of Literary Translation into English*, Vol. I, *A–L*, edited by O. Classe, 637–38. London.

Gillespie, S. 2008. "Hesiod Goes Augustan: An Early English Translation of the *Theogony*." *Translation and Literature* 17 (2): 197–209.

Hermann, G., and F. Creuzer. 1818. *Briefe über Homer und Hesiodus vorzüglich über die Theogonie*. Heidelberg, Germany.

Howald, E. 1984. *Der Kampf um Creuzers Symbolik: Eine Auswahl von Dokumenten*. Hildesheim, West Germany.

Ingenkamp, H. G. 1988. "Der Höhepunkt der deutschen Plutarchrezeption: Plutarch bei Nietzsche." *Illinois Classical Studies* 13 (2): 505–29.

Irwin, D. 1979. *John Flaxman 1755–1826: Sculptor, Illustrator, Designer*. London.

Jensen, A. K., and H. Heit, eds. 2014. *Nietzsche as a Scholar of Antiquity*. London.

Kerenyi, C. 1997. *Prometheus: Archetypal Image of Human Existence*. Translated by R. Manheim. Princeton, NJ.

Lamberton, R. 1988. *Hesiod*. New Haven, CT, and London.

Latacz, J. 2014. "On Nietzsche's Philological Beginnings." In *Nietzsche as a Scholar of Antiquity*, edited by A. K. Jensen and H. Heit, 3–26. London.

Lee, S., and A. Sherbo. 2004. "Cooke, Thomas (1703–1756)." In *Oxford Dictionary of National Biography*. Oxford. Accessed November 29, 2016. http://www.oxforddnb.com/view/article/6180,.

Louis, M. K. 2009. *Persephone Rises, 1860–1927: Mythography, Gender and the Creation of a New Spirituality*. Aldershot, UK.

Macaulay, T. B. 1976. *The Letters of Thomas Babington Macaulay*. Vol. III, *January 1834–August 1841*. Edited by T. Pinney. Cambridge.

Macaulay, T. B. 1999. "Minute on Indian Education." In *The Great Indian Education Debate: Documents Relating to the Orientalist-Anglicist Controversy, 1781–1843*, edited by L. Zastoupil and M. Moir, 161–73. Richmond, VA.

Marchand, S. L. 1996. *Down from Olympus: Archaeology and Philhellenism in Germany, 1750–1970*. Princeton, NJ.

Morrison, L., and S. Stone, eds. 2003. *A Mary Shelley Encyclopedia*. Westport, CT.

Most, G. W., ed. and trans. 2006. *Hesiod: Theogony, Works and Days, Testimonia*. Cambridge, MA and London.

Nietzsche, F. 1870. "Der Florentinische Tractat über Homer und Hesiod, ihr Geschlecht und ihren Wettkampf." *Rheinisches Museum für Philologie* Neue Folge, 25: 528–40.

Nietzsche, F. 1873. "Der Florentinische Tractat über Homer und Hesiod, ihr Geschlecht und ihren Wettkampf. (Schluss)." *Rheinisches Museum für Philologie* Neue Folge, 28: 211–49.

Nietzsche, F. 1978. *Nietzsche Werke Kritische Gesamtausgabe Abteilung 3.4: Nachgelassene Fragmente, Sommer 1872 bis Ende 1874*. Edited by G. Colli and M. Montinari. Berlin.

Nietzsche, F. 1997. *Daybreak: Thoughts on the Prejudices of Morality*. 2nd ed. Edited by M. Clark and B. Leiter. Translated by R. J. Hollingdale. Cambridge.

Nietzsche, F. 2010. *On the Genealogy of Morality*. 2nd ed. Edited by K. Ansell-Pearson. Translated by C. Diethe. Cambridge.

Panofsky, D., and E. Panofsky. 1962. *Pandora's Box: The Changing Aspects of a Mythical Symbol*. Princeton, NJ.

Porter, J. I. 2000. *Nietzsche and the Philology of the Future*. Stanford, CA.

Priestman, M. 2012. "Didactic and Scientific Poetry." In *The Oxford History of Classical Reception in English Literature*, Vol. 3, *(1660–1790)*, edited by D. Hopkins and C. Martindale, 401–25. Oxford.

Raine, K. 1979. *Blake and Antiquity*. London.

Rix, R. 2007. *William Blake and the Cultures of Radical Christianity*. Aldershot, UK.

Robertson, R. 2009. *Mock-Epic Poetry from Pope to Heine*. Oxford.

Schoeman, G. F., ed. 1868. *Die hesiodische Theogonie*. Berlin.

Shelley, M. 1994. *The Last Man*. Edited by M. D. Paley. Oxford.

Sohnle, W. P. 1972. *Georg Friedrich Creuzers "Symbolik und Mythologie," in Frankreich: Eine Untersuchung ihres Einflusses auf Victor Cousin, Edgar Quinet, Jules Michelet und Gustave Flaubert*. Göppingen, West Germany.

Stafford, F. J. 1994. *The Last of the Race: The Growth of a Myth from Milton to Darwin*. Oxford.

Swedenborg, E. 1794. *The Delights of Wisdom concerning Conjugial Love after Which Follows the Pleasures of Insanity Concerning Scortatory Love*. London.

Swedenborg, E. 2010. *Heaven and Hell*. Translated by K. C. Ryder. London.

Vasunia, P. 2015. "Barbarism and Civilization: Political Writing, History, and Empire." In *The Oxford History of Classical Reception in English Literature*, Vol. 4, *1790–1880*, edited by N. Vance and J. Wallace, 131–58. Oxford.

Vogt, E. 1962. "Nietzsche und der Wettkampf Homers." *Antike und Abendland* 11 (1): 103–13.

Voltaire. 1728. *An Essay upon the Civil Wars of France, Extracted from Curious Manuscripts and also upon the Epick Poetry of the European Nations, From Homer down to Milton*. 2nd ed. London.

Voltaire. 1733. *Henriade, avec des variantes et des notes: Et l'Essai sur le Poème Epique*. Nouvelle Edition. Londres.

Voltaire. 1824. *A Philosophical Dictionary, From the French of M. De Voltaire*. Vol. III. Translated by J. G. Gorton. London.

Weinbrot, H. D. 2007. "Pope and the Classics." In *The Cambridge Companion to Alexander Pope*, edited by P. Rogers, 76–88. Cambridge.

Williamson, G. S. 2004. *The Longing for Myth in Germany: Religion and Aesthetic Culture from Romanticism to Nietzsche*. Chicago.

CHAPTER 29

THEORIZING WITH HESIOD

Freudian Constructs and Structuralism

STEPHEN SCULLY AND CHARLES STOCKING

PART 1: HESIOD AND FREUD

Stephen Scully

Sigmund Freud briefly alludes to the *Theogony* (hereafter *Th*) when writing on Prometheus and the theft of fire (*The Standard Edition of the Complete Psychological Works of Sigmund Freud* [hereafter *SE*] 22: 185–93). There is no indication in that work or his other writings that he knew the poem well. But as fate would have it, in the last months of his life, in the last paragraph of one of his last, and unfinished, papers, he refers to the myth from memory. In poor health and in London with only a portion of his library at hand, Freud's memory proves faulty in revealing ways. Writing on childhood pathologies triggered by sexual desires, he remembers Cronus and Zeus: "At this point it is impossible to forget a primitive fragment of Greek mythology which tells how Kronos, the old Father God, swallowed his children and sought to swallow this youngest son Zeus like the rest, and how Zeus was saved by the craft of his mother and later on castrated his father" (*SE* 23: 278). In memory, he recasts what he calls "a primitive fragment of Greek mythology" as a variation of the Oedipal conflict. Hesiod's three-generation conflict is now two, with Father Cronus swallowing all of his children except for Zeus, who, saved by his mother, grows up to *castrate* his father.

This late-in-life reconstruction helps explain why the *Th* never greatly appealed to Freud. Unlike Freud's own focus on the child in the family drama, the primitive myth (as Hesiod tells it) gives equal, or greater, attention to the father's hatred of his children and his pleasure "in evil doing" (*Th* 159). Even in Sophocles' Oedipus story, Freud has little to say about Laius's (and Jocasta's) attempted murder of Oedipus, while he considers the son's murder of the father "normative development."

Notwithstanding his remote understanding of Hesiod's creation story, Freud's own "scientific myth" about the nature of the human psyche and the making of civilization, expressed most fully in *Civilization and Its Discontents* (1930, *SE* 21), has intriguing parallels with the *Th*. By "science" Freud meant his own study of human psychology. For him, "myth" refers to his constructs (1) of human evolution: "I perceived ever more clearly that the events of human history . . . are no more than a reflection of the dynamic conflicts between ego, the id, and the superego" (*SE* 20: 72); and (2) of primordial instincts: "The theory of the instincts is so to say our mythology. Instincts are mythical entities, magnificent in their indefiniteness. In our work we can never for a moment disregard them, yet we are never sure that we are seeing them clearly" (*SE* 22: 95).

What Hesiod's poem and Freud's construct have in common is a shared narrative of familial violence preceding social order and the need to tame a primordial Eros. Rather than direct influence here, one might think of the modern work as a cultural palimpsest, with Freud's thinking, as Richard Armstrong describes it, tapping into "the uncanny after-work generated by the archive of ancient culture, . . . reflect[ing] . . . the cultural logic, the values, the textual maneuvers, and nuances, and even the psychological interests of the ancient world" (2005: 5).

In *Civilization and Its Discontents*, Freud sees the advent of culture as deeply antinatural, requiring a taming of the "crude and primary instinctual impulses" (*SE* 21: 79–82). "It is impossible," he writes, "to overlook the extent to which civilization is built up upon a renunciation of instinct, how much it presupposes precisely the nonsatisfaction (by suppression, repression or some other means?) of powerful instincts" (97). At best, civilized man sublimates these impulses; at worst, he represses them. In its most extreme form, this redirection gives the impression that the sexual life of civilized man becomes, like his hair, an unnecessary appendage (cf. 101–5). The painful repression of the Love Instinct is necessitated by the necessary taming of the Death Instinct, an annihilating impulse best summarized in the expression *homo homini lupus*, which must be suppressed at all costs in man. In social terms, Freud portrayed it as the myth of the Primal Horde, a communal Oedipal story wherein a horde of sons kills en masse a domineering father and, then, out of a sense of guilt, forms a pact that is intended "to prevent a repetition of the deed" (132).

Freud's narrative is clearly at its core a "city" creation myth; sublimation and containment of an individual's instincts can only be achieved, in the end, at the communal level:

> Human life in common is only made possible when a majority comes together which is stronger than any separate individual and which remains united against all separate individuals. . . . This replacement of the power of the individual by the power of the community constitutes the decisive step of civilization. The essence of it lies on the fact that the members of the community restrict themselves in their possibilities of satisfaction, whereas the individual knew no such restrictions. (95)

While essential for the health and well-being of all humankind, the move to community and civilization comes at a great cost: "Civilization . . . obtains mastery over the individual's . . . desire for aggression by weakening and disarming it and by setting up an agency within him to watch over it, like a garrison in a conquered city" (123–24). As Freud asked, if the methods for the development of the individual and for "the evolution of civilization" are the "same, would not the diagnosis be justified that many systems of civilization—or epochs of it—possibly even the whole of humanity—have become 'neurotic' under the pressure of civilizing trends?" (141). Cultural repression is hard for all human beings, but especially so for women. In what we must regard as a culturally determined perception and not a universal trait, Freud believed that women obstruct that path to civilization; "represent[ing] the interests of the family and of sexual life," they "are forced into the background by the claims of civilization [and] adopt a hostile attitude towards it," as they are "little capable" of sublimating primal instincts (103). As indicated above, none of this thinking stems directly from Hesiod's *Th*, although similar views of the primal female's hostility to civilization are depicted in Gaia's desire to destroy Zeus when she creates Typhoeus. In these different faces, the patriarchal ideology of city myths has a long history, reaching back three thousand years.

In broad outline, the *Th* and Freud's modern "scientific" version imagine a similar need for the Olympians, or humankind, to escape from the natural conditions into which they were born. When discussing *Civilization and Its Discontents*, Jonathan Lear (1990: 14) points out that Hesiod's political terms *Eris* and *Neikos* (Discord and Quarrel, which Lear renders Hate and Quarrel) would have been better opposites for Freud's Love Instinct than his biological Death Instinct. For Freud, as for Hesiod, the biological struggle between life and death is secondary to a social and psychic conflict between interpersonal union and harmony on the one hand and strife and hatred on the other. For both mythographers, stability, permanence, and harmony are only obtainable if the social order can become as free from the biological imperative as possible. But they differ importantly in specifics.

In Hesiod, as noted, the father initiates the violence against the son. Also, unlike Freud's myth of a primal horde, in which the father-slaying children create the first social contract en masse, in the *Th* Zeus's creation of a new civic order can only be achieved by a mythic solution, and that is by his swallowing Metis and becoming the sole parent of Athena. But it is in their respective views of the endpoint that the two myths diverge most severely. For Freud, civilization is a malaise, an uneasiness (as the current title has it, *Das Unbehagen in der Kultur*), or, even worse if we choose Freud's original title, *Das Unglück in der Kultur, The Unhappiness in Civilization*. This dis-ease stems from man's conflicted state, at once drawn to and horrified by instincts that he must sublimate or repress. For Hesiod, by contrast, the beginning of evolution is beset by evils, manifest by both paternal and maternal acts of violence, and the creation of Olympus, an enclosed space within the larger world, is a welcome enclave. In the *Th*, anything that is good in the universe comes late, and more often than not it is associated with life within that enclave: good governance, cherished customs, and the pleasing chorus-song and dance of the like-minded Muses. Unlike Freud, Hesiod does not consider a universal solution to this conflict but a spatial one wherein Zeus on Olympus, and honey-tongued kings in the city agora, can create a place that keeps at bay disruptive gods like Discord, Lies, and

Quarrels (*Th* 80–93). In the *Th*, even this is not achievable within the marriage of Zeus and Hera.

Nevertheless, almost a century ago now, Freud helped us to look upon Greek myths as expressions, often buried, of the human psyche. His "scientific myths," individually and collectively, illustrate how secular modernism replaces divine cosmogonies with biological and psychological "truths." In creating this truth, the "science" of his myths is inherently reductionist, as Freud looks for primal causes, reducing the prismatic, open-ended expansiveness of mythic stories. The postulate of Instincts, he writes, "provide[s] that simplification, without either ignoring or doing violence to the facts, for which we strive in scientific work" (*SE* 21: 119). Unlike ancient allegorists who sought to save myths by deflecting attention away from their sordid literalness, Freud's reductionist tendencies embrace the violent emotions in myth, finding in them an expression of psychic truth that later, more "sophisticated" Western narratives paper over. Even so, his scientific use of myth reduces complexity of symbol and character to useful didacticism.

By contrast, the *Th* and Greek myth in general are open-ended and multidirectional. The familial triangle of father, mother, and son is filled with violence and attraction from every possible direction and emotion; a son can be attracted to or repelled by the father, as can a mother or father toward a child or partner. To that extent, myths like Hesiod's *Th* are bolder than Freud's Oedipal complex, in that they depict a wider variety of emotions that wreak havoc upon the biological family. They are also more expansive in their imaginings of both civilization' glories and a woman's place within the civic order. Witness the "new females" of the *Th*: Athena, Eunomia, Dike, Eirene, Thalia, the Muses, and so forth. Perhaps this less restrictive, Hesiodic view of civilization is closer to that of Freudian revisionists, like Herbert Marcuse (1955: 5), who can imagine a nonrepressive civilization: "[T]he very achievements of repressive civilization seem to create the preconditions for the gradual abolition of repression."[1] Reductionist and scientific as Freud's modern myth-making is, and as poorly as he remembered the "primitive fragment" of old, his *Civilization and Its Discontents* vividly renders a narrative by which we can richly interpret Hesiod's myth.

In this chapter I have focused on Freud and social thought, but of course Freud's primary concern was with psychoanalysis as a means to bring to the light of a day the nonrational impulses and hidden tensions of an individual's unconscious. Psychoanalytic applications to literary analysis often focus on childhood psychosexual development, and this is precisely what Richard Caldwell does so well in his psychoanalytical studies of the *Th*, broadly interpreted in the context of the "Greek myth of origin and succession" (see esp. 1989: 126–85). His focus is almost exclusively familial, with little attention to the social, as he considers the succession myth from the perspective of a child's transition from an initial, symbiotic state with his mother to separation and individuation, leading to various Oedipal and primal horde models of succession in the figures of Kronos and Zeus. His analysis culminates with a study of Hesphaistos exhibiting both pre-Oedipal and Oedipal strategies with his mother and an attempted Oedipal revolt against his father.

REFERENCES

Armstrong, R. 2005. *A Compulsion for Antiquity: Freud and the Ancient World.* Ithaca, NY.

Caldwell, R. 1976. "Psychoanalysis, Structuralism and Greek Mythology." In *Phenomenology, Structuralism, Semiology,* edited by H. Garvin, 209–30. Lewisburg, PA.

Caldwell, R. 1989. *The Origins of the Gods: A Psychoanalytic Study of Greek Theogonic Myth.* Oxford.

Caldwell, R. 1990. "Psychoanalytic Interpretations of Greek Myth." In *Approaches to Greek Myth,* edited by L. Edmunds, 342–89. London.

Freud, Sigmund. 1956–1974. *The Standard Edition of the Complete Psychological Works of Sigmund Freud.* 24 vols. Translated under the general editorship of James Strachey. London.

Lear, J. 1990. *Love and Its Place in Nature: A Philosophical Interpretation of Freudian Psychoanalysis.* New York.

Marcuse, H. 1955. *Eros and Civilization: A Philosophical Inquiry into Freud.* Boston.

Roazen, P. 1968. *Freud: Political and Social Thought.* New York.

Segal, C. 1978. "Pentheus and Hippolytus on the Couch and on the Grid." *Classical World* 72: 129–48.

Tauber, F. 2012. "Freud's Social Theory: Modernist and Postmodernist Revisions." *History of the Human Sciences* 25: 43–72.

PART 2: HESIOD AND STRUCTURALISM

Charles Stocking

In articulating the relationship between Greece and modern philosophy, Jacques Derrida had famously asserted that we are "today on the eve of Platonism" (1981b: 107–8, 2010: 17–42; Leonard 2010: 1–16). A close analysis of the relationship between the classical tradition and modern intellectual history indicates that before the "eve of Platonism," there was also what we might call a "dawn of Hesiodism." That is to say, at the beginning of the twentieth century Hesiodic poetry served as part of a dominant historical narrative, which is captured well by the notion of the "dawn." This is a narrative in which Hesiod represents that point after the darkness of the "Dark Age" of Greece, but before the "enlightened" era of philosophy and democracy in which "we," that is, "we and the Greeks," still live today (see Detienne 2007; Derrida 2010). Overall, classical scholars in the first half of the twentieth century seem to have placed Hesiodic poetry in a liminal position between Homeric poetry and philosophy, between the irrational and the rational, between *muthos* and *logos* (see Cornford 1912; Gigon 1945; Fränkel 1951; Havelock 1963). Yet, as I argue here, while Hesiodic poetry was being positioned as an influential source for ancient Greek philosophy, it was also playing an equally important role in shaping structuralist discourse throughout the twentieth and twenty-first centuries.[2]

It is generally agreed that the movement known as "structuralism" began with Ferdinand de Saussure and his *Course in General Linguistics*, posthumously published in 1916 (see Lévi-Strauss 1963; Benveniste 1966: 91–98; Jameson 1972; Dosse 1997: 43–51). There are two key concepts from the *Course* that are important for understanding the role that Hesiodic poetry played in structuralist discourse. First is Saussure's account of the arbitrary relationship between signifier and signified in producing the linguistic sign (Saussure 1983: 64–79). Second is his argument that all sciences should be understood to operate along two modes of analysis, an axis of "synchrony" and an axis of "diachrony." Although Saussure was a famously successful historical linguist, he ultimately presented a preference for the synchronic over the diachronic mode, and he further argued that the two modes should remain distinct in absolute terms (Saussure 1983: 120). As a result, when structural linguistics began to serve as the model for other disciplines in mid-twentieth-century Europe, the question of how to deal with history and politics became a major point of debate.

Hesiodic poetry entered structuralist discourse precisely in response to the problem of history and structure. In 1959 Jean-Pierre Vernant delivered his seminal paper on the Hesiodic myth of races at an important interdisciplinary conference in Cerisy, *Entretiens sur les notions de genèse et de structure*. This conference occurred just one year after the publication of Claude Lévi-Strauss's *Structural Anthropology*, a work with hegemonic ambitions for structural linguistics. The conference was designed primarily as a response to Lévi-Strauss and others, who championed synchrony over diachrony. In the opening comments, Lucien Goldmann specifically cited G. W. F. Hegel and Karl Marx as the founding fathers of a "genetic structuralism," which prefigured the linguistic structuralism of Saussure (Goldmann 1965: 10–11). Thus, Vernant's own arguments on the relationship between history and structure in Hesiod had important implications for the role of politics in the structural movement more generally (cf. Dosse 1997: 158–65; Leonard 2005: esp. 60–68).

Vernant's approach to Hesiod presents important convergences and divergences from the synchronic structuralism of Lévi-Strauss and others. The first major point in Vernant's paper at Cerisy is that in "mythic thought," genealogy itself is a reflection of structure (Vernant 1965: 98). This first general claim seems to reiterate Lévi-Strauss's argument regarding the "double structure of myth" based on *langue* and *parole* (Lévi-Strauss 1963: 209). A second point of apparent convergence with a Lévi-Straussian model is the argument that the Hesiodic myth does not present a diachronic model of decline. Rather, the different races are defined by the contrasting values of *dikē* and *hubris*, thereby reflecting the "permanent structures of human society and the divine world" (Vernant 1965: 102).[3] In Vernant's reading, the temporal becomes atemporal through binary opposition—another key feature of the application of linguistic structuralism (cf. Lévi-Strauss 1963: 33). Finally, Vernant accounts for the arrangement and description of the different generations in the *Works and Days* (hereafter *WD*) according to George Dumézil's model of trifunctionality, in which the contrasts between the races can be described in terms of the "religious function," the "warrior function," and the "productive function." Later Vernant would renege on the trifunctional aspect of his reading (see Dosse 1997: 32–36, 184–85).

But despite these affinities with the more general structuralist discourse, Vernant's analysis is *not* a Lévi-Straussian form of structuralism, as first noted by Pietro Pucci (1971: 108). According to Lévi-Strauss, a myth should be analyzed based on all its variants as one synchronic system (Lévi-Strauss 1963: 218). Yet Vernant's own structural analysis is developed out of a specific problem found in the Hesiodic version, namely the imposition of the race of heroes (*WD* 156–76). This unique addition to the myth prevents one from reading the narrative as a matter of strict generational decline. It is precisely this type of individual development relative to a broader conception of the myth for which a Lévi-Straussian analysis cannot account (see Pucci 1971; Gros 2016; Judet de la Combe 2016).

Although Vernant subsumes history under structure in his study of the Hesiodic races, he ultimately reintroduces a historical perspective at the level of poetic context. For Vernant, the binary opposition between *dikē* and *hubris* is not part of a structural opposition that defines myth in general. Rather, the binarism itself in the Hesiodic myth is a product of the poet's own agency in response to the moral, social, and political ambiguity of the early archaic period (Vernant 1965: 122). After this stage of ambiguity, according to Vernant, there is a critical shift: "In a later stage of rationalization, one tries to go beyond the ambiguity. A logic of ambivalence will be substituted for a logic of alternatives, of the exclusion of opposites, which will lead to the principle of contradiction" (1965: 122). The oppositional pairing between *dikē* and *hubris* may therefore be viewed as part of a more general historical trend toward "rationality." In many ways, therefore, Vernant's argument on Hesiod and structuralism prefigures his later work, *The Origins of Greek Thought* (1982), in which he argues for a correlation between the origins of the polis and the origins of philosophy. Hesiodic poetry therefore represents a unique moment of historical transition for Vernant because the religious and moral sentiment in Hesiodic poetry presents the type of binary oppositions that will come to define the future "rationality" of the Greeks. For Lévi-Strauss, structuralism was uniquely ahistorical. But for Vernant, the history of structural thought begins with Hesiod.

In the wake of the "Genesis and Structure" conference, the categories of history and structure would eventually cease being viewed in the antagonistic terms first established by Saussure. Many intellectuals considered Michel Foucault to be the future champion of a new form of "structuralist history," although he himself denied that analytic category (cf. Foucault 1970: 226, 1972: 11). Like Vernant and his colleagues, Foucault made structure itself a part of history. In fact, unbeknownst to many Anglophone classicists today, the early history of Greece, and Hesiodic poetry in particular, were critical aspects of Foucault's early reformulation of historical knowledge itself.

Foucault's inaugural lectures at the Collège de France from 1970 to 1971 offered extensive discussion of Hesiod in relation to questions of justice, truth, and history (Foucault 2013). In the first of those lectures, "Discourse on Language," Foucault specifically states that "a division emerged between Hesiod and Plato, separating true discourse from false" (1972: 218). Where classical scholars had sought continuities between Hesiodic poetry and later philosophy such that Hesiod served as a type of precursor to rationality,

Foucault considered Hesiod a turning point that specifically marked discontinuity rather than continuity in the Western intellectual tradition.

Foucault's positing of a Hesiodic "break" seems to be directly inspired by the work of Marcel Detienne. In *The Masters of Truth in Archaic Greece* (orig. pub. 1967), Detienne offers a poetic prehistory to the concept of truth in the Greek philosophical tradition. It is Hesiodic poetry above all that manifests this prehistory, with its special emphasis on the power of *alētheia*, "truth." When the Muses, daughters of Mnemosyne, appear to the poet in the *Theogony* (hereafter *Th*), we are presented with a fundamental difference between poetic and philosophic notions of truth in their famously ambiguous assertion, "We know how to say many false things similar to true sayings. But we know, when we wish, how to sing true things" (*Th* 27–28). For Detienne, what is fundamental in the Muses' claim is the final assertion, the ability to sing true things, *alēthea* (*Th* 28). Linguistically and contextually, this term for truth may be interpreted in terms of a negative relation with *Lēthē*, forgetfulness, such that truth and memory constitute a "single religious power" in the mouth of the Muses (Detienne 1996: 45). At the same time, this poetic power of truth is defined by ambiguity because the Muses are also able to "say many false things similar to true sayings" (*Th* 27; Detienne 1996: 85). Consequently, it is this very same type of ambiguity, in opposition to a principle of noncontradiction, which Vernant had asserted was characteristic of the Hesiodic era (cf. 1965: 122). Ultimately, Detienne argues that what might seem to be a point of apparent continuity between poetry and philosophy, with their common focus on truth, "constitutes one of the clearest indications of the fundamental break between rational and religious thought" (1996: 136). In this regard, Detienne's work anticipates Foucault's own efforts to offer a new method in the study of history—one that questions "everything considered immortal in man" (Foucault 1977a: 153).

Where Detienne focused strictly on the poetic prehistory of rational truth, however, Foucault was more interested in the precise practices that would bring about that shift from performative to objectivized truth. In his lectures, Foucault devotes special attention to juridical procedures in antiquity as an occasion for the production of truth. According to Foucault, Hesiod occupies a unique transitional position in this history of juridical procedures in ancient Greece, between the Homeric age and the classical period. Foucault follows Glotz and Gernet in arguing for agonistic arbitration in Homeric poetry (Glotz 1904; Gernet 1955; Leonard 2005: 72–79; Foucault 2013). In Hesiod, by contrast, Foucault argues that two new forms of legal procedures emerged, and he cites the opening comments of the *WD* as a case in point. Hesiod requests that "we settle (διακρινώμεθα) our dispute by straight judgments which come from Zeus" (*WD* 35–36), rather than appeal to the "gift-devouring kings who wish to make judgment (δικάσσαι) on a case such as this" (*WD* 39). Following Gernet, Foucault compares this episode with the Gortyn inscription in order to mark out two competing forms of judicial practice: the justice of *krinein* and the justice of *dikazein* (Foucault 2013: 87; Gernet 1917: 448–51). In contrast to *dikazein*, Foucault argues that the Hesiodic appeal to the justice of Zeus, settled through the act of *krinein*, is a form of absolute arbitration that seeks to move beyond the realm of force relations (2013: 102–3, 2014: 45–47). According to Foucault, the decision reached by *krinein* is not dependent on the performance of the two parties involved in the dispute, but depends instead on an abstract notion of justice, *dikaion* and its personification *Dikē*. Following Vernant's arguments, Foucault suggests that Hesiodic poetry gives a degree of immanence to the concept of justice such that it has its own agency, which deals with practices that go beyond those of the parties involved in legal disputes. Justice now concerns economic and social relations more generally (cf. *WD* 248–66; Foucault 2013: 94–95, 104–6). In this regard, it is the abstraction of justice, separated out from its own performative context in legal disputes, that would in turn pave the way for a nonperformative, objectivized concept of truth.[4]

Although Foucault seems to begin with Detienne's argument for discontinuity in the Hesiodic model of truth, where "a division emerged between Hesiod and Plato," Foucault's emphasis on an additional division, between Homeric and Hesiodic justice, ultimately serves to re-emphasize points of continuity between Hesiod and modernity. In his analysis of Hesiodic justice, Foucault concludes, "It is still very far from what is true discourse for us, but, through multiple transformations, ours derives from it. We belong to this dynasty of *krinein*" (2013: 96). As such, Foucault's analysis of justice in Hesiod offers a type of prehistory for the "regimes of truth" he would later argue for in *Discipline and Punish* and other works (see Foucault 1995: 23, 1977b: 13–14). Thus, despite Foucault's own arguments against "origins" and "continuity" in so much of his writing, it would appear that Foucault, like Vernant before him, cannot help but begin with Hesiod in his own effort to detail what he would later describe as the "history of the present" (see Foucault 1995: 30–31).

Nevertheless, Foucault's lectures at the Collège de France still present an important shift in the approach both to Hesiodic poetry and to the larger structural discourses of that time. Foucault places a much greater emphasis on specific techniques and practices as a means of constructing the larger structures of truth and knowledge. In this respect, he introduces the question of power into structuralist discourse, and it is the relationship between power and practice that begins to undermine the approach of those who sought to uncover purely synchronic systems informed by the Saussurian linguistic model.

Just as Detienne and Vernant were responsible for introducing Hesiod into structuralist discourse, so we can also trace the broader intellectual shift from structure to practice in one of their most influential works, *Cunning Intelligence in Greek Culture and Society* (1978), originally published (1974) just three years after Foucault's inaugural lectures on knowledge and truth in archaic and classical Greece. It was also published two years after Bourdieu's *Outline of a Theory of Practice*, a work that sought to offer a formal theory of "la pratique" in response to linguistic structuralism.[5] Like Foucault and Bourdieu, neither Detienne nor Vernant accepted the Lévi-Straussian vision of linguistic structuralism wholeheartedly (cf. Detienne and Vernant 1971; Vernant 1979; Detienne 1986). According to Detienne and Vernant, it was the concept of *mētis* that denied the type of will-to-system implicit in the structuralist method, because "[*mētis*] always appears more or less below the surface, immersed as it were in *practical operations*, which even when they use it, show no concern to make its nature explicit, or to justify its *procedures*" (Detienne and Vernant 1978: 3; emphasis added). Because *mētis* comes to represent a practical knowledge, it undermines the static, binary model implied by linguistic structuralism, oscillating between the opposite poles of "being" and "becoming," between synchrony and diachrony (see Detienne and Vernant 1978: 5). *Mētis* is shown to play the most prominent role in the *Th*, where it is used time and again as a key countermeasure to physical force in the story of divine succession (Detienne and Vernant 1978: 12–13, 57–130). In many respects, therefore, Detienne and Vernant's analysis of *mētis* reflects well the theories of power developed by Foucault and Bourdieu. Although Bourdieu and Foucault worked in different fields with different sets of questions, for both, power cannot be understood as a reified entity, nor can it be understood as a matter of physical force and coercion. Instead, power itself is produced indirectly through strategies and practices, as a relational and comparative phenomenon rather than a limited good (see Bourdieu 1977: 117; Foucault 1982: 217). The presence of *mētis* in Hesiod presents just such a concept of power by articulating unequal relations, while also providing agents within the poem with a means to overcome those relations.

Indeed, Hesiodic *mētis* proved vital for advancing and refining the theory of practice more generally. Influenced by the work of Detienne and Vernant, Michel de Certeau published a hugely influential work titled *The Practice of Everyday Life* (orig. pub. 1980), which sought to offer a new way to understand the notion of practice. With both Foucault and Bourdieu, de Certeau observed, the theorizing of practice involved an analysis that was either directly or indirectly viewed only from the perspective of the strong as a means of constructing and expressing unequal power relations, whether as a result of Foucault's "panoptic procedures" or through Bourdieu's "strategies" generated out of "habitus" (see de Certeau 1984: 45–61). By contrast, de Certeau's project was to uncover the ways in which the weak in society also actively made use of practices in the face of unequal power relations. To that end, de Certeau offered a critical distinction between "strategies" and "tactics." A strategy reflects "the calculus of force relationships which becomes possible when a subject of will and power can be isolated from an environment. A strategy circumscribes a place that is *proper*" (de Certeau 1984: xix). A tactic by contrast lacks a proper place, "it has no base where it can capitalize on its advantages, prepare its expansions, and secure independence with respect to circumstances" (xix). And he further explains that "a tactic is defined by the absence of power just as a strategy is organized by the postulation of power" (38). Ultimately, de Certeau suggests that this notion of tactic as "art of the weak" is most fully expressed in Detienne and Vernant's account of *mētis* as a form of practical intelligence, which creates the maximal number of effects through a minimal use of force (de Certeau 1984: 80–90). As such, Hesiodic *mētis* not only inaugurates a key concept in Greek cultural history, but it also serves, according to de Certeau, as a "virtual philosopher's stone" with much broader, universal application (83).

The role that Hesiod has played in the more general theorizing of power seems to have had its final culmination in one of Jacques Derrida's last works, *Rogues* (2005). In recent years Derrida's engagement with classical antiquity has been well acknowledged (cf. Miller 1998, 2007, 2015; Leonard 2005, 2010). Yet despite Derrida's ever-present engagement with ancient Greek literature, Derrida never directly addressed Hesiodic poetry until *Rogues*. In some sense, Derrida's *Rogues* represents the relationship between Hesiodic poetry and structuralism coming full circle. On the one hand, the 1959 conference at Cerisy, where Vernant first discussed Hesiod and structuralism, was also one of Derrida's first major forays into the structuralist debates, with his paper " 'Genesis and Structure' and Phenomenology." On the other hand, *Rogues* presents us with one of Derrida's last lectures from a conference at Cerisy in 2002, which was in fact dedicated to Derrida. Thus, for Derrida to discuss Hesiod in his last lecture at Cerisy only solidifies the role that Hesiodic poetry has constantly played in the history of structuralist discourse.

A full account of Derrida's philosophy is well beyond the scope of this chapter, but it is necessary to discuss briefly Derrida's analysis and use of structuralism in order to fully appreciate the role that Hesiod played in Derrida's thought. Where many argued against structuralism based on extralinguistic aspects of cultural and historical analysis, Derrida argued that the critique of structuralism was already a fundamental feature of structuralist discourse based on its own linguistic foundations. For Derrida, the Saussurian emphasis on the *arbitrary* relationship between signifier and signified and the theory of linguistic structuralism that it entailed presented a profound moment in the history of philosophy, where the search for absolute meaning became impossible: "The absence of the transcendental signified extends the domain and the interplay of signification ad infinitum" (1972: 249). This "signification ad infinitum" is eventually defined by Derrida through the neologism *différance*—a process of endless deferral of meaning through the difference that is generated between signifier and signified (cf. 1981a: 21–30 and 1982: 3–27). At the same time, however, Derrida shows that it is also impossible to conceptualize this process of *différance* without a basic presupposition regarding the "transcendental signified." In particular, Derrida demonstrates how the critique of the notion of a transcendental signified cannot be applied to the very signifier "sign." "For the signification 'sign' has always been comprehended and determined, in its sense, as sign-of, signifier referring to a signified, signifier different from its signified" (Derrida 1972: 250). On the one hand, semiotics makes it such that meaning is always undergoing a process of *différance*. On the other hand, for *différance* to take effect, one must necessarily have in place a presupposition regarding the very opposite of that process. Late in his career Derrida, relying on the Indo-Europeanist Émile Benveniste, termed the opposite of that process "ipseity" a notion of "selfness" (see Benveniste 1969: 88–91; Derrida 2009: 66). *Différance* therefore denies *ipseity* at the same time that it depends on it. This is the paradox of deconstruction. "The paradox is that the metaphysical reduction of the sign [i.e. reducing sign to thought] needed the opposition it was reducing [i.e. between sign and thought]. The opposition is part of the system, along with the reduction" (Derrida 1972: 251). Every positing of meaning must both assert and undermine that meaning; every structure already contains within it the possibility of its own deconstruction.

The deconstructive approach was first applied to Hesiod by Pietro Pucci in *Hesiod and the Language of Poetry* (1977). In that work Pucci offered a new reading of the famous and highly problematic speech of the Muses (*Th* 26–28). For Pucci, the Muses' speech presents both the audience and poet with a semiotic paradox. On the one hand, we have a clear rationalist account of a distinction between truth and falsehood, while "lies similar/identical to the truth" also indicates that a difference in signifieds is not indicated by a difference in signifiers. Thus, only the Muses would have access to what Derrida would refer to as the "transcendental signified," while mortals are forever trapped in a play of *différance*. The same semiotic ambiguity applies to the double Eris, the different forms of justice, and to Pandora and mortal women. Pucci's analysis has come under criticism for various reasons (see Clay 1988; Ferrari 1988). Nevertheless, it offers an important step in advancing the arguments on Hesiod and the history of thought beyond previous accounts. Where Vernant argued that structural opposition in Hesiod was a response to the ambiguity of the Hesiodic age, Pucci argued, following Derrida, that such ambiguity is in fact an inherent feature of structuralist thinking more generally (see Pucci 1977: 131–34). Where many philologists and philosophers sought to place Hesiodic poetry within the developmental model from *muthos* to Logos, Pucci is one of the first to show how problematic that structural opposition is. Rather than view Hesiod as "transitional," Pucci sees the role of ambiguity and structure in Hesiodic poetry as a function of the more general operation of logocentrism that is at work in all forms of discourse, oral and written, ancient and modern (Pucci 1977: 25–27).

Of course one possible criticism that might be leveled at a Derridean-inspired approach to Hesiod is that it de-historicizes and de-politicizes our interpretation of Hesiodic poetry. Indeed, a more general criticism of Derrida's philosophy has been that his earlier, linguistically inspired work did not engage in politics compared with his later work. Yet in *Rogues* Derrida insisted that "the thinking of the political has always been a thinking of *différance* and the thinking of *différance* always a thinking of the political" (2005: 39; see also Leonard 2005, 2010). It is not without significance, therefore, that Derrida, like so many others, referred to Hesiod when he applied deconstruction directly to the realm of politics in *Rogues*.

Derrida begins *Rogues* with the question of the relationship between "force" and "law" and the role of this relationship in a "democracy to come." Given our discussion in the chapter thus far, it is clear that Hesiodic poetry is immediately relevant to the history of this discourse. On the one hand, Vernant had introduced the opposition between justice and violence, *Dikē* and *Hubris,* in one of Derrida's first major conference appearances, namely at the conference *Entretiens sur les notions de genèse et de structure* in Cerisy. Foucault took up the question of the history of justice in Hesiod, and through Detienne and Vernant's work on *mētis* and its deployment by de Certeau, we see that the question of force in the *Th* has already been used to discuss modern social relations as well. Derrida, however, introduces Hesiod into his own musings on force and law by way of double indirection, through Aristotle's *Metaphysics* quoting Homer, where Odysseus insists: "No good thing is a multitude of lords; let there be one lord, one king" (Aristotle, *Metaphysics* 1076a; Homer, *Iliad* 2.204). Derrida quotes the Homeric passage in full, which concludes, "one king, to whom the son of crooked-counseling Cronos has vouchsafed the scepter and judgments, in order to counsel his people" (*Iliad* 2.205–6). Derrida reads "son of crooked-counseling Cronos" as an implicit reference to the myth of succession in Hesiod's *Th*:

Among the guardians of his son Zeus, himself a combination of ruse and force, are Kratos and Bia, power and violent force. This theogonic mythology of sovereignty belongs to, if it does not actually inaugurate, a long cycle of political theology that is at once paternalistic and patriarchal, and thus masculine, in the filiation father-son-brother. I would also call it ipsocentric. (Derrida 2005: 17)

Here, Derrida refers to Zeus's unique ability to combine force and intelligence as two opposing qualities (cf. Detienne and Vernant 1978: 57–130). Ultimately, however, Derrida insists that Zeus's sovereignty is defined by the iteration of force and power, as demonstrated by the Children of Styx, who sit eternally by Zeus's side (*Th* 383–88). When Derrida calls this myth of sovereignty and succession ipsocentric, he seems to suggest that the quality of force is something that always turns in on itself, as in the story of succession. This notion of ipsocentric violence in Derrida's musings on Hesiod was directly influenced by the work of Freud, whose writings were closely akin to Hesiodic themes (see Derrida 2005: 15–17; Scully in this chapter). According to Derrida, force (*kratos*) as a manifestation of ipseity "puts an end to time, as well as to language" (2004: 17). In contrast to this Hesiodic notion of ipsocentric sovereignty, Derrida posits: "Democracy is what it is only in the *différance* by which it defers itself and differs from itself" (2005:38). Democracy is *différance* according to Derrida, first because it relies on the same notion of sovereignty and force, *kratos*, as found in the Hesiodic myth (Derrida 2005: 23). But at the same time, the notion of sovereignty depends on a basic assertion of oneness and indivisibility that is impossible with democracy because this very notion of sovereignty must be distributed and deferred between self and others. Just as semiotics posits and challenges a "transcendental signified," so democracy is always a "democracy to come" because it is constantly engaged in the process of questioning and challenging the very concept of sovereignty upon which it relies. In effect, Derrida de-historicizes, but does not de-politicize Hesiodic poetry. Like Derrida, Vernant too had seen sovereignty as the most salient feature of Hesiodic poetry. But Vernant considered this sovereignty in historical terms as a Mycenaean reflex, which marked a point of discontinuity with the subsequent co-development of philosophy and democratic politics (Vernant 1982: 102–18). Derrida, by contrast, prevents one from making any such arguments for either historical continuity or discontinuity by arguing that the Hesiodic account of sovereignty gives expression to a more general problematic of power (*kratos*) that would serve as the foundation of future democracies, ancient and modern alike.[6]

Overall, therefore, in the work of Foucault, de Certeau, and Derrida, and in their interactions with contemporary classicists, we see a common focus on Hesiodic notions of justice, truth, and power—key concepts that can be categorized under the broader notion of "the political" (cf. Leonard 2005; Azoulay 2014). Indeed, Hesiodic poetry seems to have been a way to reintroduce both history and politics back into structuralist discourse.[7] Scholars such as Paul Allen Miller and Miriam Leonard have clearly demonstrated how classical Greek literature has always already been intimately involved in the broader philosophical and political dialogues of postwar French thought (Miller 1998, 2007; Leonard 2005, 2010). Through this brief, but certainly not exhaustive survey, we see that Hesiodic poetry exerted an influence on the French intellectual tradition in a manner equal to Plato and Tragedy. Indeed, it is perhaps Hesiodic poetry's unique historical positioning, after the "Dark Ages" of Greece, at the "dawn" of Greek rationality and democracy, that caused contemporary theorists to return to Hesiod time and again. Strangely, one area, as far as I can tell, in which Hesiodic poetry exerted less influence is that of the psychoanalytic tradition after Freud, including Lacan and the "French Feminists." The absence of Hesiod in twentieth-century French psychoanalysis is doubly strange, first because, as Scully has shown, Freud's own writings present especially strong Hesiodic themes, and second, because the psychoanalytic tradition was a key part of structuralist discourse (see Scully in this chapter and Dosse 1997: 91–125). Such lack of attention from the later psychoanalytic tradition might be the result of the distinctly historicizing perspective on Hesiod throughout the twentieth century, which might have been considered contrary to the more universal claims of psychoanalysis (cf. Leonard 2005: 22–95 on Vernant and the Oedipus debate). That narrative of historical "transition" for Hesiodic poetry, between the "Dark Ages" and "rationality," however, has certainly changed, and we are now coming to understand that the "Dark Ages" were not so dark (cf. Mazarakis Ainian 2011). Hopefully, as our own interpretations of Hesiod, history, and politics in the ancient world change and develop, Hesiodic poetry may continue to play an equally influential role in shaping future intellectual traditions.

NOTES

1. For modernist and postmodernist revisions of Freud's social theory, see Tauber (2012); for Freudian revisionists taming Freud's tragic view of civilization's repressiveness, see Roazen (1968: 268–69).
2. Special thanks are owed to Froma Zeitlin, Paul Allen Miller, Miriam Leonard, Giulia Sissa, Joshua Katz, Alex Purves, Cléo Carastro, Paulin Ismard, and Stephen Scully, who generously read and offered valuable commentary on earlier versions of this chapter. The topics and themes that are addressed only briefly here are discussed in greater depth in Stocking (2017).
3. For adjustments to Vernant's reading with a greater focus on the diachronic aspects, see Clay (2003: 82–85); Calame (2009: 84–85); and Judet de la Combe (2016: 245–50).
4. For the methodological difficulties in Foucault's treatment of Hesiodic poetry, see Stocking (2017).
5. Bourdieu makes reference to Hesiodic poetry throughout his works, but never in systematic fashion, on which see Bourdieu (1977: 175–76, 1990: 99–100, 2001: 6–7).
6. For a philological intervention in Derrida's philosophic treatment of *kratos*, see Stocking (2017). In many respects, Zeus's own *kratos* in the *Th* may be viewed not as a function of "ipseity" in the Derridean sense, but alterity. Thus, for instance, Stephen Scully observes: "It is worth noting that *no component* of Zeus' power in the *Theogony* is innate. It *all* comes from others, male and female, whom Zeus has either included into his rule or liberated from oppression" (2015: 35; emphasis in original).
7. One might be inclined to call figures such as Foucault, de Certeau, and Derrida "poststructuralists," yet that category itself is highly problematic and foreign to French intellectual discourse, on which see Angermuller (2015).

REFERENCES

Angermuller, J. 2015. *Why There Is No Poststructuralism in France:. The Making of an Intellectual Generation.* London.

Azoulay, V. 2014. "Repolitiser la cité grecque, trente ans après." *Annales. Histoire, Sciences Sociales* 69 (3): 689–719.

Benveniste, É. 1966. *Problèmes de linguistique générale 1.* Paris.

Benveniste, É. 1969. *Le vocabulaire des institutions européenne.* Paris.

Bourdieu, P. 1977. *Outline of a Theory of Practice.* Translated by R. Nice. Cambridge. Originally published as *Esquisse d'une théorie de la pratique* (Genève, 1972).

Bourdieu, P. 1990. *In Other Words: Essays Towards a Reflexive Sociology.* Translated by M. Adamson. Stanford, CA. Originally published as *Chose dites* (Paris, 1987).

Bourdieu, P. 2001. *Masculine Domination.* Translated by R. Nice. Stanford, CA. Originally published as *La domination masculine* (Paris, 1998).

Calame, C. 2009. *Poetic and Performative Memory in Ancient Greece.* Washington, DC.

Clay, J. S. 1988. "What the Muses Sang: *Theogony* 1–115." *Greek, Roman, and Byzantine Studies* 29: 323–33.

Clay, J. S. 2003. *Hesiod's Cosmos.* Cambridge.

Cornford, F. M. 1912. *From Religion to Philosophy: A Study in the Origins of Western Speculation.* New York.

de Certeau, M. 1984. *The Practice of Everyday Life.* Translated by S. Randall. Berkeley. Originally published as *L'invention de quotidian*, Vol. 1, *Arts de faire* (Paris, 1980).

Derrida, J. 1972. "Structure, Sign, and Play in the Discourse of the Human Sciences." In *The Structuralist Controversy: The Languages of Criticism and the Sciences of Man*, edited by R. Macksey and E. Donato, 247–72. Baltimore, MD.

Derrida, J. 1981a. *Positions.* Translated by A. Bass. Chicago. Originally published as *Positions: Entretiens avec Henri Ronse, Julia Kristeva, Jean-Louis Houdebine, Guy Scarpetta* (Paris, 1972).

Derrida, J. 1981b. "Plato's Pharmacy." In *Dissemination*, translated by B. Johnson, 61–171. Chicago. Originally published as "La Pharmacie de Platon," In *La Dissémination*, 79–196 (Paris, 1972).

Derrida, J. 1982. *Margins of Philosophy.* Translated by A. Bass. London. Originally published as *Marges—de la philosophie* (Paris, 1972).

Derrida, J. 2005. *Rogues: Two Essays on Reason.* Translated by P-A. Brault and M. Naas. Stanford, CA. Originally published as *Voyous: Deux essais sur la raison* (Paris, 2003).

Derrida, J. 2009. *The Beast and the Sovereign.* Vol. 1. Translated by G. Bennington. Chicago. Originally published as *Séminaire La bête et le souverain, tome 1* (Paris, 2008).

Derrida, J. 2010. "We Other Greeks," translated by M. Naas. In *Derrida and Antiquity*, edited by M. Leonard, 17–42. Oxford.

Detienne, M. 1963. *Crise Agraire et Attitude Religieuse Chez Hésiode.* Bruxelles, Belgium.

Detienne, M. 1978. *Cunning Intelligence in Greek Culture and Society.* Translated by J. Lloyd. Hassocks. Originally published as *Les ruses de l'intelligence: La mètis des grecs* (Paris, 1974).

Detienne, M. 1986. *The Creation of Mythology.* Translated by M. Cook. Chicago. Originally published as *L'invention de la mythologie* (Paris, 1981).

Detienne, M. 1996. *The Masters of Truth in Archaic Greece.* Translated by J. Lloyd. New York. Originally published as *Les maîtres de vérité dans la Grèce archaïque* (Paris, 1967).

Detienne, M. 2007. *The Greeks and Us: A Comparative Anthropology of Ancient Greece.* Translated by J. Lloyd. Cambridge. Originally published as *Les grecs et nous: une anthropologie comparée de la Grèce ancienne* (Paris, 2005).

Detienne, M., and J.-P. Vernant. 1971. "Eurydice, la femme-abeille: Le regard des historiens." *Le Monde*, November 5.

Detienne, M., and J.-P. Vernant. 1978. *Cunning Intelligence in Greek Culture and Society.* Translated by J. Lloyd. Sussex. Originally published as *Les ruses de l'intelligence: la métis des Grecs* (Paris 1974).

Dosse, F. 1997. *History of Structuralism.* Vol. 1, *The Rising Sign.* Translated by D. Glassman. Minneapolis, MN. Originally published as *Histoire du structuralisme* (Paris, 1991–1992).

Ferrari, G. 1988. "Hesiod's Mimetic Muses and the Strategies of Deconstruction." In *Post-Structuralist Classics*, edited by A. Benjamin, 45–78. London.

Foucault, M. 1970. *The Order of Things. An Archaeology of the Human Sciences.* New York. Originally published as *Les mots et les choses. Une archéologie des sciences humaines* (Paris, 1966).

Foucault, M. 1972. *The Archaeology of Knowledge and the Discourse on Language.* Translated by A. M. Sheridan Smith. New York. Originally published as *L'archéologie du savoir* (Paris, 1969).

Foucault, M. 1977a. "Nietzsche, Genealogy, History." In *Language, Counter-Memory, Practice*, edited by D. F. Bouchard, 139–64. Ithaca, NY. Originally published as "Nietzsche, la généalogie, l'histoire," in *Hommage à Jean Hyppolite*, ed. S. Bachelard et al., 145–72 (Paris, 1971).

Foucault, M. 1977b. "The Political Function of the Intellectual." *Radical Philosophy* 17: 12–14.

Foucault, M. 1982. "The Subject and Power." In *Michel Foucault: Beyond Structuralism and Hermeneutics*, edited by H. Dreyfus and P. Rabinow, 205–26. Chicago.

Foucault, M. 1995. *Discipline and Punish: The Birth of the Prison.* Translated by A. Sheridan. New York. Originally published as *Surveiller et punir: Naissance de la prison* (Paris, 1975).

Foucault, M. 2000. "Truth and Juridical Forms." In *Power: Essential Works of Foucault 1954–1984*, edited by J. E. Faubian and translated by R. Hurley, III:1–89. New York.

Foucault, M. 2013. *Lectures on the Will to Know: Lectures at the Collège de France, 1970–1971 and Oedipal Knowledge.* Edited by D. Defert. Translated by G. Burchell. New York. Originally published as *Leçons sur la volonté de savoir: Cours au collège de France, 1970–1971* (Paris, 2011).

Foucault, M. 2014. *Wrong-doing, Truth-Telling: The Function of Avowal in Justice.* Edited by F. Brion and B. E. Harcourt. Translated by S. W. Sawyer. Chicago.

Fränkel, H. 1975. *Early Greek Poetry and Philosophy.* Translated by M. Hadas. New York. Originally published as *Dichtung und Philosophie des frühen Griechentums* (New York, 1951).

Gernet, L. 1917. *Recherche sur le développement de la pensée juridique et morale en Grèce.* Paris.

Gernet, L. 1955. *Droit et société dans la Grèce ancienne.* Paris.

Gigon, O. 1945. *Der Ursprung der griechischen Philosophie: Von Hesiod bis Parmenides.* Basel, Switzerland.

Glotz, G. 1904. *L'ordalie dans la Grèce primitive.* Paris.

Goldmann, L. Introduction Générale to *Entretiens sur les notions de genèse et de structure*, edited by M. de Gandillac, L. Goldmann, and J. Piaget, 7–22. Paris.

Gros, A. 2016. "Jean-Pierre Vernant et l'analyse structural: Le mythe hésiodique des races." *L'homme: Revue française d'anthropologie* 218: 219–38.

Havelock, E. A. 1963. *Preface to Plato.* Cambridge, MA.

Humphreys, S. C. 2009. "The Historical Anthropology of Thought: Jean-Pierre Vernant and Intellectual Innovation in Ancient Greece." *Focaal* 55: 103–12.

Jameson, F. 1972. *The Prison-house of Language*. Princeton, NJ.

Judet de la Combe, P. 2016. "Le mythe hésiodique des races, oeuvre de langage." *L'homme. Revue française d'anthropologie* 218: 239–52.

Leonard, M. 2005. *Athens in Paris: Ancient Greece and the Political in Postwar French Thought*. Oxford.

Leonard, M., ed. 2010. *Derrida and Antiquity*. Oxford.

Lévi-Strauss, C. 1963. *Structural Anthropology*. Translated by C. Jacobsen and B. G. Schoepf. New York. Originally published as *Anthropologie Structurale* (Paris, 1958).

Lévi-Strauss, C. 1966. *The Savage Mind*. Chicago. Originally published as *La pensée sauvage* (Paris, 1962).

Mazarakis Ainian, A., ed. 2011. *The "Dark Ages" Revisited: Acts of an International Symposium in Memory of William D. E. Coulson, University of Thessaly, Volos, 14–17 June 2007*. Volos, Greece.

Miller, P. A. 1998. "The Classical Roots of Poststructuralism: Lacan, Derrida, and Foucault." *International Journal of the Classical Tradition* 5 (2): 204–25.

Miller, P. A. 2003. "The Trouble with Theory: A Comparatist Manifesto." *Symplokē: A Journal for the Intermingling of Literary, Cultural and Theoretical Scholarship* 11: 8–22.

Miller, P.A. 2004. "Jean-Pierre Vernant." In *The Encyclopedia of Modern French Thought*, edited by C. J. Murray, 637–39. New York.

Miller, P.A. 2007. *Postmodern Spiritual Practices: The Construction of the Subject and the Reception of Plato in Lacan, Derrida, and Foucault*. Columbus, OH.

Miller, P.A. 2015. "Placing the Self in the Field of Truth: Irony and Self-Fashioning in Ancient and Postmodern Rhetorical Theory." *Arethusa* 48 (3): 313–37.

Pucci, P. 1971. "Lévi-Strauss and Classical Culture." *Arethusa* 4 (2): 103–17.

Pucci, P. 1977. *Hesiod and the Language of Poetry*. Baltimore, MD.

Saussure, F. de 1983. *Course in General Linguistics*. Edited by C. Balley and A. Sechehaye, with the collaboration of A. Riedlinger. Translated by R. Harris. London.

Scully, S. 2015. *Hesiod's Theogony: From Near Eastern Creation Myths to Paradise Lost*. Oxford.

Stocking, C. H. 2017. "Hesiod in Paris: Justice, Truth, and Power between Past and Present." *Arethusa* 50 (3): 385–427.

Vernant, J.-P. 1965. "Genèse et structure dans le mythe Hésiodique des races." In *Entretiens sur les notions de genèse et de structure*, edited by M. de Gandillac, L. Goldmann, and J. Piaget, 95–124. Paris.

Vernant, J.-P. 1979. *Myth and Society in Ancient Greece*. Translated by J. Lloyd. Brighton, UK. Originally published as *Mythe et société en Grèce ancienne* (Paris, 1974).

Vernant, J.-P. 1982. *The Origins of Greek Thought*. Ithaca, NY. Originally published as *Les origines de la pensée grecque* (Paris, 1962).

Vernant, J.-P. 1983. *Myth and Thought among the Greeks*. London. Originally published as *Mythe et pensée chez les grecs: Études de psychologie historique* (Paris, 1965).

Vernant, J.-P. 1989. "De la psychologie historique à une anthropologie de la Grèce Ancienne." *Mètis* 4 (2): 305–14.

CHAPTER 30

··

THE RECEPTION OF HESIOD IN THE TWENTIETH AND TWENTY-FIRST CENTURIES

··

THOMAS E. JENKINS

ANY analysis of the reception of Hesiod in the twentieth and twenty-first centuries faces special difficulties, strikingly so when compared to Homer. Indeed, the booming reception of Homer has, in a strange and circuitous way, doomed a similar boom for Hesiod. It was not always so. As Hugo Koning has traced in his study of the reception of Hesiod in antiquity, much of the ancient reception of Hesiod can be traced *specifically* to Hesiod's identity as the complementary half of the archaic dyad of Homer/Hesiod: the farmer, not the warrior; the populist, not the aristocrat; the reasonable teacher, not the manipulative artist (2010: 269). Thus, ancient thinkers and artists most often thought about Hesiod when thinking about Homer, and Hesiod's reception—in such texts as Virgil and Plutarch—demonstrates the pervasive influence of Homer in shaping Hesiod's afterlife in antiquity.

Hesiod and Homer do *not* figure in the contemporary popular imagination—in video games, say—as any sort of dyad, and thus Hesiod's chances to ride the coattails of Homer are greatly diminished. More challenging, perhaps, are the very structures of Hesiod's two greatest poems: *Theogony* (hereafter *Th*) is, by design and perhaps necessity, largely governed by the logic of a catalog, and *Works and Days* (hereafter *WD*) famously resists easy classification, lurching as it does from mythological tales, to abuse of poor Perses, to a breathless run of instructions for agriculture. (See, e.g., Clay 2003: 2: "[For many] the *Works and Days* presents an apparent jumble of myths, fables, proverbs, advice, as well as fairly incoherent precepts on farming and sailing.") Homer, by contrast, offers to a modern artist two famously gripping narratives, one concerning the most enduring of human ills—war—and the other presenting a fantastic voyage of *nostos*, "homecoming." The Homeric epics thus seem modern and accessible in their narrative structure; Hesiod's poems inaugurate ancient genres with no clear modern parallels. (An exception might be made for Hesiod's "character sketches" of various gods and Titans;

George O'Connor's *The Olympians* [2010a and 2010b; collected in a six-book boxed set in 2014], for instance, offers up descriptions of the immortals covered by Hesiod—Zeus and Demeter, among them—and is clearly composed with pedagogical value in mind.)

In terms of extended narrative, a reception history of Hesiod over the last century thus relies on a handful of episodes, mostly from *Th*: Prometheus and Pandora, the Titanomachy, the Muses, Helicon. *WD* has found comparatively little artistic favor in the past century (which exactly reverses its fortunes in antiquity, as Koning has demonstrated with his "commemograms" [2010: 20–21]). Hesiod's minor poems have made nary a splash. What follows, then, is necessarily an idiosyncratic survey of receptions that can be plausibly traced to Hesiod and *not* through Hesiod's numerous intermediaries (such as Aeschylus in *Prometheus Bound*), though the line is understandably blurry. The following does not aim at comprehensiveness—the number of video games that feature, for example, Titans, boggles the mind—but I hope to trace here some main lines of reception and to outline what artists have attempted to do with Hesiod's difficult poetry, in terms of both ideology and aesthetics.

The myth of Pandora, found in both major poems, presents especial difficulties for contemporary artists. It may be reasonably reckoned as an exemplary narrative of Western misogyny (see especially Zeitlin 1996; also Lye in this volume, pp. 180–85) and thus perhaps not an ideal teaching text for impressionable boys and girls. The Canadian/Scottish TV series *Mythic Warriors* (1998–1999), which served up twenty-four half-hour episodes of Greek mythology, confronted understandable difficulties in its Pandora-themed episode, and its creators innovated some especially surprising twists. The episode in question (season 1, episode 10) begins in a remarkably Hesiodic vein: we are introduced to both Prometheus and his brother Epimetheus, who vie with each other in creating animals, mankind apparently among them. When these wretched humans shiver during a storm, Prometheus (disobeying Zeus's orders) blesses them with the gift of fire, which he steals from Hephaestus, laboring under a suspiciously proximate volcano. Zeus, enraged, chains Prometheus to a rock and prepares his ultimate revenge: Pandora. To Pandora is vouchsafed a box, which, in a moment of almost Promethean forethought, she buries. But voices taunt her in her dreams, and at night she escapes to the backyard, opens the box, and unleashes onto the world the following ghoulish evils: Deceit, Jealousy, Hate, War, and Despair. (These are the modern, cartoon equivalents to Eris's children at *Th* 226–31, including Toil, Forgetfulness, Hunger, Pain, War, and Slaughter; they are also a poetic reflex of the sorts of attributes associated with Pandora at *WD* 78 and 90–104.)

The consequent desolation of the planet is a highlight of the episode. One would imagine that to its target audience of schoolchildren, it's a genuinely scary narrative, as humans fall victim to war, plague, and bitter infighting. Particularly affecting is the scene in which Pestilence poisons a clear spring where an adorably antlered deer is otherwise minding its cervine business; the mere touch of this brackish water slays the deer, which succumbs to a pestilential death. (The parallels to Disney's *Bambi* are clear enough; there is little more affecting in cartoons than the death of a deer.) Given her responsibility for an apocalypse—and for the death of a deer—it would be difficult, it seems, to rehabilitate Pandora as any sort of paragon of virtue. But lo! Pandora's subsequent discovery of *Elpis* (here, "Hope") is given a particularly sentimental treatment, as winged Hope zooms into the hearts of men everywhere and reverses the carnage of the previous week or so. Indeed, a voice-over instructs the viewer that this Hope actually enables further developments in civilization; far from being the root of all Evil, Pandora is in fact the mother of all social progress. Zeus, impressed, praises Pandora's grit ("I was wrong about you; I never thought you'd find Hope among all those evils") and frees Prometheus. Epimetheus, however, poses a shrewd theological inquiry to Zeus: "But if you wanted to punish man, why did you put Hope in the chest?" An excellent question. The answer? Zeus's sense of "fair play." To stirring musical strains, the episode concludes.

I dwell on *Mythic Warriors*' "Pandora" episode at some length because it shows the difficulties that modern "receivers" of Hesiod often face: the transparent misogyny of Hesiod's Pandora episode is difficult even to confront, much less to finesse. Texts aimed squarely at schoolchildren propose various solutions; for example, Joan Holub's *Do Not Open! The Story of Pandora's Box* (2014) elides the creation of Pandora (a common conceit) and instead concentrates on the *box* as punishment for humans, not Pandora per se ("The people were not thankful. The gods decided / to teach them a lesson," 5). Though the box is clearly marked "Do Not Open" (amusingly, by a manufacturer's tag), Pandora's curiosity gets the better of her; she dreams of candy, music, jewels. The inevitable opening of the box releases on the world "trouble bugs," which fill the planet with a panoply of troubles, including sickness and sadness. Pandora's second discovery arcs toward a happier ending, however: the newly released Hope kisses away the "bug bites" and everyone feels much, much better. The final page thus sums up the moral of Pandora's story: "Sometimes bad things happen. But we hope things will get better. And we hope for good things to happen." By concentrating on Hope, and by eliding Pandora's genesis, Holub helps to make the story palatable to modern children (of an appropriate level of reading comprehension).

Similarly, Kate McMullan's *Keep a Lid on It, Pandora!* (2012), pitched at a somewhat higher level of reading skill, is unapologetically revisionist. The book is narrated by the god Hades, who explicitly labels Zeus's version of the legend (from the fictitious *The Big Fat Book of Greek Myths*) "total claptrap" (9). (An excerpt from *The Big Fat Book of Greek Myths* is included in the appendix; it is in fact a fairly faithful précis of Hesiod's Pandora episodes from both *Th* and *WD*. Antiquity and modernity thus jostle each other side by side.) According to Hades, disease, pain, and greed in fact existed "long before Pandora showed up," and Pandora's only real flaw, then, was "curiosity," a curiosity propelled by her virtues of pluck and intelligence (9). McMullan cannily blends various versions of myth in the genesis of Pandora, here sculpted out of marble, in a nod to Ovid's Pygmalion myth (65). After Pandora's birth, the narrative constructs the heroine as protagonist of her own labors, much like those of Hercules or Apuleius's Psyche. She overcomes unexpected obstacles (such as the attempted treachery of Zeus in disguise: "Say, that's a fine-looking box you're holding. What's in it?," 85). Zeus, again in disguise, attempts a similar tactic as the charlatan seer Zorba the Great, "the world's best guesser." (Zorba unhelpfully guesses that the box contains a delicious lemon cake; 95). All of Zeus's machinations fail, however, and further complications follow; Pandora becomes a best-selling author, but is finally tricked into opening the box when Zeus cannily disguises it as a first-aid kit (160–61). McMullan here relieves Pandora of any charge of ethical blameworthiness: yes, she opened the box, but with the *intent* of helping a wounded old man. The list of evils unleashed on the world is age-appropriate to the novel's readership: pimples, homework, dandruff, and that most vile plague upon childrenkind, low-spurting drinking fountains (162–63). In the ensuing debate over Pandora's transgression, it transpires, moreover, that Pandora didn't actually open the box; she was merely *trying* to open it when it was snatched from her hands by her ally Hades, leaving her with just the lid. McMullan's narrative thus exculpates Pandora both morally *and* physically from the genesis of evil; all vestiges of misogyny have been stamped out. A final instruction to the reader? "So don't go blaming all your troubles on the world's first girl" (169).

A different sort of reception of Pandora—but that likewise concerns its appropriateness for schoolchildren—can be found in Russell Kirk's essay "The Dissolution of Liberalism," originally published in 1955 (Kirk 2007). A founding father of modern American conservative thought, Kirk begins his short, apocalyptic article with a cursory analysis of myth writ large:

> "Myth" is not a falsehood; on the contrary, the great and ancient myths are profoundly true. The myth of Prometheus will always be a high poetic representation of an ineluctable truth, and so will the myth of Pandora. . . . Nor is myth simply a work of fancy: true myth is only represented, never created, by a poet. Prometheus and Pandora were not invented by the solitary imagination of Hesiod. Real myths are the product of a moral experience of a people, groping towards divine love and wisdom. (Kirk 2007: 23)

For Kirk, Hesiod transmits a body of collected wisdom poetry, and like all collective wisdom, that wisdom must be honored as an attempt by a civilization to become wiser and holier; the inclusion of "divine love" seems Christianizing and not particularly archaic. It's unclear, however, what "ineluctable truth" Kirk has in mind when contemplating Pandora: to many readers at many times, that "truth" seems to be of Woman's cozy kinship with evil. (Recall, for instance, Hesiod's description of Pandora as "a beautiful evil . . . from whom comes the deadly race and tribe of women, a great woe for mortal men" [*Th* 585–92]). To his credit, Kirk later expands on his challenging line of argument; in a separate essay ("The Moral Imagination," originally published in 1981), Kirk inveighs against child-friendly literature that attempts to overtly teach "tolerant, kindly, cooperative behavior" (2007: 214). For Kirk, this sort of clumsily didactic pabulum—such as "Dick and Jane"—fails to seize the imagination and thus flops entirely. Though he admits that Greek and Norse myths might not always seem "proper" for kids, they do more than "Dick and Jane" to "bring about an early apprehension of norms" (214). So schoolchildren shouldn't be ingesting dime-store pulp fiction, but rather Hesiod: "The story of Pandora, or of Thor's adventure with the old woman and her cat, gives any child an insight into the conditions of existence—dimly grasped at the moment, perhaps, but gaining in power as the years pass—that no utilitarian 'real-life situation' fiction can match. Because they are eternally valid, Hesiod and the saga-singers are modern." (214). One reading of this argument is that the myth of Pandora posits both pre- and postlapsarian worlds, in ways strikingly similar to Judeo-Christian narratives, and that children need to be reminded that evil is a permanent characteristic of our current existence. In agitating for myth to be served "straight up," Kirk warns against literary treatments (like the later Hesiodic reception of McMullan, above) that are specifically written for children and that sugarcoat the disquieting aspects of myth and (for that matter) the world. For Kirk, such receptions only adulterate myth. Instead, expressions of collective genius such as Hesiod must be transmitted to the young without intermediaries, shame, or delay.

Art that aims to reframe or rehabilitate Pandora—such as Albert Lewin's 1951 cinematic misfire *Pandora and the Flying Dutchman* (MGM)—struggles with the misogynist import of the original Greek. This odd film, which blends Greek and nautical myth in (at best) an unwieldy whole, follows the adventures of an American femme fatale in Spain, here named Pandora Reynolds (played by Ava Gardner). Even as would-be lovers commit suicide around her, this Pandora crosses paths with Hendrick van der Zee, an incarnation of the Flying Dutchman, who, at their meeting, is painting the ancient Greek Pandora, "box" in hand (see figure 30.1).

FIGURE 30.1 Still from *Pandora and the Flying Dutchman*. Dir. Albert Lewin. Metro-Goldwyn-Mayer. 1951. A shot of van der Zee's painting of the Hesiodic Pandora, holding her famous "box."

After van der Zee explains, in remarkably Hesiodic terms, the origins of the ancient Pandora, Pandora Reynolds attacks the painting; unperturbed, van der Zee refigures the painted Pandora as an "egghead" (his term, somewhat lamentably), since Pandora should figure as an Everywoman, not a Specific Woman (see figure 30.2). (Part of the artiness of the film is Lewin's allusion here to the work of the Italian metaphysical painter Giorgio de Chirico, who similarly dots his landscapes with egghead humanoids [Renger 2013: 288]). As van der Zee explains, the ancient Pandora's "curiosity cost us our earthly paradise," a formulation that constructs Pandora as the prototype of film noir's dangerous and independent femmes fatales—including Pandora Reynolds herself.

But Lewin then ironizes this trope. After a slow-paced love affair, Pandora vows that she would in fact die for van der Zee, thus relieving him of the curse of the Flying Dutchman. Though at least one critic views Lewin's film as an "outstanding expression of modern Romanticism" (Russell 2011), it's more clearly an honorable (if ultimately unsuccessful) attempt at rehabilitating Pandora's image, and sexual powers, for a modern age and in a modern genre.

In general, artists struggle with the more outré and frank aspects of Hesiod's texts. Russell Kirk's warnings notwithstanding, there are innumerable children's books dedicated to overviews of Greek mythology and necessarily rewritten with various levels

FIGURE 30.2 Still from *Pandora and the Flying Dutchman*. Dir. Albert Lewin. Metro-Goldwyn-Mayer. 1951. A shot of van der Zee's reconstructed painting of Pandora, now in the style of Giorgio de Chirico, with Pandora as a universalizing "egghead."

of tact and omission. (In a sense, this continues, in a pedagogical vein, the finessing of Hesiod already begun in antiquity in, for instance, Pseudo-Apollodorus's *Library*.) Misogyny is not the only problem for modern adapters of Hesiod; the same sorts of sex and violence that make for terrific video games (see below) create other difficulties in children's literature. Heather Alexander's *A Child's Introduction to Greek Mythology* (2011) makes some child-friendly (and Kirk-unfriendly) accommodations to modern sensibilities; in her version of the *Th*, there's a certain Hollywood sheen to the courtship of lonely Gaia and dashing Uranus [*sic*] ("[Uranus] was large and beautiful, and his stars twinkled and made Mother Earth happy," 10), and the romance culminates in a marriage and twelve bouncing babies ("the Titans"). The union sours because of Uranus's "cruel and mean" behavior toward his children (10); Cronus, at the urging of his mother, "destroys" Uranus (10), then Cronus later eats his own children (no concession to squeamish young minds, here), and Alexander even includes the "all-seeing, multi-handed Hecatoncheires" (13) during the subsequent Titanomachy. The genesis of Aphrodite—from Uranus's castrated genitals—is, however, a problem. Alexander rather skirts the matter: "Having appeared from the foam of the sea, she had no known parents" (26), which is true enough, though that adaptation doesn't exactly capture the flavor of *Th* 188–93. Alexander's list of suggested reading (96) does not, unsurprisingly, include the *Th* itself, but a miscellany of *other* books for children, including *D'Aulaires' Book of Greek Myths* (1962, repr. 1992) and other more recent re-versions. (For instance, on Aphrodite's genesis on a cushion of foam, the D'Aulaires completely punt the origin myth: "Nobody knew from where she had come [1992: 30]." O'Connor, in his *Olympians*, innovates a clever circumlocution: "Some of the essence of Ouranos flowed to the sea" [2010a: 8].)

We have seen that it is easy to read *Th* as a misogynist poem, and not simply because of the Pandora episode; Zeus's ingestion of Metis is just one more instance of the male usurpation of female power. There are, however, a few complications. One is Gaia, who is sympathetically referenced throughout the *Th*, and especially at *Th* 126–87, a passage that catalogs the multiple progeny of her (to put it mildly) dysfunctional relationship with her son Ouranos. Gaia's status as a fecund "Mother Earth" has engendered (so to speak) some surprising modern receptions, most notably in Johann Jakob Bachofen's *Mutterrecht* (Mother-right; originally published in 1861, translated in 1967). Though Bachofen does not specifically refer to *Th*, he clearly has Hesiod's worldview in mind: "How natural we now find Hesiod's world, with its dominant mother lavishing eternal loving care on an ever dependent son" (81). Bachofen's emphasis on a primal matriarchy, overthrown by a patriarchy, has been mapped onto a different, modern debate, that of our collective filial responsibility toward the planet itself. Thus, on the suggestion of William Golding, iconoclastic scientist James Lovelock (1979) named his theory of a "living," reactive Earth after Gaia, and Golding himself repaid the favor by waxing lyrical about Gaia in his Nobel Prize acceptance speech in 1983:

> Now we, if not in the spirit, have been caught up to see our earth, our mother, Gaia Mater, set like a jewel in space. We have no excuse now for supposing her riches

inexhaustible nor the area we have to live on limitless because unbounded. We are the children of that great blue white jewel. Through our mother we are part of the solar system and part, through that, of the whole universe. In the blazing poetry of the fact we are children of the stars.

Golding's language here is explicitly classical; he first affixes the Latin epithet *mater* to Gaia, and thus makes good his earlier allusion to humanity's "rape of our planet." His rhapsody on the jewel of Gaia—set among the stars—preserves the cosmological heft of the original *Th* while recontextualizing it within modern research on solar systems and planetary ecology. The brilliant website TVTropes.com—which catalogs the clichés of contemporary film-driven fiction—divides the contemporary manipulation of Gaia into three broad categories of thought: *Gaia's Vengeance* (in which Gaia explicitly unleashes revenges on malevolent mortals); *Gaia's Vengeance, Metaphorical* (a more subtle, symbolic version of the previous vengeance, often manifesting itself through, e.g., killer bees and sharks); and *Gaia's Avenger*, in which monstrous avatars fight on behalf of their earthy mother.[1]

Explicitly feminist revisions of Hesiod are few and far between. Theresa Hak Kyung Cha's *Dictee*, an experimental novel from 1982, is divided into nine sections, one for each Muse; as Kun Jong Lee has elucidated, *Dictee* figures Hesiod's original *Th* as a primary document of Western patriarchy, and Cha's own novel is thus a "feminist, subversive, and interventionist response to the call of the *Theogony*," one that privileges figures of female resistance (e.g., Demeter) and competes with Hesiod's own fragmentary *Catalogue of Women* (Lee 2006: 79). In this way, Cha's novel doesn't revise Hesiod (along the lines of the receptions above), but rather presents an *alternative* to Hesiod and thereby exposes the original poem's ideological bias against women. (In this way, *Dictee* possesses some similarities to contemporary literary receptions of ancient epic, including Atwood's *Penelopiad* and Le Guin's *Lavinia*, for which see Jenkins 2015: 184–201). The generally positive view of Athena in Hesiod's *Th*—who is lauded for her valor and excellence in the (notionally) male sphere of war (*Th* 925–26)—has been a possible avenue of feminist reclamation; in his version of the Titanomachy, O'Connor pits a hulking mountain of a male Titan against the smaller—but smarter—Athena. In addition to possessing a dubious moral compass, this Titan, Pallas, is also sexist: "You're very brave to face me, girl, or very stupid," he sneers (2010b: 33). Quite rightly, Pallas (the Titan) is clobbered by Athena the goddess, and O'Connor's retelling of Athena's life—including her patronage of the hero Perseus and her triumphant contest with Arachne—continues the generally laudatory narrative of this complicated female figure.

Hesiod's Titanomachy (*Th* 621–884) has had a vibrant afterlife in the popular imagination, one largely fueled by blockbuster films and equally blockbuster video games. If somewhat lacking in nuance, such receptions do adequately convey the core elements of the battle between gods and Titans: strength (*Th* 686) and strife (*Th* 710). The most famous of modern receptions, the motion picture *The Clash of the Titans* (1981), has a storyline involving Perseus and Medusa and prominently features one Titan, the notoriously non-humanoid "Kraken." A reboot of *Clash of the Titans*, still featuring the Titan

Kraken, was released in 2010 and starred Sam Worthington as Perseus; in this version, the clash is rather between Hades and Zeus than between Olympians and Titans per se, as Hades attempts a power grab from his elder brother. Whether by chance or design, the sequel—*Wrath of the Titans* (2012)—is far more Hesiodic then the original film or its reboot; here, Zeus is involved in a deadly battle against the newly awakened Kronos, a sort of elemental magma monster. (Further machinations involving Hades and Ares aren't particularly Hesiodic, but the film does figure Kronos as the "major boss battle" of the film.)

In a brief, fascinating article, Ted Gellar-Goad (2014) posits some reasons modern films and video games focus on (what might be termed) "second" Titanomachies, the release of the imprisoned Titans *back* to earth after the events of the *Th*. This phenomenon may be traced, ultimately, to modern American concerns over generational shifts: nearly all of these *new* Titanomachies feature not two generations of combatants, but three, as half-mortal/half-divine heroes are stirred into the mix. (Gellar-Goad thus locates the political spin of these films as products of a post–baby boomer age, as a new, fledgling generation takes on the mantle from the increasingly aging "Olympians" of World War II.) The emphasis on imprisonment might also be (in Gellar-Goad's view) a nod to anxieties about America's treatment of prisoners at Guantanamo Bay (and the ethics of imprisonment), while the Titans' frequent incarnations as elementals— such as *Wrath of the Titans*'s lava-esque Kronos (see figure 30.3)—could dovetail with

FIGURE 30.3 Still from *Wrath of the Titans*. Dir. Jonathan Liebesman. Warner Bros. 2012. A shot of the Titan Kronos, here re-envisioned as an elemental monster of lava.

Millennial concerns over climate change and global warming. Such Titanomachies are thus "mapped on" to urgent American political concerns, particularly those involving a deep generational divide.

A visually spectacular evocation of Hesiod's *Th* may be found in Tarsem Singh's otherwise empty fantasia on mythological themes, *Immortals* (2011). The opening moments are truly eye-popping. A dream sequence and voice-over briefly relate the plot of the Titanomachy and tellingly include the detail of the ending: after the attack of the Hundred-Handers, the Titans are sent under the earth "in distressing bonds" (*Th* 718), to live out their immortal punishment.

In Singh's treatment, the Titans are imprisoned in a giant bronze cube—perhaps a nod to the punishment of villains in "the Phantom Zone" in the *Superman* film franchise—and remain forever standing, forever surly, forever dangerous (see figures 30.4 and 30.5). (Or seemingly; an insurrection led by mad King Hyperion results in the freeing of the Titans and enables another full-blown Titanomachy. Zeus eventually imprisons the Titans again, with Theseus's help.) Though little about *Immortals* flows directly from Hesiod—a non-Hesiodic Bow of Epirus is the main catalyst of the plot—the film's fascination with a "war between the gods" is clearly inspired by Hesiod's poem.

One detail of Hesiod's *Th* has its own weird reception history: the shadowy Hundred-Handers who side with the Olympians against the Titans (*Th* 713–21). For video-game designers who require new and interesting monsters in their games, the Hekatonkheires are terrifically tempting, even if current video chips (and artists!) can't quite handle one hundred hands and fifty heads. The iOS/Android game *Dark Summoner* (2012) features Hekatonkheires with four heads and eight hands—sufficient for 879 attack points—while the Hecatoncheir, a "boss" in *Final Fantasy XIII*, features a truly alarming

FIGURE 30.4 Still from *Immortals*. Dir. Tarsem Singh. Universal Pictures. 2011. A bird's-eye view of the imprisoned Titans, losers of the Titanomachy.

FIGURE 30.5 Still from *Immortals*. Dir. Tarsem Singh. Universal Pictures. 2011. A close-up of the imprisoned Titans—and an ominous precursor to a second Titanomachy.

number of hands, though still somewhat less than one hundred. A demonic version of a Hecatoncheir—kelly green and sort of cuddly—appears in Nintendo's *Megami Tensei* series, while the Playstation game *Lord of Arcana* offers a more standard, burly, ogre. It is worth noting that such receptions elide the most striking feature of Hesiod's *Th*: that these fantastically scary "monsters" side, in the end, with the forces of "good" (i.e., the Olympians). In other words, Hesiod's emphasis on justice and righteousness proves that even outwardly hideous monsters are moral where it counts: on the inside. (O'Connor, in *Olympians: Zeus*, doubles down on sympathy for the Hundred-Handers; Zeus even politely introduces them as his uncles [2010a: 51].) A twist on Hesiod's moralizing can be found in the 2015 platforming game *Apotheon*, styled as a black figure vase, and starring the player as a heroic challenger to the callous, wicked gods of Olympus. In this way, millennial gamers can enjoy a battle of the gods from the "wrong" point of view: as righteous god-slayers.

Curiously, the best (and most interesting) reception of Hesiod's Titanomachy can be found in Disney's animated *Hercules* (1997), with music and lyrics by Alan Menken and David Zippel. The film begins with a portentous, rumbling voice-over that recalls to mind the staid and mind-numbing documentaries of mid-century Western classrooms. Delightfully, the Muses—here figured as an African American gospel choir—*literally* take over the narrative and thus dramatize the opening gambit of the *Th*, in which they abruptly address Hesiod himself (*Th* 25–28), in terrifically abusive terms. Hesiod's Muses then notoriously instruct him that "we know how to say many false things similar to genuine ones, and we know how—when we wish!—to proclaim things that are true." This baffling proclamation has attracted a number of scholarly responses, helpfully collected by Stoddard (2004: 84–86), who argues that the distinction isn't between falsity and truthfulness, per se, but in how the gods see mortal things (by definition changeable and finite, and therefore similar to false) and immortal truths (like the gods themselves, unchangeable and thus qualitatively different from mortal truths). A more straight-forward interpretation, however, is that adopted by Disney's team, as they ingeniously map ancient religiosity onto modern American fundamentalism: there is secular truth (changeable, finite, political) and the more urgent "Gospel Truth," a truth which (then and now) must paradoxically be credited only through faith. Thus Disney's Muses re-late the story of the Titanomachy—including the elemental Titans—while admitting, "Although, honey, it may seem imposs'ble / That's the gospel truth!"

This conflation of Hesiod and Christianity incited a predictable backlash among right-leaning Christian reviewers, already worried about the film's implicit valoriza-tion of polytheism. As Rob Smithouser writes for "Plugged In," a Christian media web-site, the film dangerously conflates Christianity and paganism before an audience of impressionable children: "But what makes things even worse is that this film teaches mythological 'history' in a rousing three-part musical number called 'The Gospel Truth'. Young viewers may be further confused by references to 'praying to the gods' and Herc[ules]'s longing to 'please the gods'. Whether intentional or not, Disney reduces Christianity to the level of folklore by blending spiritual counterfeits with biblical or-thodoxy."[2] A blogger, Forgiven83, on christianchat.com, is even more blunt: "The song 'gospel truth' is wicked to the core, brainwashing kids to hate the truth of God's Word. How can 'mythology' be anything near 'the gospel truth.'"[3] For a certain segment of the American viewing public, then, Hesiod's Muses, as exemplary of pre-Christian, poly-theistic religion, represent all that is wrong with the study, and admiration, of classical mythology.

In contradistinction to popular art, movies, and comic books, there is surprisingly little twentieth century "high art" dedicated to the *Th* per se. George Braque's amazing *Théogonie* (1932, published as a book in 1955) is a happy exception. An illustrated version of Hesiod's epic, this *Théogonie* is thoroughly surreal, a sort of fantasia executed with sweeping, simple arabesque lines, and obviously indebted to cubism (Wye 2004: 68). The very binding of the printed edition plays with the fetishized "primitivism" of Hesiod, replete with capitalized, epigraphic Greek—*ΘΕΟΓΟΝΙΑ / ΗΣΙΟΔΟΣ*. (The letters are illustrated by two doves flying in different directions, perhaps an allusion to Hesiod's divine inspiration.) This primitive take on Hesiod is taken even further with the back binding, as "fragments" of marbled rock appear to glint through the otherwise drab brown cover. The metaphor is clear: Hesiod as literally foundational, the artistic ped-estal of the West. The inside of the book features a beautiful text, in Greek, of the *Th* with over two dozen drawings on the right-hand pages. Some, in the manner of the Cubists, feature abstractly or geometrically drawn humanoids; the first image depicts a pastoral scene of a Muse—labeled in Greek—giving a laurel staff to Hesiod (cf. *Th* 30–31). She is thus literally handing off inspiration from the divine to the human, intermediated by the sacred space of nature. (On Braque's attraction to the scene of Hesiod and the Muses, see Bowness 2000: 206; also for Braque's "obsession" with the *Th*, as revealed in over a hundred extant sketches.) A duet of Themis and Hera embracing (or dancing?)

features prominently in the first third of the work, while the underappreciated Nereid Doris (*Th* 240) receives a surprising solo treatment. Cubist horses clearly comment on their similarities to their equine brethren on geometric vases—antiquity and the avant garde collide, here—while a portrait of Artemis is one of the highlights of the collection. Here the goddess is placed among the static stars, but she herself is a flurry of legs, arms, and breasts, as if art can't capture in a single moment every aspect of her quicksilver, numinous self.

WD, relatively neglected in the twentieth century, has enjoyed something of a renaissance among artists and thinkers concerned with eco-criticism and other environmentally motived analyses. In Angus Fletcher's reading, for instance, *WD* explores "how resources are to be allocated for human survival" and investigates the tension among ownership of land, habitation, and environmental wisdom. Indeed, Hesiod's poem cuts to the very essence of human conflict (and in that way mirrors the strife in the *Iliad*): "Hesiod's poem is almost a classic reminder that we humans need the skill to navigate our conflicts over possession" (Fletcher 2009: 231). For Australian poet Peter Porter, in his "On First Looking into Chapman's Hesiod," *WD* speaks to deep parallels between the lands of Australia and Ascra. As the narrator of the poem terms it: "In [*WD*] I saw . . . something strange / and balking—Australia, my own country / and its edgy managers—in the picture of / Euboean husbandry, terse family feuds/ and the minds of gods tangential to the earth" (Porter 1975: 21, lines 11–13). For Porter, both countries share a similar geography and a similar mythology: of an iron age, of course, but also one of gold—of ancestral pioneers with a manifest destiny, of an earth to conquer, tame, and plough. More tellingly, both regions feature an especially pronounced urban/rural split, as the narrator, for all of the earthy pleasures of the Outback/Boeotia, pines rather for "the permanently upright city where / speech is nature and plants conceive in pots" (since Porter had exiled himself to England, this phrase presumably maps onto the metaphor of London = Athens). In a passionate essay, "On Sitting Back and Thinking About Porter's Boeotia," fellow poet and intellectual Les Murray (1992) traces the development of all of Western (indeed, global) civilization back to the tension between Boeotia and Athens, the former a polis that prized religiosity, kinship, and the land, while the latter valued aristocracy, debate, and abstraction.[4] (In the radical *agora*, abstraction even birthed the famously gab-filled democracy.) Whereas Porter, an expatriate, clearly turns his back on Boeotian Australia, Murray argues that Australians need to confront their cultural arc head on: "[O]ur culture *is* still in its Boeotian phrase, and any distinctiveness we have *is* still firmly anchored in the bush" (Murray 1992: 61). For Murray, this Boeotian-ness, flowing from Hesiod to inheritors such as Virgil, Dante, and Whitman, is cause for celebration rather than lament; this aspect of identity resists cultural and intellectual centralization ("the centre of Boeotia is every place held sacred by any Boeotian" [1992: 64]) and might, at a later point, help to reconcile the two seeming opposites, of Athens and Boeotia, the metropolis and the outback. In this way, a country with deep roots in agriculture and indigenous cultures looks back to Hesiod's *WD* as a blueprint not only for daily life, but for spiritual and intellectual life as well.

As for ripped-from-the headlines Hesiodic reception, social media have (as of 2017) engaged with Hesiod only by fits and starts. There is, for instance, a smattering of slender fan fiction based on the films *Clash* (or *Wrath) of the Titans*. This fiction mostly continues the focus on the relationships between the gods (though a few posts concentrate rather on the domestic stresses in the marriage of Perseus and Andromeda).[5] The Twitter hashtag #hesiod is a sort of butterfly net for all things Hesiodic, including book reviews, artwork, and, well, musings; it's also a virtual treasury of aphorisms from *WD*, which function almost disconcertingly well as 140-character tweets. For example, on investing mistakes to avoid, from Equilibrium on February 17, 2012: "Poor timing. 'Observe due measure, for right timing is in all things the most important factor.'" The quote is from *WD* 694, and is quoted also in Elaine Marmel's *Microsoft Project 2007 Bible* (83); Marmel goes on to humorously praise Hesiod as "that classic Greek project manager," which reinscribes Hesiod, and modern capitalism, within a strict system of labor and temporality. Meanwhile, *WD* has popped up in other new media: an audiobook version of Lattimore's translation of *WD*—narrated by Charlton Griffin (2007)—is recited in an exceedingly dramatic vein. A modern attempt at rehabilitating *WD*—from conservative pundit and former US secretary of education William J. Bennett—asserts, rather broadly, that Hesiod is "loved at home and abroad," and observes that this didactic poem is "full of wisdom and advice" (2011: 112). (He also strangely terms the work a "letter.") In the subsequent excerpt in *The Book of Man*, Bennett wisely skips the myth of Pandora and instead presents inspiring paragraphs on the value of labor and farming, adapted from *WD* 298–319, 381–82, 410–413, 492–503, and 574–81. In this way, Hesiod is appropriated, here at "home," as a sort of prototype of *The Old Farmer's Almanac*, a classic American text of self-reliance and heartland common sense.

In sum: Hesiod's contemporary "divorce" from Homer has largely freed him from invidious comparisons concerning artistry and even (ancient) ideology and has allowed artists to engage Hesiod independently as a creator, artist, and thinker. While the didacticism of *WD* has been a challenge to rework into modern forms—allusions and sound bites have worked best—*Th*'s handful of extended narratives has seen a huge variety of receptions, from children's literature, to video games, to films, to novels, and more. In particular, *Th*'s exciting battle sequences have provided fodder for blockbuster filmmaking, and one doubts that particular trend will end anytime soon. Hesiod's sometimes troubling ideological biases—particularly his distressing views on Pandora and marriage—have elicited ellipsis, revision, and revulsion, which make for a particularly intriguing reception history; at the same time, Hesiod's status as the "first" major religious prophet in Greece has produced some surprising responses within contemporary, fundamentalist religious communities. It's a truism in reception theory that receptions tell as much about the receiving societies as about the producing societies, and the emphases of the past one hundred years—on creationism, sex, violence, and labor—demonstrate a multitude of enduring social concerns, as we moderns glide, or lurch, through the twenty-first century.

Notes

1. http://tvtropes.org/pmwiki/pmwiki.php/Main/GaiasVengeance (accessed July 17, 2017).
2. http://www.pluggedin.com/videos/1999/q1/hercules (accessed March 30, 2015).
3. http://christianchat.com/bible-discussion-forum/2461-walt-disney-corruption.html (accessed July 17, 2017).
4. This is perhaps a play on Tertullian's famous rhetorical question, "What does Jerusalem have to do with Athens?" (*Prescriptions Against Heretics*, 7), in which piety is mapped onto Jerusalem and philosophical inquiry (or sophistry) is mapped onto Athens.
5. https://www.fanfiction.net/movie/Immortals (accessed July 17, 2017).

References

Alexander, H. 2011. *A Child's Introduction to Greek Mythology*. New York.

Bachofen, J. J. 1967. *Myth, Religion, and Mother Right: Selected Writings of Johann Jakob Bachofen*. Translated by R. Manheim. (Reprint, Princeton, NJ, 1992).

Bennett, W. J. 2011. *The Book of Man: Readings on the Path to Manhood*. Nashville, TN.

Bowness, S. 2000. "Braque's Etchings for Hesiod's 'Theogony' and Archaic Greece Revived." *Burlington Magazine* 142 (1165): 204–14.

Brabant, M. 2007. "Ancient Greek Gods' New Believers." *BBC News*, January 21. http://news.bbc.co.uk/2/hi/europe/6285397.stm.

Clay, J. S. 2003. *Hesiod's Cosmos*. Cambridge.

D'Aulaire, I., and E. Parin d'Aulaire. 1962. *D'Aulaires' Book of Greek Myths*. (Reprint, Delacorte, 1992).

Fletcher, A. 2009. *A New Theory for American Poetry: Democracy, the Environment, and the Future of Imagination*. Cambridge, MA.

Gellar-Goad, T. H. M. 2014. "Rehash of the Titans: Sequels to the Titanomachy on the American Screen (Part 2)." Accessed June 29, 2015. http://apaclassics.org/blogs/t-h-m_gellar-goad/rehash-of-titans-sequels-titanomachy-american-screen-part-2.

Golding, W. 1983. Nobel Lecture. Nobel Media AB 2014. Accessed February 12, 2015. http://www.nobelprize.org/nobel_prizes/literature/laureates/1983/golding-lecture.html.

Lattimore, R., trans. 2007. *Hesiod: The Works and Days*. Read by C. Griffin. Audio Connoisseur. Audiobook.

Holub, L., and D. Jones. 2014. *Do Not Open! The Story of Pandora's Box*. New York.

Jenkins, T. E. 2015. *Antiquity Now: The Classical World in the Contemporary American Imagination*. Cambridge.

Kirk, R. 2007. *The Essential Russell Kirk: Selected Essays*. Edited by G. A. Panichas. Wilmington, DE.

Koning, H. H. 2010. *Hesiod: The Other Poet; Ancient Reception of a Cultural Icon*. Mnemosyne Supplement 325. Leiden, Netherlands.

Lee, K. J. 2006. "Rewriting Hesiod, Revisioning Korea: Theresa Hak Kyung Cha's *Dictee* as a Subversive Hesiodic *Catalogue of Women*." *College Literature* 33 (3): 77–99.

Lovelock, J. E. 1979. *Gaia: A New Look at Life on Earth*. Oxford.

Marmel, E. J. 2007. *Microsoft Project 2007 Bible*. Indianapolis, IN.

McMullan, K., and D. Zilber. 2012. *Keep a Lid on It, Pandora!* Mankato, MN.

Murray, L. 1992. "On Sitting Back and Thinking about Porter's Boeotia." In *The Paperbark Tree: Selected Prose*, 56–65. London.

O'Connor, G. 2010a. *Olympians: Zeus*. New York.

O'Connor, G. 2010b. *Olympians: Athena*. New York.

Porter, P. 1975. *Living in a Calm Country*. Oxford.

Renger, A. 2013. "Pandora-Eve-Ava: Albert Lewin's Making of A 'Secret Goddess.'" In *Ancient Worlds in Film and Television: Gender and Politics*, edited by A. Renger and M. Winkler, 271–98. Leiden.

Russell, L. 2011. "Pandora & the Flying Dutchman." Accessed June 29, 2015. http://www.culturecourt.com/F/Art/Pandora_and_the_Flying_Dutchman.htm.

Stoddard, K. 2004. *The Narrative Voice in the Theogony of Hesiod*. Mnemosyne Supplement 255. Leiden.

Wolfe, A. 2007. "Contempt." *New Republic*, July 2. http://www.newrepublic.com/article/contempt.

Wye, D. 2004. *Artists and Prints: Masterworks from The Museum of Modern Art*. New York.

Zeitlin, F. 1996. "Signifying Difference: The Case of Hesiod's Pandora." In *Playing the Other: Gender and Society in Classical Greek Literature*, 53–86. Chicago.

Index

Index Locorum Antiquorum